D0955995

Oxford Primary Thesaurus

Chief Editor: Susan Rennie
Literacy Consultant: Kate Ruttle

OXFORD
UNIVERSITY PRESS

OXFORD
UNIVERSITY PRESS

Great Clarendon Street, Oxford OX2 6DP

Oxford University Press is a department of the University of Oxford.
It furthers the University's objective of excellence in research,
scholarship, and education by publishing worldwide in

Oxford New York

Auckland Cape Town Dar es Salaam Hong Kong Karachi
Kuala Lumpur Madrid Melbourne Mexico City Nairobi
New Delhi Shanghai Taipei Toronto

With offices in

Argentina Austria Brazil Chile Czech Republic France Greece
Guatemala Hungary Italy Japan Poland Portugal Singapore
South Korea Switzerland Thailand Turkey Ukraine Vietnam

Oxford is a registered trade mark of Oxford University Press
in the UK and in certain other countries

British Library Cataloguing in Publication Data available

ISBN: 978-0-19-911516-7

10 9 8 7 6 5 4 3 2 1

Printed in Italy by Rotolito Lombarda

Contents

Preface

The *Oxford Primary Thesaurus* has been specially written for primary school children aged 7 to 11. It will be particularly useful for pupils at Key Stage 2 (YR3–6) of the Primary National Strategy, or at P4–7 of the Scottish National Guidelines. It is also designed to complement the *Oxford Primary Dictionary* which is aimed at the same age range.

A special feature of this edition is the **Become a Word Explorer** section at the back of the thesaurus. This includes advice on using synonyms and other types of language, and tips on how to make writing more varied and colourful through the use of a thesaurus.

Susan Rennie

Introduction
What is a thesaurus for?

Here are three good reasons to use your thesaurus:

✓ to *find a more interesting word*

What words can you use besides *kick* for striking a football? Look up **kick** and **ball** to find some other verbs to describe footwork.

✓ to *find the right word*

What do you call the home of a fox? Is a young otter known as a *cub* or a *pup*? Look up **animal** to find the answers.

✓ to *give you ideas for writing*

Imagine you are describing a giant's castle. Look up **castle** for ideas for the setting, then **big** to find adjectives to describe how *colossal* and *mammoth* everything is in a giant's world.

What is the difference between a thesaurus and a dictionary?

A **dictionary** tells you what a word means, whereas a **thesaurus** tells you what other words have the same meaning, or are related to the word in some way. A dictionary gives you a **definition** of a word; a thesaurus gives you **synonyms** of a word.

For example, if you look up **clothes** in a dictionary, it will tell you that clothes are things that you wear. But a thesaurus will give you some other words for clothes (*garments, dress, attire*) and will list particular types of clothes (*jeans, kilt, pyjamas*).

You often use a dictionary to check the meaning of something you have read or heard. You use a thesaurus to find ways to write or say something yourself.

How to use this thesaurus

headword

word class

synonyms

label

numbered senses

Word Web panel

example sentence

cross reference

opposites (antonyms)

special synonyms

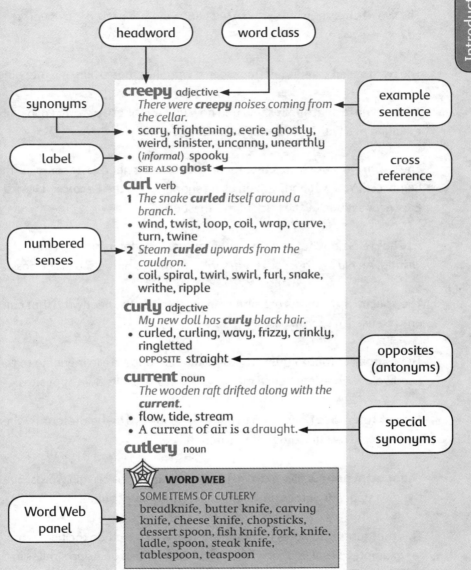

creepy adjective
*There were **creepy** noises coming from the cellar.*
- scary, frightening, eerie, ghostly, weird, sinister, uncanny, unearthly
- (*informal*) spooky
SEE ALSO **ghost**

curl verb
1 *The snake **curled** itself around a branch.*
- wind, twist, loop, coil, wrap, curve, turn, twine
2 *Steam **curled** upwards from the cauldron.*
- coil, spiral, twirl, swirl, furl, snake, writhe, ripple

curly adjective
*My new doll has **curly** black hair.*
- curled, curling, wavy, frizzy, crinkly, ringletted
OPPOSITE straight

current noun
*The wooden raft drifted along with the **current**.*
- flow, tide, stream
- A current of air is a draught.

cutlery noun

WORD WEB
SOME ITEMS OF CUTLERY
breadknife, butter knife, carving knife, cheese knife, chopsticks, dessert spoon, fish knife, fork, knife, ladle, spoon, steak knife, tablespoon, teaspoon

The **headword** is the word you look up. Headwords are given in alphabetical order.

The **word class** (part of speech) tells you whether a word is a *noun*, *verb*, *adjective*, *adverb*, or *preposition*.

The **numbered senses** tell you when a word has more than one meaning.

The **example sentences** show you how you might use a word. Each meaning of a word has a separate example sentence.

The **synonyms** are words that mean the same, or nearly the same, as the headword. You will find help on using synonyms in the **Become a Word Explorer** section at the back of this thesaurus.

A **label** tells you that certain synonyms are only for *informal* or *formal* writing. An *old use* label tells you that a word was only used in the past.

The **special synonyms** are similar in meaning to the headword, but can only be used in special cases.

The **opposites** (antonyms) are words that are opposite in meaning to the headword. Sometimes, each meaning of a word has its own opposites.

A **cross reference** points you to another headword in the thesaurus where you will find useful words or information.

The **special panels** give extra help or information for certain words. See the next page for details about the different types of panel.

This thesaurus also notes common **similes** which include the headword, for example *as cool as a cucumber*. You will find help on using similes in the **Become a Word Explorer** section at the back of the thesaurus.

pecial panels

hroughout this thesaurus, you will see special tinted boxes which give extra elp on finding and using words. There are three types of panel, each marked y a special symbol: **Overused word**, **Word Web**, and **Writing tips**.

 Overused word panels

The **overused word** panels offer more interesting alternatives for common words like *big*, *happy*, *nice*, and *sad*. If you use these words too often, your writing will seem dull and boring.

Here is a complete list of all the **overused word panels** in this thesaurus.

bad	hard	old
beautiful	like	sad
big	little	say
bit	look	small
eat	lovely	strong
good	move	walk
happy	nice	

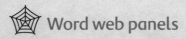

Word web panels

As well as exploring *alternative* words, you can explore *related* words. The **word web** panels give lists of words related to a topic word, such as **anim[e]** or **castle**. These can be useful for both project work and for story writing.

accommodation	chess	expression
aircraft	church	eye
alien	cloth	fairy
amphibian	clothes	family
animal	coin	farm
anniversary	colour	fighter
armed services	communication	figure of speech
armour	competition	fish
art	computer	flower
artist	cook	food
astronaut	cricket	football
athletics	criminal	fossil
bear	crockery	fruit
bee	cutlery	furniture
bicycle	dance	game
bird	day	ghost
blue	desert	glasses
boat	detective	green
body	dinosaur	group
bone	disaster	hair
book	dog	hat
brown	dragon	herb
building	drawing	horse
car	drink	hospital
card	drum	house
castle	education	ice
cat	entertainer	illness
cave	explorer	injury

Writing tips panels

Writing tips can help you to create more colourful descriptions by suggesting ways to describe how people, things, or animals look, move, or sound. Other **writing tips** offer suggestions for creating dialogue or for using idioms.

You will find more ideas for your writing in the **Become a Word Explorer** section at the back of this thesaurus.

afraid	exclamation	sky
angry	eye	smell
animal	face	sound
ball	feel	surprised
bell	food	tooth
bird	hair	un-
boat	light	voice
body	nose	water
building	planet	weather
clothes	river	writing
colour	sea	

abandon verb
1 *The robbers **abandoned** the stolen car.*
- leave, desert, forsake, leave behind, strand
- (*informal*) dump, ditch
2 *We **abandoned** our picnic because of the rain.*
- cancel, give up, scrap, drop, abort, discard

abduct verb
*The pirates **abducted** two members of the crew.*
- kidnap

ability noun
*Skin has a natural **ability** to heal itself.*
- capability, competence, aptitude, talent, expertise, skill

able adjective
1 *Will you be **able** to come to my party?*
- allowed, permitted, free, willing
  OPPOSITE unable
2 *Penguins are very **able** swimmers.*
- competent, capable, accomplished, expert, skilful, proficient, talented, gifted
  OPPOSITE incompetent

abnormal adjective
*It's **abnormal** to have snow in June.*
- unusual, exceptional, extraordinary, peculiar, odd, strange, weird, bizarre, unnatural, freak
  OPPOSITE normal

abolish verb
*I wish someone would **abolish** homework!*
- get rid of, do away with, put an end to, eliminate
  OPPOSITE create

about preposition
*There are **about** two hundred children in the school.*
- approximately, roughly, close to, around
to be about something
*The film is **about** a dog called Scruff.*
- concern, deal with, involve

above preposition
*The witch flew **above** the rooftops on her broom.*
- over, higher than

abroad adverb
*We're planning to go **abroad** next summer.*
- overseas, to a foreign country

abrupt adjective
1 *The book came to a very **abrupt** end.*
- sudden, hurried, hasty, quick, unexpected
  OPPOSITE gradual
2 *The sales assistant had a very **abrupt** manner.*
- blunt, curt, sharp, rude, gruff, impolite, tactless, unfriendly
  OPPOSITE polite

absence noun
*There's an **absence** of salt in the soup.*
- lack, want, need, deficit
  OPPOSITE presence

absent adjective
*Why were you **absent** from school yesterday?*
- away, missing
- To be absent from school without a good reason is to play truant.
  OPPOSITE present

absent-minded adjective
*The **absent-minded** witch had forgotten the spell.*
- forgetful, careless, inattentive, vague
  OPPOSITE alert

absolute adjective
*The hypnotist asked for **absolute** silence.*
- complete, total, utter, perfect

a
b
c
d
e
f
g
h
i
j
k
l
m
n
o
p
q
r
s
t
u
v
w
x
y
z

absolutely adverb
*This floor is **absolutely** filthy!*
- completely, thoroughly, totally, utterly, wholly, entirely

absorb verb
*A sponge **absorbs** water.*
- soak up, suck up, take in, fill up with, hold, retain

absorbed adjective
to be absorbed in something
*I was so **absorbed in** my book that I forgot the time.*
- be engrossed in, be interested in, be preoccupied with, concentrate on, think about

absorbing adjective
*'101 Dalmatians' is an **absorbing** book.*
- interesting, fascinating, intriguing, gripping, enthralling, engrossing, captivating

absurd adjective
*The idea that little green men live on Mars is **absurd**.*
- ridiculous, silly, ludicrous, preposterous, foolish, laughable, nonsensical, idiotic, senseless, stupid, unreasonable, illogical
- (informal) daft
OPPOSITE sensible, reasonable

abundant adjective
*Birds have an **abundant** supply of food in the summer.*
- ample, plentiful, generous, profuse, lavish, liberal
OPPOSITE meagre, scarce

abuse verb
1 *The rescued dog had been **abused** by its owners.*
- mistreat, maltreat, hurt, injure, damage, harm, misuse
2 *The referee was **abused** by players from both teams.*
- be rude to, insult, swear at
- (informal) call someone names

abuse noun
1 *They campaigned against the **abuse** of animals.*
- mistreatment, misuse, damage, harm, injury
2 *A spectator yelled **abuse** at the referee.*
- insults, name-calling, swear words

accelerate verb
*The bus **accelerated** when it reached the motorway.*
- go faster, speed up, pick up speed
OPPOSITE slow down

accent noun
1 *My mum speaks English with a Jamaican **accent**.*
- pronunciation, intonation, tone
2 *Play the first note of each bar with a strong **accent**.*
- beat, stress, emphasis, rhythm, pulse

accept verb
1 *I **accepted** the offer of a lift to the station.*
- take, receive, welcome
OPPOSITE reject
2 *The club **accepted** my application for membership.*
- approve, agree to, consent to
OPPOSITE reject
3 *Do you **accept** responsibility for the damage?*
- admit, acknowledge, recognize, face up to
OPPOSITE deny
4 *They had to **accept** the umpire's decision.*
- agree to, go along with, tolerate, put up with, resign yourself to

acceptable adjective
1 *Would a pound be **acceptable** as a tip?*
- welcome, agreeable, appreciated, pleasant, pleasing, worthwhile
2 *She said my handwriting was not **acceptable**.*
- satisfactory, adequate, appropriate, permissible, suitable, tolerable, passable
OPPOSITE unacceptable

access noun

*The **access** to the lighthouse is over those rocks.*
- entrance, way in, approach

access verb

*Can I **access** my email on this computer?*
- get at, obtain, reach, make use of

accident noun

1 *There has been an **accident** at a fireworks display.*
- misfortune, mishap, disaster, calamity, catastrophe
- A person who is always having accidents is accident-prone.

2 *A motorway **accident** is causing traffic delays.*
- collision, crash, smash
- An accident involving a lot of vehicles is a pile-up.
- A railway accident may involve a derailment.

3 *It was pure **accident** that led us to the secret passage.*
- chance, luck, a fluke

by accident

*I found the piece of paper **by accident**.*
- by chance, accidentally, coincidentally, unintentionally

accidental adjective

1 *The damage to the building was **accidental**.*
- unintentional, unfortunate, unlucky

2 *The professor made an **accidental** discovery.*
- unexpected, unforeseen, unplanned, fortunate, lucky, chance
  OPPOSITE deliberate

accommodate verb

1 *The hotel can **accommodate** thirty guests.*
- house, shelter, lodge, provide for, cater for, put up, take in, hold

2 *If you need anything, we'll try to **accommodate** you.*
- serve, assist, help, aid, oblige, supply, please

accommodation noun

> **WORD WEB**
>
> *Have you booked your holiday **accommodation** yet?*
> - housing, lodgings, quarters, premises, shelter, rooms
>   PLACES WHERE PEOPLE NORMALLY LIVE
>   bedsit, flat, house
>   KINDS OF HOLIDAY ACCOMMODATION
>   apartment, bed and breakfast, boarding house, chalet, guest house, hotel, motel, self-catering, timeshare, youth hostel
> - Accommodation for students is in a hall of residence or (*informal*) digs.
> - Accommodation for the armed services is in barracks or a billet.
>   SEE ALSO **building**, **house** noun

accompany verb

*A guide **accompanied** us through the jungle.*
- escort, go with, follow, attend, travel with, tag along with

accomplish verb

*She **accomplished** her goal of sailing round the world.*
- achieve, finish, complete, carry out, perform, succeed in, fulfil

account noun

1 *I wrote an **account** of our camping trip in my diary.*
- report, record, description, history, narrative, story, chronicle, log
- (*informal*) write-up

2 *Money was of no **account** to him.*
- importance, significance, consequence, interest, value

account verb

to account for

*Can you **account for** your strange behaviour?*
- explain, give reasons for, justify, make excuses for

accumulate verb
1 *Our family has **accumulated** a lot of rubbish.*
- collect, gather, amass, assemble, heap up, pile up, hoard
  OPPOSITE scatter
2 *Dust had **accumulated** on the mantelpiece.*
- build up, grow, increase, multiply
  OPPOSITE decrease

accurate adjective
1 *The detective took **accurate** measurements of the room.*
- careful, correct, exact, meticulous, minute, precise
  OPPOSITE inexact, rough
2 *Is this an **accurate** account of what happened?*
- faithful, true, reliable, truthful, factual
  OPPOSITE inaccurate, false

accuse verb
accuse of
*Miss Sharp **accused** her opponent **of** cheating.*
- charge with, blame for, condemn for, denounce for
  OPPOSITE defend

accustomed adjective
accustomed to
*Martians are not **accustomed to** rain.*
- acclimatized to, familiar with, used to

ache noun
*The **ache** in my tooth is getting worse.*
- pain, soreness, throbbing, discomfort, pang, twinge
  SEE ALSO **pain**

ache verb
*My legs **ached** from the long walk.*
- hurt, be painful, be sore, throb, pound, smart

achieve verb
1 *He **achieved** his ambition to play rugby for Wales.*
- accomplish, attain, succeed in, carry out, fulfil

2 *The singer **achieved** success with her first CD.*
- acquire, win, gain, earn, get, score

achievement noun
*To climb Mount Everest would be an **achievement**.*
- accomplishment, attainment, success, feat, triumph

acknowledge verb
1 *The queen did not **acknowledge** her cousin's claim to the throne.*
- admit, accept, concede, grant, recognize
  OPPOSITE deny
2 *Please **acknowledge** my email.*
- answer, reply to, respond to

acquire verb
*Where can I **acquire** a copy of this book?*
- get, get hold of, obtain
- To acquire something by paying for it is to buy or purchase it.

across preposition
*We could see their camp **across** the river.*
- on the other side of, over, beyond

act noun
1 *Rescuing the boy from the river was a brave **act**.*
- action, deed, feat, exploit, operation
2 *The best **act** at the circus involved three clowns.*
- performance, sketch, item, turn

act verb
1 *We must **act** as soon as we hear the signal.*
- do something, take action
2 *Give the medicine time to **act**.*
- work, take effect, have an effect, function
3 *Stop **acting** like a baby!*
- behave, carry on
4 *I **acted** the part of a pirate in the play.*
- perform, play, portray, represent, appear as

action noun
1 *The driver's **action** prevented an accident.*
- act, deed, effort, measure, feat
2 *The fruit ripens through the **action** of the sun.*
- working, effect, mechanism
3 *The film was packed with **action**.*
- drama, excitement, activity, liveliness, energy, vigour, vitality
4 *He was killed in **action** in the Second World War.*
- battle, fighting

active adjective
1 *Mr Aziz is very **active** for his age.*
- energetic, lively, dynamic, vigorous, busy
2 *My uncle is an **active** member of the football club.*
- enthusiastic, devoted, committed, dedicated, hard-working
OPPOSITE inactive

activity noun
1 *The town centre was full of **activity**.*
- action, life, busyness, liveliness, excitement, movement, animation
2 *My mum's favourite **activity** is gardening.*
- hobby, interest, pastime, pursuit, job, occupation, task

actor, actress nouns
*A company of **actors** performed a play in the school hall.*
- performer, player
- The most important actor in a play or film is the lead or the star.
- The other actors are the supporting actors.
- All the actors in a play or film are the cast or the company.

actual adjective
*Did you see the **actual** crime?*
- real, true, genuine, authentic
OPPOSITE imaginary, supposed

actually adverb
*What did the teacher **actually** say to you?*
- really, truly, definitely, certainly, genuinely, in fact

acute adjective
1 *She felt an **acute** pain in her knee.*
- intense, severe, sharp, piercing, sudden, violent
OPPOSITE mild, slight
2 *There is an **acute** shortage of food.*
- serious, urgent, crucial, important, vital
OPPOSITE unimportant
3 *Clearly the aliens had an **acute** intelligence.*
- keen, quick, sharp, clever, intelligent, shrewd, smart, alert
OPPOSITE stupid

adapt verb
1 *I'll **adapt** the goggles so that they fit you.*
- alter, change, modify, convert, reorganize, transform
2 *Our family **adapted** quickly to life in the country.*
- become accustomed, adjust, acclimatize

add verb
*The poet **added** an extra line in the last verse.*
- join on, attach, append, insert

to add to
*The herbs **add to** the flavour of the stew.*
- improve, enhance, increase

to add up
1 *Can you **add up** these figures for me?*
- count up, find the sum of, find the total of
- (*informal*) tot up
2 (*informal*) *Her story just doesn't **add up**.*
- be convincing, make sense

additional adjective
*There are **additional** toilets downstairs.*
- extra, further, more, supplementary

address verb
*The head **addressed** us in assembly.*
- speak to, talk to, make a speech to, lecture to

a
b
c
d
e
f
g
h
i
j
k
l
m
n
o
p
q
r
s
t
u
v
w
x
y
z

adequate adjective

1 *A sandwich will be **adequate**, thank you.*
- enough, sufficient, ample

2 *Your work is **adequate**, but I'm sure you can do better.*
- satisfactory, acceptable, tolerable, competent, passable, respectable
OPPOSITE inadequate

adjust verb

1 *You need to **adjust** the TV picture.*
- correct, modify, put right, improve, tune

2 *She **adjusted** the central heating thermostat.*
- alter, change, set, vary, regulate

to adjust to
*I found it hard to **adjust to** my new school at first.*
- adapt to, get used to, get accustomed to, become acclimatized to, settle in to

admiration noun

*I'm full of **admiration** for her work.*
- praise, respect, approval
OPPOSITE contempt

admire verb

1 *I **admire** her skill with words.*
- think highly of, look up to, value, have a high opinion of, respect, applaud, approve of, esteem
OPPOSITE despise

2 *The travellers stopped to **admire** the view.*
- enjoy, appreciate, be delighted by

admission noun

1 *We were surprised by his **admission** of guilt.*
- confession, declaration, acknowledgement, acceptance
OPPOSITE denial

2 ***Admission** to the castle is by ticket only.*
- entrance, entry, access, admittance

admit verb

1 *The hospital **admitted** all the victims of the accident.*
- receive, take in, accept, allow in, let in
OPPOSITE exclude

2 *Did he **admit** that he told a lie?*
- acknowledge, agree, accept, confess, grant, own up
OPPOSITE deny

adopt verb

1 *Our school has **adopted** a healthy eating policy.*
- take up, accept, choose, follow, embrace

2 *We have **adopted** a stray kitten.*
- foster, take in

adore verb

1 *Rosie **adores** her big sister.*
- love, worship, idolize, dote on

2 *(informal) I **adore** chocolate milk shakes!*
- love, like, enjoy
OPPOSITE hate, detest

adult adjective

*An **adult** zebra can run at 80km an hour.*
- grown-up, mature, full-size, fully grown
OPPOSITE young, immature

advance noun

1 *You can't stop the **advance** of science.*
- progress, development, growth, evolution

2 *This computer is a great **advance** on our old one.*
- improvement

advance verb

1 *As the army **advanced**, the enemy fled.*
- move forward, go forward, proceed, approach, come near, press on, progress, forge ahead, gain ground, make headway, make progress
OPPOSITE retreat

2 *Mobile phones have **advanced** in the last few years.*
- develop, grow, improve, evolve, progress

advantage noun

*We had the **advantage** of the wind behind us.*
- assistance, benefit, help, aid, asset
OPPOSITE disadvantage, drawback

adventure noun
1 *He told us about his latest **adventure**.*
- enterprise, exploit, venture, escapade
2 *They travelled the world in search of **adventure**.*
- excitement, danger, risk, thrills

adventurous adjective
1 *I dreamed of being an **adventurous** explorer.*
- bold, daring, heroic, enterprising, intrepid
2 *She has led a very **adventurous** life.*
- exciting, eventful, dangerous, challenging, risky
OPPOSITE unadventurous

advertise verb
*We made a poster to **advertise** the cake sale.*
- publicize, promote, announce, make known
- (*informal*) plug

advice noun
*The website gives **advice** on building a bird table.*
- guidance, help, directions, recommendations, suggestions, tips, pointers

advise verb
1 *What did the doctor **advise**?*
- recommend, suggest, advocate, prescribe
2 *He **advised** me to rest.*
- counsel, encourage, urge

aeroplane noun SEE **aircraft**

affair noun
*The theft of the jewels was a mysterious **affair**.*
- event, happening, incident, occurrence, occasion, thing

affairs
*I don't discuss my private **affairs** on the phone.*
- business, matters, concerns, questions, subjects, topics

affect verb
1 *Global warming will **affect** our climate.*
- have an effect or impact on, influence, change, modify, alter
2 *The bad news **affected** us deeply.*
- disturb, upset, concern, trouble, worry

affectionate adjective
*She gave him an **affectionate** kiss.*
- loving, tender, caring, fond, friendly, devoted
OPPOSITE unfriendly

afford verb
*I can't **afford** a new bike just now.*
- have enough money for, pay for, manage, spare

afraid adjective
1 *We felt **afraid** as we approached the haunted house.*
- frightened, scared, terrified, petrified, alarmed, fearful, anxious, apprehensive
OPPOSITE brave
2 *Don't be **afraid** to ask questions.*
- hesitant, reluctant, shy

to be afraid of
*Zoe was **afraid of** large hairy spiders.*
- be frightened of, be scared of, fear, dread

WRITING TIPS

- Someone who FEELS AFRAID might: blanch, go or turn pale, have goosebumps, quake in their boots, shudder, stand frozen or rooted to the spot, tremble like a leaf
- Something which MAKES YOU AFRAID might: give you goosebumps, make your hair stand on end, make your knees tremble, strike fear into you or your heart

---

again adverb
*Would you like to come round **again** next week?*
- another time, once more, once again

against preposition
I signed a petition against cruelty to animals.
- in opposition to, opposed to, hostile to

age noun
The book is set in the age of the Vikings.
- period, time, era, epoch, days

age verb
1 *The woman had aged since we last saw her.*
- become older, look older
2 *The wine is left to age in the cellar.*
- mature, develop

agent noun FOR SECRET AGENTS
SEE **spy** noun

aggressive adjective
Bats are not aggressive creatures.
- hostile, violent, provocative, quarrelsome, bullying, warlike
OPPOSITE friendly

agile adjective
Mountain goats are extremely agile.
- nimble, graceful, sure-footed, sprightly, acrobatic, supple, swift
OPPOSITE clumsy, stiff

agitated adjective
I felt agitated before my music exam.
- nervous, anxious, edgy, restless, fidgety, flustered, ruffled, disturbed, upset, unsettled
OPPOSITE calm, cool

agony noun
He screamed in agony when he broke his leg.
- pain, suffering, torture, torment, anguish, distress

agree verb
1 *I'm glad that we agree.*
- be united, think the same, concur
OPPOSITE disagree
2 *I agree that you are right.*
- accept, acknowledge, admit, grant, allow
OPPOSITE disagree

3 *I agree to pay my share.*
- consent, promise, be willing, undertake
OPPOSITE refuse

to agree on
We agreed on a price.
- decide, fix, settle, choose, establish

to agree with
1 *I don't agree with animal testing.*
- support, advocate, argue for, defend
2 *Onions don't agree with me.*
- suit

agreement noun
1 *There was agreement on the need for longer holidays.*
- consensus, unanimity, unity, consent, harmony, sympathy, conformity
OPPOSITE disagreement
2 *The two sides signed an agreement.*
- alliance, treaty
- An agreement to end fighting is an armistice or truce.
- A business agreement is a bargain, contract, or deal.

ahead adverb
1 *They sent a messenger ahead with the news.*
- in advance, in front, before
2 *I stared ahead, trying to see through the mist.*
- forwards, to the front

aid noun
1 *We can climb out with the aid of this rope.*
- help, support, assistance, backing, cooperation
2 *They agreed to send more aid to the poorer countries.*
- donations, subsidies, contributions

aid verb
The local people aided the police in their investigation.
- help, assist, support, back, collaborate with, cooperate with, contribute to, lend a hand to, further, promote, subsidize

a
b
c
d
e
f
g
h
i
j
k
l
m
n
o
p
q
r
s
t
u
v
w
x
y
z

aim noun
*What was the **aim** of the experiment?*
- ambition, desire, dream, goal, hope, intention, objective, purpose, target, wish

aim verb
1 *She **aims** to be a professional dancer.*
- intend, mean, plan, propose, want, wish, seek
2 *He **aimed** his bow and arrow at the target.*
- point, direct, take aim with, line up, level, train, focus

air noun
1 *We shouldn't pollute the **air** we breathe.*
- atmosphere
2 *This room needs some **air**.*
- fresh air, ventilation
3 *She was singing a traditional **air**.*
- song, tune, melody
4 *There was an **air** of mystery about the place.*
- feeling, mood, look, appearance, sense

air verb
1 *He opened the window to **air** the room.*
- freshen, refresh, ventilate
2 *I have a right to **air** my opinions.*
- express, make known, make public, reveal, voice

aircraft noun

> **WORD WEB**
>
> SOME TYPES OF AIRCRAFT
> aeroplane, airliner, airship, biplane, bomber, fighter, glider, helicopter, hot-air balloon, jet, jumbo jet, seaplane
>
> PARTS OF AIRCRAFT
> cabin, cargo hold, cockpit, engine, fin, flap, flight deck, fuselage, joystick, passenger cabin, propeller, rotor, rudder, tail, tailplane, undercarriage, wing
>
> PLACES WHERE AIRCRAFT TAKE OFF AND LAND
> aerodrome, airfield, airport, airstrip, helipad, heliport, landing strip, runway

> PEOPLE WHO FLY IN AIRCRAFT
> pilot, aviator, balloonist; co-pilot, cabin crew, flight attendant, passengers

airy adjective
*Our hotel room was pleasantly light and **airy**.*
- fresh, breezy, ventilated
OPPOSITE stuffy, close

alarm verb
*The barking dog **alarmed** the sheep.*
- frighten, startle, scare, panic, agitate, distress, shock, surprise, upset, worry
OPPOSITE reassure

alarm noun
1 *Did you hear the **alarm**?*
- signal, alert, warning, siren
2 *The sudden noise filled me with **alarm**.*
- fright, fear, panic, anxiety, apprehension, distress, nervousness, terror, uneasiness

alarming adjective
*We have received some **alarming** news.*
- frightening, scary, terrifying, shocking, startling

alert adjective
*The guards were told to stay **alert** at all times.*
- vigilant, watchful, sharp, observant, attentive, awake, careful, on the alert, on the lookout, ready, wary, wide awake
- A phrase meaning 'to stay alert' is to keep your eyes peeled.
OPPOSITE inattentive

alert verb
*We **alerted** them to the danger.*
- make aware, warn, notify, inform, signal, tip off

alien adjective
1 *The desert landscape looked **alien** to us.*
- strange, foreign, unfamiliar, different, exotic
OPPOSITE familiar

a
b
c
d
e
f
g
h
i
j
k
l
m
n
o
p
q
r
s
t
u
v
w
x
y
z

2 *They saw the lights of an **alien** spaceship.*
- extraterrestrial

alien noun

WORD WEB

*I wrote a story about **aliens** from Mars.*
- extraterrestrial, alien life-form, spaceman or spacewoman, starman or starwoman

AN ALIEN FROM ANOTHER PLANET MIGHT BE
humanoid, insect-like, lizard-like, reptilian, intelligent, primitive, super-intelligent, telepathic

BODY PARTS AN ALIEN MIGHT HAVE
antenna, blotches, scales, slime, sucker, tentacle, webbing

TRANSPORT AN ALIEN MIGHT USE
alien vessel, flying saucer, mothership, pod, spacecraft, spaceship, starship, time-machine, transporter beam

- An alien might call someone from Earth an Earthling.
SEE ALSO **planet, space**

alight adjective
*The bonfire was still **alight**.*
- burning, lit, on fire, ignited

alike adjective
*All the houses in the street looked **alike**.*
- similar, the same, identical, indistinguishable, comparable, uniform

alive adjective
*Fortunately, my goldfish was still **alive**.*
- living, live, existing, in existence, surviving, breathing, flourishing
OPPOSITE dead

alliance noun
*The two countries formed an **alliance**.*
- partnership, union, association, federation, league
- An alliance between political parties is a coalition.

allocate verb
*I **allocated** some pocket money for buying presents.*
- allot, assign, set aside, reserve, earmark

allow verb
1 *They don't **allow** skateboards in the playground.*
- permit, let, authorize, approve of, agree to, consent to, give permission for, license, put up with, stand, support, tolerate
OPPOSITE forbid
2 *Have you **allowed** enough time for the journey?*
- allocate, set aside, assign, grant, earmark

all right adjective
1 *The survivors appeared to be **all right**.*
- well, unhurt, unharmed, uninjured, safe
2 *The food in the hotel was **all right**.*
- satisfactory, acceptable, adequate, reasonable, passable
3 *Is it **all right** to play music in here?*
- acceptable, permissable

ally noun
*The two countries work together as **allies**.*
- friend, partner
OPPOSITE enemy

almost adverb
1 *I have **almost** finished the crossword.*
- nearly, practically, just about, virtually, all but, as good as, not quite
2 ***Almost** a hundred people came to the concert.*
- about, approximately, around

alone adjective, adverb
1 *Did you go to the party **alone**?*
- on your own, by yourself, unaccompanied
2 *Zoe had no friends and felt very **alone**.*
- lonely, friendless, isolated, solitary, lonesome, desolate

also adverb
*We need some bread, and **also** more butter.*
- in addition, besides, additionally, too, furthermore, moreover

alter verb
*They have **altered** the route for the cycle race.*
- change, adjust, adapt, modify, transform, amend, make different, revise, vary

alternative noun
*I lost my bus money and had no **alternative** but to walk.*
- choice, option

altogether adverb
1 *I'm not **altogether** satisfied.*
- completely, entirely, absolutely, quite, totally, utterly, wholly, fully, perfectly, thoroughly
2 *Our house has five rooms **altogether**.*
- in all, in total, all told

always adverb
1 *The sea is **always** in motion.*
- constantly, continuously, endlessly, eternally, for ever, perpetually, unceasingly
2 *This bus is **always** late.*
- consistently, continually, invariably, persistently, regularly, repeatedly

amateur noun
*All the players in this team are unpaid **amateurs**.*
OPPOSITE professional

amaze verb
*It **amazes** me to think that the Earth is billions of years old.*
- astonish, astound, startle, surprise, stun, shock, stagger, dumbfound
- (*informal*) flabbergast

amazed adjective
*I was **amazed** by the number of emails I received.*
- astonished, astounded, stunned, surprised, dumbfounded, speechless, staggered
- (*informal*) flabbergasted

amazing adjective
*The Northern Lights are an **amazing** sight.*
- astonishing, astounding, staggering, remarkable, surprising, extraordinary, incredible, breathtaking, phenomenal, sensational, stupendous, tremendous, wonderful, mind-boggling

ambition noun
1 *She had great **ambition** when she was young.*
- drive, enthusiasm, enterprise, push, zeal
2 *My **ambition** is to play tennis at Wimbledon.*
- goal, aim, intention, objective, target, desire, dream, wish, hope, aspiration

ambitious adjective
1 *If you're **ambitious**, you will probably succeed.*
- enterprising, enthusiastic, committed, go-ahead, keen
OPPOSITE unambitious
2 *I think your plan is too **ambitious**.*
- grand, big, large-scale

amend verb
*I **amended** the letter to make it clearer.*
- change, alter, adjust, modify, revise

among preposition
*We played hide-and-seek **among** the bushes.*
- between, amid, in, in the middle of, surrounded by

amount noun
1 *Mum wrote a cheque for the correct **amount**.*
- sum, total, whole
2 *There's a large **amount** of paper in the cupboard.*
- quantity, measure, supply, volume, mass, bulk

a
b
c
d
e
f
g
h
i
j
k
l
m
n
o
p
q
r
s
t
u
v
w
x
y
z

a
b
c
d
e
f
g
h
i
j
k
l
m
n
o
p
q
r
s
t
u
v
w
x
y
z

amount verb
to amount to
*What does the bill **amount to**?*
- add up to, come to, total, equal, make

amphibian noun

WORD WEB

SOME ANIMALS WHICH ARE AMPHIBIANS
bullfrog, frog, newt, salamander, toad, tree frog
FOR OTHER ANIMALS
SEE **animal**

ample adjective
1 *The car has an **ample** boot.*
- big, large, spacious, roomy
OPPOSITE small
2 *We had an **ample** supply of food.*
- abundant, plentiful, generous, substantial, considerable, profuse, lavish, liberal
OPPOSITE meagre
3 *No more juice, thanks—that's **ample**.*
- plenty, sufficient, lots, more than enough
- (*informal*) heaps, masses, loads, stacks
OPPOSITE insufficient

amuse verb
*I think this joke will **amuse** you.*
- make you laugh, entertain, cheer up, divert
- (*informal*) tickle

amusement noun
1 *What's your favourite **amusement**?*
- pastime, recreation, entertainment, diversion, game, hobby, interest, leisure activity, sport
2 *We tried not to show our **amusement**.*
- merriment, hilarity, laughter, mirth

amusing adjective
*I didn't find his jokes very **amusing**.*
- funny, witty, humorous, comic, comical, hilarious, diverting, entertaining
OPPOSITE unamusing, serious

analyse verb
*We **analysed** the results of our experiment.*
- examine, study, investigate, scrutinize

ancestor noun
*Our family's **ancestors** came from France.*
- forebear, forefather, predecessor
OPPOSITE descendant

ancestry noun
*She was proud of her African **ancestry**.*
- origins, descent, heredity, heritage, blood, extraction, pedigree, stock

ancient adjective
1 *Does that **ancient** car still go?*
- old, old-fashioned, antiquated, out of date, obsolete
2 *In **ancient** times, our ancestors were hunters.*
- early, primitive, prehistoric, remote, long past, olden
- The times before written records were kept are prehistoric times.
- The ancient Greeks and Romans lived in classical times.
OPPOSITE modern

anger noun
*I was filled with **anger** when I read her letter.*
- rage, fury, indignation
- (*old use*) wrath, ire
- An outburst of anger is a tantrum or a temper.

anger verb
*His cruelty towards his dog **angered** me.*
- enrage, infuriate, incense, madden, annoy, irritate, exasperate, antagonize, provoke
- (*informal*) make your blood boil, make you see red
OPPOSITE pacify

angle noun
1 *He wore a top hat set at a slight **angle**.*
- slope, slant, tilt

2 *Let's look at the problem from a different **angle**.*
- viewpoint, point of view, perspective

angry adjective
*Miss Potts turns purple when she gets **angry**.*
- cross, furious, enraged, infuriated, irate, livid, annoyed, incensed, exasperated, fuming, indignant, raging, seething
- (*informal*) mad
- To become angry is to lose your temper.

OPPOSITE calm

angry adjective

WRITING TIPS
- Someone who *GETS ANGRY* might: blow a fuse, blow their top, fly off the handle, have a face like thunder, have steam coming out of their ears, hit the roof, see red

FOR THINGS AN ANGRY PERSON MIGHT SAY

SEE **exclamation**

animal noun

WORD WEB
*Wild **animals** roam freely in the safari park.*
- creature, beast, brute
- A word for wild animals in general is wildlife.
- A scientific word for animals is fauna.

VARIOUS KINDS OF ANIMAL
amphibian, arachnid, bird, fish, insect, invertebrate, mammal, marsupial, mollusc, reptile, rodent, vertebrate
- An animal that eats meat is a carnivore.
- An animal that eats plants is a herbivore.
- An animal that eats many things is an omnivore.
- Animals that sleep most of the winter are hibernating animals.
- Animals that are active at night are nocturnal animals.

SOME ANIMALS THAT LIVE ON LAND
aardvark, antelope, ape, armadillo, baboon, badger, bat, bear, beaver, bison, buffalo, camel, cheetah, chimpanzee, chinchilla, chipmunk, deer, dormouse, elephant, elk, fox, gazelle, gibbon, giraffe, gnu, gorilla, grizzly bear, hare, hedgehog, hippopotamus, hyena, jackal, jaguar, kangaroo, koala, lemming, lemur, leopard, lion, llama, lynx, mongoose, monkey, moose, mouse, ocelot, opossum, orang-utan, otter, panda, panther, platypus, polar bear, porcupine, rabbit, rat, reindeer, rhinoceros, skunk, squirrel, stoat, tapir, tiger, vole, wallaby, weasel, wildebeest, wolf, wolverine, wombat, yak, zebra

FOR ANIMALS COMMONLY KEPT AS PETS
SEE **pet**
SEE ALSO **amphibian, bird, fish, insect, reptile**

SOME ANIMALS THAT LIVE IN THE SEA
dolphin, porpoise, seal, sea lion, walrus, whale

SOME EXTINCT ANIMALS
dinosaur, dodo, quagga
SEE ALSO **dinosaur**

PARTS OF AN ANIMAL'S BODY
antler, claw, fang, foreleg, hindleg, hoof, horn, jaws, mane, muzzle, paw, snout, tail, trotter, tusk, whisker, fur, coat, fleece, hide, pelt

MALE AND FEMALE ANIMALS
- A male elephant or whale is a bull and a female is a cow.
- A male fox is a dog and a female is a vixen.
- A male goat is a billy goat and a female is a nanny goat.
- A male hare or rabbit is a buck and a female is a doe.
- A male horse is a stallion and a female is a mare.
- A female lion is a lioness.
- A female pig is a sow.
- A male sheep is a ram and a female is a ewe.
- A female tiger is a tigress.
- A male wolf is a dog and a female is a bitch.

SEE ALSO **cat, cattle, deer, dog**

YOUNG ANIMALS
- A young beaver is a kit.
- A young fox or lion is a cub.
- A young goat is a kid.
- A young hare is a leveret.
- A young horse is a foal, colt (male), or filly (female).
- A young pig is a piglet.
- A young otter or seal is a pup.
- A young sheep is a lamb.

SEE ALSO **cat**, **cattle**, **deer**, **dog**

HOMES OF WILD ANIMALS
den, lair
- A badger lives in a sett.
- A beaver or otter lives in a lodge.
- A fox lives in an earth.
- A rabbit lives in a burrow or warren.
- A squirrel lives in a drey.

SOUNDS MADE BY ANIMALS
bark, bay, bellow, buzz, gnash, growl, grunt, hiss, howl, jabber, purr, roar, snap, snarl, snort, snuffle, squeak, trumpet, whimper, whine, yap, yelp, yowl
- A sheep bleats.
- A donkey brays.
- A frog croaks.
- Cattle low or moo.
- A cat mews or miaows.
- A horse neighs or whinnies.

FOR NAMES FOR GROUPS OF ANIMALS
SEE **group**

WRITING TIPS

You can use these words to describe an *animal*.
- to describe *HOW AN ANIMAL MOVES*:
bound, creep, crouch, dart, gallop, gambol, leap, lumber, nuzzle, pad, paw, pounce, roam, scuttle, skip, slink, slither, spring, stamp, stampede, trot, waddle
*The jaguar **padded** along silently.*
- to describe *AN ANIMAL'S BODY*:
agile, nimble, sinewy, wiry; lumbering, majestic, mighty, muscular, powerful

*The cheetah stretched its long, **sinewy** body.*
- to describe *AN ANIMAL'S SKIN* or *COAT*:
coarse, fluffy, furry, glistening, glossy, hairy, leathery, matted, prickly, scaly, shaggy, shiny, silky, sleek, slimy, slippery, smooth, spiky, thick, thorny, tough, wiry, woolly; mottled, piebald, spotted, striped
*The otters' coats were **smooth** and **silky**.*

anniversary noun

WORD WEB
- The anniversary of the day you were born is your birthday.
- The anniversary of the day someone was married is their wedding anniversary.

SPECIAL ANNIVERSARIES
centenary (100 years), sesquicentenary (150 years), bicentenary (200 years), tercentenary (300 years), quatercentenary (400 years), quincentenary (500 years), millenary (1000 years)

SPECIAL WEDDING ANNIVERSARIES
silver wedding (25 years), ruby wedding (40 years), golden wedding (50 years), diamond wedding (60 years)

announce verb

1 *The head **announced** that sports day was cancelled.*
- declare, state, proclaim, report

2 *The DJ **announced** the next record.*
- present, introduce, lead into

announcement noun

1 *The head reads the **announcements** in assembly.*
- notice

2 *The prime minister issued an **announcement**.*
- statement, declaration, proclamation, pronouncement

3 *I heard the **announcement** on TV.*
- report, bulletin, news flash

annoy verb
1 *I was **annoyed** that I missed the bus.*
- irritate, bother, displease, exasperate, anger, upset, vex, trouble, worry
OPPOSITE please

2 *Please don't **annoy** me while I'm working.*
- pester, bother, harass, badger, nag, plague, trouble, try
- (*informal*) bug

annoyance noun
1 *Mrs Grant's face showed her **annoyance**.*
- irritation, anger, exasperation, vexation

2 *Is the dog an **annoyance** to you?*
- nuisance, bother, trouble, worry

annoying adjective
*My brother has a lot of **annoying** habits.*
- irritating, exasperating, maddening, provoking, tiresome, trying, vexing, troublesome

anonymous adjective
1 *An **anonymous** donor gave the school some money.*
- unnamed, nameless, unidentified, unknown

2 *I received an **anonymous** letter.*
- unsigned

answer noun
1 *Did you get an **answer** to your letter?*
- reply, response, acknowledgement, reaction
- A quick or angry answer is a retort

2 *The **answers** to the quiz are on the next page.*
- solution, explanation

answer verb
1 *You haven't **answered** my question.*
- give an answer to, reply to, respond to, react to, acknowledge

2 *'I'm quite well,' I **answered**.*
- reply, respond, return
- To answer quickly or angrily is to retort.

to answer back
*She doesn't like it when I **answer back**.*
- argue, protest, object

anthology noun SEE **collection**

anticipate verb
*I **anticipate** that the result will be a draw.*
- expect, predict, forecast, foretell

antiquated adjective
*That washing machine is really **antiquated**.*
- ancient, aged, old-fashioned, out of date, outdated, obsolete
OPPOSITE new, up-to-date

antique adjective
*The palace was full of **antique** furniture.*
- old, old-fashioned
- Antique cars are veteran or vintage cars

anxiety noun
1 *We waited for news with a growing sense of **anxiety**.*
- apprehension, concern, worry, fear, nervousness, dread, tension, strain, stress, uncertainty, doubt,
OPPOSITE calmness

2 *In his **anxiety** to win, he started before the gun went off.*
- eagerness, keenness, desire, impatience, enthusiasm

anxious adjective
1 *Are you **anxious** about your exams?*
- nervous, worried, apprehensive, concerned, uneasy, fearful, edgy, fraught, tense, troubled
- (*informal*) uptight, jittery
OPPOSITE calm

2 *I'm **anxious** to do my best.*
- eager, keen, impatient, enthusiastic, willing

apologetic adjective
*The shopkeeper was **apologetic** about his mistake.*
- sorry, repentant, remorseful, regretful, penitent, contrite
OPPOSITE unrepentant

a
b
c
d
e
f
g
h
i
j
k
l
m
n
o
p
q
r
s
t
u
v
w
x
y
z

a
b
c
d
e
f
g
h
i
j
k
l
m
n
o
p
q
r
s
t
u
v
w
x
y
z

apologize verb
*The ogre **apologized** for being rude.*
- make an apology, say sorry, express regret, repent, be penitent

appal verb
*They were **appalled** by conditions in the prison.*
- disgust, revolt, shock, sicken, horrify, distress

appalling adjective
1 *He suffered **appalling** injuries in the accident.*
- distressing, dreadful, frightful, gruesome, horrible, horrific, horrifying, shocking, sickening, revolting

2 *This handwriting is **appalling**—I can barely read it.*
- bad, awful, terrible, deplorable, disgraceful, unsatisfactory, atrocious
- (informal) abysmal

apparent adjective
*There was no **apparent** reason for the crash.*
- obvious, evident, clear, noticeable, detectable, perceptible, recognizable, conspicuous, visible
- OPPOSITE concealed

appeal verb
to appeal for
*The prisoners **appealed for** our help.*
- request, beg for, plead for, cry out for, entreat, ask earnestly for, pray for

to appeal to
*That kind of music doesn't **appeal to** me.*
- attract, interest, fascinate, tempt

appeal noun
1 *Did you hear their **appeal** for help?*
- request, call, cry, entreaty
- An appeal signed by a lot of people is a petition.

2 *Baby animals always have great **appeal**.*
- attractiveness, interest, charm, fascination

appear verb
1 *Snowdrops **appear** in the spring.*
- come out, emerge, become visible, come into view, develop, occur, show, crop up, spring up, surface

2 *Our visitors didn't **appear** until midnight.*
- arrive, come, turn up
- (informal) show up

3 *It **appears** that the baby is asleep.*
- seem, look

4 *I once **appeared** in a musical.*
- act, perform, take part, feature

appearance noun
1 *They were startled by the **appearance** of the ghost.*
- approach, arrival, entrance, entry

2 *Mr Hogweed had a grim **appearance**.*
- air, aspect, bearing, look

appetite noun
1 *When I was ill, I completely lost my **appetite**.*
- hunger

2 *Explorers have a great **appetite** for adventure.*
- desire, eagerness, enthusiasm, passion, keenness, wish, urge, taste, thirst, longing, yearning, craving, lust, zest

appetizing adjective
*The **appetizing** smell of baking filled the house.*
- delicious, tasty, tempting, mouth-watering
- SEE ALSO food

applaud verb
*The audience laughed and **applauded**.*
- clap, cheer
- OPPOSITE boo

application noun
1 *Have you sent in our **application** for a refund?*
- request, claim

2 *The job needs a lot of patience and **application**.*
- effort, commitment, dedication, perseverance, persistence, devotion

apply verb

1 *The nurse told me to **apply** the ointment generously.*
- administer, put on, lay on, spread

2 *My brother has **applied** for a new job.*
- make an application for, ask for, request

3 *The rules **apply** to all our members.*
- be relevant, relate, refer

4 *The vet **applied** all her skill to save the animal's life.*
- use, employ, exercise, utilize

appoint verb

1 *The school governors **appointed** a new teacher.*
- choose, select, elect, vote for, settle on

2 *We **appointed** a time for our meeting.*
- arrange, decide on, fix, settle, determine

appointment noun

1 *I have an **appointment** to meet the bank manager.*
- arrangement, engagement, date

2 *The team are waiting for the **appointment** of a new captain.*
- naming, selection, choice, choosing, election

3 *My uncle got a new **appointment** overseas.*
- job, post, position, situation

appreciate verb

1 *He **appreciates** good music.*
- enjoy, like, love

2 *I **appreciate** her good qualities.*
- admire, respect, regard highly, approve of, value, esteem
- OPPOSITE despise

3 *I **appreciate** that you can't afford much.*
- realize, recognize, understand, comprehend, know, see

4 *Dad hopes that the value of our house will **appreciate**.*
- grow, increase, go up, mount, rise

apprehensive adjective

*Are you **apprehensive** about your exams?*
- worried, anxious, nervous, tense, edgy, uneasy, troubled, frightened, fearful

approach verb

1 *The lioness **approached** her prey.*
- draw near to, move towards, come near to, advance on

2 *I **approached** the head to ask if we could have a party.*
- speak to, contact, go to

3 *The volunteers **approached** their work cheerfully.*
- begin, undertake, embark on, set about

approach noun

1 *We could hear the **approach** of heavy footsteps.*
- arrival, advance, coming

2 *Dad made an **approach** to the bank manager for a loan.*
- application, appeal, proposal

3 *I like her positive **approach**.*
- attitude, manner, style, way

4 *The easiest **approach** to the castle is from the west.*
- access, entry, entrance, way in

appropriate adjective

*It's not **appropriate** to wear jeans to a wedding.*
- suitable, proper, fitting, apt, right, tactful, tasteful, well-judged
- OPPOSITE inappropriate

approval noun

1 *We cheered to show our **approval**.*
- appreciation, admiration, praise, high regard, acclaim, respect, support
- OPPOSITE disapproval

2 *The head gave her **approval** to our plan.*
- agreement, consent, authorization, assent, go-ahead, permission, support, blessing
- OPPOSITE refusal

approve verb

*The head **approved** my request for a day off school.*

- agree to, consent to, authorize, allow, accept, pass, permit, support, back

OPPOSITE refuse

to approve of

*Her family did not **approve of** her marriage.*

- like, favour, welcome, appreciate, admire, value, praise, commend, applaud, respect, esteem

OPPOSITE condemn

approximate adjective

*What is the **approximate** length of the journey?*

- estimated, rough, inexact, near

OPPOSITE exact

approximately adverb

*The film will finish at **approximately** five o'clock.*

- roughly, about, around, round about, close to, nearly, more or less

apt adjective

1 *He is **apt** to be careless with money.*
- likely, liable, inclined, prone
2 *Your comments on my essay were very **apt**.*
- appropriate, suitable, proper, fitting, right, well-judged, pertinent
- (*informal*) spot on
3 *She turned out to be a very **apt** pupil.*
- clever, quick, bright, sharp

aptitude noun

*He has a remarkable **aptitude** for music.*

- talent, gift, ability, skill, expertise, potential, bent

arch verb

*The cat **arched** its back.*
- curve, bend, bow

arch noun

*They saw the **arch** of a rainbow in the sky.*
- curve, arc, bend, bow

archer noun SEE arrow

arctic adjective SEE polar

area noun

1 *From the plane we saw a big **area** of desert.*
- expanse, stretch, tract
- A small area is a patch.
- An area of water or ice is a sheet.
2 *I live in an urban **area**.*
- district, locality, neighbourhood, region, zone, vicinity

arena noun FOR PLACES WHERE SPORT TAKES PLACE

SEE sport

argue verb

1 *You two are always **arguing** over something.*
- quarrel, disagree, differ, fall out, fight, have an argument, squabble, wrangle, bicker

OPPOSITE agree

2 *We **argued** over the price of the cloth.*
- bargain, haggle
3 *He **argued** that it was my turn to walk the dog.*
- claim, assert, try to prove, maintain, reason, suggest

to argue about something

*We could **argue** for hours **about** football.*

- debate, discuss

argument noun

1 *They was an **argument** over who should pay for the meal.*
- disagreement, quarrel, dispute, row, clash, controversy, debate, difference, fight, squabble, altercation
2 *Did you follow the **argument** of the book?*
- line of reasoning, theme, outline, gist

arid adjective

*No plants could grow in the **arid** soil.*

- dry, parched, barren, waterless, lifeless, infertile, sterile, unproductive

OPPOSITE fruitful

arise verb

1 *We can phone for help if the need **arises**.*
- occur, emerge, develop, ensue, appear, come into existence, come up, crop up, happen

2 *(old use) '**Arise**, Sir Lancelot!' said the King.*
- stand up, get up

arm noun

*The skeleton held out a bony **arm**.*

FOR PARTS OF YOUR BODY

SEE **body**

arm verb

*The boys **armed** themselves with sticks.*
- equip, supply, provide

armed services plural noun

> **WORD WEB**
>
> THE PRINCIPAL ARMED SERVICES ARE
> air force, army, navy
> - Men and women in the services are troops.
> - A new serviceman or servicewoman is a recruit.
> - A young person training to be in the armed services is a cadet.
>
> VARIOUS GROUPS IN THE ARMED SERVICES
> battalion, brigade, company, corps, fleet, garrison, legion, patrol, platoon, regiment, squad, squadron
>
> SERVICEMEN AND SERVICEWOMEN INCLUDE
> aircraftman, aircraftwoman, commando, marine, paratrooper, sailor, soldier
> SEE ALSO **soldier**

armour noun

> **WORD WEB**
>
> PARTS OF A MEDIEVAL KNIGHT'S ARMOUR
> breastplate, cuirass (breast and back plate), gauntlet, greave (shin guard), habergeon (sleeveless coat), helmet, visor
> - Armour made of linked rings is chain mail.

> - An outfit of armour is a suit of armour.
> SEE ALSO **knight**

arms plural noun

*The bandits were equipped with **arms**.*
- weapons, guns, firearms, ammunition

army noun SEE **armed services**

aroma noun

*The **aroma** of lavender filled the air.*
- smell, scent, odour, fragrance, perfume

around preposition

1 *The mermaid wore a coral necklace **around** her neck.*
- about, round, encircling, surrounding

2 *There were **around** a hundred people in the audience.*
- about, approximately, roughly, more or less

arouse verb

*The plan to build a supermarket **aroused** strong feelings.*
- cause, generate, evoke, stir up, excite, stimulate, incite, provoke, lead to, produce, set off, whip up
OPPOSITE calm, quell

arrange verb

1 *The books are **arranged** in alphabetical order.*
- sort, order, put in order, group, organize, categorize, classify, collate, display, sort out, set out, lay out, line up

2 *Do you need any help **arranging** the party?*
- plan, organize, prepare, set up, see to

arrangement noun

1 *They have improved the **arrangement** of the garden.*
- layout, organization, design, planning

2 *Did you change the **arrangement** of my CDs?*
- order, grouping, display, distribution, spacing

3 *We have an **arrangement** to use the swimming pool.*
- agreement, deal, bargain, contract, scheme

arrest verb

1 *The police **arrested** two men yesterday.*
- seize, capture, detain, apprehend, hold, take prisoner, take into custody, catch
- (*informal*) nick

2 *Doctors are trying to **arrest** the spread of the disease.*
- stop, prevent, halt, hinder, check, delay

arrive verb

*When is the train due to **arrive**?*
- appear, come, turn up, show up, get in
- When a plane arrives it lands or touches down.

to arrive at

*We **arrived at** the castle before midnight.*
- get to, reach

arrogant adjective

*His **arrogant** manner annoys me.*
- boastful, conceited, proud, haughty, self-important, bumptious, pompous, snobbish, superior, vain
- (*informal*) cocky, snooty, stuck-up
- OPPOSITE modest

arrow noun

- The spine of an arrow is the shaft.
- The point of an arrow is the arrowhead.
- Arrows are shot using a bow.
- A holder for several arrows is a quiver.
- The sport of shooting arrows at a target is archery.
- Someone who practises archery is an archer.

art noun

1 *The **art** of writing letters is disappearing fast.*
- skill, craft, technique, talent, knack, trick

2 *She took a course in **art** and design.*
- artwork, fine art

art noun

 WORD WEB

SOME ARTS AND CRAFTS
animation, basketry, batik, beadwork, carpentry, carving, collage, crochet, cross-stitch, decoupage, drawing, embroidery, enamelling, engraving, etching, graphics, illustration, jewellery, knitting, metalwork, modelling, mosaics, needlework, origami, painting, patchwork, photography, pottery, printing, quilting, screen printing, sculpture, sewing, sketching, spinning, stained glass, stamping, stencilling, tapestry, weaving, woodwork
FOR PEOPLE WHO WORK IN ARTS AND CRAFTS
SEE **artist**

article noun

1 *Have you any **articles** for the jumble sale?*
- item, object, thing

2 *Did you read my **article** in the magazine?*
- essay, report, piece of writing

artificial adjective

1 *Organic gardeners don't use **artificial** fertilizers.*
- man-made, synthetic, unnatural, manufactured
- OPPOSITE natural

2 *She had an **artificial** flower in her buttonhole.*
- fake, false, imitation, unreal, bogus, counterfeit
- OPPOSITE genuine, real

3 *Captain Hook gave us an **artificial** smile.*
- pretended, sham, affected, simulated
- (*informal*) put on
- OPPOSITE genuine, natural

artist noun

 WORD WEB

SOME ARTISTS AND CRAFTSPEOPLE
animator, blacksmith, carpenter,

cartoonist, designer, draughtsman, draughtswoman, embroiderer, engraver, goldsmith, graphic designer, illustrator, knitter, mason, painter, photographer, potter, printer, quilter, sculptor, silversmith, weaver
FOR PERFORMING ARTISTS
SEE **entertainer**

artistic adjective
Mum's flower arrangements are very **artistic**.
- creative, imaginative, aesthetic, attractive, beautiful, tasteful
OPPOSITE ugly

ascend verb
1 It took the rescuers a long time to **ascend** the mountain.
- climb, go up, mount, move up, scale
2 The plane began to **ascend**.
- lift off, take off
3 The eagle **ascended** into the air.
- fly up, rise, soar
OPPOSITE descend

ascent noun
The bus moved slowly up the steep **ascent**.
- climb, rise, slope, hill, gradient, incline, ramp
OPPOSITE descent

ashamed adjective
He was **ashamed** because of what he had done.
- sorry, remorseful, repentant, embarrassed, shamefaced, abashed, mortified apologetic, penitent
- (informal) red-faced
OPPOSITE unashamed, unrepentant

ashes plural noun
Next morning, the **ashes** of the bonfire were still glowing.
- embers, cinders

ask verb
1 I **asked** them to be careful with the parcel.
- beg, entreat, appeal to, implore, plead with

2 'Are you ready?' I **asked**.
- demand, enquire, inquire, query, question
3 I'm going to **ask** you to my party.
- invite
- (formal) request the pleasure of your company

to ask for
1 The musician **asked for** silence.
- request, appeal for, call for, demand, order, seek
2 He was **asking for** trouble!
- encourage, attract, cause, provoke, stir up

asleep adjective
I didn't hear the phone because I was **asleep**.
- sleeping, dozing, having a nap, napping
- (formal) slumbering
- A patient asleep for an operation is anaesthetized or under sedation.
- An animal asleep for the winter is hibernating.
OPPOSITE awake

to fall asleep
We waited until the giant **fell asleep**.
- drop off, doze, nod off
- To fall asleep quickly is to go out like a light.

aspect noun
1 The book describes some **aspects** of life in ancient Rome.
- part, feature, element, angle, detail, side, facet
2 The ruined tower had an unfriendly **aspect**.
- appearance, look, manner, air, expression, face, countenance
3 The front room has a southern **aspect**.
- outlook, view, prospect

assault noun
The old lady was the victim of a serious **assault**.
- attack, mugging

assault verb
It's a serious crime to **assault** a policeman.
- attack, strike, hit, beat up, mug

a
b
c
d
e
f
g
h
i
j
k
l
m
n
o
p
q
r
s
t
u
v
w
x
y
z

assemble verb
1 *A crowd **assembled** to watch the rescue.*
- gather, come together, converge, accumulate, crowd together, flock together, meet, convene
OPPOSITE disperse

2 *We **assembled** our luggage at the front door.*
- collect, gather, bring together, pile up, put together

3 *The general **assembled** his troops.*
- round up, rally, muster

assembly noun
*There was a large **assembly** of people in the market square.*
- gathering, meeting, crowd, throng
- An assembly for worship is a service.
- A large assembly to show support for something, often out of doors, is a rally.
- An assembly to discuss political matters is a council or parliament.
- An assembly to discuss and learn about a particular topic is a conference or congress.

assent noun
*The pirates gave their **assent** to the plan.*
- agreement, approval, consent, go-ahead, permission
OPPOSITE refusal

assert verb
*The prisoner **asserted** that he was innocent.*
- state, claim, contend, declare, argue, insist, maintain, proclaim, insist, protest, swear, testify

assess verb
*The test will **assess** your knowledge of French.*
- evaluate, determine, judge, estimate, measure, gauge, value, weigh up

asset noun
*Good health is a great **asset**.*
- advantage, benefit, help, blessing

assign verb
*He **assigned** the difficult jobs to the older children.*
- allocate, allot, give, consign, hand over, distribute, share out

assignment noun
*The spy was given a tough **assignment**.*
- job, task, pice of work, mission, project, duty, responsibility

assist verb
*We were asked to **assist** the gardener with the weeding.*
- help, aid, support, cooperate with, collaborate with
OPPOSITE hinder

assistance noun
1 *Do you need **assistance** with your luggage?*
- help, aid, support, encouragement

2 *We bought new sports equipment with the **assistance** of a local firm.*
- backing, collaboration, cooperation, sponsorship, subsidy, support

assistant noun
*The magician was training a new **assistant**.*
- helper, partner, colleague, associate, supporter

associate verb
to associate one thing with another
*I **associate** Christmas **with** holly and snow.*
- connect with, identify with, link with, relate to
to associate with someone
*I don't think you should **associate with** those people!*
- be friends with, go about with, mix with

association noun
1 *We have started a junior tennis **association**.*
- club, society, group, league, fellowship, partnership, union, alliance
- A political association is a party.
- A business association is a company or organization.

2 *The **association** between the two men lasted many years.*

- friendship, relationship, link, partnership, closeness

assorted adjective
*I bought a bag of sweets with **assorted** flavours.*

- various, different, mixed, diverse, miscellaneous, several

assortment noun
*There was an **assortment** of sandwiches to choose from.*

- variety, mixture, selection, array, choice, collection, diversity

assume verb
1 *I **assume** you'd like some chocolate.*

- suppose, presume, imagine, believe, guess, expect, gather, suspect, think

2 *The bandit **assumed** a disguise.*

- put on, adopt, dress up in, wear

assure verb
*I **assure** you that I will take care of your dog.*

- promise, give your word to

astonish verb
*It **astonished** us to learn that the house was haunted.*

- amaze, astound, surprise, stagger, shock, dumbfound, leave speechless, startle, stun, take aback, take by surprise
- (*informal*) flabbergast, take your breath away

astonishing adjective
*The volcano was an **astonishing** sight.*

- amazing, astounding, staggering, remarkable, surprising, extraordinary, incredible, breathtaking, phenomenal, sensational, stupendous, tremendous, wonderful

astound verb SEE astonish

astounding adjective SEE astonishing

astronaut noun

WORD WEB

*The **astronauts** climbed aboard the space shuttle.*

- spaceman or spacewoman

THINGS AN ASTRONAUT MIGHT USE OR WEAR
spacesuit, jet pack, oxygen tank; gloves, helmet, moonboots or spaceboots, visor

PLACES AN ASTRONAUT MIGHT VISIT
alien planet, moonbase, spacelab, space shuttle, space station, starbase
SEE ALSO **moon, planet, space**

astronomy noun FOR WORDS USED IN ASTRONOMY
SEE **space**

athlete noun FOR EVENTS IN WHICH ATHLETES TAKE PART
SEE **athletics**

athletic adjective
*You need to be **athletic** to run in a marathon.*

- fit, active, energetic, strong, muscular, powerful, robust, sturdy, vigorous, well-built
- (*informal*) sporty
OPPOSITE feeble, puny

athletics noun

WORD WEB

SOME ATHLETIC EVENTS
cross-country, decathlon, discus, heptathlon, high jump, hurdles, javelin, long jump, marathon, pentathlon, pole vault, relay race, running, shot, sprinting, steeplechase, triathlon, triple jump
FOR OTHER SPORTS
SEE **sport**

atmosphere noun
1 *The **atmosphere** on Mars is unbreathable.*

- air, sky

2 *There was a happy **atmosphere** at the party.*
- feeling, mood, spirit

atrocious adjective
*Everyone was shocked by the **atrocious** crime.*
- wicked, terrible, dreadful, abominable, brutal, savage, barbaric, bloodthirsty, callous, cruel, diabolical, evil, fiendish, horrifying, merciless, outrageous, sadistic, terrible, vicious, villainous

attach verb
***Attach** this label to the parcel.*
- fasten, fix, join, tie, bind, secure, connect, link, couple, stick, affix, add, append
OPPOSITE detach

attached adjective
attached to
*The twins are very **attached to** each other.*
- fond of, close to, dear to, devoted to, loyal to, affectionate towards, friendly towards, loving towards
OPPOSITE hostile

attack noun
1 *The pirates' **attack** took us by surprise.*
- assault, strike, charge, rush, raid, ambush, invasion, onslaught
- An attack with big guns or bombs is a blitz or bombardment.
- An attack by planes is an air raid.
2 *The newspaper published an **attack** on his character.*
- criticism, outburst, abuse, tirade
3 *I had a sneezing **attack** in assembly.*
- bout, fit, spasm
- (*informal*) turn

attack verb
1 *The travellers were **attacked** by highwaymen.*
- assault, beat up, mug, set on, assail
- To attack someone else's territory is to invade or raid it.
- To attack someone from a hidden place is to ambush them.
- To attack the enemy with bombs or heavy guns is to bombard them.

- To attack by rushing at the enemy is to charge.
- To attack a place suddenly is to storm it.
- If an animal attacks you, it might savage you.
2 *He **attacked** her reputation.*
- abuse, criticize, denounce
OPPOSITE defend

attain verb
*The team **attained** a total of twelve gold medals.*
- get, obtain, reach, achieve, accomplish, gain

attempt verb
*They will **attempt** to reconstruct a Viking ship.*
- try, endeavour, strive, seek, aim, make an effort

attempt noun
*The pole vaulter cleared the bar at the first **attempt**.*
- try, effort
- (*informal*) shot, go

attend verb
*Are you going to **attend** the end-of-term concert?*
- go to, appear at, be present at
to attend to
1 *Please **attend** carefully **to** my instructions.*
- listen to, pay attention to, follow carefully, heed, mark, mind, note, notice, observe, think about
2 *Who will **attend to** the washing up?*
- deal with, see to
3 *The nurses **attended to** the wounded.*
- take care of, care for, look after, help, mind, tend

attention noun
1 *Please give your full **attention** to the teacher.*
- concentration, consideration, thought, observation, awareness, heed, concern
2 *The survivors need urgent medical **attention**.*
- treatment, care

attentive adjective
Drivers should be attentive at all times.
- alert, paying attention, watchful, vigilant, observant, careful, listening, on the alert, on the lookout, sharp-eyed, wary, wide awake

attitude noun
I'm trying to take a more positive attitude to life.
- outlook, approach, behaviour, stance, frame of mind, disposition, view, position, manner, mood

attract verb
1 *Do you think our exhibition will attract people?*
- interest, appeal to, fascinate, tempt, entice
2 *Baby animals attract big crowds at the zoo.*
- draw, pull in
OPPOSITE repel

attractive adjective
1 *Miranda was a very attractive young woman.*
- beautiful, pretty, good-looking, handsome, gorgeous, glamorous, striking, fetching, charming, lovely, delightful, pleasing, fascinating, captivating, enchanting
SEE ALSO **beautiful**
OPPOSITE unattractive, repulsive
2 *There are some attractive bargains in the sale.*
- appealing, agreeable, interesting, desirable, tempting, irresistible

audible adjective SEE **hear**

audience noun
The audience were enthralled by the jugglers.
- crowd, spectators
- The audience for a TV programme is the viewers.
- The audience for a radio programme is the listeners.

authentic adjective
1 *That is an authentic painting by Picasso.*
- genuine, real, actual
OPPOSITE counterfeit
2 *The book is an authentic account of life at sea.*
- accurate, truthful, reliable, true, honest, dependable, factual
OPPOSITE false

author noun SEE **writer**

authority noun
1 *I have the head's authority to go home early.*
- permission, consent, approval
2 *The king had the authority to execute the prisoners.*
- power, right, influence
3 *My uncle is an authority on steam trains.*
- expert, specialist

automatic adjective
1 *We took our car through the automatic car wash.*
- automated, mechanical, programmed, computerized
2 *My sneezing was an automatic response to the pepper.*
- instinctive, involuntary, impulsive, spontaneous, reflex, natural, unconscious, unthinking

available adjective
1 *There are no more seats available.*
- obtainable, free
2 *Is there a phone available in the library?*
- accessible, ready, usable, at hand, handy, within reach, convenient
OPPOSITE unavailable

average adjective
It was an average kind of day at school.
- everyday, ordinary, normal, typical, usual, regular, commonplace, familiar
OPPOSITE unusual, extraordinary

avid adjective
My sister is an avid reader.
- keen, eager, enthusiastic, passionate, ardent, fervent, zealous

avoid verb
1 *The driver tried hard to **avoid** the collision.*
- get out of the way of, avert, dodge, keep clear of, steer clear of, fend off, shun

2 *The outlaws **avoided** capture for months.*
- elude, evade, run away from, escape from

3 *How did you manage to **avoid** the washing up?*
- get out of, shirk

await verb
*I **await** your reply to my letter.*
- wait for, look out for, be ready for, expect, hope for

awake adjective
*Hester lay **awake** all night worrying.*
- wide awake, restless, sleepless, conscious, astir
- Not being able to sleep is to be suffering from insomnia.

OPPOSITE asleep

awaken verb
1 *Mum **awakened** us at seven.*
- wake, waken, rouse, arouse, call, alert

2 *The dragon will **awaken** at dawn.*
- wake up, become conscious, stir

award noun
*Kirsty got a national **award** for gymnastics.*
- prize, trophy, medal

award verb
*My friend was **awarded** first prize in the competition.*
- give, present, grant

aware adjective
aware of
*The spy was **aware of** the dangers of the mission.*
- acquainted with, conscious of, familiar with, informed about

OPPOSITE ignorant of

awful adjective
1 *The weather was **awful** last weekend.*
- bad, dreadful, terrible, appalling, dire, abysmal
- (*informal*) rubbish, lousy

2 *The teacher complained about our **awful** behaviour.*
- disgraceful, shameful, disobedient, naughty

3 *Cinderella's stepmother was an **awful** woman.*
- unpleasant, disagreeable, nasty, horrid, detestable, unkind, unfriendly

4 *The country was shocked by the **awful** crime.*
- horrifying, shocking, atrocious, abominable, outrageous

5 *I feel **awful** about forgetting your birthday.*
- sorry, ashamed, embarrassed, guilty, remorseful

FOR OTHER WAYS TO DESCRIBE SOMETHING BAD
SEE **bad**

awfully adverb
*It's **awfully** stuffy in this room.*
- very, extremely, dreadfully, terribly, extraordinarily, exceptionally

awkward adjective
1 *The parcel was an **awkward** shape.*
- bulky, inconvenient, unmanageable, unwieldy

OPPOSITE convenient

2 *The giant was very **awkward** with his knife and fork.*
- clumsy, unskilful, bungling

OPPOSITE skilful

3 *We found ourselves in a very **awkward** situation.*
- difficult, troublesome, trying, perplexing, tough

OPPOSITE straightforward, easy

4 *Are you trying to be **awkward**?*
- obstinate, stubborn, uncooperative, unhelpful, exasperating

OPPOSITE cooperative

5 *I felt **awkward** as I didn't know anyone at the party.*
- embarrassed, uncomfortable, uneasy, out of place

OPPOSITE comfortable, at ease

Bb

baby noun
- infant, child
- A baby who has just been born is a new-born.
- A baby just learning to walk is a toddler.
- The time when someone is a baby is their babyhood.

FOR NAMES OF BABY ANIMALS
  SEE **animal**

babyish adjective
My brother thinks that dolls are **babyish**.
- childish, immature, infantile
OPPOSITE grown-up, mature

back noun
We always sit at the **back** of the bus.
- end, rear, tail end
- The back of a ship is the stern.
- The back of an animal is the hindquarters, rear, or rump.
- The back of a piece of paper is the reverse.
OPPOSITE front

back adjective
The **back** door of the cabin was locked.
- end, rear, tail
- The back legs of an animal are its hind legs.
OPPOSITE front

back verb
1 A big lorry was **backing** into our driveway.
- go backwards, reverse
2 I'm **backing** the blue team to win the race.
- bet on, put money on
3 The council is **backing** the plan to build a skate park.
- support, sponsor, endorse

to back away
When the dog growled, the robber **backed away**.
- back off, retreat, give way, retire, recoil
OPPOSITE approach

to back out of something
The injured player may have to **back out of** the final.
- drop out of, withdraw from

to back someone up
Will you **back me up** if I need help?
- support, second

background noun
1 I drew a mermaid with the sea in the **background**.
OPPOSITE foreground
2 The first chapter deals with the **background** to the war.
- circumstances of, history of, lead-up to
3 My mother's family has a Swedish **background**.
- tradition, upbringing, ancestry

bad adjective
This has been a **bad** week for all of us.
- awful, horrible, terrible
OPPOSITE good, fine, excellent

bad adjective

⚠️ **OVERUSED WORD**

Try to vary the words you use for **bad**. Here are some other words you could use.
- for a **BAD PERSON**:
wicked, evil, cruel, malevolent, malicious, vicious, villainous, mean, nasty, beastly, monstrous, corrupt, deplorable, detestable, immoral, infamous, shameful, sinful
Gobo was a **detestable** king who was loathed by his subjects.
- A bad person is a scoundrel, rogue, or rascal.
- A bad character in a story or film is a villain or (informal) baddy.
OPPOSITE good, virtuous

a b c d e f g h i j k l m n o p q r s t u v w x y z

27

a
b
c
d
e
f
g
h
i
j
k
l
m
n
o
p
q
r
s
t
u
v
w
x
y
z

- for a *BAD ACCIDENT* or *BAD ILLNESS*:
serious, severe, grave, distressing,
acute
Ingrid has a **severe** *case of chickenpox.*
OPPOSITE minor
- for *BAD BEHAVIOUR*:
naughty, mischievous, disobedient,
disgraceful, wrong
That **mischievous** *kitten drank my
milk!*
OPPOSITE exemplary, angelic
- for a *BAD EXPERIENCE* or *BAD NEWS*:
unpleasant, unwelcome,
disagreeable, horrible, awful, terrible,
dreadful, horrific, appalling,
shocking, hideous, disastrous,
ghastly, frightful, abominable,
diabolical
The letter contained **disagreeable**
news.
- Another word for a bad
experience is an ordeal.
OPPOSITE good, excellent
- for a *BAD HABIT* or something that is
BAD FOR YOU:
harmful, damaging, dangerous,
undesirable, detrimental, injurious
Fizzy drinks can be **harmful** *to your
teeth.*
- for a *BAD PERFORMANCE* or *BAD WORK*:
poor, inferior, weak, unsatisfactory,
inadequate, incompetent, awful,
hopeless, terrible, useless, worthless,
abysmal, shoddy
(*informal*) rubbish
The worst part of the film is the
incompetent *acting.*
- for a *BAD SMELL* or *BAD TASTE*:
disgusting, revolting, repulsive,
sickening, nauseating, repugnant,
foul, loathsome, offensive, vile
A **nauseating** *smell wafted from the
kitchen.*
OPPOSITE pleasant, appetizing
- for *BAD TIMING*:
inconvenient, unsuitable,
unfortunate, inappropriate
You've caught me at an **inconvenient**
moment.
OPPOSITE convenient, opportune
- for *BAD WEATHER*:
harsh, hostile, unfavourable, adverse,
miserable
(*informal*) lousy

Penguins face **hostile** *weather in the
Antarctic.*
OPPOSITE fine, favourable
- for food that has *GONE BAD*:
mouldy, rotten, off, decayed, sour,
spoiled, rancid
The strawberries have started to go
mouldy.
OPPOSITE fresh
- to *FEEL BAD* about something:
guilty, ashamed, sorry, remorseful,
repentant
Scrooge feels **repentant** *by the end of
the story.*
OPPOSITE unashamed, unrepentant

bad-tempered adjective
Trolls are always **bad-tempered**
before breakfast.
- cross, grumpy, irritable, moody,
quarrelsome, fractious, ill-tempered,
short-tempered, cantankerous,
crotchety, snappy, testy, sullen
OPPOSITE good-tempered, cheerful

bag noun
I put my wet clothes in a plastic **bag**.
- sack, carrier, holdall, satchel,
handbag, shoulder bag
- A bag you carry on your back is a
backpack or rucksack.

baggage noun
We loaded our **baggage** *onto a trolley.*
- luggage, bags, cases, suitcases,
belongings, things
- (*informal*) gear, stuff

baggy adjective
The clown wore a pair of **baggy**
trousers.
- loose, loose-fitting, roomy

bake verb FOR WAYS TO COOK THINGS
SEE **cook** verb

balance noun
to lose your balance
Rick **lost his balance** *and fell off the
branch.*
- totter, wobble

bald adjective
*The ogre had a **bald** patch on the top of his head.*
- bare, hairless
- OPPOSITE hairy

ball noun
1 *Wind the string into a **ball**.*
- sphere, globe, orb
- A small ball of something is a pellet or globule.

2 *We kicked a **ball** about in the playground.*
- FOR GAMES PLAYED WITH A BALL
- SEE **sport**

ball noun

✎ WRITING TIPS

You can use these words to describe **how a ball moves** or **how you hit or throw a ball**:
- arc, bounce, bowl, dribble, drive, fling, header, hurl, kick, lob, pitch, scoop, spin, strike, swerve, toss, volley; belt, blast, smash, sock, swipe, wham

*The ball **dribbled** into the back of the net.*

*Murray **smashed** the ball across the court.*

---

ban verb
*Rollerblades are **banned** from the playground.*
- forbid, prohibit, bar, exclude, outlaw
- OPPOSITE allow, permit

band noun
1 *The king was surrounded by a **band** of courtiers.*
- company, group, gang, party, troop, crew

2 *I play piano in the junior jazz **band**.*
- group, ensemble, orchestra

3 *The team captain wears a red arm **band**.*
- strip, stripe, ring, line, belt, hoop

bandage noun
*You need a **bandage** on that knee.*
- dressing, plaster, gauze, lint

bandit noun
***Bandits** used to live in these mountains.*
- robber, brigand, thief, outlaw, desperado, highwayman, pirate, buccaneer

bang noun
1 *There was a loud **bang** as the balloon burst.*
- blast, boom, crash, thud, thump, pop, explosion, report
- FOR OTHER TYPES OF NOISE
- SEE **sound** noun

2 *He got a **bang** on the head from the low ceiling.*
- bump, blow, hit, knock, thump, punch, smack, whack, clout
- (*informal*) wallop

bang verb
*Miss Crabbit **banged** her fist on the desk and scowled.*
- hit, thump, strike, bash, slam, wham

banish verb
*The king's brother was **banished** forever.*
- exile, expel, deport, send away, eject

bank noun
1 *The temple was built on the **banks** of the River Nile.*
- edge, side, shore, margin, brink

2 *We rolled our Easter eggs down a grassy **bank**.*
- slope, mound, ridge, embankment

banner noun
*The turrets were decorated with colourful **banners**.*
- flag, standard, streamer, pennant

banquet noun
*There was a **banquet** on the queen's birthday.*
- dinner, feast

bar noun
1 *Did you eat the whole **bar** of chocolate?*
- block, slab, chunk, wedge
- A bar of gold or silver is an ingot.
- A bar of soap is a cake.

2 *The window had iron **bars** across it.*
- rod, pole, rail, stake, beam, girder

bar verb

1 *Two athletes were **barred** from competing in the race.*
- ban, prohibit, exclude, keep out

2 *A fallen tree **barred** our way.*
- block, hinder, impede, obstruct, stop, check

bare adjective

1 *I put suncream on my **bare** arms and legs.*
- naked, nude, exposed, uncovered, unclothed, undressed

2 *The wolf had a **bare** patch on its back.*
- bald, hairless

3 *We slept outside on the **bare** mountain.*
- barren, bleak, treeless

4 *Inside, the dungeon was cold and **bare**.*
- empty, unfurnished, vacant

5 *There wasn't a **bare** patch of wall left.*
- blank, plain, clear, empty

6 *There is only room to pack the **bare** essentials.*
- basic, minimum

barely adverb

*We **barely** had time to get dressed.*
- hardly, scarcely, only just

bargain noun

1 *We made a **bargain** with the captain to take us ashore.*
- deal, agreement, promise, pact

2 *That camera you bought was a **bargain**.*
- good buy, special offer
- (*informal*) snip, steal

bargain verb

*He refused to **bargain** with the pirates for his life.*
- argue, do a deal, haggle, negotiate

barge verb

to barge into

1 *A woman **barged into** me with her shopping trolley.*
- bump into, collide with, veer into

2 *A messenger **barged** breathlessly **into** the room.*
- push into, rush into, storm into

bark verb

*The guard dog began to **bark** fiercely.*
- woof, yap, yelp, growl

FOR OTHER ANIMAL NOISES
SEE **animal**

barrage noun

1 *We heard a distant **barrage** of gunfire.*
- bombardment, volley

2 *The celebrity faced a **barrage** of questions.*
- mass, stream, flood, onslaught

barrel noun

*The smugglers carried **barrels** of gunpowder.*
- cask, drum, tub, keg, butt

barren adjective

*Pictures show the surface of Mars as a **barren** landscape.*
- dry, dried-up, arid, bare, waste, lifeless, sterile
- OPPOSITE fertile, lush

barrier noun

1 *Spectators were asked to stay behind the **barrier**.*
- wall, fence, railing, barricade
- A barrier across a road is a roadblock.

2 *His shyness was a **barrier** to making friends.*
- obstacle, hurdle, drawback, handicap, hindrance, stumbling block

base noun

1 *The footprints stop at the **base** of the pyramid.*
- bottom, foot

2 *The dolls' house comes with a wooden **base**.*
- foundation, support
- A base under a statue is a pedestal or plinth.

3 *The mountaineers returned to their **base**.*
- headquarters, camp, depot

basement noun
- cellar, vault
- A room underneath a church is a crypt.
- An underground cell in a castle is a dungeon.

a
b
c
d
e
f
g
h
i
j
k
l
m
n
o
p
q
r
s
t
u
v
w
x
y
z

FOR OTHER PARTS OF A BUILDING
SEE **building**

basic adjective
1 *These are the **basic** moves in ice-skating.*
- main, chief, principal, key, central, essential, fundamental, crucial
2 *My knowledge of French is very **basic**.*
- elementary, simple
OPPOSITE advanced

basically adverb
Basically, I think you're right.
- essentially, in essence, at heart, fundamentally

basin noun
*Fill a **basin** with soapy water.*
- sink, bowl, dish

basis noun
*What is the **basis** of your argument?*
- base, core, foundation

basket noun
- A basket of food is a hamper.
- A basket on a bicycle is a pannier.
- A small basket of strawberries is a punnet.

bat noun
- In golf, you hit the ball with a club.
- In snooker, you hit it with a cue.
- In tennis, you hit it with a racket.
- In hockey, you hit it with a stick.

batch noun
*Mum made a fresh **batch** of pancakes.*
- lot, bunch, amount, quantity

bathe verb
1 *It was too cold to **bathe** in the sea.*
- swim, go swimming, splash about, take a dip
- To walk about in shallow water is to paddle.
- To walk through deep water is to wade.
2 *The nurse gently **bathed** the wound.*
- clean, cleanse, wash, rinse

batter verb
*The prisoner **battered** his fists against the door.*
- beat, pound, thump, pummel

battle noun
*The **battle** between our countries raged for many years.*
- fight, clash, conflict, action, engagement, hostilities, struggle
SEE ALSO **fight** noun

bay noun
*Dolphins were swimming in the **bay**.*
- cove, inlet, gulf, harbour, sound

be verb
1 *I'll **be** at home all morning.*
- stay, continue, remain
2 *The concert will **be** in March.*
- take place, happen, come about, occur
3 *She wants to **be** a famous writer.*
- become, develop into

beach noun
*We found these shells on the **beach**.*
- sands, seashore, seaside, shore
FOR THINGS YOU MIGHT SEE OR DO ON A BEACH
SEE **seashore, seaside**

bead noun
1 *Sylvia wore a string of coral **beads**.*
FOR ITEMS OF JEWELLERY
SEE **jewel, jewellery**
2 *The explorer wiped **beads** of sweat from his brow.*
- blob, drop, droplet, drip, pearl

beam noun
1 *Wooden **beams** ran across the ceiling.*
- bar, timber, joist, plank, post, rafter, boom, spar, strut, support
2 *A **beam** of sunlight entered the cave.*
- ray, shaft, stream, gleam
- A strong narrow beam of light used in various devices is a laser.

beam verb
1 *In the photo, we are all **beaming** at the camera.*
- smile, grin
OPPOSITE frown, scowl
2 *The satellite will **beam** a signal back to Earth.*
- transmit, send out, broadcast, emit

bean noun SEE **vegetable**

a
b
c
d
e
f
g
h
i
j
k
l
m
n
o
p
q
r
s
t
u
v
w
x
y
z

a
b
c
d
e
f
g
h
i
j
k
l
m
n
o
p
q
r
s
t
u
v
w
x
y
z

bear verb

1 *The rope won't **bear** my weight.*
- carry, support, hold, take

2 *The messenger **bore** a letter from the king.*
- bring, carry, convey, transport, take, transfer

3 *The gravestone **bears** an old inscription.*
- display, show, have

4 *The stench in the cave was too much to **bear**.*
- put up with, cope with, stand, suffer, tolerate, endure, abide

5 *The lioness has **borne** three cubs.*
- give birth to

bear noun

> **WORD WEB**
>
> SOME TYPES OF BEAR
> black bear, brown bear, grizzly bear, polar bear
> - Animals rather like bears are the koala and giant panda.
> - A toy bear is a teddy bear.
> FOR OTHER ANIMALS
> SEE **animal**

bearable adjective

*The temperature at midday is high, but **bearable**.*
- tolerable, endurable, acceptable
OPPOSITE unbearable

bearings plural noun

*We lost our **bearings** in the fog.*
- sense of direction, orientation, position, whereabouts

beast noun

*In the darkness, they heard a wild **beast** howl.*
- animal, creature
- You might call a large or frightening beast a brute or monster.
FOR MYTHOLOGICAL BEASTS
SEE **myth**

beat verb

1 *It's cruel to **beat** an animal with a stick.*
- hit, strike, thrash, batter, whip, lash, flog
- (*informal*) whack, wallop
FOR OTHER WAYS OF HITTING
SEE **hit** verb

2 *I **beat** my brother at chess for the first time.*
- defeat, conquer, vanquish, win against, get the better of, overcome, overwhelm, rout, thrash, trounce
- (*informal*) hammer

3 ***Beat** the eggs, milk, and sugar together.*
- whisk, whip, blend, mix, stir

4 *Can you feel your heart **beating**?*
- pound, thump, palpitate

to beat someone up
*The bully threatened to **beat me up**.*
- assault, attack

beat noun

1 *Can you feel the **beat** of your heart?*
- pulse, throb

2 *Reggae music has a strong **beat**.*
- rhythm, accent, stress

beautiful adjective

> ⚠️ **OVERUSED WORD**
>
> Try to vary the words you use for beautiful. Here are some other words you could use.
> - for a *BEAUTIFUL PERSON*:
> attractive, good-looking, pretty, gorgeous, glamorous, radiant, elegant, enchanting, dazzling, stunning, magnificent, resplendent
> *The fairy queen looked **radiant** by moonlight.*
> - A man who is pleasing to look at is good-looking or handsome.
> OPPOSITE ugly, unattractive
> - for a *BEAUTIFUL DAY* or *BEAUTIFUL WEATHER*:
> fine, excellent, glorious, marvellous, sunny, superb, splendid, wonderful
> *It was a **glorious** day for a bicycle trip.*
> OPPOSITE dull, gloomy, drab

- for a *BEAUTIFUL SIGHT*:
  glorious, magnificent, picturesque, scenic, spectacular, splendid
  *The Northern Lights are a **spectacular** sight.*
- for a *BEAUTIFUL SOUND*:
  harmonious, mellifluous, melodious, sweet-sounding
  *The nightingale has a **sweet-sounding** song.*
  OPPOSITE grating

beauty noun
*The film star was famous for her **beauty**.*
- attractiveness, prettiness, loveliness, charm, allure, magnificence, radiance, splendour
  OPPOSITE ugliness

beckon verb
*The guard was **beckoning** me to approach.*
- signal, gesture, motion, gesticulate

become verb
1 *I soon **became** frustrated with the video game.*
- begin to be, turn, get
2 *Eventually, the tadpoles will **become** frogs.*
- grow into, change into, develop into, turn into
3 *That style of hat **becomes** you.*
- look good on, suit, flatter

bed noun
1 *The children slept on hard, wooden **beds**.*
- bunk, mattress
- A bed for a baby is a cot, cradle, or crib.
- Two single beds one above the other are bunk beds.
- A bed on a ship or train is a berth.
- A bed made of net or cloth hung up above the ground is a hammock.
2 *We planted daffodils in the flower **beds**.*
- plot, patch, border
3 *These creatures feed on the **bed** of the ocean.*
- bottom, floor
  OPPOSITE surface

bedraggled adjective
*After its swim, the puppy was wet and **bedraggled**.*
- messy, scruffy, untidy, dishevelled, dirty, wet
  OPPOSITE smart, spruce

bee noun

> **WORD WEB**
>
> SOME TYPES OF BEE
> bumblebee, drone, honeybee, worker, queen
> - A young bee after it hatches is a larva.
> - A group of bees is a swarm or a colony.
> - A place where bees live is a hive.
> FOR OTHER INSECTS
> SEE **insect**

before adverb
1 *Have you used a camera **before**?*
- previously, in the past, earlier, sooner
  OPPOSITE later
2 *Those people were **before** us in the queue.*
- in front of, ahead of, in advance of
  OPPOSITE after

beg verb
*He **begged** me not to let go of the rope.*
- ask, plead with, entreat, implore, beseech

begin verb
1 *The hunters **began** their search at dawn.*
- start, commence, embark on, set about
  OPPOSITE end, finish, conclude
2 *When did the trouble **begin**?*
- start, commence, arise, emerge, appear, originate, spring up
  OPPOSITE end, stop, cease

beginner noun
*This swimming class is for **beginners**.*
- learner, starter, novice
- A beginner in a trade or a job is an apprentice or trainee.
- A beginner in the police or armed services is a cadet or recruit.

a
b
c
d
e
f
g
h
i
j
k
l
m
n
o
p
q
r
s
t
u
v
w
x
y
z

a
b
c
d
e
f
g
h
i
j
k
l
m
n
o
p
q
r
s
t
u
v
w
x
y
z

beginning noun
*The house was built at the **beginning** of last century.*
- start, opening, commencement, introduction, establishment, foundation, initiation, launch, dawn
- The beginning of the day is dawn or daybreak.
- The beginning of a journey is the starting point.
- The beginning of a stream or river is the origin or source.
- A piece of writing at the beginning of a book is an introduction, preface, or prologue.
- A piece of music at the beginning of a musical or opera is a prelude or overture.
- OPPOSITE end, conclusion

behave verb
*Our neighbour is **behaving** very strangely.*
- act, react, perform
to behave yourself
*We promised to **behave ourselves** in the car.*
- be good, be on your best behaviour

behaviour noun
*I give my puppy treats for good **behaviour**.*
- actions, conduct, manners, attitude

being noun
*They looked like **beings** from another planet.*
- creature, individual, person, entity

belch verb
*The chimney **belched** clouds of black smoke.*
- discharge, emit, send out, gush, spew

belief noun
1 *She was a woman of strong religious **beliefs**.*
- faith, principle, creed, doctrine
2 *It is my **belief** is that he stole the money.*
- opinion, view, conviction, feeling, notion, theory

believable adjective
*None of the characters in the book are **believable**.*
- credible, plausible
- OPPOSITE unbelievable, implausible

believe verb
1 *I don't **believe** anything he says.*
- accept, have faith in, rely on, trust
- OPPOSITE disbelieve, doubt
2 *I **believe** they used to live in Canada.*
- assume, feel, know, presume, reckon, suppose, think

bell noun

> **WRITING TIPS**
> You can use these words to describe how a bell sounds:
> - chime, clang, jangle, jingle, peal, ring, tinkle, toll
> *The bell on the door **jingled** when I entered the shop.*

belong verb
1 *This ring **belonged** to my grandmother.*
- be owned by
2 *Do you **belong** to the sports club?*
- be a member of, be connected with

belongings plural noun
*Don't leave any **belongings** on the bus.*
- possessions, property, goods, things

below preposition
1 *We saw goldfish swimming **below** the surface.*
- under, underneath, beneath
2 *The temperature never fell **below** 20 degrees.*
- less than, lower than
- OPPOSITE above

belt noun
1 *The prince wore a **belt** of pure gold.*
- girdle, sash, strap, band
2 *We walked through a **belt** of woodland.*
- strip, band, line, stretch

beneath preposition

*The tunnel ran **beneath** the castle.*

* under, underneath, below
OPPOSITE above, over

bench noun

*We sat on a **bench** in the park.*

* seat, form
* A long seat in a church is a pew.
FOR OTHER TYPES OF SEAT

SEE **seat** noun

bend verb

*This drinking straw **bends** in the middle.*

* curve, turn, twist, curl, coil, loop, arch, warp, wind
* A word for things which bend easily is flexible or (*informal*) bendy.
OPPOSITE straighten

to bend down

*I **bent down** to tie my shoelaces.*

* stoop, bow, crouch, duck, kneel

bend noun

*Watch out for the sharp **bend** in the road.*

* curve, turn, angle, corner, twist, zigzag

beneficial adjective

*Drinking water is **beneficial** to your health.*

* favourable, useful, advantageous, salutary
OPPOSITE harmful, detrimental

benefit noun

*What are the **benefits** of regular exercise?*

* advantage, reward, gain, good point
OPPOSITE disadvantage, drawback

benefit verb

*The rainy weather will **benefit** gardeners.*

* help, aid, assist, be good for, profit
OPPOSITE hinder, harm

benevolent adjective

*The lady greeted us with a **benevolent** smile.*

* friendly, kind, warm-hearted, sympathetic, generous, charitable, benign
OPPOSITE malevolent

bent adjective

1 *After the crash, the car was a mass of **bent** metal.*

* curved, twisted, coiled, looped, buckled, crooked, arched, folded, warped
* (*informal*) wonky

2 *The witch had a **bent** back and walked with a stick.*

* crooked, hunched, curved, arched, bowed
OPPOSITE straight

beside preposition

*You can sit **beside** me if you like.*

* next to, alongside, by, close to, near

beside the point

*The fact that you're ill is **beside the point**.*

* irrelevant, neither here nor there, unimportant

besides adverb

1 *No-one knows the secret, **besides** you and me.*

* as well as, in addition to, apart from, other than

2 *It's too cold to go out. **Besides**, it's dark now.*

* also, in addition, additionally, furthermore, moreover

besiege verb

1 *The Greeks **besieged** Troy for 10 long years.*

* blockade, cut off, isolate

2 *The film star was **besieged** by reporters.*

* surround, mob, plague, harass

best adjective

1 *She is our **best** goalkeeper.*

* top, leading, finest, foremost, supreme, star, outstanding, unequalled, unrivalled
OPPOSITE worst

a
b
c
d
e
f
g
h
i
j
k
l
m
n
o
p
q
r
s
t
u
v
w
x
y
z

2 *We did what we thought was best.*
- most suitable, most appropriate

bet noun
I had a bet that our team would win.
- gamble, wager
- (*informal*) flutter

bet verb
1 *I bet you 50 pence that it will snow tomorrow.*
- gamble, wager, stake, risk
2 *I bet my brother forgets my birthday.*
- feel sure, be certain, expect

betray verb
1 *He betrayed us by telling the enemy our plan.*
- be disloyal to, be a traitor to, cheat, conspire against, double-cross
- Someone who betrays you is a traitor.
- To betray your country is to commit treason.
2 *The look in her eyes betrayed her true feelings.*
- reveal, show, indicate, disclose, divulge, expose, tell

better adjective
1 *Which of these songs do you think is better?*
- superior, finer, preferable
2 *I had a cold, but I'm better now.*
- recovered, cured, healed, improved, well

between preposition
Let's divide the chocolate between us.
- among, amongst

beware verb
Beware! There are thieves about.
- be careful! watch out! look out! take care! be on your guard!
beware of
Beware of the bull.
- watch out for, avoid, mind, heed, keep clear of

bewilder verb
We were bewildered by the directions on the map.
- confuse, puzzle, baffle, bemuse, mystify, perplex, fox
- (*informal*) flummox

beyond preposition
The village lies just beyond those hills.
- after, past, the other side of

biased adjective
A referee should not make a biased decision.
- prejudiced, partial, one-sided, partisan, unfair
OPPOSITE impartial

bicycle noun

| WORD WEB |
- push bike
  (*informal*) bike
- A person who rides a bicycle is a cyclist.
  SOME TYPES OF BICYCLE
  mountain bike, racing bike, reclining or recumbent bike, road bike, tandem, trailer bike
- A cycle with one wheel is a unicycle.
- A cycle with three wheels is a tricycle or (*informal*) trike.
- A cycle without pedals is a scooter.
- A type of bicycle used in the past was a penny-farthing.
  THE MAIN PARTS OF A BICYCLE ARE
  brakes, brake lever, chain, crossbar, gearshift, handlebars, pedals, saddle

bid noun
1 *There were several bids for the painting at the auction.*
- offer, price, tender
2 *His bid to beat the world record failed.*
- attempt, effort, try, go

big adjective
The giant owned three pairs of big boots.
- large, huge, great, massive, enormous, gigantic, colossal, mammoth
- (*informal*) whopping, ginormous, humungous
OPPOSITE small, little, tiny

a b c d e f g h i j k l m n o p q r s t u v w x y z

big adjective

OVERUSED WORD

Try to vary the words you use for **big**. Here are some other words you could use.

- for a *BIG PERSON* or *BIG CREATURE*:
  burly, giant, hefty, hulking, mighty, monstrous, towering
  *The **mighty** robot clanked as it moved.*

- for a *BIG OBJECT*:
  bulky, heavy, hefty, weighty
  *What could be inside that **bulky** envelope?*

- for a *BIG ROOM* or *BIG BOX*:
  roomy, sizeable, spacious
  Inside, the spaceship was surprisingly **roomy**.
  OPPOSITE cramped

- for a *BIG DISTANCE*:
  immense, infinite, vast
  *A **vast** stretch of ocean lay before them.*

- for a *BIG AMOUNT* or *BIG HELPING*:
  ample, considerable, substantial
  *We each got an **ample** helping of porridge.*
  OPPOSITE meagre, paltry

- for a *BIG DECISION* or *BIG MOMENT*:
  grave, important, serious, significant
  *Yesterday was the most **significant** day in my short life.*
  OPPOSITE unimportant, minor

bill noun

My granny offered to pay the **bill**.

- account, invoice, statement, charges

billow verb

1 *Smoke **billowed** from the mouth of the cave.*
- pour, swirl, spiral

2 *The sheets on the washing line **billowed** in the wind.*
- swell, bulge, puff, balloon

bind verb

*We **bound** the sticks together with some rope.*
- attach, fasten, tie, secure, join, connect, lash, rope

bird noun

WORD WEB

- A female bird is a hen.
- A male bird is a cock.
- A young bird is a chick, fledgling, or nestling.
- A family of chicks is a brood.
- A group of birds is a colony or flock.
- A group of flying birds is a flight or skein.
- A person who studies birds is an ornithologist.

SOME COMMON BRITISH BIRDS
blackbird, bluetit, bullfinch, bunting, chaffinch, crow, cuckoo, dove, greenfinch, jackdaw, jay, linnet, magpie, martin, nightingale, pigeon, raven, robin, rook, skylark, sparrow, starling, swallow, swift, thrush, tit, wagtail, waxwing, woodpecker, wren, yellowhammer

BIRDS OF PREY
buzzard, eagle, falcon, hawk, kestrel, kite, merlin, osprey, owl, sparrowhawk, vulture

FARM AND GAME BIRDS
chicken, duck, goose, grouse, partridge, pheasant, quail, turkey
- Birds kept by farmers are called poultry.

SEA AND WATER BIRDS
albatross, auk, bittern, coot, cormorant, crane, curlew, duck, gannet, goose, guillemot, gull, heron, kingfisher, kittiwake, lapwing, mallard, moorhen, oystercatcher, peewit, pelican, penguin, puffin, seagull, snipe, stork, swan, teal

BIRDS FROM OTHER COUNTRIES
bird of paradise, budgerigar, canary, cockatoo, flamingo, humming bird, ibis, kookaburra, macaw, mynah bird, parakeet, parrot, toucan

BIRDS WHICH CANNOT FLY
emu, kiwi, ostrich, peacock, penguin

a
b
c
d
e
f
g
h
i
j
k
l
m
n
o
p
q
r
s
t
u
v
w
x
y
z

a
b
c
d
e
f
g
h
i
j
k
l
m
n
o
p
q
r
s
t
u
v
w
x
y
z

PARTS OF A BIRD'S BODY
beak, bill; claw, talon; breast, crown, throat; crest, feather, down, plumage, plume, wing
SEE ALSO **feather**

SOME TYPES OF BIRD HOME
nest, nesting box; aviary, coop, roost

SOUNDS MADE BY BIRDS
cackle, caw, cheep, chirp, chirrup, cluck, coo, crow, gabble, honk, peep, pipe, quack, screech, squawk, trill, tweet, twitter, warble
- A turkey gobbles.
- An owl hoots.

SPECIAL NAMES
- A female peacock is a peahen.
- A young duck is a duckling.
- A young goose is a gosling.
- A young swan is a cygnet.
- An eagle's nest is an eyrie.
- A place where rooks nest is a rookery.

FOR NAMES FOR GROUPS OF BIRDS
SEE **group**

WRITING TIPS

You can use these words to describe a **bird**.
- to describe *HOW A BIRD MOVES*:
circle, dart, flit, flutter, fly, glide, hop, hover, peck, perch, preen, skim, soar, swoop, waddle, wheel
*A pair of swallows **flitted** among the rooftops.*
- to describe *A BIRD'S FEATHERS*:
bedraggled, downy, drab, fluffy, gleaming, iridescent, ruffled, smooth, speckled
*The peacock displayed its **iridescent** tail.*

bit noun

1 *Mum divided the cake into eight **bits**.*
- piece, portion, part, section, segment, share, slice

2 *These jeans are a **bit** long for me.*
- a little, slightly, rather, fairly, somewhat, quite

⚠️ **OVERUSED WORD**

Try to vary the words you use for **bit**. Here are some other words you could use.
- for a *LARGE BIT* of something:
chunk, lump, hunk, wedge, slab
***Chunks** of rock came tumbling down the mountain.*
- for a *SMALL BIT* of something:
fragment, scrap, chip, particle, speck, pinch, touch, dab, atom, iota
(*informal*) smidgen
*The map was drawn on a **scrap** of old paper.*
- for a *BIT OF FOOD*:
morsel, crumb, bite, nibble, taste, mouthful
*Please try a **morsel** of chocolate mousse.*
- for a *BIT OF LIQUID*:
drop, dash, drib, splash, spot
*Add a **splash** of vinegar to the sauce.*

bite verb

1 *I **bit** a chunk out of my apple.*
- munch, nibble, chew, crunch, gnaw
- (*informal*) chomp

FOR OTHER WAYS TO EAT
SEE **eat**

2 *Take care. These animals can **bite**.*
- nip, pinch, pierce, wound
- When an animal tries to bite you it snaps at you.
- When an insect bites you it stings you.
- A fierce animal mauls or savages its prey.

bitter adjective

1 *The medicine had a **bitter** taste.*
- sour, sharp, acid, acrid, tart
OPPOSITE sweet

2 *His brother was still **bitter** about the quarrel.*
- resentful, embittered, disgruntled, aggrieved
OPPOSITE contented

3 *The wind blowing in from the sea was bitter.*
- biting, cold, freezing, icy, piercing, raw, wintry
- (*informal*) perishing
OPPOSITE mild

bizarre adjective
'Whiskers' is a bizarre name for a goldfish!
- odd, strange, peculiar, weird, extraordinary, outlandish
OPPOSITE ordinary

black adjective, noun
The pony had a shiny black coat.
- coal-black, jet-black, pitch-black, ebony, raven
- You can also describe a black night as pitch-dark.
- Someone in a bad mood is said to look as black as thunder.
- Common similes are as black as coal and as black as night.

blame verb
Don't blame me if you miss the bus.
- accuse, criticize, condemn, reproach, scold

bland adjective
This cheese has a really bland taste.
- mild, dull, weak, insipid
OPPOSITE strong, pungent

blank adjective
1 *There are no blank pages left in my jotter.*
- empty, bare, clean, plain, unmarked, unused
2 *The old woman gave us a blank look.*
- expressionless, faceless, vacant

blank noun
Fill in the blanks to complete the sentence.
- space, break, gap

blanket noun
1 *The baby was wrapped in a woollen blanket.*
- cover, sheet, quilt, rug, throw
2 *A blanket of snow covered the lawn.*
- covering, layer, film, sheet, mantle

blast noun
1 *A blast of cold air came through the door.*
- gust, rush, draught, burst
2 *They heard the blast of a trumpet.*
- blare, noise, roar
3 *Many people were injured in the blast.*
- explosion, shock

blatant adjective
Do you expect me to believe such a blatant lie?
- barefaced, flagrant, obvious, shameless, brazen, unabashed

blaze noun
Firefighters fought the blaze for hours.
- fire, flames, inferno

blaze verb
Within a few minutes the campfire was blazing.
- burn brightly, flare up

bleak adjective
1 *The countryside was bleak and barren.*
- bare, barren, desolate, empty, exposed, stark
2 *The future looks bleak for the club.*
- gloomy, hopeless, depressing, dismal, grim, miserable
OPPOSITE promising

blemish noun
This peach has a blemish on the skin.
- fault, flaw, defect, imperfection, mark, spot, stain

blend verb
1 *Blend the flour with a tablespoon of water.*
- beat together, mix, stir together, whip, whisk
2 *The paint colours blend well with each other.*
- go together, match, fit, harmonize
OPPOSITE clash

blessing noun
1 *The author gave the film her blessing.*
- approval, backing, support, consent, permission
OPPOSITE disapproval

a
b
c
d
e
f
g
h
i
j
k
l
m
n
o
p
q
r
s
t
u
v
w
x
y
z

2 *A warm hat is a **blessing** in cold weather.*
- benefit, advantage, gift, asset, comfort
  OPPOSITE curse, evil

blight noun
*The tower block is a **blight** on the landscape.*
- menace, nuisance, affliction, curse, evil, plague

blind adjective
*Polar bear cubs are born **blind**.*
- sightless, unsighted, unseeing
- A common simile is as blind as a bat.
  OPPOSITE sighted, seeing

blind to
*The captain was **blind to** his own faults.*
- ignorant of, unaware of, oblivious to
  OPPOSITE aware of

bliss noun
*Having a whole day off school was sheer **bliss**.*
- joy, delight, pleasure, happiness, heaven, ecstasy
  OPPOSITE misery

blissful adjective
*We spent a **blissful** week camping outdoors.*
- joyful, delightful, happy, heavenly, ecstatic
  OPPOSITE miserable

blob noun
*The alien left **blobs** of green slime on the carpet.*
- drop, lump, spot, dollop, daub, globule

block noun
1 *A **block** of ice fell from the glacier.*
- chunk, hunk, lump, piece
2 *There must be a **block** in the drainpipe.*
- blockage, jam, obstacle, obstruction

block verb
1 *A tall hedge **blocked** our view of the house.*
- obstruct, hamper, hinder, interfere with

2 *A mass of leaves had **blocked** the drain.*
- clog, choke, jam, plug, stop up, congest
- (*informal*) bung up

blockage noun
*Dad spent ages clearing the **blockage** in the drain.*
- block, obstacle, obstruction

bloodcurdling adjective
*We heard a **bloodcurdling** scream in the night.*
- terrifying, frightening, horrifying, fearful, spine-chilling, hair-raising

bloodshed noun
*In ancient times, this was a scene of **bloodshed**.*
- killing, massacre, slaughter, butchery, carnage

bloodthirsty adjective
*The **bloodthirsty** pirates rattled their swords.*
- brutal, cruel, barbaric, murderous, inhuman, pitiless, ruthless, savage, vicious

bloody adjective
1 *Why is your handkerchief all **bloody**?*
- blood-stained, blood-soaked
2 *The Battle of Skull Rock was short but **bloody**.*
- gory, gruesome, bloodthirsty, violent

bloom noun
*The pear tree was covered in white **blooms**.*
- flower, blossom, bud

bloom verb
*The daffodils **bloomed** early this year.*
- blossom, flower, open
  OPPOSITE fade

blossom noun
Blossom usually refers to a mass of flowers rather than a single flower.
*I love to see the cherry **blossom** in spring.*
- blooms, buds, flowers

blot noun

*The old map was covered with ink **blots**.*

- spot, blotch, mark, blob, splodge, smudge, smear, stain

blot verb

to blot something out

*The new tower block **blots out** the view.*

- conceal, hide, mask, obliterate, obscure

blotch noun

*The dragon had green skin with purple **blotches**.*

- patch, blot, spot, mark, blob, splodge, splash, stain

blow noun

1 *He was knocked out by a **blow** on the head.*

- knock, bang, bash, hit, punch, clout, slap, smack, swipe, thump
- (*informal*) wallop, whack

2 *Losing the hockey match was a terrible **blow**.*

- shock, upset, setback, disappointment, catastrophe, misfortune, disaster, calamity

blow verb

*The wind was **blowing** from the east.*

- blast, gust, puff, fan
- To make a shrill sound by blowing is to whistle.

to blow out

*I **blew out** the candles on my birthday cake.*

- extinguish

to blow up

1 *I need to **blow up** the tyres on my bike.*

- inflate, pump up, swell, fill out

2 *The soldiers tried to **blow up** the enemy hideout.*

- blast, bomb, destroy

3 *Do you think they could **blow up** this photograph?*

- enlarge

blue adjective, noun

WORD WEB

SOME SHADES OF BLUE
azure, cobalt, indigo, navy blue, sapphire, sky-blue, turquoise

bluff verb

*I tried to **bluff** my way through the interview.*

- deceive, trick, fake, fool, lie
- (*informal*) con

blunder noun

*Forgetting her birthday was a terrible **blunder**.*

- mistake, error, fault, slip, slip-up, gaffe
- (*informal*) howler

blunt adjective

1 *This pencil is **blunt**.*

- dull, worn, unsharpened
- OPPOSITE sharp, pointed

2 *Her reply to my question was very **blunt**.*

- abrupt, frank, direct, outspoken, plain, tactless
- OPPOSITE tactful

blur verb

1 *The steamy windows **blurred** the view.*

- cloud, darken, obscure, smear

2 *The accident **blurred** her memory.*

- confuse, muddle

blurred adjective

*The background of the photograph is all **blurred**.*

- indistinct, vague, blurry, fuzzy, hazy, out of focus
- OPPOSITE clear, distinct

blush verb

*The actor **blushed** with embarrassment.*

- flush, go red, colour

blustery adjective

*It was a typical, **blustery** day in autumn.*

- gusty, windy, blowy, squally
- OPPOSITE calm

a
b
c
d
e
f
g
h
i
j
k
l
m
n
o
p
q
r
s
t
u
v
w
x
y
z

board noun
The table top was made from a wooden **board**.
- plank, panel, beam, timber

board verb
*We **boarded** the plane for New York.*
- get on, enter, embark

boast verb
*The knight was always **boasting** about his fencing skills.*
- brag, show off, crow, gloat, swagger
- (*informal*) blow your own trumpet

boastful adjective
*Giants are **boastful** creatures and brag about everything.*
- arrogant, big-headed, conceited, vain, bumptious
- (*informal*) cocky, swanky
- OPPOSITE modest, humble

boat noun

WORD WEB

*Several fishing **boats** were moored in the harbour.*
- ship, craft, vessel

SOME TYPES OF BOAT OR SHIP
barge, canoe, catamaran, cruise liner, dhow, dinghy, dugout, ferry, freighter, gondola, hovercraft, hydrofoil, junk, launch, lifeboat, motor boat, oil tanker, paper boat, punt, raft, rowing boat, schooner, skiff, speedboat, steamship, tanker, trawler, tug, yacht

MILITARY BOATS OR SHIPS
aircraft carrier, battleship, destroyer, frigate, gunboat, minesweeper, submarine, warship

SOME BOATS USED IN THE PAST
brigantine, clipper, coracle, cutter, galleon, galley, man-of-war, paddle steamer, schooner, trireme, windjammer

WORDS FOR PARTS OF A BOAT OR SHIP
boom, bridge, bulwark, cabin, crow's nest, deck, engine room, fo'c'sle or forecastle, funnel, galley, helm, hull, keel, mast, poop, porthole, propeller, quarterdeck, rigging, rudder, sail, tiller

SPECIAL NAMES
- The front part of a boat is the bow or prow.
- The back part of a boat is the stern.
- The left-hand side of a boat is called port.
- The right-hand side of a boat is called starboard.
- A shed where boats are stored is a boathouse.

WRITING TIPS
You can use these words to describe **how a boat moves**:
- cut through the waves or water, drift, float, glide, lurch, pitch, roll, sail, steam, tack
*The tiny raft **pitched** from side to side in the storm.*

bob verb
*A plastic duck **bobbed** up and down in the water.*
- bounce, dance, toss, wobble

body noun

WORD WEB
- The study of the human body is anatomy.
- The main part of your body except your head, arms, and legs is your trunk or torso.
- The shape of your body is your build, figure, or physique.
- A person's dead body is a corpse.
- The dead body of an animal is a carcass.

OUTER PARTS OF THE HUMAN BODY
abdomen, ankle, arm, armpit, breast, buttocks, calf, cheek, chest, chin, ear, elbow, eye, finger, foot, forehead, genitals, groin, hand, head, heel, hip, instep, jaw, knee, kneecap, knuckle, leg, lip, mouth, navel, neck, nipple, nose, pores, shin, shoulder, skin, stomach, temple, thigh, throat, waist, wrist

INNER PARTS OF THE HUMAN BODY
arteries, bladder, bowels, brain,

eardrum, glands, gullet, gums, guts, heart, intestines, kidneys, larynx, liver, lung, muscles, nerves, ovaries, pancreas, prostate, sinews, stomach, tendons, tongue, tonsil, tooth, uterus, veins, windpipe, womb

FOR BONES IN YOUR BODY

SEE **bone**

FOR PARTS OF ANIMAL BODIES

SEE **animal**

WRITING TIPS

You can use these words to describe a person's **body**:

- athletic, beefy, brawny, burly, hefty, hulking, muscular, sinewy, squat, stocky, stout; fat, flabby, plump, rotund, well-rounded; lean, petite, short, slight, slender, svelte, thin; bony, gangly, gaunt, lanky, puny, scraggy, scrawny, skinny, spindly, tall, wiry

*Sid had turned into a **lean** and **lanky** teenager.*

SEE ALSO **thin**

---

bog noun

*We felt our boots sinking into the **bog**.*
- swamp, quagmire, quicksand, fen

boil verb

1 *Would you like your egg **boiled** or fried?*

FOR WAYS TO COOK FOOD

SEE **cook** verb

2 *The water must be **boiling** before you add the pasta.*
- bubble, seethe, steam

boisterous adjective

*Baby dragons can be loud and **boisterous**.*
- lively, noisy, rowdy, unruly, wild, disorderly

OPPOSITE restrained, calm

bold adjective

1 *It was a **bold** move to attack the fortress.*
- brave, courageous, daring, adventurous, audacious, confident, enterprising, fearless, heroic, valiant, intrepid, plucky

OPPOSITE cowardly

2 *The poster uses large letters in **bold** colours.*
- striking, strong, bright, loud, showy, conspicuous, eye-catching, noticeable, prominent

OPPOSITE inconspicuous, subtle

bolt verb

1 *Did you remember to **bolt** the door?*
- fasten, latch, lock, secure, bar

2 *The horses **bolted** when they heard the thunder.*
- dash away, dart, flee, sprint, run away, rush off

3 *Don't **bolt** your food.*
- gobble, gulp, guzzle, wolf down

FOR OTHER WAYS TO EAT

SEE **eat**

bond noun

1 *The prisoner tried to escape from his **bonds**.*
- chains, fetters, ropes, handcuffs, manacles, shackles, restraints

2 *There was a special **bond** between the twins.*
- attachment, connection, tie, link, relationship

bone noun

WORD WEB

- The bones of your body are your skeleton.

SOME BONES IN THE HUMAN BODY

backbone or spine, collarbone, cranium or skull, pelvis, ribs, shoulder blade, vertebrae

bonus noun

*I got a **bonus** on top of my pocket money last week.*
- extra, supplement, reward, tip, handout

a
b
c
d
e
f
g
h
i
j
k
l
m
n
o
p
q
r
s
t
u
v
w
x
y
z

book noun

 WORD WEB

- A book with hard covers is a hardback.
- A book with soft covers is a paperback.
- A book which is typed or handwritten but not printed is a manuscript.
- A thin book in paper covers is a booklet, leaflet, or pamphlet.
- A book which is part of a set is a volume.
- A large, heavy book is a tome.
- The person who writes a book is the author.
- A book which sells a lot of copies is a bestseller.

SOME TYPES OF PRINTED BOOK
album, annual, anthology, atlas, dictionary, directory, encyclopedia, guidebook, manual, picture book, prayer book, reading book, reference book, story book, textbook, thesaurus

BOOKS YOU CAN WRITE OR DRAW IN
diary, exercise book, jotter, notebook, scrapbook, sketchbook

SOME PARTS OF A BOOK
appendix, bibliography, blurb, chapters, contents page, cover, foreword, illustrations, index, introduction, preface, prologue, title page

FOR WAYS TO DESCRIBE A BOOK OR STORY
SEE **writing**

book verb

1 *Have you **booked** a seat on the train?*
- order, reserve

2 *I've **booked** the disco for the party.*
- arrange, engage, organize

boom verb

1 *Miss Barker's voice **boomed** along the corridor.*
- shout, roar, bellow, blast, thunder, resound, reverberate

2 *Business was **booming** in the Riverbank Cafe.*
- be successful, do well, expand, flourish, grow, prosper, thrive

boost verb

*Winning the cup really **boosted** the team's morale.*
- raise, uplift, improve, increase, bolster, help, encourage, enhance
- OPPOSITE lower, dampen

boot noun FOR TYPES OF SHOE OR BOOT

SEE **shoe**

border noun

1 *The town is on the **border** between France and Germany.*
- boundary, frontier

2 *I drew a thin line around the **border** of the picture.*
- edge, margin, perimeter
- A decorative border round the top of a wall is a frieze.
- A border round the bottom of a skirt is a hem.
- A decorative border on fabric is a frill, fringe, or trimming.

bore verb

*They **bored** a hole right through the outer wall.*
- drill, pierce, sink, tunnel

boring adjective

*The film was so **boring** I fell asleep.*
- dull, dreary, tedious, tiresome, unexciting, uninteresting, dry, monotonous, uninspiring, insipid, unimaginative, uneventful, humdrum
- OPPOSITE interesting, exciting

borrow verb

*Can I **borrow** your pencil?*
- use, take, obtain, acquire, cadge
- (informal) scrounge
- OPPOSITE lend

boss noun

*There is a new **boss** at the football club.*
- head, chief, manager, leader, director
- (informal) gaffer

bossy adjective
*Stop being so **bossy** towards your sister.*
- domineering, bullying, dictatorial, officious, tyrannical
- An informal name for a bossy person is bossy boots.

bother verb
1 *Would it **bother** you if I played some music?*
- disturb, trouble, upset, annoy, irritate, pester, worry, vex, exasperate
- (*informal*) bug, hassle
2 *Don't **bother** to phone tonight.*
- make an effort, take trouble, concern yourself, care, mind

bother noun
*It's such a **bother** to remember the password.*
- nuisance, annoyance, irritation, inconvenience, pest, trouble, difficulty, problem
- (*informal*) hassle

bottle noun
*Bring a **bottle** of water with you.*
- flask, flagon, jar, pitcher
- A bottle for serving water or wine is a carafe or decanter.
- A small bottle for perfume or medicine is a phial.

bottle verb
to bottle something up
*It's not healthy to **bottle up** your anger.*
- hold in, cover up, conceal, suppress
- OPPOSITE show, express

bottom noun
1 *We camped at the **bottom** of the mountain.*
- foot, base
- OPPOSITE top, peak
2 *The wreck sank to the **bottom** of the sea.*
- bed, floor
- OPPOSITE surface
3 *A wasp stung me on the **bottom**.*
- backside, behind, buttocks, rear, rump, seat
- (*informal*) bum

bottom adjective
*I got the **bottom** mark in the maths test.*
- least, lowest
- OPPOSITE top

bough noun
*The robin perched on a **bough** of the tree.*
- branch, limb

bounce verb
*The ball **bounced** twice before it reached the net.*
- rebound, ricochet, spring, leap

bound adjective
1 *It's **bound** to rain at the weekend.*
- certain, sure
2 *I felt **bound** to invite my cousin to the party.*
- obliged, duty-bound, committed, compelled, forced, required
3 *The accident was **bound** to happen.*
- destined, doomed, fated

bound for
*The space rocket was **bound for** Jupiter.*
- going to, heading for, making for, travelling towards, off to

bound verb
*The puppies **bounded** across the lawn.*
- leap, bounce, jump, spring, skip, gambol, caper, frisk

boundary noun
*The lamp-post marks the **boundary** of Narnia.*
- border, frontier, edge, end, limit, perimeter, dividing line

bouquet noun
*She presented me with a **bouquet** of fresh flowers.*
- bunch, posy, sprig, spray
- SEE ALSO **flower** noun

bout noun
1 *She's recovering from a **bout** of flu.*
- attack, fit, period, spell
- (*informal*) turn
2 *A judo **bout** is between two contestants.*
- contest, match, round, fight, battle, combat

a
b
c
d
e
f
g
h
i
j
k
l
m
n
o
p
q
r
s
t
u
v
w
x
y
z

bow noun

1 *The captain stood at the **bow** of the ship.*
- front, prow

FOR OTHER PARTS OF A BOAT OR SHIP

SEE **boat**

2 *The archer raised his **bow** and arrow.*

FOR WORDS TO DO WITH ARCHERY

SEE **arrow**

bow verb

1 *The prisoner **bowed** his head in shame.*
- lower, bend, duck

2 *The knight knelt and **bowed** in front of the king.*
- The corresponding movement of a woman is to curtsy.

bowl noun

*There was a **bowl** of fresh fruit on the table.*
- basin, dish, vessel
- A large bowl for serving soup is a tureen.

bowl verb

*Can you **bowl** a faster ball next time?*
- throw, pitch, fling, hurl, toss

FOR OTHER WAYS TO THROW A BALL

SEE **ball**

box noun
- case, chest, crate, carton, packet
- A small box for jewellery or treasure is a casket.
- A large box for luggage is a trunk.

boy noun
- lad, youngster, youth
- (*informal*) kid

brag verb

*Flo is still **bragging** about her swimming medal.*
- show off, boast, gloat, crow
- (*informal*) blow your own trumpet
- A person who is always bragging is a braggart.

brain noun

*You'll need to use your **brain** to solve this riddle.*
- intelligence, intellect, mind, reason, sense, wit

branch noun

1 *A robin perched on a **branch** of the tree.*
- bough, limb

2 *I've joined the local **branch** of the Kennel Club.*
- section, division, department, wing

branch verb

*Follow the track until it **branches** into two.*
- divide, fork

brand noun

*Which **brand** of ice-cream do you like?*
- make, kind, sort, type, variety, label
- The sign of a particular brand of goods is a trademark.

brandish verb

*Captain Hook **brandished** his cutlass at the crew.*
- flourish, wield, flaunt, wave

brave adjective

*It was **brave** of you to save the cat from drowning.*
- courageous, heroic, valiant, fearless, daring, gallant, intrepid, plucky
- A common simile is as brave as a lion.

OPPOSITE cowardly

bravery noun

*The police dog was awarded a medal for **bravery**.*
- courage, heroism, valour, fearlessness, daring, nerve, gallantry, grit, pluck
- (*informal*) guts, bottle

OPPOSITE cowardice

brawl noun

*We could hear a **brawl** on the street outside.*
- fight, quarrel, scuffle, tussle
- (*informal*) scrap

brawny adjective

*The wrestler was big and **brawny**.*
- muscular, sinewy, athletic, burly, beefy

OPPOSITE puny, scrawny

breach noun

1 *Handling the ball is a **breach** of the rules.*
- breaking, violation

- You can also talk about an offence against the rules.
- **2** *The storm caused a **breach** in the sea wall.*
- break, split, crack, gap, hole, opening, fracture, rupture, fissure

break noun

- **1** *Can you see any **breaks** in the chain?*
- breach, crack, hole, gap, opening, split, rift, puncture, rupture, fracture, fissure
- **2** *Let's take a **break** for coffee.*
- interval, pause, rest, lull, time-out
- (*informal*) breather

break verb

- **1** *The vase fell off the shelf and **broke**.*
- smash, shatter, fracture, chip, crack, split, snap, splinter
- (*informal*) bust
- **2** *The burglar was arrested for **breaking** the law.*
- disobey, disregard, violate, flout
- **3** *In her last race, she **broke** the world record.*
- beat, better, exceed, surpass, outdo

to break down
*Our car **broke down** on the motorway.*
- fail, go wrong, stop working
- (*informal*) pack in, conk out

to break off
*We'll **break off** for lunch at one o'clock.*
- have a rest, pause, stop

to break out
*A flu epidemic **broke out** just after Christmas.*
- begin, spread, start

to break out of
*The prisoner tried to **break out of** jail.*
- escape from, break loose from, abscond from

to break up
*After the speeches, the crowd began to **break up**.*
- disperse, scatter, separate, split up, disintegrate

breakable adjective
*Be careful! The parcel has **breakable** things in it.*
- fragile, delicate, brittle, frail
OPPOSITE unbreakable

breakdown noun

- **1** *There has been a **breakdown** in the peace talks.*
- failure, collapse, fault
- **2** *Can you give me a **breakdown** of the figures?*
- analysis

break-in noun
*There was a **break-in** at the local bank.*
- burglary, robbery, theft, raid

breakthrough noun
*Scientists have made a **breakthrough** in medicine.*
- advance, leap forward, discovery, development, revolution, progress
OPPOSITE setback

breath noun
*There wasn't a **breath** of wind in the air.*
- breeze, puff, waft, whiff, whisper, sigh

breathe verb

- To breathe in is to inhale.
- To breathe out is to exhale.
- To breathe heavily when you have been running is to pant or puff.
- The formal word for breathing is respiration.

breathless adjective
*Leo was **breathless** after the race.*
- out of breath, gasping, panting, puffing, tired out, wheezing

breathtaking adjective
*The view from the summit was **breathtaking**.*
- spectacular, stunning, staggering, astonishing, overwhelming, awe-inspiring

breed verb

- **1** *Salmon swim upstream to **breed** every year.*
- reproduce, have young, multiply, procreate, spawn
- **2** *Bad hygiene **breeds** disease.*
- cause, produce, generate, encourage, promote, cultivate, induce

breed noun
*What **breed** of dog is that?*
- kind, sort, type, variety
- The evidence of how a dog has been bred is its pedigree.

a
b
c
d
e
f
g
h
i
j
k
l
m
n
o
p
q
r
s
t
u
v
w
x
y
z

breezy adjective

This morning the weather was bright and breezy.
- windy, blowy, blustery, gusty, fresh, draughty
  SEE ALSO **weather** noun

brew verb

1 *I'm just going to brew some tea.*
- make, prepare
- When you brew beer it ferments.

2 *It looks like a storm is brewing.*
- develop, form, loom, build up, gather, threaten

brew noun

The wizard stirred an evil-smelling brew.
- mixture, concoction

bridge noun

- A bridge you can walk over is a footbridge.
- A bridge to carry water is an aqueduct.
- A long bridge carrying a road or railway is a viaduct.

brief adjective

1 *We paid a brief visit to our cousins on the way home.*
- short, quick, hasty, fleeting, temporary

2 *Give me a brief account of what happened.*
- short, concise, abbreviated, condensed, compact, succint
  OPPOSITE long, lengthy

bright adjective

1 *We saw the bright lights of the town in the distance.*
- shining, brilliant, blazing, dazzling, glaring, gleaming
  OPPOSITE dull, dim, weak

2 *Bright colours will make the poster stand out.*
- strong, intense, vivid
- Colours that shine in the dark are luminous colours.
  OPPOSITE dull, faded, muted

3 *Her teachers thought she was very bright.*
- clever, intelligent, gifted, sharp, quick-witted
- (*informal*) brainy

- A common simile is as bright as a button.
  OPPOSITE stupid, dull-witted

4 *Miranda gave me a bright smile.*
- cheerful, happy, lively, merry, jolly, radiant
  OPPOSITE sad, gloomy

5 *The day was cold, but bright.*
- sunny, fine, fair, clear, cloudless
  OPPOSITE dull, cloudy, overcast

brighten verb

It was a cloudy morning, but it brightened after lunch.
- become sunny, clear up, improve

to brighten up

A new coat of paint will brighten up the room.
- cheer up, light up, enliven

brilliant adjective

1 *The fireworks gave off a brilliant light.*
- bright, blazing, dazzling, glaring, gleaming, glittering, glorious, shining, splendid, vivid
  OPPOSITE dim, dull

2 *Brunel was a brilliant engineer.*
- clever, exceptional, outstanding, gifted, talented
  OPPOSITE incompetent, talentless

3 (*informal*) *I saw a brilliant film last week.*
- excellent, marvellous, outstanding, wonderful, superb
- (*informal*) fantastic, fabulous
  SEE ALSO **good**

brim noun

I filled my glass to the brim.
- top, rim, edge, brink, lip

bring verb

1 *Can you bring the shopping in from the car?*
- carry, fetch, deliver, bear, transport

2 *You can bring a friend to the party.*
- invite, conduct, escort, guide, lead

3 *The war has brought great sorrow to our people.*
- cause, produce, lead to, result in, generate

a
b
c
d
e
f
g
h
i
j
k
l
m
n
o
p
q
r
s
t
u
v
w
x
y
z

to bring something about

*The new coach **brought about** some changes.*

- cause, effect, create, introduce, be responsible for

to bring someone up

*In the story, Tarzan is **brought up** by apes.*

- rear, raise, care for, foster, look after, nurture, educate, train

to bring something up

*I wish you hadn't **brought up** the subject of money.*

- mention, talk about, raise, broach

brink noun

*We stood on the **brink** of a deep crater.*

- edge, lip, rim, verge, brim

brisk adjective

1 *Mr Hastie went for a **brisk** walk every evening.*

- lively, fast-paced, energetic, invigorating, vigorous, refreshing, bracing

  OPPOSITE slow, leisurely

2 *The flower shop does a **brisk** trade around Easter.*

- busy, lively, bustling, hectic

  OPPOSITE quiet, slack, slow

brittle adjective

*The bones of the skeleton were dry and **brittle**.*

- breakable, fragile, delicate, frail

  OPPOSITE soft, flexible

broad adjective

1 *The streets in the city were **broad** and straight.*

- wide, open, large, roomy, spacious, vast, extensive

  OPPOSITE narrow

2 *Just give me a **broad** outline of what happened.*

- general, rough, vague, loose, indefinite, imprecise

  OPPOSITE specific, detailed

broadcast noun

*We listened to a radio **broadcast**.*

- programme, show, transmission
- A broadcast on the Internet is a webcast.

broadcast verb

*The concert will be **broadcast** live on TV.*

- televise, transmit, relay, air, screen

broaden verb

*I'm **broadening** my interests by listening to jazz.*

- widen, extend, enlarge, expand, increase, develop, diversify

brochure noun

*We got some holiday **brochures** from the travel agent.*

- leaflet, pamphlet, booklet, catalogue

broken adjective

1 *Don't use that computer—it's **broken**.*

- faulty, defective, damaged, out of order

  OPPOSITE working

2 *After losing all his money, Forbes was a **broken** man.*

- crushed, defeated, beaten, spiritless

brood verb

1 *The hen was **brooding** her clutch of eggs.*

- hatch, incubate, sit on

2 *He was still **brooding** over what I had said.*

- fret, mope, worry, dwell on

brown adjective, noun

WORD WEB

SOME SHADES OF BROWN
beige, bronze, buff, chestnut, chocolate, dun, fawn, khaki, russet, sepia, tan, tawny

browse verb

1 *I like **browsing** through toy catalogues.*

- flick through, leaf through, scan, skim

2 *The cattle were **browsing** in the meadow.*

- graze, feed

bruise verb
*I fell and **bruised** my knee.*
- mark, hurt, injure
  FOR OTHERS TYPES OF INJURY
  SEE **injury**

brush verb
1 *Jill spent ages **brushing** her hair for the party.*
- groom, comb, tidy
2 *A bird **brushed** against my cheek as it flew past.*
- touch, contact, rub, scrape

to brush up
*I must **brush up** my French before we go to Paris.*
- revise, improve, go over, refresh your memory of
- (*informal*) swot up

brutal adjective
*The bandits launched a **brutal** attack.*
- savage, vicious, cruel, barbaric, bloodthirsty, callous, ferocious, inhuman, merciless, pitiless, ruthless, sadistic
  OPPOSITE gentle, humane

bubble noun
- The bubbles in a fizzy drink are called effervescence.
- The bubbles made by soap or detergent are lather or suds.
- Bubbles on top of a liquid are foam or froth.
- The bubbles on top of beer are the head.

bubble verb
*A green liquid **bubbled** in the witch's cauldron.*
- boil, seethe, gurgle, froth, foam

bubbly adjective
1 ***Bubbly** drinks get up my nose.*
- fizzy, sparkling, effervescent
2 *Sophie has a bright and **bubbly** personality.*
- cheerful, lively, vivacious, spirited, animated

bucket noun
*We took **buckets** and spades to the seaside.*
- pail, can

buckle noun
*The pirate wore a belt with a large silver **buckle**.*
- clasp, fastener, fastening, clip, catch

buckle verb
1 *Please **buckle** your seat belts.*
- fasten, secure, clasp, clip, do up, hook up
2 *The bridge **buckled** when the giant stepped onto it.*
- bend, warp, twist, crumple, cave in, collapse

bud noun
***Buds** are appearing on the apple trees.*
- shoot, sprout

budding adjective
*My sister is a **budding** actor.*
- promising, aspiring, potential, would-be
- (*informal*) wannabe
  OPPOSITE experienced

budge verb
*The window was stuck and wouldn't **budge**.*
- give way, move, shift, stir

budget verb
to budget for
*Have you **budgeted for** a holiday this year?*
- allow for, plan for, provide for

buffet noun
1 *You can buy a sandwich in the **buffet**.*
- cafeteria, snack bar, cafe, bar
  FOR OTHER PLACES TO EAT
  SEE **restaurant**
2 *We will be serving a **buffet** for lunch.*
  FOR TYPES OF MEAL
  SEE **meal**

bug noun
1 *Birds help to control **bugs** in the garden.*
- insect, pest
2 (*informal*) *I can't get rid of this stomach **bug**.*
- infection, virus, germ, disease, illness

a
b
c
d
e
f
g
h
i
j
k
l
m
n
o
p
q
r
s
t
u
v
w
x
y
z

3 *There are a few **bugs** in the computer program.*
- fault, error, defect, flaw
- (*informal*) gremlin

bug verb

1 *The spy **bugged** their telephone conversations.*
- tap, listen in to, intercept

2 (*informal*) *I wish you'd stop **bugging** me with questions.*
- bother, annoy, pester, trouble, harass

build verb

*Dad is going to **build** a shed in the garden.*
- construct, erect, put together, put up, set up, assemble

to build up

1 *I'm **building up** a collection of DVDs.*
- accumulate, assemble, collect, put together

2 *We felt the tension **building up** in the crowd.*
- increase, intensify, rise, grow, mount up, escalate

build noun

*Charlotte was a girl of slender **build**.*
- body, form, frame, figure, physique
SEE ALSO **body**

building noun

WORD WEB

*The new **building** will have seven storeys.*
- construction, structure, dwelling
- A person who designs buildings is an architect.

BUILDINGS WHERE PEOPLE LIVE
apartment, barracks, bungalow, castle, cottage, farmhouse, flat, fort, fortress, house, mansion, palace, skyscraper, tenement, terrace, tower, villa
SEE ALSO **house** noun

BUILDINGS WHERE PEOPLE WORK
factory, garage, lighthouse, mill, shop, store, warehouse

BUILDINGS WHERE PEOPLE WORSHIP
abbey, cathedral, chapel, church, monastery, mosque, pagoda, shrine, synagogue, temple
SEE ALSO **church**

OTHER TYPES OF BUILDING
cabin, cafe, cinema, college, gallery, hotel, inn, library, museum, observatory, police station, post office, power station, prison, pub or public house, restaurant, school, shed, theatre

PARTS YOU MIGHT FIND INSIDE A BUILDING
balcony, basement, cellar, conservatory, corridor, courtyard, crypt, dungeon, foyer, gallery, lobby, porch, quadrangle, room, staircase, veranda
SEE ALSO **room**

PARTS YOU MIGHT FIND OUTSIDE A BUILDING
arch, balustrade, bay window, bow window, buttress, chimney, colonnade, column, dome, dormer window, drainpipe, eaves, foundations, gable, gutter, masonry, parapet, pediment, pillar, pipes, roof, tower, turret, vault, wall, window, windowsill

FOR PARTS OF A CASTLE
SEE **castle**

WRITING TIPS

You can use these words to describe a **building**:
- airy, compact, cramped, crumbling, forbidding, grand, imposing, ramshackle, ruined, run-down, spacious, sprawling, squalid, stark, stately

bulge noun

*There was a large **bulge** in the robber's sack.*
- bump, hump, lump, swelling, protuberance

a
b
c
d
e
f
g
h
i
j
k
l
m
n
o
p
q
r
s
t
u
v
w
x
y
z

bulge verb

*The creature had eyes which **bulged** out of its head.*
- stick out, swell, puff out, protrude

bulk noun

1 *The sheer **bulk** of the iceberg was staggering.*
- size, dimensions, magnitude, mass, largeness, immensity

2 *We spent the **bulk** of our holiday lazing on the beach.*
- most, most part, greater part, majority

bulky adjective

*The parcel is too **bulky** to go through the letterbox.*
- big, large, hefty, substantial, sizeable, cumbersome, unwieldy
OPPOSITE small, compact

bully verb

*Some of the children were afraid of being **bullied**.*
- persecute, torment, intimidate, terrorize, push around

bump verb

1 *The baby **bumped** his head on the table.*
- hit, strike, knock, bang

2 *My bicycle **bumped** up and down over the cobbles.*
- bounce, shake, jerk, jolt

to bump into

1 *The taxi **bumped into** the car in front of it.*
- collide with, bang into, run into, crash into

2 *I **bumped into** one of my friends in the bookshop.*
- meet, come across, run into

bump noun

1 *We felt a **bump** as the plane landed.*
- thud, thump, bang, blow, knock

2 *How did you get that **bump** on your head?*
- lump, swelling, bulge

bumpy adjective

1 *The car jolted up and down on the **bumpy** road.*
- rough, uneven, irregular, lumpy
OPPOSITE smooth, even

2 *We had a **bumpy** ride in a jeep over muddy tracks.*
- bouncy, jerky, jolting, lurching, choppy

bunch noun

1 *The jailer jangled a **bunch** of keys.*
- bundle, cluster, collection, set

2 *She picked a **bunch** of flowers.*
- bouquet, posy, spray

3 *(informal) They're a friendly **bunch** of people.*
- group, set, circle, band, gang, crowd

bundle noun

*I found a **bundle** of old newspapers.*
- bunch, batch, pile, stack, collection, pack, bale

bundle verb

1 *We **bundled** up the papers that were on the desk.*
- pack, tie, fasten, bind

2 *The police **bundled** him into the back of their car.*
- move hurriedly, push, jostle

burden noun

1 *Each mule was carrying a heavy **burden**.*
- load, weight, cargo

2 *The captain has the **burden** of organizing the players.*
- responsibility, obligation, duty, pressure, stress, trouble, worry

burden verb

*I won't **burden** you with my own problems.*
- bother, worry, trouble, distress, encumber, lumber
- (informal) saddle

burglar noun

*The **burglars** must have got in through the window.*
- robber, thief, intruder

burglary noun SEE **stealing**

burn verb

1 *We could see the campfire **burning** in the distance.*

- be alight, be on fire, blaze, flame, flare, flicker
- To burn without flames is to glow or smoulder.

2 *The captain ordered them to **burn** the enemy ship.*

- set fire to, incinerate, reduce to ashes
- To start something burning is to ignite, kindle, or light it.
- To burn something slightly is to char, scorch, or singe it.
- To hurt someone with boiling liquid or steam is to scald them.
- To burn a dead body is to cremate it.
- To burn a mark on an animal is to brand it.

burning adjective

*I had a **burning** desire to open the casket.*

- strong, intense, exteme, acute, eager, fervent, passionate

burrow noun

*The field was full of rabbit **burrows**.*

- hole, tunnel
- A piece of ground with many burrows is a warren.
- A fox's burrow is called an earth.
- A badger's burrow is called an earth or set.

FOR OTHER ANIMAL HOMES

SEE **animal**

burrow verb

*Rabbits have been **burrowing** under the fence.*

- tunnel, dig, excavate, mine

burst verb

*The balloon **burst** when my brother sat on it.*

- puncture, rupture, break, give way, split, tear

bury verb

1 *The document was **buried** under a pile of old letters.*

- cover, conceal, hide, secrete

2 *They say the old witch was **buried** in that graveyard.*

- inter, entomb

bush noun

*Birds often build their nests in **bushes**.*

- shrub

bushy adjective

*The troll had **bushy** green eyebrows.*

- hairy, thick, dense, shaggy, bristly

business noun

1 *My uncle runs a restaurant **business**.*

- company, firm, organization

2 *The new bookshop does a lot of **business**.*

- trade, trading, buying and selling, commerce

3 *What sort of **business** do you want to go into?*

- work, job, career, employment, industry, occupation, profession, trade

4 *He left early to attend to some urgent **business**.*

- matter, issue, affair, problem, point, concern, question

bustle verb

*Miss Flyte **bustled** about the kitchen making tea.*

- rush, dash, hurry, scurry, scuttle, fuss

busy adjective

1 *Mum is **busy** making my birthday cake just now.*

- occupied, engaged, employed, working, slaving away, beavering away
- (informal) hard at it, up to your eyes
- A common simile is as busy as a bee.
OPPOSITE idle

2 *Christmas is a very **busy** time for shops.*

- active, hectic, frantic, lively
OPPOSITE quiet, restful

3 *Is the town always this **busy** on Saturdays?*

- crowded, bustling, hectic, lively, teeming
OPPOSITE quiet, peaceful

butt verb

*The Minotaur **butted** Theseus against the wall.*

- hit, bump, knock, push, ram, shove

a
b
c
d
e
f
g
h
i
j
k
l
m
n
o
p
q
r
s
t
u
v
w
x
y
z

to butt in
*Please don't **butt in** when I'm talking.*
- interrupt, cut in

buy verb
*I'm saving up to **buy** a skateboard.*
- get, pay for, purchase, acquire
OPPOSITE sell

buzz noun, verb FOR VARIOUS SOUNDS
SEE **sound** noun

Cc

cabin noun
1 *The outlaws hid in a **cabin** in the woods.*
- hut, shack, shed, lodge, chalet, shelter
2 *The crew assembled in the captain's **cabin**.*
- berth, quarters, compartment

cable noun
1 *The tent was held down with strong **cables**.*
- rope, cord, line, chain
2 *Don't trip over the computer **cable**.*
- flex, lead, wire, cord

cadet noun
*My cousin is a **cadet** in the police force.*
- recruit, trainee, beginner, learner

cafe noun
*We had lunch in a **cafe** overlooking the river.*
- cafeteria, coffee shop, tearoom, snack bar, buffet, canteen, bistro, brasserie
FOR OTHER PLACES TO EAT
SEE **restaurant**

cage noun
- A large cage or enclosure for birds is an aviary.
- A cage or enclosure for poultry is a coop.
- A cage or enclosure for animals is a pen.
- A cage or box for a pet rabbit is a hutch.

cake adjective
*Do you prefer carrot **cake** or chocolate cake?*
- sponge, flan
- A small individual cake is a cupcake or fairy cake.

caked adjective
*My trainers are **caked** with mud.*
- coated, covered, plastered, mired

calamity noun
*The fire in the warehouse was a **calamity**.*
- disaster, catastrophe, tragedy, misfortune, mishap, blow

calculate verb
*I **calculated** that it would take an hour to walk home.*
- work out, compute, figure out, reckon, add up, count, total
- To calculate something roughly is to estimate.

call noun
1 *We heard a **call** for help from inside the cave.*
- cry, exclamation, scream, shout, yell
2 *Grandad made an unexpected **call**.*
- visit, stop, stay
3 *There's not much **call** for suncream in winter.*
- demand, need

call verb
1 *'Stop that racket!' **called** the janitor.*
- cry out, exclaim, shout, yell
FOR OTHER WAYS TO SAY SOMETHING
SEE **say**
2 *It was too late at night to **call** my friends.*
- phone, ring, telephone
3 *The headteacher **called** me to her office.*
- summon, invite, send for, order

4 The doctor **called** to see if I was feeling better.
- visit, pay a visit, drop in, drop by

5 They **called** the baby Jessica.
- name, baptize, christen, dub

6 What is your new book going to be **called**?
- name, title, entitle

to call something off
It was so rainy that we **called off** the barbecue.
- cancel, abandon, postpone

to call someone names
It's not funny to **call** people **names**.
- insult, be rude to, make fun of, mock

calm adjective

1 The weather was too **calm** to fly our kites.
- still, quiet, peaceful, tranquil, serene, windless
  OPPOSITE stormy, windy

2 The sea was **calm**, and we had a pleasant voyage.
- smooth, still, flat, motionless, tranquil
  OPPOSITE rough, choppy

3 I tried to stay **calm** before my judo exam.
- cool, level-headed, patient, relaxed, sedate, unemotional, unexcitable, untroubled
  OPPOSITE anxious, nervous

camel noun
- A camel with a single hump is a dromedary camel.
- A camel with two humps is a bactrian camel.

camp noun
From the hill we saw a **camp** in the field below us.
- campsite, camping ground, base
- A military camp is an encampment.

campaign noun

1 Will you join our **campaign** to save the whale?
- movement, crusade, drive, fight, effort, struggle

2 The army launched a **campaign** to recapture the city.
- operation, offensive, action, war

cancel verb
We had to **cancel** the race because of the weather.
- abandon, call off, scrap, drop
- (informal) scrub, ditch, axe
- To cancel something after it has already begun is to abort it.
- To put something off until later is to postpone it.
- To cancel items on a list is to cross out, delete, or erase them.

candidate noun
- A candidate for a job is an applicant.
- A candidate in an examination is an entrant.
- A person competing with others in a contest is a competitor, contender, or contestant.

canopy noun
We sheltered from the rain under a **canopy**.
- awning, cover, shade

cap noun

1 The tennis players wore **caps** because it was sunny.

FOR VARIOUS KINDS OF HAT

SEE **hat**

2 Who left the **cap** off the toothpaste?
- cover, lid, top

cap verb
Mount Everest is always **capped** with snow.
- cover, top, crown

capable adjective
She is a **capable** ballet dancer.
- competent, able, accomplished, proficient, skilful, skilled, gifted, talented
  OPPOSITE incompetent

to be capable of
Do you think the professor is **capable of** murder?
- be able to do, be equal to, be up to
  OPPOSITE be incapable of

a
b
c
d
e
f
g
h
i
j
k
l
m
n
o
p
q
r
s
t
u
v
w
x
y
z

a
b
c
d
e
f
g
h
i
j
k
l
m
n
o
p
q
r
s
t
u
v
w
x
y
z

capacity noun
1 *Alice has a great **capacity** for making friends.*
- ability, power, potential, capability, competence, talent
- (*informal*) knack
2 *What is the **capacity** of this glass?*
- size, volume, space, extent, room
3 *She spoke in her **capacity** as team leader.*
- position, function, role, office

cape noun
1 *We could see the island from the **cape**.*
- headland, promontory, point, head
2 *The lady wore a **cape** of black velvet.*
- cloak, shawl, wrap, robe
- (*old use*) mantle

capital noun
1 *Paris is the **capital** of France.*
- chief city, centre of government
2 *We have enough **capital** to start a new business.*
- funds, money, finance, cash, assets, savings, means, resources

capital letter
*Start a new sentence with a **capital letter**.*
- block capital, block letter

capsize verb
*The canoe **capsized** when it hit a rock.*
- overturn, tip over, turn over, keel over
- (*informal*) turn turtle

capsule noun
1 *This **capsule** contains poison.*
- pill, tablet, lozenge
2 *The space **capsule** is designed to orbit Mars.*
- module, craft, pod
FOR OTHER WORDS TO DO WITH SPACE TRAVEL
SEE **space**

captain noun
*The **captain** brought his ship safely into harbour.*
- commander, commanding officer, master, skipper

captive noun
*The **captives** were thrown into the dungeon.*
- prisoner, convict
- A person who is held captive until some demand is met is a hostage.

captive adjective
*The pirates held the crew **captive** for ten days.*
- imprisoned, captured, arrested, detained, jailed
OPPOSITE free, released

captivity noun
*The hostages have been released from **captivity**.*
- imprisonment, confinement, detention, incarceration
OPPOSITE freedom

capture verb
1 *The bank robbers were **captured** by police this morning.*
- catch, arrest, apprehend, seize, take prisoner
- (*informal*) nab, nick
2 *The castle has never been **captured** by enemy forces.*
- occupy, seize, take, take over, win

car noun

> **WORD WEB**
> *Our **car** is getting repaired in the garage.*
> - motor car, motor, vehicle (*American*) automobile
> - An informal name for an old, noisy car is a banger.
>
> SOME TYPES OF CAR
> convertible, coupé, estate, four-wheel drive, hatchback, (*trademark*) Jeep, (*trademark*) Land Rover, limousine or (*informal*) limo, (*trademark*) Mini, patrol car or police car, people carrier, racing car, saloon, sports car
> - Very early cars are veteran or vintage cars.
>
> THE MAIN PARTS OF A CAR ARE
> body, bonnet, boot, bumper, chassis, doors, engine, exhaust pipe, fuel tank, gearbox, headlamps, lights, mirrors, roof, tyres, undercarriage, wheels, windscreen, wings

THE MAIN CONTROLS IN A CAR ARE
accelerator, brake, choke, clutch,
gear lever, handbrake, ignition key,
indicators, steering wheel,
windscreen wipers
FOR OTHER VEHICLES
SEE **vehicle**

carcass noun
*The lions fed on the **carcass** of the
antelope.*
• body, corpse, cadaver, remains

card noun

WORD WEB

1 *Did you send her a birthday **card**?*

CARDS TO SEND ON SPECIAL OCCASIONS
birthday card, Christmas card,
Diwali card, Easter card, get well
card, greetings card, Hannukah
card, invitation, notelet, picture
postcard, sympathy card, thank you
card, Valentine

2 *The magician shuffled the pack of
cards.*

SOME CARD GAMES
beggar-my-neighbour, blackjack,
bridge, canasta, cribbage, go fish,
old maid, patience, poker, pontoon,
rummy, snap, solitaire, whist
• A complete set of playing cards is
a pack.
• All the cards with the same sign
on them are a suit.
THE SUITS IN A PACK OF CARDS ARE
clubs, diamonds, hearts, spades
NAMES FOR SPECIAL CARDS ARE
king, queen, jack or knave, ace,
joker
• The king, queen, and jack are
called court cards.

care noun
1 *The old wizard's face was full of **care**.*
• worry, anxiety, trouble, concern,
burden, responsibility, sorrow, stress
2 *I took great **care** with my handwriting.*
• attention, concentration,
thoroughness, thought,
meticulousness
OPPOSITE carelessness

3 *Jake left his pet hamster in my **care**.*
• charge, keeping, protection, safe
keeping, supervision
to take care
*Please **take care** crossing the road.*
• be careful, be on your guard, look
out, watch out
to take care of someone or **something**
*My granny **takes care of** me after
school.*
• care for, look after, mind, watch over,
attend to, tend

care verb
*Do you **care** which team wins the
World Cup?*
• mind, bother, worry, be interested, be
troubled, be bothered, be worried
to care for someone or **something**
1 *The veterinary hospital **cares for** sick
animals.*
• take care of, look after, attend to,
tend, nurse
2 *I don't really **care for** broccoli.*
• like, be fond of, be keen on, love

career noun
*Max had a successful **career** as a racing
driver.*
• job, occupation, profession, trade,
business, employment, calling
FOR VARIOUS CAREERS
SEE **job**

carefree adjective
*We spent two **carefree** weeks on
holiday.*
• easygoing, relaxing, light-hearted,
untroubled, stress-free, peaceful,
restful
• (*informal*) laid-back
OPPOSITE tense, stressful, hectic

careful adjective
1 *You must be more **careful** with your
spelling.*
• accurate, conscientious, thorough,
thoughtful, meticulous, painstaking,
precise
OPPOSITE careless, inaccurate

a
b
c
d
e
f
g
h
i
j
k
l
m
n
o
p
q
r
s
t
u
v
w
x
y
z

2 *Dad kept a **careful** watch on the bonfire.*
- attentive, cautious, watchful, alert, wary, vigilant

OPPOSITE careless, inattentive

to be careful

*Please **be careful** with those scissors.*
- take care, be on your guard, look out, watch out

careless adjective

1 *This is a very **careless** piece of work.*
- messy, untidy, thoughtless, inaccurate, slapdash, shoddy, scrappy, sloppy, slovenly

OPPOSITE careful, accurate

2 *I was **careless** and cut my finger.*
- inattentive, thoughtless, absent-minded, heedless, irresponsible, negligent, reckless

OPPOSITE careful, attentive

caress noun

*The mother bear gave each cub a **caress**.*
- hug, kiss, embrace, pat, stroke, touch

caress verb

*The woman gently **caressed** her child's hair.*
- stroke, touch, smooth

cargo noun

*Some planes carry **cargo** instead of passengers.*
- goods, freight, merchandise

carnival noun

*The whole village comes out for the annual **carnival**.*
- fair, festival, fête, gala, parade, procession, show, celebration, pageant

carpentry noun

*You need saws and other tools for **carpentry**.*
- woodwork, joinery

carriage noun FOR TYPES OF VEHICLE
SEE **vehicle**

carry verb

1 *I helped Mum to **carry** the shopping to the car.*
- take, transfer, lift, fetch, bring, lug

2 *Aircraft **carry** passengers and goods.*
- transport, convey

3 *The rear axle **carries** the greatest weight.*
- bear, support, hold up

to carry on

*We **carried on** in spite of the rain.*
- continue, go on, persevere, persist, keep on, remain, stay, survive

to carry something out

*The soldiers **carried out** the captain's orders.*
- perform, do, execute, accomplish, achieve, complete, finish

cart noun FOR TYPES OF VEHICLE
SEE **vehicle**

carton noun

*I put a **carton** of juice in my lunch-box.*
- box, pack, package, packet

carve verb

1 *The statue was **carved** out of stone.*
- sculpt, chisel, hew

2 *Mum **carved** the chicken for Sunday dinner.*
- cut, slice

cascade noun

*The stream poured over the rock in a **cascade**.*
- torrent, waterfall

case noun

1 *I loaded my **case** into the boot of the car.*
- suitcase, trunk
- A number of suitcases that you take on holiday is your baggage or luggage

2 *What's in those **cases** in the attic?*
- box, chest, crate, carton, casket

3 *This has been a clear **case** of mistaken identity.*
- instance, occurrence, example, illustration

4 *It was one of Sherlock Holmes's most famous **cases**.*
- inquiry, investigation

5 *She presented a good **case** for abolishing hunting.*
- argument, line of reasoning

cash noun
*How much **cash** do you have?*
- money, change, loose change, ready money, coins, notes, currency

cast verb
1 *The child **cast** a penny into the wishing-well.*
- throw, toss, drop, fling, lob, sling

2 *The statue was **cast** in bronze.*
- form, mould, shape

castle noun

WORD WEB

CASTLES AND OTHER FORTIFIED BUILDINGS
château, citadel, fort, fortress, motte and bailey, palace, stronghold, tower

PARTS OF A CASTLE
bailey, barbican, battlement, buttress, courtyard, donjon, drawbridge, dungeon, gate, gateway, keep, magazine, moat, motte, parapet, portcullis, postern, rampart, tower, turret, wall, watchtower

casual adjective
1 *It was just a **casual** remark, so don't take it too seriously.*
- accidental, chance, unexpected, unintentional, unplanned
  OPPOSITE deliberate

2 *The restaurant had a **casual** atmosphere.*
- easy-going, informal, relaxed
  OPPOSITE formal

3 *The teacher complained about our **casual** attitude.*
- apathetic, careless, slack, unenthusiastic
  OPPOSITE enthusiastic

casualty noun
*Police are reporting heavy **casualties** from the fire.*
- death, fatality, injury, loss, victim

cat noun

WORD WEB
- A male cat is a tom.
- A young cat is a kitten.
- A cat with streaks in its fur is a tabby.
- An informal word for a cat is moggy or pussy.
- A child's word for a cat is pussy.
- A word meaning 'to do with cats' is feline.

SOME BREEDS OF CAT
Abyssinian, Burmese, chinchilla, Manx, Persian, Siamese

SOME WILD ANIMALS OF THE CAT FAMILY
bobcat, cheetah, jaguar, leopard, lion, lynx, ocelot, puma, tiger, wild cat
SEE ALSO **animal**

catastrophe noun
*The drought is a **catastrophe** for the farmers.*
- disaster, calamity, misfortune, mishap, tragedy

catch verb
1 *My friends yelled at me to **catch** the ball.*
- clutch, grab, grasp, grip, hang on to, hold, seize, snatch, take

2 *One of the anglers **caught** a fish.*
- hook, net, trap

3 *The police hoped to **catch** the thief red-handed.*
- arrest, capture, corner
- (informal) nab

4 *I hope you don't **catch** my cold.*
- become infected by, contract, get
- (informal) go down with

5 *You must hurry if you want to **catch** the bus.*
- be in time for, get on

to catch on
*Their latest record didn't **catch on**.*
- become popular, do well, succeed
- (informal) make it

to catch up with someone
*If we run we'll **catch up with** them.*
- gain on, overtake

a b c d e f g h i j k l m n o p q r s t u v w x y z

a
b
c
d
e
f
g
h
i
j
k
l
m
n
o
p
q
r
s
t
u
v
w
x
y
z

catch noun
1 *The angler got a large **catch** of salmon.*
- haul

2 *The car is so cheap that there must be a **catch**.*
- problem, obstacle, snag, difficulty, disadvantage, drawback, trap, trick

3 *All the windows are fitted with safety **catches**.*
- fastening, latch, lock, bolt, hook

catching adjective
*Chickenpox is **catching**.*
- contagious, infectious

category noun
*I won first prize in the under-10s **category**.*
- group, section, class, division, set

cater verb
to cater for
*The hotel can **cater for** a hundred guests.*
- cook for, provide food for, serve, supply

cattle plural noun
- Male cattle are bulls, steers, or oxen.
- Female cattle are cows.
- Young male cattle are calves or bullocks.
- Young female cattle are calves or heifers.
- A word meaning 'to do with cattle' is bovine.
- Farm animals in general are livestock.

cause noun
1 *What was the **cause** of the trouble?*
- origin, source, start
- You can also talk about the reasons for the trouble.

2 *You've got no **cause** to complain.*
- grounds, basis, motive

3 *The sponsored walk is for a good **cause**.*
- purpose, object

cause verb
*A single spark from the fire could **cause** an explosion.*
- bring about, create, generate, lead to, give rise to, result in, provoke, arouse

caution noun
1 *We decided to proceed with **caution**.*
- care, attention, watchfulness, wariness, vigilance

2 *The traffic warden let him off with a **caution**.*
- warning, reprimand, telling-off
- (*informal*) ticking-off

cautious adjective
*My grandad is a **cautious** driver.*
- careful, attentive, watchful, wary, vigilant, hesitant
- OPPOSITE reckless

cave noun

> **WORD WEB**
> *The **cave** walls were covered with prehistoric paintings.*
> - cavern, pothole, underground chamber
> - A man-made cave with decorative walls is a grotto.
> THINGS YOU MIGHT SEE IN A CAVE
> cave painting, stalactite, stalagmite
> - The entrance to a cave is the mouth.
> - The top of a cave is the roof and the bottom is the floor.
> - Prehistoric people who lived in caves were cavemen and cavewomen, or troglodytes.
> - Someone who enjoys exploring caves is a potholer.

cave verb
to cave in
*The miners had a lucky escape when the roof **caved in**.*
- collapse, fall in

cavity noun
*The map was lodged in a secret **cavity** in the wall.*
- hole, hollow, space, chamber

cease verb
*The fighting **ceased** at midnight.*
- come to an end, end, finish, stop, halt
- OPPOSITE begin

ceaseless adjective

*The **ceaseless** noise of traffic kept me awake all night.*

- constant, continual, continuous, never-ending, non-stop, incessant, interminable, endless, everlasting, permanent, perpetual, unending, persistent, relentless
OPPOSITE brief

celebrate verb

1 *Let's **celebrate**!*

- enjoy yourself, have a good time, be happy, rejoice

2 *What shall we do to **celebrate** Granny's birthday?*

- commemorate, observe, keep

celebrated adjective

*Beatrix Potter is a **celebrated** author of children's books.*

- famous, well-known, respected, renowned, eminent, distinguished, notable, outstanding, popular, prominent
OPPOSITE unknown

celebration noun

*We had a big **celebration** for my cousin's wedding.*

- festivity, party, feast, festival, banquet, jamboree

celebrity noun

*The awards were handed out by a TV **celebrity**.*

- famous person, personality, public figure, VIP, star, idol

cellar noun

*We keep our bikes and sports gear in the **cellar**.*

- basement, vault
SEE ALSO **basement**

cemetery noun

*A famous author is buried in the local **cemetery**.*

- graveyard, burial ground, churchyard
- A place where dead people are cremated is a crematorium.

central adjective

1 *We are now in the **central** part of the building.*

- middle, core, inner, interior
OPPOSITE outer

2 *Who are the **central** characters in the story?*

- chief, crucial, essential, fundamental, important, main, major, principal, vital
OPPOSITE unimportant

centre noun

*The library is in the **centre** of the town. The burial chamber is in the **centre** of the pyramid.*

- middle, heart, core, inside, interior
- The centre of a planet or a piece of fruit is the core.
- The centre of an atom or a living cell is the nucleus.
- The centre of a wheel is the hub.
- The point at the centre of a see-saw is the pivot.
- The edible part in the centre of a nut is the kernel.
OPPOSITE edge, outside, surface

ceremony noun

1 *We watched the **ceremony** of the opening of parliament.*

- rite, ritual, formalities
- A ceremony where someone is given a prize is a presentation.
- A ceremony where someone is given a special honour is an investiture.
- A ceremony to celebrate something new is an inauguration or opening.
- A ceremony where someone becomes a member of a society is an initiation.
- A ceremony to make a church or other building sacred is a dedication.
- A ceremony to remember a dead person or a past event is a commemoration.
- A ceremony held in a church is a service.
FOR CEREMONIES WHICH CAN BE HELD IN A CHURCH
SEE **church**

a
b
c
d
e
f
g
h
i
j
k
l
m
n
o
p
q
r
s
t
u
v
w
x
y
z

2 *They had a quiet wedding without a lot of ceremony.*
- formality, pomp, pageantry, spectacle

certain adjective

1 *My mum was certain she would win the cookery competition.*
- confident, convinced, positive, sure, determined
- OPPOSITE uncertain

2 *We have certain proof that the painting is a forgery.*
- definite, clear, convincing, absolute, unquestionable, reliable, trustworthy, undeniable, infallible, genuine, valid
- OPPOSITE unreliable

3 *The damaged plane faced certain disaster.*
- inevitable, unavoidable
- OPPOSITE possible

4 *Her new book is certain to be a bestseller.*
- bound, sure

for certain
> *I'll give you the money tomorrow for certain.*
- certainly, definitely, for sure, without doubt, sure

to make certain
> *Please make certain that you switch off the lights.*
- make sure, ensure

certainly adverb
> *Baby dragons are certainly not timid.*
- definitely, undoubtedly, unquestionably, assuredly, without a doubt

certificate noun
> *At the end of the course, you will receive a certificate.*
- diploma, document, licence

chain noun

1 *The anchor was attached to a chain.*
- One ring in a chain is a link.
- A chain used to link railway wagons together is a coupling.

2 *The police formed a chain to keep the crowd back.*
- line, row, cordon

3 *Holmes described the chain of events that led to the murder.*
- series, sequence, succession, string

chair noun FOR FURNITURE TO SIT ON
SEE **seat** noun

challenge verb
I challenged Jo not to eat sweets for a week.
- dare, defy

champion noun

1 *She is the current world champion at ice-skating.*
- title-holder, prizewinner, victor, winner, conqueror

2 *Martin Luther King was a champion of civil rights.*
- supporter, advocate, defender, upholder, patron, backer

championship noun
Fifteen schools took part in the karate championship.
- competition, contest, tournament

chance noun

1 *They say there's a chance of rain later.*
- possibility, likelihood, probability, prospect, danger, risk

2 *I haven't had a chance to reply yet.*
- opportunity, time, occasion

3 *The director took a chance in hiring an unknown actor.*
- gamble, risk

by chance
> *I found the house quite by chance.*
- by accident, accidentally, by coincidence
- An unfortunate chance is bad luck or a misfortune.
- A fortunate chance is good luck or a fluke.

change verb

1 *They've changed the programme for the concert.*
- alter, modify, rearrange, reorganize, adjust, adapt, vary

2 *The town has changed a lot since Victorian times.*
- alter, become different, develop, grow, move on

3 *Can I change these jeans for a bigger size, please?*
- exchange, replace, switch, substitute
- (*informal*) swap

to change into
Tadpoles change into frogs.
- become, turn into, be transformed into

change noun
There has been a slight change of plan.
- alteration, modification, variation, difference, break
- A change to something worse is a deterioration.
- A change to something better is an improvement or a reform.
- A very big change is a revolution or transformation or U-turn.
- A change in which one person or thing is replaced by another is a substitution.

changeable adjective
The weather has been changeable today.
- variable, unsettled, unpredictable, unreliable, inconsistent, erratic, unstable
- If your loyalty is changeable you are fickle.
OPPOSITE steady

channel noun
1 *The rainwater runs along this channel.*
- ditch, duct, gully, gutter, furrow, trough
2 *How many TV channels do you get?*
- station

chaos noun
After the earthquake, the city was in chaos.
- confusion, disorder, mayhem, uproar, tumult, pandemonium, anarchy, bedlam, muddle, shambles
OPPOSITE order

chaotic adjective
Alice finds that life in Wonderland is chaotic.
- confused, disorderly, disorganized, muddled, topsy-turvy, untidy, unruly, riotous
OPPOSITE orderly, organized

chapter noun
I read a chapter of my book last night.
- part, section, division
- One section of a play is an act or scene.
- One part of a serial is an episode or instalment.

character noun
1 *Her character is quite different from her sister's.*
- personality, temperament, nature, disposition, make-up, manner
2 *Our neighbour is a well-known character in our street.*
- figure, personality, individual, person
3 *Which character would you like to play in Peter Pan?*
- part, role

characteristic noun
The Martians had some odd physical characteristics.
- feature, peculiarity, attribute, trait, distinguishing feature

characteristic adjective
Windmills are a characteristic feature of this area.
- typical, distinctive, recognizable, particular, special, unique, singular

charge noun
1 *The admission charge is five euros.*
- price, rate
- The charge made for a ride on public transport is the fare.
- The charge made to post a letter or parcel is the postage.
- A charge made to join a club is a fee or subscription.
- A charge made for certain things by the government is a duty or a tax.
- A charge made to use a private road, bridge, or tunnel is a toll.
2 *The robbers face several criminal charges.*
- accusation, allegation
3 *Many soldiers were killed in the charge.*
- assault, attack, onslaught, raid

a
b
c
d
e
f
g
h
i
j
k
l
m
n
o
p
q
r
s
t
u
v
w
x
y
z

4 *My best friend left her hamster in my charge.*
- care, keeping, protection, custody, trust

to be in charge of something
An experienced sailor was in charge of the crew.
- manage, lead, command, direct, supervise, run

charge verb
1 *The library charges ten pence for a photocopy.*
- ask for, make you pay

2 *A man has been charged with attempted robbery*
- accuse (of)

3 *The cavalry charged the enemy line.*
- attack, assault, storm, rush

charitable adjective
Christmas is a time to be charitable to others.
- generous, considerate, caring, kind, benevolent, compassionate, unselfish

OPPOSITE selfish, uncaring

charm noun
1 *In the painting, the girl's face is full of youthful charm.*
- attractiveness, appeal, charisma

2 *The sorcerer recited a magic charm.*
- spell, incantation

FOR OTHER WORDS TO DO WITH MAGIC SEE **magic** noun

3 *The boy carried a crystal as a lucky charm.*
- trinket, talisman, mascot, amulet

charm verb
Winnie the Pooh has charmed readers all over the world.
- bewitch, captivate, delight, enchant, entrance, fascinate, please

charming adjective
We drove through some charming scenery.
- delightful, attractive, pleasant, pleasing, likeable, appealing

chart noun
1 *The explorer stopped to consult his chart.*
- map

2 *This chart shows the average rainfall for each month.*
- diagram, graph, table

charter verb
We chartered a minibus for our trip.
- hire, lease, rent

chase verb
The wolves chased a deer through the forest.
- pursue, run after, follow, track, trail, hunt

chasm noun
From the bridge, we looked down at a deep chasm.
- hole, ravine, crevasse, canyon, gorge, abyss, gulf, fissure, pit, rift

chat, chatter verbs SEE **talk** verb

chatty adjective
Frank is usually shy, but today he's quite chatty.
- talkative, communicative

OPPOSITE silent

cheap adjective
1 *We got a cheap flight to London.*
- inexpensive, affordable, bargain, cut-price, discount, reasonable

2 *These tyres are made from cheap rubber.*
- inferior, shoddy, second-rate, worthless, trashy
- (*informal*) tacky, tatty

OPPOSITE superior, good-quality

cheat verb
1 *She was cheated into buying a fake diamond ring.*
- deceive, trick, swindle, double-cross, hoax
- (*informal*) con, diddle, fleece, fool, rip off

2 *Anyone who cheats in the quiz will be disqualified.*
- copy, crib

cheat noun
Don't trust him—he's a cheat.
- cheater, deceiver, swindler, fraud, impostor, hoaxer

check verb
1 *Have you **checked** your work carefully?*
- examine, inspect, look over, scrutinize

2 *The heavy snow **checked** their progress towards the Pole.*
- hamper, hinder, block, obstruct, delay, hold back, slow, slow down, halt, stop

check noun
*I need to run some **checks** on your computer.*
- test, examination, inspection, check-up

cheeky adjective
*Don't be so **cheeky**!*
- disrespectful, facetious, flippant, impertinent, impolite, impudent, insolent, insulting, irreverent, mocking, rude, saucy, shameless
OPPOSITE respectful

cheer verb
1 *We **cheered** when our team scored a goal.*
- clap, applaud, shout, yell
OPPOSITE jeer

2 *The good news **cheered** us.*
- comfort, console, gladden, delight, please, encourage, uplift
OPPOSITE sadden

to cheer up
*The weather had **cheered up** by the afternoon.*
- become more cheerful, brighten

cheerful adjective
*The sun was shining, and we set out in a **cheerful** mood.*
- happy, good-humoured, light-hearted, merry, jolly, joyful, joyous, glad, pleased, optimistic, lively, elated, animated, bright, buoyant, jovial, gleeful, chirpy
OPPOSITE sad

chemist noun
- pharmacist
- (old use) apothecary, alchemist
- A chemist's shop is a dispensary or pharmacy.

chequered adjective
*The tablecloth had a **chequered** pattern.*
- check, criss-cross
- Scottish cloth with a chequered pattern is tartan.

cherish verb
*I will **cherish** this letter forever.*
- treasure, value, prize, keep safe, look after

chess noun

> **WORD WEB**
>
> THE PIECES USED IN PLAYING CHESS ARE
> bishop, castle or rook, king, knight, pawn, queen
> SOME TERMS USED IN PLAYING CHESS
> castle, check, checkmate, mate, move, stalemate, take
> FOR OTHER BOARD GAMES
> SEE **game**

chest noun
*I found some old books in a **chest** in the attic.*
- box, crate, case, trunk

chew verb
*Are you still **chewing** that toffee?*
- eat, gnaw, munch
FOR OTHER WAYS TO EAT
SEE **eat**

chicken noun
- A female chicken is a hen.
- A male chicken is a rooster.
- A young chicken is a chick.
- A group of chickens is a brood.
- A farm which keeps chickens is a poultry farm.

chief noun
*The pirates chose Redbeard as their **chief**.*
- leader, ruler, head, commander, captain, chieftain, master, governor, president, principal
- (informal) boss

a
b
c
d
e
f
g
h
i
j
k
l
m
n
o
p
q
r
s
t
u
v
w
x
y
z

chief adjective
1 The **chief** ingredients in a trifle are jelly, custard, and cream.
- main, central, key, principal, crucial, basic, essential, important, vital, major, primary, foremost, fundamental, indispensable, necessary, significant, predominant, prominent
OPPOSITE unimportant, minor, trivial
2 Albert was Queen Victoria's **chief** advisor.
- head, senior

chiefly adverb
Kangaroos are found **chiefly** in Australia.
- mainly, mostly, predominantly, primarily, principally, especially

child noun
1 The book festival is aimed especially at **children**.
- boy or girl, infant, juvenile, youngster, youth, lad or lass
- (informal) kid, tot, nipper
2 How many **children** do you have?
- son or daughter, descendant, offspring
- A child who expects to inherit a title or fortune from parents is an heir or heiress.
- A child whose parents are dead is an orphan.
- A child looked after by a guardian is a ward.
SEE ALSO **baby**

childhood noun
Neil spent much of his **childhood** by the sea.
- infancy, youth, boyhood or girlhood
- The time when someone is a baby is their babyhood.
- The time when someone is a teenager is their adolescence or teens.
OPPOSITE adulthood

childish adjective
It's **childish** to make rude noises.
- babyish, immature, juvenile, infantile
OPPOSITE mature

chill verb
Chill the pudding before serving it.
- freeze, cool, make cold, refrigerate
OPPOSITE warm

chilly adjective
1 It's a **chilly** evening, so wrap up well.
- cold, cool, frosty, icy, crisp, fresh, raw, wintry
- (informal) nippy
OPPOSITE warm
2 The librarian gave me a very **chilly** look.
- unfriendly, hostile, unwelcoming, unsympathetic
OPPOSITE friendly

chime verb
The church clock **chimed** at midnight.
- ring, sound, strike, peal, toll
FOR SOUNDS MADE BY A BELL
SEE **bell**

chimney noun
- A chimney on a ship or steam engine is a funnel.
- A pipe to take away smoke and fumes is a flue.

chink noun
1 We peeped through a **chink** in the wall.
- crack, crevice, gap, hole, space, opening, rift, cut, split, slit, slot
2 I could hear the **chink** of coins in his pocket.
- clink, ring, tinkle
FOR OTHER KINDS OF SOUND
SEE **sound** noun

chip noun
1 There were **chips** of broken glass on the pavement.
- bit, piece, fragment, scrap, sliver, splinter, flake, shaving
2 This mug's got a **chip** in it.
- crack, nick, notch, flaw

chip verb
I **chipped** a cup while I was washing up.
- crack, nick, notch, damage

choice noun
1 My bike had a flat tyre, so I had no **choice** but to walk.
- alternative, option

2 *She wouldn't be my **choice** as team captain.*

- preference, selection, pick, vote

3 *The greengrocer has a good **choice** of vegetables.*

- range, selection, assortment, array, mixture, variety, diversity

choke verb

1 *This tie is so tight it's **choking** me.*

- strangle, suffocate, stifle, throttle

2 *Thick fumes made the firefighters **choke**.*

- cough, gasp

choose verb

1 *We had a show of hands to **choose** a winner.*

- select, appoint, elect, vote for

2 *I **chose** the blue shoes to go with my dress.*

- decide on, select, pick out, opt for, plump for, settle on, single out

3 *Lola **chose** to stay at home.*

- decide, make a decision, determine, prefer, resolve

chop verb

1 ***Chop** the celery into large chunks.*

- cut, split

2 *They **chopped** down the undergrowth to make a path.*

- hack, slash
- To chop down a tree is to fell it.
- To chop off an arm or leg is to amputate it.
- To chop a branch off a tree is to lop it.
- To chop food into small pieces is to dice or mince it.

chorus noun

1 *I'm singing in the **chorus** in the school musical.*

- choir

2 *I forgot the words to the song, so I just sang the **chorus**.*

- refrain

chubby adjective

*The baby chicks are fluffy and **chubby**.*

- plump, tubby, podgy, dumpy

chunk noun

*I bit a **chunk** out of my apple.*

- piece, portion, lump, block, hunk, slab, wedge

church noun

WORD WEB

PLACES WHERE CHRISTIANS WORSHIP
abbey, cathedral, chapel, meeting house, parish church

FOR PLACES WHERE PEOPLE OF OTHER RELIGIONS WORSHIP

SEE **building**

PARTS OF A CHURCH
aisle, belfry, chancel, cloister, crypt, nave, spire, steeple, transept, vestry

THINGS YOU MIGHT SEE IN A CHURCH
altar, crucifix, font, lectern, pews, pulpit

SERVICES WHICH MAY BE HELD IN A CHURCH
baptism or christening, communion, confirmation, funeral, mass, wedding

cinders plural noun

*The **cinders** from the fire were still glowing.*

- ashes, embers

circle noun

1 *We arranged the chairs in a **circle**.*

- ring, round, hoop, loop, band
- A flat, solid circle is a disc.
- A three-dimensional round shape is a sphere.
- An egg shape is an oval or ellipse.

FOR OTHER SHAPES

SEE **shape** noun

- The distance round a circle is the circumference.
- The distance across a circle is the diameter.
- The distance from the centre to the circumference is the radius.
- A circular movement is a revolution or rotation.
- A circular trip round the world is a circumnavigation.
- A circular trip of a satellite round a planet is an orbit.

2 *She has a wide **circle** of friends.*

- group, set, crowd

a b **c** d e f g h i j k l m n o p q r s t u v w x y z

circle verb
*The vultures **circled** overhead.*
- turn, go round, revolve, rotate, wheel

circular adjective
*The flying saucer was **circular** in shape.*
- round, ring-shaped, disc-shaped

circulate verb
1 *Blood **circulates** in the body.*
- go round, move round

2 *I asked friends to **circulate** our newsletter.*
- distribute, send round, issue

circumference noun
*There is a fence around the **circumference** of the field.*
- perimeter, border, boundary, edge, fringe

circumstances plural noun
*He described the **circumstances** which led to the accident.*
- situation, conditions, background, causes, context, details, facts, particulars

citizen noun
*The **citizens** of New York are proud of their city.*
- resident, inhabitant

city noun
- The chief city of a country or region is the metropolis.
- An area of houses outside the central part of a city is the suburbs.
- A word meaning 'to do with a town or city' is urban.
- A word meaning 'to do with a city and its suburbs' is metropolitan.
  SEE ALSO **town**

civilization noun
*We are studying the **civilization** of ancient Egypt.*
- culture, society, achievements, attainments

civilized adjective
*Trolls seldom behave in a **civilized** manner.*
- polite, well-behaved, well-mannered, orderly, cultured, sophisticated, refined
OPPOSITE uncivilized

claim verb
1 *You can **claim** your prize for the raffle here.*
- ask for, request, collect, demand, insist on

2 *The professor **claims** to be an expert on dinosaurs.*
- declare, assert, allege, maintain, argue, insist

clamber verb
*We **clambered** over the rocks towards the sea.*
- climb, scramble, crawl, move awkwardly

clammy adjective
*The walls of the dungeon were cold and **clammy**.*
- damp, moist, dank, slimy, sticky

clang, clank nouns, verbs FOR VARIOUS SOUNDS
SEE **sound** noun

clap verb
1 *The audience **clapped** loudly at the end of the concert.*
- applaud, cheer

2 *Suddenly, a hand **clapped** me on the shoulder.*
- slap, hit, pat, smack

clarify verb
*Can you **clarify** what you want us to do?*
- explain, make clear, simplify, throw light on
OPPOSITE confuse

clash noun
1 *The **clash** of cymbals made me jump.*
- crash, bang, ringing

2 *There was a **clash** between rival supporters at the match.*
- argument, confrontation, conflict, fight, scuffle
- (*informal*) scrap

clash verb

1 *The cymbals clashed.*
- crash, resound
2 *Two good films clash on TV tonight.*
- coincide, happen at the same time
3 *Demonstrators clashed with the police.*
- argue, fight, get into conflict, squabble

clasp verb

1 *My little brother clasped my hand.*
- grasp, grip, hold, squeeze, cling to
2 *She clasped him in her arms.*
- embrace, hug

clasp noun

The cloak was held in place by a gold clasp.
- fastener, fastening, brooch, clip, pin, buckle, hook

class noun

1 *There are 26 children in our class.*
- form, set, stream
- The other pupils in your class are your classmates.
2 *There are many different classes of plants.*
- category, group, classification, division, set, sort, type, kind, species
3 *The ancient Romans divided people into social classes.*
- level, rank, status

classic adjective

Notice that **classic** means **excellent of its kind**, while **classical** means either **to do with the ancient Greeks and Romans**, or **to do with serious music written in the past.**

That was a classic tennis final this year.
- excellent, first-class, first-rate, top-notch, exceptional, fine, great, admirable, masterly, model, perfect
OPPOSITE ordinary

classified adjective

The spy gave classified information to the enemy.
- confidential, secret, top secret, private

classify verb

We classified the leaves according to their shape.
- group, organize, put into sets, sort, class, grade

claw verb

We could hear the monster clawing at the door.
- scratch, scrape, tear, savage

clean adjective

1 *Can you bring me a clean cup, please?*
- spotless, washed, scrubbed, swept, tidy, immaculate, hygienic, sanitary
- An informal word meaning 'very clean' is squeaky-clean.
- A common simile is as clean as a whistle.
OPPOSITE dirty
2 *I began my diary on a clean piece of paper.*
- blank, unused, unmarked, empty, bare, fresh, new
OPPOSITE used
3 *This plaster will keep the wound clean.*
- sterile, sterilized, uninfected
4 *You can get clean water from this tap.*
- pure, clear, fresh, unpolluted, uncontaminated
5 *The referee said he wanted a clean fight.*
- fair, honest, honourable, sporting, sportsmanlike
OPPOSITE dishonourable

clean verb

1 *We cleaned the house from top to bottom.*
I tried to clean the mud off my boots.
- wash, wipe, mop, scour, scrub, polish, dust, sweep, vacuum, rinse, wring out, hose down, sponge, shampoo, swill
- To clean clothes is to launder them.
OPPOSITE dirty, mess up

a
b
c
d
e
f
g
h
i
j
k
l
m
n
o
p
q
r
s
t
u
v
w
x
y
z

2 *The nurse **cleaned** the wound with an antiseptic wipe.*
- cleanse, bathe, disinfect, sanitize, sterilize
  OPPOSITE infect, contaminate

clear adjective

1 *We saw fish swimming in the **clear** pool.*
- clean, pure, colourless, transparent
- A common simile is as clear as crystal.
- A simile which means the opposite is as clear as mud.
  OPPOSITE opaque

2 *It was a beautiful **clear** day.*
- bright, sunny, cloudless, unclouded
- A clear night is a moonlit or starlit night.
  OPPOSITE cloudy, overcast

3 *The instructions on the map were quite **clear**.*
- plain, understandable, intelligible, lucid, unambiguous
  OPPOSITE ambiguous, confusing

4 *The actor spoke his words with a **clear** voice.*
- distinct, audible
- A common simile is as clear as a bell.
  OPPOSITE muffled

5 *The signature on this letter is not **clear**.*
- legible, recognizable, visible
  OPPOSITE illegible

6 *My camera takes nice **clear** pictures.*
- sharp, well defined, focused
  OPPOSITE unfocused

7 *Are you sure that your conscience is **clear**?*
- innocent, untroubled, blameless
  OPPOSITE guilty

8 *There's a **clear** difference between a male blackbird and a female.*
- obvious, definite, noticeable, conspicuous, perceptible, pronounced
  OPPOSITE imperceptible

9 *They made sure the road was **clear** for the ambulance.*
- open, empty, free, passable, uncrowded, unobstructed
  OPPOSITE congested

clear verb

1 *I **cleared** the weeds from the flower bed.*
- get rid of, remove, eliminate, strip

2 *The plumber **cleared** the blocked drain.*
- unblock, unclog, clean out, open up
- To clear a channel is to dredge it.

3 *I **cleared** the misty windows.*
- clean, wipe, polish

4 *If the fire alarm goes, **clear** the building.*
- empty, evacuate

5 *The fog **cleared** slowly.*
- disappear, vanish, disperse, evaporate, melt away

6 *The forecast said that the weather will **clear**.*
- become clear, brighten, fair up

7 *He was **cleared** of all the charges against him.*
- acquit, free, release

8 *The runners **cleared** the first hurdle.*
- go over, get over, jump over, pass over, vault

to clear up
*Please **clear up** this mess before you go.*
- clean up, tidy up, put right, put straight

clench verb

1 *The warrior **clenched** his teeth and gripped his sword.*
- close tightly, squeeze together, grit

2 *She **clenched** the coin tightly in her hand.*
- clasp, hold, grasp, grip

clever adjective

1 *Dr Hafiz is very **clever** and can read hieroglyphics.*
- intelligent, bright, gifted, able, knowledgeable
- (*informal*) brainy, smart
  OPPOSITE unintelligent
- An informal name for a clever person is a brainbox.
- An uncomplimentary synonym is clever clogs or smartypants.

2 *The elves were very **clever** with their fingers.*
- accomplished, capable, gifted, skilful, talented

a b **c** d e f g h i j k l m n o p q r s t u v w x y z

- If you are clever at a lot of things, you are versatile.
  OPPOSITE unskilful
3 They are **clever** enough to get away with it.
- quick, sharp, shrewd, smart
- Uncomplimentary synonyms are artful, crafty, cunning, wily.
  OPPOSITE stupid

client noun
The shop has a growing number of overseas **clients**.
- customer, user, buyer, consumer

cliff noun
The car rolled over the edge of a **cliff**.
- crag, precipice, rock face

climate noun SEE **weather** noun

climax noun
The **climax** of the film is a stunning car chase.
- high point, highlight, peak, crisis
  OPPOSITE anticlimax

climb verb
1 It took us several hours to **climb** the mountain.
- ascend, clamber up, go up, scale
2 The plane **climbed** into the clouds.
- lift off, soar, take off
3 The road **climbs** steeply up to the castle.
- rise, slope

to climb down
1 It's harder to **climb down** the rock than to get up it.
- descend, get down from
2 We all told him he was wrong, so he had to **climb down**.
- admit defeat, give in, surrender

climb noun
It's a steep **climb** up to the castle.
- ascent, hill, gradient, rise, slope, incline

cling verb
to cling to someone or **something**
1 The baby koala **clung to** its mother.
- clasp, grasp, clutch, embrace, hug
2 Ivy **clings to** the wall.
- adhere to, fasten on to, stick to

clip verb
1 The sheets of paper were **clipped** together.
- pin, staple
2 Dad **clipped** the hedges in the back garden.
- cut, trim
- To cut unwanted twigs off a tree or bush is to prune it.

cloak noun
The girl wrapped her **cloak** tightly around herself.
- cape, coat, wrap
- (old use) mantle

clock noun FOR INSTRUMENTS USED TO MEASURE TIME
SEE **time**

clog verb
The dead leaves are **clogging** the drain.
- block, choke, congest, obstruct, bung up, jam, stop up

close adjective
1 Our house is **close** to the shops.
- near, nearby, not far
- To be actually by the side of something is to be adjacent.
  OPPOSITE far, distant
2 Anisha and I are **close** friends.
- intimate, dear, devoted, fond, affectionate
3 The police made a **close** examination of the stolen car.
- careful, detailed, painstaking, minute, thorough
  OPPOSITE casual
4 It was an exciting race because it was so **close**.
- equal, even, level, well-matched
5 Open the window—it's very **close** in here.
- humid, muggy, stuffy, clammy, airless, stifling, suffocating
  OPPOSITE airy

close verb
1 Don't forget to **close** the lid.
- shut, fasten, seal, secure
2 The road has been **closed** to traffic for the parade.
- barricade, block, obstruct, stop up

a
b
c
d
e
f
g
h
i
j
k
l
m
n
o
p
q
r
s
t
u
v
w
x
y
z

a
b
c
d
e
f
g
h
i
j
k
l
m
n
o
p
q
r
s
t
u
v
w
x
y
z

3 *The band **closed** the concert with my favourite song.*
- finish, end, complete, conclude, stop, terminate
- (*informal*) wind up

clot verb
*If you cut yourself, the blood will **clot** and form a scab.*
- thicken, solidify

cloth noun

WORD WEB
*The curtains were made of striped cotton **cloth**.*
- fabric, material
- A word for cloth in general is textiles.

SOME KINDS OF CLOTH

canvas, corduroy, cotton, denim, felt, flannel, jersey, linen, lycra, muslin, nylon, polyester, rayon, satin, silk, taffeta, tweed, velvet, wool

clothe verb
to be clothed in
*The bridesmaids were **clothed in** white.*
- be dressed in, be wearing

clothes plural noun

WORD WEB
*What **clothes** are you taking on holiday?*
- clothing, garments, outfits, dress, attire, garb, finery
  (*informal*) gear, togs, get-up
- A set of clothes to wear is a costume, outfit, or suit.
- An official set of clothes worn for school or work is a uniform.

SOME ITEMS OF CLOTHING

blouse, caftan, camisole, chador or chuddar, dhoti, dress, dungarees, frock, gown, jeans, jersey, jodhpurs, jumper, kilt, kimono, leggings, miniskirt, pinafore, polo shirt, pullover, robe, sari, sarong, shirt, shorts, skirt, slacks, smock, suit, sweater, sweatshirt, trousers, trunks, T-shirt, tunic, waistcoat

OUTER CLOTHES

anorak, apron, blazer, cagoule, cape, cardigan, cloak, coat, dressing gown, duffel coat, fleece, gilet, hoodie, greatcoat, jacket, mackintosh, oilskins, overalls, overcoat, parka, poncho, raincoat, shawl, stole, tracksuit, windcheater

UNDERWEAR

boxer shorts, bra, briefs, crop top, drawers, knickers, pants, petticoat, slip, socks, stockings, tights, underpants, vest

CLOTHES FOR SLEEPING IN

nightdress or (*informal*) nightie, pyjamas

CLOTHES WORN IN THE PAST

corset, doublet, frock coat, gauntlet, ruff, toga

ACCESSORIES WORN WITH CLOTHES

belt, braces, cravat, earmuffs, glove, sash, scarf, shawl, tie
SEE ALSO **hat**, **shoe**

PARTS OF A GARMENT

bodice, button, buttonhole, collar, cuff, hem, lapel, pocket, seam, sleeve, waistband, zip

THINGS USED TO DECORATE CLOTHES

beads, frills, fringes, lace, ruffles, sequins, tassels

WRITING TIPS

You can use these words to describe **clothes**:
- baggy, casual, chic, dowdy, drab, fashionable, fine, flashy, flattering, frilly, frumpy, glamorous, ill-fitting, loose, luxurious, old-fashioned, ornate, ragged, roomy, shabby, skimpy, smart, sporty, stylish, tattered or in tatters, threadbare, tight-fitting, trendy, worn

cloud noun
*A **cloud** of steam billowed from the kettle.*
- billow, puff, haze, mist

cloudy adjective
1 *The day was cold and **cloudy**.*
• dull, overcast, grey, dark, dismal, gloomy, sunless
SEE ALSO **weather** noun
OPPOSITE cloudless
2 *We couldn't see any fish in the **cloudy** water.*
• muddy, murky, hazy, milky
OPPOSITE clear, transparent

club noun
1 *The warrior brandished a wooden **club**.*
• stick, baton, truncheon
2 *Would you like to join our book **club**?*
• group, society, association, organization, circle, union

club verb
*The giant **clubbed** Jack on the head.*
• hit, strike, thump, whack, batter
• (*informal*) bash
FOR OTHER WAYS OF HITTING
SEE **hit** verb

clue noun
1 *I don't know the answer. Can you give me a **clue**?*
• hint, suggestion, indication, pointer, tip, idea
2 *'This footprint is an important **clue**,' said the detective.*
• piece of evidence, lead
SEE ALSO **detective**

clump noun
*The owl flew into a **clump** of trees on the hill.*
• group, thicket, cluster, collection
• A clump of grass or hair is a tuft.

clumsy adjective
*The **clumsy** gnome was always breaking things.*
• careless, awkward, ungainly, inept
• An informal name for a clumsy person is butterfingers.
OPPOSITE graceful

cluster noun
*A **cluster** of people waited outside the cinema.*
• crowd, bunch, collection, assembly, gathering, knot
SEE ALSO **group**

clutch verb
*The mountaineer **clutched** his rope.*
• catch, clasp, cling to, grab, grasp, grip, hang on to, hold on to, seize, snatch

clutches plural noun
*The evil wizard had us in his **clutches**.*
• grasp, power, control

clutter noun
*We'll have to clear up all this **clutter**.*
• mess, muddle, junk, litter, rubbish, odds and ends

coach noun
1 *We went to Cardiff by **coach**.*
• bus
FOR OTHER VEHICLES
SEE **vehicle**
2 *Their football team has a new **coach**.*
• trainer, instructor

coach verb
*He was **coached** by a former champion.*
• train, teach, instruct

coarse adjective
1 *The blanket was made of **coarse** woollen material.*
• rough, harsh, scratchy, bristly, hairy
OPPOSITE soft
2 *We were shocked by their **coarse** table manners.*
• rude, offensive, impolite, improper, indecent, crude, vulgar
OPPOSITE polite, refined

coast noun
*After the disaster, oil was washed up along the **coast**.*
• coastline, shore
SEE ALSO **seashore**

coast verb
*I **coasted** down the hill on my bike.*
• cruise, freewheel, glide

coat noun
1 *The detective was wearing a thick winter **coat**.*
FOR COATS AND OTHER GARMENTS
SEE **clothes**
2 *The fox had a reddish brown **coat**.*
• hide, pelt, skin, fur, hair

a
b
c
d
e
f
g
h
i
j
k
l
m
n
o
p
q
r
s
t
u
v
w
x
y
z

a
b
c
d
e
f
g
h
i
j
k
l
m
n
o
p
q
r
s
t
u
v
w
x
y
z

- A sheep's coat is a fleece.
- **3** *The front door needs a **coat** of paint.*
- layer, coating, covering

coat verb

*We ate marshmallows **coated** with chocolate.*

- cover, spread, smear, glaze

coax verb

*Sam **coaxed** the hamster back into its cage.*

- persuade, tempt, entice

code noun

1 *There is a strict **code** of conduct for using the pool.*

- rules, regulations, laws

2 *The message was written in a secret **code**.*

- To put a message in code is to encode or encrypt it.
- To understand a message in code is to decode, decipher, or (*informal*) crack it.

coil noun

*The snake twisted itself into a **coil**.*

- spiral, twist, curl, twirl, screw, corkscrew, whirl, whorl, roll, scroll
- A coil of wool or thread is a skein.

coil verb

*The snake **coiled** itself round a branch.*

- curl, loop, roll, spiral, turn, twist, twirl, wind, writhe

coin noun

 WORD WEB

*Do you have a 50 pence **coin**?*

- piece, bit

SOME TYPES OF COIN USED IN THE PAST
doubloon, ducat, farthing, florin, guinea, shilling, sovereign

- A person who studies or collects coins is a numismatist.

coin verb

*We **coined** a new name for our group.*

- invent, make up, think up, create, devise, produce

coincide verb

*My birthday **coincides** with the school holidays.*

- clash, fall together, happen together

coincidence noun

by coincidence

*We met in town **by coincidence**.*

- by accident, by chance, accidentally, unintentionally, by a fluke

cold adjective

1 *Wrap up warm in this **cold** weather.*

- freezing, chilly, frosty, icy, raw, arctic, bitter, cool, crisp, snowy, wintry
- (*informal*) perishing
- A common simile is as cold as ice.
OPPOSITE hot, warm

2 *I tried to shelter from the **cold** wind.*

- biting, bitter, keen, penetrating, piercing

3 *I was **cold** in spite of my woolly hat.*

- freezing, frozen, chilly, chilled, shivering, shivery
- To be so cold that you become ill is to suffer from hypothermia.
OPPOSITE hot, warm

4 *The cyclops gave us a **cold** stare from his one eye.*

- unfriendly, unkind, unfeeling, distant, cool, heartless, indifferent, reserved, stony, uncaring, unemotional, unsympathetic
OPPOSITE warm, friendly

collaborate verb

*Several zoos **collaborated** on the rhino project.*

- cooperate, work together

collapse verb

1 *Many buildings **collapsed** in the earthquake.*

- fall down, fall in, cave in, give way, crumple, buckle, disintegrate, tumble down

2 *Some of the runners **collapsed** in the heat.*

- faint, pass out, fall over, keel over

colleague noun

*The police officer discussed the plan with her **colleagues**.*

- associate, partner, teammate, co-worker, workmate

collect verb

1 *Squirrels **collect** nuts for the winter.*

- gather, accumulate, hoard, heap, pile up, store up, stockpile, amass

2 *A crowd **collected** to watch the fire.*

- assemble, gather, come together, converge
  OPPOSITE scatter, disperse

3 *We **collected** a large sum for charity.*

- raise, take in

4 *She **collected** the car from the garage.*

- fetch, get, obtain, bring
  OPPOSITE drop off, hand in

collection noun

*Would you like to see my fossil **collection**?*

- assortment, set, accumulation, array, hoard, pile
- A collection of books is a library.
- A collection of poems or short stories is an anthology.

collective nouns noun FOR

COLLECTIVE NOUNS

SEE **group**

college noun FOR PLACES WHERE

PEOPLE STUDY

SEE **education**

collide verb

to collide with

*The runaway trolley **collided with** a wall.*

- bump into, crash into, run into, smash into, hit, strike

collision noun

*The **collision** dented the front wheel of my bike.*

- bump, crash, smash, knock, accident
- A collision involving a lot of vehicles is a pile-up.

colloquial adjective

*The book is written in a **colloquial** style.*

- everyday, informal, conversational, slangy
  OPPOSITE formal

colony noun

1 *New Zealand was once a British **colony**.*

- possession, territory, settlement

2 *I found a **colony** of ants in the garden.*

FOR NAMES FOR GROUPS OF INSECTS

SEE **group**

colossal adjective

*A **colossal** statue towered above us.*

- huge, enormous, gigantic, immense, massive, giant, mammoth, monumental, towering, vast
  OPPOSITE small, tiny

colour noun

WORD WEB

*What do you call that **colour**?*

- hue, shade, tint, tone, tinge
  NAMES OF VARIOUS COLOURS
  black, blue, brown, cream, gold, golden, green, grey, lavender, orange, pink, purple, red, silver, turquoise, violet, white, yellow
- The colours red, yellow, and blue are known as primary colours.
  FOR SHADES OF COLOURS
  SEE **black, blue, brown, green, red, white, yellow**

WRITING TIPS

You can use these words to describe a colour.

- to describe *A PALE COLOUR*:
  delicate, faded, light, muted, neutral, pastel, washed-out
- to describe *A STRONG COLOUR*:
  bright, fluorescent, garish, loud, neon, vibrant, zingy

colour verb

*I **coloured** my dolls' house pink.*

- paint, dye, tint

colourful adjective

1 *The rose garden is **colourful** in the summer.*

- multicoloured, showy, vibrant, bright, brilliant, gaudy
  OPPOSITE colourless

a
b
c
d
e
f
g
h
i
j
k
l
m
n
o
p
q
r
s
t
u
v
w
x
y
z

a
b
c
d
e
f
g
h
i
j
k
l
m
n
o
p
q
r
s
t
u
v
w
x
y
z

2 *The book gives a **colourful** account of life on an island.*
- exciting, interesting, lively, vivid, striking, rich, picturesque
OPPOSITE dull

colourless adjective

1 *The flask contained a **colourless** liquid.*
- uncoloured, clear, transparent, neutral, pale
- Something which has lost its colour is bleached or faded.

2 *All the characters in the book are **colourless**.*
- dull, boring, uninteresting, unexciting, drab, dreary, lacklustre
OPPOSITE colourful, interesting

column noun

1 *The roof of the temple was supported by stone **columns**.*
- pillar, post, support, shaft

2 *A **column** of soldiers wound its way across the desert.*
- line, file, procession, row, string

3 *I sometimes read the sports **column** in the newspaper.*
- article, piece, report, feature

comb verb

1 *I **combed** my hair and put it in a ponytail.*
- arrange, groom, tidy, untangle

2 *The police **combed** the house in search of clues.*
- search thoroughly, hunt through, scour, ransack, rummage through

combat noun

*Two hundred warriors were killed in **combat**.*
- battle, war, warfare, fighting
SEE ALSO **fight** noun

combat verb

*There's a new campaign to **combat** crime in the city.*
- fight, oppose, resist, stand up to, tackle, battle against, grapple with

combine verb

1 *We **combined** our pocket money to buy a kite.*
- put together, add together, join, merge, unite, amalgamate
OPPOSITE divide

2 *Combine the mixture with water to make a paste.*
- mix, stir together, blend, mingle, bind
OPPOSITE separate

come verb

1 *We expect our guests to **come** in the afternoon.*
- arrive, appear, visit
OPPOSITE go

2 *When you hear a cuckoo, you know that summer is **coming**.*
- advance, draw near

to come about
*Can you tell me how the accident **came about**?*
- happen, occur, take place, result

to come across
*I **came across** an old friend of mine.*
- find, discover, chance upon, meet, bump into

to come round or **to come to**
*How long did it take me to **come round** after the operation?*
- become conscious, revive, wake up

to come to
1 *Tell me when you **come to** the last chapter.*
- reach, get to, arrive at

2 *What did the repair bill **come to**?*
- add up to, amount to, total

comfort noun

1 *My teddy bear was a **comfort** to me when I was ill.*
- reassurance, consolation, encouragement, support, relief

2 *If I had a million pounds, I could live in **comfort**.*
- ease, luxury, contentment, well-being, prosperity, luxury, affluence

comfort verb

*The coach tried to **comfort** the team after they lost.*
- cheer up, console, reassure, encourage, hearten, sympathize with, soothe

comfortable adjective

1 *The bed was so **comfortable** that Goldilocks fell fast asleep.*
- cosy, snug, relaxing, easy, soft, warm, roomy, padded, plush
- (*informal*) comfy
OPPOSITE uncomfortable
2 *We'll need **comfortable** clothes for travelling.*
- casual, informal, loose-fitting
3 *Our cat leads a **comfortable** life.*
- contented, happy, pleasant, agreeable, well-off, prosperous, luxurious, affluent

comic, comical adjectives
*We laughed at his **comic** remarks.*
- amusing, humorous, funny, hilarious, witty, diverting
- (*informal*) hysterical
- To be comical in a cheeky way is to be facetious.
- To be comical in a silly way is to be absurd, farcical, ludicrous, or ridiculous.
- To be comical in a hurtful way is to be sarcastic.

command noun

1 *The general gave the **command** to attack.*
- order, instruction, commandment, edict
2 *Captain Nemo has **command** of the whole crew.*
- charge, control, authority (over), power (over), management, supervision
3 *My sister has a good **command** of Spanish.*
- knowledge, mastery, grasp, understanding, ability (in), skill (in)

command verb

1 *The officer **commanded** his troops to fire.*
- order, instruct, direct, tell, bid
2 *The captain **commands** the ship.*
- control, direct, be in charge of, govern, head, lead, manage, administer, supervise

commander noun
*The **commander** decided to abandon the expedition.*
- leader, chief, head, officer-in-charge

commemorate verb
*This stone **commemorates** those who died in the war.*
- celebrate, honour, pay tribute to, be a memorial to, be a reminder of, remember, salute

commence verb
*The flag is a signal for the race to **commence**.*
- begin, start, embark on

commend verb
*The head **commended** us on our work.*
- congratulate, compliment, praise, applaud
OPPOSITE criticize

comment noun
*He made some nasty **comments** about his boss.*
- remark, statement, observation, opinion, mention, reference
- A hostile comment is a criticism.

commit verb
*The thieves were planning to **commit** another robbery.*
- carry out, do, perform, execute

commitment noun

1 *Our team certainly has the **commitment** to win.*
- determination, dedication, enthusiasm, keenness, passion, resolution
2 *I've made a **commitment** to join the choir.*
- promise, pledge, vow, undertaking, guarantee

committee noun
*The tennis club is run by a **committee** of volunteers.*
- board, panel, council, body, cabinet

a
b
c
d
e
f
g
h
i
j
k
l
m
n
o
p
q
r
s
t
u
v
w
x
y
z

a
b
c
d
e
f
g
h
i
j
k
l
m
n
o
p
q
r
s
t
u
v
w
x
y
z

common adjective

1 *Colds are a **common** complaint in winter.*
- commonplace, everyday, frequent, normal, ordinary, familiar, well known, widespread
  OPPOSITE rare

2 *'Good morning' is a **common** way to greet people.*
- typical, usual, regular, routine, standard, customary, conventional, habitual, traditional
  OPPOSITE uncommon

3 *My friends and I have a **common** interest in music.*
- shared, mutual, joint

commonplace adjective

*Computers are now **commonplace** in schools.*
- common, everyday, frequent, usual, normal, ordinary, routine, familiar

commotion noun

*Football supporters were causing a **commotion** outside.*
- disturbance, row, fuss, trouble, disorder, unrest, agitation, turmoil, uproar, racket, rumpus, upheaval, riot, fracas, furore, hullabaloo, brouhaha, pandemonium, bedlam

communal adjective

*The swimming pool has **communal** showers.*
- shared, public, common
  OPPOSITE private

communicate verb

1 *Steve **communicated** his boredom with a yawn.*
- express, make known, indicate, convey, disclose, announce, pass on, proclaim, publish, report

2 *Nowadays, we **communicate** by email.*
- contact each other, correspond, be in touch

communication noun

1 *Dolphins use sound for **communication**.*
- communicating, contact, understanding each other

2 *I've received an urgent **communication**.*
- message, dispatch, letter, statement, announcement

communication noun

WORD WEB

SOME FORMS OF SPOKEN COMMUNICATION
chat, conversation, dialogue, gossip, lecture, message, phonecall, rumour, speech

SOME FORMS OF WRITTEN COMMUNICATION
blog, cable, correspondence, email, fax, greetings card, letter, memo or memorandum, note, notice, postcard, telegram, text

OTHER FORMS OF COMMUNICATION
body language, Braille, hand gesture, the Internet, Morse code, radio, semaphore, sign language or signing, telepathy, television, webcast, website

community noun

*My uncle grew up in a farming **community**.*
- area, district, neighbourhood, locality

compact adjective

*This camera is light and **compact**.*
- small, portable, petite
  OPPOSITE large

companion noun

*Zak's pony was his favourite **companion**.*
- friend, partner, comrade
- (*informal*) mate, buddy, pal, chum

company noun

1 *My cousin works for a computer **company**.*
- business, firm, corporation, organization, establishment

2 *Shrek shunned the **company** of other ogres.*
- fellowship, companionship, friendship, society

compare verb
*Can you **compare** these sets of figures?*
- contrast, juxtapose, relate, set side by side

to compare with
*This copy can't **compare with** the original painting.*
- compete with, rival, emulate, equal, match

comparison noun
1 *I put the two dresses side by side for **comparison**.*
- comparing, contrast, juxtaposition
2 *There's no **comparison** between their team and ours.*
- similarity, resemblance, likeness, match

compartment noun
*The sewing box has **compartments** for needles and pins.*
- section, division, area, space

compatible adjective
*Miss Scott and her mother were not at all **compatible**.*
- well suited, well matched
OPPOSITE incompatible

compel verb
*You can't **compel** me to come with you.*
- force, make

compelling verb
*The book gives a **compelling** account of a pirate's life.*
- powerful, convincing, irresistible, persuasive, exciting, thrilling

compensation noun
*They each got £5000 in **compensation** for the accident.*
- damages, payment, repayment

compete verb
*Five schools will be **competing** in the hockey tournament.*
- participate, perform, take part, enter

to compete against
*We are **competing against** a strong team this week.*
- oppose, play against, contend with

competent adjective
*You have to be a **competent** swimmer to join the club.*
- able, capable, skilful, skilled, accomplished, proficient, experienced, expert, qualified, trained
OPPOSITE incompetent

competition noun

> **WORD WEB**
>
> SOME KINDS OF COMPETITION
> championship, contest, game, knock-out competition, match, quiz, race, rally, series, tournament, trial
> SEE ALSO **sport**

competitor noun
*The **competitors** lined up for the start of the race.*
- contestant, contender, challenger, participant, opponent, rival
- People who take part in an exam are candidates or entrants.

complain verb
*Miss Grouch spent most of her life **complaining**.*
- moan, protest, grumble, grouse, gripe, whinge, make a fuss

to complain about
*I wrote a letter **complaining about** the noise.*
- protest about, object to, criticize, find fault with
OPPOSITE praise

complaint noun
1 *They received hundreds of **complaints** about the film.*
- criticism, objection, protest, moan, grumble
2 *You have a nasty stomach **complaint**.*
- disease, illness, ailment, sickness, infection
- (informal) upset

complement verb
*That shade of green **complements** your eyes.*
- accompany, go with

complete adjective

1 *Your training as a witch is not yet complete.*
- completed, ended, finished, accomplished, concluded
- OPPOSITE unfinished

2 *Have you got a complete set of cards?*
- whole, entire, full, intact
- OPPOSITE incomplete

3 *My birthday party was a complete disaster.*
- total, utter, sheer, absolute, thorough, downright, perfect, pure

complete verb

We have completed all the tasks on the sheet.
- finish, end, conclude, carry out, perform

complex adjective

Defusing a bomb is a complex task.
- complicated, difficult, elaborate, detailed, intricate, involved
- (*informal*) fiddly
- OPPOSITE simple

complexion noun

The elf had a greenish tinge to his complexion.
- skin, colour, colouring

FOR WAYS TO DESCRIBE COMPLEXION
SEE **face** noun

complicated adjective

The plot of the film is very complicated.
- complex, intricate, involved, difficult, elaborate, convoluted
- OPPOSITE simple, straightforward

complimentary adjective

1 *My teacher made complimentary remarks on my playing.*
- appreciative, approving, admiring, positive, favourable, flattering
- OPPOSITE critical, insulting, negative

2 *We were given complimentary tickets for the game.*
- free, gratis

compliments plural noun

It was nice to get compliments about my cooking.
- praise, appreciation, approval, congratulations, tribute
- Compliments which you don't deserve are flattery.
- OPPOSITE insults

component noun

The factory makes components for cars.
- part, bit, piece, element, spare part

compose verb

Beethoven composed nine symphonies.
- create, devise, produce, make up, think up, write

to be composed of

This quilt is composed of pieces of patchwork.
- be made of, consist of, comprise

composition noun

Is the song your own composition?
- piece, work, creation
- (*formal*) opus

FOR TYPES OF MUSICAL COMPOSITION
SEE **music**

comprehend verb

The crowd couldn't comprehend what was happening.
- understand, realize, appreciate, figure out, grasp, perceive, follow

comprehensive adjective

She gave us a comprehensive account of her travels.
- complete, full, thorough, detailed, extensive, inclusive, exhaustive, wide-ranging, encyclopedic
- OPPOSITE selective

compress verb

I tried to compress all my clothes into one bag.
- press, squeeze, cram, crush, jam, squash, stuff, flatten

comprise verb

*The team **comprised** athletes from several countries.*

- be composed of, consist of, include, contain

compulsive adjective

1 *Suddenly, I felt a **compulsive** urge to laugh.*

- compelling, overwhelming, overpowering, irresistible, uncontrollable

2 *We knew that the troll was a **compulsive** liar.*

- habitual, obsessive, incurable

compulsory adjective

*The wearing of seat belts is **compulsory**.*

- required, obligatory, necessary
- OPPOSITE optional

computer noun

> **WORD WEB**
>
> SOME KINDS OF COMPUTER
>
> laptop, mainframe, notebook, palmtop, PC or personal computer, server
>
> SOME PARTS OF A COMPUTER SYSTEM
>
> CD ROM drive, DVD drive, disk drive, hard disk, keyboard, microchip, microprocessor, modem, monitor, motherboard, mouse, port, processor, screen, terminal, touchpad
>
> OTHER TERMS USED IN COMPUTING
>
> bit, bug, byte, cursor, data, database, digital, disk, gigabyte, hardware, interface, megabyte, memory, menu, network, peripheral, printout, program, software, spyware, USB, virus, window, word-processor

concave adjective SEE **curved**

OPPOSITE convex

conceal verb

1 *The dog tried to **conceal** its bone.*

- hide, cover up, bury

2 *We tried to **conceal** our hiding place.*

- disguise, mask, screen, camouflage, make invisible

3 *Don't **conceal** the truth.*

- keep quiet about, keep secret, hush up, suppress

conceited adjective

*He was so **conceited** when he won first prize!*

- boastful, arrogant, proud, vain, self-satisfied
- (*informal*) big-headed, cocky
- OPPOSITE modest

conceive verb

1 *Who **conceived** this silly plan?*

- think up, devise, invent, make up, originate, plan, produce, work out
- (*informal*) dream up

2 *I could not **conceive** how the plan would work.*

- imagine, see

concentrate verb

1 *I had to **concentrate** to hear what she was saying.*

- be attentive, think hard, focus

2 *The crowds **concentrated** in the middle of town.*

- collect, gather, converge

concept noun

*I find the **concept** of time travel fascinating.*

- idea, thought, notion

concern verb

1 *This conversation doesn't **concern** you.*

- affect, involve, be important to, matter to, be relevant to, relate to

2 *It **concerns** me that we are destroying the rain forests.*

- bother, distress, trouble, upset, worry

concern noun

1 *My private life is no **concern** of theirs.*

- affair, business

2 *Global warming is a great **concern** to us all.*

- worry, anxiety, fear

3 *She's the head of a business **concern**.*

- company, firm, enterprise, establishment

a b c d e f g h i j k l m n o p q r s t u v w x y z

concerned adjective

1 *After waiting an hour, Julia began to feel **concerned**.*
- worried, bothered, troubled, anxious, upset, distressed

2 *We're writing a letter to all those **concerned**.*
- involved, connected, related, affected

concerning preposition

*The head spoke to me **concerning** my future.*
- about, regarding, relating to, with reference to, relevant to

concert noun

*The jazz band is giving a **concert** tonight.*
- recital, peformance, show

concise adjective

*He gave the police a **concise** account of what happened.*
- brief, short, condensed, succinct
- A concise account of something is a précis or summary.
  OPPOSITE long

conclude verb

1 *We **concluded** the Christmas concert with carols.*
- end, finish, complete, round off, wind up

2 *The concert **concluded** with some carols.*
- close, terminate, culminate

3 *They **concluded** that he was guilty.*
- decide, deduce, infer, suppose, assume, gather

conclusion noun

1 *The **conclusion** of the film was a bit puzzling.*
- close, end, finale, finish, completion, culmination

2 *'What is your **conclusion**, Inspector?'*
- decision, judgement, opinion, verdict, deduction

concrete adjective

*The police are looking for **concrete** evidence.*
- real, actual, definite, firm, solid, substantial, physical, factual, objective
  OPPOSITE abstract

condemn verb

1 *The manager **condemned** the behaviour of the players.*
- criticize, disapprove of, denounce, deplore, reproach
  OPPOSITE praise

2 *The judge **condemned** the men to death.*
- sentence
  OPPOSITE acquit

condense verb

1 *I **condensed** my poem so that it fitted on one page.*
- reduce, shorten, compress, summarize
  OPPOSITE expand

2 *Steam **condenses** on a cold window.*
- become liquid, form condensation
  OPPOSITE evaporate

condescending adjective

*The princess gave us a very **condescending** look.*
- superior, patronizing, snobbish
- (*informal*) snooty, stuck-up

condition noun

1 *Is your bike in good **condition**?*
- state, order, repair

2 *A dog needs exercise to stay in good **condition**.*
- fitness, health, shape

3 *It's a **condition** of membership that you pay a subscription.*
- requirement, obligation, term

on condition that

*You can come **on condition that** you pay your own fare.*
- provided, providing that, only if

conduct verb

1 *A guide **conducted** us round the museum.*
- guide, lead, take, accompany, escort

2 *We asked the eldest girl to **conduct** our meeting.*

- lead, manage, control, run, administer, supervise, preside over, organize, handle

to conduct yourself
*The grown-ups did not **conduct** themselves well.*

- behave, act, carry on

conduct noun
*Our teacher congratulated us on our good **conduct**.*

- behaviour, manners, attitude

confer verb
1 *They **conferred** the freedom of the city on the victorious team.*

- give (to), grant (to), present (to), award (to)

2 *The king **conferred** with his advisors before making a decision.*

- consult, have a discussion, talk things over, converse

conference noun
*All the witches were invited to a grand **conference**.*

- meeting, consultation, discussion

confess verb
*The goblin **confessed** that he had stolen the gold.*

- admit, own up to, acknowledge, reveal

confidence noun
1 *We can face the future with **confidence**.*

- hope, optimism, faith
  OPPOSITE doubt

2 *I wish I had her **confidence**.*

- self-confidence, assurance, boldness, conviction

confident adjective
1 *I am **confident** that we will win.*

- certain, sure, positive, optimistic
  OPPOSITE doubtful

2 *She is a **confident** sort of person.*

- self-confident, assertive, bold, fearless, unafraid

confidential adjective
*The details of the plan are **confidential**.*

- secret, private
  OPPOSITE public

confine verb
1 *They **confined** their discussion to the weather.*

- limit, restrict

2 *Our farm animals are not **confined** indoors.*

- enclose, surround, fence in, shut in, coop up, hem in

confirm verb
1 *The strange events **confirmed** his belief in ghosts.*

- prove, justify, support, back up, reinforce
  OPPOSITE disprove

2 *I phoned to **confirm** my appointment at the dentist.*

- verify, make official
  OPPOSITE cancel

confiscate verb
*The janitor **confiscated** our ball.*

- take away, take possession of, seize

conflict noun
*There's a lot of **conflict** in their family.*

- disagreement, quarrelling, fighting, hostility, friction, antagonism, opposition, strife, unrest

conflict verb
to conflict with
*Her account of what happened **conflicts with** mine.*

- disagree with, differ from, contradict, contrast with, clash with

conflicting adjective
*My brother and I have **conflicting** tastes in music.*

- different, contrasting, contradictory, opposite, incompatible

a
b
c
d
e
f
g
h
i
j
k
l
m
n
o
p
q
r
s
t
u
v
w
x
y
z

conform verb

to conform to or **with**
The club expels anyone who doesn't conform with the rules.
- follow, keep to, obey, abide by, agree with, fit in with, submit to
OPPOSITE disobey

confront verb
I decided to confront her and demand an apology.
- challenge, stand up to, face up to
OPPOSITE avoid

confuse verb
1 *I was confused by the directions on the map.*
- puzzle, bewilder, mystify, baffle, perplex
2 *You must be confusing me with someone else.*
- mix up, muddle

confusion noun
1 *There was great confusion when the lights went out.*
- chaos, commotion, fuss, uproar, turmoil, pandemonium, bedlam, hullabaloo
2 *There was a look of confusion on her face.*
- bewilderment, puzzlement, perplexity

congeal verb
The soup had gone cold and was starting to congeal.
- clot, thicken, set, solidify

congested adjective
The roads are congested during the rush hour.
- crowded, full, jammed, clogged, blocked, obstructed
- (*informal*) snarled up
OPPOSITE clear

congratulate verb
We congratulated the winners.
- praise, applaud, compliment
OPPOSITE criticize

congregate verb
The party guests congregated in the hall.
- gather, assemble, collect, come together
OPPOSITE disperse

connect verb
1 *What's the best way to connect these wires?*
- join, attach, fasten, link, couple, fix together, tie together
OPPOSITE separate
2 *The fingerprints connected him with the crime.*
- make a connection between, associate, relate

connection noun
There is a close connection between our two families.
- association, relationship, link

conquer verb
1 *Extra troops were sent to conquer the enemy forces.*
- beat, defeat, overcome, vanquish, get the better of, overwhelm, crush, rout, thrash
2 *Gaul was conquered by Julius Caesar.*
- seize, capture, take, win, occupy, possess
3 *Several climbers have conquered Mount Everest.*
- climb, reach the top of

conqueror noun
Cheering crowds greeted the conquerors.
- victor, winner

conquest noun
The book gave an account of the Norman conquest.
- invasion, occupation, capture, possession

conscientious adjective
Elves are very conscientious workers.
- hard working, careful, dependable, reliable, responsible, dutiful, meticulous, painstaking, thorough
OPPOSITE careless

a b c d e f g h i j k l m n o p q r s t u v w x y z

conscious adjective
1 *The patient was **conscious** throughout the operation.*
- awake, alert, aware
OPPOSITE unconscious
2 *She made a **conscious** effort to improve her work.*
- deliberate, intentional, planned
OPPOSITE accidental

consecutive adjective
*It rained for three **consecutive** days.*
- continuous, running (say **three days running**), successive

consent verb
to consent to
*The head has **consented to** our request.*
- agree to, grant, approve of, authorize
OPPOSITE refuse

consequence noun
1 *He drank the potion without thinking of the **consequences**.*
- effect, result, outcome, sequel, upshot
2 *The loss of a few pence is of no **consequence**.*
- importance, significance

conservation noun
*Our group supports the **conservation** of wildlife.*
- preservation, protection, maintenance, upkeep
OPPOSITE destruction

conservative adjective
1 *Miss Frump has a very **conservative** taste in clothes.*
- old-fashioned, conventional, unadventurous, traditional
OPPOSITE progressive, up-to-date
2 *At a **conservative** estimate, the work will take six months.*
- cautious, moderate, reasonable
OPPOSITE extreme

conserve verb
*The explorers had to **conserve** their water supply.*
- save, preserve, be sparing with, use wisely, look after, protect
OPPOSITE waste

consider verb
1 *The detective **considered** the problem carefully.*
- think about, examine, contemplate, ponder on, reflect on, study, weigh up, meditate about
2 *I **consider** this to be my best work.*
- believe, judge, reckon

considerable adjective
*1000 dollars is a **considerable** sum of money.*
- big, large, significant, substantial, sizeable
OPPOSITE negligible, insignificant

considerate adjective
*It was **considerate** of you to lend me your umbrella.*
- kind, kind-hearted, helpful, obliging, sympathetic, thoughtful, unselfish, caring, charitable, neighbourly
OPPOSITE selfish

consist verb
to consist of
1 *The planet **consists** largely **of** craters.*
- be made of, be composed of, comprise, contain, include, incorporate
2 *His job **consists** mostly **of** answering the phone.*
- involve

consistency noun
*The mixture had the **consistency** of porridge.*
- texture, thickness, density

consistent adjective
1 *These plants need to be kept at a **consistent** temperature.*
- steady, constant, regular, stable, unchanging
2 *Fortunately, our goalkeeper is a **consistent** player.*
- predictable, dependable, reliable
OPPOSITE inconsistent

console verb
*He did his best to **console** me when my dog died.*
- comfort, soothe, sympathize with, support

conspicuous adjective

1 The clock tower is a **conspicuous** landmark.
- prominent, notable, obvious, eye-catching, unmistakable, visible
2 I had made some **conspicuous** mistakes.
- clear, noticeable, obvious, evident, glaring
OPPOSITE inconspicuous

constant adjective

1 There is a **constant** noise of traffic on the motorway.
- continual, continuous, never-ending, non-stop, ceaseless, incessant, interminable, endless, everlasting, permanent, perpetual, unending, persistent, relentless
OPPOSITE changeable
2 My dog has been my **constant** friend for many years.
- faithful, loyal, dependable, reliable, firm, true, trustworthy, devoted
OPPOSITE unreliable

constitute verb

In rugby, fifteen players **constitute** a team.
- make up, compose, comprise, form

construct verb

We **constructed** a tree-house in the back garden.
- build, erect, assemble, make, put together, put up, set up
OPPOSITE demolish

construction noun

1 The **construction** of the tree-house took all afternoon.
- building, erecting, erection, assembly, setting-up
2 The hut was a flimsy **construction**.
- building, structure

consult verb

1 You should **consult** the dentist about your sore tooth.
- ask, get advice from, speak to
2 If you don't know how to spell a word, **consult** your dictionary.
- refer to

consume verb

1 The birds **consumed** all the bread in ten minutes!
- eat, devour, gobble up, guzzle
2 The truck **consumed** a great deal of fuel.
- use up
3 The building was **consumed** by fire.
- destroy

contact verb

I'll **contact** you when I have some news.
- call, call on, get in touch with, communicate with, notify, speak to, talk to, correspond with, phone, ring, write to

contagious adjective

Mumps is a very **contagious** disease.
- catching, infectious

contain verb

1 This box **contains** various odds and ends.
- hold
2 A dictionary **contains** words and definitions.
- include, incorporate, comprise, consist of

container noun

Put the left-over sauce in a **container**.
- vessel, receptacle, holder, box, case, canister, carton, pot, tub, tin

contaminate verb

The river had been **contaminated** with chemicals.
- pollute, poison, infect
OPPOSITE purify

contemplate verb

1 The princess **contemplated** herself in the mirror.
- look at, view, observe, survey, watch, stare at, gaze at
2 The robbers **contemplated** what to do next.
- think about, consider, ponder, study, reflect on, weigh up, meditate about

contemporary adjective
Do you like contemporary music?
- current, fashionable, modern, up-to-date, the latest
- (*informal*) trendy
OPPOSITE old-fashioned, out-of-date

contempt noun
The knight stared at his enemy with a look of contempt.
- hatred, scorn, loathing, disgust, dislike, distaste
OPPOSITE admiration

contend verb
I contend that I was right.
- declare, claim, argue, assert, maintain
to contend with
1 *The team had to contend with strong opposition.*
- compete with, fight against, oppose, grapple with, struggle against, strive against
2 *We had to contend with bad weather and midges!*
- cope with, deal with, face, put up with

contents plural noun
The children tried to guess the contents of the mystery parcel.
- element, ingredient, part

content adjective
Fergus was perfectly content to sit reading a book.
- happy, contented, satisfied, pleased, willing
OPPOSITE unwilling

contented adjective
After her meal, the cat looked very contented.
- happy, pleased, content, satisfied, fulfilled, serene, peaceful, relaxed, comfortable, tranquil, untroubled
OPPOSITE discontented

contest noun
The tennis final was an exciting contest.
- competition, challenge, fight, bout, encounter, struggle, game, match, tournament

contest verb
Several players contested the referee's decision.
- challenge, disagree with, question, oppose, argue against, quarrel with

contestant noun
There are twenty contestants in the spelling competition.
- competitor, participant, player, contender

continual adjective
I get sick of their continual arguing.
- constant, persistent, perpetual, repeated, frequent, recurrent, eternal, unending
SEE ALSO **continuous**
OPPOSITE occasional

continue verb
1 *We continued our search until it got dark.*
- keep up, prolong, sustain, persevere with, pursue
- (*informal*) stick at
2 *This rain can't continue for long.*
- carry on, last, persist, endure, keep on, go on, linger
3 *We'll continue our meeting after lunch.*
- resume, proceed with, pick up

continuous adjective
We had continuous rain all through our holiday.
- never-ending, non-stop, ceaseless, everlasting, incessant, unbroken, unceasing, uninterrupted
- An illness which continues for a long time is a chronic illness.
SEE ALSO **continual**
OPPOSITE intermittent

contract noun
The actress has signed a contract for a new film.
- agreement, deal, undertaking
- A contract between two countries is an alliance or treaty.
- A contract to end a dispute about money is a settlement.

a b d e f g h i j k l m n o p q r s t u v w x y z

contract verb
1 *Metal **contracts** when it gets colder.*
- reduce, lessen, shrink, tighten
  OPPOSITE expand
2 *The crew **contracted** a mysterious illness.*
- catch, develop, get

contradict verb
*I didn't dare to **contradict** the witch.*
- challenge, disagree with, speak against

contraption noun
*The inventor's house was full of weird **contraptions**.*
- machine, device, gadget, invention, apparatus, contrivance, mechanism, gizmo

contrary adjective
*Griselda had always been a sulky, **contrary** child.*
- awkward, difficult, stubborn, disobedient, obstinate, uncooperative, unhelpful, wilful, perverse
  OPPOSITE cooperative

contrary to
__Contrary to__ popular belief, snakes are not slimy.
- differing from, against, opposing, in the face of, unlike

contrast verb
*We were asked to **contrast** two of our favourite poems.*
- compare, juxtapose, distinguish between
2 *Her handwriting **contrasts** with mine.*
- clash, differ (from)

contrast noun
*There is a sharp **contrast** between the two paintings.*
- difference, distinction, opposition
  OPPOSITE similarity

contribute verb
*Will you **contribute** something to our charity collection?*
- donate, give, provide
- (*informal*) chip in

to contribute to
*The sunny weather **contributed to** our enjoyment.*
- add to, help, aid, encourage, enhance

contrive verb
*They **contrived** a way to escape from the dungeon.*
- think up, plan, make up, create, invent

control noun
*The captain had complete **control** over the crew.*
- authority, power, command, government, management, direction, leadership, guidance

control verb
1 *The government **controls** the country's affairs.*
- be in control of, be in charge of, manage, run, command, direct, lead, guide, govern, administer, regulate, rule, superintend, supervise
2 *Can't you **control** that dog?*
- manage, handle, restrain
3 *They built a dam to **control** the floods.*
- check, curb, hold back, contain

controversial adjective
*The decision to award a penalty was **controversial**.*
- debatable, questionable, arguable

controversy noun
*There is much **controversy** about the election results.*
- disagreement, debate, argument, dispute, quarrelling

convalesce verb
*My aunt is **convalescing** after an operation.*
- recover, get better, improve
- (*informal*) be on the mend

convenient adjective

1 *Is there a convenient place to put my umbrella?*
- suitable, appropriate, available, nearby, accessible
OPPOSITE inconvenient

2 *Mum has a convenient tool for opening jars.*
- handy, helpful, useful, labour-saving, neat

conventional adjective

The conventional way to greet someone is to shake hands.
- customary, traditional, usual, accepted, common, normal, ordinary, everyday, routine, standard, regular, habitual, orthodox
OPPOSITE unconventional

converge verb

The two rivers converge at this point.
- come together, join, meet, merge, combine, coincide
OPPOSITE divide

conversation noun

- An informal conversation is a chat or gossip.
- A more formal conversation is a discussion.
- A very formal conversation is a conference.
- Conversation in a play or novel is dialogue.

converse verb

The travellers conversed happily for several minutes.
- chat, talk, have a conversation, engage in conversation
SEE ALSO **talk** verb

convert verb

1 *We have converted our attic into a games room.*
- change, adapt, alter, transform

2 *I never used to like football, but my cousin converted me.*
- change someone's mind, persuade, convince, win over

convex adjective SEE **curved**
OPPOSITE concave

convey verb

1 *The breakdown truck conveyed our car to a garage.*
- bring, carry, deliver, take, move, bear, transfer, transport
- To convey something by sea is to ferry or ship it.

2 *What does his message convey to you?*
- communicate, tell, reveal, indicate, signify, mean

convict noun

Four convicts have escaped from the prison.
- prisoner, criminal

convict verb

The thieves were convicted and sent to prison.
- condemn, declare guilty, sentence
OPPOSITE acquit

convince verb

The prisoner convinced them that he was innocent.
- persuade, assure, satisfy, make believe, win round

convincing adjective

I tried to think of a convincing excuse.
- persuasive, believable, credible, plausible

cook verb

WORD WEB
- To cook food for guests or customers is to cater for them.
- Cooking as a business is catering.
- The art or skill of cooking is cookery.

SOME WAYS TO COOK FOOD
bake, barbecue, boil, braise, brew, broil, casserole, deep-fry, fry, grill, poach, roast, sauté, simmer, steam, stew, toast

OTHER WAYS TO PREPARE FOOD
baste, blend, chop, dice, grate, grind, infuse, knead, liquidize, marinade, mince, mix, peel, purée, sieve, sift, stir, whisk

a
b
c
d
e
f
g
h
i
j
k
l
m
n
o
p
q
r
s
t
u
v
w
x
y
z

a
b
c
d
e
f
g
h
i
j
k
l
m
n
o
p
q
r
s
t
u
v
w
x
y
z

SOME ITEMS THAT ARE USED FOR COOKING

baking tin or tray, barbecue, blender, bowl, carving knife, casserole, cauldron, chopping board, colander, cooker, dish, food processor, frying pan, grill, ladle, liquidizer, microwave, mincer, oven, pan, pot, rolling pin, saucepan, skewer, spatula, spit, strainer, toaster, whisk, wok, wooden spoon
SEE ALSO **crockery, cutlery, kitchen**

cook noun

- The chief cook in a restaurant or hotel is the chef.
- A person who cooks food as a business is a caterer.

cool adjective

1 *The weather is **cool** for the time of year.*
- chilly, coldish
  OPPOSITE hot, warm
2 *Would you like a **cool** glass of lemonade?*
- chilled, iced, refreshing
  OPPOSITE hot
3 *Clifford remained **cool** when everyone else panicked.*
- calm, level-headed, relaxed, unexcitable, unflustered
- (*informal*) laid-back
- A common simile is as cool as a cucumber.
  OPPOSITE frantic
4 (*informal*) *Those rollerskates are really **cool**!*
- chic, fashionable, smart
- (*informal*) trendy

cooperate verb

to cooperate with
*The scouts **cooperated with** each other to build a fire.*
- work with or together with, collaborate with, aid, assist, support

cope verb
*Shall I help you, or can you **cope** on your own?*
- manage, carry on, get by, make do, survive

to cope with
*I can't **cope with** all this homework!*
- deal with, handle, manage, get through

copy noun
*That isn't the original painting—it's a **copy**.*
- replica, reproduction, duplicate, imitation, likeness
- A copy made to deceive someone is a fake or a forgery.
- A living organism which is identical to another is a clone.

copy verb
1 *I **copied** the poem into my jotter.*
- duplicate, reproduce, write out
- To copy something in order to deceive is to fake or forge it.
2 *My parrot can **copy** my voice.*
- imitate, impersonate, mimic

cord noun
*The pilot pulled the **cord** to open his parachute.*
- string, rope, tape, strap, line, cable, flex

core noun
*It is very hot at the earth's **core**.*
- centre, middle, inside, heart, nucleus

corn noun
*The farmer was growing **corn** in the field.*
- grain, cereal, wheat

corner noun
1 *I'll meet you at the **corner** of the road.*
- turn, turning, junction, crossroads, intersection
- The place where two lines meet is an angle.
2 *I sat in a quiet **corner** and read her letter.*
- alcove, recess, nook

correct adjective
1 *Your answers are all **correct**.*
- right, accurate, exact, faultless
2 *I hope he has given us **correct** information.*
- true, genuine, authentic, precise, reliable, factual

3 *What is the **correct** way to address this letter?*
- proper, acceptable, regular, appropriate, suitable
OPPOSITE wrong

correct verb

1 *I have to **correct** my spelling mistakes.*
- alter, put right, make better, improve

2 *Miss Nicol spent the day **correcting** exam papers.*
- mark

correspond verb
to correspond with

1 *Her version of the story doesn't **correspond with** mine.*
- agree with, match, be similar to, be consistent with, tally with

2 *Carol **corresponds with** a friend in Paris.*
- write to, communicate with, send letters to

corrode verb

*This acid will **corrode** metal.*
- eat away, erode, rot, rust

corrupt adjective

***Corrupt** officials had accepted millions of pounds in bribes.*
- dishonest, criminal, untrustworthy
- (informal) bent, crooked
OPPOSITE honest

cost verb

*How much do these shoes **cost**?*
- be worth, go for, sell for

cost noun

*The bill shows the total **cost**.*
- price, charge, amount, payment, fee, figure, expense, expenditure, tariff
- The cost of travelling on public transport is the fare.

costly adjective

*It would be too **costly** to repair the car.*
- dear, expensive
OPPOSITE cheap

costume noun

*The Irish dancers were wearing national **costumes**.*
- outfit, dress, clothing, suit, attire, garment, garb
- (informal) get-up
- A costume you dress up in for a party is fancy dress.
- A set of clothes worn by soldiers or members of an organization is a uniform.
SEE ALSO **clothes**

cosy adjective

*It's good to feel **cosy** in bed when it's cold outside.*
- comfortable, snug, soft, warm, secure
OPPOSITE uncomfortable

couch noun

*My brother sat on the **couch** watching TV all weekend.*
- settee, sofa
FOR OTHER TYPES OF SEAT
SEE **seat** noun

counsel verb

*His advisors **counselled** him to surrender.*
- advise, guide, direct, encourage, recommend, urge

count verb

1 *I'm **counting** the days until my birthday.*
- add up, calculate, compute, estimate, reckon, figure out, work out, total

2 *It's playing well that **counts**, not winning.*
- be important, be significant, matter
to count on
*You can **count on** me to support you.*
- depend on, rely on, trust, bank on

countless adjective

***Countless** people watched the TV broadcast.*
- a great many, numerous, innumerable
OPPOSITE finite

a
b
c
d
e
f
g
h
i
j
k
l
m
n
o
p
q
r
s
t
u
v
w
x
y
z

a
b
c
d
e
f
g
h
i
j
k
l
m
n
o
p
q
r
s
t
u
v
w
x
y
z

country noun

1 *England and Wales are separate* **countries**.
- nation, state, land, territory
- A country ruled by a king or queen is a kingdom, monarchy, or realm.
- A country governed by leaders elected by the people is a democracy.
- A democratic country with a President is a republic.

2 *We went for a picnic in the* **country**.
- countryside, landscape, outdoors, scenery
- A word meaning 'to do with the country' is rural and its opposite is urban.
  OPPOSITE town, city

coupon noun
You can exchange these **coupons** *for a free mug.*
- token, voucher, ticket

courage noun
The rescue dogs showed great **courage**.
- bravery, boldness, daring, fearlessness, nerve, pluck, valour, heroism, grit
- (*informal*) guts
  OPPOSITE cowardice

courageous adjective
The warriors were always **courageous** *in battle.*
- brave, bold, daring, fearless, heroic, intrepid, plucky, gallant, valiant
  OPPOSITE cowardly

course noun

1 *The hot-air balloon was drifting off its* **course**.
- direction, path, route, way, progress, passage

2 *The war changed the* **course** *of history.*
- development, progression, sequence, succession

of course
Of course *you can come to my party.*
- naturally, certainly, definitely, undoubtedly

courteous adjective
I received a **courteous** *reply to my letter.*
- polite, respectful, well-mannered, civil, considerate, friendly, helpful
  OPPOSITE rude

cover verb

1 *A coat of paint will* **cover** *the graffiti.*
- conceal, disguise, hide, obscure, mask, blot out

2 *She* **covered** *her face with her hands.*
- shield, screen, protect, shade, veil

3 *The hikers are hoping to* **cover** *twenty-five miles a day.*
- progress, travel

4 *An encyclopedia* **covers** *many subjects.*
- deal with, include, contain, incorporate

5 *Will £50* **cover** *your expenses?*
- be enough for, pay for

cover noun

1 *The* **cover** *of the book was torn.*
- wrapper
- A cover for a letter is an envelope.
- A cover for a book is a jacket.
- A cover to keep papers in is a file or folder.

2 *On the bare hillside, there was no* **cover** *from the storm.*
- shelter, protection, defence, shield, refuge, sanctuary

covering noun
There was a light **covering** *of snow on the hills.*
- coating, coat, layer, blanket, carpet, film, sheet, skin, veil

cowardly adjective
It was **cowardly** *to run away.*
- timid, faint-hearted, spineless, gutless
- (*informal*) yellow, chicken
  OPPOSITE brave

cower verb
A frightened creature was **cowering** *in the corner.*
- cringe, shrink, crouch, flinch, quail

crack noun

1 *There's a* **crack** *in this cup.*
- break, chip, fracture, flaw, chink, split

2 *The outlaw hid in a **crack** between two rocks.*
- gap, opening, crevice, rift, cranny

3 *The detective heard the **crack** of a pistol shot.*
- bang, fire, explosion, snap, pop

4 *She gave the robber a **crack** on the head.*
- blow, bang, knock, smack, whack

5 *I had a **crack** at writing a poem.*
- try, attempt, shot, go

crack verb
*A brick fell down and **cracked** the pavement.*
- break, fracture, chip, split, shatter, splinter

craft noun
1 *I'd like to learn the **craft** of weaving.*
- art, skill, technique, expertise, handicraft
  FOR NAMES OF ARTS AND CRAFTS
  SEE **art**

2 *All sorts of craft were in the harbour.*
- boats, ships, vessels
  FOR TYPES OF BOAT OR SHIP
  SEE **boat**

crafty adjective
*The evil sorceress had a **crafty** plan.*
- cunning, clever, shrewd, scheming, sneaky, sly, tricky, wily, artful

cram verb
1 *We can't **cram** any more people in— the car is full.*
- pack, squeeze, crush, force, jam, compress

2 *My sister is **cramming** for her maths exam.*
- revise, study
- (*informal*) swot

cramped adjective
*The seating on the train was a bit **cramped**.*
- confined, narrow, restricted, tight, uncomfortable, crowded
- (*informal*) poky
  OPPOSITE roomy

crash noun
1 *I heard a loud **crash** from the kitchen.*
- bang, smash

FOR OTHER KINDS OF SOUND
SEE **sound** noun

2 *We saw a nasty **crash** on the motorway.*
- accident, collision, smash, bump
- A crash involving a lot of vehicles is a pile-up.
- A train crash may involve a derailment.

crash verb
*The car **crashed** into a lamp-post.*
- bump, smash, collide, knock

crate noun
*We packed our belongings into **crates**.*
- box, case, chest, packing case

crater noun
*The surface of the Moon is full of **craters**.*
- pit, hole, hollow, cavity, chasm, opening, abyss

crawl verb
*I saw a caterpillar **crawling** along a leaf.*
- creep, edge, inch, slither, clamber

craze noun
*This game is the latest **craze** in the playground.*
- fad, trend, vogue, fashion, enthusiasm, obsession, passion

crazy adjective
1 *The dog went **crazy** when it was stung by a wasp.*
- mad, insane, frenzied, hysterical, frantic, berserk, delirious, wild
- (*informal*) loopy, nuts

2 *It was a **crazy** idea to try to build a space rocket!*
- absurd, ridiculous, ludicrous, daft, idiotic, senseless, silly, stupid, foolhardy, preposterous
- (*informal*) bonkers, barmy, wacky
  OPPOSITE sensible

creamy adjective
*That ice cream is really **creamy**!*
- rich, smooth, thick, velvety

a b c d e f g h i j k l m n o p q r s t u v w x y z

a
b
c
d
e
f
g
h
i
j
k
l
m
n
o
p
q
r
s
t
u
v
w
x
y
z

crease noun
*Can you iron the **creases** out of this shirt?*
- wrinkle, crinkle, pucker, fold, furrow, groove, line
- A crease made deliberately in a skirt or other garment is a pleat.

crease verb
*Pack the clothes carefully, so you don't **crease** them.*
- wrinkle, crinkle, crumple, crush, pucker

create verb
1 *The cats were **creating** a racket outside.*
- make, cause, produce
2 *We have **created** a website for our chess club.*
- set up, start up, bring about, bring into existence, originate
- You write a poem or story.
- You compose music.
- You draw or paint a picture.
- You carve a statue.
- You invent or think up a new idea.
- You design a new product.
- You devise a plan.
- You found a new club or organization.
- You manufacture goods.
- You generate electricity.
- You build or construct a model or a building.
  OPPOSITE destroy

creation noun
1 *The TV programme is about the **creation** of life on earth.*
- beginning, origin, birth, generation, initiation
2 *They raised money for the **creation** of a sports centre.*
- building, construction, establishing, foundation
3 *This pizza recipe is my own **creation**.*
- concept, invention

creative adjective
*My aunt is a very **creative** person.*
- artistic, imaginative, inventive, original, inspired
  OPPOSITE unimaginative

creator noun
*Walt Disney was the **creator** of Mickey Mouse.*
- inventor, maker, originator, producer, deviser
- The creator of a design is an architect or designer.
- The creator of goods for sale is a manufacturer.

creature noun
*A wild-looking **creature** emerged from the swamp.*
- animal, beast, being
  SEE ALSO **animal**
  FOR CREATURES FOUND IN MYTHS AND LEGENDS
  SEE **myth**

credible adjective
*The detective did not find the woman's story **credible**.*
- believable, convincing, persuasive, trustworthy, likely, possible, reasonable
  OPPOSITE incredible

credit noun
*The author is finally getting the **credit** she deserves.*
- recognition, honour, praise, distinction, fame, glory, reputation
  OPPOSITE dishonour

credit verb
*It's hard to **credit** that they are brother and sister.*
- believe, accept, have faith in, trust
  OPPOSITE doubt

creed noun
*Pupils of all races and **creeds** attend the school.*
- religion, doctrine, faith, set of beliefs

creep verb
1 *I watched the lizard **creep** back into its hiding place.*
- crawl, edge, inch, slither, wriggle
2 *I **crept** out of bed without waking the others.*
- move quietly, sneak, tiptoe, slip, slink, steal

creepy adjective

*There were **creepy** noises coming from the cellar.*

- scary, frightening, eerie, ghostly, weird, sinister, uncanny, unearthly
- (*informal*) spooky
  SEE ALSO **ghost**

crest noun

1 *The bird had a large red **crest** on its head.*

- comb, plume, tuft

2 *There was a wonderful view from the **crest** of the hill.*

- top, peak, summit, crown, head, brow

crevice noun

*Moss was growing in the **crevices** in the rock.*

- crack, cranny, gap, opening, rift, split
- A deep crack in a glacier is a crevasse.

crew noun FOR WORDS FOR GROUPS OF PEOPLE

SEE **group**

cricket noun

WORD WEB

PEOPLE WHO PLAY CRICKET

batsman, bowler, cricketer, fielder or fieldsman, wicketkeeper

- The official who makes sure players keep to the rules is the umpire.

SOME OTHER TERMS USED IN CRICKET

boundary, crease, innings, maiden over, over, run, stump, wicket

crime noun

*Robbing a bank is a serious **crime**.*

- offence, lawbreaking, wrongdoing

criminal noun

WORD WEB

*These men are dangerous **criminals**.*

- lawbreaker, offender, wrongdoer (*informal*) crook
- A criminal who has been sent to prison is a convict.

SOME TYPES OF CRIMINAL

assassin, bandit, blackmailer, brigand, burglar, cat burglar, conman, gangster, highwayman, hijacker, kidnapper, mugger, murderer, outlaw, pickpocket, pirate, poacher, robber, shoplifter, smuggler, terrorist, thief, thug, vandal

criminal adjective

*The gang were involved in many **criminal** schemes.*

- illegal, unlawful, corrupt, dishonest, wrong
- (*informal*) bent, crooked
  OPPOSITE honest

cripple verb

1 *The fall may have **crippled** the horse.*

- disable, handicap, maim, lame

2 *The country was nearly **crippled** by the war.*

- ruin, destroy, crush, wreck, damage, weaken

cringe verb

*I **cringed** with embarrassment when my name was called.*

- shrink, flinch, wince, cower

crisis noun

*The election result caused a **crisis** in the country.*

- emergency, problem, difficulty, predicament

crisp adjective

1 *Fry the bacon until it's **crisp**.*

- crispy, crunchy, brittle
  OPPOSITE soft, soggy, limp

2 *It was a **crisp** winter morning.*

- cold, fresh, frosty

critical adjective

1 *Some people made **critical** comments about my hairstyle.*

- negative, disapproving, derogatory, uncomplimentary, unfavourable
  OPPOSITE complimentary

2 *This match is **critical** for our team's chances of success.*

- crucial, important, vital, serious, decisive
  OPPOSITE unimportant

a
b
c
d
e
f
g
h
i
j
k
l
m
n
o
p
q
r
s
t
u
v
w
x
y
z

criticism noun

*I think his **criticism** of my singing was unfair.*

- attack, disapproval, reprimand, reproach

criticize verb

*She **criticized** us for being so careless.*

- blame, condemn, disapprove of, find fault with, reprimand, reproach, scold, berate

  OPPOSITE praise

crockery noun

 WORD WEB

*Please put the **crockery** away.*

- china, dishes, plates

  SOME ITEMS OF CROCKERY

  bowl, butter dish, cup, dinner plate, gravy boat, milk jug, mug, plate, saucer, side plate, sugar bowl, teacup, teapot, tureen

crooked adjective

1 *The wizard bent his wand into a **crooked** shape.*

- bent, twisted, warped, knarled

  OPPOSITE straight

2 (*informal*) *The **crooked** salesman was selling fake diamonds.*

- criminal, dishonest, corrupt, illegal, unlawful
- (*informal*) bent

  OPPOSITE honest

crop noun

*We had a good **crop** of apples this year.*

- harvest, yield, produce

crop verb

*Miss Marshall was **cropping** her garden hedge.*

- cut, trim, clip, snip, shear

to crop up

*Several problems have **cropped up**.*

- arise, appear, occur, emerge, come up, turn up

cross verb

1 *There is a bus stop where the two roads **cross**.*

- criss-cross, intersect

2 *You can **cross** the river at the footbridge.*

- go across, pass over, traverse, ford, span

cross adjective

*My mum will be **cross** if we're late.*

- angry, annoyed, upset, vexed, bad-tempered, ill-tempered, irritable, grumpy, testy, irate

  SEE ALSO **angry**

  OPPOSITE pleased

crossroads noun

*When you reach the **crossroads**, turn left.*

- intersection, junction
- A junction of two motorways is an interchange.

crouch verb

*The outlaws **crouched** silently in the bushes.*

- squat, kneel, stoop, bend, duck, bob down, hunch, huddle

crowd noun

1 *A **crowd** of people waited outside the theatre.*

- gathering, group, assembly, bunch, cluster, throng, mob, multitude, crush, horde, swarm

2 *There was a huge **crowd** for the tennis final.*

- audience, spectators, gate, attendance

crowd verb

1 *People **crowded** on the pavement to watch the parade.*

- gather, collect, assemble, congregate, mass, flock, muster

2 *Hundreds of people **crowded** into the hall.*

- push, pile, squeeze, pack, cram, crush, jam, bundle, herd

crowded adjective

*The shops are always **crowded** at Christmas time.*

- full, packed, teeming, swarming, overflowing, jammed, congested

  OPPOSITE empty

a b c d e f g h i j k l m n o p q r s t u v w x y z

crown noun

*The royal **crown** was made of solid gold.*

- coronet, diadem, tiara

crown verb

*Mary was **crowned** Queen of Scots when she was a baby.*

- enthrone, anoint
- A ceremony at which a king or queen is crowned is a coronation.

crucial adjective

*We are at a **crucial** point in our chess game.*

- important, critical, decisive, vital, serious, momentous
  OPPOSITE unimportant

crude adjective

1 *The refinery processes **crude** oil.*
- raw, natural, unprocessed, unrefined
  OPPOSITE refined

2 *We made a **crude** shelter out of twigs.*
- rough, clumsy, makeshift, primitive
  OPPOSITE skilful

3 *The teacher told them to stop using **crude** language.*
- rude, obscene, coarse, dirty, foul, impolite, indecent, vulgar
  OPPOSITE polite

cruel adjective

*I think hunting is a **cruel** way to kill animals.*

- brutal, savage, vicious, fierce, barbaric, bloodthirsty, barbarous, heartless, ruthless, merciless, inhuman, sadistic, uncivilized, beastly
  OPPOSITE kind, humane, gentle

crumb noun

*We put out some **crumbs** of bread for the birds.*

- bit, fragment, scrap, morsel
  SEE ALSO **bit**

crumble verb

1 *The walls of the castle were beginning to **crumble**.*
- disintegrate, break up, collapse, fall apart, decay, decompose

2 *The farmer **crumbled** some bread into his soup.*
- crush, grind, pound, pulverize

crumpled adjective

*Your shirt is **crumpled**.*

- creased, wrinkled, crinkled, crushed

crunch verb

1 *The dog was **crunching** on a bone.*
- chew, munch, chomp, grind
  SEE ALSO **eat**

2 *I heard heavy footsteps **crunching** up the path.*
- crush, grind, pound, smash

crush verb

1 *He **crushed** his anorak into his schoolbag.*
- squash, squeeze, mangle, pound, press, bruise, crunch, scrunch
- To crush something into a soft mess is to mash or pulp it.
- To crush something into a powder is to grind or pulverize it.
- To crush something out of shape is to crumple or smash it.

2 *Our soldiers **crushed** the attacking army.*
- defeat, conquer, vanquish, overcome, overwhelm, quash, trounce, rout

crush noun

*There was a **crush** of people at the front gates.*

- crowd, press, mob, throng, jam, congestion

cry verb

1 *Someone was **crying** for help from the burning house.*
- call, shout, yell, exclaim, roar, bawl, bellow, scream, screech, shriek

2 *The baby started to **cry** when she dropped her toy.*
- sob, weep, bawl, blubber, wail, shed tears, snivel
- When someone starts to cry, their eyes well up with tears.

a
b
c
d
e
f
g
h
i
j
k
l
m
n
o
p
q
r
s
t
u
v
w
x
y
z

a
b
c
d
e
f
g
h
i
j
k
l
m
n
o
p
q
r
s
t
u
v
w
x
y
z

cry noun

*The wounded man let out a **cry** of pain.*

- call, shout, yell, roar, howl, exclamation, bellow, scream, screech, shriek, yelp

cuddle verb

*My baby brother **cuddles** a teddy bear in bed.*

- hug, hold closely, clasp, embrace, caress, nestle against, snuggle against

cue noun

*When I nod, that is your **cue** to speak.*

- sign, signal, reminder

culminate verb

to culminate in

*The concert **culminated in** a firework display.*

- finish with, conclude with, close with, build up to, terminate with

culprit noun

*Police are searching for the **culprits**.*

- criminal, offender, wrongdoer

cultivate verb

1 *Farmers have **cultivated** this land for centuries.*

- farm, work, till, plough, grow crops on

2 *We want to **cultivate** good relations with our neighbours.*

- develop, encourage, promote, try to achieve, further, improve

cultural adjective

*The festival included sporting and **cultural** events.*

- artistic, educational, intellectual

culture noun

*The exhibition is about the **culture** of ancient Greece.*

- civilization, society, traditions, customs, learning, arts

cunning adjective

*The pirates had a **cunning** plan to seize the ship.*

- clever, crafty, devious, wily, ingenious, shrewd, artful, scheming, sly, tricky

cup noun

- A tall cup with straight sides is a mug.
- A tall cup without a handle is a beaker or tumbler.
- A decorative drinking cup is a goblet.

FOR OTHER CONTAINERS FOR DRINKS SEE **drink** noun

cupboard noun

*There are some spare pillows in the **cupboard**.*

- cabinet, dresser, sideboard
- A cupboard for food is a larder.

FOR OTHER ITEMS OF FURNITURE SEE **furniture**

curb verb

*You must try to **curb** your anger.*

- control, restrain, suppress, check, hold back, limit, moderate, repress, restrict

OPPOSITE encourage

cure verb

1 *These pills will **cure** your headache.*

- ease, heal, help, improve, make better, relieve

OPPOSITE aggravate

2 *No-one can **cure** the problem with my computer.*

- correct, mend, sort, repair, fix, put an end to, put right

cure noun

*I wish they could find a **cure** for colds.*

- remedy, treatment, antidote, medicine, therapy

curiosity noun

*Babies are full of **curiosity** about the world.*

- inquisitiveness, interest
- Uncomplimentary words are nosiness, prying, and snooping.

curious adjective

1 *We were all very **curious** about the secret chamber.*

- inquisitive, inquiring, interested (in), intrigued, agog
- An uncomplimentary word is nosy.

OPPOSITE uninterested, indifferent

2 *What is that **curious** smell?*
- odd, strange, peculiar, abnormal, queer, unusual, extraordinary, funny, mysterious, puzzling, weird

curl verb
1 *The snake **curled** itself around a branch.*
- wind, twist, loop, coil, wrap, curve, turn, twine
2 *Steam **curled** upwards from the cauldron.*
- coil, spiral, twirl, swirl, furl, snake, writhe, ripple

curl noun
*The girl's hair was a mass of golden **curls**.*
- wave, ringlet, coil, loop, twist, roll, scroll, spiral

curly adjective
*My new doll has **curly** black hair.*
- curled, curling, wavy, frizzy, crinkly, ringletted
OPPOSITE straight

current noun
*The wooden raft drifted along with the **current**.*
- flow, tide, stream
- A current of air is a draught.

current adjective
1 *The shop sells all the **current** teenage fashions.*
- modern, contemporary, present-day, up to date, topical, prevailing, prevalent
OPPOSITE past, old-fashioned
2 *Have you got a **current** passport?*
- valid, usable, up to date
OPPOSITE out of date
3 *Who is the **current** prime minister?*
- present, existing
OPPOSITE past, former

curse noun
1 *Long ago, a wizard put a **curse** on the family.*
- jinx, hex
2 *When the gardener hit his finger, he let out a **curse**.*
- swearword, oath

curve noun
*Try to draw a straight line without any **curves**.*
- bend, curl, loop, turn, twist, arch, arc, bow, bulge, wave
- A curve in the shape of a new moon is a crescent.
- A curve on a road surface is a camber.

curve verb
*The road ahead **curves** round to the right.*
- bend, wind, turn, twist, curl, loop, swerve, veer, snake, meander

curved adjective
*The wall was painted with a series of **curved** lines.*
- curving, curvy, curled, looped, coiled, rounded, bulging, bent, arched, bowed, twisted, crooked, spiral, winding, meandering, serpentine, snaking, undulating
- A surface which is curved like the inside of a circle is concave.
- A surface which is curved like the outside of a circle is convex.

cushion verb
*If you fall off the swing, the mat will **cushion** your fall.*
- soften, reduce the effect of, absorb, muffle

custom noun
1 *It's our **custom** to give presents at Christmas.*
- tradition, practice, habit, convention, fashion, routine, way
2 *The shop is having a sale to attract more **custom**.*
- customers, buyers, trade, business

customary adjective
*It is **customary** to leave the waiter a tip.*
- traditional, conventional, usual, normal, common, typical, expected, habitual, routine, regular, everyday, ordinary, prevailing, prevalent
OPPOSITE unusual

a
b
c
d
e
f
g
h
i
j
k
l
m
n
o
p
q
r
s
t
u
v
w
x
y
z

a
b
c
d
e
f
g
h
i
j
k
l
m
n
o
p
q
r
s
t
u
v
w
x
y
z

customer noun
*There was a queue of **customers** at the checkout.*
- buyer, shopper, client

cut verb
1 *The woodcutter **cut** the tree trunk to make logs.*
- chop, slit, split, chip, notch, axe, hack, hew, cleave
- To cut off a limb is to amputate or sever it.
- To cut down a tree is to fell it.
- To cut branches off a tree is to lop them.
- To cut twigs off a growing plant is to prune it.
- To cut something up to examine it is to dissect it.
- To cut stone to make a statue is to carve it.
- To cut an inscription in stone is to engrave it.

2 *The cook **cut** the apples into small pieces.*
- chop, slice, dice, grate, mince, shred

3 *I'm going to get my hair **cut** in the holidays.*
- trim, clip, crop, snip, shave
- To cut wool off a sheep is to shear it.
- To cut grass is to mow it.
- To cut corn is to harvest or reap it.

4 *Josh **cut** his foot on a sharp stone.*
- gash, slash, nick, stab, pierce, wound

5 *This letter is too long—I'll need to **cut** it.*
- shorten, condense, edit

6 *The shop has **cut** its prices by 10%.*
- lower, reduce, decrease
- If you cut something by half, you halve it.

cut noun
1 *I got a nasty **cut** when I was slicing bread.*
- gash, wound, injury, nick, slash, scratch, slit, snip

2 *There has been a **cut** in the price of petrol.*
- fall, reduction, decrease

cutlery noun

WORD WEB

SOME ITEMS OF CUTLERY
breadknife, butter knife, carving knife, cheese knife, chopsticks, dessert spoon, fish knife, fork, knife, ladle, spoon, steak knife, tablespoon, teaspoon

cutting adjective
*She made a **cutting** remark about my dress.*
- sharp, hurtful, biting, stinging, vicious

cycle noun SEE **bicycle**

daily adjective
*Walking to school is part of my **daily** exercise routine.*
- everyday, regular
- OPPOSITE infrequent, irregular

dainty adjective
*The doll's hair was tied with a **dainty** little ribbon.*
- delicate, neat, charming, fine, exquisite, bijou
- (*informal*) cute, dinky
- OPPOSITE clumsy

dam noun
*Some beavers have built a **dam** in this river.*
- barrier, barrage, embankment, dike, weir

dam verb
*The river was **dammed** to make a reservoir.*
- block, check, hold back

damage verb
*Many books were **damaged** in the fire.*
- harm, spoil, mar, break, impair, weaken, disfigure, deface, mutilate, scar
- To damage something beyond repair is to destroy, ruin, or wreck it.
- To damage something deliberately is to sabotage or vandalize it.

damp adjective
1 *Don't wear those clothes if they are **damp**.*
- moist, soggy, clammy, dank
2 *I don't like this **damp** weather.*
- drizzly, foggy, misty, rainy, wet
- Weather which is both damp and warm is humid or muggy weather.
OPPOSITE dry

dampen verb
1 ***Dampen** the cloth with a little water.*
- moisten, wet
2 *Nothing could **dampen** her enthusiasm.*
- make less, decrease, reduce

dance noun

> **WORD WEB**
>
> SOME KINDS OF DANCE OR DANCING
> ballet, ballroom dancing, barn dance, belly-dancing, bolero, break-dancing, cancan, disco, flamenco, folk dance, Highland dancing, hornpipe, jazz dance, jig, jive dancing, limbo dancing, line-dancing, mazurka, morris dance, quadrille, reel, rumba, samba, Scottish country dancing, square dance, step dancing, street dance, tap dancing, tarantella
> - A person who writes the steps for a dance is a choreographer.
>
> SOME BALLROOM DANCES
> foxtrot, minuet, polka, quickstep, tango, waltz
>
> GATHERINGS WHERE PEOPLE DANCE
> ball, ceilidh, disco

dance verb
*I could have **danced** for joy.*
- caper, cavort, frisk, frolic, gambol, hop about, jig about, jump about, leap, prance, skip, whirl

danger noun
1 *Who knows what **dangers** lie ahead?*
- peril, jeopardy, trouble, crisis, hazard, menace, pitfall, threat, trap
OPPOSITE safety
2 *The forecast says there's a **danger** of frost.*
- chance, possibility, risk

dangerous adjective
1 *We were in a **dangerous** situation.*
- hazardous, perilous, risky, precarious, treacherous, unsafe, alarming, menacing
- (*informal*) hairy
2 *The police arrested him for **dangerous** driving.*
- careless, reckless
3 *A **dangerous** criminal had escaped from prison.*
- violent, desperate, ruthless, treacherous
4 *It's wicked to empty **dangerous** chemicals into the river.*
- harmful, poisonous, deadly, toxic
OPPOSITE harmless, safe

dangle verb
*There was a bunch of keys **dangling** from the chain.*
- hang, swing, sway, droop, wave about, flap, trail

dare verb
1 *I wouldn't **dare** to make a parachute jump.*
- have the courage, take the risk
2 *They **dared** me to climb the tree.*
- challenge, defy

daring adjective
*It was a very **daring** plan.*
- bold, brave, adventurous, courageous, fearless, intrepid, plucky, valiant
- A daring person is a daredevil.
OPPOSITE timid

a b c d e f g h i j k l m n o p q r s t u v w x y z

a
b
c
d
e
f
g
h
i
j
k
l
m
n
o
p
q
r
s
t
u
v
w
x
y
z

dark adjective
1 *It was a very **dark** night.*
- black, dim, murky, shadowy, gloomy, dingy
  OPPOSITE bright
2 *She wore a **dark** green coat.*
  OPPOSITE pale, light

darken verb
*The sky **darkened**.*
- become overcast, blacken, cloud over
  OPPOSITE brighten

dash noun
1 *When the storm broke, we made a **dash** for shelter.*
- run, rush, race, sprint
2 *I like just a **dash** of milk in my tea.*
- drop, small amount, splash, spot

dash verb
1 *We **dashed** home because it was raining.*
- hurry, run, rush, race, hasten, sprint, speed, tear, zoom
2 *She **dashed** her cup against the wall.*
- throw, hurl, knock, smash

data plural noun
*I entered all the **data** into the computer.*
- information, details, facts
- Data can be in the form of figures, numbers, or statistics.

date noun
*I have a **date** with some friends this evening.*
- meeting, appointment, engagement

dawdle verb
*Don't **dawdle**—we haven't got all day!*
- linger, dally, drag your feet, be slow, delay, lag behind, straggle
- (*informal*) dilly-dally
  OPPOSITE hurry

dawn noun
1 *I was woken at **dawn** by the birds singing outside.*
- daybreak, sunrise, first light
  OPPOSITE dusk, sunset
2 *It was the **dawn** of the modern age.*
- beginning, start, birth, origin

day noun
1 *Badgers sleep during the **day**.*
- daytime
  OPPOSITE night
2 *Things were different in my grandfather's **day**.*
- age, time, era, epoch, period

day noun

> **WORD WEB**
>
> VARIOUS TIMES OF THE DAY
> dawn or daybreak or sunrise, morning, noon or midday, afternoon, evening, nightfall or sunset, dusk or twilight, night, midnight

dazed adjective
*He had a **dazed** expression on his face.*
- confused, bewildered, muddled, perplexed

dazzle verb
1 *My eyes were **dazzled** by the bright lights.*
- daze, blind
2 *The acrobats **dazzled** the audience with their skill.*
- amaze, astonish, impress, fascinate, awe

dead adjective
1 *A **dead** fish floated by the side of the river.*
- deceased, lifeless
- Instead of 'the king who has just died', you can say 'the late king'.
- A dead body is a carcass or corpse.
- A common simile is as dead as a doornail.
  OPPOSITE alive
2 *Latin is a **dead** language.*
- extinct, obsolete
  OPPOSITE living
3 *This battery is **dead**.*
- flat, not working, worn out
4 *The town centre is **dead** at this time of night.*
- dull, boring, uninteresting, slow
  OPPOSITE lively

deaden verb

1 *The dentist gave me an injection to* ***deaden*** *the pain.*
- anaesthetize, lessen, reduce, suppress
  OPPOSITE increase
2 *Double glazing* ***deadens*** *the noise of the traffic.*
- dampen, muffle, quieten
  OPPOSITE amplify

deadly adjective

The witch gave her a ***deadly*** *dose of poison.*
- lethal, fatal, harmful, dangerous, destructive
  OPPOSITE harmless

deafening adjective

We complained about the ***deafening*** *noise.*
- loud, blaring, booming, thunderous, penetrating

deal verb

1 *Who is going to* ***deal*** *the cards?*
- give out, distribute, share out
2 *My uncle used to* ***deal*** *in second-hand cars.*
- do business, trade

to deal with something
1 *I can* ***deal with*** *this problem.*
- cope with, sort out, attend to, see to, handle, manage, control, grapple with, look after, solve
2 *The book* ***deals with*** *the history of Rome.*
- be concerned with, cover, explain about

deal noun

She made a ***deal*** *with the garage for her new car.*
- arrangement, agreement, contract, bargain

a good deal or **a great deal**
We went to a ***great deal*** *of trouble to do things properly.*
- a lot, a large amount

dear adjective

1 *She is a very* ***dear*** *friend.*
- close, loved, valued, beloved
  OPPOSITE distant

2 *I didn't buy the watch because it was too* ***dear***.
- expensive, costly
- (*informal*) pricey
  OPPOSITE cheap

death noun

1 *The Vikings mourned the* ***death*** *of their chief.*
- dying, end, passing
2 *The accident resulted in several* ***deaths***.
- fatality

debate noun

We had a ***debate*** *about animal rights.*
- discussion, argument, dispute
- Something which people argue about a lot is a controversy.

debate verb

1 *We* ***debated*** *whether it is right to kill animals for food.*
- discuss, argue
2 *I* ***debated*** *what to do next.*
- consider, ponder, deliberate, weigh up, reflect on

debris noun

Debris *from the crashed aircraft was scattered over a large area.*
- remains, wreckage, fragments, pieces

decay verb

Dead leaves fall to the ground and ***decay***.
- decompose, rot, disintegrate, break down

deceit noun

I saw through his ***deceit***.
- deception, trickery, dishonesty, fraud, duplicity, double-dealing, pretence, bluff, cheating, deceitfulness, lying
  OPPOSITE honesty

deceitful adjective

Don't trust him—he's a ***deceitful*** *person.*
- dishonest, underhand, insincere, duplicitous, false, cheating, hypocritical, lying, treacherous, two-faced, sneaky
  OPPOSITE honest

a b c d e f g h i j k l m n o p q r s t u v w x y z

a
b
c
d
e
f
g
h
i
j
k
l
m
n
o
p
q
r
s
t
u
v
w
x
y
z

deceive verb
*The spy had been **deceiving** them for years.*
- fool, trick, delude, dupe, hoodwink, cheat, double-cross, mislead, swindle, take in
- (*informal*) con, diddle

decent adjective
1 *I did the **decent** thing and owned up.*
- honest, honourable
2 *My friend's jokes were not **decent**.*
- polite, proper, respectable, acceptable, appropriate, suitable, fitting
OPPOSITE indecent
3 *I haven't had a **decent** meal for ages!*
- satisfactory, agreeable, good, nice
OPPOSITE bad

deception noun SEE deceit

deceptive adjective
*Appearances can be **deceptive**.*
- misleading, unreliable, false

decide verb
1 *We **decided** to finish our work instead of going out to play.*
- choose, make a decision, make up your mind, opt, elect, resolve
2 *The referee **decided** that the player was offside.*
- conclude, judge, rule
3 *The last lap **decided** the result of the race.*
- determine, settle

decision noun
1 *Can you tell me what your **decision** is?*
- choice, preference
2 *The judge announced his **decision**.*
- conclusion, judgement, verdict, findings

decisive adjective
1 *A **decisive** piece of evidence proved that he was innocent.*
- crucial, convincing, definite
OPPOSITE uncertain
2 *A referee needs to be **decisive**.*
- firm, forceful, strong-minded, resolute, quick-thinking
OPPOSITE hesitant

declare verb
*He **declared** that he was innocent.*
- announce, state, assert, make known, pronounce, proclaim, swear

decline verb
1 *Our enthusiasm **declined** as the day went on.*
- become less, decrease, diminish, lessen, weaken, dwindle, flag, wane, tail off
OPPOSITE increase
2 *Why did you **decline** my invitation to lunch?*
- refuse, reject, turn down
OPPOSITE accept

decode verb SEE ALSO code

decorate verb
1 *We **decorated** the Christmas tree with tinsel.*
- ornament, adorn, beautify, prettify, deck, festoon
- To decorate a dish of food is to garnish it.
- To decorate clothes with lace or ribbon is to trim them.
2 *Dad is going to **decorate** my bedroom next weekend.*
- paint, paper, or wallpaper
- (*informal*) do up, make over
3 *The firefighters were **decorated** for their bravery.*
- award or give a medal to, honour, reward

decorative adjective
*The book had a **decorative** design on the cover.*
- ornamental, elaborate, fancy, attractive, beautiful, colourful, pretty
OPPOSITE plain

decrease verb
1 *We **decreased** speed.*
- reduce, cut, lower, slacken
2 *Our enthusiasm **decreased** as the day went on.*
- become less, decline, decrease, diminish, lessen, weaken, dwindle, flag, wane, tail off, shrink, subside
OPPOSITE increase

decrease noun

*There has been a **decrease** in the number of sparrows this year.*

- decline, drop, fall, cut, reduction
OPPOSITE increase noun

decree verb

*The king **decreed** that the day would be a holiday.*

- order, command, declare, pronounce, proclaim

dedicate verb

*He **dedicates** himself entirely to his art.*

- commit, devote

dedicated adjective

*A group of **dedicated** fans waited at the stage door.*

- committed, devoted, keen, enthusiastic, faithful, zealous

deduce verb

*The detective **deduced** that the footprints were fresh.*

- conclude, work out, infer, reason, gather

deduct verb

*Tax is **deducted** from your salary.*

- subtract, take away, knock off
OPPOSITE add (to)

deed noun

*They thanked the rescue team for their heroic **deed**.*

- act, action, feat, exploit, effort, achievement

deep adjective

1 *The pond is quite **deep** in the middle.*
OPPOSITE shallow
2 *The letter expressed his **deep** regret.*
- intense, earnest, genuine, sincere
OPPOSITE insincere
3 *Veronica fell into a **deep** sleep.*
- heavy, sound
OPPOSITE light
4 *The actor spoke in a **deep** and sombre voice.*
- low, bass
OPPOSITE high

deer noun

- A male deer is a buck, hart, roebuck, or stag.
- A female deer is a doe or hind.
- A young deer is a fawn.
- Deer's flesh used as food is venison.

defeat verb

*The Greeks attacked and **defeated** the Trojans.*

- beat, conquer, vanquish, triumph over, win a victory over, overcome, overpower, crush, rout, trounce
- To defeat someone in chess is to checkmate them.
- To be defeated is to lose.

defeat noun

*The team suffered a humiliating **defeat**.*

- failure, humiliation, rout, trouncing
OPPOSITE victory

defect noun

*Cars are tested for **defects** before they leave the factory.*

- fault, flaw, imperfection, shortcoming, failure, weakness
- A defect in a computer program is a bug.

defective adjective

*If the goods are **defective**, take them back to the shop.*

- faulty, damaged, imperfect, out of order
OPPOSITE perfect

defence noun

1 *What was the accused woman's **defence**?*
- justification, excuse, explanation, argument, case
2 *The castle was built as a **defence** against enemy attack.*
- protection, guard, safeguard, fortification, barricade, shield

defend verb

1 *They tried to **defend** themselves against the enemy.*
- protect, guard, keep safe
OPPOSITE attack

a
b
c
d
e
f
g
h
i
j
k
l
m
n
o
p
q
r
s
t
u
v
w
x
y
z

2 He gave a speech **defending** his actions.

- justify, support, stand up for, make a case for
OPPOSITE accuse

defer verb
They **deferred** their departure until the weekend.
- delay, put off, postpone

defiant adjective
The prisoner cursed with a **defiant** look in his eye.
- rebellious, insolent, aggressive, challenging, disobedient, obstinate, quarrelsome, uncooperative, stubborn, mutinous
OPPOSITE submissive, compliant

deficient adjective
Their diet is **deficient** in vitamins.
- lacking, wanting, short of, inadequate, insufficient, unsatisfactory,
OPPOSITE adequate

define verb
A dictionary **defines** lots of words.
- explain, give the meaning of, interpret, clarify

definite adjective
1 Is it **definite** that we're going to move?
- certain, sure, fixed, settled, decided
2 The doctor saw **definite** signs of improvement.
- clear, distinct, noticeable, obvious, marked, positive, pronounced, unmistakable
OPPOSITE indefinite

definitely adverb
I'll **definitely** phone you tomorrow.
- certainly, for certain, positively, surely, unquestionably, without doubt, without fail
OPPOSITE perhaps

deflect verb
The goalkeeper was able to **deflect** the shot.
- divert, turn aside, intercept, avert, fend off, ward off

deft adjective
She applied the paint with a **deft** flick of her brush.
- skilful, agile, nimble, quick, clever, expert, proficient, adept
- (informal) nifty
OPPOSITE clumsy

defy verb
1 The rebel army decided to **defy** the king.
- disobey, refuse to obey, resist, stand up to, confront
OPPOSITE obey
2 I **defy** you to come up with a better idea.
- challenge, dare
3 The jammed door **defied** our efforts to open it.
- resist, withstand, defeat, frustrate, beat

degrading adjective
Losing by ten goals to nil was a **degrading** experience.
- shameful, humiliating, embarrassing, undignified

degree noun
The young gymnast showed a high **degree** of skill.
- standard, level, grade, measure, extent

dejected adjective
I felt **dejected** when I failed the test.
- depressed, disheartened, downhearted, unhappy, sad, low, gloomy, glum, melancholy, miserable, downcast, despondent, woeful, wretched, forlorn
- (informal) fed up, down
OPPOSITE happy, cheerful

delay verb
1 Don't let me **delay** you.
- detain, hold up, keep waiting, make late, hinder, slow down
2 They **delayed** the race because of bad weather.
- postpone, put off, defer

3 *You'll miss the bus if you **delay**.*
- hesitate, linger, pause, wait, dawdle, loiter
- (*informal*) hang about or around, drag your feet

delay noun
*There has been a **delay** with the building work.*
- hold-up, wait, pause

delete verb
*I **deleted** your email by mistake.*
- remove, erase, cancel, cross out

deliberate adjective
1 *That remark was a **deliberate** insult.*
- intentional, planned, calculated, conscious, premeditated
  OPPOSITE accidental, unintentional

2 *He walked with **deliberate** steps across the room.*
- careful, steady, cautious, slow, unhurried
  OPPOSITE hasty, careless

deliberately verb
*Did you say that **deliberately** to hurt my feelings?*
- on purpose, intentionally
  OPPOSITE accidentally, unintentionally

delicate adjective
1 *The blouse has **delicate** embroidery on the cuffs.*
- dainty, exquisite, intricate, neat

2 *Take care not to damage the **delicate** material.*
- fragile, fine, flimsy, thin

3 ***Delicate** plants should be protected from frost.*
- sensitive, tender
  OPPOSITE tough, hardy

4 *The child was born with a **delicate** constitution.*
- frail, weak, feeble, sickly, unhealthy
  OPPOSITE strong

5 *The pianist's fingers had a **delicate** touch.*
- gentle, light, soft

6 *He discussed the matter in a **delicate** way.*
- tactful, sensitive, considerate, diplomatic, careful, discreet
  OPPOSITE insensitive

7 *Can you help me with a **delicate** problem?*
- awkward, embarrassing, ticklish

delicious adjective
*The food at the banquet was **delicious**.*
- tasty, appetizing, mouth-watering, delectable
- (*informal*) scrumptious, yummy
  FOR OTHER WAYS TO DESCRIBE FOOD
  SEE **food**
  OPPOSITE horrible, disgusting

delight noun
*Imagine my **delight** when I saw my friend again!*
- happiness, joy, pleasure, enjoyment, bliss, ecstasy

delight verb
*The puppet show **delighted** the children.*
- please, charm, entertain, amuse, divert, enchant, entrance, fascinate, thrill
  OPPOSITE dismay

delighted adjective
*The **delighted** crowd cheered the winners.*
- pleased, happy, joyful, thrilled, ecstatic, elated, exultant

delightful adjective
*The poem she wrote was **delightful**.*
- lovely, pleasant, pleasing, beautiful, attractive, charming

delirious adjective
*I was **delirious** with joy when we scored a goal.*
- ecstatic, hysterical, crazy, frantic, frenzied, excited, mad, wild, beside yourself
  OPPOSITE calm

deliver verb
1 *Does anyone **deliver** mail to the island?*
- convey, bring, hand over, distribute, present, supply, take round

a
b
c
d
e
f
g
h
i
j
k
l
m
n
o
p
q
r
s
t
u
v
w
x
y
z

2 *The head **delivered** a lecture on good behaviour.*
- give, make, read out

delude verb
*He **deluded** us into thinking he was very rich.*
- deceive, fool, trick, mislead, hoax, bluff
- (*informal*) con

delusion noun
*Your belief that you are a great writer is a **delusion**!*
- fantasy, dream, self-deception

demand verb
1 *I **demanded** a refund for my train fare.*
- insist on, claim, call for, require, want
2 *'What do you want?' **demanded** a voice inside.*
- ask, enquire, inquire

demand noun
1 *The king refused the **demands** of his people.*
- request, claim, requirement
2 *There is not much **demand** for ice lollies in winter.*
- need, call

demanding adjective
1 *Toddlers can be very **demanding**.*
- difficult, trying, tiresome, insistent
2 *The expedition leader had a very **demanding** job.*
- difficult, challenging, exhausting, hard, tough, testing, taxing, onerous
- OPPOSITE easy

demolish verb
*They **demolished** a building to make way for the road.*
- destroy, flatten, knock down, level, pull down, tear down, bulldoze
- OPPOSITE build, construct

demonstrate verb
1 *The teacher **demonstrated** how warm air rises.*
- show, exhibit, illustrate
2 *Animal rights campaigners were **demonstrating** in the street.*
- protest, march, parade

demonstration noun
1 *I watched a **demonstration** of the new computer game.*
- show, display, presentation
2 *Everyone joined the **demonstration** against world poverty.*
- protest, rally, march, parade
- (*informal*) demo

demote verb
*The team may be **demoted** to a lower division.*
- put down, relegate
- OPPOSITE promote

den noun
*We built a **den** in the garden.*
- hideout, shelter, hiding place, secret place
- The den of a wild animal is its lair.

denote verb
*What does this symbol **denote**?*
- mean, indicate, signify, stand for, be a sign for, express

dense adjective
1 *The accident happened in **dense** fog.*
- thick, heavy
2 *A **dense** crowd waited in the square.*
- compact, packed, solid
3 *I'm being rather **dense** today!*
- stupid, slow

dent noun
*There was a large **dent** in the car door.*
- indentation, depression, hollow, dip, dimple

dent verb
*A football hit the car door and **dented** it.*
- make a dent in, knock in, push in

dentist noun
- A dentist who specializes in straightening teeth is an orthodontist.

FOR OTHER WORDS TO DO WITH YOUR TEETH

SEE **tooth**

deny verb
1 *The boy **denied** that he had stolen the money.*
- reject, dispute, disagree with, contradict, dismiss, oppose
OPPOSITE admit, accept
2 *Her parents don't **deny** her anything.*
- refuse, deprive of, withhold
OPPOSITE give

depart verb
1 *What time is the train due to **depart**?*
- leave, set off, get going, set out, start, begin a journey
OPPOSITE arrive, get in
2 *It looks as if the robbers **departed** in a hurry.*
- leave, exit, go away, retreat, withdraw, make off
- (*informal*) clear off, scram, scarper
OPPOSITE arrive

department noun
*Mr Taylor works in the sales **department**.*
- section, branch, division, office

depend verb
to depend on someone
*I **depend on** you to help me.*
- rely on, count on, bank on, trust
to depend on something
*My success will **depend on** good luck.*
- be decided by, rest on, hinge on

dependable adjective
*Are these friends of yours **dependable**?*
- reliable, trustworthy, loyal, faithful, trusty, honest, sound, steady
OPPOSITE unreliable

dependent adjective
dependent on
*Everything is **dependent on** the weather.*
- determined by, subject to, controlled by, reliant on

depict verb
1 *She **depicted** the landscape in watercolours.*
- draw, paint, sketch

2 *The film **depicts** the horror of war.*
- show, represent, portray, describe, illustrate, outline

deplorable adjective
*Their rudeness was **deplorable**.*
- disgraceful, shameful, scandalous, shocking, unforgivable, lamentable, reprehensible, inexcusable
OPPOSITE praiseworthy

deplore verb
*We all **deplore** cruelty to animals.*
- condemn, disapprove of, hate

deport verb
*He was **deported** from Australia.*
- exile, banish, expel, send abroad

deposit noun
1 *Dad paid the **deposit** on a new car.*
- down-payment, first instalment, initial payment
2 *There was a **deposit** of mud at the bottom of the river.*
- layer, sediment

depress verb
*The miserable weather was **depressing** us.*
- sadden, discourage, dishearten, dispirit
OPPOSITE cheer

depressed adjective
*After his friends left, he began to feel **depressed**.*
- disheartened, dejected, discouraged, downcast, downhearted, unhappy, sad, low, gloomy, glum, melancholy, miserable, despondent, desolate, in despair
- (*informal*) down
OPPOSITE cheerful

depressing adjective
*It was a **depressing** situation to be in.*
- discouraging, dispiriting, disheartening, gloomy, sad, dismal, dreary, sombre, bleak
OPPOSITE cheerful

a
b
c
d
e
f
g
h
i
j
k
l
m
n
o
p
q
r
s
t
u
v
w
x
y
z

depression noun

1 *She sank into a state of depression.*
- despair, dejection, sadness, gloom, unhappiness, hopelessness, low spirits, melancholy, misery, desolation, pessimism, glumness
OPPOSITE cheerfulness

2 *Most businesses do badly during a depression.*
- recession, slump
OPPOSITE boom

3 *The rain had collected in several depressions in the ground.*
- hollow, indentation, dent, dip, hole, pit, rut
OPPOSITE bump

deprived adjective
The charity tries to help deprived families.
- poor, needy, underprivileged
OPPOSITE wealthy, privileged

deputy noun
The sheriff appointed a new deputy.
- second-in-command, assistant, stand-in, substitute
Words with the prefix **vice** often mean 'the deputy for a particular person', e.g. **vice-captain, vice-president.**

derelict adjective
They plan to pull down those derelict buildings.
- dilapidated, crumbling, decrepit, neglected, deserted, abandoned, ruined

deride verb
The book was derided when it first came out.
- ridicule, mock, laugh at, dismiss
- (*informal*) pooh-pooh
OPPOSITE praise

derision noun
His idea was greeted with shouts of derision.
- scorn, ridicule, mockery

derive verb
1 *Bill derives a lot of pleasure from his garden.*
- get, obtain, receive, gain

2 *She derived many of her ideas from books.*
- borrow, draw, pick up, take
- (*informal*) lift

derogatory adjective
His email was full of derogatory remarks.
- critical, uncomplimentary, insulting
OPPOSITE complimentary

descend verb
1 *After admiring the view, we began to descend the mountain.*
- climb down, come down, go down, move down
- To descend through the air is to drop or fall.
- To descend through water is to sink.

2 *The road descends gradually into the valley.*
- drop, fall, slope, dip, incline
OPPOSITE ascend

to be descended from someone
She's descended from a French family.
- come from, originate from

descendant noun
- A person's descendants are their heirs or successors.
OPPOSITE ancestor

descent noun
The path makes a steep descent into the valley.
- drop, fall, dip, incline
OPPOSITE ascent

describe verb
1 *An eyewitness described how the accident happened.*
- report, tell about, depict, explain, outline

2 *Friends described him as a quiet, shy man.*
- portray, characterize, represent, present

description noun
1 *I wrote a description of our day at the seaside.*
- report, account, story

2 *Write a description of your favourite character in the play.*
- portrait, representation, sketch

descriptive adjective
*The author writes in a very **descriptive** style.*
- expressive, colourful, detailed, graphic, vivid

desert noun

 WORD WEB

THINGS YOU MIGHT SEE OR EXPERIENCE IN A DESERT

mirage, oasis, sand dune, sandstorm, whirlwind

SOME ANIMALS WHICH LIVE IN DESERTS

armadillo, camel, chameleon, coyote, desert rat, gerbil, lizard, locust, meerkat, rattlesnake, roadrunner, scorpion, tarantula, vulture

SOME PLANTS WHICH ARE FOUND IN DESERTS

cactus, date palm, grasses, prickly pear, sagebrush, tumbleweed
- A group of people travelling together across a desert is a caravan.
- People who live in the desert are often nomads.

FOR DESERT ISLANDS

SEE **island**

desert verb
*He **deserted** his friends when they needed him most.*
- abandon, leave, forsake, betray
- (*informal*) walk out on
- To desert someone in a place they can't get away from is to maroon or strand them.

deserted adjective
*By midnight, the streets of the town were **deserted**.*
- empty, unoccupied, uninhabited, vacant
OPPOSITE crowded

deserve verb
*You **deserve** a break after all your hard work.*
- be worthy of, be entitled to, have earned, merit, warrant

design noun
1 *This is the winning **design** for the new art gallery.*
- plan, drawing, outline, blueprint, sketch
- A first example of something, used as a model for making others, is a prototype.
2 *Do you like the **design** of this wallpaper?*
- style, pattern, arrangement, composition

design verb
*She **designs** all her own clothes.*
- create, develop, invent, devise, conceive, think up

desirable adjective
1 *The house has many **desirable** features.*
- appealing, attractive, interesting, tempting
OPPOSITE worthless
2 *It is **desirable** to phone before you arrive.*
- advisable, sensible, prudent, wise
OPPOSITE unwise

desire verb
*The magic mirror will show you what you most **desire**.*
- wish for, long for, want, crave, fancy, hanker after, yearn for, pine for, set your heart on, have a yen for

desire noun
*My greatest **desire** is to swim with dolphins.*
- wish, want, longing, ambition, craving, fancy, hankering, urge, yearning
- A desire for food is appetite or hunger.
- A desire for drink is thirst.
- Excessive desire for money or other things is greed.

desolate adjective
1 *Jamie felt **desolate** when his goldfish died.*
- depressed, dejected, miserable, sad, melancholy, hopeless, wretched, forlorn
OPPOSITE cheerful

a b c d e f g h i j k l m n o p q r s t u v w x y z

2 *No-one wants to live in that **desolate** place.*
- bleak, depressing, dreary, gloomy, dismal, cheerless, inhospitable, deserted, uninhabited, abandoned, godforsaken
OPPOSITE pleasant

despair noun
*The defeated knight was overcome by **despair**.*
- depression, desperation, gloom, hopelessness, misery, anguish, dejection, melancholy, pessimism, wretchedness
OPPOSITE hope

despatch noun verb SEE
dispatch noun, verb

desperate adjective
1 *The shipwrecked crew were in a **desperate** situation.*
- difficult, critical, grave, serious, severe, drastic, dire, urgent, extreme
2 *The hills were home to a band of **desperate** outlaws.*
- dangerous, violent, reckless

despicable adjective
*The pirates were known for **despicable** acts of cruelty.*
- disgraceful, hateful, shameful, contemptible, loathsome, vile

despise verb
*I **despise** people who cheat at cards.*
- hate, loathe, feel contempt for, deride, have a low opinion of, look down on, scorn, sneer at
OPPOSITE admire

despite preposition
*We went for a walk **despite** the rain.*
- in spite of, regardless of, notwithstanding
OPPOSITE because of

dessert noun
*For **dessert**, there's apple pie and ice cream.*
- pudding, sweet
- (*informal*) afters

destination noun
*The train arrived at its **destination** five minutes early.*
- terminus, stop

destined adjective
1 *It was **destined** that he would become a famous actor.*
- fated, doomed, intended, meant, certain, inevitable, unavoidable, inescapable
2 *This parcel is **destined** for Japan.*
- bound, directed, intended, headed

destiny noun
*Was it **destiny** that brought us together?*
- fate, fortune

destroy verb
1 *An avalanche **destroyed** the village.*
- demolish, devastate, crush, flatten, knock down, level, pull down, shatter, smash, sweep away
2 *He tried to **destroy** the good work we had done.*
- ruin, wreck, sabotage, undo

destruction noun
1 *The hurricane caused **destruction** all along the coast.*
- devastation, damage, demolition, ruin, wrecking
OPPOSITE creation
2 *Global warming may cause the **destruction** of many animal species.*
- elimination, annihilation, obliteration, extermination, extinction
OPPOSITE conservation

destructive adjective
*Tornadoes have a great **destructive** power.*
- damaging, devastating, catastrophic, disastrous, harmful, injurious, ruinous, violent

detach verb
*The camera lens can be **detached** for cleaning.*
- remove, separate, disconnect, take off, release, undo, unfasten, part

a b c d e f g h i j k l m n o p q r s t u v w x y z

- To detach a caravan from a vehicle is to unhitch it.
- To detach railway wagons from a locomotive is to uncouple them.
- To detach something by cutting it off is to sever it.
  OPPOSITE attach

detail noun

*Her account of what happened was accurate in every **detail**.*

- fact, feature, particular, aspect, item, point, respect

detailed adjective

*This book gives a **detailed** description of Victorian London.*

- precise, exact, specific, full, thorough, elaborate, comprehensive, exhaustive
  OPPOSITE rough, vague

detain verb

1 *The police **detained** the suspect.*
- hold, arrest, capture, imprison, restrain
  OPPOSITE release
2 *I'll try not to **detain** you for long.*
- delay, hold up, hinder, keep waiting

detect verb

*I could **detect** the smell of burning in the air.*

- identify, recognize, spot, find, discover, reveal, diagnose, track down

detective noun

WORD WEB

***Detective** Dewar solved the case of the stolen tiara.*

- investigator, sleuth
  (*informal*) private eye
  THINGS A DETECTIVE MIGHT LOOK FOR
  clues, evidence, eyewitness, fingerprints, footprints, murder weapon, tracks; criminal, crook, culprit, felon, suspect, mastermind

THINGS A DETECTIVE MIGHT DO
analyse, comb (an area), deduce, deduct, detect, dig up, ferret out, follow a hunch, follow a lead or a tip-off, interrogate or question (a witness), investigate, pursue, shadow, solve (a case), stake out (a hiding place), tail or track down (a suspect)

- An informal name for a story in which a detective solves a crime is a whodunnit.

deter verb

*How can we **deter** birds from eating the pears?*

- discourage, put off, dissuade, prevent, stop
  OPPOSITE encourage

deteriorate verb

1 *The queen's health had begun to **deteriorate**.*
- worsen, decline, degenerate, get worse, go downhill
2 *The walls will **deteriorate** if we don't maintain them.*
- decay, disintegrate, crumble
  OPPOSITE improve

determination noun

*Marathon runners show great **determination**.*

- resolve, commitment, will-power, courage, dedication, drive, grit, perseverance, persistence, spirit
- (*informal*) guts

determine verb

*Our task was to **determine** the depth of the loch.*

- calculate, compute, figure out, work out, reckon, decide

determined adjective

1 *Boudicca must have been a **determined** woman.*
- resolute, decisive, firm, strong-minded, assertive, persistent, tough
  OPPOSITE weak-minded
2 *I'm **determined** to finish the race.*
- committed, resolved

a
b
c
d
e
f
g
h
i
j
k
l
m
n
o
p
q
r
s
t
u
v
w
x
y
z

a
b
c
d
e
f
g
h
i
j
k
l
m
n
o
p
q
r
s
t
u
v
w
x
y
z

detest verb
*I **detest** the smell of boiled cabbage.*
- dislike, hate, loathe
- Informal expressions are can't bear and can't stand.
OPPOSITE love

detour noun
*I wasted time by taking a **detour**.*
- diversion, indirect route, roundabout route

detrimental adjective
*Too much water can be **detrimental** to plants.*
- damaging, harmful, destructive, adverse
OPPOSITE beneficial

devastate verb
*The earthquake **devastated** the island.*
- destroy, wreck, ruin, demolish, flatten, level

devastating adjective
*The siege had a **devastating** effect on the town.*
- overwhelming, stunning, shocking, shattering

develop verb
1 *The zoo is **developing** its education programme.*
- expand, extend, enlarge, build up, diversify
2 *Her piano playing has **developed** this year.*
- improve, progress, evolve, advance, get better
3 *The plants will **develop** quickly in the spring.*
- grow, flourish
4 *How did he **develop** that posh accent?*
- get, acquire, pick up, cultivate

development noun
1 *Were there any **developments** while I was away?*
- event, happening, incident, occurrence, change
2 *We are pleased with the **development** of our website.*
- growth, expansion, improvement, progress, spread

deviate verb
*We were forced to **deviate** from our original plan.*
- depart, diverge, differ, stray

device noun
*The TV comes with a remote control **device**.*
- tool, implement, instrument, appliance, apparatus, gadget, contraption
- (informal) gizmo

devious adjective
1 *The mad professor had a **devious** plan to take over the world.*
- cunning, deceitful, dishonest, furtive, scheming, sly, sneaky, treacherous, wily
2 *Because of the roadworks, we took a **devious** route home.*
- indirect, roundabout, winding, meandering
OPPOSITE direct

devise verb
*We need to **devise** a strategy for Saturday's game.*
- conceive, form, invent, contrive, formulate, come up with, make up, plan, prepare, map out, think out, think up

devote verb
*My brother **devotes** all his free time to football.*
- set aside, dedicate, assign, commit

devoted adjective
*She's a **devoted** supporter of our team.*
- loyal, faithful, dedicated, enthusiastic, committed
OPPOSITE apathetic

devotion noun
*Penguins show great **devotion** to their offspring.*
- attachment, fondness, loyalty, dedication, commitment

devour verb

*He **devoured** a whole plateful of sandwiches.*

- eat, consume, guzzle, gobble up, gulp down, swallow
- (*informal*) scoff, wolf down
  SEE ALSO **eat**

diagnose verb

*No-one could **diagnose** the cause of her illness.*

- identify, name, determine, detect, recognize

diagnosis noun

*What is the doctor's **diagnosis**?*

- opinion, conclusion, explanation, interpretation, verdict

diagram noun

*We drew a **diagram** of the life cycle of a frog.*

- chart, plan, sketch, outline

dial verb

*I picked up the phone and **dialled** his number.*

- phone, call, ring, telephone

dialogue noun

*The play consists of a series of **dialogues**.*

- conversation, talk, discussion, exchange, debate, chat

diary noun

*I write all about my birthday party in my **diary**.*

- journal, daily record
- A diary describing a voyage or mission is a log or logbook.
- A diary in which you insert pictures and souvenirs is a scrapbook.
- A diary published on a website is a blog.

dictate verb

to dictate to someone

*You've got no right to **dictate to** me!*

- order about, give orders to, command, bully
- (*informal*) boss about, push around, lord it over

die verb

1 *My sister's hamster **died** last week.*

- expire, pass away, perish
- (*informal*) snuff it, kick the bucket, croak
- To die of hunger is to starve.

2 *The flowers will **die** if they don't have water.*

- wither, wilt, droop, fade

to die down

*The flames will **die down** eventually.*

- become less, decline, decrease, subside, weaken, dwindle, fizzle out, wane

to die out

*When did the dinosaurs **die out**?*

- become extinct, cease to exist, come to an end, disappear, vanish

diet noun

*Koalas live on a **diet** of eucalyptus leaves.*

- food, nourishment, nutrition
- If you choose what to eat in order to lose weight, you are on a slimming diet.
- If you don't eat meat, you are on a vegetarian diet.
- If you don't eat any animal products at all, you are on a vegan diet.
  SEE ALSO **food**

differ verb

*The two men **differed** in their beliefs.*

- disagree, conflict, argue, clash, contradict each other, oppose each other, quarrel
  OPPOSITE agree

to differ from

*My style of painting **differs from** hers.*

- be different from, contrast with

difference noun

1 *Can you see any **difference** between these two colours?*

- contrast, distinction
  OPPOSITE similarity

2 *This money will make a **difference** to their lives.*

- change, alteration, modification, variation

a b c d e f g h i j k l m n o p q r s t u v w x y z

different adjective

1 *We have **different** views about global warming.*
- differing, contradictory, opposite, clashing, conflicting

2 *It's important that the teams wear **different** colours.*
- contrasting, dissimilar, distinguishable

3 *The packet contains sweets of **different** flavours.*
- various, assorted, mixed, several, diverse, numerous, miscellaneous

4 *Let's go somewhere **different** on holiday this year.*
- new, original, fresh

5 *Everyone's handwriting is **different**.*
- distinct, distinctive, individual, special, unique
- OPPOSITE identical, similar

difficult adjective

1 *This crossword is really **difficult**. We were faced with a **difficult** problem.*
- hard, complicated, complex, involved, intricate, baffling, perplexing, puzzling
- (informal) tricky, thorny, knotty
- OPPOSITE simple

2 *It is a **difficult** climb to the top of the hill.*
- challenging, arduous, demanding, taxing, exhausting, formidable, gruelling, laborious, strenuous, tough
- OPPOSITE easy

3 *Mum says I was a **difficult** child when I was little.*
- troublesome, awkward, trying, tiresome, annoying, disruptive, obstinate, stubborn, uncooperative, unhelpful
- OPPOSITE cooperative

difficulty noun

1 *The explorers were used to facing **difficulty**.*
- trouble, adversity, challenges, hardship

2 *There are some **difficulties** with your application.*
- problem, complication, hitch, obstacle, snag

dig verb

1 *We spent the afternoon **digging** the garden.*
- cultivate, fork over, turn over

2 *Rabbits **dig** holes in the ground.*
- burrow, excavate, tunnel, gouge out, hollow out, scoop out

3 *Did you **dig** me in the back?*
- poke, prod, jab

dignified adjective

*Lady Snodgrass was a very **dignified** old lady.*
- refined, stately, distinguished, noble, sedate, solemn, proper, grave, grand, august
- OPPOSITE undignified

dignity noun

1 *Their laughter spoilt the **dignity** of the occasion.*
- formality, seriousness, solemnity

2 *She handled the problem with **dignity**.*
- calmness, poise, self-control

dilute verb

*You need to **dilute** orange squash with water.*
- thin, water down, weaken
- OPPOSITE concentrate

dim adjective

1 *I could see the **dim** outline of a figure in the mist.*
- indistinct, faint, blurred, fuzzy, hazy, shadowy, vague
- OPPOSITE clear

2 *The light in the cave was rather **dim**.*
- dark, dull, dingy, murky, gloomy
- OPPOSITE bright

dimensions plural noun

*We measured the **dimensions** of the room.*
- measurements, size, extent, capacity
- FOR WORDS USED IN MEASURING
- SEE **measurement**

diminish verb

1 *Don't **diminish** his confidence by making fun of him.*
- lessen, reduce, make smaller, minimize

a
b
c
d
e
f
g
h
i
j
k
l
m
n
o
p
q
r
s
t
u
v
w
x
y
z

2 *Our water supply was **diminishing** rapidly.*
- become less, decrease, decline, subside, dwindle, wane
OPPOSITE increase

din noun
*I can't hear you because of that awful **din**!*
- noise, racket, row, clatter, hullabaloo

dine verb
*We will be **dining** at eight o'clock.*
- eat, have dinner, sup

dingy adjective
*How can we brighten up this **dingy** room?*
- dull, drab, dreary, dowdy, colourless, dismal, gloomy, murky
OPPOSITE bright

dinosaur noun

WORD WEB

SOME TYPES OF DINOSAUR
apatosaurus, archaeopteryx, brachiosaurus, diplodocus, gallimimus, iguanodon, megalosaurus, pterodactylus, stegosaurus, triceratops, tyrannosaurus rex, velociraptor

BODY PARTS WHICH A DINOSAUR MAY HAVE

dorsal plates, bony frill, fleshy fin, horn, wings, crest
- A person who studies dinosaurs and other fossils is a palaeontologist.

FOR OTHER PREHISTORIC ANIMALS

SEE **prehistoric**

---

dip verb
1 *I **dipped** my hand in the water.*
- immerse, lower, plunge, submerge, dunk
2 *The road **dips** down into the valley.*
- descend, go down, slope down

dip noun
1 *There was a **dip** in the road ahead.*
- hollow, hole, depression, slope
2 *It was so hot we decided to have a **dip** in the sea.*
- swim, bathe

dire adjective
1 *The survivors were in a **dire** situation.*
- dreadful, terrible, awful, appalling, severe, grave, drastic, extreme
2 *After weeks of drought, the garden is in **dire** need of rain.*
- urgent, desperate, pressing, sore

direct adjective
1 *It would be quicker to take the **direct** route.*
- straight, shortest
OPPOSITE indirect
2 *Please give me a **direct** answer.*
- straightforward, frank, honest, sincere, blunt, plain, outspoken, candid, unambiguous
OPPOSITE evasive

direct verb
1 *Can you **direct** me to the station?*
- guide, point, show the way, give directions to
2 *A new manager has been apppointed to **direct** the company.*
- manage, run, be in charge of, control, administer, superintend, supervise, take charge of
- To direct an orchestra is to conduct it.
3 *The conductor **directed** us to begin playing.*
- instruct, command, order, tell

direction noun
*Which **direction** did they go in?*
- way, route, course, path
directions
*I read the **directions** for building the model.*
- instructions, guidance, guidelines, plans

director noun
*Who is the **director** of the company?*
- manager, head, chief, leader, president
- (*informal*) boss

dirt noun
1 *The floor was covered in **dirt**.*
- filth, grime, mess, muck, mud, dust
2 *Chickens scratched about in the **dirt**.*
- earth, soil, clay, loam, mud

a
b
c
d
e
f
g
h
i
j
k
l
m
n
o
p
q
r
s
t
u
v
w
x
y
z

dirty adjective

1 *Those **dirty** clothes need to be washed.*
- unclean, filthy, grimy, grubby, soiled, stained, messy, mucky, muddy, sooty, foul
- (*informal*) manky, grotty
OPPOSITE clean

2 *We refused to drink the **dirty** water.*
- impure, polluted, murky, cloudy
OPPOSITE pure

3 *The other team used **dirty** tactics.*
- unfair, dishonest, illegal, mean, unsporting
OPPOSITE honest

4 *The comedian used a lot of **dirty** words.*
- rude, offensive, coarse, crude, improper, indecent, obscene
OPPOSITE decent

disability noun

*She leads a normal life in spite of her **disabilities**.*
- handicap, infirmity, incapacity

disabled adjective

*He has been **disabled** since the accident.*
- handicapped, incapacitated
OPPOSITE able-bodied
- An animal which is injured and cannot walk is lame.
- A person who cannot move part of their body is paralysed.

disadvantage noun

*It's a **disadvantage** to be small if you play basketball.*
- drawback, handicap, hindrance, inconvenience, downside, snag

disagree verb

*My sister and I often **disagree** about music.*
- argue, differ, clash, quarrel, squabble, bicker, fall out
OPPOSITE agree

to disagree with

1 *He **disagrees with** everything I say.*
- argue with, contradict, oppose, object to

2 *Broccoli **disagrees with** me.*
- have a bad effect on, upset

disagreeable adjective

*There's no need to be so **disagreeable**.*
- unpleasant, horrible, nasty, offensive, horrid, revolting
OPPOSITE pleasant

disagreement noun

*We had a **disagreement** over who should pay for the meal.*
- argument, dispute, difference of opinion, quarrel, row, clash, squabble, conflict
OPPOSITE agreement

disappear verb

1 *The markings will **disappear** as the chicks grow older.*
- become invisible, vanish, fade, clear, disperse, dissolve

2 *The thief **disappeared** around the corner.*
- run away, escape, flee, go away, withdraw
OPPOSITE appear

disappoint verb

*She didn't want to **disappoint** her fans by cancelling the show.*
- let down, fail, dissatisfy, displease, upset
OPPOSITE please, satisfy

disappointed adjective

*I'm **disappointed** that you can't come to my party.*
- saddened, unhappy, upset, let down, unsatisfied, displeased
OPPOSITE pleased, satisfied

disapprove verb

to disapprove of

*My aunt **disapproves of** watching television.*
- object to, take exception to, dislike, deplore, condemn, criticize, denounce, frown on
- (*informal*) take a dim view of
OPPOSITE approve of

disaster noun

WORD WEB

*There was a near **disaster** when the engine caught fire.*
- catastrophe, calamity, tragedy

SOME TYPES OF NATURAL DISASTER
avalanche, earthquake, epidemic, famine, fire, flood, hurricane, landslide, plague, tidal wave, tornado, tsunami, volcanic eruption

disastrous adjective
*The **disastrous** fire cost millions of pounds.*
- catastrophic, devastating, calamitous, destructive, dire, dreadful, terrible, ruinous

disc noun
*The full moon appears as a **disc** in the sky.*
SEE **circle** noun

discard verb
*I **discarded** some of my old toys.*
- get rid of, throw away, throw out, reject, cast off, dispose of, dump, scrap

discharge verb
1 *The accused man was found not guilty and **discharged**.*
- free, release, clear, acquit, let off, allow to leave, liberate
2 *The chimney **discharged** thick smoke.*
- expel, emit, give out, pour out, eject, belch, produce

disciple noun
*The religious leader had many **disciples**.*
- follower, supporter, admirer, devotee
- In Christianity, the disciples of Jesus are called the apostles.

discipline noun
***Discipline** is important in the army.*
- order, control

disclose verb
*He never **disclosed** the truth.*
- reveal, tell, make known, confess, make public
OPPOSITE conceal

discomfort noun
*He still experiences a lot of **discomfort** from his injury.*
- pain, soreness, distress, unease

disconnect verb
*We need to **disconnect** the cooker before we can move it.*
- detach, cut off, unplug, unhook

discontented adjective
*She felt very **discontented** with her job.*
- dissatisfied, miserable, unhappy, upset
- (*informal*) fed up
OPPOSITE happy, satisfied

discontinue verb
*That style of shoe has been **discontinued**.*
- stop, end, terminate
OPPOSITE introduce, establish

discount noun
*I got a **discount** on the full price.*
- deduction, reduction, cut, concession, allowance

discourage verb
1 *Don't let her criticism **discourage** you.*
- demoralize, depress
- (*informal*) put you off
2 *The burglar alarm will **discourage** thieves.*
- deter, dissuade, prevent, restrain, stop, hinder
OPPOSITE encourage

discover verb
*I **discovered** some old toys in the attic.*
- find, come across, spot, stumble across, uncover
- To discover something that has been buried is to unearth it.
- To discover something that has been under water is to dredge it up.
- To discover something you have been pursuing is to track it down.
OPPOSITE hide

discovery noun
*Scientists have made an exciting new **discovery**.*
- find, breakthrough

a
b
c
d
e
f
g
h
i
j
k
l
m
n
o
p
q
r
s
t
u
v
w
x
y
z

a
b
c
d
e
f
g
h
i
j
k
l
m
n
o
p
q
r
s
t
u
v
w
x
y
z

discreet adjective

*I asked a few **discreet** questions about her illness.*

- tactful, sensitive, delicate, careful, cautious, diplomatic, wary
  OPPOSITE tactless

discriminate verb

*It's sometimes hard to **discriminate** between poisonous mushrooms and edible ones.*

- distinguish, tell the difference

to discriminate against

*It's wrong to **discriminate against** people because of their age.*

- be biased against, be intolerant of, be prejudiced against

discrimination noun

1 *She shows **discrimination** in her choice of music.*

- good taste, good judgement

2 *The school has a policy against racial **discrimination**.*

- prejudice, bias, intolerance, unfairness
- Discrimination against people because of their sex is sexism.
- Discrimination against people because of their race is racism.

discuss verb

*I **discussed** the idea with my parents.*

- talk about, confer about, debate

discussion noun

*We had a lively **discussion** about pocket money.*

- conversation, argument, exchange of views
- A formal discussion is a conference or debate.

disease noun

*He was suffering from a serious **disease**.*

- illness, ailment, sickness, complaint, affliction
- (*informal*) bug
  SEE ALSO **illness**

diseased adjective

*Gardeners throw away **diseased** plants.*

- unhealthy, sickly, infected
  OPPOSITE healthy

disembark verb

*The passengers **disembarked** from the ferry.*

- go ashore
  OPPOSITE embark

disgrace noun

1 *He never got over the **disgrace** of being caught cheating.*

- humiliation, shame, embarrassment, dishonour

2 *The way he treats them is a **disgrace**!*

- outrage, scandal

disgraceful adjective

*We were shocked by her **disgraceful** behaviour.*

- shameful, shocking, appalling, outrageous, scandalous
  OPPOSITE honourable

disguise verb

*I tried to **disguise** my feelings.*

- conceal, hide, cover up, camouflage, mask

to disguise yourself as

*The spy **disguised himself as** a hotel porter.*

- dress up as, pretend to be

disguise noun

*I didn't recognize him in that **disguise**.*

- costume, camouflage, make-up, mask

disgust noun

*The sight of the carcass filled me with **disgust**.*

- repulsion, repugnance, distaste, dislike, horror, loathing, detestation
  OPPOSITE liking

disgust verb

*The smell of rotten eggs **disgusts** me.*

- repel, revolt, sicken, appal, offend, distress, shock, horrify
- (*informal*) put you off, turn your stomach
  OPPOSITE please

disgusting adjective
The brew in the cauldron looked ***disgusting***.
- repulsive, revolting, horrible, nasty, loathsome, repellent, repugnant, offensive, appalling, sickening, nauseating
- (*informal*) yucky, icky, gross
OPPOSITE delightful, pleasing

dish noun
1 *Mum served the trifle in a large glass* ***dish***.
- bowl, basin, plate, platter
- A dish to serve soup from is a tureen.
  SEE ALSO **crockery**
2 *What's your favourite* ***dish***?
- food, recipe, meal

dishevelled adjective
His clothes were a mess and his hair was ***dishevelled***.
- messy, untidy, scruffy, unkempt, bedraggled, slovenly,
OPPOSITE neat, tidy

dishonest adjective
1 *They were taken in by a* ***dishonest*** *salesman.*
- deceitful, cheating, corrupt, disreputable, untrustworthy, immoral, lying, swindling, thieving
- (*informal*) bent, crooked, dodgy, shady
2 *The author makes some* ***dishonest*** *claims.*
- false, misleading, untruthful, fraudulent, devious
OPPOSITE honest

dishonesty noun
The MP was accused of ***dishonesty***.
- deceit, cheating, corruption, insincerity, lying, deviousness
- (*informal*) crookedness
OPPOSITE honesty

disinfect verb
The nurse ***disinfected*** *my wound.*
- cleanse, sterilize
- To disinfect an infected area is to decontaminate it.

- To disinfect a room with fumes is to fumigate it.
OPPOSITE infect

disintegrate verb
The cloth is so old that it's starting to ***disintegrate***.
- break up, fall apart, break into pieces, crumble, decay, decompose

disinterested adjective
A referee must be ***disinterested***.
- impartial, neutral, unbiased, unprejudiced, detached, fair
OPPOSITE biased

disk noun SEE **disc**

dislike noun
His colleagues regarded him with intense ***dislike***.
- hatred, loathing, detestation, disapproval, disgust, revulsion
OPPOSITE liking

dislike verb
I ***dislike*** *people who hunt wild animals.*
- hate, loathe, detest, disapprove of
OPPOSITE like

dislodge verb
The wind ***dislodged*** *some tiles on the roof.*
- displace, move, shift, disturb

disloyal adjective
The rebels were accused of being ***disloyal*** *to the king.*
- unfaithful, treacherous, faithless, false, unreliable, untrustworthy
OPPOSITE loyal

dismal adjective
1 *How can we brighten up this* ***dismal*** *room?*
- dull, drab, dreary, dingy, colourless, cheerless, gloomy, murky
OPPOSITE bright, cheerful
2 (*informal*) *It was a* ***dismal*** *performance by the home team.*
- dreadful, awful, terrible, feeble, useless, hopeless
- (*informal*) pathetic
OPPOSITE bright, cheerful

a
b
c
d
e
f
g
h
i
j
k
l
m
n
o
p
q
r
s
t
u
v
w
x
y
z

a
b
c
d
e
f
g
h
i
j
k
l
m
n
o
p
q
r
s
t
u
v
w
x
y
z

dismantle verb
*After the school fair, we had to **dismantle** all the stalls.*
- take apart, take down
- To dismantle a tent is to strike it.
OPPOSITE assemble

dismay noun
*We listened with **dismay** to the bad news.*
- distress, alarm, shock, concern, anxiety, gloom

dismayed adjective
*I was **dismayed** by the failure of our plan.*
- distressed, discouraged, depressed, devastated, shocked, appalled
OPPOSITE encouraged

dismiss verb
1 *The teacher **dismissed** the class.*
- send away, discharge, free, let go, release
2 *The firm **dismissed** ten workers.*
- sack, give the sack, give notice to, make redundant
- (*informal*) fire
3 *The weather was so bad that we **dismissed** the idea of having a picnic.*
- discard, drop, reject

dismount verb
*The knight **dismounted** from his horse.*
- descend, get off

disobedient adjective
*She said she had never known such a **disobedient** child.*
- naughty, badly behaved, undisciplined, uncontrollable, unmanageable, unruly, ungovernable, troublesome, defiant, disruptive, mutinous, rebellious, contrary
OPPOSITE obedient

disobey verb
1 *You will be penalized if you **disobey** the rules.*
- break, ignore, disregard, defy, violate
2 *Soldiers are trained never to **disobey**.*
- be disobedient, rebel, revolt, mutiny
OPPOSITE obey

disorder noun
1 *The public meeting broke up in **disorder**.*
- disturbance, uproar, commotion, quarrelling, rioting, brawling, fighting, lawlessness, anarchy
2 *It's time I tidied up the **disorder** in my room.*
- mess, muddle, untidiness, chaos, confusion, clutter, jumble
OPPOSITE order

disorderly adjective
*The class were behaving in a **disorderly** manner.*
- badly behaved, disobedient, unruly, uncontrollable, undisciplined, ungovernable, unmanageable
OPPOSITE orderly

dispatch noun
*The messenger brought a **dispatch** from headquarters.*
- message, communication, report, letter, bulletin

dispatch verb
*The parcel has already been **dispatched**.*
- post, send, transmit

dispense verb
to dispense with
*Now that I have new trainers, I can **dispense with** the old ones.*
- get rid of, dispose of, do without, remove

disperse verb
1 *The police **dispersed** the crowd.*
- break up, send away, drive away, separate, send in different directions
2 *The crowd **dispersed** quickly after the match.*
- scatter, spread out, disappear, dissolve, melt away, vanish
OPPOSITE gather

displace verb
1 *The gales have **displaced** some of the roof tiles.*
- dislodge, put out of place, shift, disturb

2 *A brilliant new player **displaced** me in the team.*
- replace, take the place of, succeed

display verb
*We planned the best way to **display** our work.*
- demonstrate, exhibit, present, put on show, set out, show, show off
- To display something boastfully is to flaunt it.

display noun
*We set out a **display** of our art work.*
- exhibition, show, presentation, demonstration

displease verb
*I must have done something to **displease** her.*
- annoy, irritate, upset, anger, exasperate, vex

dispose verb
to dispose of something
*Let's **dispose of** this old carpet.*
- get rid of, discard, throw away, give away, scrap
- (informal) dump

to be disposed to do something
*He didn't seem **disposed to** help us.*
- be willing to, be inclined to, be ready to, be likely to

disposition noun
*Our labrador has a very friendly **disposition**.*
- character, nature, personality

dispute noun
*We settled the **dispute** about who should wash the dishes.*
- argument, disagreement, quarrel, debate, controversy, difference of opinion

disqualify verb
*Two athletes have been **disqualified** from the competition.*
- bar, prohibit

disregard verb
*I **disregarded** the doctor's advice.*
- ignore, pay no attention to, take no notice of, reject
OPPOSITE heed

disrespectful adjective
*She was very **disrespectful** towards her parents.*
- rude, bad-mannered, insulting, impolite, insolent, cheeky
OPPOSITE respectful

disrupt verb
*Bad weather has **disrupted** the tennis tournament.*
- interrupt, upset, interfere with, throw into confusion or disorder

dissatisfied adjective
*I was **dissatisfied** with my piano playing.*
- displeased, disappointed, discontented, frustrated, annoyed
OPPOSITE satisfied

dissolve verb
*Stir your tea until the sugar **dissolves**.*
- disperse, disintegrate, melt

dissuade verb
to dissuade someone from doing something
*We tried to **dissuade** him **from** going out in the storm.*
- discourage someone from, persuade someone not to, deter someone from, warn someone against
OPPOSITE persuade

distance noun
*What is the **distance** from Earth to the Sun?*
- measurement, space, extent, reach, mileage
- The distance across something is the breadth or width.
- The distance along something is the length.
- The distance between two points is a gap or interval.
FOR UNITS FOR MEASURING DISTANCE
SEE **measurement**

distant adjective
1 *I'd love to travel to **distant** countries.*
- faraway, remote, out-of-the-way, inaccessible, exotic
OPPOSITE close

2 *His **distant** manner puts me off.*
- unfriendly, unapproachable, formal, reserved, withdrawn, cool, haughty, aloof
OPPOSITE friendly

distinct adjective

1 *There is a **distinct** improvement in your handwriting.*
- definite, evident, noticeable, obvious, perceptible
OPPOSITE imperceptible

2 *It was a small photo, but the details were quite **distinct**.*
- clear, distinguishable, plain, recognizable, sharp, unmistakable, visible, well defined
OPPOSITE indistinct

3 *Organize your essay into **distinct** sections.*
- individual, separate

distinction noun

1 *There's a clear **distinction** between the real diamond and the fake.*
- difference, contrast, distinctiveness

2 *He had the **distinction** of being the team captain.*
- honour, glory, merit, credit, prestige

distinctive adjective
*We spotted the **distinctive** footprints of a yeti in the snow.*
- characteristic, recognizable, unmistakable, special, unique

distinguish verb

1 *It was impossible to **distinguish** one twin from the other.*
- tell apart, pick out, discriminate, differentiate, make a distinction, decide

2 *In the dark we couldn't **distinguish** who was walking past.*
- identify, tell, make out, determine, perceive, recognize, single out

distinguished adjective

1 *The school has a **distinguished** academic record.*
- excellent, first-rate, outstanding, exceptional
OPPOSITE ordinary

2 *He is a very **distinguished** actor.*
- famous, celebrated, well known, eminent, notable, prominent, renowned
OPPOSITE unknown, obscure

distort verb

1 *When my bike hit the kerb, it **distorted** the wheel.*
- bend, buckle, twist, warp, contort

2 *The newspaper **distorted** the facts of the story.*
- twist, slant, misrepresent

distract verb
*Don't **distract** the bus driver.*
- divert the attention of, disturb, put off

distress noun
*The trapped animal was clearly in **distress**.*
- suffering, torment, anguish, dismay, anxiety, grief, misery, pain, sadness, sorrow, worry, wretchedness

distress verb
*We could see that the bad news **distressed** her.*
- upset, disturb, trouble, worry, alarm, dismay, torment
OPPOSITE comfort

distribute verb

1 *The coach **distributed** water to the players at half-time.*
- give out, hand round, circulate, dispense, issue, share out, take round
- (informal) dish out, doll out

2 ***Distribute** the seeds evenly.*
- scatter, spread, disperse

district noun
*Granny lives in a quiet **district**.*
- area, neighbourhood, locality, region, vicinity

distrust verb
*I **distrusted** the professor from the moment I met him.*
- doubt, mistrust, question, suspect, be suspicious or wary of, be sceptical about, feel uncertain or uneasy or unsure about
OPPOSITE trust

disturb verb

1 *Don't **disturb** the baby when she's asleep.*
- bother, interrupt, annoy, pester

2 *They were **disturbed** by the bad news.*
- distress, trouble, upset, worry, alarm, frighten

3 *Please don't **disturb** the papers on my desk.*
- muddle, mix up, move around, mess about with

disused adjective

*They made the **disused** railway line into a cycle track.*
- abandoned, unused, closed down

ditch noun

*We dug a **ditch** to drain away the water.*
- trench, channel, drain, gully

dither verb

*Stop **dithering** and make up your mind!*
- hesitate, waver, be in two minds
- (*informal*) shilly-shally

dive verb

1 *The mermaid **dived** into the water.*
- plunge, jump, leap
- A dive in which you land flat on your front is a bellyflop.

2 *The eagle **dived** towards its prey.*
- pounce, swoop

diver noun

- A diver who wears a rubber suit and flippers and breathes air from a portable tank is a scuba diver or frogman.

diverse adjective

*People from many **diverse** cultures live in the area.*
- different, differing, varied, various, contrasting

diversion noun

1 *The police had set up a traffic **diversion**.*
- detour, indirect route, roundabout route

2 *There were lots of **diversions** at the holiday camp.*
- entertainment, amusement, recreation

divert verb

1 *They **diverted** the plane to another airport.*
- redirect, switch

2 *She **diverted** herself by practising handstands.*
- entertain, amuse, occupy, interest, keep happy

divide verb

1 *We **divided** the class into two groups.*
- separate, split, break up, move apart, part
  OPPOSITE combine

2 *I **divided** the cake between my friends.*
- distribute, share out, give out, allot, deal out, dispense

3 *Which way do we go? The path **divides** here.*
- branch, fork
  OPPOSITE converge

divine adjective

1 *The temple is used for **divine** worship.*
- holy, religious, sacred, spiritual

2 *The Greeks believed **divine** beings lived on Mount Olympus.*
- godlike, immortal, heavenly

3 *(informal) These fairy cakes taste **divine**!*
- excellent, wonderful, superb

division noun

1 *The map shows the **division** of Europe after the war.*
- dividing, splitting, separation, partition

2 *There was a **division** in the government.*
- disagreement, split, feud

3 *There is a movable **division** between the two classrooms.*
- partition, divider, dividing wall, screen

4 *They work in different **divisions** of the same company.*
- branch, department, section, unit

dizzy adjective
*Going on a roundabout makes me feel **dizzy**.*
- dazed, giddy, faint, reeling, unsteady

do verb
1 *My friend always knows what to **do** in a crisis.*
- act, behave, conduct yourself
2 *The vet has a lot of work to **do** this morning.*
- attend to, cope with, deal with, handle, look after, perform, undertake
3 *It took me half an hour to **do** the washing-up.*
- accomplish, achieve, carry out, complete, execute, finish
4 *I need to **do** all of these sums.*
- answer, puzzle out, solve, work out
5 *Staring at the sun can **do** damage to your eyes.*
- bring about, cause, produce, result in
6 *If you don't have lemonade, water will **do**.*
- be acceptable, be enough, be satisfactory, be sufficient, serve

to do away with
*I wish our school would **do away with** homework.*
- get rid of, abolish, eliminate, end, put an end to

to do up
*These jeans are too tight to **do up**.*
- button up, fasten

docile adjective
*Don't be afraid of the dog—he's quite **docile**.*
- tame, gentle, meek, obedient, manageable, safe, submissive
OPPOSITE fierce

dock noun
*A boat was waiting for us at the end of the **dock**.*
- harbour, quay, jetty, wharf, landing stage, dockyard, pier, port, marina

dock verb
*We can't disembark until the ship **docks**.*
- moor, tie up

doctor noun FOR PEOPLE WHO PRACTISE MEDICINE
SEE **medicine**

document noun
*The library contains many old **documents**.*
- paper, record, file, certificate, deed

dodge verb
*I just managed to **dodge** the snowball.*
- avoid, evade, side-step

dog noun

WORD WEB
- A female dog is a bitch.
- A young dog is a pup, puppy, or whelp.
- Informal words for a dog are mutt and pooch.
- An uncomplimentary word for a dog is cur.
- A dog of pure breed with known ancestors has a pedigree.
- A dog of mixed breeds is a mongrel.
- A dog used for hunting is a hound.
- A word meaning 'to do with dogs' is canine.

SOME BREEDS OF DOG
Afghan hound, Alsatian, basset hound, beagle, bloodhound, boxer, bulldog, bull terrier, cairn terrier, chihuahua, cocker spaniel, collie, corgi, dachshund, Dalmatian, Doberman, foxhound, fox terrier, Great Dane, greyhound, husky, Irish Setter, Labrador, mastiff, Pekinese or Pekingese, Pomeranian, poodle, pug, golden retriever, Rottweiler, St Bernard, Schnauzer, setter, sheepdog, spaniel, terrier, West Highland terrier, whippet, wolfhound, Yorkshire terrier
SEE ALSO **animal**

domestic adjective
1 *At weekends I do various **domestic** chores.*
- household, family
2 *Cats and dogs are popular **domestic** animals.*
- domesticated, tame

dominant adjective

1 *The captain plays a **dominant** role in the team.*
- leading, main, chief, major, powerful, principal, important, influential
OPPOSITE minor

2 *The castle is a **dominant** feature in the landscape.*
- conspicuous, prominent, obvious, large, imposing, eye-catching
OPPOSITE insignificant

dominate verb

*The visiting team **dominated** the game.*
- control, direct, monopolize, govern, take control of, take over

donate verb

*Will you **donate** something to our collection?*
- give, contribute

donation noun

*The museum relies on **donations** from the public.*
- contribution, gift, offering

done adjective

1 *All my thank-you letters are **done** now.*
- finished, complete, over

2 *The cake will be brown on top when it's **done**.*
- cooked, ready

donor noun

*A generous **donor** gave us money for new sports equipment.*
- benefactor, contributor, sponsor

doomed adjective

*The expedition was **doomed** from the start.*
- ill-fated, condemned, fated, cursed, jinxed, damned

door noun

- A door in a floor or ceiling is a hatch or trapdoor.
- The plank or stone underneath a door is the threshold.
- The beam or stone above a door is the lintel.
- The device on which most doors swing is the hinge.

dose noun

*The nurse gave me a **dose** of the medicine.*
- measure, correct amount, dosage, portion

dot noun

*She was furious when she saw **dots** of paint on the carpet.*
- spot, speck, fleck, point, mark
- The dot you always put at the end of a sentence is a full stop.

on the dot (*informal*)

*We left the house at nine o'clock **on the dot**.*
- exactly, precisely

double adjective

*You enter the room through a **double** set of doors.*
- dual, twofold, paired, twin, matching, duplicate

double noun

*She's so like you—she's almost your **double**.*
- twin
- (*informal*) lookalike, spitting image, dead ringer
- A living organism created as an exact copy of another living organism is a clone.

doubt noun

1 *Have you any **doubt** about his honesty?*
- distrust, suspicion, mistrust, hesitation, reservation, scepticism
OPPOSITE confidence

2 *There is no **doubt** that you will pass your exam.*
- question, uncertainty, ambiguity, confusion
OPPOSITE certainty

doubt verb

*There is no reason to **doubt** her story.*
- distrust, feel uncertain or uneasy or unsure about, question, mistrust, suspect, be sceptical about, be suspicious or wary of
OPPOSITE trust

a
b
c
d
e
f
g
h
i
j
k
l
m
n
o
p
q
r
s
t
u
v
w
x
y
z

a
b
c
d
e
f
g
h
i
j
k
l
m
n
o
p
q
r
s
t
u
v
w
x
y
z

doubtful adjective

1 *He looked **doubtful**, but agreed to let us go.*
- unsure, uncertain, unconvinced, hesitant, distrustful, sceptical, suspicious
  OPPOSITE certain

2 *The referee made a **doubtful** decision there.*
- questionable, debatable, arguable

downfall noun

*After the government's **downfall**, there was a general election.*
- collapse, fall, ruin

downward adjective

*We took the **downward** path into the valley.*
- downhill, descending
  OPPOSITE upward

doze verb

*Dad often **dozes** in the evening.*
- rest, sleep, nod off
- (*informal*) drop off

drab adjective

*That dress is too **drab** to wear to the party.*
- dull, dingy, dreary, cheerless, colourless, dismal, gloomy, grey
  OPPOSITE bright, cheerful

draft noun

*I jotted down a **draft** of my story.*
- outline, plan, sketch, rough version

draft verb

*I began to **draft** my story.*
- outline, plan, prepare, sketch, work out

drag verb

*The tractor **dragged** the car out of the ditch.*
- pull, tow, tug, draw, haul, lug
  OPPOSITE push

dragon noun

WORD WEB

*A fearsome **dragon** once lived in these hills.*

SOME WAYS TO DESCRIBE A DRAGON
ancient, fearsome, fiery, fire-breathing, mighty, monstrous, scaly

BODY PARTS A DRAGON MIGHT HAVE
claws, crest, forked tail or tongue, scales, spikes or spines, bat-like wings

A DRAGON'S SCALES MIGHT BE
dazzling, iridescent, patterned, shimmering

A DRAGON'S BREATH MIGHT BE
fiery, flaming, scorching, searing

THINGS A DRAGON MIGHT DO
breathe fire, puff smoke, roar, snort; change shape, fly, soar, swoop

PLACES WHERE A DRAGON MIGHT LIVE
cave, den, lair

FOR OTHER CREATURES FOUND IN MYTHS AND LEGENDS
SEE **myth**

drain noun

*Surplus water runs away along a **drain**.*
- ditch, channel, drainpipe, gutter, pipe, sewer

drain verb

1 *If they **drain** the marsh, lots of waterbirds will die.*
- dry out, remove water from

2 *She **drained** the oil from the engine.*
- draw off, empty

3 *The water slowly **drained** away.*
- trickle, ooze, seep

4 *The tough climb **drained** my energy.*
- use up, consume, exhaust

drama noun

1 ***Drama** is one of my favourite subjects.*
- acting
  SEE ALSO **theatre**

2 *I witnessed the **drama** of a real robbery.*
- action, excitement, suspense, spectacle

dramatic adjective

*We watched the **dramatic** rescue on TV.*
- exciting, eventful, thrilling, sensational, spectacular, gripping

drastic adjective

*After being without food for three days, the explorers needed to take **drastic** action.*

- desperate, extreme, radical, harsh, severe
  OPPOSITE moderate

draught noun

*I felt a **draught** of air from the open window.*

- breeze, current, movement, puff

draw verb

1 *I **drew** some pictures of the flowers in our garden.*
- sketch, trace, doodle

2 *I'm not very good at **drawing** faces.*
- depict, portray, represent

3 *The horse was **drawing** a cart.*
- pull, tow, drag, haul, tug, lug

4 *We expect tomorrow's match to **draw** a big crowd.*
- attract, bring in, pull in

5 *The two teams **drew** 1-1.*
- finish equal, tie

to draw near

*As the spaceship **drew near**, I began to get nervous.*

- approach, advance, come near

draw noun

- Kinds of prize draw are a lottery and a raffle.

drawback noun

*It's a **drawback** to be small if you play basketball.*

- disadvantage, difficulty, handicap, obstacle, inconvenience, hindrance, downside, snag

drawing noun

> **WORD WEB**
>
> SOME TYPES OF DRAWING
> caricature, cartoon, design, doodle, illustration, outline, sketch
>
> TOOLS USED FOR DRAWING
> chalk, charcoal, crayon, ink, pastel, pen, pencil
> SEE ALSO **picture** noun

dread noun

*Our teacher has a **dread** of spiders.*

- fear, horror, terror, phobia (about), anxiety (about)

dreadful adjective

1 *There has been a **dreadful** accident at sea.*
- horrible, terrible, appalling, horrendous, distressing, shocking, upsetting, tragic, grim

2 *The weather at the weekend was **dreadful**.*
- bad, awful, terrible, abysmal, abominable, dire, foul, nasty
  OPPOSITE good, pleasant

dream noun

- A bad dream is a nightmare.
- A dreamlike experience you have while awake is a daydream, fantasy, or reverie.
- Something you see in a dream or daydream is a vision.
- The dreamlike state when you are hypnotized is a trance.
- Something you think you see that is not real is a hallucination or illusion.

dream verb

*I **dreamed** that I was a mermaid.*

- daydream, imagine, fancy, fantasize

dreary adjective

1 *The newsreader had a very **dreary** voice.*
- dull, boring, flat, tedious, unexciting, uninteresting
  OPPOSITE lively

2 *When will this **dreary** weather end?*
- depressing, dismal, dull, gloomy, cheerless, murky, overcast
  OPPOSITE bright, sunny

drench verb

*The rain **drenched** me to the skin.*

- soak, wet thoroughly

dress noun

1 *What kind of **dress** are you wearing to the party?*
- frock, gown

a
b
c
d
e
f
g
h
i
j
k
l
m
n
o
p
q
r
s
t
u
v
w
x
y
z

2 *The invitation said to wear casual **dress**.*
• clothes, clothing, outfit, costume, garments
SEE ALSO **clothes**

dress verb
1 *I helped to **dress** my little brother.*
• clothe, put clothes on
OPPOSITE undress
2 *A nurse **dressed** my wound.*
• bandage, put a dressing on, bind up

dressing noun
*The nurse put a **dressing** on the wound.*
• bandage, plaster

dribble verb
1 *Careful, the baby's **dribbling** on your jumper.*
• drool
2 *Water **dribbled** out of the hole in the tank.*
• drip, trickle, leak, ooze, seep

drift verb
1 *The boat **drifted** downstream.*
• float, be carried, move slowly
2 *The crowd lost interest and **drifted** away.*
• stray, wander, meander, ramble, walk aimlessly
3 *The snow will **drift** in this wind.*
• pile up, accumulate, make drifts

drift noun
1 *The car was stuck in a snow **drift**.*
• bank, heap, mound, pile, ridge
2 *Did you understand the **drift** of the speech?*
• gist, main idea, point

drill noun
1 *There will be a fire **drill** at school next week.*
• practice, training
2 *Do you all know the **drill** for erecting a tent?*
• procedure, routine, system

drill verb
*It took a long time to **drill** through the wall.*
• bore, penetrate, pierce

drink noun

> ### WORD WEB
>
> SOME HOT DRINKS
> chocolate, cocoa, coffee, tea
>
> SOME NON-ALCOHOLIC COLD DRINKS
> barley water, cola, cordial, fruit juice, ginger beer, iced tea, lemonade, milk, milkshake, mineral water, orangeade, smoothie, sodawater, squash, tonic water, water
>
> SOME ALCOHOLIC DRINKS
> beer, brandy, champagne, cider, gin, mead, port, punch, rum, shandy, sherry, whisky, wine
> • Very strong alcoholic drinks are spirits.
>
> CONTAINERS FOR DRINKS
> beaker, bottle, can, cup, glass, goblet, mug, tankard, tumbler, wineglass
> SEE ALSO **bottle** noun, **cup**

drink verb
• To drink greedily is to gulp, guzzle, or swig.
• To drink noisily is to slurp.
• To drink a small amount at a time is to sip.
• To drink with the tongue as a cat does is to lap.

drip noun
*Dad was worried by the **drips** of oil underneath the car.*
• spot, dribble, splash, trickle

drip verb
*The oil **dripped** onto the garage floor.*
• drop, leak, dribble, splash, trickle

drive verb
1 *The dog **drove** the sheep through the gate.*
• direct, guide, herd
2 *I couldn't **drive** the spade into the hard ground.*
• push, thrust, hammer, plunge, ram
3 *When can I learn to **drive** a car?*
• control, handle, manage
4 *Lack of money **drove** him to steal.*
• force, compel, oblige

to drive someone out

*The invading soldiers **drove** the people out.*

- eject, expel, throw out
- To drive people out of their homes is to evict them.
- To drive people out of their country is to banish or exile them.

drive noun

1 *We went for a **drive** in the country.*
- ride, trip, journey, outing, excursion, jaunt

2 *Have you got the **drive** to succeed?*
- ambition, determination, keenness, motivation, energy, zeal

driver noun

*Many **drivers** go too fast.*
- motorist
- A person who drives someone's car as a job is a chauffeur.

droop verb

*Plants tend to **droop** in dry weather.*
- sag, wilt, bend, flop, be limp

drop noun

1 *Large **drops** of rain began to fall.*
- drip, droplet, spot, bead, blob

2 *Could I have another **drop** of milk in my tea?*
- dash, small quantity

3 *We expect a **drop** in the price of fruit in the summer.*
- decrease, reduction, cut

4 *There's a **drop** of two metres on the other side of the wall.*
- fall, descent, plunge

drop verb

1 *The hawk **dropped** onto its prey.*
- descend, dive, plunge, swoop

2 *I **dropped** to the ground exhausted.*
- collapse, fall, sink, subside, slump, tumble

3 *Why did you **drop** me from the team?*
- omit, eliminate, exclude, leave out

4 *They **dropped** the plan for a new bypass.*
- abandon, discard, reject, give up, scrap

to drop in

***Drop in** on your way home.*
- visit, call, pay a call

to drop out

*Why did you **drop out** of the race at the last minute?*
- withdraw, back out, pull out
- (*informal*) quit

drown verb

*The music from upstairs **drowned** our conversation.*
- overwhelm, overpower, drown out

drowsy adjective

*If you feel **drowsy**, why not go to bed?*
- sleepy, tired, weary

drug noun

*A new **drug** has been discovered for back pain.*
- medicine, remedy, treatment
- A drug which relieves pain is an analgesic or painkiller.
- A drug which calms you down is a sedative or tranquillizer.
- Drugs which make you more active are stimulants.

drum noun

WORD WEB

SOME TYPES OF DRUM
bass drum, bongo drum, kettledrum or timpani, snare drum, tabor, tambour, timpani, tom-tom
FOR OTHER MUSICAL INSTRUMENTS
SEE **music**

dry adjective

1 *Nothing will grow in this **dry** soil.*
- arid, parched, moistureless, waterless, dehydrated, desiccated, barren
- A common simile is as dry as a bone.
OPPOSITE wet

2 *He gave rather a **dry** speech.*
- dull, boring, dreary, tedious, uninteresting
OPPOSITE interesting

3 *I can't understand his **dry** sense of humour.*
- ironic, wry, witty, subtle

a
b
c
d
e
f
g
h
i
j
k
l
m
n
o
p
q
r
s
t
u
v
w
x
y
z

dry verb

1 *If it's sunny, I'll hang the clothes out to **dry**.*
- get dry, dry out

2 *Will you please **dry** the dishes?*
- wipe dry
- When you dry food to preserve it, you dehydrate it.
- When your throat feels very dry, you are parched.

dual adjective

*The building has a **dual** purpose: it can be either a cinema or a theatre.*
- double, twofold, twin, combined

dubious adjective

*I'm a bit **dubious** about getting a snake for a pet.*
- doubtful, uncertain, unsure, hesitant
- OPPOSITE certain, sure

duck noun
- A male duck is a drake.
- A young duck is a duckling.

duck verb

1 *Oliver **ducked** to avoid the snowball.*
- bend down, bob down, crouch, stoop

2 *My friends threatened to **duck** me in the pool.*
- dip, immerse, plunge, submerge

due adjective

1 *The train is **due** in five minutes.*
- expected, anticipated

2 *Subscriptions are now **due**.*
- owed, owing, payable

3 *I give her **due** credit for what she did.*
- fitting, proper, appropriate, suitable, deserved, well-earned

dull adjective

1 *I don't like the **dull** colours in this room.*
- dim, dingy, drab, dreary, dismal, faded, gloomy, sombre, subdued
- OPPOSITE bright, colourful

2 *The sky was **dull** that day.*
- cloudy, overcast, grey, sunless, murky
- OPPOSITE clear

3 *I heard a **dull** thud from upstairs.*
- indistinct, muffled, muted
- OPPOSITE distinct

4 *He's rather a **dull** student.*
- stupid, slow, unintelligent, dim, unimaginative, dense, obtuse
- (*informal*) thick
- OPPOSITE clever

5 *The play was so **dull** that I fell asleep.*
- boring, dry, monotonous, tedious, uninteresting, unexciting, lacklustre
- A common simile is as dull as ditchwater.
- OPPOSITE interesting

dumb adjective

1 *The spectators were struck **dumb** with amazement.*
- If you do not speak, you are mute or silent.
- If you cannot speak because you are surprised, confused, or embarrassed, you are speechless or tongue-tied.
- If you find it hard to express yourself, you are inarticulate.

2 (*informal*) *He's too **dumb** to understand.*
- stupid, unintelligent, dim, slow, dense, obtuse
- (*informal*) thick

dumbfounded adjective

*I was **dumbfounded** when I heard the news.*
- amazed, astonished, astounded, stunned, staggered, thunderstruck, speechless, struck dumb
- (*informal*) flabbergasted, gobsmacked

dummy adjective

*There was a **dummy** door at the side of the stage.*
- imitation, fake, copy, toy

dump verb

1 *I decided to **dump** some of my old toys.*
- get rid of, throw away, throw out, discard, dispose of, scrap

2 *Just **dump** your things in the bedroom.*
- put down, set down, deposit, place, drop, throw down, tip

duplicate noun

*We made a **duplicate** of the original document.*
- copy, photocopy, reproduction, replica

- An exact copy of a historic document or manuscript is a **facsimile**.
- A person who looks like you is your **double** or **twin**.
- A living organism which is a duplicate of another living organism is a **clone**.

durable adjective
*Denim is a very **durable** material.*
- hard-wearing, lasting, strong, tough, robust
  OPPOSITE flimsy

duration noun
*We slept in a tent for the **duration** of the holiday.*
- length, period, extent

dusk noun
*Bats begin to emerge at **dusk**.*
- twilight, nightfall, sunset, sundown
  OPPOSITE dawn

dust noun
*There was a lot of **dust** on the furniture.*
- dirt, grime, particles, powder, grit

dust verb
1 *I **dusted** the bookshelves.*
- wipe over, clean, polish
2 *Mum **dusted** the top of the cake with icing sugar.*
- powder, sprinkle

dusty adjective
*The books we found in the attic were very **dusty**.*
- dirty, grimy
  OPPOSITE clean

dutiful adjective
*She is a kind and **dutiful** daughter.*
- faithful, loyal, obedient, devoted, conscientious, reliable, responsible, trustworthy
  OPPOSITE irresponsible, lazy

duty noun
1 *I have a **duty** to help my parents.*
- responsibility, obligation
2 *I carried out my **duties** conscientiously.*
- job, task, assignment, chore
3 *The government has increased the **duty** on petrol.*
- charge, tax

dwell verb
to dwell in
*It is said that bandits **dwell in** these caves.*
- live in, inhabit, occupy, reside in
to dwell on
*Try not to **dwell on** things that happened in the past.*
- keep thinking about, worry about, brood over

dwelling noun SEE **house** noun

dwindle verb
*Our enthusiasm **dwindled** as the day went on.*
- become less, diminish, decline, decrease, lessen, subside, wane, weaken
  OPPOSITE increase

dynamic adjective
*The team has a new, **dynamic** captain.*
- energetic, lively, enthusiastic, vigorous, active, forceful, powerful
  OPPOSITE apathetic

Ee

eager adjective
*He is always **eager** to help.*
- keen, enthusiastic, desperate, anxious
  OPPOSITE unenthusiastic

early adjective
1 *The bus was **early** today.*
- ahead of time, ahead of schedule
  OPPOSITE late
2 *The **early** computers were huge machines.*
- first, old, primitive, ancient
  OPPOSITE recent, new

a
b
c
d
e
f
g
h
i
j
k
l
m
n
o
p
q
r
s
t
u
v
w
x
y
z

earn verb
1 *Bob **earns** extra pocket money washing cars.*
● work for, receive, get, make, obtain, bring in
2 *She trained hard and **earned** her success.*
● deserve, merit

earnest adjective
*He's a terribly **earnest** young man.*
● serious, sincere, solemn, thoughtful, grave
OPPOSITE casual, flippant

earth noun
*The **earth** was so dry that many plants died.*
● ground, land, soil
● Rich, fertile earth is loam.
● The top layer of fertile earth is topsoil.
● Rich earth consisting of decayed plants is humus.
● A heavy, sticky kind of earth is clay.

earthquake noun
● When there is an earthquake, you feel a shock or tremor.
● An instrument which detects and measures earthquakes is a seismograph.

ease noun
1 *She swam ten lengths of the pool with **ease**.*
● facility, skill, speed
OPPOSITE difficulty
2 *Lady Deadwood leads a life of **ease**.*
● comfort, contentment, leisure, peace, quiet, relaxation, rest, tranquillity
OPPOSITE stress

ease verb
1 *The doctor gave her some pills to **ease** her pain.*
● relieve, lessen, soothe, moderate
OPPOSITE aggravate
2 *After taking the pills, the pain began to **ease**.*
● decrease, reduce, slacken
OPPOSITE increase

3 *We **eased** the piano into position.*
● edge, guide, manoeuvre, inch, slide, slip

east noun, adjective, adverb
● The parts of a country or continent in the east are the eastern parts.
● In the past, the countries of east Asia, east of the Mediterranean, were called oriental countries.
● To travel towards the east is to travel eastward or eastwards or in an easterly direction.
● A wind from the east is an easterly wind.

easy adjective
1 *Tonight's homework is really **easy**.*
● undemanding, effortless, light
● An informal word for an easy task is a doddle.
2 *The instructions were **easy** to understand.*
● simple, straightforward, clear, plain, elementary
● A common simile is as easy as ABC.
3 *Our cat has an **easy** life.*
● carefree, comfortable, peaceful, relaxed, leisurely, restful, tranquil, untroubled
OPPOSITE difficult

eat verb
*Hannah was **eating** a cheese sandwich.*
● consume, devour
● (informal) scoff
● When cattle eat grass they are grazing.
● A person who eats a large amount is said to eat like a horse.
FOR VARIOUS THINGS TO EAT
SEE **food**

eat verb

⚠ **OVERUSED WORD**
Try to vary the words you use for **eat**. Here are some other words you could use.
● to *EAT GREEDILY* or *QUICKLY*: bolt down, gobble, gulp, guzzle, gorge, polish off, wolf down
*I was so hungry, I **wolfed down** a whole pizza.*

- to *EAT NOISILY* :
chomp, crunch, gnash, gnaw, munch, slurp
*Rabbits like to **chomp** raw carrots.*
- to *EAT IN SMALL AMOUNTS* :
nibble, peck, pick at or pick away at, taste
*Do you have any biscuits we could **nibble**?*
- to *EAT WITH ENJOYMENT* :
relish, savour, tuck into
*Mr Hogg was **savouring** a sausage roll.*
- to *EAT A FORMAL MEAL* :
banquet, dine, feast
*The guests will be **dining** in the great hall.*

ebb verb
1 *The fishermen waited for the tide to **ebb**.*
- recede, retreat, flow back, fall, go down
2 *She fell ill and her strength began to **ebb**.*
- decline, weaken, lessen, fade, wane

eccentric adjective
*What is the reason for his **eccentric** behaviour?*
- odd, peculiar, strange, weird, abnormal, unusual, curious, unconventional, unorthodox, quirky, zany
- (*informal*) way-out, dotty
- OPPOSITE conventional, orthodox

echo verb
1 *The sound **echoed** across the valley.*
- resound, reverberate
2 *'He's gone home.' 'Gone home?' she **echoed**.*
- repeat, imitate, mimic

economical adjective
1 *My uncle is very **economical** with his money.*
- careful, prudent, thrifty, frugal
- If you are economical with money in a selfish way, you are mean or miserly.
- OPPOSITE wasteful
2 *Our new car is very **economical** to run.*
- cheap, inexpensive, reasonable
- OPPOSITE expensive

ecstatic adjective
*Samantha was feeling **ecstatic** about her party.*
- elated, delighted, overjoyed, gleeful, joyful, blissful, rapturous, euphoric, exultant, delirious, fervent, frenzied

edge noun
- The edge of a cliff or other steep place is the brink.
- The edge of a cup or other container is the brim or rim.
- The line round the edge of a circle is the circumference.
- The line round the edge of any other shape is its outline.
- The distance round the edge of an area is the perimeter.
- The stones along the edge of a road are the kerb.
- Grass along the edge of a road is the verge.
- The space down the edge of a page is the margin.
- The space round the edge of a picture is a border.
- Something that fits round the edge of a picture is a frame.
- The edge of a garment is the hem.
- An edge with threads or hair hanging loosely down is a fringe.
- The edge of a crowd also is the fringe of the crowd.
- The area round the edge of a city is the outskirts or suburbs.
- The edge of a cricket field is the boundary.
- The edge of a football pitch is the touchline.

edge verb
1 *We **edged** away from the lion's den.*
- creep, inch, move stealthily, steal, slink
2 *Her bonnet was **edged** with black lace.*
- trim, hem

edgy adjective
*Horses become **edgy** during thunderstorms.*
- nervous, restless, anxious, agitated, excitable, tense, jumpy, fidgety
- (*informal*) uptight, jittery
- OPPOSITE calm

a b c d **e** f g h i j k l m n o p q r s t u v w x y z

edible adjective
*Are these toadstools **edible**?*
- eatable, fit to eat, good to eat, safe to eat

OPPOSITE poisonous, uneatable

edit verb
*The letters were **edited** before they were published.*
- revise, correct, adapt, rework, rewrite, rephrase

edition noun
*We're preparing a Christmas **edition** of our magazine.*
- copy, issue, number, version

educate verb
*The job of a school is to **educate** young people.*
- teach, train, inform, instruct, tutor

educated adjective
*She is an **educated** woman.*
- knowledgeable, learned, literate, well informed, well read, cultivated, cultured

education noun

WORD WEB

*This school is for the **education** of young witches and wizards.*
- schooling, teaching, training, instruction, tuition, tutoring, coaching
- A programme of education is the curriculum or syllabus.

PEOPLE WHO PROVIDE EDUCATION
coach, counsellor, governess, headteacher, instructor, lecturer, professor, teacher, trainer, tutor

PLACES TO RECEIVE EDUCATION
academy, college, kindergarten or nursery, playgroup, primary school, secondary school, sixth-form college, university

eerie adjective
*I heard some **eerie** sounds in the night.*
- strange, weird, uncanny, mysterious, frightening, creepy, ghostly, sinister, unearthly, unnatural
- (*informal*) scary, spooky

effect noun
1 *The **effect** of eating too much was that I became fat!*
- result, consequence, outcome, sequel, upshot
2 *Does this music have any **effect** on you?*
- impact, influence
3 *The lighting gives an **effect** of warmth.*
- feeling, impression, sense, illusion

effective adjective
1 *I wish they could find an **effective** cure for colds.*
- successful
2 *Our team needs an **effective** goalkeeper.*
- competent, able, capable, proficient, skilled
3 *He presented an **effective** argument against hunting.*
- convincing, persuasive, compelling, impressive, telling

OPPOSITE useless

efficient adjective
1 *An **efficient** worker can do the job in an hour.*
- effective, competent, able, capable, proficient
2 *Dad tried to work out an **efficient** way of heating our house.*
- economic, productive

OPPOSITE inefficient

effort noun
1 *A lot of **effort** went into making the film.*
- work, trouble, exertion, industry, labour, toil
2 *She congratulated us on a good **effort**.*
- attempt, try, endeavour, go, shot

eject verb
1 *Lava was **ejected** from the volcano when it erupted.*
- discharge, emit
2 *The caretaker **ejected** an intruder from the building.*
- remove, expel, evict, banish, kick out, throw out, turn out

elaborate adjective
*The plot of the book is so **elaborate** that I got lost halfway through.*
- complicated, complex, detailed, intricate, involved, convoluted
OPPOSITE simple

elated adjective
*We were **elated** when we won the match.*
- delighted, pleased, thrilled, joyful, ecstatic, gleeful, exultant, delirious
- (*informal*) over the moon

elbow verb
*Miss Crook **elbowed** her way to the front of the queue.*
- push, shove, nudge, jostle

elder adjective
*My **elder** brother is in the football team.*
- older

elderly adjective
*I helped the **elderly** couple to get on the bus.*
- aged, aging, old, senior
OPPOSITE young

eldest adjective
*Jane is my **eldest** sister.*
- oldest

elect verb
*We **elected** a new captain.*
- vote for, appoint

election noun
*We had an **election** to choose a new captain.*
- vote, ballot, poll

electricity noun
*The **electricity** went off in the middle of the thunderstorm.*
- power, power supply, current
- Someone whose job is to fit and repair electrical equipment is an electrician.

elegant adjective
*She always wears **elegant** clothes.*
- graceful, stylish, fashionable, chic, smart, tasteful, sophisticated
OPPOSITE inelegant

element noun
*They discussed various **elements** of the book.*
- part, component, feature, constituent

to be in your element
*Doug was **in his element** at a computer.*
- be at home, be comfortable, be happy, enjoy yourself

elementary adjective
*Anyone can solve such an **elementary** problem.*
- basic, simple, easy, fundamental, straightforward, uncomplicated
OPPOSITE advanced, complex

eligible adjective
*Children over twelve are not **eligible** to enter this race.*
- qualified, allowed, authorized, suitable
OPPOSITE ineligible

eliminate verb
*The government wants to **eliminate** crime.*
- get rid of, put an end to
- To be eliminated from a competition is to be knocked out.

elude verb
*The police chased him, but he managed to **elude** them.*
- avoid, evade, escape from, get away from

embark verb
*The passengers **embarked** in time for the ship to sail at high tide.*
- board, go aboard
OPPOSITE disembark

to embark on something
*Today we **embarked on** a big project.*
- begin, start, commence, undertake

embarrass verb
*Will it **embarrass** you if I tell people our secret?*
- humiliate, distress, mortify, make you blush

a
b
c
d
e
f
g
h
i
j
k
l
m
n
o
p
q
r
s
t
u
v
w
x
y
z

embarrassed adjective
Don't feel embarrassed—it happens to everyone!
- humiliated, ashamed, awkward, uncomfortable, bashful, distressed, flustered, mortified, self-conscious

emblem noun
The dove is an emblem of peace.
- sign, symbol

embrace verb
1 *The mother gorilla embraced her baby.*
- hug, clasp, cuddle, hold
2 *She's always ready to embrace new ideas.*
- welcome, accept, adopt, take on
3 *The syllabus embraces all aspects of the subject.*
- include, incorporate, take in

emerge verb
He didn't emerge from his bedroom until ten o'clock.
- appear, come out

emergency noun
Try to keep calm in an emergency.
- crisis, serious situation, danger, difficulty

emigrant noun
OPPOSITE immigrant

emigrate verb
During the famine, many Irish people were forced to emigrate to America.
- leave the country, move abroad
OPPOSITE immigrate

eminent adjective
An eminent scientist is giving a public lecture tonight.
- famous, great, celebrated, renowned, well known, distinguished, notable, prominent, respected
OPPOSITE unknown

emit verb
1 *The exhaust pipe emitted clouds of smoke.*
- discharge, expel, belch, blow out, give off

2 *The satellite was emitting radio signals.*
- transmit, give out, send out
OPPOSITE receive

emotion noun
His voice was full of emotion.
- feeling, passion, sentiment, fervour

emotional adjective
1 *He made an emotional farewell speech.*
- moving, touching
2 *The music for the love scenes was very emotional.*
- romantic, sentimental
3 *She's a very emotional woman.*
- passionate, intense
OPPOSITE unemotional, cold

emphasis noun
In the word 'aardvark' the emphasis is on the first syllable.
- stress, accent, weight

emphasize verb
She emphasized the important points.
- highlight, stress, focus on, dwell on, underline

employ verb
1 *The new factory plans to employ 100 workers.*
- hire, engage, give work to, take on
2 *The factory will employ the latest methods.*
- use, utilize

employee noun
100 employees will work at the new factory.
- worker
- A word for all the employees of an organization is staff or workforce.

employment noun
He's still looking for suitable employment.
- work, a job, an occupation, a profession, a trade
FOR VARIOUS KINDS OF EMPLOYMENT SEE **job**

empty adjective
1 *Please put the **empty** milk bottles outside the door.*
OPPOSITE full
2 *The house next to ours has been **empty** for weeks.*
• unoccupied, uninhabited, vacant, deserted
OPPOSITE occupied
3 *After we put up our display, there was still some **empty** space on the wall.*
• blank, bare, clear, unused

empty verb
1 ***Empty** the dirty water into the sink.*
• drain, pour out
OPPOSITE fill
2 *The building **emptied** when the fire alarm went off.*
• clear, evacuate, vacate
3 *Did you **empty** all the shopping out of the trolley?*
• remove, unload

enable verb
1 *The fine weather **enabled** us to do the job quickly.*
• allow, make it possible for, help, aid, assist
2 *A passport **enables** you to travel abroad.*
• allow, entitle, permit, authorize
OPPOSITE prevent

enchanting adjective
*The ballet dancers were **enchanting**.*
• delightful, charming, appealing, attractive, bewitching, spellbinding

enchantment noun
1 *The forest had an air of **enchantment**.*
• magic, wonder, delight, pleasure
2 *The witch recited an **enchantment**.*
• spell, incantation
SEE ALSO **magic** noun

enclose verb
1 *The documents were **enclosed** in a brown paper envelope.*
• contain, insert, wrap, bind, sheathe
2 *The animals were **enclosed** within a wire fence.*
• confine, restrict, fence in, shut in, imprison

enclosure noun
• An animal's enclosure with bars is a cage.
• An enclosure for chickens is a coop or run.
• An enclosure for cattle and other animals is a pen or corral.
• An enclosure for horses is a paddock.
• An enclosure for sheep is a fold.

encounter verb
1 *He **encountered** her outside the station.*
• meet, come across, run into, bump into, come face to face with
2 *We **encountered** some problems.*
• experience, come upon, confront, be faced with

encourage verb
1 *We went to the match to **encourage** our team.*
• inspire, support, motivate, cheer, spur on, egg on
2 *The poster **encourages** people to eat healthily.*
• persuade, urge
3 *Is advertising likely to **encourage** sales?*
• increase, boost, stimulate, further, promote, help, aid
OPPOSITE discourage

encouragement noun
*Our team needs some **encouragement**.*
• reassurance, inspiration, incitement, stimulation, urging, incentive, stimulus, support

encouraging adjective
*The results of the tests were **encouraging**.*
• hopeful, positive, promising, reassuring, optimistic, cheering, favourable

end noun
1 *The fence marks the **end** of the garden.*
• boundary, limit

a
b
c
d
e
f
g
h
i
j
k
l
m
n
o
p
q
r
s
t
u
v
w
x
y
z

2 *The **end** of the film was the most exciting part.*
- ending, finish, close, conclusion, culmination
- The last part of a show or piece of music is the finale.
- A section added at the end of a letter is a postscript.
- A section added at the end of a story is an epilogue.

3 *I was tired by the time we got to the **end** of the journey.*
- termination, destination

4 *We arrived late and found ourselves at the **end** of the queue.*
- back, rear, tail

5 *What **end** did you have in view when you started?*
- aim, purpose, intention, objective, plan, outcome, result

end verb

1 *The meeting should **end** in time for lunch.*
- finish, complete, conclude, break off, halt
- (*informal*) round off

2 *When did they **end** public executions?*
- abolish, do away with, get rid of, put an end to, discontinue, eliminate

3 *The festival **ended** with a show of fireworks.*
- close, come to an end, stop, cease, terminate, culminate, wind up

endanger verb
*Bad driving **endangers** other people.*
- put at risk, threaten
- OPPOSITE protect

endeavour verb
*Please **endeavour** to behave well.*
- try, attempt, aim, strive, make an effort

ending noun
*The **ending** of the film was the most exciting part.*
- end, finish, close, conclusion, culmination, last part
- The ending of a show or piece of music is the finale.

endless adjective
1 *Teachers need **endless** patience.*
- unending, limitless, infinite, inexhaustible, unlimited

2 *There's an **endless** procession of cars along the main road.*
- continual, continuous, constant, incessant, interminable, perpetual, unbroken, uninterrupted, everlasting, ceaseless

endurance noun
*The climb was a test of their **endurance**.*
- perseverance, persistence, determination, resolution, stamina

endure verb
1 *She had to **endure** a lot of pain.*
- bear, stand, suffer, cope with, experience, go through, put up with, tolerate, undergo

2 *These traditions have **endured** for centuries.*
- survive, continue, last, persist, carry on, keep going

enemy noun
*They used to be friends but now they are bitter **enemies**.*
- opponent, adversary, foe, rival
- OPPOSITE friend, ally

energetic adjective
1 *She's a very **energetic** person.*
- dynamic, spirited, enthusiastic, animated, active, zestful
- OPPOSITE inactive, lethargic

2 *It was a very **energetic** exercise routine.*
- lively, vigorous, brisk, fast, quick moving, strenuous
- OPPOSITE slow-paced, sluggish

energy noun
1 *The dancers had tremendous **energy**.*
- liveliness, spirit, vitality, vigour, life, drive, zest, verve, enthusiasm, dynamism
- (*informal*) get-up-and-go, zip
- OPPOSITE lethargy

2 *Wind power is a renewable source of **energy**.*
- power, fuel

enforce verb
*The umpire's job is to **enforce** the rules.*
- carry out, administer, apply, implement, put into effect, impose, insist on

engage verb
1 *The builder **engaged** extra workers in order to complete the job on time.*
- employ, hire, take on
2 *The general decided to **engage** the enemy at dawn.*
- attack, start fighting

engaged adjective
1 *The painter was **engaged** in his work.*
- busy, occupied, employed, tied up, immersed, absorbed, engrossed
2 *I tried to phone but the line was **engaged**.*
- busy, being used, unavailable
OPPOSITE free, available

engagement noun
*She has a business **engagement** this afternoon.*
- meeting, appointment, commitment, date

engine noun
*The lawnmower needs a new **engine**.*
- motor, mechanism, turbine
- A railway engine is a locomotive.

engrave verb
*An inscription was **engraved** on the stone.*
- carve, cut, etch

engrossed adjective
*Peggy was **engrossed** in her knitting.*
- absorbed, busy, occupied, preoccupied, engaged, immersed

engulf verb
*The floods **engulfed** several villages.*
- flood, drown, immerse, inundate, overwhelm, submerge, swallow up, swamp

enhance verb
*The team's victory **enhanced** their reputation.*
- improve, strengthen

enjoy verb
*I really **enjoyed** the film.*
- like, love, get pleasure from, be pleased by, admire, appreciate

enjoyable adjective
*It was an **enjoyable** party.*
- pleasant, agreeable, delightful, entertaining, amusing
OPPOSITE unpleasant

enlarge verb
*The zoo is going to **enlarge** the lion enclosure.*
- expand, extend, develop, make bigger
- To make something wider is to broaden or widen it.
- To make something longer is to extend, lengthen, or stretch it.
- To make something seem larger is to magnify it.
OPPOSITE reduce

enormous adjective
***Enormous** waves battered the ship.*
- huge, gigantic, immense, colossal, massive, monstrous, monumental, mountainous, towering, tremendous, vast
- (informal) ginormous, humungous
OPPOSITE small

enough adjective
*Is there **enough** food for ten people?*
- sufficient, adequate, ample

enquire verb
to enquire about
*I **enquired about** train times to Bristol.*
- ask for, get information about, request, investigate

enquiry noun
*The librarian helped me with my **enquiry**.*
- question, query, request, investigation, research

enrage verb
*I was **enraged** by their stupidity.*
- anger, infuriate, madden, incense, exasperate, provoke
OPPOSITE pacify

a
b
c
d
e
f
g
h
i
j
k
l
m
n
o
p
q
r
s
t
u
v
w
x
y
z

enrol verb
*I **enrolled** as a member of the drama club.*
- join, sign up, put your name down, volunteer

ensure verb
*Please **ensure** that you lock the door.*
- make certain, make sure, confirm, see

enter verb
1 *Silence fell as I **entered** the room.*
- come in, walk in
- To enter a place without permission is to invade it.
  OPPOSITE leave

2 *The arrow **entered** his shoulder.*
- go into, penetrate, pierce

3 *Can I **enter** my name on the list?*
- insert, record, register, put down, set down, sign, write, inscribe
  OPPOSITE cancel

4 *Our class decided to **enter** the competition.*
- take part in, enrol in, sign up for, go in for, join in, participate in, volunteer for
  OPPOSITE withdraw from

enterprise noun
1 *She showed **enterprise** in starting her own business.*
- drive, initiative

2 *The expedition was a very rash **enterprise**.*
- adventure, operation, project, undertaking, venture, effort, mission

enterprising adjective
*Some **enterprising** girls organized a sponsored walk.*
- adventurous, daring, intrepid, ambitious, bold, courageous, eager, energetic, enthusiastic, imaginative, industrious
  OPPOSITE unadventurous

entertain verb
1 *The storyteller **entertained** us with scary ghost stories.*
- amuse, divert, keep amused, make you laugh, please, cheer up
  OPPOSITE bore

2 *You can **entertain** friends in the private dining room.*
- receive, welcome, cater for, give hospitality to

entertainer noun

> **WORD WEB**
>
> SOME KINDS OF ENTERTAINER
> acrobat, actor, actress, ballerina, busker, clown, comedian or comic, conjuror, dancer, disc jockey or DJ, escape artist or escapologist, juggler, magician, mime artist, musician, singer, street entertainer, stunt man or stunt woman, trapeze artist, TV presenter, ventriloquist
> - A famous entertainer is a star or superstar.
> FOR TYPES OF MUSICIAN
> SEE **music**
> ENTERTAINERS IN THE PAST
> fool or jester, gladiator, minstrel

entertainment noun
*Our hosts had arranged some **entertainment** for us.*
- amusements, recreation, diversions, enjoyment, fun, pastimes

enthusiasm noun
1 *The young athletes showed plenty of **enthusiasm**.*
- keenness, keenness, ambition, commitment, drive, zeal, zest
  OPPOSITE apathy

2 *Collecting fossils is one of my **enthusiasms**.*
- interest, passion, pastime, hobby, craze, diversion, fad

enthusiast noun
*My brother is a football **enthusiast**.*
- fan, fanatic, devotee, lover, supporter, addict
- (*informal*) freak, nut

enthusiastic adjective
1 *He's an **enthusiastic** supporter of our local team.*
- keen, passionate, avid, devoted, energetic, fervent, zealous

2 *The audience burst into **enthusiastic** applause.*
- eager, excited, lively, vigorous, exuberant, hearty
  OPPOSITE apathetic

entire adjective
*Donald spent the **entire** evening watching television.*
- complete, whole, total, full

entirely adverb
*I'm not **entirely** sure that I agree with you.*
- completely, absolutely, wholly, totally, utterly, fully, perfectly, quite

entitle verb
*The voucher **entitles** you to claim a discount.*
- permit, allow, enable, authorize

entrance noun
1 *Please pay at the **entrance**.*
- entry, way in, access, door, gate
- When you go through the entrance to a building, you cross the threshold.
2 *I'll meet you in the **entrance**.*
- entrance hall, foyer, lobby, porch
3 *Her sudden **entrance** took everyone by surprise.*
- entry, arrival, appearance
  OPPOSITE exit

entrance verb
*The crowd were **entranced** by the fireworks display.*
- charm, delight, please, enchant

entrant noun
*A prize will be awarded to the winning **entrant**.*
- contestant, competitor, contender, candidate, participant

entry noun
1 *A van was blocking the **entry** to the school.*
- way in, entrance, access, door, gate
2 *Every evening I write an **entry** in my diary.*
- item, note

envelop verb
*Mist **enveloped** the top of the mountain.*
- cover, hide, mask, conceal

envious adjective
*He was **envious** of his brother's success.*
- jealous, resentful

environment noun
*Animals should live in their natural **environment**, not in cages.*
- habitat, surroundings, setting, conditions, situation
the environment
*We must do all we can to protect **the environment**.*
- the natural world, nature, the earth, the world

envy noun
*I didn't feel any **envy**, even when I saw how rich she was.*
- jealousy, resentment, bitterness

envy verb
*The evil queen **envied** Snow White's beauty.*
- be jealous of, begrudge, grudge, resent

episode noun
1 *I paid for the broken window, and I want to forget the whole **episode**.*
- event, incident, experience
2 *I missed last night's **episode** of 'Dr Who'.*
- instalment, part

equal adjective
1 *Give everyone an **equal** amount.*
- equivalent, identical, matching, similar, corresponding, fair
2 *The scores were **equal** at half-time.*
- even, level, the same, square
- To make the scores equal is to equalize.

equip verb
*All the bedrooms are **equipped** with a colour television.*
- provide, supply
- To equip soldiers with weapons is to arm them.
- To equip a room with furniture is to furnish it.

a
b
c
d
e
f
g
h
i
j
k
l
m
n
o
p
q
r
s
t
u
v
w
x
y
z

equipment noun
The shed is full of gardening equipment.
- apparatus, gear, kit, tackle, tools, implements, instruments, materials, machinery, paraphernalia, things
- Computing equipment is hardware.

equivalent adjective
A metre is equivalent to a hundred centimetres.
- matching, similar, corresponding, identical

era noun
Shakespeare lived in the Elizabethan era.
- age, period, time, epoch

erase verb
I erased the writing on the blackboard.
- delete, remove, rub out, wipe out, get rid of

erect adjective
The dog stood with its ears erect.
- upright, vertical, perpendicular

erect verb
The town hall was erected in 1890.
- build, construct, raise, put up, set up
- To erect a tent is to pitch it.

erode verb
The flood water eroded the river bank.
- wear away, eat away, destroy

errand noun
I went on an errand to the corner shop.
- job, task, assignment, trip, journey

erratic adjective
The team's performance has been erratic this season.
- inconsistent, irregular, uneven, variable, changeable, fluctuating, unpredictable
OPPOSITE consistent

error noun
1 *The accident was the result of an error by the driver.*
- mistake, fault, lapse, blunder
2 *I think there is an error in your argument.*
- flaw, inaccuracy, misunderstanding, inconsistency

- The error of leaving something out is an omission or oversight.

erupt verb
Smoke began to erupt from the volcano.
- be discharged, be emitted, pour out, issue, spout, gush, spurt, belch

escape verb
1 *Why did you let him escape?*
- get away, get out, run away, break free, break out
- (informal) give you the slip
- A performer who escapes from chains, etc., is an escape artist or escapologist.
2 *She always escapes the nasty jobs.*
- avoid, get out of, evade, dodge, shirk

escape noun
1 *The prisoner's escape was filmed by security cameras.*
- getaway, breakout, flight
2 *The explosion was caused by an escape of gas.*
- leak, leakage, seepage

escort noun
1 *The president always has an escort to protect him.*
- bodyguard, guard
2 *The actress arrived with her escort.*
- companion, partner

escort verb
The queen was escorted by a number of attendants.
- accompany, guard, protect, look after

especially adverb
I like apple pie, especially with ice-cream.
- above all, chiefly, most of all

espionage noun SEE **spy** noun

essential adjective
Fruit and vegetables are an essential part of our diet.
- important, necessary, basic, vital, principal, fundamental, chief, crucial, indispensable

establish verb

1 *He plans to **establish** a new business.*
- set up, start, begin, create, found, initiate, institute, introduce, launch, originate

2 *The police have not managed to **establish** his guilt.*
- prove, show to be true, confirm, verify

estate noun

1 *There's a new housing **estate** near our school.*
- area, development, scheme

2 *The castle is sited on a large **estate**.*
- land, grounds

3 *The millionaire left his **estate** to charity.*
- property, fortune, wealth, possessions

estimate noun

*What is your **estimate** of how much it will cost?*
- assessment, calculation, evaluation, guess, judgement, opinion
- An official estimate of the value of something is a valuation.
- An official estimate of what a job is going to cost is a quotation or tender.

estimate verb

*The builders **estimate** that the work will take four months.*
- calculate, assess, work out, compute, count up, evaluate, judge, reckon, think out

eternal adjective

1 *The magic fountain was said to give **eternal** youth.*
- everlasting, infinite, lasting, unending, timeless
- Beings with eternal life are said to be immortal.

2 *I'm sick of your **eternal** quarrelling!*
- constant, continual, never-ending, non-stop, persistent, perpetual, endless, ceaseless, incessant, unceasing

evacuate verb

1 *The firefighters **evacuated** everyone from the building.*
- remove, clear, send away, move out

2 *We were told to **evacuate** the building.*
- leave, quit, abandon, withdraw from, empty, vacate

evade verb

*Don't try to **evade** your responsibilities.*
- avoid, dodge, shirk, escape from, steer clear of, fend off
- OPPOSITE confront

even adjective

1 *You need an **even** surface for ice-skating.*
- level, flat, smooth, straight
- OPPOSITE uneven

2 *The runners kept up an **even** pace.*
- regular, steady, unvarying, rhythmical, monotonous
- OPPOSITE irregular

3 *Mr Humphreys has an **even** temper.*
- calm, cool, placid, unexcitable
- OPPOSITE excitable

4 *The scores were **even** at half time.*
- equal, level, matching, identical, the same, square
- OPPOSITE different

5 *2, 4, and 6 are **even** numbers.*
- OPPOSITE odd

even verb

to even something up

*If you join their team, that will **even up** the numbers.*
- equalize, level, balance, match, square

evening noun

*Towards **evening** it clouded over and began to rain.*
- dusk, nightfall, sundown, sunset, twilight

event noun

1 *Her autobiography describes the main **events** of her life.*
- happening, incident, occurrence

2 *There was an **event** to mark the launch of the new film.*
- function, occasion, ceremony, entertainment, party, reception

a
b
c
d
e
f
g
h
i
j
k
l
m
n
o
p
q
r
s
t
u
v
w
x
y
z

a
b
c
d
e
f
g
h
i
j
k
l
m
n
o
p
q
r
s
t
u
v
w
x
y
z

3 *The World Cup is an important **event** for football fans.*
- competition, contest, fixture, engagement, meeting, game, match, tournament

eventful adjective
*We had an **eventful** journey.*
- interesting, exciting, busy, lively, active
OPPOSITE uneventful, dull

eventual adjective
*We were happy with our **eventual** score.*
- final, ultimate, resulting, overall, ensuing

eventually adverb
*The journey took ages, but **eventually** we arrived safely.*
- finally, at last, in the end, ultimately

evergreen adjective
*Most pine trees are **evergreen**.*
OPPOSITE deciduous

everlasting adjective
*I'm sick of their **everlasting** chatter!*
- constant, continual, persistent, incessant, never-ending, non-stop, endless, ceaseless, perpetual, unending, eternal, recurrent, repeated, unceasing
- Everlasting life is immortality.
OPPOSITE occasional, transient

everyday adjective
*Don't dress up—just wear your **everyday** clothes.*
- normal, ordinary, usual, regular, customary

evict verb
*The landlord threatened to **evict** the tenants.*
- expel, eject, remove, throw out, turn out, put out

evidence noun
*This piece of paper is **evidence** that he is lying.*
- proof, confirmation
- Evidence that someone accused of a crime was not there when the crime was committed is an alibi.

- Evidence given in a law court is a testimony.
- To give evidence in court is to testify.

evident adjective
*It was **evident** that someone had been in the room.*
- clear, obvious, apparent, plain, certain, unmistakable, undeniable, noticeable, perceptible, visible

evidently adverb
*The woman was **evidently** upset.*
- clearly, obviously, apparently, plainly, undoubtedly

evil adjective
1 *The charm was used to keep away **evil** spirits.*
- malevolent, fiendish, diabolical
2 *Who would do such an **evil** deed?*
- wicked, immoral, cruel, sinful, villainous, malicious, foul, hateful, vile
OPPOSITE good

evil noun
1 *The good witch tried to fight against **evil**.*
- wickedness, badness, wrongdoing, sin, immorality, villainy, malevolence, malice
2 *They had to endure the **evils** of famine and drought.*
- disaster, misfortune, suffering, pain, affliction, curse

evolve verb
*Life **evolved** on Earth over millions of years.*
- develop, grow, progress, emerge, mature

exact adjective
1 *I gave the police an **exact** account of what happened.*
- accurate, precise, correct, true, faithful, detailed, meticulous, strict
2 *Is this an **exact** copy of the original document?*
- identical, perfect, indistinguishable
OPPOSITE inaccurate

exactly adverb
*At what time **exactly** did you leave the house?*
- precisely, specifically, accurately, correctly, strictly
- A phrase meaning 'exactly on time' is to be on the dot.
OPPOSITE roughly, inaccurately

exaggerate verb
*He tends to **exaggerate** his problems.*
- magnify, inflate, overdo, make too much of
OPPOSITE minimize

examination noun
1 *The results of the **examinations** will be announced next month.*
- test, assessment
- (*informal*) exam
2 *The judge made a thorough **examination** of the facts.*
- investigation, inspection, study, analysis, survey, review, appraisal
3 *He was sent to hospital for an **examination**.*
- check-up
- A medical examination of a dead person is a post-mortem.

examine verb
1 *The judge **examined** the evidence.*
- inspect, study, investigate, analyse, look closely at, pore over, scrutinize, probe, survey, review, weigh up, sift
2 *They were **examined** on their knowledge of history.*
- question, interrogate, quiz
- To examine someone rigorously is to grill them.

example noun
1 *Give me an **example** of what you mean.*
- instance, illustration, sample, specimen, case
2 *She's an **example** to us all.*
- model, ideal

exasperate verb
*Dad was becoming **exasperated** with his computer.*
- annoy, irritate, upset, frustrate, anger, madden, vex

exceed verb
*She **exceeded** the previous race record by two seconds.*
- beat, better, outdo, pass, surpass, go over

excel verb
*She's a good all-round athlete, but she **excels** at sprinting.*
- do best, stand out, shine

excellent adjective
*That's an **excellent** idea!*
- first-class, first-rate, outstanding, exceptional, remarkable, tremendous, wonderful, superb, great, fine, marvellous, superior, superlative, top-notch
- (*informal*) brilliant, fantastic, terrific, fabulous, sensational, super
FOR OTHER WAYS TO DESCRIBE SOMETHING GOOD
SEE **good**
OPPOSITE bad, awful, second-rate

except preposition
*Everyone got a prize **except** me.*
- apart from, but, with the exception of, excluding

exception noun
to take exception to something
*She **took exception to** what he said about her clothes.*
- dislike, object to, complain about, disapprove of, be upset by

exceptional adjective
*It is **exceptional** to have such cold weather in June.*
- unusual, extraordinary, uncommon, unexpected, amazing, rare, odd, peculiar, strange, surprising, special, abnormal, phenomenal, unheard-of, bizarre
OPPOSITE normal, usual

excerpt noun
*She recited an **excerpt** from the poem.*
- extract, passage, part, section

a
b
c
d
e
f
g
h
i
j
k
l
m
n
o
p
q
r
s
t
u
v
w
x
y
z

- A short excerpt is a quotation.
- The most interesting excerpts from something are the highlights.
- Excerpts from a film are clips.

excess noun

- If there is an excess of something so that it is hard to sell it, there is a glut.
- When a business has an excess of income over its expenses, it has a profit or a surplus.

excessive adjective

1 *I think his enthusiasm for football is* **excessive***.*

- extreme, exaggerated, fanatical

2 *Mum prepared* **excessive** *amounts of food for the party.*

- unnecessary, needless, superfluous, extravagant, wasteful, unreasonable

exchange verb

The shop will **exchange** *faulty goods.*

- change, replace
- To exchange goods for other goods without using money is to barter.
- To exchange an old thing for part of the cost of a new one is to trade it in.
- To exchange things with your friends is to swap or swop them.
- To exchange players for other players in football, etc., is to substitute them.

excite verb

The prospect of going to Italy **excited** *Miss MacKillop.*

- thrill, enthuse, stimulate, arouse, electrify, rouse, stir up
OPPOSITE calm

excited adjective

On Christmas Eve, my little brother was too **excited** *to sleep.*

- agitated, lively, enthusiastic, exuberant, thrilled, elated, eager, animated
OPPOSITE calm

excitement noun

I could hardly bear the **excitement***!*

- suspense, tension, drama, thrill

exciting adjective

The last minutes of the match were the most **exciting** *of all!*

- dramatic, eventful, thrilling, gripping, sensational, stirring, rousing, stimulating, electrifying
OPPOSITE dull, boring

exclaim verb

'Get out of my house!' she **exclaimed***.*

- call, shout, cry out, yell
FOR OTHER WAYS TO SAY SOMETHING
SEE **say**

exclamation noun

Dr Doyle gave an **exclamation** *of surprise.*

- cry, shout, yell
- An impolite exclamation is an oath or swear word.

WRITING TIPS

- Someone who is *ANGRY* or *ANNOYED* might say:
blast, bother, drat, fiddlesticks
'Fiddlesticks!' said Merlin. 'I've forgotten the spell!'
- Someone who is *SURPRISED* or *ALARMED* might say:
blimey, crikey, golly, goodness me, good gracious, good heavens, gosh, my word, yikes
'My word, is that a dinosaur bone?' asked Dr Doyle.

---

exclude verb

1 *Adults are* **excluded** *from joining our club.*

- ban, bar, prohibit, keep out, banish, reject

2 *She had to* **exclude** *dairy products from her diet.*

- leave out, omit
OPPOSITE include

excluding preposition

The gardens are open every day **excluding** *Christmas.*

- except, except for, with the exception of, apart from, bar

exclusive adjective
*They stayed at a very **exclusive** hotel.*
- select, private, snobbish, upmarket
- (*informal*) posh, fancy

excursion noun
*We went on an **excursion** to the seaside.*
- trip, journey, outing, expedition, jaunt

excuse noun
*What is your **excuse** for being so late?*
- reason, explanation, defence, justification

excuse verb
*I can't **excuse** his bad behaviour.*
- forgive, overlook, pardon
- OPPOSITE punish

to be excused something
*May I **be excused** swimming?*
- be exempt from, be let off, be released from

execute verb
1 *In some countries, criminals may still be **executed**.*
- put to death
- Someone who executes people is an executioner.
- To execute someone unofficially without a proper trial is to lynch them.

2 *She **executed** a perfect somersault.*
- perform, carry out, produce, complete, accomplish

exercise noun
1 ***Exercise** helps to keep you fit.*
- physical activity, working out, keep fit, training

2 *Doing **exercises** will improve your guitar playing.*
- practice, training, drill

exercise verb
1 *If you **exercise** regularly, you will keep fit.*
- keep fit, train, exert yourself

2 *I sometimes **exercise** our neighbour's dog.*
- take for a walk, take out, walk

3 *We must **exercise** patience.*
- show, use, apply, display, employ

exert verb
*He **exerted** all his strength to lift the box.*
- use, apply, employ

exertion noun
*The **exertion** of climbing the stairs made him sweat.*
- effort, hard work, labour, toil

exhale verb
*The doctor asked me to **exhale** slowly.*
- breathe out
- OPPOSITE inhale

exhaust noun
*The **exhaust** from cars damages the environment.*
- fumes, smoke, emissions, gases

exhaust verb
1 *The steep climb up the hill **exhausted** me.*
- tire, wear out

2 *We had **exhausted** our food supply by midday.*
- finish, go through, use up, consume
- (*informal*) polish off

exhausted adjective
*After a hard race, we lay **exhausted** on the grass.*
- tired, weary, worn out, fatigued, breathless, gasping, panting
- (*informal*) all in, done in, bushed, zonked

exhausting adjective
*Digging the garden is **exhausting** work.*
- tiring, demanding, hard, laborious, strenuous, difficult, gruelling, wearisome
- OPPOSITE easy

exhaustion noun
*He was overcome by sheer **exhaustion**.*
- tiredness, fatigue, weariness, weakness

exhibit verb
1 *Her paintings were **exhibited** in galleries all over Europe and America.*
- display, show, present, put up, set up, arrange

a b c d e f g h i j k l m n o p q r s t u v w x y z

a
b
c
d
e
f
g
h
i
j
k
l
m
n
o
p
q
r
s
t
u
v
w
x
y
z

2 *He was **exhibiting** signs of anxiety.*
- show, demonstrate, reveal
  OPPOSITE hide

exhibition noun
*We went to see an **exhibition** of paintings by Picasso.*
- display, show

exile verb
*As a result of the war, many people were **exiled** from their own country.*
- banish, expel, drive out, deport, eject, send away

exile noun
*He returned to his country after 24 years of **exile**.*
- banishment, expulsion, deportation
- A person who has been exiled is a refugee.

exist verb
1 *Some people claim that ghosts actually **exist**.*
- be real, occur

2 *We can't **exist** without food.*
- live, remain alive, survive, keep going, last, continue, endure

existence noun
1 *Do you believe in the **existence** of ghosts?*
- reality

2 *Most plants depend on sunlight for their **existence**.*
- life, survival

existing adjective
1 *There are only two **existing** species of elephants.*
- surviving, living, remaining

2 *Next year, the **existing** rules will be replaced by new ones.*
- present, current

exit noun
1 *I'll wait for you by the **exit**.*
- door, way out, doorway, gate, barrier
  OPPOSITE entrance

2 *The robbers made a hurried **exit**.*
- departure
  OPPOSITE entrance

exit verb
*The actors **exited** from the left of the stage.*
- go out, leave, depart, withdraw
  OPPOSITE enter

exotic adjective
*My aunt has travelled to many **exotic** places.*
- remote, foreign, alien, different, exciting, romantic, strange, unfamiliar, wonderful
  OPPOSITE familiar

expand verb
*Their computer business is **expanding** rapidly.*
- increase, enlarge, extend, build up, develop, make bigger
- To become larger is to grow or swell.
- To become wider is to broaden, thicken, or widen.
- To become longer is to extend, lengthen, or stretch.
  OPPOSITE contract, reduce

expanse noun
*The explorers crossed a large **expanse** of desert.*
- area, stretch, tract
- An expanse of water or ice is a sheet.

expect verb
1 *I **expect** that it will rain today.*
- anticipate, imagine, forecast, predict, foresee, prophesy

2 *She **expects** me to do everything for her!*
- require, want, count on, insist on, demand

3 *I **expect** they missed the bus.*
- believe, imagine, guess, suppose, presume, assume, think

expedition noun
- An expedition into unknown territory is an exploration.
- An expedition to carry out a special task is a mission.
- An expedition to find something is a quest.

- An expedition to worship at a holy place is a pilgrimage.
- An expedition to see or hunt wild animals is a safari.
  SEE ALSO **explorer**

expel verb

1 *A fan **expels** the stale air and fumes.*
- send out, force out

2 *He was **expelled** from school.*
- dismiss, ban, remove, throw out, send away
- To expel someone from their home is to eject or evict them.
- To expel someone from their country is to banish or exile them.
- To expel evil spirits is to exorcise them.

expense noun

*She was worried about the **expense** of the holiday.*
- cost, charges, expenditure

expensive adjective

*Houses are very **expensive** in this area.*
- dear, costly
  OPPOSITE cheap

experience noun

1 *Have you had any **experience** of singing in a choir?*
- practice, involvement, participation

2 *I had an unusual **experience** today.*
- happening, event, occurrence, incident
- An exciting experience is an adventure.
- An unpleasant experience is an ordeal.

experienced adjective

*He's an **experienced** actor who has been in many films.*
- skilled, qualified, expert, knowledgeable, trained, professional
  OPPOSITE inexperienced

experiment noun

*We carried out a scientific **experiment**.*
- test, trial
- A series of experiments is research or an investigation.

experiment verb

*They **experimented** to see if their robot would work.*
- do tests
- To experiment on or with something is to test it or try it out.

expert noun

*He's an **expert** at chess.*
- specialist, authority, genius, wizard
- (*informal*) dab hand, whizz

expert adjective

*Only an **expert** sailor could cross the ocean.*
- brilliant, capable, clever, competent, experienced, knowledgeable, professional, proficient, qualified, skilful, skilled, specialized, trained
  OPPOSITE amateur, unskilful

expertise noun

*Do you have the **expertise** to restore the painting?*
- skill, ability, competence, knowledge, know-how, training

expire verb

1 *The television licence **expires** next month.*
- finish, run out, come to an end, become invalid

2 *The animal **expired** before the vet arrived.*
- die, pass away

explain verb

1 *The doctor **explained** the procedure carefully.*
- make clear, give an explanation of, clarify, describe

2 *Can you **explain** your strange behaviour?*
- give reasons for, account for, excuse, make excuses for, justify

explanation noun

1 *They could find no **explanation** for the accident.*
- reason, excuse, justification

2 *He gave a brief **explanation** of how his invention worked.*
- account, description, demonstration

a
b
c
d
e
f
g
h
i
j
k
l
m
n
o
p
q
r
s
t
u
v
w
x
y
z

a
b
c
d
e
f
g
h
i
j
k
l
m
n
o
p
q
r
s
t
u
v
w
x
y
z

explode verb
1 *The firework **exploded** with a bang.*
- blow up, make an explosion, go off, burst, shatter

2 *The slightest movement might **explode** the bomb.*
- detonate, set off

exploit noun
*The book describes her **exploits** as a secret agent.*
- adventure, deed, feat, venture, escapade

exploit verb
*They plan to **exploit** the area as a tourist attraction.*
- make use of, take advantage of, use, develop, profit by
- (*informal*) cash in on

explore verb
1 *The spacecraft will **explore** the solar system.*
- search, survey, travel through, probe

2 *We must **explore** all the possibilities.*
- examine, inspect, investigate, look into, research, analyse, scrutinize

explorer noun

> ### WORD WEB
>
> *The **explorers** were looking for the legendary Lost City.*
> - traveller, voyager, discoverer, wanderer
>
> THINGS AN EXPLORER MIGHT FIND
> catacombs, cave, cavern, chest, hieroglyphics, inscription, labyrinth, maze, mummy, parchment, pyramid, riddle, sarcophagus, seal, secret passage, skeleton, stone tablet, temple, tomb, treasure, tunnel, underground chamber
>
> THINGS AN EXPLORER MIGHT USE OR CARRY
> binoculars, chart, compass, machete, map, penknife, rope, rucksack, telescope, tent, torch, water bottle
>
> FOR EXPLORERS IN POLAR REGIONS
> SEE **polar**
>
> FOR EXPLORERS IN SPACE
> SEE **astronaut**

explosion noun
*The **explosion** rattled the windows.*
- blast, bang
- An explosion from a volcano is an eruption.
- An explosion of laughter is an outburst.
- The sound of a gun going off is a report.

export verb
*The factory **exports** most of the cars it makes.*
- sell abroad, send abroad, ship overseas

OPPOSITE import

expose verb
1 *He yawned, **exposing** a set of white teeth.*
- uncover

2 *The truth about his past was **exposed** in the newspaper.*
- make known, publish, reveal, disclose

express verb
*He's always quick to **express** his opinions.*
- voice, communicate, convey, put into words, phrase
- To express yourself by word of mouth is to speak.
- To express yourself on paper is to write.
- To express your feelings is to give vent to them.

expression noun
1 *'Tickled pink' is a colloquial **expression**.*
- phrase, saying, term, wording
- An expression that people use too much is a cliché.

2 *Did you see her **expression** when I told her the news?*
- look, appearance, countenance, face

3 *Rhona plays the piano with great **expression**.*
- feeling, emotion, sympathy, understanding

expression noun

WORD WEB

EXPRESSIONS YOU MIGHT SEE ON A FACE
beam, frown, glare, glower,
grimace, grin, laugh, leer, long face,
poker-face, pout, scowl, smile,
smirk, sneer, wide-eyed look, wince,
yawn
SEE ALSO **face** noun

expressive adjective

1 *The old wizard gave me an* ***expressive***
look.
- meaningful, significant, revealing,
telling
2 *An actor needs to have an* ***expressive***
voice.
- lively, varied, eloquent
OPPOSITE expressionless, flat

exquisite adjective

There was some ***exquisite*** *lace on the*
collar.
- beautiful, fine, delicate, intricate,
dainty

extend verb

1 *Stopping for lunch will* ***extend*** *our*
journey by an hour.
- lengthen, make longer, prolong,
delay, draw out
OPPOSITE shorten
2 *They have recently* ***extended*** *their*
website.
- enlarge, expand, increase, build up,
develop, add to, widen the scope of
OPPOSITE reduce
3 *He sat back and* ***extended*** *his legs.*
- stretch out, hold out, put out, reach
out, stick out
4 *We* ***extended*** *a warm welcome to the*
visitors.
- give, offer

extension noun

They are building an ***extension*** *to the*
runway.
- continuation, addition

extensive adjective

The palace gardens cover an ***extensive***
area.
- big, large, broad, wide, spread out
OPPOSITE small

extent noun

1 *The map shows the* ***extent*** *of the*
island.
- area, dimensions, expanse, spread,
breadth, length, limits,
measurement
2 *After the storm we went out to see the*
extent *of the damage.*
- amount, degree, level, size, scope,
magnitude, range

exterior noun

He painted the ***exterior*** *of his house.*
- outside
OPPOSITE interior

exterminate verb

They used poison to ***exterminate*** *the*
rats.
- destroy, kill, get rid of, annihilate,
wipe out

external adjective

In ***external*** *appearance, the house was*
rather gloomy.
- exterior, outside, outer
OPPOSITE internal

extinct adjective

- An extinct species is one that has
died out or vanished.
- An extinct volcano is an inactive
volcano.

extinguish verb

We ***extinguished*** *the campfire before*
we went to bed.
- put out, quench, smother
OPPOSITE ignite

extra adjective

1 *There is an* ***extra*** *charge for taking your*
bike on the train.
- additional, further, added,
supplementary, excess
2 *There is* ***extra*** *food in the kitchen if you*
need it.
- more, spare, surplus, reserve

a
b
c
d
e
f
g
h
i
j
k
l
m
n
o
p
q
r
s
t
u
v
w
x
y
z

a
b
c
d
e
f
g
h
i
j
k
l
m
n
o
p
q
r
s
t
u
v
w
x
y
z

extract noun

*There's an **extract** from the new Jacqueline Wilson book in the magazine.*

- excerpt, passage, part, section
- A short extract is a quotation.
- Specially interesting extracts from something are the highlights.
- An extract from a newspaper is a cutting.
- An extract from a film is a clip.

extract verb

1 *The dentist decided to **extract** my tooth.*

- pull out, remove, take out, draw out, withdraw
- (*informal*) whip out

2 *The following passages are **extracted** from the book.*

- derive, get, gather, obtain, quote, select, excerpt

extraordinary adjective

*The astronauts saw many **extraordinary** sights.*

- amazing, astonishing, remarkable, outstanding, exceptional, incredible, fantastic, marvellous, miraculous, phenomenal, rare, special, strange, surprising, unheard of, unusual, weird, wonderful, abnormal, curious

OPPOSITE ordinary

extravagant adjective

*He held a large, **extravagant** party for all his friends.*

- expensive, lavish, wasteful
- Someone who spends money in an extravagant way is a spendthrift.

OPPOSITE modest

extreme adjective

1 *Polar bears can withstand **extreme** cold.*

- great, intense, severe, acute, excessive

2 *She lives on the **extreme** edge of the town.*

- farthest, furthest

eye noun

WORD WEB

PARTS OF YOUR EYE

cornea, eyeball, eyebrow, eyelash, eyelid, iris, lens, pupil, retina

- A person who tests your eyesight is an optician.
- A word meaning 'to do with eyes' is optical.
- A person with good eyesight is said to have eyes like a hawk.

WRITING TIPS

You can use these words to describe eyes:

- beady, bulbous, bulging, deep-set, glassy, heavy-lidded, hooded, protuberant, saucer-like, sunken; cloudy, misty, moist, piercing, steely, tearful, watery

*The monster had a single **bulging** red eye.*

eye verb

*The dog **eyed** the sausages hungrily.*

- look at, regard, stare at, watch, gaze at, contemplate

Ff

fabric noun

*This **fabric** will make a lovely dress for my doll.*

- cloth, material, stuff
- A plural word is textiles.

FOR KINDS OF FABRIC

SEE **cloth**

fabulous adjective

1 (*informal*) *We had a **fabulous** time at the party.*
- excellent, first-class, marvellous, outstanding, superb, tremendous, wonderful
- (*informal*) brilliant, fantastic, smashing

2 *Dragons are **fabulous** creatures.*
- fictitious, imaginary, legendary, mythical

face noun

1 *We saw the anger in the witch's **face**.*
- expression, features, look, countenance

2 *The **face** of the clock had been smashed.*
- front

3 *A cube has six **faces**.*
- side, surface

WRITING TIPS

You can use these words to describe a **face**.
- to describe its *SHAPE*:
  flat, long, oval, round, rounded; lantern-jawed, square-jawed
- to describe its *FEATURES*:
  chiselled, chubby, craggy, delicate, fine, gaunt, haggard, hollow, pinched, prominent, puffy, skeletal, sunken
  *Their faces were **gaunt** and **pinched** from hunger.*
- to describe its *SKIN* or *COLOUR*:
  clear, dark, fair, flushed, freckled, fresh, glowing, healthy, rosy, ruddy, tanned; ashen, grey, leaden, pale, pallid, pasty, sallow, sickly, unhealthy, wan; flabby, saggy, shrivelled, weather-beaten, wizened, wrinkled, wrinkly; disfigured, pimply, pock-marked, scarred, spotty
  *The old witch was **wizened** like a prune.*
- to describe *THE LOOK ON A FACE* :
  cheeky, cheerful, radiant, sunny; grave, grim, serious; sulky, sullen, surly; blank, deadpan, faceless, impassive, unmoving, vacant

---

*The guard stared ahead, his face **unmoving**.*
SEE ALSO **expression**
FOR PARTS OF A FACE
SEE **eye, nose**

face verb

1 *Stand and **face** your partner.*
- be opposite to, look towards

2 *The astronauts had to **face** many dangers.*
- cope with, deal with, face up to, stand up to, tackle, meet, encounter, confront
OPPOSITE avoid

fact noun

*It is a **fact** that dodos are now extinct.*
- reality, truth, certainty
OPPOSITE fiction

the facts

*The detective considered **the facts** in the case.*
- details, particulars, information, data
- Facts which are useful in trying to prove something are evidence.
- Facts expressed as numbers are statistics.

factual adjective

*Anne Frank wrote a **factual** account of her life during the war*
- real, true, truthful, accurate, authentic, faithful, genuine, objective, reliable
- A film or story based on a person's life is biographical.
- A film or story based on history is historical.
- A film telling you about real events is a documentary.
OPPOSITE made-up, fictional

fade verb

1 *Sunlight has **faded** the curtains.*
- make paler, bleach, blanch, whiten, dim
OPPOSITE brighten

2 *Those flowers will **fade** in a few days.*
- wither, wilt, droop, flag, shrivel
OPPOSITE flourish

a
b
c
d
e
f
g
h
i
j
k
l
m
n
o
p
q
r
s
t
u
v
w
x
y
z

3 *Gradually, the light began to fade.*
- weaken, decline, diminish, dwindle, fail, wane, disappear, melt away, vanish
  OPPOSITE increase

fail verb
1 *Their plan to steal the crown jewels failed miserably.*
- be unsuccessful, go wrong, fall through, founder, come to grief, miscarry
- (informal) flop, bomb
  OPPOSITE succeed
2 *The rocket engine failed before take-off.*
- break down, cut out, give up, stop working
3 *By late afternoon, the light had begun to fail.*
- weaken, decline, diminish, dwindle, fade, get worse, deteriorate
  OPPOSITE improve
4 *The professor failed to warn us of the danger.*
- neglect, forget, omit
  OPPOSITE remember
5 *I hope I don't fail my violin exam.*
  OPPOSITE pass

failure noun
1 *The storm caused a power failure.*
- breakdown, fault, malfunction, crash, loss, collapse, stoppage
2 *Their attempt to reach the North Pole was a failure.*
- defeat, disappointment, disaster, fiasco
- (informal) flop, wash-out
  OPPOSITE success

faint adjective
1 *The details in the photograph are very faint.*
- faded, dim, unclear, indistinct, vague, blurred, hazy, pale, shadowy, misty
  OPPOSITE clear, distinct
2 *There was a faint smell of burning in the air.*
- delicate, slight
  OPPOSITE strong
3 *We heard a faint cry for help.*
- weak, low, muffled, distant, hushed, muted, soft, thin
  OPPOSITE loud

4 *Gordon was so hungry that he felt faint.*
- dizzy, giddy, light-headed, unsteady, weak, exhausted, feeble
- (informal) woozy

faint verb
The explorers nearly fainted from exhaustion.
- become unconscious, collapse, pass out, black out
- (old use) swoon

fair adjective
1 *I think the referee made a fair decision.*
- just, proper, right, fair-minded, honest, honourable, impartial, unbiased, unprejudiced, disinterested
  OPPOSITE unfair
2 *The twins both have fair hair.*
- blond or blonde, light, golden, yellow
  OPPOSITE dark
3 *Our team has a fair chance of winning the cup.*
- reasonable, moderate, average, acceptable, adequate, satisfactory, passable, respectable, tolerable
4 *The weather should be fair today.*
- dry, fine, sunny, bright, clear, cloudless, pleasant, favourable

fair noun
1 *My sister won a teddy bear at the fair.*
- fairground, funfair, carnival, fête, gala
2 *Our school is holding a book fair next week.*
- show, exhibition, display, market, bazaar

fairly adverb
1 *The competition will be judged fairly.*
- honestly, properly, justly, impartially
2 *The ground is still fairly wet. I'm fairly certain that we are heading north.*
- quite, rather, somewhat, slightly, moderately, up to a point, reasonably, tolerably
- (informal) pretty

fairy noun

> **WORD WEB**
>
> THINGS A FAIRY MIGHT HAVE OR USE
> fairy dust, lantern, wand, wings
>
> A FAIRY'S WINGS OR CLOTHES MIGHT BE
> diaphonous, feathery, glittering,
> glowing, gossamer, lustrous, sheer,
> sparkling, translucent, transparent
>
> PLACES WHERE A FAIRY MIGHT LIVE
> dell, glen, magic forest or tree,
> glade, mound, toadstool
>
> SOME CREATURES LIKE FAIRIES
> brownie, elf, imp, leprechaun,
> nymph, pixie, sprite
>
> FOR OTHER CREATURES FOUND IN MYTHS
> AND LEGENDS
> SEE **myth**

faith noun

1 *The acrobat had complete* **faith** *in his assistant.*
* belief, trust, confidence
  OPPOSITE doubt
2 *In our school, we have pupils of many different* **faiths**.
* religion, creed, doctrine, belief

faithful adjective

1 *My dog, Scruffy, is my* **faithful** *friend.*
* loyal, devoted, reliable, trustworthy, dependable, firm, constant, close
  OPPOSITE unfaithful
2 *Is this a* **faithful** *copy of the map?*
* accurate, exact, precise, true

fake noun

That's not a real Roman coin—it's a **fake**.
* copy, imitation, reproduction, replica, forgery
* (*informal*) phoney
* An event which fakes a real event is a hoax, sham, or simulation.
* A person who pretends to be another person is an impostor.

fake verb

The spy tried to **fake** *a foreign accent.*
* imitate, copy, pretend, put on, reproduce, simulate
* To fake someone's signature is to forge it.

fall verb

1 *The acrobat* **fell** *off a ladder and broke his leg.*
* tumble, topple, crash down, pitch, plunge
2 *Snow was beginning to* **fall** *quite thickly.*
* drop, come down, descend, rain down, plummet
3 *The level of the river had* **fallen** *since March.*
* go down, subside, recede, sink, ebb
4 *The temperature in the cave* **fell** *to below freezing.*
* go down, become lower, decrease, decline, lessen, diminish, dwindle
5 *After a long siege, the town* **fell** *to the enemy.*
* give in, surrender
6 *Millions of soldiers* **fell** *in the war.*
* die, be killed, perish
* (*old use*) be slain
7 *We arrived at the camp as night was* **falling**.
* happen, occur, come, take place

to fall in
The roof of the cabin **fell in** *during the storm.*
* cave in, collapse, give way

to fall out
The twins are always **falling out** *with each other.*
* argue, disagree, quarrel, squabble, bicker

to fall through
Our holiday plans have **fallen through** *again.*
* come to nothing, fail, collapse, founder

fall noun

1 *Ellen had a* **fall** *and cut her knee.*
* tumble
2 *We noticed a sharp* **fall** *in the temperature.*
* drop, lowering
  OPPOSITE rise
3 *There has been a* **fall** *in the price of coffee.*
* decrease, reduction, decline
  OPPOSITE increase
4 *This is a story about the* **fall** *of Troy.*
* defeat, surrender

a
b
c
d
e
f
g
h
i
j
k
l
m
n
o
p
q
r
s
t
u
v
w
x
y
z

false adjective

1 *They gave us **false** information about the treasure.*

- wrong, incorrect, untrue, inaccurate, mistaken, erroneous, faulty, invalid, misleading, deceptive

OPPOSITE correct

2 *The spy was travelling with a **false** passport.*

- fake, bogus, sham, counterfeit, forged

OPPOSITE genuine, authentic

3 *Mrs Gummidge put in her **false** teeth.*

- artificial, imitation

OPPOSITE real, natural

4 *The Black Knight turned out to be a **false** ally.*

- unfaithful, disloyal, unreliable, untrustworthy, deceitful, dishonest, treacherous

OPPOSITE faithful, loyal

falter verb

1 *The horse **faltered** as it approached the jump.*

- hesitate, flinch, hold back, pause, stumble, waver, get cold feet
- To falter in your speech is to stammer or stutter.

2 *The knight's courage began to **falter**.*

- weaken, diminish, flag, wane

fame noun

*Her Olympic medal brought her international **fame**.*

- celebrity, stardom, renown, glory, reputation, name, standing, stature, prominence
- Fame that you get for doing something bad is notoriety.

familiar adjective

1 *Seagulls are a **familiar** sight on the beach.*

- common, everyday, normal, ordinary, usual, regular, customary, frequent, mundane, routine

OPPOSITE rare

2 *It seems a bit **familiar** to call her by her first name.*

- informal, friendly, intimate, relaxed, close

OPPOSITE formal, unfriendly

to be familiar with something

*Are you **familiar with** the rules of chess?*

- be acquainted with, be aware of, know

family noun

> **WORD WEB**
>
> *Some members of my **family** live in New Zealand.*
>
> - relations, relatives
> - An old-fashioned term for your family is your kin.
> - The official term for your closest relative is next of kin.
> - A group of related Scottish families is a clan.
> - A succession of people from the same powerful family is a dynasty.
> - In certain societies, a group of families living together is a tribe.
> - A single stage in a family is a generation.
> - The line of ancestors from which a family is descended is its ancestry.
> - A diagram showing how people in your family are related is a family tree.
> - The study of family history is genealogy.
> - A family of young birds is a brood.
> - A family of kittens or puppies is a litter.
>
> MEMBERS OF A FAMILY MAY INCLUDE adopted child, aunt, brother, child, cousin, daughter, father, foster-child, foster-parent, grandchild, grandparent, guardian, husband, mother, nephew, niece, parent, sister, son, spouse, step-child, step-parent, uncle, ward, wife

famished adjective

*What's for dinner? I'm **famished**!*

- hungry, ravenous, starving
- If you are slightly hungry, you are peckish.

famous adjective

*Pele is a very **famous** football player.*

- well-known, celebrated, renowned, acclaimed, notable, prominent, distinguished, eminent
- To be famous for doing something bad is to be notorious.

OPPOSITE unknown, obscure

fan noun

1 *Can you switch on the **fan**, please?*

- ventilator, blower, extractor, air-conditioner

2 *I used to be a **fan** of jazz music.*

- enthusiast, admirer, devotee, follower, supporter

fanatic noun

*My brother is a rugby **fanatic**.*

- enthusiast, addict, devotee
- (informal) freak, nut

fanatical adjective

*Wayne is **fanatical** about football.*

- enthusiastic, extreme, fervent, over-enthusiastic, passionate, rabid, zealous

OPPOSITE moderate

fanciful adjective

*I like reading **fanciful** stories about dragons.*

- fantastic, unrealistic, whimsical, imaginary, fictitious, made-up

OPPOSITE realistic

fancy adjective

*Alice bought a **fancy** hat for her friend's wedding.*

- elaborate, decorative, ornamental, ornate

OPPOSITE plain

fancy verb

1 *What do you **fancy** to eat?*

- feel like, want, wish for, desire, prefer

2 *I **fancied** I heard a noise downstairs.*

- imagine, think, believe, suppose

fantastic adjective

1 *The story is full of **fantastic** creatures.*

- fanciful, extraordinary, strange, odd, weird, outlandish, far-fetched, incredible, imaginative

OPPOSITE realistic

2 (informal) *We had a **fantastic** time at camp.*

- excellent, first-class, outstanding, superb, wonderful, tremendous, marvellous
- (informal) brilliant, fabulous, smashing

fantasy noun

*Rosie had a **fantasy** about being a mermaid.*

- dream, daydream, delusion, fancy

far adjective

1 *The castle stood in the **far** north of the country.*

- distant, faraway, remote

2 *The ferry took us to the **far** side of the river.*

- opposite, other

OPPOSITE near

fare noun

*Do you have enough money for the bus **fare**?*

- price, charge, cost, payment, fee

far-fetched adjective

*That explanation sounds **far-fetched** to me.*

- unbelievable, unlikely, improbable, unconvincing, unrealistic, incredible

OPPOSITE likely, believable

farm noun

WORD WEB
- The formal word for farming is agriculture.
- A farm which uses no artificial fertilizers or chemicals is an organic farm.
- A very small farm is a smallholding.
- A small farm growing fruit and vegetables is a market garden.

a b c d e **f** g h i j k l m n o p q r s t u v w x y z

- A small farm in Scotland is a croft.
- A large cattle farm in America is a ranch.

FARM BUILDINGS
barn, byre or cowshed, dairy, farmhouse, granary, milking parlour, outhouse, pigsty, stable

OTHER PARTS OF A FARM
barnyard or farmyard, cattle pen, fields, haystack, meadow, paddock, pasture, rick, sheep fold, silo

ITEMS OF FARM EQUIPMENT
baler, combine harvester, cultivator, drill, harrow, harvester, mower, planter, plough, tractor, trailer

PEOPLE WHO WORK ON A FARM
agricultural worker, (old use) dairymaid, farmer, farm labourer, ploughman, shepherd, stockbreeder, tractor driver

SOME FARM ANIMALS
bull, bullock, chicken or hen, cow, duck, goat, goose, horse, pig, sheep, turkey

- Birds kept on a farm are poultry.
- Animals kept for milk or beef are cattle.
- Farm animals in general are livestock.

farm verb
*The Macdonalds had **farmed** the land for centuries.*
- cultivate, work, till, plough

fascinate verb
*We were **fascinated** by the inventor's workshop.*
- interest (in), engross, captivate, enthrall, absorb, beguile, entrance, attract, charm, enchant, delight
OPPOSITE bore

fashion noun
1 *The Martians behaved in a peculiar **fashion**.*
- way, manner
2 *Zoe dresses according to the latest **fashion**.*
- trend, vogue, craze, fad, style, look

fashionable adjective
*Megan has a **fashionable** new hairstyle.*
- stylish, chic, up-to-date, popular, elegant, smart
- (*informal*) trendy, hip, in
OPPOSITE unfashionable, out-of-date

fast adjective
*The robber made a **fast** exit when he heard us coming.*
- quick, rapid, speedy, swift, brisk, hurried, hasty, high-speed, headlong, breakneck
- (*informal*) nippy
- Something which goes faster than sound is supersonic.
- A common simile is as fast as lightning.
OPPOSITE slow, unhurried

fast adverb
1 *Mr Toad was driving too **fast** in his motor car.*
- quickly, speedily, swiftly, rapidly, briskly
2 *The boat was stuck **fast** on the rocks.*
- firmly, securely, tightly
3 *Be quiet! The baby is **fast** asleep.*
- deeply, sound, completely

fasten verb
1 *They **fastened** their ropes to the rock face.*
- tie, fix, attach, connect, join, link, bind, hitch, clamp, pin, clip, tack, stick
- To fasten a boat is to anchor or moor it.
- To fasten an animal is to tether it.
2 *They **fastened** the gate with a heavy chain.*
- secure, seal, lock, bolt, make fast

fat adjective
1 *You'll get **fat** if you eat too many crisps!*
- overweight, obese, chubby, plump, podgy, dumpy, flabby, portly, stout, round, rotund
2 *The witch opened a big, **fat** book of spells.*
- thick, bulky, chunky, weighty, substantial
OPPOSITE thin

fatal adjective

1 *The knight delivered a **fatal** wound to his enemy.*
- deadly, lethal, mortal
- A fatal illness is an incurable or terminal illness.

2 *Leaving the door unlocked was a **fatal** mistake.*
- disastrous, catastrophic, dreadful, calamitous

fate noun

1 *The shipwrecked crew were in the hands of **fate**.*
- fortune, destiny, providence, chance, luck

2 *The prisoner met with a terrible **fate**.*
- death, end

fatigue noun

*Some of the runners were overcome with **fatigue**.*
- exhaustion, tiredness, weariness, weakness

fatigued adjective

*We were all **fatigued** by the time we got home.*
- exhausted, tired, worn out, weary
- (*informal*) all in

fatty adjective

*I don't like **fatty** food.*
- fat, greasy, oily

fault noun

1 *This DVD has a **fault** in it.*
- defect, flaw, malfunction, snag, problem, weakness

2 *It was my **fault** that we missed our bus.*
- responsibility, liability

faultless adjective

*The dancer's movements were **faultless**.*
- perfect, flawless, ideal, impeccable
- OPPOSITE imperfect

faulty adjective

*The TV was **faulty**, so we took it back to the shop.*
- broken, not working, defective, out of order, unusable, damaged
- OPPOSITE perfect

favour noun

1 *I asked my friend to do me a **favour**.*
- good deed, good turn, kindness, service, courtesy

2 *The captain's plan found **favour** with most of the crew.*
- approval, support, liking, goodwill

to be in favour of something

*We're all **in favour of** longer holidays.*
- agree to, approve of, support, like the idea of

favour verb

*Do you **favour** the idea of free school meals?*
- approve of, support, back, advocate, choose, like, opt for, prefer
- (*informal*) fancy, go for
- OPPOSITE oppose

favourable adjective

1 *The weather conditions are **favourable** for sailing.*
- advantageous, helpful, beneficial
- OPPOSITE unfavourable

2 *The film has received **favourable** reviews.*
- good, positive, complimentary, encouraging, enthusiastic, sympathetic, approving, agreeable
- OPPOSITE critical, hostile, negative

favourite adjective

*What is your **favourite** book?*
- best-loved, preferred, treasured, dearest, special, top

fear noun

*When Garth heard the monster, he trembled with **fear**.*
- fright, terror, horror, alarm, panic, dread, anxiety, apprehension, trepidation
- A formal word for a special type of fear is phobia.
- A fear of open spaces is agoraphobia.
- A fear of spiders is arachnophobia.
- A fear of enclosed spaces is claustrophobia.
- A fear or dislike of foreigners is xenophobia.
- OPPOSITE courage

a
b
c
d
e
f
g
h
i
j
k
l
m
n
o
p
q
r
s
t
u
v
w
x
y
z

a
b
c
d
e
f
g
h
i
j
k
l
m
n
o
p
q
r
s
t
u
v
w
x
y
z

fear verb

1 *My sister **fears** snakes and spiders.*
- be frightened of, be afraid of, be scared of, dread

2 *I **fear** we may be too late.*
- suspect, expect, anticipate

fearful adjective

1 *The young warrior had a **fearful** look in his eyes.*
- frightened, scared, terrified, afraid, panicky, nervous, anxious, timid
- OPPOSITE brave

2 *The erupting volcano was a **fearful** sight.*
- frightening, terrifying, shocking, fearsome, ghastly, dreadful, appalling, terrible

fearless adjective

*The **fearless** explorers entered the dark cave.*
- brave, courageous, daring, heroic, valiant, intrepid, plucky
- OPPOSITE cowardly

fearsome adjective

*The dragon yawned, revealing a **fearsome** set of teeth.*
- frightening, fearful, horrifying, terrifying, dreadful, awesome
- (*informal*) scary

feasible adjective

*Is it **feasible** to fly to Paris and back in a day?*
- possible, practicable, practical, achievable, realistic, workable
- OPPOSITE impractical, impossible

feast noun

*The king held a great **feast** to celebrate his birthday.*
- banquet, dinner
- (*informal*) spread

feat noun

*The trapeze artists performed many daring **feats**.*
- act, action, deed, exploit, achievement, performance

feather noun
- A large feather is a plume.

- All the feathers on a bird are its plumage.
- Soft, fluffy feathers are down.
- A feather used as a pen is a quill.

FOR WAYS TO DESCRIBE A BIRD'S FEATHERS
SEE **bird**

feature noun

1 *The room has several unusual **features**.*
- characteristic, detail, point, aspect, quality, peculiarity, trait, facet
- A person's features are their face.

FOR WAYS TO DESCRIBE FACIAL FEATURES
SEE **face** noun

2 *There was a **feature** about our school in the newspaper.*
- article, report, story, item, piece

feature verb

1 *The film **features** some thrilling car chases.*
- give prominence to, highlight, spotlight, show off

2 *A new cartoon character **features** in this film.*
- appear, take part, figure, star

fee noun

*The club charges an annual membership **fee**.*
- charge, cost, payment, price
- A fee to use a private road or bridge is a toll.

feeble adjective

1 *The elderly knight looked tired and **feeble**.*
- weak, frail, infirm, delicate, poorly, sickly, puny, weary, weedy
- OPPOSITE strong, powerful

2 *I made a **feeble** attempt to stop the ball.*
*Do you expect me to believe that **feeble** excuse?*
- weak, poor, ineffective, inadequate, unconvincing, tame, flimsy, lame

feed verb

*We have enough sandwiches to **feed** six people.*
- provide for, cater for, give food to, nourish

to feed on

*The leopard was **feeding on** its prey.*

• eat, consume, devour

feel verb

1 *I **felt** the llama's soft, woolly fur.*

• touch, caress, stroke, fondle

2 *When the candle went out, we had to **feel** our way out of the cave.*

• grope, fumble

3 *It **feels** colder today.*

• appear, seem, strike you as

4 *Older people tend to **feel** the cold.*

• notice, be aware of, be conscious of, experience, suffer from

5 *I **feel** that it's time we made a start.*

• think, believe, consider

to feel like

*Do you **feel like** going for a walk?*

• fancy, want, wish for, desire

feel verb

WRITING TIPS

You can use these words to describe **how something feels**:

• bristly, coarse, creamy, crinkly, crunchy, dry, feathery, fibrous, fine, fluffy, grainy, hairy, knobbly, lumpy, moist, papery, rough, rubbery, runny, silky, smooth, spongy, springy, squashy, sticky, stiff, stringy, velvety, watery, woolly

*The moss felt **spongy** and **springy** underfoot.*

---

feel noun

*I love the **feel** of warm sand between my toes.*

• feeling, sensation, touch

feeling noun

1 *The cat had lost all **feeling** in its paw.*

• sense of touch, sensation, sensitivity

2 *I didn't mean to hurt your **feelings**.*

• emotion, passion, sentiment

3 *I have a **feeling** that something is wrong.*

• suspicion, notion, inkling, hunch, idea, impression, fancy, intuition

4 *There was a good **feeling** at the party.*

• atmosphere, mood, air, aura

female adjective

FOR FEMALE HUMAN BEINGS

SEE **woman**

FOR FEMALE ANIMALS

SEE **animal**

OPPOSITE male

feminine adjective

*Lisa likes to dress in a **feminine** style.*

• womanly, ladylike, girlish

• (*informal*) girly

OPPOSITE masculine

fence noun

*The mansion was surrounded by a tall **fence**.*

• railing, barrier, wall, paling, stockade, hedge

fence verb

*The field was **fenced** with a thorn hedge.*

• enclose, surround, bound, encircle

fend verb

to fend for yourself

*The lion cubs will soon have to **fend for themselves**.*

• look after, take care of, care for

to fend someone or **something off**

*The knight raised his shield to **fend off** the blow.*

• repel, resist, ward off, fight off, hold off, thwart

ferment verb

*The sorcerer left the potion to **ferment** in a jar.*

• bubble, fizz, foam, seethe

ferment noun

*Before the revolution, the country was in a state of **ferment**.*

• turmoil, unrest, upheaval, agitation, excitement, commotion, turbulence, confusion, disorder, tumult

ferocious adjective

*The mansion was guarded by a **ferocious** dog.*

• fierce, fearsome, savage, wild, vicious, violent, bloodthirsty, brutal

OPPOSITE tame

a b c d e **f** g h i j k l m n o p q r s t u v w x y z

a
b
c
d
e
f
g
h
i
j
k
l
m
n
o
p
q
r
s
t
u
v
w
x
y
z

fertile adjective
*The surrounding countryside was green and **fertile**.*
- fruitful, productive, rich, fecund
OPPOSITE barren, sterile

fertilize verb
*If you want good crops, you must **fertilize** the soil.*
- enrich, feed, manure

fervent adjective
*My gran is a **fervent** supporter of the local team.*
- eager, keen, avid, ardent, committed, enthusiastic, fanatical, passionate, zealous
OPPOSITE apathetic, lukewarm

festival noun
*The town holds a **festival** every summer.*
- carnival, fiesta, fête, gala, fair, celebration, jamboree
- A celebration of a special anniversary is a jubilee.
  FOR RELIGIOUS FESTIVALS
  SEE **religion**

festive adjective
*Chinese New Year is a **festive** occasion.*
- cheerful, happy, merry, jolly, cheery, joyful, joyous, jovial, light-hearted, celebratory
OPPOSITE gloomy, sombre

fetch verb
1 *I **fetched** the shopping from the car.*
- get, bring, carry, collect, transfer, transport, convey, pick up, retrieve, obtain
2 *If we sell our car, how much will it **fetch**?*
- make, raise, sell for, go for, bring in, earn

feud noun
*There has been a **feud** between our families for years.*
- quarrel, dispute, conflict, hostility, enmity, rivalry, strife, antagonism
- A feud that lasts a long time is a vendetta.

feverish adjective
1 *I felt **feverish** with the cold.*
- When you are feverish you are hot and shivery.
- With a bad fever you may become delirious.
2 *There was **feverish** activity in the kitchen.*
- frenzied, frantic, frenetic, excited, agitated, hectic, busy, hurried, impatient, restless

few adjective
*I've only been abroad a **few** times. **Few** astronauts have walked on the Moon.*
- not many, hardly any, a small number of, a handful of
OPPOSITE many

fibre noun
*Rope is made by twisting **fibres** together.*
- thread, strand, hair, filament

fickle adjective
*Some **fickle** supporters deserted the team when they lost.*
- changeable, disloyal, unfaithful, unreliable, erratic, inconsistent, unpredictable, inconstant
OPPOSITE loyal

fiction noun
1 *Roald Dahl wrote **fiction** for both children and adults.*
  FOR VARIOUS KINDS OF LITERATURE
  SEE **writing**
2 *Her account of what happened was pure **fiction**.*
- fantasy, invention, fabrication, lies
OPPOSITE fact

fictional adjective
*Harry Potter is a **fictional** character.*
- imaginary, made-up, invented, fanciful
OPPOSITE factual, real

fictitious adjective
*The spy was using a **fictitious** name.*
- false, fake, fabricated, fraudulent, bogus, assumed, spurious, unreal
OPPOSITE genuine, real

fiddle verb

1 *Who's been **fiddling** with the DVD player?*
- tinker, meddle, tamper, play about, mess about, twiddle

2 *(informal) Mr Filch had been **fiddling** the bank account for years.*
- falsify, alter, rig
- *(informal)* cook the books

fiddly adjective

*Icing a cake can be a **fiddly** job.*
- intricate, complicated, awkward, involved
OPPOSITE simple

fidget verb

*I begin to **fidget** when I'm bored.*
- be restless, fiddle about, play about, mess about

fidgety adjective

*After waiting an hour, we began to get **fidgety**.*
- restless, unsettled, impatient, agitated, jumpy, nervy
OPPOSITE calm

field noun

1 *Cattle were grazing in the **field**.*
- meadow, pasture
- A small field for horses is a paddock.
- An area of grass in a village is a green.

2 *The **field** is too wet to play football.*
- ground, pitch, playing field

3 *Electronics is not my **field**.*
- special interest, speciality, area of study

fierce adjective

1 *The travellers were killed in a **fierce** attack by armed bandits.*
- vicious, ferocious, savage, brutal, violent, wild, cruel, merciless, ruthless, pitiless

2 *Our team will face **fierce** opposition in the final.*
- strong, keen, eager, aggressive, competitive, passionate, relentless

3 *The explorers braved the **fierce** heat of the desert sun.*
- blazing, intense, raging

fiery adjective

1 *It's best to avoid the **fiery** heat of the midday sun.*
- blazing, burning, hot, intense, fierce, raging, flaming, red-hot, glowing

2 *My great aunt has always had a **fiery** temper.*
- violent, passionate, excitable, angry, furious

fight noun

1 *The warriors faced each other for a **fight** to the death.*
- Fighting is combat or hostilities.
- A fight between armies is a battle.
- A minor unplanned battle is a skirmish.
- A series of battles is a campaign or war.
- A minor fight is a brawl, scrap, scuffle, or tussle.
- A fight arranged between two people is a duel.

2 *We support the **fight** to save the rainforest.*
- campaign, crusade, struggle

fight verb

1 *Two seagulls were **fighting** over a scrap of bread.*
- have a fight, scrap, scuffle, exchange blows, come to blows

2 *The two countries **fought** each other in the war.*
- do battle with, wage war with, attack
- Fighting with swords is fencing.
- Fighting with fists is boxing.
- Fighting in which you try to throw your opponent to the ground is wrestling.
- Fighting sports such as karate and judo are martial arts.

3 *We will **fight** the decision to close our local library.*
- protest against, oppose, resist, make a stand against, campaign against

a
b
c
d
e
f
g
h
i
j
k
l
m
n
o
p
q
r
s
t
u
v
w
x
y
z

fighter noun

WORD WEB

PEOPLE WHO FIGHT IN A WAR OR CONFLICT
guerrilla, soldier, warrior
SEE ALSO **armed services**

PEOPLE WHO FOUGHT IN PAST TIMES
archer, gladiator, knight, swordsman or swordswoman

PEOPLE WHO FIGHT AS A SPORT
boxer, fencer, kick-boxer, wrestler

figure noun

1 *Please write the **figure** '8' on the board.*
- number, numeral, digit, integer
2 *What **figure** would you put on your old bike?*
- price, value, amount, sum, cost
3 *Ballet dancers need to have a good **figure**.*
- body, build, form, shape
4 *Inside the temple were several clay **figures**.*
- statue, carving, sculpture
5 *The **figure** on page 22 shows the annual rainfall for Wales.*
- diagram, graph, illustration, drawing

figure verb

*Donald Duck **figures** in many cartoons.*
- appear, feature, take part

to figure out

*We couldn't **figure out** what the riddle meant.*
- work out, make out, understand, see

figure of speech noun

WORD WEB

SOME COMMON FIGURES OF SPEECH
alliteration, metaphor, onomatopoeia, personification, simile

file noun

1 *I keep all my award certificates in a **file**.*
- folder, binder, cover
- A file containing information, especially secret information, is a dossier.

2 *Please walk in a single **file**.*
- line, row, column, rank, queue, procession

file verb

1 *I **file** all my letters in a pink folder.*
- organize, put away, store
2 *We **filed** into the hall for assembly.*
- walk in a line, march, troop, parade

fill verb

1 *Dad **filled** the trolley with shopping.*
- load, pack, stuff, cram, top up
- To fill a tyre with air is to inflate it.
OPPOSITE empty
2 *What can I use to **fill** this hole?*
- close up, plug, seal, block up, stop up
3 *Sightseers **filled** the streets.*
- crowd, jam, block, obstruct
- (*informal*) bung up

filling noun

*The **filling** started to ooze out of my sandwich.*
- stuffing, insides, innards, padding

film noun

1 *There is a good **film** on TV tonight.*
- movie, picture, video, DVD
- A long film is a feature film.
- A short excerpt from a film is a clip.
- A script for a film is a screenplay and a writer of screenplays is a screenwriter.
- A well-known film actor is a film star.
- A theatre where films are shown is a cinema, picture house, or (*American*) movie theatre.
2 *There was a **film** of oil on the water.*
- coat, coating, layer, covering, sheet, skin
- A large patch of oil floating on water is a slick.

filth noun

*The walls of the dungeon were covered with **filth**.*
- dirt, grime, muck, mess, mud, sludge, scum, slime

filthy adjective

1 *Those trainers are **filthy**!*
- dirty, mucky, messy, grimy, grubby, muddy, soiled, stained
  OPPOSITE clean

2 *Don't drink the **filthy** water from the well.*
- cloudy, contaminated, foul, impure, polluted, slimy, smelly, stinking
  OPPOSITE pure

final adjective

1 *The **final** moments of the match were very tense.*
- last, closing, concluding
  OPPOSITE opening

2 *What was the **final** result?*
- eventual, ultimate

finally adverb

*I've **finally** managed to finish my book.*
- eventually, at last, in the end

finances plural noun

*Are your **finances** doing well?*
- money, bank account, funds, resources, assets, wealth

find verb

1 *Did you **find** any fossils on the beach?*
- come across, discover, see, spot, locate, encounter, stumble across, unearth

2 *The children never **found** the secret door again.*
- trace, track down, recover, retrieve
  OPPOSITE lose

3 *Did the doctor **find** what was wrong?*
- detect, identify, diagnose, ascertain

4 *You will **find** that building a tree house is hard work.*
- become aware, realize, learn, recognize, notice, observe

findings plural noun

*The detective told us of his **findings**.*
- judgement, conclusion, verdict, decision

fine adjective

1 *The young musicians gave a **fine** performance.*
- excellent, first-class, superb, splendid, admirable, commendable, good
  OPPOSITE bad

2 *As the weather was **fine**, we took a picnic.*
- sunny, fair, bright, clear, cloudless, pleasant
  OPPOSITE dull

3 *Spiders spin very **fine** thread for their webs.*
- delicate, fragile, thin, flimsy, slender, slim
  OPPOSITE thick

4 *The desert dunes were made of **fine** sand.*
- dusty, powdery
  OPPOSITE coarse

fine noun

*The boy had to pay a **fine** for dropping litter.*
- penalty, charge, damages

finger noun

- Your short fat finger is your thumb.
- The finger next to your thumb is your index finger, because it is the finger you point with or indicate things with.
- The next finger is your middle finger.
- The next finger is your ring finger, because you can wear a wedding or engagement ring on that finger of your left hand.
- Your small thin finger is your little finger or (Scottish) pinkie.
- The joints in your fingers are your knuckles.

finger verb

*Please don't **finger** the food on the table.*
- touch, feel, poke, fondle

finicky adjective

*Our cat is **finicky** about her food.*
- fussy, hard to please, particular
- (informal) choosy, picky

finish verb

1 *When are you likely to **finish** your homework?*
- complete, reach the end of, cease, round off

a
b
c
d
e

f

g
h
i
j
k
l
m
n
o
p
q
r
s
t
u
v
w
x
y
z

2 *The film should **finish** around nine o'clock.*
- end, stop, conclude, terminate
- (informal) wind up

3 *I've already **finished** my bag of crisps.*
- consume, use up, get through, exhaust
- (informal) polish off
OPPOSITE start

finish noun
*We stayed to watch the parade until the **finish**.*
- end, close, conclusion, completion, result, termination
OPPOSITE start

fire noun
*The campers toasted marshmallows in the **fire**.*
- blaze, flames, burning, combustion
- A very big hot fire is an inferno.
- An open fire out of doors is a bonfire.
- An enclosed fire which produces great heat is a furnace.
- An enclosed fire for cooking food is an oven.
- An enclosed fire for making pottery is a kiln.
- A team of people whose job is to put out fires is a fire brigade.
- A member of a fire brigade is a firefighter.

fire verb
1 *The clay will harden if you **fire** it in a kiln.*
- bake, harden, heat

2 *The soldier aimed his rifle and **fired** two shots.*
- shoot, discharge, let off, set off
- To fire a missile is to launch it.

3 *(informal) Miss Stark **fired** her assistant for being late for work.*
- dismiss, sack

firm noun
*Mr Perkins owns a **firm** that makes biscuits.*
- company, business, organization, enterprise

firm adjective
1 *The surface of the planet was dry and **firm**.*
- hard, solid, dense, compact, rigid, set
OPPOSITE soft

2 *Make sure the knots in the rope are **firm**.*
- secure, tight, strong, stable, fixed, sturdy, steady

3 *Zelda had a **firm** belief in the power of magic.*
- definite, certain, sure, decided, determined, resolute, unshakeable, unwavering
OPPOSITE unsure

4 *The two girls have become **firm** friends.*
- close, devoted, faithful, loyal, constant, dependable, reliable

first adjective
1 *The **first** inhabitants of the area were Picts.*
- earliest, original

2 *The **first** thing to do in an emergency is to keep calm.*
- principal, key, main, fundamental, basic, chief

at first
At first, we thought the dog was asleep.
- at the beginning, to start with, initially, originally

first-class, first-rate adjectives
*That was a **first-class** game of chess.*
- excellent, first-rate, outstanding, superb, exceptional, superior, superlative, top-notch
OPPOSITE second-rate, mediocre

fish noun

WORD WEB
SOME TYPES OF FISH
brill, carp, catfish, chub, cod, conger, cuttlefish, dace, eel, flounder, goldfish, grayling, gudgeon, haddock, hake, halibut, herring, jellyfish, lamprey, ling, mackerel, minnow, mullet, perch, pike, pilchard, piranha, plaice, roach, salmon, sardine, sawfish, shark, skate, sole, sprat, squid, starfish, stickleback, sturgeon, swordfish, trout, tuna, turbot, whitebait, whiting

FOR TYPES OF SHELLFISH
SEE **shellfish**
- Young fish are fry.
- An informal word for a very small fish is a tiddler.
- A large number of fish swimming together is a shoal.
- A person who sells fish is a fishmonger.
- The sport or job of catching fish is fishing.
- Fishing with a rod and line is angling and a person who does this is an angler.
- Fishing with nets from a boat is trawling.
- Fishing equipment is tackle.

fit adjective
1 *Cinderella's gown was **fit** for a princess.*
- suitable, appropriate, fitting, right, good enough, worthy (of)
OPPOSITE unsuitable
2 *I walk to school every day to keep **fit**.*
- healthy, well, strong, robust
- (*old use*) hale and hearty
- A common simile is as fit as a fiddle.
OPPOSITE unhealthy
3 *After a long ride, the horses were **fit** to collapse.*
- ready, liable, likely, about

fit verb
1 *We need to **fit** a new lock on the door.*
- install, put in place, position
2 *This key doesn't **fit** the lock.*
*He **fits** the description of the wanted criminal.*
- match, correspond to, go together with, tally with
3 *Her speech perfectly **fitted** the occasion.*
- be suitable for, be appropriate to, suit

fit noun
*My friend and I had a **fit** of the giggles.*
- attack, bout, outburst, spell

fitting adjective
*Scoring the winning goal was a **fitting** end to his career.*
- suitable, appropriate, apt, proper
OPPOSITE inappropriate

fix verb
1 *The soldier **fixed** a bayonet to the end of his rifle.*
- fasten, attach, connect, join, link
2 *We **fixed** the tent poles in the ground.*
- set, secure, make firm, stabilize
3 *Let's **fix** a time for the party.*
- decide on, agree on, set, arrange, settle, determine, specify, finalize
4 (*informal*) *Dad says he can **fix** my bike.*
- repair, mend, sort, put right

fix noun
(*informal*) *Can you help me? I'm in a **fix**.*
- difficulty, mess, predicament, plight
- (*informal*) jam, hole

fizz verb
*The lemonade **fizzed** when I opened the bottle.*
- hiss, bubble, foam, froth

fizzy adjective
*Could I have a bottle of **fizzy** water, please?*
- sparkling, bubbly, effervescent, gassy, foaming
OPPOSITE still

flabby adjective
*This exercise is good for **flabby** thighs.*
- fat, fleshy, sagging, slack, loose, floppy, limp
OPPOSITE firm

flag noun
*The street was decorated with **flags** for the carnival.*
- banner, pennant, streamer
- The flag of a regiment is its colours or standard.
- A flag flown on a ship is an ensign.
- Decorative strips of small flags are bunting.

flag verb
*By evening, our energy was starting to **flag**.*
- diminish, lessen, decrease, decline, weaken, slump, fade, dwindle, wane

flap verb
*The sail **flapped** in the wind.*
- flutter, sway, swing, wave about, thrash about

flare verb
to flare up
1 *The fire **flared up** when we blew on it.*
* blaze, burn brightly, flame
2 *My sister **flares up** at the slightest thing.*
* become angry, lose your temper

flash verb
*We saw a light **flash** from an upstairs window.*
* shine, beam, blaze, flare, glare, gleam, glint, flicker, glimmer, sparkle
FOR OTHER WAYS TO DESCRIBE LIGHT
SEE **light** noun

flash noun
*There were **flashes** of lightning in the sky.*
* blaze, flare, beam, ray, shaft, burst, gleam, glint, flicker, glimmer, sparkle

flat adjective
1 *You need a **flat** surface to write on.*
* even, level, smooth, plane
* A common simile is as flat as a pancake.
OPPOSITE uneven
2 *I lay **flat** on the ground.*
* horizontal, outstretched, spread out
* To be lying face downwards is to be prone.
* To be lying face upwards is to be supine.
OPPOSITE upright
3 *The robot spoke in a **flat**, electronic voice.*
* dull, boring, lifeless, uninteresting, monotonous, tedious
OPPOSITE lively
4 *The front tyre of my bike was **flat**.*
* deflated, punctured
OPPOSITE inflated
5 *Our request met with a **flat** refusal.*
* outright, straight, positive, absolute, total, utter, point-blank

flat noun FOR PLACES WHERE PEOPLE LIVE
SEE **building**

flatten verb
1 *We **flattened** the crumpled map on the desk.*
* smooth, press, roll out, iron out
2 *The earthquake **flattened** several buildings.*
* demolish, destroy, knock down, pull down, level
3 *The young plants were **flattened** by the rain.*
* squash, crush, trample

flaunt verb
*She's always **flaunting** her expensive jewellery.*
* show off, display, parade, exhibit

flavour noun
1 *I don't like the **flavour** of raw onions.*
* taste, tang
FOR WAYS TO DESCRIBE FLAVOUR
SEE **food**
2 *Which **flavour** of ice cream do you like best?*
* kind, sort, variety

flavour verb
*The sauce was **flavoured** with garlic and herbs.*
* season, spice

flaw noun
1 *Pride was the only **flaw** in his character.*
* weakness, fault, shortcoming, failing, lapse
2 *I can see a **flaw** in your argument.*
* error, inaccuracy, mistake, slip
3 *There is a tiny **flaw** in this glass.*
* imperfection, defect, blemish, break, chip, crack

fleck noun
*There were a few **flecks** of paint on the carpet.*
* spot, speck, flake, dot, dab
SEE ALSO **bit**

flee verb
*When they heard the alarm, the robbers **fled**.*
* run away, bolt, fly, escape, get away, take off, hurry off
* (*informal*) clear off, make off, scarper

a b c d e **f** g h i j k l m n o p q r s t u v w x y z

fleet noun

- A fleet of boats or small ships is a flotilla.
- A fleet of warships is an armada.
- A military fleet belonging to a country is its navy.

fleeting adjective

*I only caught a **fleeting** glimpse of the badger.*
- brief, momentary, quick, short, passing
  OPPOSITE lengthy, lasting

flesh noun

- tissue, muscle, fat
- An animal's flesh used for food is meat.
- The decaying flesh of a dead animal is carrion.

flex noun

*Don't trip over the **flex** of the iron!*
- cable, lead, wire

flexible adjective

1 *I need a pair of trainers with **flexible** soles.*
- bendable, supple, pliable, bendy, elastic, springy
  OPPOSITE rigid, inflexible
2 *My working hours are very **flexible**.*
- adjustable, adaptable, variable, open
  OPPOSITE fixed

flicker verb

*The candlelight **flickered** in the draught.*
- twinkle, glimmer, waver, flutter, blink, shimmer

flight noun

1 *He is an expert in the history of **flight**.*
- flying, aviation, aeronautics
2 *No-one saw the king's **flight** from the battlefield.*
- escape, getaway, retreat

flimsy adjective

1 *The kite was so **flimsy** that it broke apart.*
- fragile, delicate, frail, brittle, weak, wobbly, shaky, rickety,
  OPPOSITE sturdy, robust

2 *The fairy wore a dress of the **flimsiest** silk.*
- thin, fine, light, lightweight, floaty

flinch verb

*He **flinched** as an arrow flew past his head.*
- back off, draw back, falter, recoil, shrink back, start, wince

fling verb

*I **flung** a stone into the pond.*
- throw, cast, sling, toss, hurl, pitch
- (informal) chuck, bung

flip verb

*We **flipped** a coin to decide who should go first.*
- toss, flick, spin

float verb

*We watched the twigs **float** gently down the river.*
- sail, drift, glide, slip, slide, waft

flock noun FOR GROUPS OF ANIMALS
SEE group

flock verb

*People **flocked** round to see what was happening.*
- crowd, gather, collect, herd, jostle

flood noun

1 *The **flood** of water swept away the bridge.*
- deluge, inundation, rush, torrent, spate
2 *The restaurant has received a **flood** of complaints.*
- succession, barrage, storm, volley

flood verb

1 *The river burst its banks and **flooded** the valley.*
- drown, swamp, inundate, submerge, immerse, engulf
2 *We have been **flooded** with entries for our competition.*
- overwhelm, swamp, besiege

floor noun

1 *The children in the audience sat on the **floor**.*
- ground, flooring, base
- A floor on a ship is a deck.
2 *Doreen's flat is on the top **floor**.*
- storey, level, tier, stage

a
b
c
d
e
f
g
h
i
j
k
l
m
n
o
p
q
r
s
t
u
v
w
x
y
z

flop verb

1 *I was so tired that I just **flopped** onto my bed.*
- collapse, drop, fall, slump

2 *The plants will **flop** if you don't water them.*
- dangle, droop, hang down, sag, wilt

3 (*informal*) *The first film **flopped**, but the sequel was a big hit.*
- be unsuccessful, fail, founder, fall flat

floppy adjective

*The dog had long, **floppy** ears.*
- droopy, limp, saggy, soft
  OPPOSITE stiff, rigid

flounder verb

*The soldiers **floundered** through the mud.*
- struggle, stumble, stagger, fumble, wallow, blunder, falter

flourish verb

1 *My tomato plants are **flourishing** this year.*
- grow well, thrive, bloom, blossom, flower
  OPPOSITE die

2 *Sales on our website have continued to **flourish**.*
- be successful, do well, prosper, thrive, boom, succeed, progress, develop, increase
  OPPOSITE fail

3 *Ted **flourished** a newspaper to attract my attention.*
- wave, brandish, wield, shake

flow verb

*The rain water **flowed** along the gutter.*
- run, stream, pour, glide
- To flow slowly is to dribble, drip, ooze, seep, or trickle.
- To flow fast is to cascade, gush, or sweep.
- To flow with sudden force is to spurt or squirt.
- To flow over the edge of something is to overflow or spill.
- When blood flows from a wound, it bleeds.
- When the tide flows out, it ebbs.

flow noun

1 *It's hard work rowing against the **flow**.*
- current, tide, drift

2 *There was a steady **flow** of water into the pond.*
- stream, flood, cascade, gush, rush, spate

flower noun

WORD WEB
- A single flower is a bloom.
- A mass of small flowers growing together is blossom.
- Flowers in a vase are an arrangement.
- A bunch of flowers arranged for a special occasion is a bouquet, posy, or spray.
- Flowers arranged in a circle are a garland or wreath.
- A person who sells and arranges flowers is a florist.

SOME WILD FLOWERS
bluebell, buttercup, catkin, cornflower, cowslip, daisy, dandelion, foxglove, harebell, orchid, poppy, primrose

SOME POPULAR CULTIVATED FLOWERS
azalea, begonia, carnation, chrysanthemum, crocus, cyclamen, daffodil, dahlia, forget-me-not, freesia, fuschia, geranium, gladiolus, hollyhock, hyacinth, iris, lilac, lily, lupin, marigold, nasturtium, pansy, peony, petunia, phlox, rose, snowdrop, sunflower, tulip, violet, water lily

THE MAIN PARTS OF A FLOWER ARE
anther, filament, ovary, petal, pistil, pollen, sepal, stamen, stigma, style

flower verb

*Most plants **flower** in the summer.*
- bloom, blossom, bud

fluffy adjective

*Four **fluffy** ducklings were swimming in the pond.*
- feathery, downy, furry, fuzzy, hairy, woolly, shaggy, soft

fluid noun
*An oily **fluid** oozed from the pipe.*
- liquid, solution, juice, gas, vapour
OPPOSITE solid

fluke noun
*It was a **fluke** that the ball went into the net.*
- chance, accident, stroke of good luck

flush verb
*Rory **flushed** with embarrassment.*
- blush, go red, colour, redden, burn

flustered adjective
*I get **flustered** when I have to read in assembly.*
- confused, upset, bothered, agitated, unsettled, ruffled
- (*informal*) rattled
OPPOSITE calm

flutter verb
*A moth **fluttered** about the light bulb.*
- flap, beat, flicker, quiver, tremble, vibrate

fly noun FOR VARIOUS INSECTS
SEE **insect**

fly verb
1 *Two swallows were **flying** high in the sky.*
- glide, swoop, flit, hover, float
FOR WAYS TO DESCRIBE HOW BIRDS MOVE
SEE **bird**
2 *Suddenly the ladybird **flew** into the air.*
- rise, soar, mount, take off
3 *The ship was **flying** the British flag.*
- display, show, hoist, raise
4 *Doesn't time **fly**!*
- go quickly, pass quickly, rush by

foam noun
*The bath water was covered with pinkish **foam**.*
- bubbles, froth, suds, lather
- Foam made by sea water is surf or spume.

foam verb
*The mixture in the cauldron **foamed** and gurgled.*
- froth, bubble, fizz, boil, seethe, ferment, lather

focus noun
1 *Can you adjust the **focus** on your camera?*
- clarity, sharpness
2 *The new lion cubs were the **focus** of everyone's attention.*
- centre, focal point, target, core, pivot

focus verb
to focus on
*Our teacher wants us to **focus on** our spelling.*
- concentrate on, think about, examine, look at

fog noun
*The top of the mountain was covered with **fog**.*
- Thin fog is haze or mist.
- A thick mixture of fog and smoke is smog.

foggy adjective
1 *It was too **foggy** to see through the windows.*
- misty, hazy, murky, cloudy, smoggy
2 *My photo of the horses came out **foggy**.*
- blurred, fuzzy, indistinct, out of focus
OPPOSITE clear, in focus

foil verb
*The guard-dog **foiled** their plan to break into the house.*
- frustrate, thwart, block, prevent, obstruct, stop, check, halt

fold verb
***Fold** the paper along the dotted line.*
- bend, double over, crease, pleat

fold noun
1 *She smoothed the soft **folds** of her dress.*
- crease, furrow, layer
- A fold which is pressed into a garment is a pleat.
2 *The dog drove the sheep into the **fold**.*
- enclosure, pen

folder noun
*I keep all my art work in a **folder**.*
- file, binder, wallet, portfolio

a
b
c
d
e
f
g
h
i
j
k
l
m
n
o
p
q
r
s
t
u
v
w
x
y
z

follow verb

1 *Why does thunder always **follow** lightning?*
- come after, succeed, replace
OPPOSITE precede

2 *I think that car is **following** us!*
- go after, chase, pursue, track, trail, tail, stalk, hunt, shadow

3 ***Follow** this path until you reach the river.*
- go along, keep to

4 *I **followed** the instructions on the packet.*
- carry out, comply with, heed, obey, observe

5 *Which football team do you **follow**?*
- be a fan of, support

6 *We found it hard to **follow** what the creature was saying.*
- understand, comprehend, grasp, take in, catch

7 *Although we are the same age, it doesn't **follow** that we are friends.*
- mean, happen, result, ensue, arise, come about

follower noun

- Someone who follows you in a job is your successor.
- Someone who follows a person or animal to try to catch them is a hunter or pursuer.
- Someone who continually follows a person about is a stalker.
- Someone who follows a person's teaching is a disciple.
- Someone who follows a football team, etc., is a fan or supporter.

fond adjective

1 *Mrs Walker gave her pet poodle a **fond** kiss.*
- loving, tender, affectionate

2 *Anna had a **fond** hope that she would become a film star.*
- foolish, silly, unrealistic, fanciful

to be fond of
*I'm very **fond of** chocolate cake.*
- be keen on, be partial to, like, love

food noun

WORD WEB

*The banquet table was laid out with all kinds of **food**.*
- foodstuffs, rations, provisions, refreshments, eatables, nourishment, nutrition
(*informal*) grub, nosh
- The food that you normally eat or choose to eat is your diet.
- A diet which includes no meat is a vegetarian diet.
- A diet which includes no animal products is a vegan diet.
- Food which includes fish or shellfish is seafood.
- Foods made from milk, butter, cheese, or eggs are dairy foods.
- Food for farm animals is fodder.

FOR MEAT AND FOODS MADE FROM MEAT
SEE meat

SOME TYPES OF SEAFOOD
bloater, bream, caviare, cod, crab, eel, haddock, halibut, herring, kipper, lobster, mackerel, monkfish, mussels, oysters, pilchard, plaice, prawn, salmon, sardine, scampi, sea bass, shrimp, sole, sprat, trout, tuna, whelks, whitebait, whiting

SOME DAIRY FOODS
butter, cheese, cream, curds, custard, eggs, ice-cream, milk, yoghurt

FOR FRUITS AND VEGETABLES
SEE fruit, vegetable

FOODS MADE FROM FLOUR OR CEREALS
batter, biscuits, bread, bun, cornflakes, cracker, crispbread, muesli, noodles, oatcake, pancake, pastry, popcorn, porridge, ricecake, roll, scone, toast

SOME PREPARED DISHES OF FOOD
balti, bhaji, broth, casserole, chilli, chips, chop suey, chow mein, curry, dhal, fritters, goulash, houmous, hotpot, omelette, pakora, panini, pasta, pie, pizza, quiche, samosa, sandwich, soufflé, soup, stew, stir-fry, sushi

FOR TYPES OF PASTA
SEE pasta

SOME PUDDINGS AND OTHER SWEET FOODS

brownie, cake, chocolate, flan, gateau, honey, jam, jelly, marmalade, marzipan, meringue, mousse, muffin, sponge, steamed pudding, sugar, tart, treacle, trifle

SOME FLAVOURINGS AND SAUCES FOR FOOD

chilli, chutney, French dressing, garlic, gravy, herbs, ketchup, mayonnaise, mustard, pepper, pickle, salsa, salt, spice, vinegar

- Things like salt and pepper which you add to food are condiments or seasoning.

WRITING TIPS

You can use these words to describe **food**.

- to describe how it *LOOKS* or *FEELS*: chewy, creamy, crispy, crumbly, crunchy, dry, flaky, greasy, juicy, leathery, lumpy, milky, mushy, rubbery, runny, slimy, sloppy, smooth, soggy, soupy, spongy, sticky, stodgy, stringy, syrupy, velvety, watery
*The pudding was a **sloppy**, **watery** mess.*

- to describe how it *TASTES*: bitter, bland, fiery, flavourful, fresh, fruity, hot, mellow, mild, peppery, piquant, pungent, refreshing, salty, savoury, sharp, sour, spicy, strong, sugary, sweet, syrupy, tangy, tart, vinegary
*The sauce was **hot**, but not too* **spicy**.

FOR WAYS TO DESCRIBE HOW FOOD SMELLS

SEE **smell** verb

- to describe *FOOD YOU LIKE*: delicious, appetizing, tasty, tempting, mouth-watering, well-cooked (*informal*) scrummy, scrumptious, yummy
- Something specially tasty to eat is a delicacy.

- to describe *FOOD YOU DON'T LIKE*: disgusting, flavourless, indigestible, inedible, nauseating, stomach-turning, tasteless, unappetizing, uneatable; charred, mouldy, stale, undercooked (*informal*) yucky

fool noun

1 *Only a **fool** would believe that ridiculous story.*
- idiot, dope, ass, clown, halfwit, dimwit, dunce, simpleton, blockhead, buffoon, clot, dunderhead, imbecile, moron
- (*informal*) twit, chump, nitwit, nincompoop
2 (*old use*) *The king's **fool** entertained the court.*
- jester, clown

fool verb

*The spy **fooled** everyone with his disguises.*
- deceive, trick, mislead, hoax, dupe, hoodwink
- (*informal*) con, kid, have you on, take you in, pull the wool over your eyes

to fool about or **around**
*We were told not to **fool about** in the swimming pool.*
- play about, mess about, misbehave

foolish adjective

*It would be **foolish** to stand too close to the lions.*
- stupid, silly, idiotic, senseless, ridiculous, nonsensical, unwise, ill-advised, half-witted, unintelligent, absurd, crazy, mad, hare-brained
- (*informal*) daft
OPPOSITE sensible

foot noun

1 *Rhona walked on the sand in her bare feet.*
- The foot of an animal that has claws is a paw.
- The foot of a cow, deer, or horse is a hoof.
- A pig's foot is a trotter.
- A bird's feet are its claws.
- The feet of a bird of prey are its talons.

a
b
c
d
e
f
g
h
i
j
k
l
m
n
o
p
q
r
s
t
u
v
w
x
y
z

a
b
c
d
e
f
g
h
i
j
k
l
m
n
o
p
q
r
s
t
u
v
w
x
y
z

2 *We set up camp at the **foot** of the mountain.*

- base, bottom

football noun

> **WORD WEB**
>
> - Football is also known as soccer.
> - Someone who plays football is a footballer.
> - Football is played on a field or pitch in a ground, park, or stadium.
>
> MEMBERS OF A FOOTBALL TEAM
> captain, defender, fullback, forward, goalkeeper or (*informal*) goalie, midfielder, striker, substitute, sweeper, winger
>
> OTHER PEOPLE INVOLVED IN FOOTBALL
> ballboy or ballgirl, coach, linesman, manager, referee
>
> SOME MOVES A FOOTBALLER MIGHT MAKE
> chip, dribble, dummy, header, kick, mazy run, miss, pass, score, shot, tackle, volley
>
> FOR WAYS TO HIT OR KICK A BALL
> SEE **ball**
>
> SOME OTHER TERMS USED IN FOOTBALL
> corner, crossbar, deflection, dugout, equalizer, extra time, final whistle, foul, free kick, goal, goalposts, half-time, kick-off, net, offside, penalty, penalty shootout, red or yellow card, sending off, throw-in

footprint noun
*We followed the **footprints** in the snow.*

- footmark, track, print
- The track left by an animal is also called a spoor.

footstep noun
*I heard **footsteps** crunching up the garden path.*

- step, footfall, tread

forbidden adjective
*Skateboarding is **forbidden** in the playground.*

- banned, barred, prohibited, disallowed, outlawed
  OPPOSITE allowed

forbidding adjective
*The haunted tower had a dark, **forbidding** look.*

- gloomy, grim, menacing, ominous, stern, threatening, unfriendly, unwelcoming
  OPPOSITE friendly

force noun
1 *The firefighters had to use **force** to open the door.*

- strength, power, might, muscle, vigour, effort, energy

2 *The **force** of the explosion broke all the windows.*

- impact, effect, shock, intensity

3 *The soldiers are part of a peace-keeping **force**.*

- group, unit, team, corps, army, troops

force verb
1 *The slaves were **forced** to work in the mines.*

- compel, make, order, require, oblige, pressurize, coerce

2 *The king **forced** a new law upon the country.*

- impose, inflict

3 *The firefighters had to **force** the door.*

- break open, burst open, prise open, smash, wrench
- (*informal*) yank

forceful adjective
*My great aunt has a very **forceful** personality.*

- strong, powerful, dynamic, commanding, assertive
  OPPOSITE weak

forecast noun
*The weather **forecast** is for snow tomorrow.*

- outlook, prediction

forecast verb
*Snow has been **forecast** for Tuesday.*

- foresee, foretell, predict

foreground noun
I took a photo of our house with my mum in the foreground.
- front
OPPOSITE background

foreign adjective
1 *Lots of foreign tourists visit Edinburgh in the summer.*
- overseas, international
OPPOSITE native, domestic
2 *I like travelling to foreign countries.*
- overseas, distant, faraway, exotic, remote, far-flung
3 *The idea of work was completely foreign to the princess.*
- unnatural, unfamiliar, strange, alien

foreigner noun
Many foreigners have come to live in the city.
- overseas visitor, stranger, outsider, newcomer
- A formal word is alien.
- A word describing people who come from abroad to live in a country is immigrant.

foremost adjective
Hans Christian Andersen was one of the foremost writers of fairy tales.
- best known, leading, most important, greatest, principal, chief, major

foresee verb
Do you foresee any problems with our plan?
- anticipate, expect, predict, forecast, prophesy, foretell

forest noun FOR PLACES WHERE TREES GROW
SEE **tree**

foretell verb
1 *The fortune-teller foretold that I would go on a voyage.*
- predict, prophesy, forecast, foresee
2 *The cold wind foretold a change in the weather.*
- herald, signify

forever adverb
Timmy is forever complaining about something.
- constantly, continually, always, perpetually

forge verb
1 *The blacksmith forged a new horseshoe.*
- cast, hammer out, beat into shape
2 *That signature has been forged.*
- fake, copy, counterfeit
to forge ahead
After a slow start, the rowing team was forging ahead.
- advance, make progress, make headway

forgery noun
One of these paintings is a forgery.
- fake, copy, imitation, reproduction, replica
- (*informal*) phoney

forget verb
1 *I forgot my toothbrush when I packed my suitcase.*
- leave out, leave behind, overlook
2 *I forgot to switch off the computer.*
- omit, neglect, fail
OPPOSITE remember

forgetful adjective
As the professor grew older, he became more forgetful.
- absent-minded, careless, inattentive, oblivious, vague, dreamy, lax

forgive verb
Please forgive me for being so rude.
- excuse, pardon, let off, overlook, spare

fork verb
The path ahead widened and then forked into two.
- split, branch, divide

forlorn adjective
Asha felt forlorn after her friends had left.
- sad, unhappy, lonely, dejected, miserable, sorrowful
OPPOSITE cheerful

form noun

1 *I made out the **form** of a man through the mist.*
- shape, figure, outline, silhouette

2 *Ice is a **form** of water.*
- kind, sort, type, variety

3 *My brother moves up into a higher **form** next term.*
- class, year, grade, set

4 *If you want to join the club, sign this **form**.*
- document, paper, sheet, questionnaire

form verb

1 *The sculptor **formed** the clay into the shape of a bird.*
- shape, mould, model, fashion, work, cast

2 *My friends and I have **formed** a chess club.*
- set up, establish, found, create, start

3 *Icicles had **formed** on the roof of the cave.*
- appear, develop, grow, emerge, take shape

formal adjective

1 *I was invited to the **formal** opening of the museum.*
- official, ceremonial

2 *The letter was written in a very **formal** style.*
- correct, proper, conventional, dignified, solemn
- OPPOSITE informal, casual

former adjective

*In **former** times, the castle was surrounded by a moat.*
- earlier, previous, past, bygone

formula noun

*The inventor was working on a new **formula** for toothpaste.*
- recipe, prescription

forsake verb

*Ben knew that his old sheepdog would never **forsake** him.*
- abandon, desert, leave

fort noun

*A few soldiers were left to defend the **fort**.*
- fortress, fortification, stronghold, castle, citadel, tower
- SEE ALSO **castle**

fortify verb

1 *The townspeople built fences to **fortify** the town.*
- defend, protect, secure, reinforce

2 *A good breakfast will **fortify** you for the morning.*
- strengthen, support, sustain, bolster, boost, invigorate
- OPPOSITE weaken

fortunate adjective

*We were **fortunate** to have good weather.*
- lucky, in luck
- OPPOSITE unfortunate, unlucky

fortune noun

1 *By good **fortune**, I stumbled across a secret doorway.*
- chance, luck, accident, fate

2 *The millionairess left her **fortune** to charity.*
- wealth, riches, possessions, property, assets, estate
- (informal) millions

fortune-teller noun

*The **fortune-teller** gazed in her crystal ball.*
- clairvoyant, soothsayer, seer

forward adjective

1 *We need to do some **forward** planning for the camping trip.*
- advance, early, future

2 *Would it be too **forward** to send him an email?*
- bold, cheeky, brash, familiar, impudent, presumptuous

forwards adverb

1 *The queue moved **forwards** very slowly.*
- on, onwards, along

2 *Will you all face **forwards**, please.*
- to or toward the front, ahead
- OPPOSITE backwards

a b c d e f g h i j k l m n o p q r s t u v w x y z

fossil noun

WORD WEB

*Isla found a **fossil** on the beach.*
SOME TYPES OF FOSSIL
ammonite, dinosaur bone, petrified wood, trilobyte
- A person who looks for fossils is a fossil-hunter.
- A person who studies fossils is a palaeontologist.

foster verb
*My aunt has decided to **foster** a child.*
- bring up, rear, raise, care for, look after, take care of
- To adopt a child is to make the child legally a full member of your family.

foul adjective
1 *The knight fainted at the **foul** smell of the dragon's breath.*
- disgusting, revolting, repulsive, rotten, stinking, offensive, unpleasant, loathsome, nasty, horrible, vile
OPPOSITE pleasant
2 *The walls and floor of the dungeon were **foul**.*
- dirty, unclean, filthy, mucky, messy
OPPOSITE clean, pure
3 *The player was sent off for using **foul** language.*
- rude, offensive, insulting, abusive, improper, indecent, obscene
4 *The referee blew her whistle for a **foul** tackle.*
- illegal, prohibited, unfair
OPPOSITE fair

found verb
*The school was **founded** a hundred years ago.*
- establish, set up, start, begin, create, originate, initiate, institute

foundation noun
1 *There's no **foundation** for the rumour they are spreading.*
- basis, grounds
2 *It's a hundred years since the **foundation** of the museum.*
- founding, beginning, establishment, setting up

founder verb
1 *The ship struck a rock and **foundered**.*
- go under, sink, submerge
2 *The project **foundered** because of lack of money.*
- fail, fall through, collapse, come to nothing
- (*informal*) fold, flop, bomb

fountain noun
*A **fountain** of water shot into the air.*
- jet, spout, spray, spring

fox noun
- A female fox is a vixen.
- A young fox is a cub.
- A fox lives in an earth.

fox verb
*The last clue in the crossword **foxed** me completely.*
- puzzle, baffle, bewilder, mystify, perplex
- (*informal*) flummox, floor

fraction noun
*Only a **fraction** of an iceberg shows above the water.*
- bit, part, portion

fracture verb
*Steve fell his bike and **fractured** his wrist.*
- break, crack, split, splinter

fracture noun
*The X-ray showed a **fracture** in the bone.*
- break, breakage, crack, split, fissure

fragile adjective
*Fossil dinosaur bones are very **fragile**.*
- breakable, delicate, frail, brittle, easily damaged, weak
OPPOSITE strong

fragment noun
1 *I dug up a **fragment** of broken pottery.*
- bit, piece, chip, sliver, shard
2 *She overheard **fragments** of their conversation.*
- part, portion, scrap, snippet

fragrant adjective
*The room was **fragrant** with the smell of roses.*
- sweet-smelling, perfumed, scented, aromatic

frail adjective
1 *My grandad felt **frail** after his illness.*
- weak, infirm, feeble
2 *That step-ladder looks a bit **frail**.*
- flimsy, fragile, delicate, rickety, unsound
OPPOSITE strong, robust

frame noun
1 *The **frame** of the house is made of timber.*
- framework, structure, shell, skeleton
2 *I put the photo of my friend in a **frame**.*
- mount, mounting, surround, border, setting, edging

frank adjective
*We had a very **frank** discussion about money.*
- honest, direct, sincere, genuine, candid, outspoken, plain, blunt, straightforward, truthful
OPPOSITE insincere

frantic adjective
1 *I was **frantic** with worry when our kitten got lost.*
- beside yourself, fraught, desperate, distraught, hysterical, worked up, berserk
2 *There was **frantic** activity on the day of the wedding.*
- excited, hectic, frenzied, feverish, wild, mad
OPPOSITE calm

fraud noun
1 *The bank manager was found guilty of **fraud**.*
- deceit, deception, dishonesty, swindling, cheating
2 *The prize draw was just a **fraud**—no-one won anything.*
- swindle, trick, hoax, pretence, sham
- (*informal*) con, scam
3 *The salesman turned out to be a **fraud**.*
- cheat, swindler, trickster, hoaxer
- (*informal*) con man, phoney

fraudulent adjective
*Beware of **fraudulent** email messages.*
- dishonest, illegal, criminal, corrupt, swindling, bogus, sham
- (*informal*) crooked, phoney
OPPOSITE honest

frayed adjective
*The old woman wore a cloak of **frayed** tartan cloth.*
- tattered, ragged, worn, threadbare

free adjective
1 *You are **free** to wander anywhere in the building.*
- able, allowed, permitted, at liberty
OPPOSITE restricted
2 *After ten years in jail, the prisoners were **free** at last.*
- freed, liberated, released, emancipated, at large, on the loose
- A common simile is as free as a bird.
OPPOSITE imprisoned, enslaved
3 *I got a **free** drink with my sandwich.*
- complimentary, free of charge, gratis, on the house
4 *Are you **free** this weekend?*
- available, unoccupied
OPPOSITE busy, occupied
5 *The bathroom is **free** now.*
- available, unoccupied, vacant, empty
OPPOSITE engaged
6 *Uncle Jack is very **free** with his money.*
- generous, lavish, liberal
OPPOSITE mean

free verb
1 *The soldiers **freed** the prisoners of war.*
- release, liberate, set free, deliver
- To free slaves is to emancipate them.
- To free prisoners by paying money to the captors is to ransom them.
OPPOSITE imprison
2 *We **freed** the dogs and let them run about.*
- loose, turn loose, let go, untie, unchain
OPPOSITE confine
3 *The escapologist tried to **free** his arms from the chains.*
- undo, untangle, work loose

freedom noun
*The animals have a lot of **freedom** in the safari park.*
- liberty, independence

freeze verb
1 *Water begins to **freeze** at 0°C.*
- become ice, ice over, harden, solidify
2 *If you **freeze** food, you can store it for a long time.*
- deep-freeze, chill, refrigerate
3 *Season ticket prices have been **frozen** for another year.*
- fix, hold, peg, keep as they are

freezing adjective
*It's **freezing** cold outside in winter.*
- chilly, frosty, icy, wintry, raw, bitter

frequent adjective
1 *I send **frequent** email messages to my friends.*
- numerous, constant, continual, recurring, recurrent, repeated, countless
OPPOSITE infrequent
2 *Badgers are **frequent** visitors to the garden.*
- regular, habitual, common, familiar, persistent
OPPOSITE rare

frequent verb
*Office workers **frequent** the park at lunchtime.*
- visit, attend, haunt

fresh adjective
1 *This pudding is made with **fresh** fruit.*
- natural, raw, unprocessed
2 *The shop bakes **fresh** bread every day.*
- new
OPPOSITE old, stale
3 *Sally went outside to get some **fresh** air.*
- clean, cool, crisp, refreshing
OPPOSITE stuffy
4 *Have you put **fresh** sheets on the bed?*
- new, clean, laundered, washed
OPPOSITE dirty
5 *Having a shower makes me feel nice and **fresh**.*
- refreshed, revived, restored, invigorated
6 *We need some **fresh** ideas for our magazine.*
- new, original, different, novel, innovative
OPPOSITE old

fret verb
*My sister is **fretting** about her piano exam.*
- worry, fuss, agonize, become stressed, get worked up

friction noun
1 *You can make fire from the **friction** of rubbing sticks together.*
- rubbing, chafing, abrasion
2 *There was some **friction** between the two teams.*
- conflict, disagreement, hostility, rivalry, antagonism, discord, quarrelling

friend noun
*I am inviting four **friends** to my birthday party.*
- companion, comrade
- (*informal*) mate, pal, buddy, chum
- A friend you play games with is a playmate.
- A friend you work with or live with is your partner.
- A friend you write to but don't normally meet is a penfriend.
- A friend you know only slightly is an acquaintance.
OPPOSITE enemy

friendly adjective
1 *Our neighbour's pet dog is very **friendly**.*
- affectionate, loving, good-natured, likeable, amiable, approachable, kind-hearted, kindly, amicable, genial, sociable, outgoing, sympathetic
2 *Those two are very **friendly** with each other.*
- close, familiar, intimate
- (*informal*) pally, chummy
3 *I like this cafe—it has a very **friendly** atmosphere.*
- warm, welcoming, hospitable, cordial, neighbourly
OPPOSITE unfriendly

a
b
c
d
e
f
g
h
i
j
k
l
m
n
o
p
q
r
s
t
u
v
w
x
y
z

friendship noun
*Their **friendship** has lasted for many years.*
- closeness, affection, fondness, familiarity, intimacy, attachment, comradeship, fellowship
- A formal friendship between countries or parties is an alliance.
OPPOSITE hostility

fright noun
1 *The girl jumped up in **fright** and began to scream.*
- fear, terror, alarm, horror, panic, dread
2 *The explosion gave us an awful **fright**!*
- scare, shock, surprise, start, turn, jolt

frighten verb
*Sorry—I didn't mean to **frighten** you.*
- scare, terrify, startle, alarm, shock, panic, petrify

frightened adjective
*Mia always felt **frightened** in the dark.*
- afraid, scared, terrified, alarmed, fearful, panicky, petrified
SEE ALSO **afraid**

frightening adjective
*The ghost story she told was quite **frightening**.*
- terrifying, horrifying, scary, alarming, nightmarish, chilling, spine-chilling, hair-raising, bloodcurdling, chilling, eerie, sinister, fearsome
- (*informal*) creepy, spooky

frill noun
1 *My party dress has a **frill** round the hem.*
- ruffle, ruff, flounce, fringe
2 *Our hotel was basic with no **frills**.*
- extra, luxury

fringe noun
1 *My scarf has a beaded **fringe** at each end.*
- border, edging, frill, trimming
2 *We live on the **fringe** of the town.*
- edge, border, margin, outskirts

frisky adjective
*The new lion cubs in the zoo are very **frisky**.*
- playful, lively, high-spirited, sprightly

fritter verb
to fritter away
*Luke **frittered away** his pocket money on sweets.*
- waste, squander, spend unwisely, use up

frivolous adjective
1 *We were in a **frivolous** mood before we went on holiday.*
- playful, lively, high-spirited, jaunty
2 *Don't waste my time asking **frivolous** questions.*
- foolish, silly, ridiculous, shallow, superficial, pointless, unimportant, trivial, petty
OPPOSITE serious

frock noun FOR ITEMS OF CLOTHING
SEE **clothes**

frog noun
- A young frog or toad is a tadpole.
- Frogs' eggs are frogspawn.
- The sound a frog makes is a croak or ribbet.

frolic verb
*Lambs were **frolicking** in the field.*
- jump about, leap about, bound, caper, prance, gambol, romp, skip

front noun
1 *We stood at the **front** of the queue.*
- head, start, beginning, lead, top
2 *The **front** of the house was painted white.*
- face, facing, frontage, facade
- The front of a ship is the bow or prow.
- The front of a picture is the foreground.
OPPOSITE back

front adjective
1 *The **front** runners came into sight round the corner.*
- first, leading, most advanced
OPPOSITE back

2 *The horse had injured one of its **front** legs.*
- fore
  OPPOSITE back, rear, hind

frontier noun
*We crossed the **frontier** between France and Belgium.*
- border, boundary

frosty adjective
1 *It was a clear, **frosty** night.*
- cold, crisp, icy, freezing, wintry
2 *The shopkeeper gave us a **frosty** stare.*
- unfriendly, unwelcoming, cold, cool, stony
  OPPOSITE warm

froth noun
*I like a lot of **froth** on my hot chocolate.*
- foam, bubbles, head
- The froth on top of soapy water is lather or suds.
- Dirty froth is scum.

frown noun
*On Christmas Eve, Scrooge had a **frown** on his face.*
- scowl, glare, grimace, glower, black look

FOR OTHER FACIAL EXPRESSIONS

SEE **expression**

frown verb
*The witch **frowned** when her spell didn't work.*
- scowl, glare, grimace, glower, knit your brow, look sullen

frugal adjective
1 *Mr Skinflint was always **frugal** with his money.*
- thrifty, sparing, economical, prudent
  OPPOSITE wasteful, spendthrift
2 *Cinderella ate a **frugal** meal of bread crusts.*
- meagre, paltry, plain, simple
  OPPOSITE lavish

fruit noun

WORD WEB

SOME COMMON VARIETIES OF FRUIT
apple, apricot, avocado, banana, bilberry, blackberry or bramble, blackcurrant, blueberry, cherry, coconut, cranberry, damson, date, fig, gooseberry, grape, guava, kiwi fruit, loganberry, lychee, mango, melon, nectarine, pawpaw or papaya, peach, pear, pineapple, plum, pomegranate, quince, raspberry, redcurrant, rosehip, sloe, strawberry, tomato

CITRUS FRUITS
clementine, grapefruit, kumquat, lemon, lime, mandarin, orange, satsuma, tangerine

DRIED FRUITS
currant, prune, raisin, sultana
- Rhubarb is not a fruit, although it is often eaten like one.
- A person who sells fruit and vegetables is a greengrocer.

fruitful adjective
*Did you have a **fruitful** shopping trip?*
- successful, productive, useful, worthwhile, profitable, rewarding
  OPPOSITE fruitless

fruitless adjective
*They spent a **fruitless** morning searching for clues.*
- unsuccessful, unprofitable, unproductive, futile, pointless, useless, vain
  OPPOSITE fruitful, successful

frustrate verb
1 *It was **frustrating** to have to wait in the long queue.*
- exasperate, discourage, dispirit, irritate
2 *Our plan for the day was **frustrated** by the weather.*
- block, foil, thwart, defeat, check, hinder, prevent

fry verb
FOR WAYS TO COOK THINGS
SEE **cook** verb

a b c d e **f** g h i j k l m n o p q r s t u v w x y z

fugitive noun
*Police searched everywhere for the **fugitives**.*
- runaway, escapee, outlaw, deserter
- Someone who is a fugitive from war or persecution is a refugee.

fulfil verb
1 *She **fulfilled** her ambition to play at Wimbledon.*
- achieve, realize, accomplish, attain, carry out, complete, succeed in
2 *To join the club, you must **fulfil** these conditions.*
- meet, satisfy, conform to

full adjective
1 *My suitcase is **full** to the brim.*
- filled, loaded, topped up
  OPPOSITE empty
2 *The shopping centre was **full** on Saturday.*
- busy, crowded, jammed, packed, crammed, congested
  OPPOSITE empty
3 *The detective gave a **full** account of his findings.*
- complete, detailed, comprehensive, thorough, exhaustive
  OPPOSITE incomplete
4 *The horses were galloping at **full** speed.*
- top, maximum, greatest, highest
  OPPOSITE minimum
5 *The wedding dress has a very **full** skirt.*
- wide, broad, loose
  OPPOSITE tight

fun noun
*We had great **fun** at the beach on our holiday.*
- amusement, diversion, enjoyment, entertainment, games, jokes, laughter, merriment, play, pleasure, recreation, sport

to make fun of someone
*It was cruel to **make fun of** her when she fell over.*
- jeer at, laugh at, mock, ridicule, taunt, tease

function noun
1 *The **function** of a vet is to cure sick animals.*
- duty, role, task, job, responsibility, purpose
2 *The hall is being used for an official **function**.*
- event, occasion, party, reception

function verb
*This camera doesn't **function** properly.*
- work, go, operate, run, perform

fundamental adjective
*He taught me the **fundamental** rules of chess.*
- basic, elementary, essential, important, main, necessary, principal

funds plural noun
*The school used some of its **funds** to buy a minibus.*
- money, cash, savings, capital, reserves

funny adjective
1 *There are some very **funny** jokes in the film.*
- amusing, humorous, comic, comical, hilarious, witty, entertaining, diverting
- (*informal*) hysterical, priceless
  OPPOSITE serious
2 *There's a **funny** smell in here.*
- strange, odd, peculiar, curious, puzzling, weird, queer, bizarre

fur noun
*Arctic foxes have thick white **fur** in the winter*
- hair, coat, hide, pelt

furious adjective
1 *The manager was **furious** when his team lost.*
- angry, mad, enraged, infuriated, incensed, livid, fuming, raging, seething
2 *The elves worked at a **furious** rate to finish their work.*
- frantic, hectic, frenzied, extreme, intense
  OPPOSITE calm

furniture noun

WORD WEB

SOME ITEMS OF FURNITURE
armchair, bed, bookcase, bureau, chair, chest of drawers, coffee table, couch, cupboard, desk, dresser, dressing table, filing cabinet, settee, sideboard, sofa, sofabed, stool, table, wardrobe
- The soft covering on a chair or sofa is upholstery.
- Old and valuable pieces of furniture are antiques.

furrow noun
*The tractor wheels had made deep **furrows** in the mud.*
- groove, rut, ditch, channel, trench

furry adjective
*A small, **furry** creature was curled inside the box.*
- hairy, fleecy, woolly, fuzzy, downy, feathery

further adjective
*Look on our website for **further** information.*
- more, extra, additional, supplementary

furtive adjective
*The spy cast a **furtive** glance around the room.*
- secretive, stealthy, surreptitious, underhand, crafty, sneaky, sly

fury noun
1 *The **fury** of the creature showed in its eyes.*
- anger, rage, wrath, indignation
2 *There was no shelter from the **fury** of the storm.*
- ferocity, fierceness, intensity, severity, violence, turbulence, savagery

fuse verb
*The metals had **fused** together into a solid mass.*
- blend, combine, merge, unite, join, melt

- To fuse metals together when you are making or mending something is to solder or weld them.

fuss noun
*There was a lot of **fuss** when the queen arrived.*
- bother, commotion, excitement, trouble, hullabaloo

fuss verb
*Please don't **fuss**!*
- worry, fret, bother, get worked up

fussy adjective
1 *Our cat is **fussy** about her food.*
- finicky, hard to please, particular
- (*informal*) choosy, picky
- An informal name for a fussy person is a fusspot.
2 *I don't like clothes with **fussy** designs.*
- fancy, elaborate, ornate, florid

futile adjective
*They made a **futile** attempt to put out the fire.*
- fruitless, pointless, unsuccessful, useless, ineffectual, vain, wasted
OPPOSITE successful

future noun
*She has a bright **future** as a tennis player.*
- outlook, prospects
OPPOSITE past

fuzzy adjective
1 *The TV picture has gone **fuzzy**.*
- blurred, bleary, unfocused, unclear, indistinct, hazy, cloudy
OPPOSITE clear
2 *Mia was wearing a **fuzzy** cardigan.*
- fluffy, frizzy, furry, woolly, fleecy

a b c d e **f** g h i j k l m n o p q r s t u v w x y z

Gg

a
b
c
d
e
f
g
h
i
j
k
l
m
n
o
p
q
r
s
t
u
v
w
x
y
z

gadget noun
My pocket torch is a handy little gadget.
- tool, instrument, implement, device, contraption, gizmo

gain verb
1 *Martha gained a reputation as an excellent cook.*
- get, acquire, obtain, earn, win
OPPOSITE lose
2 *We gained our target of raising £200.*
- reach, get to, arrive at, achieve, attain

game noun
1 *My favourite game is hide-and-seek.*
- amusement, pastime, sport, activity, recreation
2 *The big game is on this Saturday.*
- match, contest, competition, tournament

 WORD WEB

SOME BOARD AND TABLE GAMES
backgammon, bagatelle, battleships, billiards, bingo, cards, chess, Chinese checkers, cribbage, dice, dominoes, draughts, go, hangman, lotto, ludo, ping-pong, pool, snakes and ladders, snooker, solitaire, table tennis, tiddlywinks

FOR NAMES OF CARD GAMES
SEE **card**

PARTY GAMES
charades, hide-and-seek, I-spy, musical chairs, pass the parcel

PLAYGROUND AND OTHER OUTDOOR GAMES
conkers, hopscotch, leapfrog, marbles, skittles, tag
FOR MORE INDOOR AND OUTDOOR GAMES
SEE **sport**

gang noun
1 *The sea was swarming with gangs of pirates.*
- group, band, crowd, pack, set, mob
2 *A gang of workmen dug a hole in the road.*
- team, unit, crew, squad, party

gap noun
1 *The animals escaped through a gap in the fence.*
- opening, space, hole, breach, break, crack, rift
2 *She returned to work after a gap of two years.*
- break, interval, interruption, pause, lull

gaping adjective
The meteor left a gaping hole in the ground.
- wide, broad, yawning, vast, cavernous

garden noun
- A small area of garden is a plot or patch.
- A rented garden for growing vegetables is an allotment.
- A garden planted with trees is an orchard.
- A formal word for gardening is horticulture.
- A word meaning 'to do with gardens or gardening' is horticultural.
FOR TOOLS USED FOR GARDENING
SEE **tool**

garment noun SEE **clothes**

gas noun
The mixture gave off an evil-smelling gas.
- vapour, fumes

gash noun
*The broken glass made a nasty **gash** in my foot.*
- cut, slash, wound, slit

gasp verb
*At the end of the race we lay **gasping** for breath.*
- gulp, pant

gate noun
*People waited at the **gate** to be let in.*
- gateway, doorway, entrance, portal

gather verb
1 *A crowd **gathered** to watch the performers.*
- assemble, collect, come together, congregate
  OPPOSITE disperse
2 *The captain **gathered** her team to give them a talk.*
- bring together, round up, muster
3 *We **gathered** daisies to make into chains.*
- pick, pluck, collect, harvest
4 *I **gather** that you've been on holiday.*
- understand, hear, learn, believe

gathering noun
*There was a family **gathering** for granny's birthday.*
- assembly, meeting, crowd, party, get-together

gaudy adjective
*The newsreader wore a rather **gaudy** tie.*
- flashy, showy, loud, glaring, garish, lurid

gaunt adjective
*The sorceress had a **gaunt** face and stringy hair.*
- haggard, drawn, thin, skinny, scraggy, scrawny, wasted, skeletal

gauge verb
*They're trying to **gauge** the size of the volcano.*
- measure, calculate, judge, assess, estimate, reckon

gaze verb
*The dog **gazed** hungrily at the food.*
- stare, look, gape

gear noun
*We put our fishing **gear** in the back of the car.*
- equipment, stuff, things, paraphernalia, tackle

gem noun
*The crown was made of solid gold, studded with **gems**.*
- jewel, precious stone
  FOR NAMES OF GEM STONES
  SEE **jewel, jewellery**

general adjective
1 *There was a **general** air of gloom about the abbey.*
- widespread, extensive, broad, sweeping, overall, prevalent
2 *I've only got a **general** idea of where we are.*
- rough, approximate, indefinite, vague, loose

generally adverb
*I **generally** travel to school by bus.*
- usually, normally, as a rule, chiefly, mostly, mainly, commonly, on the whole

generate verb
*Our website has **generated** a lot of interest.*
- create, produce, bring about, give rise to

generous adjective
1 *It was **generous** of you to give me your seat.*
- unselfish, charitable, kind-hearted
  OPPOSITE selfish
2 *We each got a **generous** helping of ice-cream.*
- ample, large, lavish, plentiful
  OPPOSITE meagre

genial adjective
*The housekeeper greeted us with a **genial** smile.*
- friendly, kind, warm, warm-hearted, kindly, good-natured, pleasant, agreeable, cordial
  OPPOSITE unfriendly

a b c d e f g h i j k l m n o p q r s t u v w x y z

a
b
c
d
e
f
g
h
i
j
k
l
m
n
o
p
q
r
s
t
u
v
w
x
y
z

genius noun

*Nila is a **genius** at maths.*
- expert, master, mastermind, wizard, ace

gentle adjective

1 *The vet is very **gentle** with sick animals.*
- kind, tender, good-tempered, humane

2 *Grasses swayed in the **gentle** breeze.*
- light, slight, mild, soft, faint
OPPOSITE strong

3 *There is a **gentle** slope to the top of the hill.*
- slight, gradual, easy
OPPOSITE steep

genuine adjective

1 *Is that a **genuine** diamond?*
- real, actual, true, authentic
OPPOSITE fake

2 *Your friend seems like a very **genuine** person.*
- honest, sincere, frank, earnest
OPPOSITE false

gesture noun

*She opened her arms in a **gesture** of welcome.*
- sign, signal, motion, movement

get verb

1 *We're **getting** a goldfish for our class.*
- acquire, obtain, buy, purchase

2 *Can you **get** me another blanket, please?*
- bring, fetch, collect, pick up, retrieve

3 *Cara **got** a medal for swimming.*
- receive, gain, earn, win, achieve

4 *What time did you **get** home?*
- arrive at, reach, come to
OPPOSITE leave

5 *It was starting to **get** dark outside.*
- become, grow, turn

6 *I **got** a stomach bug on holiday last year.*
- catch, develop, pick up, come down with

7 *You'll never **get** Oscar to eat celery.*
- persuade, urge, influence, coax

8 *I don't **get** the point of that film.*
- understand, follow, comprehend, grasp

to get on or along

*How are you **getting on** with playing guitar?*
- manage, fare, cope, prosper, succeed

to get out of

*My brother **got out of** doing the washing up.*
- avoid, evade, shirk

to get over

*He hasn't **got over** the accident yet.*
- get better from, recover from, shake off, survive

ghastly adjective

*The boy's face turned a **ghastly** shade of green.*
- appalling, awful, dreadful, frightful, grim, grisly, horrible, horrifying, shocking, monstrous, terrible

ghost noun

WORD WEB

*Meldrop House was haunted by several **ghosts**.*
- spirit, spectre, phantom, ghoul, apparition, shade, wraith (*informal*) spook
- A ghost that makes a lot of noise is a poltergeist.

A GHOST OR GHOSTLY EXPERIENCE MIGHT BE
bloodcurdling, chilling, grisly, gruesome, hair-raising, macabre, nightmarish, spine-chilling, spine-tingling.

THINGS A GHOST MIGHT DO
flit, float, glide, glow, haunt a person or place, hover, lurk, materialize, pass through walls, rattle chains, shimmer, vanish, waft

NOISES A GHOST MIGHT MAKE
cackle, clang, clank, creak, groan, hoot, howl, moan, screech, sigh, sob, wail

PLACES A GHOST MIGHT BE FOUND
catacombs, crypt, haunted house or mansion, graveyard, sepulchre, tomb, vault

OTHER THINGS THAT MIGHT BE IN A
HAUNTED HOUSE
bats, candles, cellar, cobwebs,
dungeon, gargoyle, mummy, owl,
secret door or passage, skeleton,
skull, trap door, turret

ghostly adjective
*The candlelight cast **ghostly** shadows
on the wall.*
- spectral, phantom, ghoulish,
unearthly, eerie, sinister, uncanny
- (*informal*) spooky, creepy

giant noun
*The castle belonged to a fearsome
giant.*
FOR CREATURES FOUND IN MYTHS AND
LEGENDS
SEE **myth**

giant adjective
*A **giant** tree towered above us.*
- gigantic, huge, enormous, massive,
immense, mammoth, colossal,
monstrous
SEE ALSO **big**
OPPOSITE **tiny**

giddy adjective
*I felt **giddy** when I stood at the edge of
the cliff.*
- dizzy, faint, unsteady

gift noun
1 *I received some nice **gifts** on my
birthday.*
- present
2 *Elsa has a **gift** for music.*
- talent, ability, flair, knack, genius

gifted adjective
*There are some **gifted** players in the
team.*
- talented, able, accomplished,
capable, skilful, expert

gigantic adjective
*The dragon reared its **gigantic** head.*
- huge, giant, enormous, massive,
colossal, immense, mammoth,
monstrous
- (*informal*) whopping, humungous
OPPOSITE **tiny**

giggle verb
*Ailsa and I couldn't stop **giggling**.*
- snigger, titter, chuckle, laugh

girl noun
- A synonym used in some parts of
Britain is *lass*.
- Old-fashioned words are *damsel,
maid*, and *maiden*.

give verb
1 *Santa Claus **gave** each child a present.*
- deal out, distribute, issue, supply,
offer, present, hand over, pass, award
2 *Will you **give** something to our
collection for charity?*
- contribute, donate
3 *The giant **gave** a loud sneeze.*
- utter, emit, let out
4 *We are **giving** a concert at the end of
term.*
- present, put on, lay on, organize,
arrange
5 *Will this branch **give** if I sit on it?*
- collapse, give way, bend, break,
buckle
to give in
*The boxer **gave in** after a long fight.*
- surrender, yield, submit, quit
to give up
*He **gave up** trying to start the car.*
- abandon, stop, cease, quit

glad adjective
*I'm **glad** to hear that you're feeling
better.*
- pleased, happy, delighted, thrilled
OPPOSITE **sad**

glamorous adjective
*She looked very **glamorous** in a long
black dress.*
- beautiful, attractive, gorgeous,
elegant, stylish, fashionable

glance verb
*The bus driver **glanced** quickly at his
watch.*
- look quickly, peek, peep, glimpse

glare verb
*The troll **glared** at us from under his
bushy eyebrows.*
- stare, frown, scowl, glower

a
b
c
d
e
f
g
h
i
j
k
l
m
n
o
p
q
r
s
t
u
v
w
x
y
z

a
b
c
d
e
f
g
h
i
j
k
l
m
n
o
p
q
r
s
t
u
v
w
x
y
z

glare noun
1 *The **glare** of the lights dazzled me.*
- dazzle, blaze, brightness, brilliance
2 *Miss Frump silenced the children with an angry **glare**.*
- stare, scowl, glower, frown, nasty look

glasses plural noun

WORD WEB
*She put on her **glasses** to read the letter.*
- spectacles
OTHER INSTRUMENTS WITH LENSES
binoculars, magnifying glass, microscope, telescope
- An old word for a telescope is a spyglass.

gleam noun
*I saw a **gleam** of moonlight between the clouds.*
- glimmer, glint, flash, ray, shaft

gleam verb
*The lights **gleamed** on the water.*
- glimmer, glint, glisten, shimmer, shine

glide verb
*The boat **glided** gently across the lake.*
- move smoothly, slide, slip, drift, float, coast

glimmer verb
*The city lights **glimmered** in the distance.*
- gleam, glint, glow, glisten, shimmer, flicker, blink

glimpse verb
*I **glimpsed** a deer running through the forest.*
- catch sight of, spot, spy, sight

glimpse verb
*We caught a **glimpse** of a whale in the sea.*
- peek, peep, glance, sighting, view

glint verb
*Sunlight **glinted** on the windows.*
- flash, glitter, sparkle, twinkle

glisten verb
*The pavement **glistened** with frost.*
- gleam, shine, glint, shimmer, glimmer

glitter verb
*The jewels **glittered** under the bright lights.*
- sparkle, twinkle, shimmer, glimmer, glint, glisten, flash, shine

gloat verb
*He was **gloating** about winning the poetry prize.*
- boast, brag, crow, show off

global adjective
*The Internet is a **global** network of computers.*
- worldwide, international, universal

globe noun
1 *I'd like to travel all round the **globe**.*
- world, planet, earth
2 *The fortune-teller used a crystal **globe**.*
- ball, sphere, orb

gloom noun
1 *We could hardly see in the **gloom** of the cave.*
- darkness, dimness, shade, shadow, murk
- The gloomy light late in the evening is dusk or twilight.
2 *There was an air of **gloom** in the abandoned tower.*
- depression, sadness, unhappiness, melancholy, misery, despair

gloomy adjective
1 *It was cold and **gloomy** in the cellar.*
- dark, dingy, dim, dismal, dreary, sombre, cheerless, murky, shadowy
OPPOSITE bright
2 *Eeyore was feeling **gloomy** again.*
- depressed, sad, unhappy, glum, miserable, melancholy, low, downcast, dejected
- (*informal*) down in the dumps
OPPOSITE cheerful

glorious adjective
*Look at that **glorious** sunset!*
- magnificent, splendid, stunning, spectacular, superb, magnificent, wonderful, marvellous

glossy adjective
*The bear had a thick, **glossy** coat of black fur.*
- shiny, sleek, silky, shining, gleaming, lustrous
OPPOSITE dull

glove noun FOR ITEMS OF CLOTHING
SEE **clothes**

glow noun
*The soft **glow** of burning candles lit the room.*
- brightness, shine, gleam, radiance

glow verb
*The embers of the bonfire were still **glowing**.*
- shine, gleam, burn
- Something that glows in the dark is luminous or phosphorescent.

glower verb
*The jailer **glowered** at the prisoners.*
- glare, scowl, frown, stare angrily

glue noun
*Put a blob of **glue** on each corner of the paper.*
- adhesive, paste, gum

glue verb
__Glue__ the edges of the box together.
- stick, paste, bond, seal

glum adjective
*Why are you looking so **glum**?*
- depressed, sad, unhappy, gloomy, miserable, melancholy, low, downcast, dejected
OPPOSITE cheerful

gnarled adjective
*The branches of the tree were **gnarled** with age.*
- bent, twisted, crooked, distorted, knobbly, knotty

gnaw verb
*The wolves **gnawed** at a pile of bones.*
- chew, bite, nibble, munch

go verb
1 *A carriage was **going** slowly along the road.*
- move, progress, proceed
SEE ALSO **move** verb
2 *My granny has always wanted to **go** to China.*
- travel, journey
3 *Some of the guests had already **gone**.*
- leave, depart, get away, withdraw
4 *By morning, the ice had all **gone**.*
- disappear, vanish
5 *The canal **goes** all the way from Inverness to Fort William.*
- extend, lead, reach, stretch, run
6 *The mountaineer's face **went** blue with cold.*
- become, turn, grow
7 *Is that old grandfather clock still **going**?*
- function, operate, work, run
8 *Cups and saucers **go** on the bottom shelf.*
- belong, be kept, be placed
9 *Time **goes** slowly when you're stuck indoors.*
- pass, go by, elapse

to go back
*Sarah has **gone back** to the house.*
- return, retreat, retrace your steps

to go in for
*I'm not **going in for** the race this year.*
- enter, take part in, participate in

to go off
1 *A bomb **went off** nearby.*
- explode, blow up, detonate
2 *The milk will **go off** if it's not in the fridge.*
- turn sour, go bad, rot

to go on
1 *What's **going on** over there?*
- happen, occur, take place
2 *Please **go on** with your story.*
- carry on, continue, keep going, proceed

to go with
*Do these shoes **go with** my dress?*
- match, suit, blend with

a b c d e f g h i j k l m n o p q r s t u v w x y z

---

go noun
Would you like to have a go on my computer?
- try, turn, chance, opportunity
- (*informal*) shot, bash, stab

goal noun
1 *The goal of the society is to protect wildlife.*
- aim, ambition, intention, object, objective, purpose, target
2 *We managed to get a goal just before half-time.*
- Three goals scored by the same player is known as a hat-trick.

gobble verb
Ladybirds love to gobble greenfly.
- guzzle, gulp, bolt, devour

god, goddess noun
Zeus was one of the gods of ancient Greece.
- deity
- A word meaning 'to do with a god or goddess' is divine.

gold noun
- Something that is made of gold is golden or gilded.
- A thin covering of gold is gilt.

good adjective
That is a really good idea!
- excellent, fine, lovely, nice, wonderful
- (*informal*) fantastic, great, super, cool
OPPOSITE bad

⚠ **OVERUSED WORD**
Try to vary the words you use for **good**. Here are some other words you could use.
- for a **GOOD PERSON**:
honest, worthy, honourable, moral, decent, virtuous, noble, kind, humane, charitable, merciful
The virtuous knight defeated the evil queen.
OPPOSITE evil, wicked

- A good character in a story or film is a hero or heroine or (*informal*) goody.
- for **GOOD BEHAVIOUR**:
well-behaved, obedient, angelic, exemplary
The twins are surprisingly well-behaved.
- A common simile is as good as gold.
OPPOSITE naughty, disobedient
- for a **GOOD FRIEND**:
true, loyal, loving, reliable, trusty, trustworthy
My dog, Rusty, is a loyal companion.
- for a **GOOD FEELING** or **GOOD MOOD**:
happy, cheerful, light-hearted, positive, contented
Mr Fox was in a cheerful mood after his tea.
- for a **GOOD EXPERIENCE** or **GOOD NEWS**:
pleasant, enjoyable, delightful, agreeable, pleasing
OPPOSITE unpleasant, disagreeable
The girls had an enjoyable time at the party.
The letter contained some pleasing news.
- for a **GOOD PERFORMER** or **GOOD WORK**:
capable, skilful, clever, able, talented, competent, commendable, sound
My friend, Chris, is a talented dancer.
OPPOSITE poor, awful
- for **GOOD FOOD** or a **GOOD MEAL**:
delicious, healthy, nourishing, nutritious, tasty, well-cooked, wholesome, substantial, hearty
The crew ate a hearty breakfast together.
- for a **GOOD EXCUSE** or **GOOD REASON**:
acceptable, valid, proper, satisfactory, legitimate
I hope you have a valid excuse for being late.
OPPOSITE poor, unacceptable
- for **GOOD TIMING**:
convenient, suitable, fortunate, appropriate, opportune
Is this a convenient time for a chat?
OPPOSITE inconvenient, unsuitable

- for *GOOD WEATHER*:
fine, favourable
*We are hoping for **fine** weather tomorrow.*
OPPOSITE harsh, adverse

goodbye noun
*The astronauts said **goodbye** to their families.*
- farewell
- (*informal*) cheerio
- A formal phrase meaning 'to say goodbye' is to bid farewell.

good-looking adjective
*I think your cousin is quite **good-looking**.*
- attractive, handsome, pretty
OPPOSITE ugly

goods plural noun
*The smugglers hid the stolen **goods** in a cave.*
- property, merchandise, wares, cargo

gorgeous adjective
*The gardens look **gorgeous** in the summer.*
- beautiful, glorious, dazzling, stunning, splendid, superb, glamorous, handsome

gossip verb
*Two neighbours were **gossiping** over the fence.*
- chatter, tell tales
- (*informal*) natter

gossip noun
1 *Don't believe all the **gossip** you hear.*
- chatter, rumour, hearsay, scandal
- (*informal*) tittle-tattle
2 *Our next-door neighbour is a dreadful **gossip**.*
- busybody, chatterbox, telltale, scandalmonger

gouge verb
*The builders **gouged** a hole in the wall.*
- dig, hollow out, scoop out, excavate

govern verb
*The ancient Romans **governed** a vast empire.*
- rule, run, administer, direct, command, manage, be in charge of

gown noun
*The mermaid wore a **gown** made of seaweed and pearls.*
- dress, robe, frock

grab verb
*The cowboy **grabbed** the reins of the runaway horse.*
- seize, grasp, catch, clutch, grip, get hold of, snatch

graceful adjective
*The gymnast made a **graceful** landing.*
- elegant, beautiful, stylish, smooth, flowing, agile, nimble
OPPOSITE clumsy, graceless

gracious adjective
*The film star waved and gave a **gracious** smile.*
- polite, courteous, good-natured, pleasant, agreeable, civil

grade noun
*My sister has reached the top **grade** in judo.*
- class, standard, level, stage, rank, degree

grade verb
*Eggs are **graded** according to size.*
- group, sort, classify

gradual adjective
*There's been a **gradual** change in the weather.*
- steady, slow, gentle, moderate, regular, even
OPPOSITE sudden

grain noun
1 *Some **grains** of sand stuck to my toes.*
- bit, particle, speck, granule
2 *The **grain** will be made into bread.*
- cereals, corn

grand adjective
1 *The wedding was a **grand** occasion.*
- magnificent, splendid, stately, impressive, big, great, important, imposing
2 (*informal*) *Keep going—you're doing a **grand** job!*
- excellent, fine, good, first-class

a
b
c
d
e
f
g
h
i
j
k
l
m
n
o
p
q
r
s
t
u
v
w
x
y
z

grant verb
The king **granted** the prisoners their freedom.
- give, allow, permit, award

grapple verb
The guard **grappled** with the thief, but he got away.
- struggle, wrestle, fight, tussle

grasp verb
1 The climber **grasped** the end of the rope.
- clutch, grab, grip, seize, catch, snatch, take hold of, hang on to
2 The ideas were quite difficult to **grasp**.
- understand, comprehend, follow, take in

grasp noun
Rita has a good **grasp** of mathematics.
- understanding, comprehension, knowledge, mastery

grass noun
People were told not to walk on the **grass**.
- lawn, turf, green

grate verb
1 I **grated** the cheese onto the pizza.
- shred, grind
2 The chalk **grated** on the blackboard.
- scrape, scratch

to grate on
That man's voice **grates on** my nerves.
- annoy, irritate, jar on

grateful adjective
I'm **grateful** for your help.
- thankful, appreciative, obliged, indebted
OPPOSITE ungrateful

gratitude noun
We sent some flowers to show our **gratitude**.
- thanks, appreciation

grave adjective
1 They looked **grave** when they heard the news.
- grim, sad, serious, thoughtful
OPPOSITE cheerful
2 She made a **grave** mistake.
- crucial, important, serious, vital
OPPOSITE trivial

grave noun SEE **tomb**

graveyard noun
He was buried in the local **graveyard**.
- burial ground, cemetery, churchyard

graze verb
I **grazed** my knee when I fell off my bike.
- scrape, cut, scratch, scuff

greasy adjective
I don't like **greasy** food.
- fatty, oily

great adjective
1 The inventor had made a **great** discovery.
- important, significant, major, leading, noteworthy
OPPOSITE insignificant, minor
2 Mozart was a **great** composer.
- famous, notable, celebrated, eminent, distinguished, outstanding, brilliant
3 Their voices echoed round the **great** hall.
- big, huge, large, enormous, vast, immense, gigantic, extensive, cavernous
OPPOSITE small
4 Beth took **great** care over her knitting.
- considerable, extreme, exact
OPPOSITE little
5 (informal) That is a **great** idea!
- very good, excellent, marvellous, outstanding, superb, tremendous, wonderful
- (informal) brilliant, fantastic, super, smashing, terrific
OPPOSITE bad, awful

greed noun
The king wanted more gold to satisfy his **greed**.
- avarice, selfishness, hunger, craving, gluttony

greedy adjective
1 The boys were so **greedy** that they ate all the cakes.
- gluttonous
- (informal) piggish
- A common simile is as greedy as a pig.

2 *Mr Skimp is very **greedy** with his money.*
- selfish, miserly, tight-fisted, grasping
  OPPOSITE generous

green adjective, noun

> **WORD WEB**
>
> SOME SHADES OF GREEN
> emerald, jade, khaki, lime, olive, pea-green

greens plural noun SEE **vegetable**

greet verb
*My aunt **greeted** us with a friendly wave.*
- welcome, hail, receive, salute

grey adjective
1 *The old wizard had a bushy **grey** beard.*
- silver, silvery, grizzly, hoary, whitish

2 *The mother's face was **grey** with worry.*
- ashen, pale, leaden, wan

3 *The day began cold and **grey**.*
- dull, cloudy, overcast

grief noun
*He couldn't hide his **grief** at his friend's death.*
- sorrow, sadness, mourning, unhappiness, distress, anguish, heartache
  OPPOSITE joy

grieve verb
1 *The family is still **grieving** over her death.*
- mourn, lament, sorrow, weep
  OPPOSITE rejoice

2 *It **grieves** me to leave so soon.*
- sadden, upset, distress, hurt
  OPPOSITE please

grim adjective
1 *The judge wore a **grim** expression on his face.*
- stern, severe, harsh, bad-tempered, sullen
  OPPOSITE cheerful

2 *The detective made the **grim** discovery of the body.*
- unpleasant, horrible, dreadful, terrible, hideous, shocking, gruesome, grisly
  OPPOSITE pleasant

grime noun
*There was nearly an inch of **grime** on the floor.*
- dirt, filth, muck, mire, mess

grimy adjective
*Don't wipe those **grimy** feet on the carpet!*
- dirty, filthy, grubby, mucky, soiled
  OPPOSITE clean

grin noun, verb
*Mark arrived with a silly **grin** on his face.*
- smile, beam, smirk
- A large grin is a broad, wide, or cheesy grin.

grind verb
1 ***Grind** the spices into a fine powder.*
- crush, pound, powder, pulverize, mill

2 *This tool is used for **grinding** knives.*
- sharpen, file, hone, whet

grip verb
1 ***Grip** the handle tightly.*
- grasp, seize, clutch, clasp, hold

2 *The audience was **gripped** by the film.*
- fascinate, engross, absorb, enthrall

grisly adjective
*We found the **grisly** remains of a dead sheep.*
- gruesome, gory, ghastly, hideous, nasty, revolting, sickening

grit noun
1 *I've got some **grit** in my shoe.*
- gravel, dust, sand

2 *The marathon runners showed real **grit**.*
- bravery, courage, toughness, spirit, pluck
- (informal) guts

groan verb
*The wounded soldier **groaned** with pain.*
- cry out, moan, sigh, wail

a
b
c
d
e
f
g
h
i
j
k
l
m
n
o
p
q
r
s
t
u
v
w
x
y
z

a
b
c
d
e
f
g
h
i
j
k
l
m
n
o
p
q
r
s
t
u
v
w
x
y
z

groove noun
*Thick **grooves** had been carved in the stone wall.*
- channel, furrow, rut, cut, scratch, slot

grope verb
*I **groped** in the dark for the light switch.*
- fumble, feel about, flounder

gross adjective
1 *That is a **gross** exaggeration!*
- extreme, glaring, obvious, sheer, blatant, outright

2 *Most ogres have **gross** table manners.*
- offensive, rude, coarse, vulgar

ground noun
1 *I planted some seeds in the **ground**.*
- earth, soil, land

2 *The **ground** was too wet to play on.*
- field, pitch, park, stadium, arena

group noun
1 *Japan consists of a **group** of islands.*
- collection, set, batch, cluster, clump

2 *A **group** of children was waiting at the bus stop.*
- crowd, bunch, gathering, band, body, gang

3 *The book **group** meets once a month.*
- club, society, association, circle

4 *We sorted the fossils into different **groups**.*
- category, class, type, kind, sort

WORD WEB

WORDS FOR GROUPS OF PEOPLE
- a band of musicians
- a class of pupils
- a company or troupe of actors
- a congregation of worshippers in church
- a coven of witches
- a crew of sailors
- a gang of workers
- a horde of invaders
- a team of players

WORDS FOR GROUPS OF ANIMALS
- an army or colony of ants
- a band of gorillas
- a brood of chicks
- a covey of partridges
- a flock of sheep or birds
- a gaggle of geese
- a herd of cattle or elephants
- a litter of pigs or puppies
- a pack of wolves
- a pride of lions
- a school or pod of dolphins or whales
- a shoal of fish
- a swarm of insects
- a troop of monkeys

WORDS FOR GROUPS OF THINGS
- a battery of guns
- a bunch of flowers
- a clump of trees
- a clutch of eggs in a nest
- a constellation or galaxy of stars
- a convoy or fleet of ships

grow verb
1 *I've **grown** an inch taller since last summer.*
- get bigger, put on growth, spring up, sprout

2 *The number of children in the school has **grown**.*
- increase, develop, enlarge, expand, build up
- OPPOSITE decrease

3 *Our neighbour **grows** orchids in her greenhouse.*
- cultivate, produce, raise, farm

4 *It is **growing** dark outside.*
- become, get, turn

grown-up adjective
*The female cheetah has two **grown-up** cubs.*
- adult, mature, fully grown
- OPPOSITE young

growth noun
1 *There's been a **growth** of interest in golf for kids.*
- increase, rise, spread, expansion, development, enlargement

2 *The doctor examined the **growth** on my foot.*
- lump, swelling, tumour

grub noun
*I found a **grub** on the cabbage leaf.*
• larva, maggot, caterpillar

grubby adjective
*My hands were **grubby** from working in the garden.*
• dirty, filthy, grimy, messy, mucky, soiled
OPPOSITE clean

grudge noun
*Captain Hook bore a **grudge** against Peter Pan.*
• grievance, bitterness, resentment, hard feelings, ill-will, spite

gruelling adjective
*The marathon is a **gruelling** race.*
• hard, tough, demanding, exhausting, challenging, difficult, laborious, strenuous, backbreaking, punishing
OPPOSITE easy

gruesome adjective
*The battlefield was a **gruesome** sight.*
• grisly, gory, ghastly, hideous, monstrous, revolting, sickening, appalling, dreadful, frightful, shocking, abominable

gruff adjective
*The ogre spoke in a **gruff** voice.*
• harsh, rough, hoarse, husky, throaty

grumble verb
*You're always **grumbling** about the weather!*
• complain, moan, groan, protest, whine, gripe

grumpy adjective
*Marge was **grumpy** because she had a headache.*
• bad-tempered, cross, irritable, testy, tetchy, cantankerous
• (informal) grouchy
OPPOSITE good-humoured

guarantee verb
*I **guarantee** that you will enjoy the show.*
• promise, assure, pledge, vow

guard verb
*The cave was **guarded** by a one-eyed giant.*
• protect, defend, stand guard over, patrol, safeguard, shield, watch over

guard noun
*A **guard** was on duty at the gate.*
• sentry, sentinel, warder, lookout, watchman

guardian noun
*The **guardian** of the treasure was a fierce dragon.*
• defender, protector, keeper, minder, custodian

guess noun
*My **guess** is that it will rain tomorrow.*
• estimate, prediction, feeling, hunch

guess verb
1 *There was a prize for **guessing** the weight of the cake.*
• estimate, judge, work out, guage, predict, reckon
2 *I **guess** you must be tired after your journey.*
• suppose, imagine, expect, assume, think

guest noun
*We are having **guests** for tea on Sunday.*
• visitor, caller, company

guide noun
1 *Our **guide** showed us around the zoo.*
• courier, escort, leader, chaperon
2 *We bought a useful **guide** to the city.*
• guidebook, handbook, manual

guide verb
*The explorers used the stars to **guide** them at night.*
• direct, lead, steer, conduct, escort, show the way

guilt noun
1 *The prisoner admitted his **guilt**.*
• guiltiness, responsibility, liability, blame, wrongdoing
OPPOSITE innocence
2 *You could see the look of **guilt** on her face.*
• shame, remorse, regret, penitence, disgrace, dishonour

a
b
c
d
e
f
g
h
i
j
k
l
m
n
o
p
q
r
s
t
u
v
w
x
y
z

a
b
c
d
e
f
g
h
i
j
k
l
m
n
o
p
q
r
s
t
u
v
w
x
y
z

guilty adjective

1 *The prisoner was found **guilty** of the crime.*

- responsible, to blame, at fault, in the wrong, liable

OPPOSITE innocent

2 *You have a **guilty** look on your face!*

- ashamed, guilt-ridden, remorseful, sorry, conscience-stricken, repentant, shamefaced, sheepish

OPPOSITE unrepentant

gulp verb

*Peter **gulped** down the cake in one go.*

- swallow, bolt, gobble, guzzle, devour

FOR OTHER WAYS TO EAT

SEE **eat**

gulp noun

*Amanda took a long **gulp** of lemonade.*

- swallow, mouthful
- (*informal*) swig

gun noun FOR VARIOUS WEAPONS

SEE **weapon**

gurgle verb

*The mountain stream **gurgled** over the rocks.*

- burble, babble

gush noun

*There was a **gush** of water from the pipe.*

- rush, stream, torrent, rush, cascade, flood, jet, spout, spurt

gush verb

*Water **gushed** from the broken pipe.*

- rush, stream, flow, pour, flood, spout, spurt, squirt

gust noun

*A **gust** of wind carried the kite into the sky.*

- blast, rush, puff, squall, flurry

guzzle verb

*The seagulls **guzzled** all the bread.*

- gobble, gulp, bolt, devour

FOR OTHER WAYS TO EAT

SEE **eat**

Hh

habit noun

1 *It's her **habit** to go for a walk each morning.*

- custom, practice, routine, rule

2 *My dog has a **habit** of scratching his ear.*

- mannerism, way, tendency, inclination, quirk

hack verb

*The explorers **hacked** their way through the jungle.*

- chop, cut, hew, slash, lop

haggard adjective

*The warriors looked **haggard** after the battle.*

- drawn, gaunt, thin, pinched, wasted, shrunken, wan

OPPOSITE healthy

haggle verb

*The men **haggled** over the price of the gems.*

- bargain, negotiate, argue, wrangle

hair noun

 WORD WEB

*Rapunzel's **hair** reached down to the ground.*

- locks, tresses
  (*informal*) mop
- A single piece of hair is a strand.
- A bunch of hair is a hank, lock, or tress.
- False hair is a hairpiece, toupee, or wig.
- An area without hair is a bald patch.
- The way hair is cut is a hairstyle or (*informal*) hairdo or (*formal*) coiffure.
- Hair is cut or styled by a hairdresser or hairstylist.
- Men's hair is also cut by a barber.

SOME HAIRSTYLES

Afro, bob, braids, bun, bunches, chignon, corn rows, crew-cut, curls, dreadlocks, fishtail, French braid or plait, fringe, Mohican, perm, pigtail, plaits, ponytail, quiff, ringlets, short back and sides, sideburns, skinhead, topknot

HAIR ON AN ANIMAL

bristles, coat, down, fleece, fur, mane, whiskers

✎ **WRITING TIPS**

You can use these words to describe **hair**.

- to describe its COLOUR :
  auburn, blond (male) or blonde (female), brunette, (*informal*) carroty, dark, fair, flaxen, ginger, grey, grizzled, hoary, mousy, platinum blonde, raven, red, silver
- to describe how it LOOKS or FEELS:
  bushy, coarse, curly, dishevelled, fine, frizzy, glossy, greasy, lank, limp, ringletted, shaggy, shiny, silky, spiky, straggly, straight, stringy, tangled, thick, tousled, tuggy, unkempt, wavy, windswept, wispy
  *The elderly knight had a **grizzled**, **straggly** beard.*

FOR WAYS TO DESCRIBE ANIMAL HAIR
SEE **animal**

hairy adjective
*Mammoths were like elephants with thick **hairy** coats.*
- shaggy, bushy, bristly, woolly, fleecy, furry, fuzzy, long-haired, hirsute

hall noun
1 *The **hall** was full for the concert.*
- assembly hall, auditorium, concert hall, theatre
2 *You can use the coat stand in the **hall**.*
- entrance hall, hallway, lobby, foyer

halt verb
1 *The car **halted** at the red light.*
- stop, come to a halt, draw up, pull up, wait

2 *A traffic jam **halted** the traffic.*
- stop, check, obstruct
3 *Work **halted** when the whistle went.*
- end, cease, terminate, break off
OPPOSITE start, go

halve verb
1 ***Halve** the tomatoes and scoop out the seeds.*
- cut in half, divide into halves, split in two
2 *The workforce has been **halved** in the last five years.*
- cut by half, reduce by half

hammer verb
*I **hammered** on the door, but no one answered.*
- strike, beat, knock, batter, pummel, pound

hamper verb
*Bad weather **hampered** the rescuers.*
- hinder, hold up, obstruct, impede, restrict, handicap, frustrate
OPPOSITE help

hand noun
- When you clench your hand you make a fist.
- The flat part of the inside of your hand is the palm.
- Work that you do with your hands is manual work.

hand verb
*The postman **handed** me several letters.*
- give, pass, present, offer, deliver
to hand something down
*This brooch has been **handed down** from generation to generation.*
- pass down, pass on, bequeath

handicap noun
1 *Lack of experience can be a **handicap** in some jobs.*
- disadvantage, drawback, hindrance, obstacle, problem, difficulty, limitation
OPPOSITE advantage
2 *He was born with a visual **handicap**.*
- disability, impairment

handicap verb
*The search was **handicapped** by bad weather.*
- hamper, hinder, hold up, restrict, impede

OPPOSITE help

handle noun
*The door **handle** is broken.*
- grip, handgrip, knob, shaft
- The handle of a sword is the hilt.

handle verb
1 *Please don't **handle** the exhibits.*
- touch, feel, hold, stroke, fondle, finger, grasp

2 *The referee **handled** the game well.*
- manage, control, conduct, deal with, cope with, tackle

handsome adjective
1 *Prince Charming was very **handsome**.*
- attractive, good-looking, nice-looking, gorgeous
- (*informal*) dishy

OPPOSITE ugly, unattractive

2 *They sold their house for a **handsome** profit.*
- big, large, substantial, sizeable

OPPOSITE slight

handy adjective
1 *This **handy** gadget is for peeling potatoes.*
- useful, helpful, convenient, practical

OPPOSITE awkward

2 *I always keep my umbrella **handy**.*
- accessible, available, close at hand, nearby, ready

OPPOSITE inaccessible

hang verb
1 *A monkey was **hanging** from the tree branch.*
- dangle, be suspended, swing, sway

2 *The dog had hair **hanging** down over his eyes.*
- droop, drape, flop, trail, cascade

3 *I **hung** the picture on the wall.*
- fix, attach, fasten, stick, peg

4 *Smoke **hung** in the air.*
- float, hover, drift, linger, cling

to hang about or around
*Don't **hang about**, we'll miss the bus.*
- delay, dawdle, linger, loiter

to hang on (*informal*)
*Try to **hang on** a bit longer.*
- carry on, continue, stay, remain, persist, keep going, persevere

to hang on to something
1 *Hang on to the rope.*
- hold, grip, grasp

2 *Hang on to your bus ticket.*
- keep, retain, save

haphazard adjective
*The books were shelved in a **haphazard** fashion.*
- random, unplanned, arbitrary, disorderly, chaotic, higgledy-piggledy

OPPOSITE orderly

happen verb
*Did anything interesting **happen** today?*
- take place, occur, arise, come about, crop up, emerge, result

happening noun
*There have been strange **happenings** here lately.*
- event, occurrence, incident, phenomenon

happiness noun
*The bride's face glowed with **happiness**.*
- joy, joyfulness, delight, jubilation, pleasure, contentment, gladness, cheerfulness, merriment, ecstasy, bliss

OPPOSITE sorrow

happy adjective

> ⚠️ **OVERUSED WORD**
> Try to vary the words you use for happy. Here are some other words you could use.
> - for a *HAPPY MOOD* or *HAPPY PERSON*: cheerful, joyful, jolly, merry, light-hearted, contented, gleeful, delighted
> *The girls look really **cheerful** in the photograph.*

a b c d e f g h i j k l m n o p q r s t u v w x y z

- A common simile is **as happy as a lark**.

  OPPOSITE unhappy, sad

- for a **VERY HAPPY MOOD**:
  thrilled, ecstatic, elated, overjoyed
  (*informal*) over the moon, thrilled to bits, tickled pink
  *Sandy was **ecstatic** when she won first prize.*

- for a **HAPPY TIME** or **HAPPY EXPERIENCE**:
  enjoyable, joyous, glorious, blissful, heavenly, idyllic
  *They spent a **glorious** summer on the island.*

- for a **HAPPY COINCIDENCE**:
  lucky, fortunate, favourable
  *By a **lucky** coincidence, we took the same train.*

  OPPOSITE unfortunate

- to be **HAPPY TO DO SOMETHING**:
  pleased, glad, willing, delighted
  *I would be **glad** to help organize the party.*

  OPPOSITE unwilling

harass verb
*I keep being **harassed** with junk email.*

- pester, trouble, bother, annoy, disturb, plague, torment, badger, hound, hassle

harbour noun
*Several yachts were tied up in the **harbour**.*

- port, dock, mooring, quay, pier, wharf

hard adjective

OVERUSED WORD
Try to vary the words you use for **hard**. Here are some other words you could use.

- for **HARD GROUND** or a **HARD SURFACE**:
  solid, firm, dense, compact, rigid, stiff
  *The ground was **solid** and covered with frost.*

- Common similes are **as hard as nails** and **as hard as a rock**.
  OPPOSITE soft

- for a **HARD PULL** or **HARD PUSH**:
  strong, forceful, heavy, powerful, violent
  *The climber gave the rope a **hard** pull.*
  OPPOSITE light

- for **HARD WORK**:
  tough, gruelling, strenuous, tiring, exhausting, laborious, backbreaking
  *Digging the tunnel was **strenuous** work.*
  OPPOSITE easy

- for a **HARD WORKER**:
  energetic, keen, diligent
  *The elves are very **diligent** workers.*
  OPPOSITE lazy

- for a **HARD PERSON** or **HARD TREATMENT**:
  strict, stern, harsh, severe, cruel, hard-hearted, heartless, unfeeling, unkind
  *Cinderella's sisters were **heartless** and selfish.*
  OPPOSITE mild

- for a **HARD PROBLEM** or **HARD QUESTION**:
  difficult, complicated, complex, intricate, perplexing, puzzling, baffling, knotty, thorny
  *None of us could solve the **complex** riddle.*
  OPPOSITE simple

hard adverb
1 *Ros is working **hard** at learning French.*
- strenuously, energetically, diligently, keenly, intently
2 *It has been raining **hard** all afternoon.*
- heavily, steadily
- (*informal*) cats and dogs

harden verb
*We left the cement to **harden**.*
- set, solidify, stiffen
- If you harden clay in a kiln, you bake or fire it.
  OPPOSITE soften

hardly adverb
*I could **hardly** see in the fog.*
- barely, scarcely, only just, with difficulty

hardship noun
*They suffered years of **hardship** during the war.*
- suffering, trouble, difficulty, distress, misery, misfortune, need, want

a b c d e f g **h** i j k l m n o p q r s t u v w x y z

a
b
c
d
e
f
g
h
i
j
k
l
m
n
o
p
q
r
s
t
u
v
w
x
y
z

hardy adjective

*You must be **hardy** to go camping in winter.*

- tough, strong, robust, sturdy, hearty, rugged

OPPOSITE tender

harm verb

1 *His captors didn't **harm** him.*

- hurt, injure, ill-treat, wound

2 *Too much direct sunlight may **harm** this plant.*

- damage, spoil, ruin

harm noun

*I didn't mean to cause him any **harm**.*

- damage, hurt, injury, pain

OPPOSITE benefit

harmful adjective

*Junk food can be **harmful** to your health.*

- damaging, dangerous, destructive, injurious, unhealthy

OPPOSITE harmless, beneficial

harmless adjective

1 *You can drink the potion—it is quite **harmless**.*

- safe, non-toxic, innocuous

OPPOSITE harmful, dangerous

2 *It was just a bit of **harmless** fun.*

- innocent, inoffensive

harsh adjective

1 *The trumpet sounded loud and **harsh**.*

- rough, rasping, grating, jarring, shrill, raucous

OPPOSITE soft, gentle

2 *We blinked in the **harsh** light.*

- bright, brilliant, dazzling, glaring

OPPOSITE soft, subdued

3 *The rescue team braved the **harsh** weather.*

- severe, strict, cruel, hard, tough, bleak

OPPOSITE mild

4 *The coach had some **harsh** words to say.*

- strong, sharp, unkind, unfriendly

harvest noun

*There was a good **harvest** of apples this year.*

- crop, yield, return
- Things grown on a farm are produce.
- A plentiful harvest is a bumper harvest.

haste noun

*The elves worked with great **haste**.*

- hurry, rush, speed, urgency

hasty adjective

1 *The robbers made a **hasty** exit.*

- fast, hurried, quick, sudden, swift, rapid, speedy

OPPOSITE slow

2 *The king regretted his **hasty** decision.*

- rash, reckless, impatient, foolhardy, thoughtless

OPPOSITE careful

hat noun

WORD WEB

SOME KINDS OF HAT
balaclava, baseball cap, bearskin, beret, boater, bonnet, bowler, cap, deerstalker, fez, helmet, mitre, mortarboard, panama hat, skull cap, sombrero, sou'wester, stetson, sun-hat, tam-o'-shanter, top hat, trilby, turban

hatch verb

*The gang **hatched** a plot to rob a bank.*

- plan, develop, conceive, think up, devise
- (*informal*) cook up, dream up

hate verb

1 *Eddie **hates** broccoli and peas.*

- dislike, detest, despise, loathe

2 *I **hate** to bother you.*

- be sorry, be reluctant, regret

OPPOSITE like, love

hate noun

*Washing dishes is one of my pet **hates**.*

- dislike

OPPOSITE like, love

hatred noun
*The evil wizard stared with **hatred** in his eyes.*
- hate, loathing, dislike, hostility, enmity, contempt, detestation
OPPOSITE love

haughty adjective
*Celia sniffed and gave us a **haughty** look.*
- proud, arrogant, conceited, lofty, superior, pompous, disdainful
- (*informal*) stuck-up
OPPOSITE modest

haul verb
*Eric **hauled** his bike out of the shed.*
- drag, pull, tow, draw

haunt verb
FOR THINGS A GHOST MIGHT DO
SEE **ghost**

have verb
1 *I **have** my own CD player.*
- own, possess
2 *Our house **has** three bedrooms.*
- consist of, comprise, include, incorporate
3 *We are **having** a barbecue at the weekend.*
- hold, organize, provide, host, throw
4 *Dad **had** trouble finding a place to park.*
- experience, go through, meet with, run into, face, suffer
5 *The girls **had** a great time at the party.*
- experience, enjoy
6 *The BBC has **had** lots of email messages.*
- receive, get, be given, be sent
7 *Sharon **had** the last toffee.*
- take, consume, eat
8 *One of the giraffes has **had** a baby.*
- give birth to, bear, produce
9 *I **have** to be home by six o'clock.*
- must, need to, ought to, should

haven noun
*The lake is a **haven** for wild birds.*
- refuge, shelter, retreat, sanctuary

havoc noun
*The pixies were causing **havoc** in the kitchen.*
- chaos, mayhem, disorder, disruption

hazard noun
*The road through the mountains is full of **hazards**.*
- danger, risk, threat, trap, pitfall, snag

hazardous adjective
*They made the **hazardous** journey to the South Pole.*
- dangerous, risky, unsafe, perilous, precarious
OPPOSITE safe

haze noun
*I could hardly see through the **haze**.*
- fog, mist, cloud, steam, vapour

hazy adjective
1 *The things in the distance were rather **hazy**.*
- blurred, misty, unclear, dim, faint
2 *He's only got a **hazy** knowledge of history.*
- uncertain, vague
OPPOSITE clear

head noun
1 *My dad hit his **head** on the attic ceiling.*
- skull, crown
- (*informal*) nut
FOR OTHER PARTS OF YOUR BODY
SEE **body**
2 *Can you add up these figures in your **head**?*
- brain, mind, intellect, intelligence
3 *There is a new **head** of the music department.*
- chief, leader, manager, director, controller
- (*informal*) boss
4 *The girls waited at the **head** of the queue.*
- front, lead, top
OPPOSITE back, rear

head verb
*The professor was chosen to **head** the expedition.*
- lead, be in charge of, direct, command, manage, oversee, supervise

to head for
*At the end of the day we **headed for** home.*
- go towards, make for, aim for

heading noun
*Each chapter had a different **heading**.*
- title, caption, headline

headlong adjective
*We made a **headlong** dash to get under cover.*
- quick, hurried, hasty, breakneck

headquarters plural noun
*The spy contacted **headquarters** for instructions.*
- base, head office
- (*informal*) HQ

headteacher noun
*The **headteacher** runs the school.*
- headmaster or headmistress, principal

heal verb
1 *It took two months for my leg to **heal** properly.*
- get better, mend, recover
2 *Part of a vet's job is to **heal** sick animals.*
- cure, make better, treat, restore

health noun
*The puppies are in excellent **health**.*
- condition, fitness, shape, strength, vigour, wellbeing

FOR VARIOUS MEDICAL TREATMENTS
SEE **medicine**

healthy adjective
1 *Neil has always been a **healthy** child.*
- well, fit, strong, sturdy, vigorous, robust
- (*informal*) in good shape
OPPOSITE ill
2 *Porridge makes a very **healthy** breakfast.*
- health-giving, wholesome, invigorating
OPPOSITE unhealthy

heap noun
*There was an untidy **heap** of clothes on the floor.*
- mound, pile, stack, mountain, collection, mass

heap verb
*We **heaped** up all the rubbish in the corner.*
- pile, stack, collect, bank, mass

hear verb
1 *Did you **hear** what she said?*
- catch, listen to, make out, pick up, overhear, pay attention to
- A sound that you can hear is audible.
- A sound that you cannot hear is inaudible.
2 *Have you **heard** the news?*
- be told, discover, find out, learn, gather

heart noun
1 *Have you no **heart**?*
- compassion, feeling, sympathy, tenderness, affection, humanity, kindness, love
2 *The hotel is located right in the **heart** of the city.*
- centre, middle, hub
3 *They tried to get to the **heart** of the problem.*
- core, essence

heartless adjective
*How could she be so **heartless**?*
- hard-hearted, callous, cruel, inhuman, unfeeling, unkind, pitiless, ruthless
OPPOSITE kind

hearty adjective
1 *He gave me a **hearty** slap on the back.*
- strong, forceful, vigorous
OPPOSITE feeble
2 *The girls had a **hearty** appetite after their walk.*
- big, healthy
OPPOSITE poor
3 *Our friends gave us a **hearty** welcome.*
- enthusiastic, sincere, warm
OPPOSITE unenthusiastic

heat noun
1 *The cat basked in the **heat** of the fire.*
- warmth, hotness, glow
2 *Last summer, the **heat** made me feel ill.*
- hot weather, high temperatures, closeness
- A long period of hot weather is a heatwave.

heave verb
*The men **heaved** the sacks onto a lorry.*
- haul, drag, pull, draw, tow, tug, hoist, lug, lift, raise, throw

heavy adjective
1 *The box was too **heavy** for me to lift.*
- weighty, massive, dense, bulky

2 *Digging the garden is **heavy** work.*
- hard, tough, gruelling, back-breaking, strenuous

3 *This book makes **heavy** reading.*
- serious, intense, demanding

4 *The rain has caused **heavy** flooding.*
- severe, extreme, torrential

5 *Both sides suffered **heavy** losses in the battle.*
- large, substantial, considerable

6 *A **heavy** mist hung over the landscape.*
- dense, thick
- OPPOSITE light

with a heavy heart
*She said goodbye **with a heavy heart**.*
- unhappily, sadly, sorrowfully, gloomily, in low spirits

hectic adjective
*The days before the wedding were **hectic**.*
- busy, frantic, feverish, frenzied, chaotic
- (*informal*) manic
- OPPOSITE quiet, leisurely

heed verb
*The sailors didn't **heed** the captain's warning.*
- listen to, pay attention to, take notice of, attend to, regard, obey, follow, mark, mind, note
- OPPOSITE ignore

hefty adjective
1 *The postman was carrying a **hefty** parcel.*
- big, large, weighty, massive, bulky

2 *The wrestler was a **hefty** man.*
- strong, sturdy, muscular, powerful, brawny, burly, hulking
- (*informal*) beefy
- OPPOSITE slight

height noun
*The plane was flying at its normal **height**.*
- altitude, elevation

help noun
1 *Thank you for your **help**.*
- aid, assistance, support, guidance, cooperation, advice
- OPPOSITE hindrance

2 *Would a torch be of any **help** to you?*
- use, benefit

help verb
1 *Could you please **help** me with my luggage?*
- aid, assist, cooperate with
- (*informal*) give a hand to

2 *The Red Cross is an organization that **helps** people in need.*
- be helpful to, support, serve, stand by

3 *This medicine will **help** your cough.*
- make better, cure, ease, relieve, improve
- OPPOSITE aggravate, worsen

4 *I can't **help** coughing.*
- stop, avoid, prevent, refrain from

helpful adjective
1 *The staff were friendly and **helpful**.*
- obliging, cooperative, kind, considerate, thoughtful, sympathetic
- OPPOSITE unhelpful

2 *The shop assistant gave us some **helpful** advice.*
- useful, valuable, worthwhile, beneficial, profitable
- OPPOSITE worthless

helping noun
*I got a huge **helping** of ice cream.*
- serving, portion, plateful, amount, share, ration

helpless adjective
*Kittens are born blind and **helpless**.*
- powerless, weak, feeble, dependent, defenceless, vulnerable
- OPPOSITE independent, strong

a
b
c
d
e
f
g
h
i
j
k
l
m
n
o
p
q
r
s
t
u
v
w
x
y
z

a
b
c
d
e
f
g
h
i
j
k
l
m
n
o
p
q
r
s
t
u
v
w
x
y
z

hem verb **to hem someone in**

*The bus was **hemmed in** by some parked cars.*

- shut in, box in, encircle, enclose, surround

herb noun

WORD WEB

SOME COMMON HERBS
basil, camomile, caraway, chervil, chicory, chive, coriander, cumin, dill, fennel, fenugreek, hyssop, lemon balm, liquorice, lovage, marjoram, mint, oregano, parsley, peppermint, rosemary, sage, tarragon, thyme

herd noun FOR GROUPS OF ANIMALS
SEE **group**

heroic adjective

*The firefighters made a **heroic** effort to put out the blaze.*

- bold, brave, courageous, daring, fearless, noble, selfless, valiant
OPPOSITE cowardly

hesitant adjective

*The puppy was **hesitant** about going outside.*

- uncertain, unsure, doubtful, cautious, tentative, timid, shy, wary
OPPOSITE confident

hesitate verb

*I **hesitated** for a moment before ringing the doorbell.*

- pause, delay, wait, hold back, dither, falter, waver
- (*informal*) think twice

hidden adjective

1 *The giant kept his gold **hidden** in a wooden chest.*
- concealed, out of sight, unseen, invisible, covered, disguised
OPPOSITE visible

2 *There's a **hidden** message in the riddle.*
- secret, mysterious, obscure, coded, cryptic
OPPOSITE obvious

hide verb

1 *Quick!—someone's coming—we'd better **hide**.*
- go into hiding, take cover, take refuge, keep out of sight, lie low, go to ground

2 *They **hid** the jewels in a secret drawer.*
- conceal, secrete, bury
- (*informal*) stash
OPPOSITE expose

3 *The clouds **hid** the sun.*
- blot out, cover, screen, shroud, veil, mask
OPPOSITE uncover

4 *I tried to **hide** my feelings.*
- disguise, keep secret, suppress, camouflage, cloak
OPPOSITE show

hideous adjective

*The troll had a **hideous** grin on his face.*

- repulsive, revolting, ugly, grotesque, monstrous, ghastly, gruesome, horrible, appalling, dreadful, frightful
OPPOSITE beautiful

high adjective

1 *The castle was surrounded by a **high** wall.*
- tall, towering, elevated, lofty
OPPOSITE low

2 *Sir Grinalot was a knight of **high** rank and status.*
- senior, top, leading, important, prominent, powerful
OPPOSITE low, junior

3 *House prices are very **high** at the moment.*
- expensive, dear, costly, excessive
OPPOSITE low

4 *A **high** wind was blowing.*
- strong, powerful, forceful, extreme
OPPOSITE gentle

5 *The pixie spoke in a **high** squeaky voice.*
- high-pitched, sharp, shrill, piercing
- A high singing voice is soprano or treble.
OPPOSITE deep

highlight noun
*The **highlight** of the holiday was spotting a wild dolphin.*
- high point, high spot, best moment, climax

highly adverb
*It is **highly** unusual to see foxes during the day.*
- very, extremely, exceptionally, considerably, decidedly

hike verb, noun
*We often go **hiking** across the moors.*
- trek, walk, ramble, tramp

hilarious adjective
*The boys thought the cartoon was **hilarious**.*
- funny, amusing, comical
- (*informal*) hysterical

hill noun
1 *From the top of this **hill** you can see for miles.*
- mount, peak, ridge
- A small hill is a hillock or mound.
- The top of a hill is the summit.
2 *Jenny pushed her bike up the steep **hill**.*
- slope, rise, incline, ascent, gradient

hinder verb
*The snowstorm **hindered** the rescue attempt.*
- hamper, hold up, obstruct, impede, slow down, stand in the way of, restrict, handicap
OPPOSITE help

hindrance noun
*The sharks were a **hindrance** to the divers.*
- obstacle, obstruction, handicap, inconvenience, difficulty, disadvantage, drawback
OPPOSITE help

hint noun
1 *I don't know the answer—can you give me a **hint**?*
- clue, indication, sign, suggestion, inkling
2 *The magazine offers handy **hints** for decorating.*
- tip, pointer

hint verb
*Mum **hinted** that we might be getting a puppy.*
- give a hint, suggest, imply, indicate

hire verb
- If you hire a bus or aircraft you charter it.
- If you hire someone to do a. job you engage or employ them.
- If you hire a building for a time you lease or rent it.

historic adjective
Take care not to confuse **historic**, which means famous or important in history, with **historical**, which simply refers to anything that happened in the past.
*The first landing on the Moon was a **historic** event.*
- famous, notable, celebrated, important, renowned, momentous, significant, major
OPPOSITE unimportant

historical adjective
See note at **historic.**
*Robin Hood may have been a **historical** character.*
- real, real-life, true, actual, authentic
OPPOSITE fictitious

history noun
1 *Dr Rice is an expert on Egyptian **history**.*
- heritage, past, antiquity, past times, olden days
2 *He wrote a **history** of the First World War.*
- account, chronicle, record
- The history of a person's life is their biography.
- The history of your own life is your autobiography or memoirs.

hit noun
1 *Matt got a nasty **hit** on the head.*
- bump, blow, bang, knock, whack
- A hit with your fist is a punch.
- A hit with your open hand is a slap or smack.

a
b
c
d
e
f
g
h
i
j
k
l
m
n
o
p
q
r
s
t
u
v
w
x
y
z

- A hit with a bat or club is a drive, stroke, or swipe.

2 *Their new CD was an instant **hit**.*
- success, triumph
- (*informal*) winner

hit verb

1 *Auntie Flo **hit** the burglar on the head with her umbrella.*
- strike, knock, bang, bash, thump, bump, crack, rap, slam, swipe, slog, cuff
- (*informal*) whack, wham, wallop, sock, clout, clobber, belt, biff
- (*old use*) smite
- To hit with your fist is to punch.
- To hit with the palm of your hand is to slap or smack.
- To punish someone by hitting them is to beat them.
- To hit someone with a stick is to club them.
- To hit your toe on something is to stub it.
- To kill an insect by hitting it is to swat it.
- To hit something repeatedly is to batter, buffet, or pound it.
- To hit something gently is to tap it.

FOR WAYS TO HIT A BALL

SEE **ball**

2 *The drought has **hit** many farms in the area.*
- affect, damage, harm, hurt

hoard noun

*Hamish keeps a **hoard** of sweets in his desk.*
- cache, store, stock, supply, pile, stockpile
- A hoard of treasure is a treasure trove.

hoard verb

*Squirrels **hoard** nuts for the winter.*
- store, collect, gather, save, put by, pile up, stockpile
- (*informal*) stash away

hoarse adjective

*Mr Barker's voice was **hoarse** from shouting.*
- rough, harsh, husky, croaky, throaty, gruff, rasping, gravelly

hoax noun

*The telephone call was a **hoax**.*
- joke, practical joke, prank, trick, spoof
- (*informal*) con, scam

hobby noun

*My favourite **hobby** is snorkelling.*
- pastime, pursuit, interest, activity, recreation

hoist verb

*The crane **hoisted** the crates onto a ship.*
- lift, pull up, raise, heave, winch up

hold noun

*The vet took a firm **hold** on the dog's collar.*
- grip, grasp, clutch, clasp

hold verb

1 *Please **hold** the dog's lead.*
- clasp, grasp, grip, cling to, hang on to, clutch, seize

2 *Can I **hold** the baby?*
- embrace, hug, cradle

3 *They **held** the suspect until the police arrived.*
- confine, detain, keep

4 *Will the ladder **hold** my weight?*
- bear, support, carry, take

5 *If our luck **holds**, we could reach the final.*
- continue, last, carry on, persist, stay

6 *She **holds** strong opinions.*
- believe in, maintain, stick to

to hold out

1 *The robot **held out** one of his arms.*
- extend, reach out, stick out, stretch out

2 *Our supplies won't **hold out** much longer.*
- keep going, last, carry on, continue, endure

to hold something up

1 *Please **hold up** your hand.*
- lift, put up, raise

2 *The accident **held up** the traffic.*
- delay, hinder, slow down

hole noun

1 *The meteor created a massive **hole** in the ground.*
- pit, hollow, crater, dent, depression, cavity, chasm, abyss

2 *The rabbits escaped through a **hole** in the fence.*
- gap, opening, breach, break, cut, slit, gash, split, tear, vent

holiday noun

*We spent our summer **holiday** in Ireland.*
- vacation, break, leave, time off

hollow adjective

*Tennis balls are **hollow**.*
- empty, unfilled
- OPPOSITE solid

hollow noun

*The ball rolled into a **hollow** in the ground.*
- dip, dent, depression, hole, pit, crater
- A hollow between two hills is a valley.

hollow verb

*We **hollowed** out a pumpkin to make a Halloween lantern.*
- dig, excavate, gouge, scoop

holy adjective

1 *The pilgrims knelt to pray in the **holy** shrine.*
- sacred, blessed, revered

2 *The pilgrims were **holy** people.*
- religious, spiritual, devout, pious, godly, saintly

home noun

*The hurricane forced people to flee their **homes**.*
- house, residence, dwelling, abode, lodging
- A home for the sick is a convalescent home or nursing home.
- A place where a bird or animal lives is its habitat.
- SEE ALSO **house** noun
- FOR HOMES OF WILD ANIMALS
- SEE **animal**

homely adjective

*The hotel was small with a **homely** atmosphere.*
- friendly, informal, cosy, familiar, relaxed, easygoing, comfortable, simple

honest adjective

1 *He's an **honest** boy, so he gave the money back.*
- good, honourable, law-abiding, moral, trustworthy, upright, virtuous
- OPPOSITE dishonest

2 *Please give me your **honest** opinion.*
- sincere, genuine, truthful, direct, frank, candid, plain, straightforward, unbiased
- OPPOSITE insincere

honour noun

1 *Her success brought **honour** to the school.*
- credit, good reputation, good name, respect, praise, acclaim

2 *It's an **honour** to meet you.*
- privilege, distinction

honour verb

*The winners were **honoured** at a special ceremony.*
- praise, celebrate, salute, give credit to, pay tribute to, glorify

honourable adjective

1 *The knight was an **honourable** man.*
- good, honest, sincere, noble, principled, moral, righteous, trustworthy, upright, virtuous, worthy, decent, fair, trusty

2 *It was an **honourable** thing to do.*
- noble, admirable, praiseworthy, decent
- OPPOSITE unworthy

hook verb

1 *Dad **hooked** the trailer to the car.*
- attach, fasten, hitch, connect, couple

2 *The angler **hooked** an enormous fish.*
- catch, land, take

hop verb

*The goblins **hopped** about in excitement.*
- jump, leap, skip, spring, prance, caper, bound, dance

a
b
c
d
e
f
g
h
i
j
k
l
m
n
o
p
q
r
s
t
u
v
w
x
y
z

hope verb

I hope to see you again soon.
- wish, trust, expect, look forward

hope noun

1 *Her dearest hope was to see her family again.*
- ambition, dream, desire, wish

2 *There's hope of better weather tomorrow.*
- prospect, expectation, likelihood

hopeful adjective

1 *I am feeling hopeful about tomorrow's match.*
- optimistic, confident, positive, expectant
OPPOSITE pessimistic

2 *The future is beginning to look more hopeful.*
- promising, encouraging, favourable, reassuring
OPPOSITE discouraging

hopeless adjective

1 *The shipwrecked crew were in a hopeless situation.*
- desperate, wretched, beyond hope
OPPOSITE hopeful

2 *I'm hopeless at ice-skating.*
- bad, poor, incompetent
- (*informal*) useless, rubbish
OPPOSITE good, competent

horde noun

Hordes of people were queuing for tickets.
- crowd, throng, mob, swarm, gang, group

horizontal adjective

Lay the pole on the ground in a horizontal position.
- flat, level
OPPOSITE vertical

horrible adjective

What a horrible smell!
- awful, terrible, dreadful, appalling, unpleasant, disagreeable, offensive, objectionable, disgusting, repulsive, revolting, horrendous, horrid, nasty, hateful, odious, loathsome, beastly, ghastly
OPPOSITE pleasant

horrific adjective

The film has some horrific scenes of battle.
- horrifying, terrifying, shocking, gruesome, dreadful, appalling, ghastly, hideous, atrocious, grisly, sickening

horrify verb

We were horrified by the sight of the monster.
- appal, shock, terrify, frighten, alarm, scare, sicken, disgust

horror noun

1 *Ingrid screamed in horror when she saw the snake.*
- terror, fear, fright, alarm, dread

2 *The film depicts the full horror of war.*
- awfulness, hideousness, gruesomeness, ghastliness, frightfulness

horse noun

WORD WEB
- A male horse is a stallion and a female is a mare.
- A young horse is a foal, colt (male), or filly (female).
- An uncomplimentary word for a horse is nag.
- A poetic word for a horse is steed.
- A word meaning 'to do with horses' is equine.
- A cross between a donkey and a horse is a mule.

SOME TYPES OF HORSE
bronco, carthorse, Clydesdale, mustang, piebald, pony, racehorse, Shetland pony, shire horse, warhorse

NOISES MADE BY A HORSE
neigh, snicker, snort, whinny

WAYS A HORSE CAN MOVE
canter, gallop, trot, walk

PARTS OF A HORSE'S HARNESS
bit, blinker, bridle, girth, halter, noseband, pommel, rein, saddle, spurs, stirrups, trace

SPORTS AND ACTIVITIES INVOLVING HORSES

gymkhana, horse-racing, jousting, rodeo, polo, showjumping, steeplechase

- A person who rides a horse in a race is a jockey.
- A word meaning 'to do with horse riding' is equestrian.
- Soldiers who fight on horseback are cavalry.
- An old word for a cavalry horse was a charger.

hospital noun

 WORD WEB

PLACES WHERE PEOPLE GO FOR MEDICAL TREATMENT

clinic, convalescent home, hospice, infirmary, nursing home, sanatorium

PARTS OF A HOSPITAL

accident and emergency, dispensary, intensive care unit, operating theatre, outpatients, pharmacy, X-ray department, ward

SEE ALSO **medicine**

hostile adjective

1 *The warriors shook their weapons in a **hostile** manner.*
- aggressive, antagonistic, unfriendly, unwelcoming, warlike, malevolent
  OPPOSITE friendly
2 *The North Pole has a very **hostile** climate.*
- harsh, unfavourable, adverse, bad
  OPPOSITE favourable

hostility noun

*The **hostility** between the two players was obvious.*
- dislike, enmity, hate, hatred, aggression, antagonism, bad feeling, detestation, ill-will, unfriendliness, malice
  OPPOSITE friendship

hot adjective

1 *The weather has been **hot** this summer.*
- warm, balmy, blazing, roasting, scorching, blistering, sweltering, stifling
  OPPOSITE cold, cool
2 *Careful—the soup's really **hot**.*
- burning, boiling, baking hot, piping hot, scalding, searing, sizzling, steaming
  OPPOSITE cold, cool
3 *I like curry, but only if it's not too **hot**.*
- spicy, peppery, fiery
  OPPOSITE mild
4 *My sister, Diana, has a **hot** temper.*
- fierce, fiery, violent, passionate, raging, angry, intense
  OPPOSITE calm, mild

house noun

 WORD WEB

WORDS FOR THE PLACE YOU LIVE IN

abode, dwelling, home, lodging, quarters, residence

BUILDINGS WHERE PEOPLE LIVE

apartment, bungalow, chalet, cottage, council house, croft, detached house, farmhouse, flat, hovel, hut, igloo, lodge, manor, manse, mansion, rectory, semi-detached house, shack, shanty, tenement, terraced house, thatched house, vicarage, villa

FOR ROOMS IN A HOUSE

SEE **room**

house verb

*The farm animals are **housed** indoors during the winter.*
- accommodate, lodge, shelter, take in, quarter, board

hover verb

1 *A flock of seagulls **hovered** overhead.*
- fly, flutter, float, hang, drift
2 *He **hovered** outside the room, afraid to knock.*
- linger, pause, wait about, hesitate, dally, loiter, dither
- (*informal*) hang about

however adverb

1 *I couldn't lift the stone, **however** hard I tried.*
- no matter how

2 *Spiders' silk is thin; **however**, it is also strong.*
- nevertheless, nonetheless, yet, still, even so

howl verb

1 *The injured boy **howled** in pain.*
- cry, yell, scream, yelp, shriek, wail

2 *They heard wolves **howling** in the night.*
- bay, yowl

huddle verb

*The penguins **huddled** together to get warm.*
- crowd, gather, flock, cluster, squeeze, pack, nestle, cuddle, snuggle
OPPOSITE scatter

hue noun

*The alien's face turned a strange **hue** of green.*
- colour, shade, tint, tone, tinge
FOR VARIOUS COLOURS
SEE **colour** noun

hug verb

*Ellie was **hugging** her favourite teddy bear.*
- cuddle, clasp, embrace, cling to, hold close, squeeze

huge adjective

*Elephants are **huge** animals.*
- enormous, gigantic, massive, colossal, giant, immense, vast, mighty, mammoth, monumental, hulking, great, big, large
- (*informal*) whopping, ginormous, humungous
OPPOSITE small, little, tiny

hum verb

*We heard insects **humming** in the air.*
- buzz, drone, murmur, purr, whirr

humans plural noun

***Humans** have smaller brains than whales.*
- human beings, the human race, humanity, mankind, people

humane adjective

*A **humane** society should treat animals well.*
- kind, compassionate, sympathetic, civilized, benevolent, kind-hearted, charitable, loving, merciful
OPPOSITE cruel

humble adjective

1 *The gentle giant was both **humble** and kind.*
- modest, meek, unassuming, polite, respectful, submissive
OPPOSITE proud

2 *Hansel and Gretel lived a **humble** cottage.*
- simple, modest, plain, ordinary, commonplace, lowly
OPPOSITE grand

humid adjective

*I don't like this **humid** weather.*
- muggy, clammy, close, sticky, steamy, sweaty
OPPOSITE fresh

humiliate verb

*He **humiliated** her in front of her friends.*
- embarrass, disgrace, shame, make ashamed, humble, crush, degrade
- (*informal*) put you in your place, take you down a peg

humiliating adjective

*The team suffered a **humiliating** defeat.*
- embarrassing, crushing, degrading, humbling, undignified
OPPOSITE glorious

humorous adjective

*My friend told me a **humorous** story.*
- amusing, funny, comic, witty, entertaining
OPPOSITE serious

humour noun

1 *I liked the **humour** in the film.*
- comedy, wit, amusement, jokes

2 *The ogre was in a very bad **humour**.*
- mood, temper, disposition, frame of mind, spirits

hump noun

*Camels have **humps** on their backs.*
- bump, lump, bulge, swelling

hunch noun

*The detective had a **hunch** about the murder case.*
- feeling, intuition, inkling, guess, impression, suspicion, idea

hunch verb

*Will **hunched** his shoulders to keep out the cold.*
- arch, bend, curve, hump, shrug, curl up

hunger noun

*After a week without food, the crew were faint with **hunger**.*
- lack of food, starvation, famine
- Bad health caused by not having enough food is malnutrition.

hungry adjective

*Our dog always seems to be **hungry**.*
- starving, famished, ravenous
- (*informal*) peckish

hunt noun

*Police have begun the **hunt** for clues.*
- search, quest, chase, pursuit (of)

hunt verb

1 *Some Native Americans tribes used to **hunt** buffalo.*
- chase, pursue, track, trail, hound, stalk
- An animal which hunts other animals for food is a predator.

2 *I **hunted** in the attic for our old photos.*
- search, seek, look, rummage, ferret, root around

hurdle noun

1 *The horse jumped over the **hurdle** easily.*
- fence, barrier, jump, barricade, obstacle

2 *The biggest **hurdle** facing the team is lack of experience.*
- difficulty, problem, handicap, hindrance, snag, stumbling block

hurl verb

*I **hurled** the ball as far as I could.*
- throw, fling, pitch, toss, cast, sling, launch
- (*informal*) chuck

hurry verb

1 *If you want to catch the bus, you'd better **hurry**.*
- be quick, hasten, make speed
- (*informal*) get a move on, step on it
OPPOSITE dawdle

2 *Alice saw the White Rabbit **hurrying** past.*
- rush, dash, fly, speed, hurtle, scurry
OPPOSITE amble, stroll

3 *It's no good trying to **hurry** a donkey.*
- quicken, speed up, urge on
OPPOSITE slow down

hurry noun

*In our **hurry**, we forgot the tickets.*
- rush, haste, speed, urgency

hurt verb

1 *Be careful not to **hurt** yourself with the scissors.*
- harm, injure, damage, wound, maim
- To hurt someone deliberately is to torment or torture them.

2 *My feet **hurt**.*
- be sore, be painful, ache, throb, sting, smart

3 *Your letter **hurt** me deeply.*
- upset, distress, offend, grieve

hurtful adjective

*That was a very **hurtful** remark.*
- upsetting, unkind, cruel, mean, painful, spiteful, nasty

hurtle verb

*The train **hurtled** along at top speed.*
- rush, speed, race, dash, fly, charge, tear, shoot, zoom

husband noun

*Hugh is Mrs Hart's fourth **husband**.*
- Another word for a person's husband or wife is their spouse.

hush verb

*The speaker tried his best to **hush** the crowd.*
- silence, quieten, settle, still, calm

a
b
c
d
e
f
g
h
i
j
k
l
m
n
o
p
q
r
s
t
u
v
w
x
y
z

to hush something up
*They tried to **hush up** the scandal.*
• cover up, hide, conceal, keep quiet, keep secret, suppress

husky adjective
*The wizard spoke in a **husky** voice.*
• hoarse, throaty, gruff, rasping, gravelly, rough, croaky

hut noun
*The walkers came across a **hut** in the forest.*
• shed, shack, cabin, den, shelter, shanty, hovel

hygienic adjective
*Always use a **hygienic** surface for chopping food.*
• sanitary, clean, disinfected, sterilized, sterile, germ-free, healthy
OPPOSITE unhygienic

hysterical adjective
1 *The fans became **hysterical** when the band appeared.*
• crazy, frenzied, mad, delirious, raving, wild, uncontrollable
2 *(informal) We laughed at the **hysterical** jokes in the film.*
• hilarious, funny, amusing, comical

Ii

ice noun

WORD WEB
VARIOUS FORMS OF ICE
black ice, floe, frost, glacier, iceberg, ice sheet, icicle

WAYS TO DESCRIBE ICE
brittle, cracked, frozen solid, glacial, glassy, gleaming, glinting, hard, packed, slippery or (informal) slippy, smooth, treacherous
THINGS YOU MIGHT DO ON ICE
glide, skate, skid, slide, slip, slither
SPORTS THAT ARE PLAYED ON ICE
curling, figure skating, ice skating, ice hockey, speed skating
• Ice sports are played on an ice rink.

icy adjective
1 *You need to dress warmly in **icy** weather.*
• cold, freezing, frosty, wintry, arctic, bitter, biting
2 ***Icy** roads are dangerous.*
• frozen, slippery, glacial, glassy
• (informal) slippy

idea noun
1 *I've got a great **idea**!*
• plan, scheme, proposal, suggestion, inspiration
2 *She has some funny **ideas** about life.*
• belief, notion, opinion, view, theory, concept, conception, hypothesis
3 *What's the main **idea** of this poem?*
• point, meaning, intention, thought
4 *Give me an **idea** of what you are planning.*
• clue, hint, inkling, impression

ideal adjective
*It's **ideal** weather for a picnic.*
• perfect, excellent, the best, faultless, suitable

identical adjective
*The twins were wearing **identical** clothes.*
• matching, similar, alike, indistinguishable
OPPOSITE different

identify verb
1 *The police asked if I could **identify** the thief.*
• recognize, name, distinguish, pick out, single out

2 *The doctor couldn't **identify** what was wrong.*
- diagnose, discover, spot
- (*informal*) put a name to

to identify with
*Can you **identify with** the hero of the story?*
- sympathize with, feel for, understand
- (*informal*) put yourself in the shoes of

idiotic adjective
*That was an **idiotic** thing to do.*
- stupid, silly, foolish, unwise, senseless, ridiculous, half-witted, unintelligent, crazy, mad, hare-brained
- (*informal*) daft
- OPPOSITE sensible

idle adjective
1 *The ogre was an **idle**, foul-smelling creature.*
- lazy, indolent, slothful, work-shy
- OPPOSITE hard-working

2 *The computers lay **idle** all week.*
- inactive, unused, inoperative
- OPPOSITE busy, active

idol noun
1 *The floor of the temple was littered with broken **idols**.*
- god, deity, image, statue

2 *He was a pop **idol** of the fifties.*
- star, celebrity, icon, pin-up, favourite

idolize verb
*Kirsty **idolizes** her big brother.*
- adore, love, worship, be devoted to, look up to

ignite verb
*The matches were wet and would not **ignite**.*
- light, catch fire, burn, kindle, spark

ignorant adjective
*Trolls are often described as **ignorant** creatures.*
- uneducated, simple, stupid

ignorant of
*Detective Miles was **ignorant of** the facts in the case.*
- unaware of, unfamiliar with, unacquainted with
- OPPOSITE aware of

ignore verb
***Ignoring** the weather, Lynn went for a walk.*
- disregard, take no notice of, overlook, neglect, spurn, snub
- (*informal*) turn a blind eye to

ill adjective
1 *I missed school for a week when I was **ill**.*
- sick, unwell, poorly, sickly, ailing, infirm, unfit, indisposed, diseased, infected, nauseous, queasy, off colour, peaky
- (*informal*) under the weather

  FOR COMMON ILLNESSES
  SEE **illness**
  OPPOSITE healthy, well

2 *Did the plants suffer **ill** effects in the frost?*
- bad, harmful, adverse, damaging
- OPPOSITE good

illegal adjective
*Stealing is **illegal**.*
- unlawful, against the law, banned, prohibited, criminal, forbidden, wrong
- OPPOSITE legal

illegible adjective
*The signature on the letter was **illegible**.*
- unreadable, indecipherable, unclear, indistinct
- OPPOSITE legible, readable

illness noun

WORD WEB

*What kind of **illness** is he suffering from?*
- abnormality, affliction, ailment, attack, complaint, condition, disability, disease, disorder, health problem, infection, infirmity, sickness (*informal*) bug, upset
- A sudden illness is an attack or fit.
- A period of illness is a bout.
- A general outbreak of illness in a particular area is an epidemic.

---

a
b
c
d
e
f
g
h
i
j
k
l
m
n
o
p
q
r
s
t
u
v
w
x
y
z

a
b
c
d
e
f
g
h
i
j
k
l
m
n
o
p
q
r
s
t
u
v
w
x
y
z

SOME COMMON ILLNESSES
allergy, appendicitis, asthma, bronchitis, chickenpox, chill, cold, cough, diarrhoea, eczema, fever, flu, glandular fever, hay fever, headache, indigestion, influenza, jaundice, laryngitis, measles, migraine, mumps, stomach-ache, tonsillitis, ulcer, whooping cough
FOR WAYS TO TREAT ILLNESS
SEE **medicine**

illustrate verb

1 I used some photos to **illustrate** my story.
- depict, picture, portray
2 The accident **illustrates** the importance of road safety.
- show, demonstrate, make clear

illustration noun

1 I like cookery books with lots of **illustrations**.
- picture, photograph, drawing, sketch, diagram
2 I'll give you an **illustration** of what I mean.
- example, instance, demonstration, specimen

image noun

1 The film contained frightening **images** of war.
- picture, portrayal, depiction, representation
2 The temple contained **images** of the gods.
- figure, idol, statue, carving
3 You can see your **image** in the mirror.
- reflection, likeness
4 Alice is the **image** of her mother.
- double, twin

imaginary adjective

The story takes place in an **imaginary** universe.
- imagined, non-existent, unreal, made up, invented, fanciful, fictitious, fictional
OPPOSITE real

imagination noun

Use your **imagination** to draw an alien spaceship.
- creativity, inventiveness, ingenuity, inspiration, originality, vision, artistry, fancy

imaginative adjective

Roald Dahl wrote highly **imaginative** stories.
- creative, inventive, inspired, original, artistic, fanciful, ingenious, clever
OPPOSITE unimaginative, dull

imagine verb

1 **Imagine** what it would be like to visit Mars.
- picture, visualize, pretend, think up, dream up, fancy, conjure up
2 I **imagine** you'd like something to eat.
- suppose, assume, presume, believe, guess

imitate verb

Parrots can **imitate** the human voice.
- copy, reproduce, mimic, mirror, echo, simulate, impersonate, follow, match
- (informal) send up, take off

imitation adjective

The coat was made from **imitation** leather.
- artificial, synthetic, fake, sham, mock
OPPOSITE real, genuine

imitation noun

This is an **imitation** of a Viking helmet.
- copy, replica, reproduction, duplicate
- An imitation made to deceive someone is a fake or a forgery.

immature adjective

Tess is quite **immature** for her age.
- childish, babyish, infantile, juvenile
OPPOSITE mature

immediate adjective

1 Please can I have an **immediate** reply.
- instant, instantaneous, prompt, speedy, swift, urgent, quick, direct
- (informal) snappy
OPPOSITE slow

2 *Are you friends with your **immediate** neighbours?*
- closest, nearest, adjacent, next
OPPOSITE distant

immediately adverb
*You must fetch a doctor **immediately**!*
- at once, now, straight away, right away, instantly, promptly, directly

immense adjective
*The giant wiggled one of his **immense** toes.*
- huge, great, massive, enormous, colossal, vast, giant, gigantic, mighty, mammoth, monumental
- (*informal*) whopping, ginormous, humungous
OPPOSITE tiny

immobile adjective
*The knight stood **immobile** at the castle gate.*
- unmoving, motionless, stationary, still
OPPOSITE mobile

immoral adjective
*It would be **immoral** to steal the money.*
- wrong, wicked, bad, sinful, dishonest, corrupt
OPPOSITE moral, right

immortal adjective
*The ancient Greeks believed their gods were **immortal**.*
- undying, ageless, eternal, everlasting
OPPOSITE mortal

impact noun
1 *The crater was caused by the **impact** of a meteor.*
- crash, collision, smash, blow, bump, bang, knock, jolt
2 *Computers have a big **impact** on our lives.*
- effect, influence

impair verb
*Very loud noise can **impair** your hearing.*
- damage, harm, injure, weaken

impartial adjective
*Referees must be **impartial**.*
- neutral, detached, objective, unbiased, unprejudiced, disinterested, independent, fair, fair-minded, just, even-handed, open-minded
OPPOSITE biased

impatient adjective
1 *As time went on, Henry grew more and more **impatient**.*
- restless, agitated, anxious, edgy, fidgety, irritable, snappy, testy, jumpy
OPPOSITE patient
2 *The crowd were **impatient** for the show to begin.*
- anxious, eager, in a hurry, keen
- (*informal*) itching

imperfect adjective
*The items on this shelf are **imperfect**.*
- damaged, faulty, defective, flawed, broken, incomplete
OPPOSITE perfect

impertinent adjective
*The elf made some rather **impertinent** remarks.*
- rude, cheeky, impolite, impudent, insolent, disrespectful
OPPOSITE respectful, polite

implement noun
*The shed is full of garden **implements**.*
- tool, appliance, device, utensil, gadget, instrument
SEE ALSO **tool**

implore verb
*Jack **implored** the giant not to eat him.*
- beg, entreat, plead with

imply verb
*Are you **implying** that I am a liar?*
- suggest, hint, indicate

impolite adjective
*It would be **impolite** to refuse the invitation.*
- rude, bad-mannered, discourteous, disrespectful, insulting
OPPOSITE polite

a
b
c
d
e
f
g
h
i
j
k
l
m
n
o
p
q
r
s
t
u
v
w
x
y
z

a
b
c
d
e
f
g
h
i
j
k
l
m
n
o
p
q
r
s
t
u
v
w
x
y
z

import verb
*The UK **imports** tea and coffee.*
- bring in, ship in
OPPOSITE export

important adjective
1 *The World Cup is an **important** sporting event.*
- major, significant, big, central, momentous, outstanding, historic
2 *I have some **important** business to attend to.*
- serious, urgent, pressing, weighty, vital, essential, crucial
3 *The prime minister is an **important** person.*
- prominent, powerful, influential, notable, eminent, distinguished
OPPOSITE unimportant, minor

impose verb
*The government **imposed** a tax on fuel.*
- introduce, enforce, fix, inflict, prescribe, set

to impose on
*I don't want to **impose on** you.*
- inconvenience, intrude on, take advantage of

imposing adjective
*The castle is an **imposing** building.*
- grand, great, impressive, stately, magnificent, splendid, majestic, dignified, striking
OPPOSITE insignificant

impossible adjective
*We used to think that space travel was **impossible**.*
- impractical, unthinkable, unrealistic, unachievable, unworkable, out of the question
OPPOSITE possible

impress verb
*Frank **impressed** the coach with his football skills.*
- make an impression on, influence, leave its mark on, stick in your mind

impression noun
1 *I had the **impression** that something was wrong.*
- feeling, idea, sense, notion, suspicion, hunch
2 *The film made a big **impression** on them.*
- effect, impact, influence, mark
3 *My sister does a good **impression** of the Queen.*
- imitation, impersonation,
- (*informal*) send-up

impressive adjective
*The film includes some **impressive** special effects.*
- striking, effective, powerful, remarkable, spectacular, exciting, inspiring
OPPOSITE unimpressive, uninspiring

imprison verb
*The thief was **imprisoned** for two years.*
- send to prison, jail, lock up, incarcerate, confine, detain
- (*informal*) put away, send down, put under lock and key
OPPOSITE liberate

improve verb
1 *Her work **improved** during the term.*
- get better, advance, progress, develop, move on
OPPOSITE deteriorate
2 *Has he **improved** since his illness?*
- get better, recover, recuperate, pick up, rally, revive
OPPOSITE get worse
3 *How can I **improve** this story?*
- make better, enhance, refine, amend, revise, correct, upgrade

improvement noun
1 *Your handwriting shows signs of **improvement**.*
- getting better, advance, progress, development, recovery, upturn
2 *The author made some **improvements** to the book.*
- amendment, correction, revision, modification, enhancement

impudent adjective
*The pixie had an **impudent** grin on his face.*
* cheeky, insolent, rude, impolite, impertinent, disrespectful
OPPOSITE respectful, polite

impulse noun
*I had a sudden **impulse** to sing out loud.*
* desire, instinct, urge

impulsive adjective
*She regretted her **impulsive** decision to dye her hair.*
* hasty, rash, reckless, sudden, spontaneous, thoughtless, unthinking, impetuous
OPPOSITE deliberate

inaccessible adjective
*The caves were in an **inaccessible** part of the island.*
* unreachable, isolated, remote, out-of-the-way, hard to find
OPPOSITE accessible

inaccurate adjective
*That spelling of my surname is **inaccurate**.*
* wrong, incorrect, mistaken, false, inexact, untrue
OPPOSITE accurate

inadequate adjective
*They had brought an **inadequate** supply of matches.*
* insufficient, not enough, limited, scarce, scanty, meagre
OPPOSITE adequate

inappropriate adjective
*It's **inappropriate** to call the teacher by her first name.*
* unsuitable, improper, out of place, unfitting, unseemly
OPPOSITE appropriate

inaudible adjective SEE **hear**

incapable adjective
incapable of
*Mr Havers is **incapable of** making a decision.*
* unable to, incompetent at, unfit to, unsuited to, ineffective at
OPPOSITE capable of

incident noun
*There was an amusing **incident** at school this morning.*
* event, happening, occurrence, episode, affair

incidental adjective
*Tell us the main story without the **incidental** details.*
* unimportant, minor, inessential, secondary, subordinate
OPPOSITE essential

incline noun
*The house was at the top of a steep **incline**.*
* hill, slope, rise, gradient

inclined adjective
to be inclined to
*Ogres are **inclined to** eat too much.*
* be disposed to, have a habit of, be liable to, tend to

include verb
*Does the cost **include** postage and packing?*
* contain, incorporate, comprise, involve, take in, allow for, take into account, cover
OPPOSITE exclude

income noun
*What is your average monthly **income**?*
* pay, salary, wages, earnings
OPPOSITE expenditure

incompetent adjective
*The actor was so **incompetent** that he forgot his lines.*
* unskilful, inept, ineffective, unsatisfactory, useless, hopeless
OPPOSITE competent

a b c d e f g h i j k l m n o p q r s t u v w x y z

a
b
c
d
e
f
g
h
i
j
k
l
m
n
o
p
q
r
s
t
u
v
w
x
y
z

incomplete adjective
The new football stadium is still **incomplete**.
• unfinished, uncompleted, not ready
OPPOSITE complete

inconsiderate adjective
It's **inconsiderate** *to play the radio so loudly.*
• selfish, unthinking, thoughtless, insensitive, rude, tactless, unkind, uncaring
OPPOSITE considerate

inconsistent adjective
1 *His performance has been* **inconsistent** *this season.*
• changeable, unreliable, variable, unpredictable, erratic, fickle
2 *The stories of the two witnesses are* **inconsistent**.
• contradictory, conflicting, different
OPPOSITE consistent

inconspicuous adjective
The spy wore plain clothes to be **inconspicuous**.
• unnoticed, unobtrusive, camouflaged, out of sight
OPPOSITE conspicuous

inconvenient adjective
The guests arrived at an **inconvenient** *moment.*
• awkward, difficult, unsuitable, unfortunate, untimely, inopportune
OPPOSITE convenient

incorporate verb
The show **incorporates** *some well-known tunes.*
• include, contain, embrace, take in
OPPOSITE exclude

incorrect adjective
Nine out of ten of his answers were **incorrect**.
• wrong, mistaken, inaccurate, false
OPPOSITE correct

increase verb
1 *They've* **increased** *the size of the tennis courts.*
• make bigger, enlarge, expand, develop, add to, widen, broaden

2 *She* **increased** *the cooking time in the recipe.*
• extend, lengthen, prolong
3 *The police* **increased** *their efforts to find the murderer.*
• intensify, step up
4 *Will you be* **increasing** *the bus fares?*
• put up, raise
5 *Can you* **increase** *the volume of the TV?*
• turn up, amplify, boost
6 *The number of cars on the roads continues to* **increase**.
• grow, mount, go up, rise, soar, build up, escalate, multiply
FOR OPPOSITES
SEE **decrease** verb

incredible adjective
1 *Do you expect us to believe that* **incredible** *story?*
• unbelievable, unlikely, improbable, far-fetched, absurd, implausible
OPPOSITE credible
2 *The Forth Bridge is an* **incredible** *feat of engineering.*
• extraordinary, amazing, astounding, magnificent, marvellous, spectacular

independence noun
The islanders value their **independence**.
• freedom, liberty, autonomy
OPPOSITE dependence

independent adjective
1 *My granny is a very* **independent** *person.*
• free, liberated, self-sufficient, self-reliant
OPPOSITE dependent
2 *Luxembourg is an* **independent** *country.*
• autonomous, self-governing
3 *We need an* **independent** *opinion on the matter.*
• impartial, neutral, objective, unbiased
OPPOSITE biased

indicate verb

1 *The usher **indicated** where we should sit.*
- point to or out, specify, show, reveal, make known

2 *A red light **indicates** danger.*
- mean, stand for, denote, express, signal, signify, communicate, convey

indication noun

*He gave no **indication** that he felt ill.*
- sign, signal, hint, clue, inkling, evidence, warning, symptom, token

indifferent adjective

1 *I felt **indifferent** as I watched the game.*
- uninterested, detached, uncaring, unenthusiastic, unmoved, uninvolved, unconcerned
- OPPOSITE enthusiastic

2 *The food in the restaurant was **indifferent**.*
- mediocre, ordinary, unexciting, average
- OPPOSITE excellent

indignant adjective

*The player was **indignant** when he was sent off.*
- annoyed, angry, cross, affronted, offended, outraged, piqued

indirect adjective

*The bus took an **indirect** route into town.*
- roundabout, winding, meandering, rambling, zigzag
- OPPOSITE direct

indistinct adjective

1 *The photo was rather **indistinct**.*
- unclear, blurred, blurry, fuzzy, hazy, vague, indefinite, obscure, shadowy
- OPPOSITE clear

2 *They heard **indistinct** sounds of people talking.*
- muffled, mumbled, muted, faint, weak, inaudible, unintelligible, incoherent
- OPPOSITE distinct

individual adjective

*Her singing has an **individual** style.*
- characteristic, distinct, distinctive, special, unique, personal, singular

individual noun

*Who was that odd **individual**?*
- person, character, man, woman

induce verb

1 *I couldn't **induce** her to come to the party.*
- persuade, convince, prevail on, coax, tempt

2 *Some headaches are **induced** by stress.*
- cause, produce, provoke, bring on, lead to, give rise to

indulge verb

*They **indulged** their children too much.*
- spoil, pamper, mollycoddle

to indulge in

*I **indulged in** a nice hot bath.*
- enjoy, revel in, wallow in

indulgent adjective

*They are very **indulgent** towards their grandchildren.*
- tolerant, patient, permissive, lenient, easygoing, generous, liberal
- OPPOSITE strict

industry noun

1 *Many people in the area work in the car **industry**.*
- business, trade, commerce, manufacturing, production

2 *The elves' workshop was a hive of **industry**.*
- hard work, effort, energy, diligence, application, busyness
- OPPOSITE laziness

ineffective adjective

*He was an **ineffective** captain of the team.*
- incompetent, inadequate, unsuccessful, inept,
- (*informal*) useless, hopeless
- OPPOSITE effective

a
b
c
d
e
f
g
h
i
j
k
l
m
n
o
p
q
r
s
t
u
v
w
x
y
z

a b c d e f g h **i** j k l m n o p q r s t u v w x y z

inefficient adjective
1 *Our old vacuum cleaner was very inefficient.*
• ineffective, unproductive, useless, slow, sloppy
2 *The car is inefficient in its use of fuel.*
• wasteful, uneconomical, extravagant
OPPOSITE efficient

inevitable adjective
If it rains, it is inevitable that the pitch will get wet.
• certain, sure, definite, unavoidable, inescapable

inexpensive adjective
We bought some inexpensive clothes in the market.
• cheap, low-priced, low-cost, cut-price, affordable
OPPOSITE expensive

infamous adjective
Dick Turpin was an infamous highwayman.
• notorious, villainous, wicked

infant noun
He had blond, curly hair as an infant.
• baby, small child, tot, toddler

infect verb
A virus may have infected the water supply.
• contaminate, pollute, poison

infection noun
The infection spread rapidly.
• disease, virus, contagion, contamination

infectious adjective
Chickenpox is highly infectious.
• contagious, catching

infer verb
Note that **infer** and **imply** are not synonyms.
What can you infer from the tone of her letter?
• conclude, deduce, gather, assume, guess, work out

inferior adjective
1 *The clothes were of inferior quality.*
• poor, bad, second-rate, mediocre, cheap, shoddy
2 *Officers can give orders to those of inferior rank.*
• lesser, lower, junior, subordinate
OPPOSITE superior

infested adjective
The attic was infested with mice.
• swarming, teeming, crawling, overrun, plagued

infiltrate verb
Spies infiltrated the enemy's camp.
• enter secretly, penetrate

infinite adjective
You need infinite patience to train a puppy.
• endless, limitless, unlimited, boundless, never-ending, unending, inexhaustible
OPPOSITE finite

infirm adjective
Most of the patients are elderly and infirm.
• frail, weak, feeble, poorly, ill, unwell
• People who have to stay in bed are bedridden.
OPPOSITE healthy

inflammation noun
This ointment will soothe the inflammation.
• swelling, redness, soreness, infection

inflate verb
The tyres need to be inflated.
• blow up, pump up
OPPOSITE deflate

inflict verb
I hate seeing anyone inflict pain on an animal.
• administer, deal out, apply, impose

influence noun
Rock music had a big influence on her life.
• effect, impact, power, dominance, guidance, authority, control

influence verb

*The money he was offered **influenced** his decision.*

- affect, have an effect on, direct, guide, control, motivate

influential adjective

*She knows some very **influential** people.*

- important, leading, powerful, significant

OPPOSITE unimportant

inform verb

*Please **inform** us if you move house.*

- tell, let you know, notify, advise

informal adjective

1 *The party will be a very **informal** event.*
- casual, relaxed, easygoing, friendly, homely, natural

2 *Emails are usually written in an **informal** style.*
- colloquial, familiar, chatty, personal

OPPOSITE formal

information noun

*There is more **information** on our website.*

- details, particulars, facts, data, advice, guidance, knowledge
- (*informal*) info

informative adjective

*That book you lent me was very **informative**.*

- helpful, useful, instructive, illuminating, revealing

OPPOSITE unhelpful

infuriate verb

*He was **infuriated** by the umpire's decision.*

- anger, enrage, incense, madden, exasperate

ingenious adjective

*It seemed like an **ingenious** plan.*

- clever, brilliant, inspired, inventive, imaginative, original, crafty, cunning, shrewd

inhabit verb

*People **inhabited** the caves thousands of years ago.*

- live in, occupy, dwell in, reside in, populate, settle in

inhabitant noun

*The island has fewer than thirty **inhabitants**.*

- resident, dweller, native, occupier, occupant
- An inhabitant of a particular city or country is a citizen.
- The inhabitants of a place are its population.

inhabited adjective

*Is the island **inhabited**?*

- occupied, lived-in

OPPOSITE uninhabited

inherit verb

*She **inherited** the farm from her uncle.*

- succeed to, be left, come into

inherited adjective

*Eye colour is an **inherited** characteristic.*

- hereditary, passed down

inhuman adjective

*I think it's **inhuman** to hunt animals.*

- barbaric, cruel, inhumane, merciless, heartless

OPPOSITE humane

initial adjective

*My **initial** reaction was to run away and hide.*

- first, earliest, preliminary, opening, introductory

OPPOSITE final, eventual

initially adverb

***Initially**, I didn't like swimming.*

- at first, in the beginning, to begin with, to start with, at the outset

initiative noun

*You must use your **initiative** on the treasure hunt.*

- resourcefulness, inventiveness, originality, enterprise

a
b
c
d
e
f
g
h
i
j
k
l
m
n
o
p
q
r
s
t
u
v
w
x
y
z

a
b
c
d
e
f
g
h
i
j
k
l
m
n
o
p
q
r
s
t
u
v
w
x
y
z

injection noun
*The nurse gave me an **injection**.*
- inoculation, vaccination
- (*informal*) jab

injure verb
*Was anyone **injured** in the accident?*
- hurt, harm, wound
- To injure someone causing permament damage is to maim them.

injury noun

 WORD WEB

*She escaped without any serious **injury**.*
- wound, harm, hurt
SOME TYPES OF INJURY
bite, bruise, burn, cut, fracture, gash, graze, scald, scratch, sprain, sting, strain

inner adjective
1 *A passageway led to the **inner** chamber.*
- central, inside, interior, internal, middle
2 *She tries to hide her **inner** feelings.*
- innermost, inward, personal, private, intimate, secret, hidden, concealed
OPPOSITE outer

innocent adjective
1 *The jury found the man **innocent**.*
- guiltless, blameless, free from blame
OPPOSITE guilty
2 *Baby tigers look so **innocent**.*
- angelic, harmless, faultless, virtuous, pure, simple, inexperienced, naïve
OPPOSITE wicked

innumerable adjective
*There are **innumerable** stars in the sky.*
- countless, numberless, uncountable, untold

inquire verb
to inquire into
*Detectives are **inquiring into** the robbery.*
- look into, investigate, examine, explore

inquiry noun
*There will be an official **inquiry** about the accident.*
- investigation, inspection, examination

inquisitive adjective
*Chimpanzees are naturally **inquisitive**.*
- curious, questioning, inquiring, probing
FOR UNCOMPLIMENTARY SYNONYMS
SEE **nosy**

insane adjective
1 *It was rumoured that the king had gone **insane**.*
- mentally ill, mad, crazy, deranged, demented, disturbed, unhinged
- (*informal*) off your head, out of your mind
OPPOSITE sane
2 *It would be **insane** to swim in the sea in January!*
- crazy, mad, daft, senseless, stupid, foolish, idiotic
OPPOSITE sensible, wise

inscription noun
*The professor read the **inscription** on the tomb.*
- engraving, carving, writing

insect noun

WORD WEB

SOME TYPES OF INSECT
ant, aphid, bee, beetle, bluebottle, bumble-bee, butterfly, cicada, cockroach, crane fly or daddy-long-legs, cricket, dragonfly, earwig, firefly, flea, fly, glow-worm, gnat, grasshopper, greenfly, hornet, horsefly, ladybird, locust, louse, mantis, mayfly, midge, mosquito, moth, stick insect, termite, tsetse fly, wasp, weevil
SEE ALSO **bee**
FOR NAMES FOR GROUPS OF INSECTS
SEE **group**
LIFE STAGES OF SOME INSECTS
caterpillar, chrysalis, grub, larva, maggot, pupa

PARTS OF INSECTS' BODIES
head, thorax, abdomen; antennae, legs, wings

SOME CREATURES SIMILAR TO INSECTS
centipede, earthworm, mite, slug, spider, woodlouse, worm

insecure adjective

1 *Be careful—that scaffolding is* **insecure**.
- unsafe, unsteady, unstable, loose, shaky, wobbly, dangerous, hazardous, precarious

2 *Colin felt* **insecure** *on his first day at school.*
- anxious, nervous, worried, apprehensive, uneasy, uncertain, unconfident
OPPOSITE secure

insensitive adjective

I'm sorry if my comments were **insensitive**.
- thoughtless, tactless, unfeeling, uncaring, unsympathetic, callous
OPPOSITE sensitive

insert verb

Please **insert** *a coin in the slot.*
- put in, place, push in, stick in, install, implant

inside adjective

The **inside** *doors are all painted green.*
- indoor, inner, interior, internal
OPPOSITE outside

inside noun

The **inside** *of the nest was lined with feathers.*
- interior, inner surface, centre, core, heart, middle
OPPOSITE outside

insignificant adjective

The author made a few **insignificant** *changes.*
- unimportant, minor, trivial, negligible, slight, meaningless
OPPOSITE significant

insincere adjective

The butler welcomed us with an **insincere** *smile.*
- false, pretended, hypocritical, dishonest, deceitful, deceptive, lying
- (*informal*) two-faced
OPPOSITE sincere

insist verb

Griselda **insisted** *that she was not a witch.*
- declare, state, assert, maintain, stress, emphasize, swear, vow, claim

to insist on
The magician **insisted on** *silence before he began.*
- demand, require

insolent adjective

The boy gave the teacher an **insolent** *stare.*
- rude, impudent, disrespectful, impolite, impertinent, arrogant, brazen
- (*informal*) cheeky
OPPOSITE polite, respectful

inspect verb

They **inspected** *the damage done by the storm.*
- check, examine, investigate, look over, study, survey, scrutinize

inspection noun

There will be a safety **inspection** *this afternoon.*
- check, check-up, examination, review, survey

inspiration noun

1 *What was the* **inspiration** *behind your story?*
- impulse, motivation, stimulus

2 *The scientist had a sudden* **inspiration**.
- idea, thought

inspire verb

The crowd **inspired** *the team to play well.*
- motivate, prompt, stimulate, encourage, stir, arouse, spur on

a
b
c
d
e
f
g
h
i
j
k
l
m
n
o
p
q
r
s
t
u
v
w
x
y
z

install verb

We are getting a new bathroom installed.

- put in, set up, fix, place, position, establish

OPPOSITE remove

instalment noun

I missed the first instalment of 'Dr Who'.

- episode, part

instance noun

Give me an instance of what you mean.

- example, illustration, case, sample

instant adjective

Gardeners don't expect instant results.

- immediate, quick, rapid, fast, prompt, snappy, speedy, swift, direct

instant noun

The shooting star was gone in an instant.

- moment, second, split second, flash
- (*informal*) tick, jiffy

instinct noun

The detective always followed his own instincts.

- impulse, inclination, intuition, hunch, feeling, urge

instinctive adjective

Most people have an instinctive fear of sharks.

- intuitive, natural, innate, inherent, automatic, involuntary, reflex, spontaneous, impulsive, unconscious, unthinking

OPPOSITE deliberate, conscious

instruct verb

1 *All the staff are instructed in first aid.*
- teach, train, coach, tutor
2 *The police officer instructed the cars to wait.*
- tell, order, direct, command

instructions plural noun

Please follow the instructions carefully.

- directions, guidelines, orders, commands

instructor noun

The swimming instructor also teaches life-saving.

- teacher, trainer, coach

instrument noun

Dentists use special instruments to check your teeth.

- tool, implement, utensil, appliance, device, gadget, contraption

FOR MUSICAL INSTRUMENTS

SEE **music**

insufficient adjective

The plants died because they had insufficient water.

- inadequate, deficient, not enough, too little, scant, scanty

OPPOSITE enough, excessive

insult verb

He was insulted not to be invited to the wedding.

- offend, outrage, be rude to, hurt, injure, slight, snub

insult noun

It is considered an insult to refuse a gift.

- rudeness, offence, affront, slight, slur, snub

insulting adjective

She made an insulting comment about my clothes.

- offensive, rude, impolite, derogatory, scornful

OPPOSITE complimentary

intact adjective

The vase has remained intact for centuries.

- unbroken, whole, undamaged, unharmed, complete, perfect
- (*informal*) in one piece

a b c d e f g h i j k l m n o p q r s t u v w x y z

integrate verb

*They decided to **integrate** the two orchestras.*

- bring together, combine, join, merge, unite, unify, amalgamate

OPPOSITE separate verb

integrity noun

*Do you have any reason to doubt his **integrity**?*

- honesty, honour, loyalty, trustworthiness, reliability, goodness, sincerity, virtue, fidelity

OPPOSITE dishonesty

intelligence noun

1 *The robot shows some signs of **intelligence**.*

- cleverness, understanding, comprehension, reason, sense, wisdom, brainpower, wits
- (*informal*) brains

2 *The spy was sent to gather secret **intelligence**.*

- information, knowledge, data, facts, reports

intelligent adjective

*The aliens from Planet Zog are highly **intelligent**.*

- clever, bright, smart, quick, sharp, perceptive, shrewd, able, brilliant, rational, thinking
- (*informal*) brainy

OPPOSITE unintelligent, stupid

intelligible adjective

*The language of the Martians was not **intelligible**.*

- understandable, comprehensible, meaningful, straightforward, unambiguous, clear, legible, plain, lucid

OPPOSITE incomprehensible

intend verb

1 *What do you **intend** to do?*

- plan, aim, mean, have in mind, plot, propose

2 *The class is **intended** for non-swimmers.*

- design, set up, aim (at)

intense adjective

1 *I felt a sudden, **intense** pain in my chest.*

- extreme, acute, severe, sharp, great, strong, violent

OPPOSITE slight, mild

2 *The contest aroused **intense** feelings.*

- deep, passionate, powerful, strong, profound

OPPOSITE mild

intensive adjective

*Police carried out an **intensive** search of the area.*

- detailed, thorough, concentrated

OPPOSITE superficial

intent adjective

*He read the letter with an **intent** look on his face.*

- concentrating, absorbed, engrossed, preoccupied, interested

intent on

*The detective was **intent on** solving the mystery.*

- determined to, resolved to, eager to, fixed on, bent on

intention noun

*It's his **intention** to play cricket for Australia.*

- aim, objective, target, goal, ambition, plan, intent

intentional adjective

*He was penalized for an **intentional** foul.*

- deliberate, conscious, calculated, planned, intended, wilful

OPPOSITE accidental

intercept verb

*The defender managed to **intercept** the pass.*

- check, stop, catch, cut off, head off, deflect

interest verb

*Politics doesn't **interest** me at all.*

- appeal to, attract, capture your imagination, excite, fascinate, stimulate, absorb

OPPOSITE bore

a
b
c
d
e
f
g
h
i
j
k
l
m
n
o
p
q
r
s
t
u
v
w
x
y
z

a
b
c
d
e
f
g
h
i
j
k
l
m
n
o
p
q
r
s
t
u
v
w
x
y
z

interest noun

1 *The dog showed no **interest** in the bone.*
- curiosity, attention, concern, involvement

2 *The information was of no **interest** to anyone.*
- importance, significance, consequence, value

3 *My **interests** include judo and playing the trombone.*
- hobby, pastime, pursuit, activity, diversion

interesting adjective
*Everyone wanted to hear about our **interesting** adventures.*
- fascinating, absorbing, enthralling, intriguing, engrossing, stimulating, riveting, gripping, entertaining, diverting

OPPOSITE boring, dull

interfere verb
to interfere in
*Don't **interfere in** other people's affairs.*
- intervene in, intrude in, meddle in, pry into, encroach on, butt in on

to interfere with
*The bad weather **interfered with** our plans.*
- hamper, hinder, get in the way of, obstruct

interior adjective, noun
SEE **inside** adjective, noun

intermediate adjective
*Should I join the **intermediate** or the advanced class?*
- middle, midway, halfway, transitional

internal adjective
*Scoop out the **internal** parts of the tomato.*
- inner, inside, interior
OPPOSITE external

international adjective
*Interpol is an **international** police organization.*
- global, worldwide, intercontinental

interpret verb
*Can you **interpret** this old writing?*
- explain, make sense of, make clear, translate, clarify, decipher, decode

interrogate verb
*The police **interrogated** the suspect for several hours.*
- question, interview, examine, cross-examine
- (*informal*) quiz, grill

interrupt verb

1 *Please don't **interrupt** while I am speaking.*
- intervene, interject, break in, butt in, cut in

2 *Heavy rain **interrupted** the tennis match.*
- stop, suspend, disrupt, break off, cut short

3 *The new houses will **interrupt** the view.*
- get in the way of, obstruct, spoil

interruption noun
*He wrote for an hour without any **interruption**.*
- break, pause, stop, gap, halt, disruption, suspension

interval noun

1 *There will be a short **interval** after the first act.*
- break, pause, wait, delay, lapse, lull
- Another word for an interval in a play or film is interlude or intermission.
- An interval in a meeting is a recess.
- An interval when you take a rest is a breather or breathing space.

2 *There were signs at regular **intervals** along the road.*
- space, gap, distance

intervene verb
*A man **intervened** to stop the fight.*
- step in, interfere, interrupt, butt in

interview verb
*He **interviewed** the author about her new book.*
- question, talk to, interrogate, examine

intimate adjective
1 *They have been **intimate** friends for years.*
- close, cherished, dear, friendly, informal
  OPPOSITE distant
2 *The newspaper printed **intimate** details about her life.*
- personal, private, confidential, secret

intimidate verb
*You can't **intimidate** me into telling a lie.*
- bully, threaten, frighten, menace, scare, terrify, terrorize, persecute

intrepid adjective
*The **intrepid** explorers finally reached the North Pole.*
- daring, bold, fearless, courageous, brave, valiant, heroic, plucky

intricate adjective
*The clock has an **intricate** mechanism.*
- complex, complicated, elaborate, sophisticated, involved
  OPPOSITE simple

intriguing adjective
*The results of the experiment are **intriguing**.*
- interesting, attractive, fascinating, captivating, beguiling

introduce verb
1 *Let me **introduce** you to my friend.*
- present, make known
2 *The director stood up to **introduce** the film.*
- give an introduction to, announce, lead into
3 *They are **introducing** a new bus service next year.*
- set up, start, begin, create, establish, initiate, bring in

introduction noun
- Something which happens as an introduction to a bigger event is a prelude.
- An introduction to a book is a preface.
- An introduction to a play is a prologue.

- A piece played as an introduction to a concert or opera is an overture.

intrude verb
to intrude on
*I don't mean to **intrude on** your privacy.*
- break in on, encroach on, interrupt, butt in on, interfere with, intervene in

intruder noun
*Some **intruders** broke into the building last night.*
- trespasser, prowler, burglar

invade verb
*The Vikings **invaded** many parts of Europe.*
- attack, enter, occupy, overrun, march into, raid

invalid adjective
1 *The ticket is **invalid** because it is out of date.*
- unacceptable, unusable, worthless
2 *That is an **invalid** argument.*
- false, unsound, unreasonable, illogical, irrational, unconvincing
  OPPOSITE valid

invaluable adjective
*Reena is an **invaluable** member of the hockey team.*
- indispensable, irreplaceable, crucial, essential, useful, valuable
  OPPOSITE worthless

invasion noun
*Fortunately, the Martian **invasion** never happened.*
- attack, raid

invent verb
*James Dewar **invented** the thermos flask.*
- create, devise, think up, conceive, design, originate

invention noun
1 *This computer program is my own **invention**.*
- creation, design, discovery
- (informal) brainchild
2 *Her account of what happened was pure **invention**.*
- fantasy, fiction, lies, deceit

a
b
c
d
e
f
g
h
i
j
k
l
m
n
o
p
q
r
s
t
u
v
w
x
y
z

inventive adjective
*Roald Dahl's stories are full of **inventive** characters.*
- creative, original, imaginative, ingenious, inspired

inventor noun
*James Dewar was the **inventor** of the thermos flask.*
- creator, designer, originator, discoverer

investigate verb
*Police are **investigating** the cause of the accident.*
- examine, explore, inquire into, look into, study, consider, follow up, probe, research, scrutinize
- (*informal*) go into

investigation noun
*An **investigation** showed how the accident happened.*
- examination, inquiry, inspection, study, review, survey

invigorating adjective
*We went for an **invigorating** walk before breakfast.*
- refreshing, stimulating, reviving, bracing, healthy
OPPOSITE tiring

invisible adjective
*The wizard was **invisible** when he wore his magic cloak.*
- out of sight, unseen, unnoticed, hidden, concealed, covered, obscured, camouflaged, disguised, undetectable, unnoticeable, inconspicuous
OPPOSITE visible

invite verb
*Our neighbours **invited** us round for tea.*
- ask, request your company, welcome, summon

inviting adjective
*An **inviting** smell came from the kitchen.*
- attractive, appealing, pleasant, welcoming, agreeable, appetizing, tempting
OPPOSITE repulsive

involve verb
1 *My job **involves** a lot of travel.*
- include, comprise, require, demand, necessitate, mean
2 *Protecting the environment **involves** us all.*
- affect, concern, interest, touch

involved adjective
1 *The film has a long and **involved** plot.*
- complex, complicated, elaborate, intricate, confusing, difficult, convoluted
OPPOSITE simple
2 *Are you **involved** in the theatre?*
- concerned, participating, engaged, caught up, mixed up

irrational adjective
*My aunt has an **irrational** fear of hamsters.*
- unreasonable, illogical, senseless, nonsensical, absurd, crazy
OPPOSITE rational

irregular adjective
1 *The bricks were arranged in an **irregular** pattern.*
- varying, erratic, haphazard, random, unpredictable, fitful
OPPOSITE regular
2 *It is highly **irregular** to eat pizza with a spoon!*
- abnormal, unusual, exceptional, unconventional, improper
OPPOSITE normal

irrelevant adjective
*Some of the information in the book is **irrelevant**.*
- inappropriate, unnecessary, inessential, pointless, unrelated, unconnected, beside the point
OPPOSITE relevant

irresistible adjective
*I had an **irresistible** urge to burst out laughing.*
- overwhelming, overpowering, uncontrollable, unavoidable, powerful, compelling

irresponsible adjective
*It's **irresponsible** to drive too fast.*
- reckless, rash, thoughtless, inconsiderate, uncaring, unthinking, negligent
- OPPOSITE responsible

irritable adjective
*After a bad night, he woke in an **irritable** mood.*
- bad-tempered, grumpy, short-tempered, cross, impatient, snappy, touchy, testy, prickly, peevish
- (*informal*) stroppy, shirty
- OPPOSITE good-humoured, cheerful

irritate verb
*The noise from next door began to **irritate** me.*
- annoy, bother, exasperate, anger, provoke, madden, vex
- (*informal*) get on your nerves, bug

island noun

WORD WEB
- A small island is an islet.
- A coral island is an atoll.
- A group of islands is an archipelago.
- An uninhabited island is a desert island.
- An island which is not on a map is uncharted.
- A person who is stranded on a desert island is a castaway.

ON A DESERT ISLAND YOU MIGHT BE
cast adrift, beached, marooned, shipwrecked, stranded, washed ashore

THINGS YOU MIGHT FIND OR USE ON A DESERT ISLAND
beach, cave, driftwood, flotsam, footprints, lagoon, message in a bottle, palm trees, raft, shelter, tree-house

isolated adjective
1 *They sheltered in an **isolated** cave in the mountains.*
- remote, out-of-the-way, secluded, outlying, inaccessible, cut off, deserted
- OPPOSITE accessible
2 *There have been a few **isolated** cases of cheating.*
- single, uncommon, unusual, abnormal, exceptional, unique
- OPPOSITE common

issue verb
1 *They **issued** blankets to the refugees.*
- give out, distribute, supply
2 *They have **issued** a new set of stamps.*
- bring out, put out, produce, publish, release, circulate, print
3 *Green smoke **issued** from the dragon's nostrils.*
- come out, emerge, appear, flow out, gush, erupt

issue noun
1 *The new **issue** of the magazine comes out this week.*
- edition, number, instalment, copy
2 *They print stories about local **issues** in the magazine.*
- matter, subject, topic, affair, concern, question, problem

itch noun
1 *I had an annoying **itch** on my foot.*
- tickle, tingling, prickle
2 *Olga had a great **itch** to travel.*
- desire, longing, urge, wish, yearning, ache, impulse

item noun
1 *I bought a few **items** in the jumble sale.*
- thing, object, article
2 *There was an **item** about our school in the paper.*
- article, piece, report, feature

a
b
c
d
e
f
g
h
i
j
k
l
m
n
o
p
q
r
s
t
u
v
w
x
y
z

Jj

jab verb
*A passer-by **jabbed** me in the ribs.*
- poke, prod, elbow, nudge, stab, thrust

jagged adjective
*This dinosaur had **jagged** teeth.*
- rough, uneven, ragged, spiky, toothed, serrated
- OPPOSITE smooth

jail noun SEE prison

jam noun
1 *We got stuck in a **jam** on the motorway.*
- traffic jam, hold-up, tailback, blockage
2 (*informal*) *I'm in a bit of a **jam**.*
- difficulty, mess, predicament, plight
- (*informal*) fix, tight corner

jam verb
1 *Someone had **jammed** the door open.*
- prop, wedge, stick
2 *The roads are **jammed** at rush hour.*
- block, clog, obstruct, congest
- (*informal*) bung up
3 *I **jammed** my things into a backpack.*
- cram, pack, stuff, squeeze, squash, crush, ram, crowd

jangle verb
*Silver bracelets **jangled** on her wrists.*
- jingle, chink, clink, tinkle

jar noun
*We collected some tadpoles in a glass **jar**.*
- pot, jug, pitcher, vase

jar verb
1 *He **jarred** his back badly when he fell.*
- jolt, jerk, shake, shock
2 *Those paint colours **jar** with each other.*
- clash, conflict, be at odds

jaunty adjective
*The seven dwarves whistled a **jaunty** tune.*
- cheerful, lively, bright, jolly, perky, breezy, sprightly
- OPPOSITE gloomy

jealous adjective
*Cinderella's sisters were **jealous** of her beauty.*
- envious, resentful, grudging

jeer verb
*Some of the audience whistled and **jeered**.*
- boo, hiss, sneer, taunt, mock, scoff, ridicule
- OPPOSITE cheer

jerk verb
*The rider **jerked** on the horse's reins.*
- pull, tug, yank, pluck, wrench, tweak

jerky adjective
*The stagecoach drew to a **jerky** halt.*
- jolting, jumpy, shaky, bouncy, bumpy, uneven
- OPPOSITE steady

jester noun
*The king's **jester** kept the court amused.*
- fool, joker, clown

jet noun
*A **jet** of water shot high in the air.*
- spout, spurt, squirt, gush, stream, fountain

jewel, jewellery nouns

 WORD WEB

SOME ITEMS OF JEWELLERY
anklet, bangle, beads, bindi, bracelet, brooch, chain, charm, choker, clasp, crown, cufflinks, earring, engagement ring, locket, necklace, pendant, pin, ring, tiara, tie pin, wedding ring

STONES OR GEMS USED TO MAKE JEWELLERY

agate, amber, amethyst, aquamarine, carnelian or cornelian, coral, diamond, emerald, garnet, jade, jasper, jet, lapis lazuli, onyx, opal, pearl, ruby, sapphire, topaz, turquoise

METALS USED TO MAKE JEWELLERY

gold, platinum, silver

jingle verb
Some coins jingled in his back pocket.
- jangle, chink, clink, tinkle

job noun
1 *My sister wants a job as a TV reporter.*
- post, position, profession, occupation, employment, trade, work, career
- The job you particularly want to do is your mission or vocation.

2 *Whose job is it to do the washing-up?*
- duty, task, assignment, chore, errand

job noun

WORD WEB

SOME JOBS PEOPLE DO

actor, architect, artist, astronaut, banker, barber, bookseller, builder, bus driver, chef, cleaner, coach, cook, curator, dancer, dentist, detective, diver, doctor, editor, electrician, engineer, explorer, farmer, firefighter, fisherman, flight attendant, florist, footballer, gardener, hairdresser, imam, janitor, joiner, journalist, lawyer, librarian, mechanic, midwife, miner, minister, model, musician, nurse, office worker, optician, painter, pharmacist, photographer, pilot, plumber, police officer, politician, postman, priest, professor, programmer, psychiatrist, rabbi, receptionist, reporter, sailor, scientist, secretary, shepherd, shopkeeper, singer, soldier, solicitor, surgeon, tailor, teacher, traffic warden, train driver, TV presenter, undertaker, vet, waiter or waitress, writer, zookeeper

jog verb
1 *He jogs round the park every morning.*
- go jogging, run, trot

2 *A boy sitting next to me jogged my elbow.*
- nudge, prod, jolt, knock, bump, jar, jostle

3 *The photograph may jog her memory.*
- prompt, stir, arouse, set off, stimulate

join verb
1 *Our families joined together to buy the present.*
- combine, come together, merge, unite, amalgamate
- OPPOSITE separate

2 *Join one piece of rope to the other.*
- connect, fasten, attach, fix, link, put together, tack on
- OPPOSITE detach

3 *The two roads join here.*
- meet, merge, converge
- OPPOSITE divide

4 *I joined the crowd going into the cinema.*
- follow, go with, tag along with
- OPPOSITE leave

5 *We have joined a local sports club.*
- become a member of, enrol in, sign up for
- To join the army is to enlist.
- OPPOSITE leave, resign from

join noun
If you look hard, you can still see the join.
- joint, connection, link, mend, seam

joint adjective
The preparation of the meal was a joint effort.
- combined, shared, common, communal, cooperative, united, collective, mutual
- OPPOSITE individual

joke noun
Do you know any good jokes?
- jest, quip, crack, witticism, wisecrack
- (*informal*) gag

a
b
c
d
e
f
g
h
i
j
k
l
m
n
o
p
q
r
s
t
u
v
w
x
y
z

a
b
c
d
e
f
g
h
i
j
k
l
m
n
o
p
q
r
s
t
u
v
w
x
y
z

joke verb
Those two are always laughing and joking.
• jest, clown, have a laugh, make jokes

jolly adjective
We had a jolly time on holiday.
• cheerful, merry, happy, joyful, pleasant, enjoyable
OPPOSITE gloomy

jolt verb
The car jolted over the bumps in the road.
• jerk, jog, bump, bounce, shake, shudder

jostle verb
The film star was jostled by photographers.
• push, shove, hustle, press, crowd in on

jot verb
to jot down
I quickly jotted down some ideas.
• make a note of, write down, take down, note, scribble

journal noun
1 *The newsagent sells a few journals.*
• magazine, newspaper, paper, periodical, publication
2 *The captain kept a journal of the voyage.*
• diary, log, record, account, chronicle

journalist noun
She works as a journalist on the local paper.
• reporter, correspondent, columnist, writer

journey noun
On their journey, the astronauts will pass the Moon.
• voyage, trip, expedition, travels, tour, route

jovial adjective
Our guests were in a jovial mood.
• cheerful, happy, jolly, good-humoured, merry, joyful
OPPOSITE sad

joy noun
I remember the sheer joy of scoring a goal!
• happiness, joyfulness, delight, cheerfulness, gladness, mirth, glee, jubilation, gaiety, rejoicing, bliss, ecstasy, elation
OPPOSITE sorrow

joyful adjective
The wedding was a joyful occasion.
• happy, cheerful, merry, joyous, jolly, jovial, good-humoured
OPPOSITE sad

judge noun
• A judge in a local court is a magistrate.
• A judge in a competition is an adjudicator.
• A judge in a sport is a referee or umpire.

judge verb
1 *The umpire judged that the ball was out.*
• rule, decide, decree, adjudicate
2 *Who's judging the flower show this year?*
• decide on, assess, evaluate, appraise
3 *He judged the coin to be about 1000 years old.*
• reckon, suppose, consider, gauge, guess, estimate

judgement noun
1 *What is the judgement of the court?*
• decision, finding, ruling, verdict, decree
2 *His comments show a lack of judgement.*
• wisdom, common sense, understanding, discrimination
3 *In my judgement, you're making a big mistake.*
• opinion, view, belief, assessment, estimate

juice noun
Squeeze the juice from the lemons.
• liquid, fluid, sap

jumble noun

*There was a **jumble** of clothes on the floor.*

- mess, muddle, clutter, chaos, confusion, disorder

jumble verb

*Please don't **jumble** the pages.*

- muddle, mix up, mess up, disorganize, shuffle
- OPPOSITE arrange

jump verb

1 *Suddenly a rabbit **jumped** in front of us.*

- leap, spring, bound, bounce, hop
- When a cat jumps it pounces.

2 *All the horses **jumped** the first hurdle.*

- leap over, vault, clear

3 *The loud bang made them all **jump**.*

- start, flinch, jolt

jump noun

1 *With a **jump**, the grasshopper landed on the leaf.*

- leap, spring, bound, vault, hop

2 *The horse easily cleared the last **jump**.*

- hurdle, fence, gate, barrier, obstacle

junction noun

*There are traffic lights at the road **junction**.*

- intersection, crossing, interchange

jungle noun

WORD WEB

*One of my dreams is to be a **jungle** explorer.*

- rainforest, tropical forest

THINGS YOU MIGHT SEE IN THE JUNGLE
canopy, foliage, forest floor, swamp, undergrowth

SOME ANIMALS WHICH LIVE IN THE JUNGLE
alligator, ant, anteater, armadillo, bird of paradise, butterfly, chameleon, crocodile, gorilla, hummingbird, jaguar, leopard, macaw, monkey, mosquito, parrot, piranha, porcupine, snake, tarantula, tiger, toucan, tree frog

---

SOME PLANTS WHICH ARE FOUND IN THE JUNGLE
banana tree, cacao, creeper or liana, mangrove, orchid, palm tree, rubber tree
SEE ALSO **explorer**

---

junior adjective

1 *I'm a member of the **junior** hockey team.*

- younger

2 *He's only a **junior** employee in the firm.*

- low-ranking, minor, lesser, subordinate
- OPPOSITE senior

junk noun

*The garage is full of old **junk**.*

- rubbish, clutter, garbage, jumble, trash, waste, scrap, odds and ends

just adjective

*It was a **just** punishment, considering the crime.*

- fair, fitting, appropriate, deserved, proper, reasonable, justified
- OPPOSITE unjust, unfair

justice noun

1 *The prisoners demanded to be treated with **justice**.*

- fairness, justness, fair play, right, honesty, impartiality
- OPPOSITE injustice

2 *They were tried in a court of **justice**.*

- law

justify verb

*How can you **justify** spending so much money?*

- defend, excuse, account for, explain

jut verb

to jut out

*A large nail **jutted out** from the wall.*

- stick out, project, protrude, extend, overhang

a
b
c
d
e
f
g
h
i
j
k
l
m
n
o
p
q
r
s
t
u
v
w
x
y
z

juvenile adjective

1 *This part of the library is for **juvenile** fiction.*
- children's, young people's
  OPPOSITE adult

2 *His jokes are really **juvenile**.*
- childish, babyish, immature
  OPPOSITE mature

Kk

keen adjective

1 *Rhona is a **keen** hockey player.*
- enthusiastic, eager, fervent, avid, devoted, committed, motivated
- A common simile is as keen as mustard.
  OPPOSITE unenthusiastic

2 *A carving knife should have a **keen** edge.*
- sharp, razor-sharp, cutting
  OPPOSITE blunt

3 *Owls must have **keen** eyesight.*
- sharp, acute, piercing
  OPPOSITE poor

4 *A **keen** wind was blowing from the east.*
- bitter, cold, icy, penetrating
  OPPOSITE mild

keep verb

1 *Let's **keep** the rest of the cake for later.*
- save, conserve, preserve, retain, hang on to, hold on to, guard, store

2 *Please **keep** still.*
- stay, remain

3 *A man in the audience **kept** coughing.*
- persist in, go on, carry on, continue

4 *You're late. What **kept** you?*
- delay, detain, hold up, keep waiting

5 *Where do you **keep** the knives and forks?*
- store, house, put, stow

6 *Will the milk **keep** until tomorrow?*
- last, be usable, stay good

7 *It costs money to **keep** a pet.*
- support, maintain, provide for, pay for

to keep something up
Keep up the good work!
- carry on, continue, maintain

key noun
*Have you found the **key** to the riddle?*
- answer, solution, explanation, clue

keyboard noun FOR KEYBOARD INSTRUMENTS
SEE **music**

kidnap verb
*In the story, a boy is **kidnapped** by bandits.*
- abduct, capture, seize, carry off, snatch

kill verb
*Several people were **killed** in the explosion.*
- (*informal*) bump off, do away with
- (*old use*) slay
- To kill someone deliberately is to murder them.
- To kill someone brutally is to butcher them.
- To kill large numbers of people is to massacre or slaughter them.
- To kill someone as a punishment is to execute them or put them to death.
- To kill someone for political reasons is to assassinate them.

kind noun
*What **kind** of music do you like to play?*
- sort, type, variety, style, category, class, set

kind adjective
*It was very **kind** of you to help me.*
- kind-hearted, caring, good-natured, kindly, affectionate, warm, genial, loving, sweet, gentle, lenient, amiable, friendly, generous, sympathetic, thoughtful, obliging,

considerate, understanding, compassionate, unselfish, giving, gracious, merciful, benevolent, charitable, humane, neighbourly

OPPOSITE unkind

king noun

*Neptune is the mythological **king** of the sea.*

- monarch, sovereign

kingdom noun

*King Brian the Bald ruled over a vast **kingdom**.*

- realm, monarchy

kiss noun

*The princess gave the frog a **kiss** on the cheek.*

- (*informal*) peck

kit noun

*I've forgotten my games **kit**.*

- gear, outfit, equipment, paraphernalia, tools, tackle

kitchen noun

WORD WEB

EQUIPMENT YOU MIGHT FIND IN A KITCHEN

apron, blender, bread bin, cooker, crockery, cutlery, dishwasher, draining board, food processor, freezer, fridge, grill, kettle, liquidizer, microwave, mixer, oven, oven gloves, refrigerator, scales, sink, toaster

FOR OTHER THINGS USED FOR COOKING

SEE **cook** verb, **cutlery**

kitten noun SEE **cat**

knack noun

*George has a **knack** for taking photographs.*

- skill, talent, gift, flair

knead verb

***Knead** the dough until it is smooth.*

- work, press, squeeze, pummel

knife noun

WORD WEB

SOME KINDS OF KNIFE

cleaver, dagger, dirk, machete, penknife, scalpel

FOR KITCHEN KNIVES

SEE **cutlery**

knight noun

WORD WEB

THINGS A MEDIEVAL KNIGHT MIGHT WEAR OR CARRY

armour, baldric (leather belt), coat of arms, falcon or hawk, lance, mace (metal club), pennant, shield, surcoat, sword, tabard, tunic

FOR PARTS OF A SUIT OF ARMOUR

SEE **armour**

- A fight between knights on horseback was a joust.
- A series of sporting contests between knights was a tournament.
- A boy training to be a knight was first a page and then a squire.
- An expedition made by a knight was a quest.

knob noun

1 *The **knob** had fallen off the door.*
- handle
2 *Melt a **knob** of butter in a pan.*
- lump, piece, bit

knobbly adjective

*Crocodiles have thick and **knobbly** skin.*

- lumpy, bumpy, gnarled

knock verb

*I **knocked** my head as I came out of the car.*

- bump, bang, hit, strike, thump
- (*informal*) bash

knot verb

*The sailors **knotted** the two ropes together.*

- tie, bind, fasten, join, entwine, lash

OPPOSITE untie

a
b
c
d
e
f
g
h
i
j
k
l
m
n
o
p
q
r
s
t
u
v
w
x
y
z

know verb
1 *Do you **know** how to mend a puncture?*
• understand, have knowledge of, comprehend
2 *As soon as she saw the unicorn, she **knew** what it was.*
• recognize, realize, appreciate, be aware of
3 *Do you **know** Stewart well?*
• be acquainted with, be familiar with, be a friend of

knowledge noun
1 *She has a good **knowledge** of Italian.*
• understanding, grasp, command, familiarity (with)
2 *An encyclopedia contains a lot of **knowledge**.*
• information, data, facts, learning, know-how, wisdom, scholarship

knowledgeable adjective
*My dad is very **knowledgeable** about guitars.*
• familiar (with), well informed, educated, learned
OPPOSITE ignorant

label noun
*The washing instructions are on the **label**.*
• tag, ticket, sticker

label verb
*I've **labelled** all the boxes, so we'll know what's in them.*
• put a label on, tag, mark, name, identify

laborious adjective
*It was a **laborious** climb to the top of the hill.*
• hard, tough, strenuous, difficult, stiff, tiring, exhausting, gruelling
OPPOSITE easy

labour noun
1 *The workers were paid for their **labour**.*
• work, effort, industry, exertion, toil
2 *The factory took on extra **labour**.*
• workers, employees

labour verb
*They **laboured** to get the job finished on time.*
• work hard, exert yourself, toil
• (*informal*) slave away

lack noun
*The judge dismissed the case because of a **lack** of evidence.*
• absence, shortage, scarcity, want
• A general lack of food is a famine.
• A general lack of water is a drought.
OPPOSITE abundance

lack verb
*The game **lacked** excitement.*
• be short of, be without, want, need, require, miss

lady noun SEE **woman**

lag verb
*One runner was **lagging** behind the others.*
• straggle, trail, fall behind, drop behind, dawdle, linger, loiter

lair noun
*The hunters tracked the animal back to its **lair**.*
• den, refuge, shelter, hideout, hiding place

lake noun
*We rowed across the **lake**.*
• pond, pool
• (*Scottish*) loch
• A salt-water lake is a lagoon.
• A lake used to supply water is a reservoir.

lame adjective

1 *The **lame** horse had to be withdrawn from the race.*
- disabled, handicapped, crippled, limping

2 *I didn't believe her **lame** excuse.*
- feeble, flimsy, poor, unconvincing, inadequate, weak, tame

lamp noun SEE **light** noun

land noun

1 *The castle is surrounded by several acres of **land**.*
- grounds, estate, property

2 *The **land** here is good for growing strawberries.*
- ground, soil, earth

3 *China is a **land** with an ancient history.*
- country, nation, state, region, territory

land verb

1 *The plane **landed** exactly on time.*
- touch down, arrive
  OPPOSITE take off

2 *The ship will **land** at Dover.*
- dock, berth, come ashore

3 *How did these papers **land** on my desk?*
- arrive, turn up, end up, wind up, settle

landscape noun

*We sat on the hill and admired the **landscape**.*
- countryside, scenery, view, scene, outlook, prospect

lane noun SEE **road**

language noun

1 *The scroll was written in an ancient **language**.*
- tongue, speech, dialect

2 *The author uses very poetic **language**.*
- wording, phrasing, vocabulary, expression, style
- The words of a language are its vocabulary.
  SEE ALSO **writing**

lap noun

1 *My cat, Snowy, likes to sit on my **lap**.*
- knees, thighs

2 *The cars were on the last **lap** of the race.*
- circuit, round, loop

lapse noun

1 *They made a mistake because of a **lapse** in concentration.*
- failure, error, fault, slip, flaw, weakness, shortcoming

2 *I've started swimming again after a **lapse** of a year.*
- break, gap, interval, interruption, lull, pause

large adjective

1 *Elephants are **large** animals.*
- big, huge, enormous, colossal, giant, gigantic, immense, great, massive, bulky, heavy, hefty, weighty, mighty, towering
- (*informal*) whopping, ginormous

2 *The cook gave me a **large** helping of pudding.*
- ample, generous, plentiful, abundant, lavish

3 *Is this room **large** enough for dancing in?*
- spacious, roomy, sizeable

4 *The gales caused damage over a **large** area.*
- wide, broad, extensive, widespread, vast

5 *The meeting was attended by a **large** number of people.*
- considerable, substantial
  OPPOSITE small

largely adverb

*The driver was **largely** to blame for the accident.*
- mainly, chiefly, mostly, principally, to a large extent

last adjective

1 *Z is the **last** letter of the alphabet.*
- final, closing, concluding, terminating, ultimate
  OPPOSITE first

2 *Did you see the **last** Harry Potter film?*
- latest, most recent
  OPPOSITE next

last noun

at last
*The holidays are here **at last**!*
- finally, eventually, in the end

last verb
1 *Let's hope the fine weather **lasts**.*
- carry on, continue, keep on, stay, remain, persist, endure, hold
2 *The plants won't **last** long without water.*
- hold out, keep going, live, survive

late adjective
1 *The bus is **late**.*
- delayed, overdue
OPPOSITE early, punctual, on time
2 *Mr Pettigrew showed us a portrait of his **late** wife.*
- dead, deceased, departed, former

lately adverb
*There has been a lot of snow **lately**.*
- recently, latterly, of late

later adjective
*We'll study that poem in a **later** class.*
- future, following, subsequent

later adverb
*I'm busy now, but I'll phone you **later**.*
- afterwards, in a while, subsequently, next

laugh verb
1 *The childen **laughed** when the clown fell over.*
- chuckle, chortle, giggle, titter, burst out laughing, roar or scream with laughter, roll or fall about laughing, guffaw
- (*informal*) have hysterics, be in stitches
2 *It's rude to **laugh** at his way of singing.*
- make fun of, mock, ridicule, scoff at, tease, deride

laughter noun
*We heard bursts of **laughter** coming from the kitchen.*
- laughing, amusement, hilarity, mirth, merriment

launch verb
1 *The space shuttle will be **launched** tomorrow.*
- send off, set off, blast off, fire
2 *The new website was **launched** in the summer.*
- begin, start, set up, open, establish, found, initiate

lavatory noun
*The girls' **lavatories** are at the end of the corridor.*
- toilet, bathroom, WC, cloakroom, washroom
- (*informal*) loo

lavish adjective
*The king put on a **lavish** feast for his birthday.*
- generous, extravagant, sumptuous, luxurious, opulent, grand, abundant, copious, plentiful, bountiful
OPPOSITE meagre, paltry

law noun
- A law passed by parliament is an act.
- A proposed law to be discussed by parliament is a bill.
- The laws of a game are regulations or rules.
- A regulation which must be obeyed is a commandment, decree, edict, or order.

lay verb
1 *He **laid** the parchment carefully on his desk.*
- put down, set down, place, position, spread, deposit, leave
2 *Please **lay** the table for dinner.*
- set out, arrange

layer noun
1 *The walls needed two **layers** of paint.*
- coat, coating, covering, thickness, film, sheet, skin
2 *You can see various **layers** of rock in the cliff.*
- seam, stratum

laze verb
*We spent the day **lazing** in the garden.*
- be lazy, idle, loaf, lounge, lie about, relax, loll

lazy adjective
*My **lazy** little brother stayed in bed all day!*
- idle, inactive, lethargic, slack, slothful, indolent
- An informal name for a lazy person is lazybones.

a b c d e f g h i j k l m n o p q r s t u v w x y z

lead verb

1 *The rescuers **led** the climbers to safety.*
- guide, conduct, escort, usher, steer, pilot, shepherd
- OPPOSITE follow

2 *Dr Martez will **lead** the expedition to Peru.*
- be in charge of, direct, command, head, manage, supervise

3 *The British cyclist **led** from the start of the race.*
- be in front, be in the lead, head the field

4 *The animals in the zoo **lead** a peaceful life.*
- have, pass, spend, experience

lead noun

1 *The team followed the captain's **lead**.*
- example, guidance, leadership, direction

2 *The Australian swimmer is in the **lead**.*
- first place, front position

3 *Charlie was given the **lead** in the play.*
- chief part, starring role, title role

4 *Keep the dog on a **lead**.*
- leash, strap, chain, tether, rein

5 *Don't trip over the electrical **lead**.*
- cable, flex, wire

leader noun

*The **leader** of the pirates was Captain Cutlass.*
- head, chief, commander, captain, director, principal, ruler
- (*informal*) boss
- The leader of a group of wrongdoers is the ringleader.

leaf noun

1 *Deciduous trees lose their **leaves** in autumn.*
- A mass of leaves is foliage or greenery.

2 *A single **leaf** had been torn out of the book.*
- page, sheet

leak noun

*The plumber mended a **leak** in the water tank.*
- crack, hole, opening, drip
- A leak in a tyre is a puncture.

leak verb

1 *The juice had **leaked** all over my schoolbag.*
- escape, drip, seep, ooze, trickle

2 *Details of a secret plan were **leaked** to the newspaper.*
- reveal, disclose, make known, pass on, give away, let out

lean verb

1 *I **leaned** against the wall.*
- recline, rest, prop yourself, support yourself

2 *The yacht **leaned** to one side in the wind.*
- slope, tilt, tip, incline, slant, list, bank

lean adjective

*The athlete has a strong, **lean** figure.*
- slim, slender, thin, wiry
- OPPOSITE fat

leap verb

*The dog **leaped** in the air to catch the ball.*
- jump, spring, bound, vault

learn verb

1 *We are **learning** about the Vikings this term.*
- discover, find out, gather, grasp, pick up

2 *I've got to **learn** the words of this song.*
- learn by heart, memorize, master

learner noun

*This swimming class is for **learners** only.*
- beginner, starter, novice
- Someone learning things at school or college is a pupil or student.
- Someone learning a trade is an apprentice or trainee.

least adjective

1 *Who got the **least** number of points?*
- fewest, lowest

2 *The **least** amount of this poison is deadly.*
- slightest, smallest, tiniest

leave verb

1 *Do you have to **leave** now?*
- go, go away, depart, withdraw, take your leave, go out, set off, say goodbye
- (*informal*) take off, disappear
  OPPOSITE arrive

2 *The doctor **left** the room in a hurry.*
- exit, go out of, depart from, quit, vacate
  OPPOSITE enter

3 *Don't **leave** me here on my own!*
- abandon, desert, forsake

4 *The crew **left** the sinking ship.*
- evacuate, get out of

5 *My sister has **left** her job at the bank.*
- give up, quit, resign from
- (*informal*) walk out of

6 ***Leave** the milk bottles by the front door.*
- place, position, put down, set down, deposit

7 *I'll just **leave** all the arrangements to you.*
- pass on, hand over, refer, entrust

8 *Lady Bigwig **left** all her money to charity.*
- bequeath, hand down, will, endow

to leave someone or **something out**
*Eric was **left out** of the basketball team.*
- miss out, omit, exclude, reject

leave noun

1 *The prime minister is away on **leave**.*
- holiday, vacation, time off

2 *Will you give me **leave** to speak?*
- permission, freedom, liberty

lecture noun

1 *There is a **lecture** about dinosaurs at the museum today.*
- talk, lesson, speech, address

2 *The teacher gave us a **lecture** on how to behave.*
- reprimand, warning
- (*informal*) telling off

ledge noun
*The climbers rested on a **ledge** of rock.*
- shelf, projection
- A ledge under a window is a windowsill.

left adjective
- The left side of a ship when you face forwards is the port side.
  OPPOSITE right

leg noun

1 *Boris fell and bruised his **leg**.*
FOR PARTS OF YOUR BODY
SEE **body**

2 *The rowers completed the first **leg** of the race.*
- part, stage, section, phase, stretch

legal adjective
*Is it **legal** to park here on Sundays?*
- lawful, legitimate, permissible, permitted, allowed
  OPPOSITE illegal

legend noun
*I like reading **legends** about ancient heroes.*
- myth, story, folk tale, fairy tale, fable, tradition

FOR CREATURES FOUND IN MYTHS AND LEGENDS
SEE **myth**

legendary adjective
*Unicorns are **legendary** beasts.*
- mythical, fabulous, fabled, fictional, fictitious, invented, made-up
  OPPOSITE real

legible adjective
*Although the letter is old, the handwriting is **legible**.*
- readable, clear, distinct, neat
  OPPOSITE illegible

legitimate adjective
*Are you the **legitimate** owner of this car?*
- legal, proper, rightful, authorized, licensed, permitted

leisure noun
*Grandad has plenty of **leisure** since he retired.*
- free time, spare time, relaxation, recreation, rest

leisurely adjective
*We went for a **leisurely** stroll in the park.*
- gentle, relaxed, relaxing, unhurried, restful, slow
OPPOSITE fast

lend verb
*Can you **lend** me some money until the weekend?*
- loan, advance, let you have
OPPOSITE borrow

length noun
1 *My heart sank when I saw the **length** of the queue.*
- extent, size
2 *We only had to wait a short **length** of time.*
- space, period, stretch

lengthen verb
1 *Is it possible to **lengthen** these curtains?*
- extend, make longer, increase, stretch
2 *The days **lengthen** in spring.*
- draw out, get longer, stretch out
OPPOSITE shorten

lengthy adjective
*There was a **lengthy** argument over who was to blame.*
- long, drawn out, extended, prolonged, time-consuming
OPPOSITE short

lenient adjective
*The teacher was **lenient** and let us off.*
- easygoing, soft-hearted, tolerant, forgiving, indulgent, kind, merciful
OPPOSITE strict

lessen verb
1 *The nurse used ointment to **lessen** the pain.*
- minimize, reduce, relieve
2 *The strong winds **lessened** during the night.*
- diminish, decrease, dwindle, subside, weaken, ease off, tail off, die away or down
OPPOSITE increase

lesson noun
*My piano **lesson** is on Friday afternoon.*
- class, period, tutorial, instruction

let verb
1 *Abby's parents **let** her go to the party.*
- allow, give permission to, permit, consent to, agree to
OPPOSITE forbid
2 *Our friends are **letting** their house for the summer.*
- lease, rent out, hire out

lethal adjective
*This bottle contains a **lethal** potion.*
- deadly, fatal, mortal, poisonous

letter noun
1 *There are twenty-six **letters** are in the alphabet.*
- character, symbol, sign, figure
- The letters a, e, i, o, u, and sometimes y are vowels.
- The other letters are consonants.
2 *Did you remember to sign your **letter**?*
- note, message, communication
- Letters people send each other are correspondence.

level adjective
1 *You need a **level** field for playing rounders.*
- even, flat, horizontal, smooth
OPPOSITE uneven
2 *At half-time the scores were **level**.*
- equal, even, the same, matching
- (*informal*) neck-and-neck

level verb
1 *Dad **levelled** the garden to make a lawn.*
- even out, flatten, smooth
2 *A serious earthquake **levelled** the town.*
- knock down, demolish, destroy, devastate

level noun
1 *The water had reached a high **level**.*
- height
2 *The lift takes you up to the sixth **level**.*
- floor, storey, tier
3 *What **level** have you reached in judo?*
- grade, standard, stage, rank, degree

a b c d e f g h i j k l m n o p q r s t u v w x y z

a
b
c
d
e
f
g
h
i
j
k
l
m
n
o
p
q
r
s
t
u
v
w
x
y
z

lever verb
*Slowly, I **levered** open the lid of the chest.*
- prise, wrench, force

liable adjective
1 *You're **liable** to make mistakes when you're tired.*
- likely, inclined, disposed, prone, ready
OPPOSITE unlikely
2 *If you break anything, you'll be **liable** for the cost.*
- responsible, answerable, accountable

liberal adjective
1 *We each got a **liberal** helping of ice cream.*
- generous, ample, plentiful, lavish, abundant, copious, bountiful
OPPOSITE meagre, miserly
2 *She has a **liberal** attitude towards most things.*
- broad-minded, easygoing, lenient, tolerant, permissive
OPPOSITE strict

liberate verb
*The prisoners were **liberated** at the end of the war.*
- free, release, set free, emancipate, discharge, let go, set loose
OPPOSITE imprison

liberty noun
1 *The animals have **liberty** to wander around the park.*
- freedom, independence
2 *The king granted the prisoners their **liberty**.*
- liberation, release, emancipation

licence noun
*He has a **licence** to practise as a doctor.*
- permit, certificate, authorization, warrant

license verb
*Are you **licensed** to drive this vehicle?*
- permit, allow, authorize, entitle

lid noun
*Can you help me get the **lid** off this jar?*
- cap, cover, covering, top

lie noun
*He accused the newspaper of printing **lies**.*
- deceit, falsehood, dishonesty
- (*informal*) fib
OPPOSITE truth

lie verb
1 *It's twelve o'clock and he's still **lying** in bed!*
- recline, stretch out, lounge, sprawl, rest
- To lie face down is to be prone.
- To lie face upwards is to be supine.
2 *The castle **lies** in a valley.*
- be sited, be situated, be located, be found
3 *I don't trust her—I think she's **lying**.*
- deceive someone, bluff
- (*informal*) fib

life noun
1 *My hamster, Fluffy, leads a very easy **life**.*
- existence, being, way of life
2 *Our **lives** depended on finding water.*
- survival
3 *You seem to be full of **life** today!*
- energy, liveliness, vigour, vitality, spirit, sprightliness, animation
4 *I'm reading a **life** of Elvis Presley.*
- life story, autobiography, biography

lift verb
1 *The removal men **lifted** the piano carefully.*
- pick up, raise, elevate, pull up, hoist
2 *The plane **lifted** off the ground.*
- rise, ascend, soar

light noun

WORD WEB

SOME KINDS OF NATURAL LIGHT
daylight, moonlight, starlight, sunlight, twilight

SOURCES OF ARTIFICIAL LIGHT
bulb, candle, chandelier, floodlight, fluorescent lamp, headlamp or headlight, lamp, lantern, laser, neon light, searchlight, spotlight, street light, torch

VARIOUS FORMS OF LIGHT
beam, flash, flicker, glow, halo, lustre, radiance, ray, reflection, shaft

WRITING TIPS

You can use these words to describe **light**.

- to describe *HOW LIGHT APPEARS*:
  bright, brilliant, harsh, luminous, lustrous, strong; diffused, dim, muted, soft, warm
- *LIGHT* may:
  beam, blaze, dazzle, flash, flicker, glare, gleam, glimmer, glint, glisten, glitter, glow, shimmer, shine, sparkle, twinkle

light adjective
1 *The artist worked in a **light** and airy studio.*
- bright, well-lit, illuminated
  OPPOSITE dim, gloomy
2 *She was wearing **light** blue jeans.*
- pale
  OPPOSITE dark
3 *The parcel looks big, but it is quite **light**.*
- lightweight, portable, weightless, slight
- A common simile is as light as a feather.
  OPPOSITE heavy
4 *A **light** wind rippled the surface of the water.*
- gentle, faint, slight
  OPPOSITE strong
5 *We had a **light** meal before we went out.*
- small, modest, simple, insubstantial
  OPPOSITE heavy, substantial
6 *I brought a book for some **light** reading.*
- undemanding, entertaining, lightweight
  OPPOSITE serious

light verb
1 *We **lit** the candles on my birthday cake.*
- ignite, kindle, set alight, set fire to, switch on
  OPPOSITE extinguish
2 *The fireworks **lit** the sky.*
- light up, brighten, illuminate, shed light on, shine on
  OPPOSITE darken

like preposition
*The witch's hand looked **like** a knobbly tree.*
- similar to, the same as, resembling, identical to
  OPPOSITE unlike

like verb

⚠ **OVERUSED WORD**

Try to vary the words you use for **like**. Here are some other words you could use.

- to *LIKE A PERSON* or *ANIMAL*:
  admire, adore, be attached to, be fond of, care for, cherish, esteem, hold dear, love
  (*informal*) have a soft spot for
  *Lauren is very **attached** to her new puppy.*
- to *LIKE SOMETHING* or *LIKE DOING SOMETHING*:
  appreciate, be interested in, be keen on, be partial to, delight in, enjoy, prefer, relish
  *Alex is very **partial** to chocolate cake. What sort of films do you **enjoy**?*
  OPPOSITE dislike

likely adjective
*It's **likely** that the shop will be closed tomorrow.*
- probable, expected, anticipated, predictable, foreseeable
  OPPOSITE unlikely

likeness noun
1 *There's a strong **likeness** between the two sisters.*
- resemblance, similarity, correspondence
  OPPOSITE difference

a
b
c
d
e
f
g
h
i
j
k
l
m
n
o
p
q
r
s
t
u
v
w
x
y
z

2 *This photo is a good **likeness** of my grandfather.*
- image, representation, picture, portrait, copy

liking noun
*Ray has a **liking** for classical music.*
- fondness, taste, love, affection, preference
- OPPOSITE dislike

limb noun
- Your limbs are your arms and legs.
- Birds have wings.
- Seals, whales, and dolphins have flippers.
- An octopus has tentacles.
- The limbs of a tree are its boughs or branches.

limit noun
1 *There is a **limit** of twenty pupils for this class.*
- maximum, restriction, threshold, ceiling, cut-off point
- A limit on time is a deadline or time limit.

2 *The fence marks the **limit** of the school grounds.*
- border, boundary, edge, perimeter, frontier

limit verb
*I had to **limit** the invitations to my party.*
- put a limit on, restrict, control, ration

limited adjective
1 *The crew had a **limited** supply of water.*
- restricted, short, inadequate, insufficient, rationed, finite, fixed

2 *It was hard to move about in the **limited** space.*
- small, cramped, narrow, confined
- OPPOSITE limitless

limp verb
*She **limped** off the pitch with an injured ankle.*
- hobble, hop, falter, stumble

limp adjective
*The leaves on the plant are looking **limp**.*
- drooping, floppy, sagging, wilting, soft, flabby, slack
- OPPOSITE rigid

line noun
1 *I drew a pencil **line** across the page.*
- stroke, rule, underline, stripe, streak, band, bar, dash
- A line that is cut into a surface is a groove, score, or scratch.
- A line on a person's skin is a wrinkle.
- A deep groove or wrinkle is a furrow.
- A line on fabric is a crease

2 *There was a long **line** of people waiting at the bus stop.*
- queue, row, file, column, rank, procession, chain
- A line of police officers forming a barrier is a cordon.
- A line of schoolchildren walking in pairs is a crocodile.

3 *The clothes were drying on the washing **line**.*
- cord, rope, string, thread, wire, cable, flex, lead

linger verb
1 *The smell of burning wood **lingered** in the air.*
- continue, remain, stay, last, persist
- OPPOSITE disappear

2 *Don't **linger** outside in this cold weather.*
- hang about, wait about, loiter, dawdle, dally, delay
- OPPOSITE hurry

link noun
*The two schools have close **links** with each other.*
- relationship, association, connection, bond, tie

link verb
*They **linked** the trailer to the tractor.*
- attach, connect, fasten, join, couple
- OPPOSITE separate

a b c d e f g h i j k l m n o p q r s t u v w x y z

lion noun

- A female lion is a lioness.
- A young lion is a cub.
- A group of lions is a pride.
- The fur collar on a male lion is its mane.

liquid adjective

*Pour the **liquid** jelly into a mould.*

- runny, watery, wet, fluid, flowing, running, sloppy
- To make something liquid by heating it is to melt it.
- Liquid metal or rock is molten.

OPPOSITE solid

liquid noun

*The flask contained a frothy green **liquid**.*

- fluid, solution, juice, liquor
- The liquid inside a plant is sap.

list noun

- A list of people's names is a roll or register.
- A list of people who have tasks to do is a rota.
- A list of books in the library or of goods for sale is a catalogue.
- A list of topics mentioned in a book is an index.
- A list of things to choose from is a menu.
- A list of things to do or remember is a checklist.

list verb

1 *I helped to **list** the books in the library.*

- record, write down, catalogue, index, register

2 *The damaged ship **listed** to one side.*

- lean, tilt, tip, slope, incline

listen verb

to listen to something

*The spy **listened** carefully **to** the instructions.*

- pay attention to, take notice of, attend to, heed
- To listen secretly to a private conversation is to eavesdrop.

literature noun

1 *The bookshop specializes in children's **literature**.*

- books, writings

FOR VARIOUS KINDS OF LITERATURE

SEE **writing**

2 *The travel agent gave us some **literature** to read.*

- brochures, leaflets, pamphlets, handouts

litter noun

*The street was covered with **litter**.*

- rubbish, waste, refuse, garbage, junk, clutter, mess, odds and ends

litter verb

*The desk was **littered** with scrunched-up paper.*

- scatter, strew

little adjective

⚠ **OVERUSED WORD**

Try to vary the words you use for little. Here are some other words you could use.

- for something *LITTLE IN SIZE*:
  compact, mini, miniature, minute, petite, small, tiny
  (*informal*) teeny
  (*Scottish*) wee
  *The camera is so **tiny** it will fit in your pocket.*
  OPPOSITE big, large

- for someone *LITTLE IN AGE*:
  small, young
  (*Scottish*) wee
  *My granny lived in India when she was **young**.*
  OPPOSITE big, old

- for a *LITTLE TIME* or a *LITTLE WHILE*:
  brief, fleeting, passing, short
  *It was a **short** while before our friends arrived.*
  OPPOSITE lengthy, long

- for *LITTLE FOOD* or *LITTLE MONEY*:
  hardly any, insufficient, meagre, paltry, scarcely any
  *There was **scarcely any** food left in the house.*
  OPPOSITE ample, plenty

a
b
c
d
e
f
g
h
i
j
k
l
m
n
o
p
q
r
s
t
u
v
w
x
y
z

a
b
c
d
e
f
g
h
i
j
k
l
m
n
o
p
q
r
s
t
u
v
w
x
y
z

a little
1 *Would you like a **little** milk in your tea?*
- some, a bit of, a spot of, a touch of
2 *I'm feeling a **little** tired now.*
- a bit, slightly, rather, somewhat

live adjective
*The fishermen caught a **live** octopus in their nets.*
- alive, living, breathing
OPPOSITE dead

live verb
*Will these plants **live** through the winter?*
- stay alive, survive, exist, flourish, last, continue, remain
OPPOSITE die
to live in a place
*They **live in** a basement flat.*
- inhabit, occupy, dwell in, reside in
to live on
*Koalas **live on** eucalyptus leaves.*
- eat, feed on

lively adjective
1 *The toddlers were in a **lively** mood.*
- active, energetic, animated, spirited, boisterous, excited, vivacious, sprightly, frisky, chirpy, perky
OPPOSITE inactive
2 *The city centre is always **lively** at night.*
- busy, bustling, crowded, exciting, buzzing
OPPOSITE quiet, dead

livid adjective
*Gary was **livid** when he saw the damage to his bike.*
- angry, furious, fuming, incensed, enraged, seething, raging

living adjective
1 *Miss Millicent had no **living** relatives.*
- alive
OPPOSITE dead
2 *There are no dinosaurs still **living**.*
- existing, surviving
OPPOSITE extinct

living noun
1 *He makes a **living** from painting.*
- income, livelihood
2 *What does she do for a **living**?*
- job, occupation, profession, trade, career

load noun
1 *Camels can carry heavy **loads**.*
- burden, weight
2 *The lorry delivered its **load** to the supermarket.*
- cargo, consignment, goods, freight

load verb
1 *We **loaded** the suitcases into the car.*
- pack, pile, heap, stow
2 *He arrived **loaded** with shopping bags.*
- weigh down, burden, saddle

loan noun
*She needs a **loan** to pay for her holiday.*
- advance
- A system which allows you to pay for something later is credit.
- A loan to buy a house is a mortgage.

loathe verb
*My brother **loathes** the colour pink.*
- hate, detest, dislike, despise
OPPOSITE love, adore

local adjective
*Our **local** shop delivers newspapers.*
- neighbourhood, nearby, neighbouring

locate verb
1 *I can't **locate** the book you asked for.*
- find, discover, track down, detect, unearth, lay your hands on
OPPOSITE lose
2 *The art gallery is **located** in the city centre.*
- place, position, put, situate, set up, build, establish, station

location noun
*The pilot made a note of his **location**.*
- position, situation, whereabouts, place, spot

lock noun

1 *There was a heavy lock on the lid of the chest.*
- fastening, clasp, padlock, bolt, latch

2 *The princess cut a lock from her hair.*
- tress, curl, tuft

lock verb

Make sure you lock the door when you go out.
- fasten, secure, bolt, close, shut, seal

lodge verb

1 *Where are you lodging at present?*
- live, stay, reside, dwell

2 *The animals are lodged indoors in the winter.*
- house, accommodate, board, put up

3 *The ball was lodged in a tree.*
- get caught, get stuck, jam, wedge, fix, embed

log noun

1 *They collected logs to burn on the fire.*
FOR VARIOUS TYPES OF WOOD
SEE **wood**

2 *The astronauts kept a log of their voyage.*
- diary, journal, record, account

logical adjective

The robot always gave a logical answer.
- rational, reasonable, sensible, sound, valid, intelligent, clear, lucid, methodical, systematic
OPPOSITE illogical

lone adjective

A lone rider galloped past.
- single, solitary, unaccompanied, isolated

lonely adjective

1 *Cara felt lonely while her friends were away.*
- alone, friendless, lonesome, solitary, abandoned, neglected, forlorn, forsaken

2 *The climbers sheltered in a lonely hut.*
- deserted, isolated, remote, secluded, out-of-the-way

long adjective

It seemed a long time before the bus came.
- lengthy, prolonged, extended, extensive, long-lasting
OPPOSITE short

long verb

to long for something
I'm longing for a drink.
- yearn for, crave, want, wish for, desire, fancy, hunger for, pine for, hanker after, itch for
- (*informal*) be dying for

look verb

1 *If you look carefully, you'll see an owl in the tree.*
- watch, observe, view, regard, keep your eyes open

2 *My pet snake looks a bit hungry.*
- appear, seem

to look after someone or **something**
We looked after their house when they went on holiday.
- care for, keep an eye on, mind, tend, watch over, guard, protect
- To look after sick people is to nurse them.

to look for something
He spent ages looking for his keys.
- hunt for, search for, seek

to look out
If you don't look out, you'll get wet.
- beware, pay attention, take care, watch out, keep an eye open

⚠️ **OVERUSED WORD**

Try to vary the words you use for look. Here are some other words you could use.
- to *LOOK QUICKLY*:
glance, glimpse, peek, peep
The secret agent glanced at her watch.
- to *LOOK CAREFULLY* or *INTENTLY*:
stare, peer, study, scrutinize, examine, inspect, take a good look at
The fossil hunters peered at the rocks.

a b c d e f g h i j k **l** m n o p q r s t u v w x y z

a
b
c
d
e
f
g
h
i
j
k
l
m
n
o
p
q
r
s
t
u
v
w
x
y
z

- to *LOOK ANGRILY* :
  glare, glower, grimace, frown, scowl
  *The grumpy knight **glowered** at his servant.*
- To look steadily is to gaze.
- To look in amazement is to gape.
- To look over a wide area is to scan or survey it.

look noun

1 *Did you have a **look** at what she was wearing?*
- glance, glimpse, peep, sight, view

2 *The guard had an unfriendly **look**.*
- appearance, bearing, manner, air, expression, face

lookout noun

***Lookouts** were posted along the wall.*
- sentry, guard, sentinel, watchman

loom verb

1 *A figure **loomed** out of the mist.*
- appear, emerge, arise, take shape

2 *The haunted mansion **loomed** above us.*
- rise, tower, stand out, hang over

loop noun

*Make a **loop** in the string and then tie a knot.*
- coil, hoop, circle, ring, noose, bend, curl, kink, twist

loop verb

*The cowboy **looped** the reins round a fence post.*
- coil, wind, curl, bend, turn, twist

loose adjective

1 *Some of the cobbles on the road are **loose**.*
- insecure, unfixed, movable, unsteady, shaky, wobbly
  OPPOSITE firm, secure

2 *The fire was started by a **loose** wire.*
- disconnected, unattached, detached

3 *These jeans are **loose** around the waist.*
- slack, baggy, roomy, loose-fitting
  OPPOSITE tight

4 *The chickens wander **loose** about the farm.*
- free, at large, at liberty, on the loose, unconfined, unrestricted
  OPPOSITE confined

loosen verb

*Can you **loosen** these knots?*
- undo, unfasten, untie, free, loose, slacken, release, ease
  OPPOSITE tighten

loot noun

*The thieves buried their **loot** in a safe place.*
- haul, plunder, takings

loot verb

*Rioters **looted** the shops.*
- raid, ransack, rob, steal from, pillage, plunder

lorry noun FOR TYPES OF VEHICLE
SEE **vehicle**

lose verb

1 *Debbie has **lost** one of her gloves.*
- be unable to find, mislay, misplace
  OPPOSITE find

2 *Unfortunately, we **lost** the game on Saturday.*
- be defeated, get beaten, suffer a defeat
  OPPOSITE win

loss noun

1 *She is suffering from a **loss** of memory.*
- failure, disappearance, deprivation

2 *The farmer was upset by the **loss** of his sheepdog.*
- death, decease, passing

lot noun

*We are having another **lot** of visitors this weekend.*
- group, batch, set, crowd, collection

a lot of

*My brother needs **a lot of** help with his spelling.*
- a large amount of, a good or great deal of, plenty of

lots of

*There are **lots of** toys to choose from in the shop.*

- a great number of, many, numerous, plenty (of)
- (*informal*) loads of, tons of, masses of, oodles of, hundreds of

loud adjective

1 *The whole house was kept awake by the **loud** music.*
- noisy, blaring, booming, deafening, rowdy, resounding, thunderous, penetrating, piercing
- A noise which is loud enough to hear is audible.
OPPOSITE quiet, soft

2 *The tourists wore rather **loud** shirts.*
- bright, gaudy, garish, showy, flashy
OPPOSITE muted, subdued

lounge verb

*They **lounged** in the garden all day.*
- relax, be lazy, idle, laze, sprawl, lie around, loll, take it easy, waste time

lovable adjective

*Our friends have a **lovable** new kitten.*
- adorable, dear, sweet, charming, likeable, lovely, appealing, attractive, cuddly, enchanting, endearing
OPPOSITE hateful

love noun

*She often mentions her **love** of the outdoors.*
- liking, passion, fondness, affection, devotion, admiration, adoration
- (*informal*) soft spot (for)

love verb

1 *They **love** each other and want to get married.*
- be in love with, care for, adore, cherish, hold dear, treasure, worship, idolize
- A relationship between two people who love each other is a romance.

2 *My friend, Dot, **loves** knitting.*
- like, have a passion for, be fond of, be partial to, enjoy
OPPOSITE hate

lovely adjective

> **OVERUSED WORD**
>
> Try to vary the words you use for **lovely**. Here are some other words you could use.
>
> - for a *LOVELY PERSON*:
> charming, delightful, lovable, likeable, dear, sweet, enchanting, endearing
> *Jemma is a **charming** girl.*
> - for a *LOVELY DAY* or *LOVELY VIEW*:
> fine, glorious
> *It's a **glorious** day for a bicycle trip.*
> - for a *LOVELY EXPERIENCE*:
> pleasant, pleasing, enjoyable
> *The girls had an **enjoyable** time camping.*
> OPPOSITE nasty
> - for something that *LOOKS LOVELY*:
> appealing, attractive, beautiful, pretty
> *The roses look **attractive** in that vase.*

loving adjective

*Erin gave her teddy bear a **loving** hug.*
- affectionate, kind, friendly, warm, tender, fond, devoted, passionate
OPPOSITE unfriendly

low adjective

1 *The garden is surrounded by a **low** wall.*
- short, shallow, sunken

2 *They were soldiers of **low** rank in the army.*
- junior, inferior, lowly, modest, humble

3 *We spoke in **low** whispers.*
- quiet, soft, muted, subdued, muffled

4 *The tuba plays **low** notes.*
- bass, deep
OPPOSITE high

lower verb

1 *The supermarket **lowered** its prices.*
- reduce, cut, bring down, decrease, lessen,
- (*informal*) slash

2 *Please **lower** the volume of your radio.*
- quieten, turn down

3 *At the end of the Olympic Games, they **lower** the flag.*
- take down, let down, dip
- OPPOSITE raise

loyal adjective
*Sir Valiant had always been a **loyal** knight.*
- true, trusty, faithful, steadfast, reliable, dependable, devoted, constant, sincere
- OPPOSITE disloyal

luck noun
1 *He found the secret entrance by **luck**.*
- accident, chance, coincidence, fluke, fate, destiny
2 *She had a bit of **luck** today.*
- good fortune, success

lucky adjective
1 *I got the right answer by a **lucky** guess.*
- accidental, chance, unintentional, unplanned
2 *Some **lucky** person won a million pounds.*
- fortunate, favoured, successful
- OPPOSITE unlucky

ludicrous adjective
*They laughed at such a **ludicrous** idea.*
- ridiculous, absurd, laughable, idiotic, foolish, crazy, daft, senseless

luggage noun
*The **luggage** can go in the boot of the car.*
- baggage, cases, suitcases, bags

lull verb
*She **lulled** the baby by rocking it gently.*
- calm, soothe, hush, quieten, pacify, subdue

lull noun
*There was a brief **lull** in the conversation.*
- pause, break, gap, interval, calm
- (informal) let-up

lumber verb
1 *A rhinoceros **lumbered** towards them.*
- move clumsily, trundle, trudge, tramp, blunder, shamble

2 *(informal) Why am I **lumbered** with the washing up?*
- burden
- (informal) saddle

lump noun
1 ***Lumps** of sticky clay stuck to his boots.*
- chunk, piece, cluster, clump, wad, mass, hunk, wedge, block
- A round lump of something is a ball.
- A lump of gold is a nugget.
- A lump of earth is a clod.
- A lump of blood is a clot.
2 *I could feel a **lump** where I'd bumped my head.*
- bump, swelling, bulge, protrusion

lump verb
to lump things together
*The books and CDs were all **lumped** together.*
- put together, combine, merge, bunch up

lunge verb
*Robin **lunged** at the sheriff with his sword.*
- thrust, charge, rush, dive, pounce, throw yourself

lurch verb
1 *The bus passengers **lurched** from side to side.*
- reel, sway, rock, stagger, stumble, totter
2 *The ship **lurched** as the waves pounded it.*
- pitch, roll, heave, lean, list

lure verb
*Spiders **lure** insects into their webs.*
- attract, entice, tempt, coax, draw, invite, persuade
- Something used to lure an animal into a trap is bait.

lurk verb
*The jaguar **lurked** in wait for its prey.*
- skulk, loiter, prowl, crouch, hide, lie in wait, lie low

lush adjective
*Rainforests have **lush** vegetation.*
- rich, dense, thick, rampant, abundant

luxurious adjective

*The dress was trimmed with **luxurious** lace.*

- grand, lavish, lush, rich, expensive, costly, deluxe, plush, magnificent, splendid, sumptuous
  OPPOSITE simple, austere

luxury noun

*The millionaire lived a life of **luxury**.*

- affluence, wealth, richness, splendour, comfort, ease
  OPPOSITE poverty

machine noun

*Do you know how this **machine** works?*

- apparatus, appliance, device, engine, contraption

mad adjective

1 *You must be **mad** to go out on a day like this.*

- crazy, daft, insane, senseless, stupid, foolish, idiotic
- (*informal*) out of your mind, potty, nuts
  OPPOSITE sensible, wise

2 *The emperor was **mad** with rage.*

- angry, furious, beside yourself, frenzied, hysterical

3 (*informal*) *Sandra is **mad** about horses.*

- enthusiastic, fanatical, passionate

magazine noun

*I bought a **magazine** to read on the train.*

- journal, periodical, paper, comic

magic adjective

1 *My uncle taught me some **magic** tricks.*

- conjuring

2 *The castle was surrounded by a **magic** spell.*

- magical, supernatural

magic noun

> **WORD WEB**
>
> *Do you believe in magic?*
>
> - sorcery, witchcraft, wizardry, spells, charms, enchantments
>
> PEOPLE WHO USE MAGIC
> enchanter or enchantress, magician, sorceror or sorceress, warlock, witch, wizard
> SEE ALSO **fairy**
>
> THINGS WHICH A SORCEROR MIGHT DO
> bewitch, enchant, cast or undo a spell, become invisible or vanish, brew a potion, put a curse on you
>
> THINGS WHICH A SORCEROR MIGHT HAVE OR USE
> apprentice, cauldron, charm, elixir, magic potion, magic spell or incantation, talisman, wand
> FOR MAGICAL CREATURES
> SEE **myth**

magical adjective SEE **magic** adjective

magician noun

1 *The **magician** pulled a scarf out of his hat.*

- conjuror

2 *King Arthur was helped by the **magician**, Merlin.*

- sorcerer, witch, wizard

magnificent adjective

1 *The mountain scenery was **magnificent**.*

- beautiful, glorious, splendid, spectacular, impressive, majestic

2 *The film star lived in a **magnificent** house.*

- grand, imposing, stately
- (*informal*) posh

a b c d e f g h i j k **l m** n o p q r s t u v w x y z

3 *That was a **magnificent** meal!*
- excellent, first-class, marvellous, superb
- (*informal*) fabulous, fantastic
- OPPOSITE ordinary

magnify verb
*Objects are **magnified** through binoculars.*
- enlarge, make larger
- (*informal*) blow up
- OPPOSITE reduce, minimize

mail noun
*The **mail** arrived early this morning.*
- post, delivery, letters and parcels

mail verb
*Can you **mail** this letter for me?*
- post, send, dispatch

maim verb SEE injure

main adjective
1 *What was the **main** point of the story?*
- central, chief, most important, basic, essential, fundamental, primary, predominant
2 *This is the **main** shopping area in the town.*
- major, principal, biggest, foremost, largest, leading, prime
- OPPOSITE minor, unimportant

mainly adverb
*Chimpanzees eat **mainly** fruit and vegetables.*
- largely, mostly, chiefly, principally, predominantly, primarily

maintain verb
1 *The referee tried to **maintain** order.*
- keep, preserve
2 *A team of gardeners **maintain** the grounds.*
- look after, take care of, keep in order
3 *How much does it cost to **maintain** a family?*
- support, keep, provide for
4 *He still **maintains** that he's innocent.*
- claim, declare, assert, insist, state, contend

majestic adjective
*The town was dominated by the **majestic** castle.*
- grand, magnificent, splendid, impressive, stately, imposing, noble

major adjective
1 *There are delays on all the **major** roads into the city.*
- chief, principal, primary, leading
2 *Writing her first novel was a **major** achievement.*
- big, great, considerable, significant, important
- OPPOSITE minor

majority noun
the majority of
*The **majority of** children walk to school.*
- the greater number of, the bulk of, most
- OPPOSITE minority

make verb
1 *We **made** a shelter out of leaves and branches.*
- build, construct, assemble, put together, produce, manufacture
2 *Those two are always **making** trouble.*
- cause, bring about, give rise to, provoke
3 *They **made** me captain.*
- appoint, elect, nominate
4 *They've **made** the attic into a games room.*
- change, turn, convert, modify, transform, alter
5 *She'll **make** a good actress when she's older.*
- become, grow into, turn into, change into
6 *The regulations were **made** to protect children.*
- establish, fix, decide on, agree
7 *You **made** me jump!*
- cause you to
8 *We can't **make** her go if she doesn't want to.*
- force, compel, order
9 *He **made** a lot of money last year.*
- gain, get, obtain, acquire, receive, earn, win

a b c d e f g h i j k l **m** n o p q r s t u v w x y z

10 *The ship finally **made** land.*
- reach, arrive at, get to, get as far as

11 *What time do you **make** it?*
- calculate, estimate, reckon

12 *2 and 2 **make** 4.*
- add up to, come to, total

13 *I'll **make** you an offer for your old bike.*
- propose, suggest

14 *Have you **made** your bed this morning?*
- arrange, tidy

to make off
*The thieves **made off** in a stolen car.*
- leave, escape, get away, run away, disappear
- (*informal*) clear off

to make someone or **something out**
*I can't **make out** why everything went wrong.*
- understand, work out, comprehend, fathom, make sense of

to make up
*I **made up** a new flavour of ice-cream.*
- create, invent, think up, concoct

make noun
*What **make** of computer do you have?*
- brand, model, label

male adjective FOR MALE HUMAN BEINGS
SEE **man**
FOR MALE ANIMALS
SEE **animal**
OPPOSITE female

malicious adjective
*Someone had spread a **malicious** rumour.*
- malevolent, hostile, malign, spiteful, vindictive, vicious, hurtful

mammal noun FOR VARIOUS KINDS OF ANIMAL
SEE **animal**

man noun
- A polite word for a man is gentleman.
- Informal words are bloke, chap, fellow, and guy.
- A married man is a husband.
- A man who has children is a father.
- An unmarried man is a bachelor.

- A man whose wife has died is a widower.
- A man on his wedding day is a bridegroom.
- A man who is engaged to be married is a fiancé.
- Words for a young man are boy, lad, and youth.

manage verb
1 *His eldest son **manages** the business now.*
- be in charge of, run, direct, lead, control, govern, rule, supervise, oversee, preside over

2 *I can't **manage** any more work this week.*
- cope with, deal with, take on, carry out

3 *We'll have to **manage** without the car.*
- cope, make do, get along, get by

manager noun
*If you have a problem, talk to the **manager**.*
- chief, director, proprietor
- (*informal*) boss

mania noun
*A **mania** for the pop group swept the country.*
- craze, hysteria, obsession, passion, fixation, fad

manipulate verb
1 *He **manipulated** the dials on the robot.*
- operate, work, handle, control
- (*informal*) twiddle

2 *She uses her charm to **manipulate** people.*
- take advantage of, use, exploit, impose on

manner noun
1 *They did the work in an efficient **manner**.*
- way, style, fashion, method

2 *I was put off by her frosty **manner**.*
- behaviour, conduct, attitude, disposition, air, look, bearing

manners
*Trolls have no **manners** at all!*
- politeness, courtesy, graces

manoeuvre noun
1 *Parking a bus is a difficult **manoeuvre**.*
- move, operation
2 *The opposing team used a clever **manoeuvre**.*
- strategy, tactic, trick, dodge, plan, plot, scheme

manoeuvre verb
*How do you **manoeuvre** a hot-air balloon?*
- guide, move, pilot, steer, navigate

manufacture verb
*The factory **manufactures** pine furniture.*
- make, build, assemble, fabricate

many adjective
*I've been on an aeroplane **many** times.*
- a lot of, plenty of, numerous, frequent, countless, innumerable, untold
- (*informal*) umpteen, lots of
OPPOSITE few

map noun
*The travel agent gave us a free **map** of Paris.*
- chart, diagram, plan
- A book of maps is an atlas.
- A person who draws maps is a cartographer.

mar verb
*The film was **marred** by a terrible soundtrack.*
- spoil, ruin, harm, impair, tarnish

march verb
*The brass band **marched** down the High Street.*
- parade, file, troop, stride, pace

margin noun
*Don't write in the **margin** of the paper.*
- border, edge

marginal adjective
*There is a **marginal** difference between the two signatures.*
- slight, small, minimal, minor, unimportant, negligible, borderline
OPPOSITE great

mark noun
1 *There were muddy paw **marks** all over the kitchen floor.*
- spot, stain, blemish, blotch, blot, smear, smudge, streak
- A mark left by a pen or pencil is a scribble.
- A mark left by fingers is a fingermark.
- A mark on your skin that you are born with is a birthmark.
2 *They stood in silence as a **mark** of respect.*
- sign, token, indication, symbol, emblem
3 *What **mark** did you get in the spelling test?*
- score, grade

mark verb
1 *Please be careful not to **mark** the photographs.*
- stain, smudge, dirty, blot
2 *The teacher had a pile of essays to **mark**.*
- correct, grade, assess
3 *There will be trouble, you **mark** my words!*
- mind, heed, attend to, listen to, note, take note of

marked adjective
*There's a **marked** difference in style between the paintings.*
- noticeable, considerable, pronounced, clear, obvious, distinct, decided
OPPOSITE slight, minor

market noun SEE **shop**

marriage noun
1 *My grandparents celebrated 40 years of **marriage**.*
- matrimony, wedlock
2 *Today is the anniversary of their **marriage**.*
- wedding
SEE ALSO **wedding**

marry verb

In what year did your grandparents ***marry***?

- get married, wed
- (*informal*) tie the knot, get hitched
- A couple who have promised to marry are engaged to each other.
- A man who is engaged to be married is a fiancé and the woman he is engaged to is his fiancée.

marsh noun

Wading birds are found in coastal ***marshes***.

- swamp, bog, wetland, marshland, fen

marvel noun

the ***marvels*** *of modern science*

- wonder, miracle

marvel verb

to marvel at

The crowd ***marvelled at*** *the juggler's skill.*

- admire, wonder at, be amazed by, be astonished by

marvellous adjective

1 *The professor showed us his* ***marvellous*** *inventions.*
- amazing, remarkable, extraordinary, incredible, miraculous, astonishing, phenomenal
  OPPOSITE ordinary
2 *We had a* ***marvellous*** *day at the zoo.*
- excellent, superb, tremendous, wonderful, splendid
- (*informal*) brilliant, fantastic, terrific, super, smashing
  OPPOSITE bad, awful

masculine adjective

The singer had a deep, ***masculine*** *voice.*

- male, manly, macho, virile
  OPPOSITE feminine

mash verb

Mash *the potatoes until they're smooth.*

- crush, pound, pulp, smash, squash
- To make something into powder is to grind or pulverize it.

mask verb

The entrance was ***masked*** *by an overhanging tree.*

- conceal, hide, cover, obscure, screen, veil, shroud, camouflage

mass noun

She sifted through the ***mass*** *of papers on her desk.*

- heap, pile, mound, stack, collection, quantity, accumulation
- (*informal*) load

massacre verb SEE **kill**

massive adjective SEE **huge**

master noun

1 *We played a game in which I was* ***master*** *of the castle.*
- lord, ruler, governor, chief
2 *Sherlock Holmes was a* ***master*** *of disguises.*
- expert (at), genius, ace, wizard

master verb

1 *Have you* ***mastered*** *chess yet?*
- grasp, learn, understand
- (*informal*) get the hang of, get to grips with
2 *I've managed to* ***master*** *my fear of heights.*
- overcome, conquer, defeat, triumph over, get the better of, control, curb, subdue, tame

match noun

1 *The semi-final was a really exciting* ***match***.
- game, contest, competition, fixture, tournament, tie
2 *The hat and gloves are a good* ***match***.
- combination, pair

match verb

Does this tie ***match*** *my shirt?*

- go with, suit, fit with, blend with, tone in with
  OPPOSITE contrast with

a
b
c
d
e
f
g
h
i
j
k
l
m
n
o
p
q
r
s
t
u
v
w
x
y
z

a
b
c
d
e
f
g
h
i
j
k
l
m
n
o
p
q
r
s
t
u
v
w
x
y
z

matching adjective
*The bed cover comes with a **matching** pillowcase.*
- coordinating, corresponding, complimentary, twin
  OPPOSITE contrasting

mate noun (informal)
1 *Gary is one of my best **mates**.*
- friend
- (informal) pal, chum, buddy
2 *He's got a job as a plumber's **mate**.*
- assistant, helper, apprentice

material noun
1 *I'm collecting **material** for the school magazine.*
- information, facts, data, ideas, notes
2 *The cleaning **materials** are in the cupboard.*
- stuff, substances, things
3 *The kite is made of lightweight **material**.*
- cloth, fabric
  FOR KINDS OF FABRIC
  SEE **cloth**

mathematics noun

> 🕸 **WORD WEB**
> *This computer game makes **mathematics** fun!*
> - sums
>   (informal) maths
>   BRANCHES OF MATHEMATICS
>   algebra, arithmetic, geometry, statistics
>   THINGS YOU MIGHT DO IN MATHS
>   adding, calculating, counting, dividing, measuring, multiplying, subtracting
>   SOME INSTRUMENTS USED FOR MATHS
>   calculator, compasses, computer, dividers, ruler, set square
>   FOR OTHER WORDS USED IN MATHS
>   SEE **measurement, shape** noun

matted adjective
*The dog's coat was dirty and **matted**.*
- knotted, tangled, uncombed

matter noun
1 *The manager will deal with this **matter**.*
- affair, concern, issue, business, situation, incident, subject, topic, thing
2 *Peat consists mainly of plant **matter**.*
- material, stuff, substance
3 *What's the **matter** with the car?*
- problem, difficulty, trouble, worry

matter verb
*Will it **matter** if I'm late?*
- be important, count, make a difference

mature adjective
1 *The zoo has two **mature** gorillas.*
- adult, fully grown, well developed
  OPPOSITE young
2 *He acts very **mature** for his age.*
- grown-up, responsible, sensible
  OPPOSITE immature, childish

maximum adjective
*What is the **maximum** speed of the rocket?*
- greatest, top, highest, fullest, biggest, largest
  OPPOSITE minimum

maximum noun
*The heat is at its **maximum** at midday.*
- highest point, peak, top, upper limit, ceiling

maybe adverb
***Maybe** you'll be picked for the football team.*
- perhaps, possibly
  OPPOSITE definitely

maze noun
*We were lost in a **maze** of underground tunnels.*
- labyrinth, network, web, tangle

meadow noun
*Cows were grazing in the **meadow**.*
- field, pasture

meagre adjective
*The prioners were given **meagre** rations of food.*

- scant, sparse, poor, scanty, inadequate, insufficient, skimpy, paltry
- (*informal*) measly, stingy
OPPOSITE generous, ample

meal noun

> **WORD WEB**
>
> MEALS YOU HAVE AT VARIOUS TIMES OF DAY
>
> breakfast, brunch, dinner, (*informal*) elevenses, high tea, lunch or luncheon, supper, tea
> - A big formal meal is a banquet or feast.
> - A quick informal meal is a snack.
> - A meal you eat out of doors is a barbecue or picnic.
> - A meal where you help yourself to food is a buffet.
> - A meal you buy ready cooked is a takeaway.
>
> VARIOUS COURSES OF A MEAL
>
> starter, main course; dessert, pudding, sweet, (*informal*) afters
> SEE ALSO **food**

mean adjective
1 *Scrooge was too **mean** to buy any presents.*

- selfish, miserly, uncharitable
- (*informal*) stingy, tight-fisted, penny-pinching
OPPOSITE generous

2 *That was a **mean** trick to play.*

- unkind, unpleasant, nasty, spiteful, vicious, cruel, malicious
OPPOSITE kind

mean verb
1 *A red traffic light **means** that cars have to stop.*

- indicate, signify, denote, express, imply, convey, communicate, stand for, symbolize

2 *I **mean** to get better at swimming this year.*

- intend, plan, aim, propose, want

meaning noun
*What is the **meaning** of this riddle?*

- sense, significance, explanation, interpretation, definition

meaningful adjective
*The two friends exchanged a **meaningful** look.*

- pointed, suggestive, signifcant, expressive
OPPOSITE meaningless

means plural noun
1 *Email is a popular **means** of communication.*

- method, mode, medium, channel, course, way

2 *They don't have the **means** to buy a house.*

- money, resources, funds, finance, income, wherewithal

measure verb
***Measure** the height of the wall.*

- calculate, gauge, assess, survey
- To measure the weight of something is to weigh it.

measure noun
1 *At least we now know the **measure** of the problem.*

- size, extent, magnitude

2 *They are taking **measures** to improve the park.*

- step, action, course, procedure, means

measurement noun

> **WORD WEB**
>
> *What are the **measurements** of this room?*
> - dimensions, size, extent, proportions
>
> UNITS FOR MEASURING DISTANCE
>
> millimetre, centimetre, metre, kilometre; inch, foot, yard, mile
> - The distance of an object in space is measured in light years.
> - The depth of the sea is measured in fathoms.
>
> UNITS FOR MEASURING AREA
>
> square centimetre or metre, hectare; square inch or foot, acre

a
b
c
d
e
f
g
h
i
j
k
l
m
n
o
p
q
r
s
t
u
v
w
x
y
z

UNITS FOR MEASURING VOLUME
millilitre, litre, kilolitre; pint, quart, gallon

UNITS FOR MEASURING WEIGHT
milligram, gram, kilo or kilogram, tonne; ounce, pound, stone, ton

UNITS FOR MEASURING TIME
second, minute, hour, day, week, month, year, decade, century

UNITS FOR MEASURING SPEED
kilometres per hour, miles per hour

- The speed of a boat or ship is measured in knots.

UNITS FOR MEASURING TEMPERATURE
degrees Celsius, degrees centigrade, degrees Fahrenheit

OTHER MEASUREMENTS USED IN COOKING
cup or cupful, dessertspoon, pinch, spoonful, teaspoon, tablespoon

meat noun

 WORD WEB

SOME KINDS OF MEAT
bacon, beef, chicken, duck, game, gammon, goose, ham, lamb, mutton, pork, turkey, veal, venison

CUTS OR JOINTS OF MEAT
breast, brisket, chop, cutlet, fillet, leg, loin, rib, rump, sirloin, steak

FOODS MADE FROM MEAT
burger, chop, corned beef, cutlet, haggis, hamburger, kebab, meatball, mince, pasty, paté, pie, rissole, sausage, sausage roll

medal noun

*Our team won a bronze **medal** in the relay race.*
- award, prize, trophy
- A person who wins a medal is a medallist.

meddle verb

1 *He is always **meddling** in other people's affairs.*
- interfere, intrude, intervene, pry
- (*informal*) poke your nose in

2 *Don't **meddle** with my things.*
- fiddle about, tinker

medicine noun

 WORD WEB

1 *Did you take your cough **medicine**?*
- drug, medication, treatment, remedy
- An amount of medicine taken at one time is a dose.
- Medicine which a doctor gives you is a prescription.

2 *My cousin is studying herbal **medicine**.*
- therapy, treatment, healing

SOME TYPES OF MEDICINE
anaesthetic, antibiotic, antidote, antiseptic, gargle, herbs, painkiller, sedative, tincture, tonic, tranquillizer

FORMS IN WHICH YOU TAKE MEDICINE
capsule, inhaler, injection, lotion, lozenge, ointment, pill, tablet

INSTRUMENTS AND OTHER THINGS USED IN MEDICINE
bandage, dressing, forceps, gauze, lint, plaster, poultice, scalpel, sling, splint, stethoscope, syringe, thermometer, tweezers

PLACES WHERE YOU CAN GET MEDICAL TREATMENT
clinic, doctor's surgery, health centre, hospital, infirmary, nursing home, sickbay

SOME FORMS OF ALTERNATIVE MEDICINE
acupuncture, aromatherapy, herbal medicine, homeopathy, reflexology

PEOPLE WHO PRACTISE MEDICINE
- A person trained to heal sick people is a doctor or physician.
- A person trained to look after sick people is a nurse.
- Someone who performs medical operations is a surgeon.
- A person who puts you to sleep during operations is an anaesthetist.
- A person who takes X-rays is a radiologist.
- A person who tests your eyes is an optician.
- People who look after your teeth are dentists and hygienists.
- A person who practises herbal medicine is a herbalist.

- A specialist in children's health is a paediatrician.
- A specialist in mental illnesses is a psychiatrist.
- A person who treats you using massage and exercise is a physiotherapist.

mediocre adjective
*I thought the film was rather **mediocre**.*
- ordinary, average, commonplace, indifferent, second-rate, run-of-the-mill, undistinguished, uninspiring
OPPOSITE outstanding

medium adjective
*The man was of **medium** height.*
- average, middle, middling, standard, moderate, normal

medium noun
*The Internet is a great **medium** of communication.*
- means, mode, method, way, channel

meek adjective
*Koalas look **meek**, but they have fierce claws.*
- gentle, mild, tame, submissive, modest, docile, quiet, humble
OPPOSITE aggressive

meet verb
1 *I **met** an old friend at the party.*
- come across, encounter, run into, see
- (*informal*) bump into
2 *My parents **met** me at the station.*
- greet, pick up, welcome
3 *We're **meeting** outside the cinema at eight.*
- gather, assemble, collect, muster, rally
4 *The two roads **meet** here.*
- come together, merge, connect, join, cross, intersect
5 *She **meets** all the requirements for the job.*
- fulfil, satisfy, match, answer, comply with

meeting noun
*The bandits held a **meeting** to discuss their plan.*
- gathering, assembly, council, forum, congress, conference
- A large outdoor public meeting is a rally.
- A formal meeting with a king or queen is an audience.

melancholy adjective
*The princess sat alone with a **melancholy** look on her face.*
- sad, unhappy, miserable, gloomy, mournful, sorrowful, sombre, cheerless, woeful, dejected, depressed
OPPOSITE cheerful

melody noun
*The pianist played my favourite **melody**.*
- tune, air, theme

melt verb
*The ice began to **melt** in the sun.*
- thaw, soften, unfreeze
- To melt frozen food is to defrost it.
- To melt ore to get metal from it is to smelt it.
- Rock or metal that has melted through great heat is molten.
OPPOSITE freeze

member noun
to be a member of something
*Are you a **member of** the book club?*
- belong to, subscribe to

memorable adjective
*The concert should be a **memorable** event.*
- unforgettable, notable, noteworthy, impressive, remarkable, outstanding
OPPOSITE ordinary

memorize verb
*I have to **memorize** my words for the play.*
- learn, learn by heart, remember
OPPOSITE forget

memory noun
*She has happy **memories** of her childhood in Wales.*
- recollection, remembrance, reminiscence, reminder, impression

menace noun
1 *Sharks can be a **menace** to divers.*
- danger, threat
2 *That cat is an absolute **menace**!*
- nuisance, annoyance, irritation, inconvenience

mend verb
*Workmen were **mending** the pavement.*
- fix, repair, put right, restore, renovate, patch

mention verb
1 *Please don't **mention** the idea to anyone.*
- refer to, speak about, touch on, hint at
2 *You **mentioned** that you spoke Japanese.*
- say, remark, reveal, disclose
- (*informal*) let out
3 *The director **mentioned** all the cast.*
- name, acknowledge, list

mercy noun
*The evil queen showed no **mercy**.*
- compassion, humanity, sympathy, pity, leniency, kindness, charity
OPPOSITE cruelty

merge verb
1 *They plan to **merge** the two schools.*
- join together, combine, integrate, put together, unite, amalgamate
2 *Two streams **merge** here to form a river.*
- come together, converge, join, meet
OPPOSITE separate

merit noun
*She's a writer of great **merit**.*
- excellence, quality, distinction, worth, talent, virtue, value

merit verb
*The project **merits** our full attention.*
- deserve, justify, be entitled to, earn, rate, warrant

merry adjective
*The postman was whistling a **merry** tune.*
- cheerful, happy, jolly, bright, joyful, light-hearted, lively, spirited
OPPOSITE gloomy

mess noun
1 *Please clear up this **mess**.*
- muddle, untidiness, chaos, disorder, confusion, clutter, jumble, litter, dirt
- (*informal*) shambles
2 *Zoe made a **mess** of her audition.*
- disaster, botch
- (*informal*) hash
3 *They got into a **mess** over money.*
- difficulty, problem, dilemma, plight
- (*informal*) fix, jam

mess verb
to mess about
*We spent the day **messing about** on the beach.*
- play about, fool around, lounge about
- (*informal*) muck about
to mess things up
*I hope you haven't **messed up** my CDs.*
- confuse, mix up, muddle, jumble, make a mess of, tangle
to mess something up
*I think I **messed up** my interview.*
- bungle, botch
- (*informal*) make a hash of

message noun
*Did you get my **message**?*
- note, letter, communication
FOR TYPES OF MESSAGE
SEE **communication**
FOR SECRET MESSAGES
SEE **code**

messy adjective
*My bedroom is really **messy**!*
- muddled, untidy, disorderly, chaotic, dirty, filthy, grubby, mucky
- (*informal*) higgledy-piggledy
OPPOSITE neat

metal noun

WORD WEB

SOME COMMON METALS
aluminium, brass, bronze, copper, gold, iron, lead, magnesium, mercury, nickel, pewter, platinum, silver, steel, tin, zinc

- A bar of metal is an ingot.
- A lump of metal is a nugget.
- Somethings that looks or sounds like metal is metallic.

method noun

*My granny has a secret **method** for making jam.*

- technique, way, procedure, process
- A specially skilful method for doing something is a knack.

methodical adjective

*Inspector Dixon is always very **methodical**.*

- organized, orderly, systematic, meticulous, careful, deliberate, efficient, businesslike, painstaking
OPPOSITE careless

middle adjective

*The **middle** lane is reserved for buses.*

- central, inner, inside, midway

middle noun

*A scarecrow stood in the **middle** of the field.*

- centre, core, heart, midpoint
- The middle of a wheel is the hub.
- The middle part of an atom or cell is the nucleus.

might noun

*I banged at the door with all my **might**.*

- strength, power, energy, force, vigour

mighty adjective

*The dragon let out a **mighty** roar.*

- powerful, forceful, vigorous, ferocious, violent, great, enormous, hefty
OPPOSITE weak

mild adjective

1 *He's a **mild** person who never complains.*
- amiable, docile, easygoing, gentle, good-tempered, harmless, kind, lenient, merciful, placid, soft-hearted
2 *The weather has been **mild** for this time of year.*
- pleasant, warm, temperate
OPPOSITE severe

milk noun

- Foods made from milk are dairy products.
SEE ALSO **food**

milky adjective

*The flask contained a **milky** liquid.*
- whitish, cloudy, misty, chalky, opaque
OPPOSITE clear

mimic verb

*My dad is good at **mimicking** famous people.*
- do impressions of, imitate, impersonate, pretend to be
- (*informal*) take off
- If you mimic people specially to make fun of them, you caricature or parody them.

mind noun

1 *Her **mind** was as sharp as ever.*
- brain, intelligence, intellect, head, sense, understanding, wits, judgement, mental powers, reasoning
2 *Are you sure you won't change your **mind**?*
- wishes, intention, fancy, inclination, opinion, outlook, point of view

mind verb

1 *Will you **mind** my bag for a minute?*
- guard, look after, watch, care for
- (*informal*) keep an eye on
2 ***Mind** the step.*
- look out for, watch out for, beware of, pay attention to, heed, note
3 *They won't **mind** if I'm late.*
- bother, care, worry, be upset, take offence, object, disapprove

a
b
c
d
e
f
g
h
i
j
k
l
m
n
o
p
q
r
s
t
u
v
w
x
y
z

a
b
c
d
e
f
g
h
i
j
k
l
m
n
o
p
q
r
s
t
u
v
w
x
y
z

mine noun
- A coal mine is a colliery or pit.
- A place where coal is removed from the surface of the ground is an opencast mine.
- A place where stone or slate is removed is a quarry.

mingle verb
*The secret agent **mingled** with the crowd.*
- mix in, circulate, blend, combine, merge, fuse

miniature adjective
*A piccolo looks like a **miniature** flute.*
- tiny, minute, diminutive, small-scale, baby, mini
  SEE ALSO **small**

minimum adjective
*Set the oven to the **minimum** temperature.*
- least, smallest, littlest, lowest
  OPPOSITE maximum

minor adjective
*I only had a **minor** part in the play.*
- small, unimportant, insignificant, inferior, subordinate, trivial, petty
  OPPOSITE major

minute adjective
*You can hardly see the **minute** crack.*
- tiny, minuscule, microscopic, negligible
  OPPOSITE large

miraculous adjective
*The patient made a **miraculous** recovery.*
- amazing, astonishing, astounding, extraordinary, incredible, marvellous, unbelievable, wonderful, mysterious, inexplicable

misbehave verb
*My puppy has been **misbehaving** again!*
- behave badly, be naughty, be disobedient, get up to mischief
  OPPOSITE behave

miscellaneous adjective
*The bag contained **miscellaneous** balls of wool.*
- assorted, various, different, mixed

mischief noun
*The twins are always getting up to **mischief**.*
- naughtiness, bad behaviour, disobedience, playfulness, roguishness

miserable adjective
1 *You look **miserable**—what's the matter?*
- sad, unhappy, sorrowful, gloomy, glum, downhearted, despondent, dejected, depressed, melancholy, mournful, tearful
  OPPOSITE cheerful, happy
2 *The poor animals lived in **miserable** conditions.*
- distressing, uncomfortable, wretched, pitiful, pathetic, squalid
  OPPOSITE comfortable
3 *The weather was cold and **miserable**.*
- dismal, dreary, depressing, unpleasant
  OPPOSITE pleasant

miserly adjective
*He was too **miserly** to donate any money.*
- mean, selfish
- (*informal*) grasping, stingy, tight-fisted, penny-pinching
  OPPOSITE generous

misery noun
*The slaves must have led a life of **misery**.*
- sadness, sorrow, unhappiness, grief, distress, despair, anguish, wretchedness, suffering, torment, heartache, depression
  OPPOSITE happiness

misfortune noun
*I heard about her family's **misfortune**.*
- bad luck, trouble, hardship, adversity, affliction, setback, mishap
  OPPOSITE good luck

mishap noun

*Dad had a slight **mishap** with the car.*
- accident, problem, difficulty, setback

mislay verb

*I seem to have **mislaid** my purse.*
- lose

OPPOSITE find

misleading adjective

*The directions he gave were quite **misleading**.*
- confusing, unreliable, deceptive, ambiguous, unclear

miss verb

1 *I **missed** the bus.*
- be too late for

2 *The arrow **missed** the target.*
- fall short of, go wide of

3 *If we leave now, we should **miss** the traffic.*
- avoid

4 *I **missed** dad when he was in hospital.*
- long for, yearn for, pine for

to miss something out

*I **missed out** the boring bits of the story.*
- leave out, omit, ignore, overlook, skip

missile noun SEE **weapon**

missing adjective

*She found the **missing** keys in a drawer.*
- lost, mislaid, misplaced, absent, straying

mission noun

1 *Her **mission** in life was to help those in need.*
- aim, purpose, objective, task, job, campaign

2 *The astronauts are on a **mission** to Mars.*
- expedition, journey, voyage, exploration

mist noun

1 *We drove slowly through the **mist**.*
- fog, haze, cloud, drizzle

2 *I can't see for the **mist** on my glasses.*
- condensation, steam

mistake noun

*This piece of writing is full of **mistakes**.*
- error, inaccuracy, blunder, slip, slip-up, lapse
- A spelling mistake is a misspelling.
- A mistake where something is left out is an omission.
- A mistake in a printed book is a misprint.

mistake verb

*She **mistook** my meaning entirely.*
- misunderstand, get wrong, mix up

mistrust verb

*Do you have any reason to **mistrust** him?*
- distrust, have doubts about, suspect

OPPOSITE trust

misty adjective

1 *If it's **misty** outside, take a torch.*
- foggy, hazy

2 *I can't see through the **misty** window.*
- steamy, cloudy, smoky, opaque

3 *We saw a **misty** shape approaching.*
- faint, fuzzy, blurred, dim, indistinct, shadowy, vague

OPPOSITE clear

misunderstand verb

*I think you **misunderstood** what I said.*
- mistake, get wrong, miss the point of

OPPOSITE understand

mix verb

***Mix** the ingredients in a bowl.*
- combine, blend, mingle

to mix something up

*Please don't **mix up** my CDs.*
- muddle, jumble, confuse
- To mix up playing cards is to shuffle them.

mixed adjective

*Add a teaspoon of **mixed** herbs.*
- assorted, various, different, miscellaneous

OPPOSITE separate

mixture noun

1 *Put the cake **mixture** in a baking tin.*
- mix, blend, combination
- A mixture of metals is an alloy.

a b c d e f g h i j k l **m** n o p q r s t u v w x y z

- A mixture of two different species of plant or animal is a hybrid.
2 *There's an odd **mixture** of things in the drawer.*
- assortment, collection, variety, jumble
- A confused mixture is a mishmash.

moan verb
1 *The wounded warrior **moaned** in pain.*
- cry, groan, sigh, wail, howl, whimper
2 *Ned's always **moaning** about the food.*
- complain, grumble, grouse, whine
- (*informal*) whinge

mob noun
*An angry **mob** stormed the gates of the castle.*
- crowd, horde, throng, mass, rabble, gang, pack, herd, bunch

mob verb
*Autograph hunters **mobbed** the popstar.*
- crowd round, swarm round, surround, besiege, hem in, jostle

mobile adjective
1 *A **mobile** library visits once a fortnight.*
- movable, travelling
- Something that you can carry about is portable.
2 *A week after the injury, he was **mobile** again.*
- moving about, active
- (*informal*) up and about
OPPOSITE immobile

mock verb
*It was mean of them to **mock** his singing.*
- jeer at, laugh at, make fun of, scoff at, sneer at, ridicule, scorn, deride
- (*informal*) take the mickey out of

model adjective
1 *We went to an exhibition of **model** railways.*
- miniature, toy
2 *She's a **model** pupil.*
- ideal, perfect

model noun
1 *I'm building a **model** of a space rocket.*
- copy, replica, toy

2 *This is the latest **model** of skateboard.*
- design, type, version
3 *She's a **model** of good behaviour.*
- example, ideal

model verb
*The artist **models** figures in clay.*
- make, mould, shape, construct, fashion

moderate adjective
*Her first book was a **moderate** success.*
- average, fair, modest, medium, reasonable, passable, tolerable
OPPOSITE exceptional

moderately adverb
*He answered the questions **moderately** well.*
- fairly, reasonably, quite, rather, somewhat
- (*informal*) pretty

modern adjective
1 *All the equipment in their kitchen was **modern**.*
- up to date, contemporary, advanced, the latest
OPPOSITE out of date
2 *She always dresses in **modern** clothes.*
- fashionable, stylish, modish
- (*informal*) trendy, hip
OPPOSITE old-fashioned

modest adjective
1 *He's very **modest** about his success.*
- humble, quiet, reserved, shy, bashful, coy
OPPOSITE conceited
2 *There has been a **modest** increase in sales.*
- moderate, reasonable, average, medium

modify verb
*We've had to **modify** our travel plans.*
- adapt, alter, change, adjust, refine, revise, vary

moist adjective
1 *The walls of the dungeon were **moist**.*
- damp, wet, watery, clammy, dank
2 *Tropical plants grow well in a **moist** atmosphere.*
- humid, muggy, steamy, rainy
OPPOSITE dry

a b c d e f g h i j k l **m** n o p q r s t u v w x y z

moisture noun

*There is still a lot of **moisture** on the ground.*

- wetness, dampness, damp, dew, condensation, humidity

moment noun

1 *I'll be ready in a **moment**.*
- minute, second, instant, flash
- (*informal*) jiffy, tick

2 *It was a great **moment** in the history of space travel.*
- time, occasion, period

momentary adjective

*He felt a **momentary** stab of pain.*

- brief, short, fleeting, temporary
OPPOSITE permanent

monarch noun SEE **ruler**

money noun

*How much **money** do you have with you?*

- cash, currency, funds, finance
- (*informal*) dough, dosh
- A large amount of money is a fortune, riches, or wealth.

monster noun

*A sea **monster** reared its head above the waves.*

- beast, giant, ogre, brute

monstrous adjective

1 *The town was engulfed by a **monstrous** wave.*
- huge, gigantic, enormous, immense, massive, colossal, great, hulking, mighty, towering, vast

2 *The nation was shocked by the **monstrous** crime.*
- horrifying, shocking, wicked, evil, hideous, horrible, terrible, atrocious, dreadful, gruesome, outrageous, scandalous

mood noun

*What sort of **mood** is he in today?*

- temper, humour, state of mind, disposition

moody adjective

*She's been **moody** and withdrawn for weeks.*

- sulky, sullen, grumpy, bad-tempered, temperamental, touchy, miserable, gloomy, glum
OPPOSITE cheerful

moon noun

 WORD WEB

FORMS IN WHICH WE SEE THE MOON
crescent moon, full moon, new moon; moonbeam, moonlight

THINGS YOU MIGHT FIND OR DO ON THE MOON
crater, moon dust, moon rock, moonscape, moonwalk

- A word meaning 'to do with the Moon' is lunar.
SEE ALSO **astronaut**, **space**

moor noun

*The tower stood on a windswept **moor**.*

- moorland, heath, fell

moor verb

*We **moored** the boat in the harbour.*

- tie up, secure, fasten, anchor, berth, dock

moral adjective

*She tried her best to lead a **moral** life.*

- good, honest, truthful, upright, decent, honourable, principled, ethical, virtuous, righteous
OPPOSITE immoral

moral noun

*The **moral** of this story is that crime doesn't pay.*

- lesson, message, meaning

morale noun

*The new coach has improved the team's **morale**.*

- confidence, spirit, state of mind, attitude, mood

more adjective

*The soup needs **more** pepper.*

- extra, further, added, additional
OPPOSITE less

a b c d e f g h i j k l **m** n o p q r s t u v w x y z

morning noun

*The expedition set off in the early **morning**.*

- daybreak, dawn, first light, sunrise

FOR OTHER TIMES OF THE DAY

SEE **day**

morsel noun

*They hadn't eaten a **morsel** of food all day.*

- bite, crumb, mouthful, taste, nibble, piece, scrap, fragment

mortal adjective

1 *All human beings are **mortal**.*

OPPOSITE immortal

2 *The knight had received a **mortal** wound.*

- deadly, fatal, lethal

mostly adverb

*I spend my money **mostly** on books and CDs.*

- mainly, largely, chiefly, primarily, generally, usually, normally, typically, principally, predominantly

motion noun

*He summoned the waiter with a **motion** of his hand.*

- gesture, movement

motivate verb

*What **motivated** you to write a book?*

- prompt, drive, stimulate, urge, provoke, spur, influence, induce

motive noun

*The police can find no **motive** for the crime.*

- cause, motivation, reason, purpose, grounds

motor noun

*The toy train had an electric **motor**.*

- engine

motto noun

*Her **motto** has always been, 'keep smiling'.*

- catchphrase, proverb, saying, slogan, golden rule

mould verb

*The sculptor **moulded** the figures from clay.*

- shape, form, fashion, model, cast

mouldy adjective

*All I found in the fridge was some **mouldy** cheese.*

- rotten, rotting, decaying, musty, damp

mound noun

1 *Her desk was covered with **mounds** of paper.*

- heap, pile, stack, mass

2 *There used to be a castle on top of that **mound**.*

- hill, hillock, rise, hump
- An ancient mound of earth over a grave is a barrow.

mount verb

1 *She **mounted** the pony and rode off.*

- get on, jump onto

2 *The butler slowly **mounted** the stairs.*

- go up, climb, ascend

3 *The gallery is **mounting** a new exhibition.*

- put up, set up, display

4 *The tension began to **mount** in the crowd.*

- grow, increase, rise, intensify

mountain noun

WORD WEB

- The top of a mountain is the peak or summit.
- A line of mountains is a range.
- A long, narrow mountain is a ridge.
- A mountain with a hole at the top caused by an eruption is a volcano.

THINGS YOU MIGHT SEE ON OR NEAR A MOUNTAIN

avalanche, boulder, cave, cliff, crag, crevice, glacier, gorge, ledge, mountain pass, mountain stream, precipice, rocks, slope, valley or (*Scottish*) glen

SOME WORDS TO DESCRIBE A MOUNTAIN

barren, craggy, forbidding, jagged, lofty, massive, misty, rocky, rugged, snow-capped, soaring, towering, treacherous

- An area of land with many mountains is said to be mountainous.

mourn verb

*He was still **mourning** the loss of his friend.*

- grieve for, lament for

mouth noun

1 *The crocodile slept with its **mouth** wide open.*

- jaws
- A dog's nose and mouth is its muzzle.
- A word meaning 'to do with your mouth' is oral.

2 *They lived in a village at the **mouth** of the river.*

- outlet
- A wide river mouth is an estuary or (*Scottish*) firth.

3 *The **mouth** of the cave was hidden by trees.*

- entrance, opening

move noun

1 *Don't make a **move**!*

- movement

2 *The spy was watching their every **move**.*

- action, step, deed, manoeuvre

3 *Is it my **move** next?*

- turn, go, chance, opportunity

move verb

 OVERUSED WORD

Try to vary the words you use for move. Here are some other words you could use.

- to *MOVE FROM ONE PLACE TO ANOTHER*:
  carry, remove, transfer, transport, shift
  *They **shifted** the piano into the front room.*

- to *MOVE FROM A POSITION*:
  go, leave, depart, quit, budge
  *The camel stared and refused to **budge**.*

- to *MOVE RESTLESSLY*:
  toss, turn, stir, twist, shake, fidget, twitch, flap
  *Please stop **twitching** in your seat.*

- to *MOVE FROM SIDE TO SIDE*:
  sway, swing, wave, wag, wiggle
  *The knight **swung** a sword above his helmet.*

- to *MOVE ALONG*:
  travel, walk, proceed
  *Few people **travel** on these roads after dark.*

- to *MOVE ALONG QUICKLY*:
  hurry, dash, race, run, rush, hasten, hurtle, career, fly, speed, sweep, shoot, zoom
  *A boy went **careering** past on a scooter.*
  SEE ALSO **run** verb

- to *MOVE ALONG SLOWLY*:
  amble, stroll, saunter, dawdle, crawl, drift
  *Gerald the tortoise **sauntered** down the path.*

- to *MOVE TOWARDS SOMETHING*:
  advance, approach, come, proceed, progress
  *The lookout saw a pirate ship **approaching**.*

- to *MOVE BACK* or *MOVE AWAY*:
  back, retreat, reverse, withdraw
  *The serpent **retreated**, hissing, into its lair.*

- to *MOVE DOWNWARDS*:
  drop, descend, fall, sink, swoop
  *A pair of vultures **swooped** down from the sky.*

- to *MOVE UPWARDS*:
  rise, ascend, climb, mount, soar, arise
  *A hot-air balloon **mounted** into the air.*

- to *MOVE GRACEFULLY*:
  flow, glide, dance
  *Some swans **glided** gently across the pond.*

- to *MOVE CLUMSILY*:
  stumble, stagger, flounder, lurch, lumber, shuffle, totter, trundle, trip
  *The ogre **stumbled** up the narrow steps.*

- to *MOVE STEALTHILY*:
  creep, crawl, edge, inch, slink
  *The secret agent **edged** carefully along the wall.*

FOR WAYS TO DESCRIBE HOW AN ANIMAL OR BIRD MOVES

SEE **animal, bird**

a b c d e f g h i j k l **m** n o p q r s t u v w x y z

a
b
c
d
e
f
g
h
i
j
k
l
m
n
o
p
q
r
s
t
u
v
w
x
y
z

movement noun
1 *The robot made a sudden, jerky **movement**.*
• motion, move, action, gesture
2 *Has there been any **movement** in their attitude?*
• progress, development, change, shift
3 *She was involved in the peace **movement**.*
• organization, group, party, campaign

movie noun SEE **film**

moving adjective
*The story was so **moving** that I started to cry.*
• emotional, inspiring, stirring, touching
• (*informal*) tear-jerking

muck noun
*They cleared the **muck** out of the stable.*
• dirt, filth, grime, mud, sludge, dung, manure

mucky adjective
*My football boots are all **mucky**.*
• dirty, messy, muddy, grimy, grubby, filthy, foul, soiled, squalid
OPPOSITE clean

mud noun
*The tractor left a trail of **mud** on the road.*
• dirt, muck, mire, sludge, clay, soil

muddle noun
1 *There was a **muddle** over the date of the party.*
• confusion, misunderstanding
• (*informal*) mix-up
2 *There was a **muddle** of clothes on the floor.*
• jumble, mess, tangle

muddle verb
1 *Who **muddled** the papers on my desk?*
• mix up, mess up, disorder, jumble up, shuffle, tangle
OPPOSITE tidy
2 *They got **muddled** and took the wrong turning.*
• confuse, bewilder, puzzle, perplex

muddy adjective
1 *Take off your **muddy** shoes before you come in.*
• dirty, messy, mucky, filthy, caked, soiled
OPPOSITE clean
2 *I got filthy walking across the **muddy** ground.*
• boggy, marshy, waterlogged, wet, sodden
OPPOSITE dry, firm

muffle verb
1 *We **muffled** ourselves up to play in the snow.*
• wrap, cover
2 *She tried to **muffle** her sneeze.*
• stifle, smother, suppress, silence, deaden, dull

muffled adjective
*They heard **muffled** voices from the next room.*
• faint, indistinct, unclear, muted, deadened
OPPOSITE clear

mug noun SEE **cup**

muggy adjective
*The weather is often **muggy** before a storm.*
• humid, close, clammy, sticky, moist, damp, oppressive
OPPOSITE fresh

multiply verb
*Her problems seemed to be **multiplying**.*
• increase, grow, spread, mount up

mumble verb
*We couldn't hear the actor as he was **mumbling**.*
• mutter, talk indistinctly

munch verb
*Kim sat **munching** popcorn all through the film.*
• chew, crunch
FOR OTHER WAYS TO EAT
SEE **eat**

murder verb SEE **kill**

murky adjective

*A creature loomed out of the **murky** waters of the loch.*

- dark, clouded, cloudy, dim, dull, dingy, gloomy, grey, foggy, misty
OPPOSITE clear

murmur verb

*We heard voices **murmuring** in the room above.*

- mutter, mumble, whisper

muscular adjective

*The wrestler had a **muscular** body.*

- brawny, beefy, athletic, sinewy, strapping, strong, well-built
OPPOSITE puny, weak

music noun

 WORD WEB

VARIOUS KINDS OF MUSIC
blues, classical music, country and western, dance music, disco music, folk music, gospel, hip hop, jazz, orchestral music, pop music, punk, ragtime, rap, reggae, rock, soul, swing

TYPES OF MUSICAL COMPOSITION
anthem, ballad, carol, concerto, folk song, fugue, hymn, lullaby, march, melody, musical, opera, operetta, sonata, song, symphony, tune

MUSICAL INSTRUMENTS

FAMILIES OF MUSICAL INSTRUMENTS
brass, keyboard, percussion, strings, woodwind

STRINGED INSTRUMENTS THAT CAN BE PLAYED WITH A BOW
cello, double bass, viola, violin or fiddle

STRINGED INSTRUMENTS PLAYED BY PLUCKING OR STRUMMING
banjo, cittern, guitar, harp, lute, lyre, mandolin, sitar, ukulele, zither

BRASS INSTRUMENTS
bugle, cornet, euphonium, flugelhorn, French horn, trombone, trumpet, tuba

OTHER INSTRUMENTS PLAYED BY BLOWING
bagpipes, bassoon, clarinet, cor anglais, flute, harmonica or mouth organ, oboe, piccolo, recorder, saxophone

KEYBOARD INSTRUMENTS
accordion, harmonium, harpsichord, keyboard, organ, piano, synthesizer

PERCUSSION INSTRUMENTS
bass drum, bongo drum, castanets, cymbals, drum, glockenspiel, gong, kettledrum, maracas, marimba, rattle, snare drum, tabor, tambour, tambourine, timpani, tom-tom, triangle, tubular bells, vibraphone, xylophone

PEOPLE WHO PLAY VARIOUS INSTRUMENTS
bugler, cellist, clarinettist, drummer, fiddler, flautist, guitarist, harpist, lutenist, oboist, organist, percussionist, pianist, piper, timpanist, trombonist, trumpeter, violinist

SOME OTHER MUSICIANS
accompanist, composer, conductor, instrumentalist, singer, vocalist

FOR TYPES OF SINGING VOICE
SEE **sing**

GROUPS OF MUSICIANS
band, choir or chorus, duet or duo, ensemble, group, orchestra, quartet, quintet, trio

MUSICAL TERMS

TERMS USED IN MUSIC
chord, counterpoint, discord, harmony, melody, note, octave, pitch, rhythm, scale, semitone, tempo, theme, tone, tune

NAMES OF NOTES AND SIGNS IN WRITTEN MUSIC
clef, crotchet, flat, key signature, minim, natural, quaver, semibreve, semiquaver, sharp, stave, time signature

musical adjective

*Helena has a very **musical** voice.*

- tuneful, melodic, melodious, harmonious, sweet-sounding

a
b
c
d
e
f
g
h
i
j
k
l
m
n
o
p
q
r
s
t
u
v
w
x
y
z

musty adjective
*There was a **musty** smell in the cellar.*
- damp, dank, mouldy, stale, stuffy, airless
OPPOSITE fresh

mute adjective
*We stared in **mute** amazement at the volcano.*
- silent, speechless, dumb, tongue-tied

mutilate verb
*His right hand was **mutilated** by a firework.*
- maim, disfigure, injure, wound, mangle

mutiny noun
*The crew were plotting a **mutiny** against the captain.*
- rebellion, revolt, uprising

mutter verb
*The goblin sat **muttering** to himself in the corner.*
- mumble, murmur, whisper

mutual adjective
*It is in our **mutual** interest to work together.*
- joint, common, shared, reciprocal

mysterious adjective
*They uncovered a **mysterious** sign on the wall.*
- strange, puzzling, baffling, mystifying, perplexing, obscure, unexplained, incomprehensible, inexplicable, curious, weird

mystery noun
*What really happened was a **mystery**.*
- puzzle, riddle, secret

mystify verb
*We were **mystified** by the curious message.*
- puzzle, baffle, bewilder, perplex

myth noun

WORD WEB
CREATURES FOUND IN MYTHS AND LEGENDS
basilisk, brownie, chimera, centaur, cyclops, dragon, dwarf,

elf, fairy, genie, giant, gnome, goblin, gremlin, gryphon, imp, kelpie, leprechaun, mermaid, nymph, ogre, phoenix, pixie, sea monster, selkie, serpent, sphinx, siren, sprite, troll, unicorn, vampire, werewolf, winged horse, yeti
SEE ALSO **dragon, fairy**

mythical adjective
*The unicorn is a **mythical** beast.*
- fabulous, fanciful, imaginary, invented, fictional, legendary, mythological, non-existent, unreal
OPPOSITE real

nag verb
*He was always **nagging** her to work harder.*
- badger, pester, scold

naive adjective
*He's so **naive** that he believes her promises.*
- innocent, inexperienced, unsophisticated, artless, gullible, simple

naked adjective
*He walked **naked** into the bathroom.*
- bare, nude, unclothed, undressed
OPPOSITE clothed

name noun
- The official names you have are your first names or forenames, and surname.

- Names a Christian is given at baptism are Christian names.
- A false name is an alias.
- A name people use instead of your real name is a nickname.
- A false name an author uses is a pen name or pseudonym.
- The name of a book or film is its title.

name verb

*The zoo **named** the new lion cubs, Kiara and Kovu.*

- call
- To name someone at the ceremony of baptism is to baptize or christen them.

nap noun

*Granny always takes a **nap** on Sunday afternoons.*

- rest, sleep, doze, lie-down, siesta
- (*informal*) snooze, forty winks

narrate verb

*The famous actor **narrated** the story of his life.*

- tell, recount, relate

narrative noun

*The sailor wrote an exciting **narrative** of his voyage.*

- account, history, story, tale, chronicle
- (*informal*) yarn

narrow adjective

*The rabbit squeezed through a **narrow** opening in the fence.*

- thin, slender, slim
- OPPOSITE wide

nasty adjective

1 *Ogres have a thoroughly **nasty** temper.*
- unkind, unpleasant, unfriendly, disagreeable, objectionable, odious, mean, malicious, cruel, spiteful, vicious

2 *A **nasty** smell wafted from the laboratory.*
- unpleasant, offensive, disgusting, repulsive, revolting, horrible, foul, rotten, sickening
- OPPOSITE agreeable, pleasant

3 *The weather suddenly turned **nasty**.*
- unpleasant, rough, stormy, squally

FOR OTHER WAYS TO DESCRIBE SOMETHING YOU DON'T LIKE
SEE **bad**

nation noun

*People from many **nations** compete in the Olympic Games.*

- country, state, land, race, population

national adjective

*The programme will be broadcast on **national** television.*

- nationwide
- OPPOSITE local

natural adjective

1 *Karen has a **natural** gift for music.*
- born, inborn, instinctive, intuitive, native

2 *It's only **natural** to be nervous before an exam.*
- normal, common, understandable, reasonable, predictable
- OPPOSITE unnatural

nature noun

1 *I like TV programmes about **nature**.*
- natural history, wildlife

2 *The old sheepdog has a very kind **nature**.*
- character, disposition, personality, manner

3 *I collect coins, medals, and things of that **nature**.*
- kind, sort, type, description, variety

naughty adjective

*The puppies were quite **naughty** when they were young.*

- bad, badly behaved, disobedient, mischievous, uncontrollable, unmanageable, troublesome, unruly
- OPPOSITE well behaved

to be naughty
- misbehave, behave badly, disobey

navigate verb

*The captain **navigated** his ship between the dangerous rocks.*

- steer, direct, guide, manoeuvre, pilot

navy noun SEE **fleet**

near adjective
1 *We get on well with our **near** neighbours.*
- next-door, nearby, close, adjacent, surrounding
2 *My birthday is **near**.*
- approaching, coming
- (*informal*) round the corner
3 *We sent cards to all our **near** relatives.*
- close, dear, familiar, intimate
OPPOSITE distant

nearly adverb
*Thank goodness, it's **nearly** dinner time!*
- almost, practically, virtually, just about, approaching

neat adjective
1 *Please leave the room as **neat** as possible.*
- clean, orderly, tidy, uncluttered, immaculate
- (*informal*) spick and span
2 *Craig always looks **neat** in his school uniform.*
- smart, elegant, spruce, trim
3 *Her handwriting is very **neat**.*
- precise, skilful, well-formed
OPPOSITE untidy

necessary adjective
*The recipe lists all the **necessary** ingredients.*
- essential, required, needed, needful, compulsory, obligatory, unavoidable
OPPOSITE unnecessary

need noun
*There's a **need** for more shops in our area.*
- call, demand, requirement

need verb
1 *I **need** a pound coin for the locker.*
- require, want, be short of, lack
2 *The charity **needs** our support.*
- depend on, rely on

needless adjective
*They went to a lot of **needless** expense.*
- unnecessary, unwanted, uncalled-for, excessive, superfluous

needlework noun

> **WORD WEB**
> *You need good eyesight for **needlework**.*
> - sewing
> SOME TYPES OF NEEDLEWORK
> appliqué, beadwork, cross-stitch, embroidery, patchwork, quilting, tapestry
> FOR OTHER ARTS AND CRAFTS
> SEE **art**

needy adjective
*They set up a fund to help **needy** children.*
- poor, deprived, badly off, hard up
OPPOSITE rich

negative adjective
*He has a very **negative** attitude to his job.*
- pessimistic, uncooperative, unenthusiastic, grudging, unhelpful, unwilling
OPPOSITE positive

neglect verb
*She's been **neglecting** her work.*
- forget, ignore, overlook, abandon, disregard, pay no attention to, shirk

negligible adjective
*There is a **negligible** difference in price.*
- tiny, slight, insignificant, unimportant, trivial
OPPOSITE considerable

negotiate verb
1 *She **negotiated** with the car salesman.*
- bargain, haggle, deal, confer
2 *The skier **negotiated** the course with ease.*
- get past, get round, manoeuvre round

neighbourhood noun
*They live in a very nice **neighbourhood**.*
- area, district, community, locality, vicinity

neighbouring adjective
The journey will take them to Mexico and neighbouring countries.
- nearby, bordering, adjacent, adjoining, surrounding, nearest, next-door

neighbourly adjective
It was very neighbourly of her to offer to feed the cat.
- friendly, helpful, kind, obliging, sociable
- OPPOSITE unfriendly

nerve noun
1 *Acrobats need to have a lot of nerve.*
- bravery, courage, daring, pluck
- (*informal*) bottle
2 *He had the nerve to ask for more money!*
- cheek, impudence, rudeness, impertinence

nervous adjective
She always feels nervous before an exam.
- anxious, worried, apprehensive, concerned, uneasy, fearful, edgy, fraught, tense, troubled
- (*informal*) uptight, jittery
- OPPOSITE calm

nestle verb
The cubs nestled against their mother.
- cuddle, curl up, snuggle

neutral adjective
1 *A referee has to be neutral.*
- impartial, unbiased, unprejudiced, even-handed
- OPPOSITE biased, prejudiced
2 *The room was decorated in neutral colours.*
- dull, drab, indefinite, colourless
- OPPOSITE vibrant, distinctive

new adjective
1 *Start on a new sheet of paper.*
- clean, fresh, unused, brand-new
- Something new and unused is in mint condition.
2 *They went to the motor show to see the new models.*
- latest, current, modern, recent, up-to-date

3 *They've found a new bug in the computer program.*
- additional, extra, unexpected, unfamiliar
4 *Haven't you got any new ideas?*
- fresh, original, novel, innovative, creative, different
- OPPOSITE old

news noun
What's the latest news?
- information, word, report, bulletin
- (*old use*) tidings

next adjective
1 *He lives in the house next to the chip shop.*
- adjacent, closest, nearest
- OPPOSITE distant
2 *If you miss this bus, you can catch the next one.*
- following, subsequent
- OPPOSITE previous

nice adjective
1 *That's not a very nice thing to say!*
- pleasant, agreeable
- OPPOSITE nasty
2 *There is a nice distinction between borrowing and stealing.*
- delicate, fine, precise, subtle

⚠ **OVERUSED WORD**

Try to vary the words you use for **nice**. Here are some other words you could use.

- for a *NICE PERSON*:
  good, kind, friendly, helpful, generous, likeable, amiable, charming, polite, genial
  Our singing teacher is very likeable.

- for a *NICE EXPERIENCE*:
  delightful, enjoyable, wonderful, marvellous, splendid
  Did you have an enjoyable time in France?

- for something that *LOOKS NICE*:
  beautiful, attractive, pleasing, lovely
  There is an attractive view from the upstairs window.

a
b
c
d
e
f
g
h
i
j
k
l
m
n
o
p
q
r
s
t
u
v
w
x
y
z

- for a *NICE SMELL* :
  agreeable, fragrant, sweet-smelling
  *The **fragrant** scent of lavender filled the garden.*
- for *NICE FOOD* :
  delicious, tasty, appetizing, satisfying
  *They serve **tasty** sandwiches in the cafe.*
- for *NICE WEATHER* :
  fine, sunny, warm
  *The weather has been **fine** all week.*
  FOR OTHER WAYS TO DESCRIBE SOMETHING YOU LIKE
  SEE **good**

night noun
*Badgers usually come out at **night**.*
- night-time, dark
- Animals which are active at night are nocturnal animals.

nimble adjective
*The elves sewed the shoes with their **nimble** fingers.*
- agile, skilful, quick, deft
  OPPOSITE clumsy

nip verb
1 *She **nipped** her finger in the door.*
- pinch, squeeze, clip, catch
2 *The dog **nipped** my leg.*
- bite, peck, snip
3 (*informal*) *I'll just **nip** along to the post office.*
- dash, run, rush
- (*informal*) pop

noble adjective
1 *The knight belonged to an ancient **noble** family.*
- aristocratic, high-born, upper-class
2 *The rescuers were congratulated for their **noble** efforts.*
- brave, heroic, courageous, honourable, worthy, virtuous, gallant
  OPPOSITE cowardly, unworthy

nod verb
*Simon **nodded** his head in agreement.*
- bob, bow, dip, lower

to nod off
*He sometimes **nods off** in front of the television.*
- fall asleep, doze off, drop off, have a nap

noise noun
*Where is that dreadful **noise** coming from?*
- din, racket, row, uproar, commotion, tumult, hullabaloo, pandemonium
  FOR VARIOUS NOISES
  SEE **sound** noun

noisy adjective
1 *The people next door were playing **noisy** music.*
- loud, blaring, booming, deafening, ear-splitting, thunderous
2 *The children are very **noisy** this morning.*
- rowdy, raucous, chattering, talkative
  OPPOSITE quiet

nominate verb
*They **nominated** her as captain.*
- appoint, elect, choose, select, name

nonsense noun
*Stop talking **nonsense**!*
- rubbish, drivel, balderdash, piffle, gibberish, claptrap, gobbledegook
- (*informal*) rot, tripe, twaddle

nonsensical adjective
*My brother came up with a **nonsensical** plan.*
- absurd, ludicrous, ridiculous, laughable, silly, stupid, crazy, foolish, illogical, irrational, insane, senseless, idiotic
- (*informal*) daft
  OPPOSITE sensible

non-stop adjective
1 *Their **non-stop** chattering annoyed her.*
- constant, continual, continuous, endless, ceaseless, incessant, never-ending
2 *They took a **non-stop** train from Glasgow to Edinburgh.*
- direct, express, fast

a b c d e f g h i j k l m n o p q r s t u v w x y z

normal adjective

1 *He had a **normal** kind of day at work.*

- average, common, customary, familiar, habitual, ordinary, predictable, regular, routine, standard, typical, unsurprising, usual

2 *No **normal** person would sleep on a bed of nails.*

- healthy, rational, reasonable, sane
OPPOSITE abnormal

north noun, adjective, adverb

- The parts of a continent or country in the north are the northern parts.
- To travel towards the north is to travel northward or northwards or in a northerly direction.
- A wind from the north is a northerly wind.
- A person who lives in the north of a country is a northerner.

nose noun

1 *Someone punched Roger on the **nose**.*

- (*informal*) hooter
- The openings in your nose are your nostrils.
- A word meaning 'to do with your nose' is nasal.
- Words for an animal's nose are muzzle and snout.

2 *I sat in the **nose** of the boat hoping to spot a dolphin.*

- front, bow, prow

WRITING TIPS

You can use these words to describe a nose:

- beak-like, bulbous, button, classical or Roman, crooked, pointed, snub, upturned

*The troll had **bushy** eyebrows and a red, **bulbous** nose.*

---

nosy adjective (*informal*)

*Stop being so **nosy** and asking all these questions!*

- inquisitive, curious, prying, snooping, intrusive
- An informal name for a nosy person is a nosy parker.

notable adjective

1 *Many **notable** artists lived and worked in Paris.*

- famous, celebrated, renowned, noted, distinguished, eminent, prominent

2 *The fireworks concert this year was a **notable** event.*

- memorable, noteworthy, significant, major, important, remarkable
OPPOSITE insignificant, minor

notch noun

*The woodsman cut a **notch** in the tree trunk.*

- cut, nick, groove, score, incision

note noun

1 *I sent a **note** thanking him for the present.*

- message, letter, communication

2 *There was a **note** of anger in her voice.*

- sound, tone, feeling, quality

note verb

1 *The detective **noted** the address on a scrap of paper.*

- jot down, make a note of, write down, record, scribble

2 *Did you **note** what she was wearing?*

- notice, see, take note of, pay attention to, heed, mark, observe

nothing noun

*Four minus four equals **nothing**.*

- nought, zero
- In cricket a score of nothing is a duck; in tennis it is love, and in football it is nil.

notice noun

*Someone put up a **notice** about the meeting.*

- sign, advertisement, placard, poster, warning

a
b
c
d
e
f
g
h
i
j
k
l
m
n
o
p
q
r
s
t
u
v
w
x
y
z

to take notice of something

*They **took** no **notice of** the warning.*
- heed, pay attention to

notice verb

1 *Did you **notice** what he was wearing?*
- note, see, take note of, pay attention to, heed, mark, observe

2 *I **noticed** a funny smell in the room.*
- become aware of, detect

noticeable adjective

1 *There has been a **noticeable** improvement in the weather.*
- definite, distinct, notable, measurable, perceptible, significant

2 *The tower is **noticeable** for miles around.*
- visible, conspicuous

3 *He spoke with a **noticeable** foreign accent.*
- obvious, pronounced, unmistakable, audible
- OPPOSITE imperceptible

notion noun

*Uncle Ollie has some strange **notions** about life.*
- belief, idea, view, thought, opinion, theory, concept

notorious adjective

*He is a **notorious** liar as well as a thief.*
- infamous, well-known, disgraceful, scandalous

nought noun SEE nothing

nourish verb

*Plants are **nourished** by water drawn up through their roots.*
- feed, sustain, support

nourishing adjective

*The penguins live on **nourishing** diet of fish and squid.*
- nutritious, wholesome, healthy, health-giving

novel adjective

*The inventor had a **novel** idea for building a robot.*
- original, new, innovative, fresh, different, imaginative, creative, unusual, unconventional
- OPPOSITE familiar

novel noun FOR VARIOUS FORMS OF WRITING

SEE **writing**

now adverb

1 *My cousins are **now** living in Melbourne.*
- at present, at the moment, currently, nowadays

2 *I'll give them a ring **now**.*
- immediately, at once, straight away, without delay, instantly

nude adjective

*The artist painted from a **nude** model.*
- naked, bare, undressed, unclothed
- OPPOSITE clothed

nudge verb

*She **nudged** me with her elbow.*
- poke, prod, shove, bump, jog, jolt

nuisance noun

*The traffic noise is a real **nuisance**.*
- annoyance, irritation, inconvenience, bother, menace, pest, drawback

numb adjective

*My toes are **numb** with cold.*
- unfeeling, deadened, frozen, insensitive, paralysed
- OPPOSITE sensitive

number noun

1 *Add the **numbers** together to get the answer.*
- figure, numeral
- Any of the numbers from 0 to 9 is a digit.
- A negative or positive whole number is an integer.
- An amount used in measuring or counting is a unit.

2 *A large **number** of people applied for the job.*
- amount, quantity, collection, crowd

3 *I've ordered the latest **number** of the magazine.*
- edition, issue

4 *The band played some well-known **numbers**.*
- song, piece, tune

numerous adjective
*There are **numerous** spelling mistakes on this page.*
- many, plenty of, countless, innumerable, untold, abundant
OPPOSITE few

nurse noun FOR PEOPLE WHO PRACTISE MEDICINE

SEE **medicine**

nurse verb
*The aid workers **nursed** the sick children.*
- look after, care for, tend, treat

nut noun

> **WORD WEB**
>
> SOME KINDS OF NUT
> almond, brazil, cashew, chestnut, coconut, hazelnut, macadamia, peanut, pecan, pistachio, walnut

Oo

oath noun
1 *The knights swore an **oath** of honour.*
- pledge, promise, vow

2 *He let out an **oath** when he banged his head.*
- swear word, curse, blasphemy

obedient adjective
*The dog seems very **obedient**.*
- well-behaved, disciplined, manageable, dutiful, docile
OPPOSITE disobedient

obey verb
1 *The dog **obeyed** his owner's commands.*
- follow, carry out, execute, implement, observe, adhere to, heed

2 *The soldiers **obeyed** without question.*
- do what you are told, take orders, be obedient, conform
OPPOSITE disobey

object noun
1 *We saw some strange **objects** in the museum.*
- article, item, thing

2 *What is the **object** of this exercise?*
- point, purpose, aim, goal, intention, objective

object verb
to object to something
*Several residents have **objected to** the plan.*
- complain about, be opposed to, disapprove of, take exception to, protest against
OPPOSITE accept, agree to

objection noun
*Do you have any **objection** to my sitting here?*
- protest, complaint, disapproval, opposition

objectionable adjective
*The drains were giving off an **objectionable** smell.*
- unpleasant, disagreeable, disgusting, foul, offensive, repellent, revolting, obnoxious, nasty
OPPOSITE acceptable

objective adjective
*He gave an **objective** account of what happened.*
- disinterested, factual, impartial, rational, unbiased, unemotional, unprejudiced
OPPOSITE subjective

a
b
c
d
e
f
g
h
i
j
k
l
m
n
o
p
q
r
s
t
u
v
w
x
y
z

objective noun
*Their **objective** was to reach the top of the hill.*
- aim, goal, intention, target, ambition, object, purpose

obligatory adjective
*The wearing of seat belts is **obligatory**.*
- compulsory, necessary, required
OPPOSITE optional

oblige verb
*Would you **oblige** me by watering the plants?*
- help, assist, do you a favour

obliged adjective
1 *He felt **obliged** to help them.*
- bound, compelled, expected, required
2 *I'm much **obliged** to you for your kindness.*
- thankful, grateful, indebted

oblong noun
- rectangle
FOR OTHER SHAPES
SEE **shape** noun

obscene adjective
*The film contains some **obscene** language.*
- offensive, rude, indecent, improper, shocking, coarse, crude, foul
OPPOSITE decent

obscure adjective
1 *An **obscure** figure emerged from the mist.*
- dim, murky, shadowy, misty, blurred, unclear, vague, indistinct
OPPOSITE clear
2 *His joke seemed rather **obscure**.*
- confusing, puzzling, incomprehensible
OPPOSITE obvious
3 *Henry Kirke White is an **obscure** poet.*
- unknown, unheard of, unimportant, forgotten, minor
OPPOSITE famous

obscure verb
*A tall hedge **obscured** the view.*
- block out, cover, hide, mask, screen, shroud
OPPOSITE reveal

observant adjective
*If you're **observant**, you might see a fox tonight.*
- alert, attentive, sharp-eyed, vigilant, watchful
OPPOSITE inattentive

observation noun
1 *They took him to hospital for **observation**.*
- study, watching, scrutiny
2 *The detective made an interesting **observation**.*
- comment, remark, statement

observe verb
1 *Astronomers **observed** the eclipse last night.*
- watch, look at, view, study
2 *I have **observed** a change in his behaviour.*
- notice, note, see, detect, spot, discern, perceive, witness
3 *It's important to **observe** the rules.*
- follow, abide by, adhere to, heed, keep to, obey
4 *My friend **observed** that I had grown taller.*
- mention, say, comment, remark, declare

obsession noun
*Football is Frank's **obsession**.*
- passion, fixation, addiction, mania

obsolete adjective
*That computer software is now **obsolete**.*
- out of date, outdated, outmoded, antiquated, dated
OPPOSITE current

obstacle noun
1 *They drove around the **obstacles** in the road.*
- obstruction, barrier, barricade
2 *His age proved to be an **obstacle**.*
- problem, difficulty, hindrance, hurdle, snag, catch

obstinate adjective

*The **obstinate** camel refused to budge.*

- stubborn, uncooperative, wilful, headstrong, pig-headed
OPPOSITE cooperative

obstruct verb

*The path was **obstructed** by a fallen tree.*

- block, jam, make impassable

obstruction noun

*The fallen tree was causing an **obstruction**.*

- blockage, barrier, barricade

obtain verb

*You must **obtain** a permit before you can park here.*

- get, get hold of, acquire
- (*informal*) pick up

obvious adjective

1 *It was silly to make so many **obvious** mistakes.*

- glaring, noticeable, pronounced

2 *The castle is an **obvious** landmark.*

- conspicuous, notable, prominent, visible
OPPOSITE inconspicuous

3 *It was **obvious** that the woman was a spy.*

- clear, evident, apparent, plain, undeniable, unmistakable
OPPOSITE hidden

occasion noun

1 *I've been to Italy on several **occasions**.*

- time, moment, instance, opportunity, chance

2 *The wedding was a happy **occasion**.*

- affair, event, happening, incident, occurrence

occasional adjective

*The weather forecast said there would be **occasional** showers.*

- intermittent, odd, scattered, irregular, infrequent
OPPOSITE frequent, regular

occasionally adverb

*The dragon **occasionally** lifted its head and roared.*

- sometimes, now and again, once in a while, every so often
OPPOSITE frequently, often

occupant noun

*The only **occupants** of the castle were a family of bats.*

- inhabitant, occupier, resident, tenant

occupation noun

1 *He's not happy with his present **occupation**.*

- job, post, employment, profession, trade, work
FOR VARIOUS OCCUPATIONS
SEE **job**

2 *Vita's favourite **occupation** is reading.*

- activity, hobby, pastime, pursuit

occupied adjective

*She's very **occupied** in her work just now.*

- absorbed, involved, engrossed, busy, engaged
OPPOSITE idle

occupy verb

1 *They **occupy** the house next door.*

- live in, reside in, dwell in, inhabit

2 *We sold the piano because it **occupied** too much space.*

- fill, take up, use up

3 *The rebel army **occupied** the town.*

- capture, seize, take over, conquer, invade

occur verb

1 *She told us what had **occurred**.*

- happen, take place, come about, arise

2 *The disease only **occurs** in certain plants.*

- develop, crop up, turn up

occurrence noun

*An eclipse of the sun is an unusual **occurrence**.*

- event, happening, incident, phenomenon

a
b
c
d
e
f
g
h
i
j
k
l
m
n
o
p
q
r
s
t
u
v
w
x
y
z

ocean noun

WORD WEB

THE OCEANS OF THE WORLD ARE
Antarctic, Arctic, Atlantic, Indian,
Pacific
FOR CREATURES THAT LIVE IN THE OCEAN
SEE **sea**

odd adjective

1 *Her behaviour seemed very **odd**.*
- strange, unusual, abnormal, peculiar, curious, puzzling, queer, unconventional, eccentric, funny, weird
  OPPOSITE normal

2 *He could only find a couple of **odd** socks.*
- left over, single, spare

3 *He does **odd** jobs to earn money.*
- occasional, casual, irregular, various

odour noun

*There's a nasty **odour** coming from the fridge.*
- A nice smell is a fragrance or perfume.
- A nasty smell is a reek, stench, or stink.
  SEE ALSO **smell** verb

offence noun

1 *The thief was punished for his **offence**.*
- crime, wrongdoing, misdeed, fault, sin
- In games, an offence is a foul or an infringement.

2 *I didn't mean to cause any **offence**.*
- hurt, anger, annoyance, displeasure, hard feelings, disgust

offend verb

1 *I hope my letter didn't **offend** you.*
- give or cause offence to, insult, upset, hurt your feelings, anger, displease, annoy, affront, disgust, vex

2 *You'll be punished if you **offend** again.*
- break the law, do wrong

offensive adjective

1 *The gas produces an **offensive** smell.*
- unpleasant, repellent, disgusting, revolting, nasty
  OPPOSITE pleasant

2 *He apologized for his **offensive** remarks.*
- insulting, impolite, rude, abusive

offer verb

1 *A reward was **offered** for the capture of the outlaws.*
- propose, put forward, suggest, make available

2 *He **offered** to help with the washing-up.*
- volunteer

offer noun

*Their **offer** of help was gratefully received.*
- proposal, suggestion

office noun

1 *The boss won't be in the **office** today.*
- workplace, bureau, department

2 *Penny will take up the **office** of treasurer.*
- post, position, appointment, role, function

officer noun FOR OFFICERS IN THE POLICE FORCE

SEE **police officer**

official adjective

*The **official** opening of the museum is next month.*
- formal, authentic, authorized, legitimate, proper, genuine, approved
  OPPOSITE unofficial

official noun

*We spoke to an **official** of the organization.*
- officer, office-holder, representative, executive

often adverb

*It **often** rains in April.*
- frequently, regularly, repeatedly, time after time, many times, again and again, constantly

oil verb
*He **oiled** the hinge to stop it squeaking.*
- grease, lubricate

oily adjective
*Fried food is too **oily** for me.*
- fatty, greasy

ointment noun
*The chemist gave her some **ointment** for the rash.*
- cream, lotion

old adjective

 OVERUSED WORD
Try to vary the words you use for *old*. Here are some other words you could use.

- for an OLD PERSON:
elderly, aged
*Bus tickets are free for **elderly** people.*
OPPOSITE young

- for an OLD BUILDING or OLD DOCUMENT:
ancient, historic, original
*The **ancient** Norman church is to be restored.*

- Something that you respect because it is old is venerable.

- for OLD CLOTHES or OLD SHOES:
worn, scruffy, shabby, threadbare
*I put on **scruffy** jeans to do some gardening.*
OPPOSITE new

- for an OLD MACHINE:
old-fashioned, out of date, antiquated, early, obsolete
*The museum has a display of **early** computers.*

- Valuable old cars are veteran or vintage cars.

- Other things which are valuable because they are old are antique.
OPPOSITE up to date, current

- for THE OLD DAYS or OLD TIMES:
past, former, earlier, previous, bygone, olden
*We did a project on how children lived in **former** times.*

- Times before written records were kept are prehistoric times.
OPPOSITE modern

old-fashioned adjective
*That hairstyle is quite **old-fashioned** now.*
- out of date, outdated, outmoded, antiquated
OPPOSITE modern, up to date

omit verb
1 *His article was **omitted** from the magazine.*
- exclude, leave out, miss out, cut, eliminate, overlook, skip
2 *Don't **omit** to turn off the lights.*
- forget, fail, neglect

one-sided adjective
*The driver gave a **one-sided** account of the accident.*
- biased, prejudiced, unbalanced, unfair

ooze verb
*The filling started to **ooze** out my sandwich.*
- leak, seep, escape, dribble, drip

opaque adjective
*The dirt had turned the window **opaque**.*
- cloudy, obscure, unclear, dull, hazy, muddy, murky
OPPOSITE transparent

open adjective
1 *The puppy escaped through the **open** door.*
- unlocked, unfastened, ajar, gaping
OPPOSITE closed
2 *The jam jar had been left **open**.*
- uncovered, unsealed
3 *There is a view of **open** country from the back window.*
- clear, unrestricted, unenclosed, extensive
OPPOSITE enclosed
4 *He was **open** about what he had done wrong.*
- frank, honest, sincere, straightforward, candid
OPPOSITE deceitful

a
b
c
d
e
f
g
h
i
j
k
l
m
n
o
p
q
r
s
t
u
v
w
x
y
z

5 *The captain faced open rebellion from the crew.*
- unconcealed, undisguised, obvious, plain
  OPPOSITE concealed

open verb
1 *Please open the door.*
- unfasten, unlock, unbolt
2 *I can't wait to open my birthday presents!*
- undo, unwrap, untie, unseal
- To open an umbrella is to unfurl it.
- To open a wine bottle is to uncork it.
- To open a map is to unfold or unroll it.
3 *The jumble sale opens at 10 a.m.*
- begin, start, commence
- (*informal*) get going
  OPPOSITE close

opening noun
1 *The sheep got out through an opening in the fence.*
- gap, hole, breach, break, split
2 *The film has a very dramatic opening.*
- beginning, start, commencement
3 *We are invited to the opening of the new sports centre.*
- launch, initiation
4 *The job offers a good opening for a keen young person.*
- chance, opportunity

operate verb
1 *This watch operates even under water.*
- work, function, go, perform
2 *Do you know how to operate this machine?*
- use, work, drive, handle, manage, deal with
3 *The surgeon operated to remove her appendix.*
- carry out an operation, perform surgery

operation noun
1 *Astronauts control the operation of the spacecraft.*
- performance, working, functioning
2 *He had an operation to remove his appendix.*
- surgery

3 *Trying to defuse a bomb is a dangerous operation.*
- task, activity, action, exercise, manoeuvre, process, procedure

opinion noun
What was your honest opinion of the film?
- view, judgement, impression, belief, attitude, point of view, thought, conclusion, assessment, notion, feeling, idea

opponent noun
The knight fought bravely against his opponent.
- enemy, foe, rival, adversary, challenger
- Your opponents in a game are the opposition.
  OPPOSITE ally

opportunity noun
1 *There were few opportunities to relax.*
- chance, occasion, moment, time
2 *The job offers a good opportunity for a keen young person.*
- opening
- (*informal*) break

oppose verb
Many people opposed the building of the new road.
- object to, disapprove of, be against, be hostile towards, argue against, fight against, attack, resist
  OPPOSITE support, defend

opposite adjective
1 *They have opposite views about politics.*
- contrasting, conflicting, contradictory, opposed, opposing, different, contrary
  OPPOSITE similar
2 *My friend lives on the opposite side of the road.*
- facing

opposite noun
She says one thing and does the opposite.
- contrary, reverse, converse

opposition noun
1 *There was fierce **opposition** to the new road.*
- hostility, resistance, disapproval, unfriendliness, scepticism
  OPPOSITE support
2 *The **opposition** were stronger than our team expected.*
- opponents, rivals

optical adjective FOR OPTICAL INSTRUMENTS
  SEE **glasses**

optimistic adjective
*She's **optimistic** about her chances of success.*
- hopeful, positive, confident, expectant, cheerful, buoyant
  OPPOSITE pessimistic

option noun
*He had the **option** of staying or leaving.*
- choice, alternative, possibility

optional adjective
*The holiday includes an **optional** tour of the city.*
- voluntary, possible
  OPPOSITE compulsory

oral adjective
*She had to take an **oral** exam in French.*
- spoken, verbal
  OPPOSITE written

orbit verb
*The earth **orbits** the sun in about 365 days.*
- circle, travel round

ordeal noun
*The shipwrecked sailor told us about his **ordeal**.*
- suffering, troubles, trial, anguish, torture, nightmare

order noun
1 *The captain gave the **order** to abandon ship.*
- command, instruction, direction
2 *I've put in an **order** for the new book.*
- request, demand, reservation, booking

3 *The police restored **order** after the riot.*
- peace, calm, control, quiet, harmony, law and order
4 *The CDs are arranged in alphabetical **order**.*
- arrangement, sequence, series, succession
5 *She keeps her bike in good **order**.*
- condition, state

order verb
1 *She **ordered** them to be quiet.*
- command, instruct, require, tell
2 *He **ordered** the new magazine.*
- request, reserve, apply for, book

orderly adjective
1 *The library has an **orderly** system for sorting books.*
- organized, ordered, tidy, neat, systematic, methodical
  OPPOSITE untidy
2 *Please form an **orderly** queue.*
- well behaved, controlled, disciplined
  OPPOSITE disorderly

ordinary adjective
1 *It was just an **ordinary** sort of day.*
- normal, typical, usual, customary, habitual, everyday
2 *This is more than just an **ordinary** robot.*
- standard, average, common, conventional, regular
3 *It was a very **ordinary** game.*
- mediocre, unexceptional, run-of-the-mill, routine
  OPPOSITE special, unusual

organization noun
1 *She works for a charitable **organization**.*
- institution, operation, enterprise, company
- (*informal*) outfit, set-up
2 *Who was responsible for the **organization** of the conference?*
- coordination, planning, arrangement, running

organize verb
1 *It took her ages to **organize** the party.*
- coordinate, plan, make arrangements for, see to, set up, run

a
b
c
d
e
f
g
h
i
j
k
l
m
n
o
p
q
r
s
t
u
v
w
x
y
z

2 *The librarian has to **organize** the books in the library.*
- arrange, put in order, classify, sort out, tidy up

origin noun
1 *We know very little about the **origin** of life on earth.*
- beginning, creation, start, birth, source, cause
OPPOSITE end noun

2 *He became very rich, despite his humble **origins**.*
- background, ancestry, descent, family, parentage, pedigree, stock

original adjective
1 *The settlers drove out the **original** inhabitants.*
- earliest, first, initial, native, aboriginal

2 *The story was very **original**.*
- inventive, new, novel, creative, fresh, imaginative, unusual, unconventional

3 *Is that an **original** work of art or a copy?*
- genuine, real, authentic, unique

originate verb
1 *Where did the idea **originate**?*
- begin, start, commence, emerge, crop up

2 *They **originated** a new style of dancing.*
- invent, create, design, conceive, introduce, launch

ornament noun
*A few **ornaments** will make the room more attractive.*
- decoration, adornment, trinket, bauble

ornamental adjective
*There were a few **ornamental** statues in the garden.*
- decorative, fancy, pretty, ornate

ornate adjective
*The furniture in the palace was very **ornate**.*
- elaborate, fancy, showy, ornamental, decorative

orthodox adjective
*She wasn't taught to play piano in the **orthodox** way.*
- conventional, accepted, customary, usual, standard, traditional, regular, established, approved, recognized, official
OPPOSITE unorthodox, unconventional

outbreak noun
1 *The townspeople feared an **outbreak** of violence.*
- outburst, upsurge (in), flare-up, spate
- An outbreak of disease that spreads quickly is an epidemic.

2 *The armies prepared for the **outbreak** of war.*
- beginning, start, onset

outburst noun
*There was an **outburst** of laughter from the next room.*
- explosion, eruption, outbreak, storm

outcome noun
*What was the **outcome** of the meeting?*
- result, consequence, effect, upshot

outcry noun
*There was an **outcry** over the closure of the hospital.*
- protest, complaint, uproar, fuss, furore

outdoor adjective
*The hotel had an **outdoor** swimming pool.*
- open-air, out of doors, outside

outer adjective
*The fishermen wore waterproof **outer** garments.*
- external, exterior, outside
OPPOSITE inner

outfit noun
1 *Katie bought a new **outfit** for the wedding.*
- clothes, costume, suit, ensemble
- (informal) get-up

2 *The puncture repair **outfit** is in the boot.*
- equipment, kit, gear

outing noun
*They've gone on their annual **outing** to London.*
- trip, excursion, expedition, jaunt

outlaw noun
*A band of **outlaws** held up the train.*
- bandit, brigand, robber, highwayman, criminal, fugitive

outlet noun
1 *The basin has an **outlet** for excess water.*
- opening, vent, channel, way out, exit, mouth
OPPOSITE inlet

2 *The company has **outlets** throughout the UK.*
- shop, store, market

outline noun
1 *We could see the **outline** of some trees in the distance.*
- profile, shape, silhouette, form, shadow

2 *He gave us a brief **outline** of his plan.*
- summary, sketch, framework, précis, rough idea

outline verb
*The detective **outlined** his plan.*
- summarize, sketch out

outlook noun
1 *The cottage has a beautiful **outlook** over the loch.*
- view, prospect, sight, vista

2 *He has a rather gloomy **outlook** on life.*
- point of view, view, attitude, frame of mind

3 *The **outlook** for the weekend is bright and sunny.*
- forecast, prediction, prospect

outrage noun
1 *There was public **outrage** at the government's decision.*
- anger, fury, disgust, indignation, horror

2 *He said it was an **outrage** that so much money has been wasted.*
- disgrace, scandal, crime, atrocity

outrageous adjective
1 *The behaviour of the trolls was **outrageous**.*
- disgraceful, scandalous, shocking, atrocious, appalling, monstrous, shameful

2 *They charge **outrageous** prices at that shop.*
- excessive, unreasonable
OPPOSITE acceptable, reasonable

outside adjective
*Lookouts were stationed on the **outside** wall of the castle.*
- exterior, external, outer

outside noun
*Insects have their skeletons on the **outside** of their bodies.*
- exterior, shell, surface
OPPOSITE inside

outsider noun
*She's lived in the village for years, but still feels like an **outsider**.*
- newcomer, stranger, alien, foreigner, immigrant, incomer

outskirts plural noun
*We live on the **outskirts** of town.*
- edge, fringe, outer areas
- The outskirts of a big town are the suburbs.
OPPOSITE centre

outspoken adjective
*She's always been **outspoken** in her views.*
- frank, honest, plain, blunt, straightforward

outstanding adjective
1 *She will be an **outstanding** tennis player in a few years.*
- excellent, exceptional, superb, extraordinary, superlative, brilliant, great, fine, distinguished, celebrated, remarkable, superior, striking, notable
OPPOSITE ordinary

2 *There are still some **outstanding** bills to pay.*
- overdue, unpaid, owing

a b c d e f g h i j k l m n o p q r s t u v w x y z

a
b
c
d
e
f
g
h
i
j
k
l
m
o
p
q
r
s
t
u
v
w
x
y
z

outward adjective
*In **outward** appearance, the castle was dark and dingy.*
- outer, outside, external, exterior, surface, visible

outwit verb
*Ewan managed to **outwit** his dad at chess.*
- outsmart, get the better of, beat, defeat

oval adjective
*The sandwiches were arranged on an **oval** platter.*
- egg-shaped, elliptical

oven noun
*The meat was roasting in the **oven**.*
- cooker, stove
- A special oven for firing pottery is a kiln.

overcast adjective
*The sky has been **overcast** all day.*
- cloudy, dull, grey, sunless, dark, leaden
  SEE ALSO **weather** noun

overcome verb
1 *He managed to **overcome** his fear of flying.*
- conquer, defeat, master, get the better of
2 *Some people in the building were **overcome** by fumes.*
- overpower, overwhelm

overflow verb
*Someone left the tap on and the bath **overflowed**.*
- spill over, run over, pour over, flood

overgrown adjective
*The back garden was completely **overgrown**.*
- unkempt, untidy, tangled, weedy, wild

overhaul verb
*The boiler was recently **overhauled**.*
- service, check over, inspect, repair, restore, refurbish

overhead adverb
*A flock of geese flew **overhead**.*
- above, high up, in the sky

overlook verb
1 *He seems to have **overlooked** one important fact.*
- miss, fail to see
2 *She's always willing to **overlook** his faults.*
- excuse, forget about, ignore, disregard, pardon, pay no attention to
- (*informal*) turn a blind eye to
3 *The front room of the house **overlooks** the garden.*
- have a view of, look on to, face

overpowering adjective
*I felt an **overpowering** urge to giggle.*
- overwhelming, powerful, strong, compelling, irresistible, uncontrollable

overrun verb
*The barn was **overrun** with rats and mice.*
- invade, take over, spread over, swarm over

overtake verb
*We **overtook** the car in front.*
- pass, leave behind, pull ahead of, outstrip

overthrow verb
*The rebels **overthrew** the President.*
- bring down, topple, oust, defeat, drive out, depose

overturn verb
1 *The boat **overturned**.*
- capsize, tip over, turn over, turn turtle
2 *She leapt to her feet, **overturning** her chair.*
- knock over, tip over, topple, upset, spill

overwhelm verb
1 *The troops were **overwhelmed** by the enemy forces.*
- defeat, overcome, overpower, crush
2 *A tidal wave **overwhelmed** the village.*
- engulf, flood, inundate, submerge, swallow up, bury

overwhelming adjective

*He was elected by an **overwhelming** majority.*

- decisive, devastating, crushing, huge, massive, great
- An overwhelming victory at an election is a landslide.

owe verb

- If you owe money to someone, you are in debt.

owing adjective

owing to

***Owing to** the rain, the match is cancelled.*

- because of, on account of, as a result of, thanks to

own verb

*It was the first bike she had **owned**.*

- be the owner of, have, possess

to own up to

*No one **owned up to** breaking the window.*

- confess to, admit to, tell the truth about
- (*informal*) come clean about

pace noun

1 *Move forward two **paces**.*
- step, stride
2 *The front runner set a fast **pace**.*
- rate, speed
- A formal word is velocity.

pacify verb

*The zookeeper managed to **pacify** the polar bear.*

- calm, quieten, soothe, humour, appease

OPPOSITE anger, annoy

pack noun

1 *There were four candles in each **pack**.*
- package, packet, bundle, bale
2 *The hikers picked up their **packs** and trudged off.*
- rucksack, backpack, haversack, knapsack

pack verb

1 *She **packed** her suitcase and called a taxi.*
- fill, load up
2 *I forgot to **pack** my hairdryer.*
- stow away, wrap up
3 *They tried to **pack** too many passengers onto the train.*
- cram, crowd, squeeze, stuff, jam, wedge

package noun

*The postman delivered a big **package**.*

- parcel, packet, bundle

pad noun

1 *She put a **pad** of cotton wool over the wound.*
- wad
- A pad to make a chair or bed comfortable is a cushion or pillow.
2 *There's a **pad** for messages next to the phone.*
- jotter, notebook, writing pad

pad verb

*The seats are **padded** with foam rubber.*

- stuff, fill, pack
- To put covers and padding on furniture is to upholster it.

padding noun

*The **padding** is coming out of this cushion.*

- stuffing, filling
- The covers and padding on furniture is upholstery.

a
b
c
d
e
f
g
h
i
j
k
l
m
n
o
p
q
r
s
t
u
v
w
x
y
z

a b c d e f g h i j k l m n o **p** q r s t u v w x y z

paddle verb

1 *The children **paddled** at the water's edge.*
- dabble, splash about
- To walk through deep water is to **wade**.

2 *He **paddled** his canoe along the canal.*
- To move a boat along with two oars is to **row** it.

page noun

1 *Several **pages** have been torn out of this book.*
- sheet, leaf

2 *He wrote two **pages** of notes.*
- side

pain noun

*Dirk felt a sudden jabbing **pain** in his foot.*
- anguish, suffering
- A dull pain is an **ache** or **soreness**.
- Severe pain is **agony**, **torment**, or **torture**.
- A slight pain is **discomfort**.
- A slight pain which doesn't last long is a **twinge**.
- A sudden pain is a **pang** or **stab**.
- Pain in your head is a **headache**.
- Pain in your teeth is **toothache**.

painful adjective

1 *My shoulder is still really **painful**.*
- sore, aching, tender, hurting, smarting, stinging, throbbing

2 *The conversation brought back many **painful** memories.*
- unpleasant, upsetting, distressing, disagreeable, traumatic
OPPOSITE painless

painless adjective

1 *The treatment is quite **painless**.*
- comfortable, pain-free

2 *This is a quick and **painless** way to make a cake.*
- easy, simple, effortless, undemanding
OPPOSITE painful

paint noun

 WORD WEB

KINDS OF PAINT FOR DECORATING
emulsion, undercoat, whitewash
- A layer of paint is a coat of paint.
- Paint which stays shiny when it dries is gloss paint.
- Paint which goes dull when it dries is matt paint.

KINDS OF PAINT FOR ARTWORK
acrylic, finger paint, oil paint, poster paint, watercolour

paint verb

1 *The bedroom walls were **painted** green.*
- colour, decorate

2 *Samantha **painted** the flowers in bright colours.*
- depict, portray, represent

painter noun

- A person who paints houses is a decorator.
- A person who paints pictures is an artist.

painting noun

- A picture painted on a wall is a fresco or a mural.
- A picture painted by a famous artist of the past is an old master.
SEE ALSO **picture** noun

pair noun

- A pair of people who go out together are a couple.
- Two people who sing or play music together are a duet.
- Two people who work together are partners or a partnership.
- Two babies born together are twins.

palace noun FOR TYPES OF BUILDING
SEE **building**

pale adjective

1 *Are you all right? You're looking a little **pale**.*
- white, pallid, pasty, wan, ashen, sallow, anaemic

- To go pale with fear is to blanch.
OPPOSITE ruddy, flushed
2 *That shade of pink is too **pale**.*
- light, pastel, faded, faint, dim, bleached, colourless
OPPOSITE bright

pamper verb
*The twins' grandparents liked to **pamper** them.*
- spoil, indulge, cosset, mollycoddle, humour

pamphlet noun
*We were given a **pamphlet** about road safety.*
- leaflet, booklet, brochure

pan noun FOR THINGS USED FOR COOKING
SEE **cook** verb

panel noun
*A **panel** of experts judged the contest.*
- group, team, board, committee

panic noun
*People fled the streets in **panic**.*
- alarm, fright, terror, frenzy, hysteria

panic verb
*If a fire starts, don't **panic**!*
- be alarmed, take fright, become hysterical
- (*informal*) lose your head, get in a flap
- To panic is also to be panic-stricken.

pant verb
*Some of the runners were **panting** by the last lap.*
- breathe quickly, gasp, wheeze, puff

pants plural noun FOR UNDERWEAR
SEE **clothes**

paper noun
1 *She started her diary on a fresh sheet of **paper**.*
- A piece of paper is a leaf or a sheet.
2 *The doctor had some important **papers** to sign.*
- document, deed, certificate
3 *The story made the front page of the local **paper**.*
- newspaper, journal
- (*informal*) rag

paper noun

WORD WEB

MATERIALS FOR WRITING OR DRAWING ON

card, cardboard, cartridge paper, notepaper, postcard, stationery, tracing paper, writing paper

EARLY MATERIALS FOR WRITING ON

papyrus, parchment, vellum

OTHER KINDS OF PAPER

greaseproof paper, tissue paper, toilet paper, wallpaper, wrapping paper

parade noun
*A circus **parade** passed along the street.*
- procession, march, spectacle, show, display
- A parade of vehicles or people or horseback is a cavalcade.
- A parade of people in costume is a pageant.

parade verb
*The brass band **paraded** through the town.*
- march, troop, file past

paralyse verb
*His right arm was **paralysed** in the accident.*
- disable, immobilize, cripple, deaden, numb

parcel noun
*The postman delivered a bulky **parcel**.*
- package, packet

parched adjective
1 *Nothing was growing in the **parched** earth.*
- dry, arid, baked, scorched, barren, sterile, waterless
2 *I need a drink of water—I'm **parched**!*
- thirsty

pardon verb
*The king decided to **pardon** the prisoners.*
- release, free, set free, let off, spare, excuse, forgive

a
b
c
d
e
f
g
h
i
j
k
l
m
n
o
P
q
r
s
t
u
v
w
x
y
z

a
b
c
d
e
f
g
h
i
j
k
l
m
n
o
p
q
r
s
t
u
v
w
x
y
z

- To pardon someone who is condemned to death is to reprieve them.

parent noun FOR FAMILY RELATIONSHIPS

SEE **family**

park noun

WORD WEB

At lunchtime, we went for a walk in the park.
- public gardens, recreation ground
- A park with fields and trees around a big house is an estate or parkland.

SOME KINDS OF PARK
adventure park, amusement park, arboretum, botanical gardens, forest park, nature reserve, playpark or playground, safari park, skate park, theme park

EQUIPMENT YOU MIGHT FIND IN A PLAYPARK
chute or slide, climbing frame, flying fox, monkey bars, rope ladder, roundabout, sandpit, seesaw, swings, trapeze

park verb
The postman parked his van around the corner.
- leave, position, station

part noun
1 *All the parts of the engine are now working properly.*
- bit, component, constituent
2 *I only saw the first part of the programme.*
- section, piece, portion, element
3 *Which part of the business do they own?*
- branch, department, division
4 *Granny lives in another part of the town.*
- area, district, region, neighbourhood, sector
5 *He's just right to act the part of Peter Pan.*
- character, role

part verb
1 *It was the first time she'd been parted from her parents.*
- separate, divide, remove
OPPOSITE join
2 *They exchanged a final kiss before parting.*
- go away, leave, depart, say goodbye
OPPOSITE meet

partial adjective
The play was only a partial success.
- limited, imperfect, incomplete
OPPOSITE complete
to be partial to
Becky is very partial to chocolate cake.
- be fond of, be keen on, enjoy, like

participate verb
Our school is participating in the mini marathon.
- take part, join in, be involved, cooperate, help, share

particle noun
The camera lens was covered with particles of dust.
- speck, grain, fragment, bit, piece, scrap, shred, sliver
SEE ALSO **bit**

particular adjective
1 *The tickets must be used on a particular day.*
- specific, certain, distinct, definite, exact
2 *She took particular care not to damage the parcel.*
- special, exceptional, unusual, extreme, marked, notable
3 *The cat's very particular about his food.*
- fussy, finicky, hard to please
- (informal) choosy, picky

particulars plural noun
The police officer took down all the particulars.
- details, facts, information, circumstances

partition noun
A partition separates the two classrooms.
- room divider, screen

partly adverb

*It was **partly** my fault that we were late.*

- in part, to some extent, up to a point
OPPOSITE entirely

partner noun

*The two women have been business **partners** for years.*

- colleague, associate, ally
- In marriage, your partner is your spouse or your husband or wife.
- An animal's partner is its mate.

party noun

1 *We had a class **party** at the end of term.*
- celebration, festivity, function, gathering, reception
- (informal) get-together, do
2 *A **party** of tourists was going round the museum.*
- group, band, crowd, gang
3 *They have formed a new political **party**.*
- alliance, association, faction, league

party noun

> **WORD WEB**
>
> SOME KINDS OF PARTY
> ball, banquet, barbecue, birthday party, ceilidh, Christmas party, cocktail party, dance, dinner party, disco, fancy-dress party, garden party, Halloween party, housewarming, picnic, pot luck, reunion, sleepover party, tea party, wedding
>
> THINGS YOU MIGHT SEE AT A PARTY
> balloons, birthday cake, birthday candles, bunting, party bags, poppers, sparklers, streamers
> FOR PARTY GAMES
> SEE **game**

pass verb

1 *We watched the parade as it **passed**.*
- go by, move past
2 *She tried to **pass** the car in front.*
- overtake, go ahead of
3 *We **passed** over the bridge.*
- go, advance, proceed, progress
4 *Could you **pass** me the sugar, please?*
- hand, give, deliver, offer, present

5 *Do you think you will **pass** your music exam?*
- be successful in, get through, succeed in
6 *How did you **pass** the time on holiday?*
- spend, use, occupy, fill, while away
7 *Three years **passed** before we met again.*
- go by, elapse
8 *The pain will soon **pass**.*
- go away, come to an end, disappear, fade

to pass out

*One of the runners **passed out** in the heat.*

- faint, lose consciousness, black out

pass noun

1 *We had a **pass** to get into the concert for free.*
- permit, licence, ticket
2 *The horses filed through a **pass** between the hills.*
- gap, gorge, ravine, canyon, valley

passage noun

1 *A secret **passage** led from the chamber to the outside.*
- passageway, corridor, tunnel
2 *The guards forced a **passage** through the crowd.*
- path, route, way
3 *A sea **passage** takes longer than going by air.*
- journey, voyage, crossing
4 *Our homework is to choose a favourite **passage** from a book.*
- episode, excerpt, extract, piece, quotation, section
5 *He hadn't changed, despite the **passage** of time.*
- passing, progress, advance

passenger noun

*The bus has seats for 55 **passengers**.*

- traveller
- Passengers who travel regularly to work are commuters.

passion noun

1 *'Romeo and Juliet' is a story of youthful **passion**.*
- love, emotion

a
b
c
d
e
f
g
h
i
j
k
l
m
n
o
P
q
r
s
t
u
v
w
x
y
z

2 *She has a **passion** for sports.*
- enthusiasm, eagerness, appetite, desire, craving, urge, zest, thirst, mania

passionate adjective
1 *The captain gave a **passionate** speech before the battle.*
- emotional, intense, moving, heartfelt
OPPOSITE unemotional
2 *He is a **passionate** follower of football.*
- eager, keen, avid, enthusiastic, fanatical, fervent
OPPOSITE apathetic

passive adjective
*Owls are normally **passive** during the daytime.*
- inactive, docile
OPPOSITE active

past noun
*In the **past**, things were different.*
- past times, old days, olden days, days gone by
- The study of what happened in the past is history.
- The things and ideas that have come down to us from the past are our heritage or traditions.
OPPOSITE future

past adjective
*Things were very different in **past** centuries.*
- earlier, former, previous, old
OPPOSITE future

pasta noun

WORD WEB
SOME TYPES OF PASTA
cannelloni, lasagne, macaroni, noodles, penne, ravioli, spaghetti, tagliatelle, tortellini
FOR OTHER KINDS OF FOOD
SEE **food**

paste noun
*I used some **paste** to stick things into my scrapbook.*
- glue, gum, adhesive

pastime noun
*Shona's favourite **pastime** is swimming.*
- activity, hobby, recreation, amusement, diversion, entertainment, relaxation, game, sport
SEE ALSO **game**, **sport**

pasture noun
*Cattle were grazing on the **pasture**.*
- field, meadow, grassland

pat verb
*Andy **patted** the Shetland pony on the head.*
- tap, touch, stroke, pet
- To touch something quickly and lightly is to dab it.
- To stroke someone with an open hand is to caress them.

patch verb
*I need some material to **patch** my jeans.*
- mend, repair
- Another way to mend holes in clothes is to darn them or stitch them up.

patchy adjective
*There will be **patchy** outbreaks of rain overnight.*
- irregular, inconsistent, uneven, varying, unpredictable

path noun
*Please keep to the **path** as you walk through the gardens.*
- pathway, track, trail, footpath, walk, walkway, lane
- A path for horse-riding is a bridleway.
- A path by the side of a road is a pavement.
- A path above a beach is an esplanade or promenade.
- A path along a canal is a towpath.
- A path between buildings is an alley.
SEE ALSO **road**

pathetic adjective

1 *The abandoned kittens were a **pathetic** sight.*
- moving, touching, pitiful, distressing, heartbreaking, sad, sorry

2 *The goalie made a **pathetic** attempt to stop the ball.*
- hopeless, useless, weak, feeble, inadequate, incompetent

patience noun

*She waited with great **patience** for an hour.*
- calmness, tolerance, self-control, endurance, restraint, perseverance, persistence, resignation

OPPOSITE impatience

patient adjective

1 *The nurse was very **patient** with the children.*
- calm, composed, even-tempered, easygoing, tolerant, lenient, mild, quiet, uncomplaining, resigned, long-suffering

2 *It took hours of **patient** work to restore the painting.*
- persevering, persistent, unhurried, untiring, steady, determined

OPPOSITE impatient

patrol verb

*Police **patrolled** the area all night.*
- guard, keep watch over, inspect, tour

patter noun, verb FOR VARIOUS SOUNDS

SEE **sound** noun

pattern noun

 WORD WEB

*Do you like the **pattern** on this wallpaper?*
- design, decoration

SOME KINDS OF PATTERN
checked, criss-cross, dotted or dotty, floral or flowery, geometric, gingham, paisley, polka dot, spotted or spotty, striped or stripey, tartan, wavy, zigzag

pause noun

*There was a **pause** while the singers got their breath back.*
- break, gap, halt, rest, lull, stop, wait, interruption, stoppage
- A pause in the middle of a performance is an interlude or interval.
- A pause in the middle of a cinema film is an intermission.

pause verb

1 *The stranger **paused** at the door before knocking.*
- hesitate, wait, delay, hang back

2 *The cyclists **paused** to let the others catch up.*
- halt, stop, rest, take a break, break off

paw noun

*The cat had a mouse under its **paw**.*
- foot
- A horse's foot is a hoof.
- A pig's feet are its trotters.
- A bird's feet are its claws.

pay verb

1 *How much did you **pay** for your new bike?*
- spend, give out, hand over
- (*informal*) fork out

2 *Who's going to **pay** the bill?*
- pay off, repay, settle, clear, refund

3 *They had to **pay** for all the damage they caused.*
- compensate, pay back

4 *Do you think the new business is likely to **pay**?*
- be profitable

5 *I'll make you **pay** for this!*
- suffer

pay noun

*We should get an increase in **pay** next year.*
- wages, salary, income, earnings
- A payment you get for doing a single job is a fee.

payment noun

- A voluntary payment to a charity is a contribution or donation.
- The payment you make to travel on public transport is the fare.

- A payment you have to make as a punishment is a fine.
- A payment made to free a hostage or prisoner is a ransom.
- A payment you get as a prize is a reward.
- A payment to join a club is a subscription.
- A voluntary payment to a waiter, etc., is a tip.
- Payment that you receive regularly from parents is pocket money.
- A payment you get if you paid too much for something is a refund.

peace noun

1 *After the war there was a period of* **peace**.
- agreement, harmony, friendliness

2 *She enjoys the* **peace** *of the countryside.*
- calmness, peacefulness, quiet, tranquillity, stillness, serenity, silence

peaceful adjective
They enjoyed a **peaceful** *day fishing.*
- calm, quiet, relaxing, tranquil, restful, serene, undisturbed, untroubled, gentle, placid, soothing, still

OPPOSITE noisy, troubled

peak noun

1 *The* **peak** *of the mountain was covered in snow.*
- summit, cap, crest, crown, pinnacle, top, tip, point

2 *She is at the* **peak** *of her career as an athlete.*
- top, height, highest point, climax

peal verb FOR SOUNDS MADE BY A BELL
SEE bell

peculiar adjective

1 *What's that* **peculiar** *smell?*
- strange, unusual, odd, curious, extraordinary, abnormal, funny, weird, bizarre

OPPOSITE ordinary

2 *He recognized her* **peculiar** *way of writing.*
- characteristic, distinctive, individual, particular, personal, special, unique, identifiable

pedigree noun
They have a complete record of the dog's **pedigree**.
- ancestry, descent, family history

peel noun
Orange **peel** *is used in marmalade.*
- rind, skin

peep, peer verbs SEE look verb

peg noun
Leave your coat and scarf on the **peg**.
- hook, knob

pelt verb

1 *The boys* **pelted** *each other with snowballs.*
- attack, bombard, shower
SEE ALSO **throw**

2 *The rain was* **pelting** *down outside.*
- pour, teem

pen noun

1 *My* **pen** *has run out of ink.*
- ballpoint, biro, felt-tipped pen, fountain pen

2 *The dog drove the sheep into the* **pen**.
- enclosure, fold

penalize verb
In football, you are **penalized** *if you handle the ball.*
- punish

penalty noun
The **penalty** *for this crime is ten years in prison.*
- punishment
OPPOSITE reward

penetrate verb

1 *The bullet had* **penetrated** *the man's chest.*
- make a hole in, pierce, bore through
- When something penetrates a tyre, it punctures it.

2 *The soldiers* **penetrated** *the enemy's defences.*
- get past, get through, infiltrate

penniless adjective
*The family was left **penniless** and without a home.*
- poor, impoverished, poverty-stricken
OPPOSITE rich

people plural noun
1 *How many **people** are you inviting?*
- persons, individuals
- People as opposed to animals are humans or human beings or mankind.
2 *The government is elected by the **people** of the country.*
- population, citizens, the public, society, nation, race

perceive verb
1 *They **perceived** a figure moving along the horizon.*
- make out, notice, become aware of, catch sight of, recognize
2 *I began to **perceive** what she meant.*
- realize, understand, comprehend, grasp

perceptive adjective
*It was very **perceptive** of you to spot my mistake.*
- observant, clever, sharp, shrewd, quick, alert
OPPOSITE unobservant

perch verb
*A robin was **perching** on top of the postbox.*
- sit, settle, rest, balance

percussion noun FOR PERCUSSION INSTRUMENTS
SEE **music**

perfect adjective
1 *Each petal on the flower was **perfect**.*
- faultless, flawless, ideal, intact, undamaged, complete, whole
2 *The dress is a **perfect** fit.*
- exact, faithful, precise, accurate, correct
OPPOSITE imperfect
3 *I received a letter from a **perfect** stranger.*
- complete, total, absolute, utter

perfect verb
*Gymnasts spend years **perfecting** their technique.*
- make perfect, improve, refine, polish

perform verb
1 *Is this your first time **performing** on stage?*
- act, appear, play, dance, sing
2 *The children **performed** a play about Cinderella.*
- present, stage, produce, put on
3 *Soldiers are expected to **perform** their duty.*
- do, carry out, execute, fulfil
- To perform a crime is to commit a crime.

performance noun
1 *Tonight's **performance** is already sold out.*
- show, production, presentation
2 *He congratulated the players on their outstanding **performance**.*
- effort, work, endeavour, exertion, behaviour, conduct

performer noun SEE **entertainer**

perfume noun
*The **perfume** of roses filled the room.*
- smell, scent, fragrance

perhaps adverb
__Perhaps__ the weather will improve soon.
- maybe, possibly
OPPOSITE definitely

peril noun
*The crew faced many **perils** on their voyage.*
- danger, hazard, risk, menace, threat
OPPOSITE safety

perimeter noun
*There is a fence round the **perimeter** of the field.*
- edge, border, boundary
- The distance round the edge of something is the circumference.

period noun
1 After a long **period** of hard work they had a rest.
- time, span, spell, stretch

2 The book is about the Victorian **period**.
- age, era, epoch

perish verb
1 Many birds **perish** in cold weather.
- die, be killed, pass away

2 The old tyres have started to **perish** with age.
- disintegrate, crumble away, rot, decay, decompose

permanent adjective
1 Sugar can do **permanent** damage to your teeth.
- lasting, long-lasting, long-term, everlasting, enduring

2 Traffic noise is a **permanent** problem in the city centre.
- never-ending, perpetual, persistent, chronic, perennial

3 She has been offered a **permanent** job in the firm.
- stable, steady, fixed, lifelong
- OPPOSITE temporary

permission noun
They had the teacher's **permission** to leave.
- consent, agreement, approval
- (informal) go-ahead

permit verb
The council doesn't **permit** fishing in the lake.
- allow, consent to, give permission for, authorize, license, grant, tolerate, admit

permit noun
You need a **permit** to fish in the river.
- licence, pass, ticket

perpetual adjective
The machine produces a **perpetual** hum.
- constant, continual, continuous, never-ending, non-stop, endless, ceaseless, incessant, persistent, unceasing, unending
- OPPOSITE temporary

perplexing adjective
'This is the most **perplexing** case I've seen,' said the detective.
- puzzling, confusing, bewildering, baffling, mystifying

persecute verb
People were **persecuted** for their religious beliefs.
- oppress, discriminate against, harass, intimidate, bully, terrorize, torment

persevere verb
The rescuers **persevered** despite the bad weather.
- continue, carry on, keep going, persist
- (informal) keep at it, stick at it
- OPPOSITE give up

persist verb
If your headache **persists**, you should see a doctor.
- continue, carry on, last, linger, remain, endure
- OPPOSITE stop

to persist in
He **persists in** wearing that awful tie!
- keep on, insist on

persistent adjective
1 There was a **persistent** drip from the tap in the kitchen.
- constant, continual, incessant, never-ending, steady, non-stop

2 That dog is very **persistent**—he won't go away.
- determined, persevering, tireless, resolute, steadfast, stubborn, obstinate

person noun
Not a single **person** has replied to my email.
- individual, human being, character, soul

personal adjective
1 The book is based on the writer's **personal** experience.
- own, individual, particular

2 The contents of the letter are **personal**.
- confidential, private, secret, intimate

personality noun

1 *Like all ogres, he has an ugly **personality**.*
- character, nature, disposition, temperament, make-up

2 *The show was introduced by a TV **personality**.*
- celebrity, star, VIP

perspire verb

*He **perspires** a lot in hot weather.*
- sweat

persuade verb

*I **persuaded** my friend to join the choir.*
- convince, coax, induce
- To persuade someone to do something is also to talk them into doing it.

OPPOSITE dissuade

persuasive adjective

*She used some very **persuasive** arguments.*
- convincing, effective, sound, strong, forceful, compelling, valid

OPPOSITE unconvincing

pessimistic adjective

*The players are **pessimistic** about their chances of winning.*
- negative, unhopeful, gloomy, despairing, resigned, cynical

OPPOSITE optimistic

pest noun

1 *I'm trying an organic method to get rid of garden **pests**.*
- Pests in general are vermin.
- An informal word for insect pests is bugs.
- A pest which lives on or in another creature is a parasite.

2 *Don't be a **pest**!*
- nuisance, bother, annoyance
- (*informal*) pain

pester verb

*Please don't **pester** me while I'm busy!*
- annoy, bother, trouble, harass, badger, hound, nag
- (*informal*) bug

pet noun

WORD WEB

SOME ANIMALS COMMONLY KEPT AS PETS

budgerigar, canary, cat, dog, ferret, fish, gerbil, goldfish, guinea pig, hamster, mouse, parrot, pigeon, rabbit, rat, tortoise

petrified adjective

*Jack stood **petrified** as the monster lumbered towards him.*
- terrified, horrified, terror-struck, paralysed, frozen

SEE ALSO **afraid**

petty adjective

*There were a lot of annoying **petty** rules.*
- minor, trivial, unimportant, insignificant

OPPOSITE important

phase noun

*Going to school is the start of a new **phase** in your life.*
- period, time, stage, step

phenomenal adjective

*The winner of the quiz had a **phenomenal** memory.*
- amazing, incredible, outstanding, remarkable, exceptional, extraordinary
- (*informal*) fantastic

OPPOSITE ordinary

phenomenon noun

1 *Snow is a common **phenomenon** in winter.*
- happening, occurrence, event, fact

2 *The six-year-old pianist was quite a **phenomenon**.*
- wonder, curiosity, marvel

phobia noun SEE **fear** noun

phone verb

*I'll **phone** you later this evening.*
- telephone, call, ring, dial

a
b
c
d
e
f
g
h
i
j
k
l
m
n
o
p
q
r
s
t
u
v
w
x
y
z

a
b
c
d
e
f
g
h
i
j
k
l
m
n
p
q
r
s
t
u
v
w
x
y
z

photograph noun

*I put my holiday **photographs** in an album.*

- photo, snap or snapshot, shot
- The photographs you get when a film is processed are prints.
- A photograph on the original film from which a print is made is a negative.
- A photograph for projecting onto a screen is a slide or transparency.

photograph verb

*Rachel **photographed** some animals in the zoo.*

- take a picture of, shoot, snap

phrase noun

*'Bon voyage' is a French **phrase** meaning 'have a good journey'.*

- expression, saying

phrase verb

*I tried to **phrase** my letter carefully.*

- express, put into words

physical adjective

1 *There's a lot of **physical** contact in rugby.*
- bodily
- Physical punishment is corporal punishment.

2 *Ghosts have no **physical** presence.*
- earthly, material, solid, substantial

pick verb

1 *They've **picked** the players for the hockey team.*
- choose, select, decide on, settle on, opt for, single out

2 *Irene **picked** some flowers from the garden.*
- gather, collect, cut

3 *I **picked** an apple off the tree.*
- pluck, pull off, take

to pick up

1 *He was too weak to **pick up** the box.*
- lift, raise, hoist

2 *I'll **pick up** some milk on the way home.*
- get, collect, fetch

picture noun

1 *There's a **picture** of a pyramid in this book.*
- illustration, image, print
- A picture which represents a particular person is a portrait.
- A picture which represents the artist himself or herself is a self-portrait.
- A picture which represents a group of objects is a still life.
- A picture which represents a country scene is a landscape.
- Pictures on a computer are graphics.
  SEE ALSO **painting, portrait**

2 *Mum took some **pictures** of us building a sandcastle.*
- photograph, snapsot, snap

picture verb

1 *The girl is **pictured** against a background of flowers.*
- depict, illustrate, represent, show, portray

2 *Can you **picture** what the world will be like in 100 years?*
- imagine, visualize

picturesque adjective

1 *They stayed in a **picturesque** thatched cottage.*
- attractive, pretty, charming, quaint
  OPPOSITE ugly

2 *She wrote a **picturesque** account of her trip to Morocco.*
- colourful, descriptive, imaginative, expressive, lively, poetic, vivid

piece noun

1 *They collected **pieces** of wood to build a raft.*
- bar, block, length, stick, chunk, lump, hunk, bit, chip, fragment, particle, scrap, shred

2 *I've only got two **pieces** of chocolate left.*
- bit, portion, part, section, segment, share, slice

3 *I always have a **piece** of fruit in my snack box.*
- item

- A piece of clothing is an article of clothing.
4 I've lost one of the **pieces** of the jigsaw.
- part, element, unit, component, constituent
5 There's a **piece** about our school in the local paper.
- article, item, report, feature

pier noun
The passengers waited at the **pier** to board the ship.
- quay, wharf, jetty, landing stage

pierce verb
The arrow had **pierced** the knight's armour.
- enter, go through, make a hole in, penetrate, bore through
- To pierce a hole through paper is to punch a hole or perforate it.
- To pierce a hole in a tyre is to puncture it.
- To pierce someone with a spike is to impale or spear them.

piercing adjective
When she saw the dragon, she let out a **piercing** scream.
- high-pitched, shrill, penetrating, loud, shattering, deafening, ear-splitting

pig noun
- An old word for pigs is swine.
- A wild pig is a wild boar.
- A male pig is a boar or hog.
- A female pig is a sow.
- A young pig is a piglet.
- A family of piglets is a litter.
- The smallest piglet in a litter is the runt.

pile noun
1 Where did this **pile** of rubbish come from?
- heap, mound, mountain, stack, hoard, mass, quantity, collection, assortment
2 I've still got **piles** of homework to do.
- plenty, a lot, a great deal
- (informal) lots, masses

pile verb
Pile everything in the corner and we'll sort it out later.
- heap, stack, collect, gather, assemble, hoard
to pile up
The bills are beginning to **pile up**.
- build up, mount up, accumulate

pill noun
Take one **pill** every four hours.
- tablet, capsule, pellet

pillar noun
The roof was supported by tall **pillars**.
- column, pier, post, prop, support

pillow noun
- A long kind of pillow is a bolster.
- A kind of pillow for a chair or sofa is a cushion.

pilot verb
He **piloted** the hot-air balloon back to safety.
- fly, steer, guide, lead, navigate

pimple noun
The troll had a **pimple** on the end of his nose.
- spot, boil, swelling

pin noun
- A decorative pin to wear is a brooch.
- A pin to fix something on a noticeboard is a drawing pin.
- A pin to fix a baby's nappy in place is a safety pin.

pinch verb
1 The baby **pinched** my arm and wouldn't let go.
- nip, squeeze, press, tweak, grip
2 (informal) Who **pinched** my calculator?
- steal, take, snatch, pilfer
- (informal) nick, swipe, make off with

pine verb
The dog **pined** when its master died.
- mope, languish, sicken, waste away
to pine for
She was **pining for** her old house by the sea.
- long for, yearn for, miss, crave, hanker after

a
b
c
d
e
f
g
h
i
j
k
l
m
n
o
p
q
r
s
t
u
v
w
x
y
z

a
b
c
d
e
f
g
h
i
j
k
l
m
n
o
P
q
r
s
t
u
v
w
x
y
z

pip noun
*Make sure there are no **pips** in the lemon juice.*
- seed

pipe noun
*The water flows away along this **pipe**.*
- tube
- A pipe used for watering the garden is a hose.
- A pipe in the street which supplies water for fighting fires is a hydrant.
- A pipe which carries oil, etc., over long distances is a pipeline.
- The system of water pipes in a house is the plumbing.

pipe verb
1 *Water is **piped** from the reservoir to the town.*
- carry, convey, channel, funnel

2 *She began to **pipe** a tune on her recorder.*
- play, blow, sound, whistle

pirate noun

WORD WEB
*The ship was overrun by bloodthirsty **pirates**.*
- buccaneer, marauder

THINGS YOU MIGHT FIND ON A PIRATE SHIP
barrels, cabin, crow's nest, deck, hammock, lantern, mast, plank, pirate flag, rigging, sail, treasure chest, wheel
- A pirate flag is a Jolly Roger or skull-and-crossbones.
- A pirate ship might sail on the high seas or the Spanish Main.
  SEE ALSO **boat**

PEOPLE YOU MIGHT FIND ON A PIRATE SHIP
cabin boy or girl, captain, captives, cook, crew, first mate, lookout, stowaway

PIRATE TREASURE MIGHT CONTAIN
doubloons or ducats, gold bullion, pieces of eight
- Goods or treasure seized by pirates is booty.
  SEE ALSO **treasure** noun

WEAPONS A PIRATE MIGHT USE
cannon, cutlass, dagger, gunpowder, musket, pistol

OTHER THINGS A PIRATE MIGHT WEAR OR CARRY
bandanna or kerchief, bottle of rum, breeches, cocked hat, earrings, eye patch, hook, parrot or cockatoo, pigtail, sea chart, spyglass or telescope, treasure map, wooden leg or peg leg

SOME WORDS TO DESCRIBE A PIRATE
barbaric, black-hearted, bloodthirsty, cut-throat, daring, dastardly, fearless, heartless, lawless, merciless, murderous, pitiless, ruthless, savage, swashbuckling, vengeful, vicious, villainous

pit noun
1 *They dug a deep **pit** to bury the treasure.*
- hole, crater, cavity, hollow, depression, pothole, chasm, abyss

2 *Coal used to be mined from the **pits** in this area.*
- mine, coal mine, colliery, quarry

pitch noun
1 *The **pitch** was waterlogged, so the match was called off.*
- ground, field, playing field

2 *She can sing at a very high **pitch**.*
- tone, frequency

pitch verb
1 *Scott **pitched** the ball back over the fence.*
- throw, toss, fling, hurl, sling, cast, lob
- (*informal*) chuck

2 *It was hard trying to **pitch** the tent in the rain!*
- erect, put up, set up

3 *He lost his balance and **pitched** headlong into the water.*
- plunge, dive, drop, topple, plummet

4 *The rowing boat **pitched** about in the storm.*
- lurch, rock, roll, toss

pitfall noun

*The author described some of the **pitfalls** of being famous.*

- difficulty, problem, hazard, danger, snag, catch, trap

pitiful adjective

1 *We could hear **pitiful** cries for help.*

- sad, sorrowful, mournful, pathetic, plaintive, heart-rending, moving, touching

2 *The goalie made a **pitiful** attempt to stop the ball.*

- hopeless, useless, feeble, inadequate, incompetent, pathetic

pity noun

*The pirates showed no **pity** towards the captives.*

- mercy, compassion, sympathy, humanity, kindness, concern, feeling
  OPPOSITE cruelty

a pity

*It's **a pity** that you have to leave so early.*

- a shame, unfortunate, bad luck

pity verb

*We **pitied** anyone who was caught up in the storm.*

- feel sorry for, feel for, sympathize with, take pity on

pivot noun

- The point on which a lever turns is the fulcrum.
- The point on which a spinning object turns is its axis.
- The point on which a wheel turns is the axle or hub.

place noun

1 *This is a good **place** to park.*

- site, venue, spot, location, position, situation

2 *They are looking for a quiet **place** to live.*

- area, district, locality, neighbourhood, region, vicinity

3 *Save me a **place** on the bus.*

- seat, space

place verb

1 *The hotel is **placed** next to the beach.*

- locate, situate, position, station

2 *You can **place** your coats on the bed.*

- put down, set down, leave, deposit, lay
- (*informal*) dump, plonk

placid adjective

1 *The dog has a **placid** nature and would make an ideal pet.*

- calm, composed, unexcitable, even-tempered
  OPPOSITE excitable

2 *The sea was **placid** at that time of the day.*

- calm, quiet, tranquil, peaceful, undisturbed, unruffled
  OPPOSITE stormy

plague noun

1 *Doctors worked hard to prevent the **plague** from spreading.*

- pestilence, epidemic, contagion, outbreak

2 *There was a **plague** of wasps this summer.*

- invasion, infestation, swarm

plague verb

1 *Stop **plaguing** me with questions!*

- bother, pester, trouble, annoy, badger, harrass
- (*informal*) nag, bug

2 *Celia has been **plagued** by bad luck recently.*

- afflict, beset, torment, hound

plain adjective

1 *The furniture in the room was very **plain**.*

- simple, modest, basic, unelaborate
  OPPOSITE elaborate

2 *Some people say she looks **plain** compared with her sister.*

- unattractive, ordinary
  OPPOSITE attractive

3 *It is **plain** to me that you are not interested.*

- clear, evident, obvious, apparent, unmistakable
  OPPOSITE unclear

a b c d e f g h i j k l m n o **p** q r s t u v w x y z

4 *She told us what she thought in very* ***plain*** *terms.*
- direct, frank, blunt, outspoken, honest, sincere, straightforward

5 *We need to wear a* ***plain*** *t-shirt for sports.*
- unpatterned, self-coloured

plain noun
- A grassy plain in a hot country is called savannah.
- The large plains of North America are the prairies.
- The large plains of Russia are the steppes.

plan noun
1 *The captain explained her* ***plan*** *to the rest of the team.*
- idea, proposal, scheme, strategy, project, suggestion, proposition
- A plan to do something bad is a plot.

2 *They looked at the* ***plans*** *for the new sports centre.*
- design, diagram, chart, map, drawing, blueprint

plan verb
1 *The outlaws* ***planned*** *an attack upon the sheriff.*
- scheme, design, devise, work out, formulate, prepare, organize
- To plan to do something bad is to plot.

2 *What do you* ***plan*** *to do next?*
- aim, intend, propose, mean

plane noun SEE aircraft

planet noun

WORD WEB

The new space probe will travel to far-off ***planets***.
- world

THE PLANETS OF THE SOLAR SYSTEM (IN ORDER FROM THE SUN) ARE

Mercury, Venus, Earth, Mars, Jupiter, Saturn, Uranus, Neptune, Pluto

- The path followed by a planet is its orbit.
- Minor planets orbiting the sun are asteroids.

- Something which orbits a planet is a satellite.
- The earth's large satellite is the Moon.

SEE ALSO **space**

WRITING TIPS

You can use these words to describe an **alien planet**:
- Earth-like, gaseous, inhospitable, uninhabitable
- to describe its SURFACE: barren, desolate, dusty, frozen, icy, molten, rocky, volcanic
- to describe its ATMOSPHERE or AIR: airless, noxious, poisonous, thin, unbreathable

plant noun

WORD WEB

SOME TYPES OF PLANT

algae, bush, cactus, cereal, evergreen, fern, flower, fungus, grass, herb, house plant, lichen, moss, pot plant, shrub, tree, vegetable, vine, weed, wildflower

SEE ALSO **flower, fruit, herb, tree, vegetable**

PARTS OF VARIOUS PLANTS

bloom, blossom, branch, bud, flower, fruit, leaf, petal, pod, root, shoot, stalk, stem, trunk, twig

- A young plant is a seedling.
- A piece cut off a plant to form a new plant is a cutting.
- A word for plants in general is vegetation.
- A person who studies plants is a botanist.
- A word meaning 'to do with plants' is botanical.

plant verb

These seeds should be ***planted*** *in the Spring.*
- sow, put in the ground

- To move a plant from where it was growing and plant it somewhere else is to transplant it.

plaster noun
The nurse put a plaster on the cut.
- dressing, sticking plaster, bandage

plate noun
1 *She piled their plates with food.*
FOR ITEMS OF CROCKERY
SEE **crockery**
2 *The robot's body was formed of metal plates.*
- panel, sheet
3 *The book includes colour plates of various flowers.*
- illustration, photo, picture

platform noun
The conductor stood on a platform to address the audience.
- dias, podium, stage, stand

play noun
1 *There was a good play on TV last night.*
- drama, performance, production
2 *It is important to balance work and play.*
- playing, recreation, amusement, fun, games, sport
FOR VARIOUS GAMES AND SPORTS
SEE **game, sport**

play verb
1 *The children went out to play.*
- amuse yourself, have fun, romp about
2 *Do you like playing basketball?*
- take part in, participate in, compete in
3 *We are playing the home team next week.*
- compete against, oppose, challenge, take on
4 *Mira played the piano at the school concert.*
- perform on
5 *My sister played Goldilocks in the school play.*
- act, take the part of, portray, represent

player noun
1 *You need four players for this game.*
- contestant, participant, competitor
2 *How many players are in the orchestra?*
- performer, instrumentalist, musician
- Someone who plays music on their own is a soloist.
FOR VARIOUS PERFORMERS
SEE **entertainer, music**

playful adjective
The kittens were in a playful mood.
- lively, spirited, frisky, mischievous, roguish, impish, joking, teasing
OPPOSITE serious

playground noun
FOR PLAYGROUND GAMES
SEE **game**

playing field noun
There is a training session on the playing field tomorrow.
- ground, pitch, sports ground

playpark noun SEE **park** noun

plea noun
The king ignored the captives' plea for mercy.
- appeal, request, entreaty, petition

plead verb
to plead with
The children pleaded with the witch to let them go.
- beg, entreat, implore, appeal to, ask, request, petition

pleasant adjective
1 *The owner of the shop is always pleasant to us.*
- kind, friendly, likeable, charming, amiable, amicable, cheerful, genial, good-natured, good-humoured, approachable, hospitable, welcoming
2 *We spent a very pleasant evening playing cards.*
- pleasing, enjoyable, agreeable, delightful, lovely, entertaining
3 *The weather is quite pleasant today.*
- fine, mild, sunny, warm
OPPOSITE unpleasant

a
b
c
d
e
f
g
h
i
j
k
l
m
n
o
p
q
r
s
t
u
v
w
x
y
z

please verb
1 *I hope my present will **please** you.*
- give pleasure to, make happy, satisfy, delight, amuse, entertain
2 *Do as you **please**.*
- want, wish

pleased adjective
*Why do you look so **pleased** today?*
- contented, delighted, elated, glad, grateful, happy, satisfied, thankful, thrilled
OPPOSITE annoyed

pleasure noun
1 *Mrs Ramsay gets a lot of **pleasure** from her garden.*
- delight, enjoyment, happiness, joy, satisfaction, comfort, contentment, gladness
- Very great pleasure is bliss or ecstasy.
2 *He talked about the **pleasures** of living in the country.*
- joy, comfort, delight

pleat noun
*It takes ages to iron the **pleats** in the skirt.*
- crease, fold, tuck

pledge noun
*The knights swore a **pledge** of loyalty to the king.*
- oath, vow, promise, word

plentiful adjective
*There is a **plentiful** supply of berries in the forest.*
- abundant, ample, generous, inexhaustible, lavish, liberal, profuse
OPPOSITE scarce

plenty noun
*Don't buy any milk—there's **plenty** in the fridge.*
- a lot, a large amount, an abundance, a profusion
- A lot more than you need is a glut or surplus.
OPPOSITE scarcity

plenty of
*We've still got **plenty of** time.*
- a lot of, lots of, ample, abundant
- (*informal*) loads of, masses of, tons of

plight noun
*He was concerned about the **plight** of the homeless.*
- predicament, trouble, difficulty, problem, dilemma

plod verb
1 *The hikers **plodded** on through the mud.*
- tramp, trudge, lumber
2 *She's still **plodding** away at her violin lessons.*
- drudge, slog, labour, persevere

plot noun
1 *Guy Fawkes was part of a **plot** against the government.*
- conspiracy, scheme, secret plan
2 *It was hard to follow the **plot** of the film.*
- story, storyline, narrative, thread
3 *They bought a **plot** of ground to build a new house.*
- area, piece, lot, patch
- A plot of ground for growing flowers or vegetables is an allotment.
- A large plot of land is a tract of land.

plot verb
1 *The gang were **plotting** a daring bank raid.*
- plan, devise, concoct, hatch
- (*informal*) cook up
2 *They were accused of **plotting** against the queen.*
- conspire, intrigue, scheme
3 *The captain **plotted** the course of the ship.*
- chart, map, mark

plough verb
1 *Tractors are used to **plough** the fields.*
- cultivate, till, turn over
2 *Are you still **ploughing** through that book?*
- wade, labour, toil

pluck verb
1 *They **plucked** the apples off the tree.*
- pick, pull off, gather, collect, harvest

2 *A seagull **plucked** the sandwich out of her hand.*
- grab, seize, snatch, jerk, pull, tug, yank

3 *The guitarist **plucked** the strings very gently.*
- To run your finger or plectrum across the strings of a guitar is to strum.
- To pluck the strings of a violin or cello is to play pizzicato.

plug noun
*They removed the **plug** in the side of the barrel.*
- stopper, cork, bung

plug verb
1 *Dad managed to **plug** the leak in the pipe.*
- stop up, block, close, fill, seal, bung up

2 *(informal) We asked the local radio station to **plug** our concert.*
- advertise, publicize, promote, push

plump adjective
*The goblin was short and **plump**, with pointy ears.*
- chubby, dumpy, fat, tubby, podgy, round, stout, portly
- OPPOSITE skinny

plunder verb
*Viking raiders **plundered** the village.*
- loot, pillage, raid, ransack, rob, steal from

plunge verb
1 *One by one, the girls **plunged** into the pool.*
- dive, jump, leap, throw yourself

2 *As the wind died down, the kite **plunged** to the ground.*
- drop, fall, pitch, tumble, plummet, swoop

3 *I **plunged** my hand in the cold water.*
- dip, lower, sink, immerse, submerge

4 *Finn **plunged** his spear into the dragon's throat.*
- thrust, stab, push, stick, shove, force

plural adjective
- OPPOSITE singular

poem noun

> **WORD WEB**
>
> *We each wrote a **poem** about the seaside.*
> - rhyme
> - Poems are poetry or verse.
> - A group of lines forming a section of a poem is a stanza.
> - A pair of rhyming lines within a poem is a couplet.
> - The rhythm of a poem is its metre.
>
> SOME KINDS OF POEM
> ballad, cinquain, clerihew, concrete poem, elegy, epic, free verse, haiku, limerick, lyric, narrative poem, nonsense verse, nursery rhyme, ode, sonnet, tanka

poetic adjective
*The opening chapter is written in a **poetic** style.*
- expressive, imaginative, lyrical, poetical
- An uncomplimentary synonym is flowery.

point noun
1 *Be careful—that knife has a very sharp **point**.*
- tip, end, spike, prong

2 *The stars looked like **points** of light in the sky.*
- dot, spot, speck, fleck

3 *He marked on the map the exact **point** where the treasure lay.*
- location, place, position, site

4 *At that **point** the rain started to come down.*
- moment, instant, time

5 *I agree with your last **point**.*
- idea, argument, thought

6 *His sense of humour is one of his good **points**.*
- characteristic, feature, attribute

7 *There is no **point** in phoning at this hour.*
- purpose, reason, aim, object, use, usefulness

8 *I think I missed the **point** of that film.*
- meaning, essence, core, gist

a
b
c
d
e
f
g
h
i
j
k
l
m
n
o
p
q
r
s
t
u
v
w
x
y
z

a
b
c
d
e
f
g
h
i
j
k
l
m
n
o
p
q
r
s
t
u
v
w
x
y
z

point verb

1 *She **pointed** the way.*
- draw attention to, indicate, point out, show, signal

2 *Can you **point** me in the right direction for the station?*
- aim, direct, guide, lead, steer

pointless adjective

*It's **pointless** to argue with him—he's so stubborn.*
- useless, futile, vain
- OPPOSITE worthwhile

poise noun

*The young actress showed great **poise** for her age.*
- calmness, composure, assurance, self-confidence

poised adjective

*The jaguar was **poised** to pounce on its prey.*
- ready, waiting, prepared, set

poison noun

- A poison to kill plants is herbicide or weedkiller.
- A poison to kill insects is insecticide or pesticide.
- The poison in a snake bite is venom.
- A substance which can save you from the effects of a poison is an antidote.

poisonous adjective

*Some of those mushrooms may be **poisonous**.*
- toxic, venomous, deadly, lethal

poke verb

*Someone **poked** me in the back with an umbrella.*
- prod, dig, jab, stab, thrust

to poke out

*The kitten's head was **poking out** of the basket.*
- stick out, project, protrude

polar adjective

WORD WEB

*The **polar** expedition will study birds and sealife.*
- Antarctic or Arctic

THINGS YOU MIGHT SEE IN POLAR REGIONS

glacier, iceberg, ice field or ice cap, moss, permafrost, pack ice, sheet ice, tundra
SEE ALSO **ice**

SOME ANIMALS WHICH LIVE IN POLAR REGIONS

albatross, arctic fox, arctic tern, narwhal, penguin, polar bear, reindeer, seal, walrus, whale, wolf

THINGS A POLAR EXPLORER MIGHT USE

goggles, huskies, ice-pick, kayak, mittens, parka, skis, ski pole, sledge, snowmobile, snowshoes

pole noun

*Four **poles** marked the corners of the field.*
- post, bar, rod, stick, shaft
- A pole that you use when walking or as a weapon is a staff.
- A pole for a flag to fly from is a flagpole.
- A pole to support sails on a boat or ship is a mast or spar.
- A pole with a pointed end to stick in the ground is a stake.
- Poles which a circus entertainer walks on are stilts.

police officer noun

*Several **police officers** were patrolling the football ground.*
- policeman or policewoman, officer, constable
- (*informal*) cop, copper
- Police officers of higher rank are sergeant, inspector, and superintendent.
- The head of a police force is the chief constable.
- Someone training for the police force is a cadet.
- Someone who investigates crimes is a detective.
SEE ALSO **detective**

policy noun

*The leaflet explains the school's **policy** on bullying.*

- approach, strategy, stance, plan of action

polish verb

*Beeswax is used to **polish** furniture.*

- rub down, shine, buff, burnish, wax

to polish something off

*The girls **polished off** a whole plate of sandwiches.*

- finish, get through, eat up

polish noun

*The silverware had been cleaned to give it a good **polish**.*

- shine, sheen, gloss, lustre, sparkle, brightness, glaze, finish

polished adjective

1 *She could see her face in the **polished** surface.*

- shining, shiny, bright, glassy, gleaming, glossy, lustrous
  OPPOSITE dull, tarnished

2 *The orchestra gave a **polished** performance.*

- accomplished, skilful, faultless, perfect, well prepared

polite adjective

*My aunt is always **polite** to visitors.*

- courteous, well-mannered, respectful, civil, well-behaved, gracious, gentlemanly or ladylike, chivalrous, gallant
  OPPOSITE rude, impolite

politics noun

WORD WEB

SOME WORDS USED IN POLITICS
alliance, ballot, cabinet, campaign, devolution, election, government, left-wing, lobby, majority, manifesto, parliament, party, policy, referendum, right-wing, vote

poll noun

*The result of the **poll** has been declared.*

- election, vote, ballot

- A vote on a particular question by all the people in a country is a referendum.
- An official survey to find out about the population is a census.

pollute verb

*The river has been **polluted** by chemicals.*

- contaminate, infect, poison

pompous adjective

*The giant spoke in a rather **pompous** manner.*

- arrogant, self-important, haughty, snobbish
- (*informal*) stuck-up
  OPPOSITE modest

pond noun SEE **pool**

pool noun

1 *The surface of the **pool** was covered with frogspawn.*

- pond
- A larger area of water is a lake or (in Scotland) a loch.
- A small shallow area of water is a puddle.
- A pool of water in the desert is an oasis.
- A pool among rocks on a seashore is a rock pool.

2 *The sports centre has an indoor and an outdoor **pool**.*

- swimming pool, swimming bath

poor adjective

1 *You can't afford luxuries if you're **poor**.*

- impoverished, poverty-stricken, penniless, needy, badly off, hard-up
  OPPOSITE rich

2 *His handwriting is very **poor**.*

- bad, inferior, inadequate, incompetent, unsatisfactory, shoddy, weak, worthless
  OPPOSITE good, superior

3 *They pitied the **poor** animals standing in the rain.*

- unlucky, unfortunate, pitiful, wretched
  OPPOSITE lucky

a
b
c
d
e
f
g
h
i
j
k
l
m
n
o
p
q
r
s
t
u
v
w
x
y
z

a b c d e f g h i j k l m n o **p** q r s t u v w x y z

poorly adjective
*He stayed at home because he felt **poorly**.*
- ill, sick, unwell, unfit
  OPPOSITE well

pop noun, verb FOR VARIOUS SOUNDS
  SEE **sound** noun

popular adjective
1 *Disney has made a lot of **popular** children's films.*
- well-liked, well-loved, celebrated, favourite
  OPPOSITE unpopular
2 *Rollerblades are very **popular** just now.*
- fashionable, widespread, current, in demand
- (*informal*) trendy
  OPPOSITE unpopular

population noun
*About ten per cent of the world's **population** is left-handed.*
- inhabitants, residents, occupants, citizens, people, community

pore verb
to pore over
*The detective **pored over** the evidence on his desk.*
- examine, study, inspect, look closely at, scrutinize

port noun
*A large cruise ship sailed into the **port**.*
- harbour, dock, anchorage
- A harbour for yachts and pleasure boats is a marina.

portable adjective
*They took a **portable** TV on holiday.*
- transportable, mobile, compact, lightweight
- A portable phone is a mobile phone.
- A portable computer is a laptop or notebook.

portion noun
*Violet asked for a large **portion** of trifle.*
- helping, serving, ration, share, quantity, piece, part, bit, slice

portrait noun
*There's a **portrait** of the Queen on every stamp.*
- picture, image, likeness, representation
- A portrait which shows a side view of someone is a profile.
- A portrait which shows just the outline of someone is a silhouette.
- A portrait which exaggerates some aspect of a person is a caricature.

portray verb
*The film **portrays** life in Victorian England.*
- depict, represent, show, describe, illustrate

pose verb
*The film star **posed** in front of the camera.*
- model, sit
to pose as someone
*The spy **posed as** a newspaper reporter.*
- impersonate, pretend to be, pass yourself off as

posh adjective (*informal*)
*We went to a **posh** restaurant for a treat.*
- smart, stylish, high-class, elegant, fashionable, up-market, luxurious, luxury, deluxe, plush
- (*informal*) classy, swanky, swish, snazzy

position noun
1 *Mark the **position** on the map.*
- location, place, point, spot, site, whereabouts
2 *He shifted his **position** to avoid getting cramp.*
- pose, posture, stance
3 *Losing all her money put her in a difficult **position**.*
- situation, state, condition, circumstances
4 *A referee should adopt a neutral **position**.*
- opinion, attitude, outlook, view
5 *Being a head teacher is an important **position**.*
- job, post, appointment, function

positive adjective

1 *The detective was **positive** that the cook was lying.*
- certain, sure, convinced, assured, confident
  OPPOSITE uncertain

2 *Miss Andrews made some **positive** comments on my singing.*
- helpful, useful, worthwhile, beneficial, constructive
  OPPOSITE negative

possess verb

1 *They don't **possess** a computer.*
- have, own

2 *What **possessed** you to take up diving?*
- make you think of, come over you

possessions plural noun

*The refugees had lost all of their **possessions**.*
- belongings, goods, property

possibility noun

*There's a **possibility** that it may rain later.*
- chance, likelihood, danger, risk

possible adjective

1 *Is it **possible** that life exists on other planets?*
- likely, probable, conceivable, credible

2 *It wasn't **possible** to shift the piano.*
- feasible, practicable, practical
  OPPOSITE impossible

possibly adverb

*'Will you finish your homework today?' '**Possibly**.'*
- maybe, perhaps

post noun

1 *The farmer put up some **posts** for a new fence.*
- pole, pillar, shaft, stake, support, prop

2 *The **post** was delivered late.*
- mail, letters, delivery

3 *Are you thinking of applying for the **post**?*
- job, position, situation, appointment, vacancy

post verb

1 *Did you **post** those letters?*
- mail, send, dispatch

2 *The names of the winners will be **posted** on the noticeboard.*
- display, put up, announce, advertise

poster noun

*We saw a **poster** about a missing cat.*
- advertisement, announcement, bill, notice, sign, placard

postpone verb

*They **postponed** the match because of bad weather.*
- put off, defer, delay
- To stop a game or meeting that you intend to start again later is to adjourn or suspend it.

pot noun

*On the table were little **pots** of jam and honey.*
- jar, dish, bowl, pan

potent adjective

1 *The magic potion is very **potent**, so you only need a single drop.*
- strong, powerful, intoxicating, pungent, heady

2 *She persuaded us with her **potent** arguments.*
- effective, forceful, strong, compelling
  OPPOSITE weak

potential adjective

1 *He's a **potential** champion.*
- budding, future, likely, possible, probable, promising

2 *These floods are a **potential** disaster for the farmers.*
- looming, threatening

potion noun

*A magic **potion** was brewing in the wizard's cauldron.*
- drug, medicine, mixture

a b c d e f g h i j k l m n o **p** q r s t u v w x y z

a
b
c
d
e
f
g
h
i
j
k
l
m
n
o
p
q
r
s
t
u
v
w
x
y
z

pottery noun

> **WORD WEB**
> • Someone who creates pottery is a potter.
> • A formal word for pottery is ceramics.
> TYPES OF POTTERY
> bone china, china, earthenware, porcelain, stoneware, terracotta
> • The kind of pottery we eat and drink from is crockery.

pouch noun
The pirate kept his gunpowder in a leather pouch.
• bag, purse, sack

poultry noun

> **WORD WEB**
> KINDS OF POULTRY
> bantam, chicken, duck, fowl, goose, guinea fowl, hen, pullet, turkey
> • A male chicken specially fattened for eating is a capon.

pounce verb
to pounce on
The cat pounced on the mouse.
• jump on, leap on, spring on, swoop down on, lunge at, ambush, attack

pound verb
Huge waves pounded the stranded ship.
• beat, hit, batter, smash
• To pound something hard until it is powder is to crush, grind, or pulverize it.
• To pound something soft is to knead, mash, or pulp it.

pour verb
1 *Water poured through the hole.*
• flow, run, gush, stream, spill, spout
2 *I poured some milk into my cup.*
• tip, serve

poverty noun
Many of the townspeople were living in poverty.
• pennilessness, hardship, need, want

• *Extreme poverty is known as* abject *poverty.*
OPPOSITE wealth

powder noun
The fairy sprinked some magic powder in the air.
• dust, particles

powdery adjective
The wind blew the powdery soil away.
• dusty, fine, loose, grainy, sandy

power noun
1 *They were amazed by the power of the robot.*
• strength, force, might, energy
2 *The storyteller has the power to enthrall an audience.*
• skill, talent, ability, competence
3 *A policeman has the power to arrest someone.*
• authority, right
4 *The empress had power over all the people.*
• authority, command, control, dominance, domination

powerful adjective
1 *Sir Joustalot was the most powerful knight in the kingdom.*
• influential, leading, commanding, dominant, high-powered
2 *The wrestler had a powerful punch.*
• strong, forceful, hard, mighty, vigorous, formidable, potent
3 *He used some powerful arguments.*
• strong, convincing, effective, persuasive, impressive
OPPOSITE powerless, weak

powerless adjective
The good fairy was powerless to undo the spell.
• helpless, ineffective, weak, feeble, defenceless

practical adjective
1 *I'll ask Katie what to do—she is always very practical.*
• down-to-earth, matter-of-fact, sensible, level-headed
OPPOSITE impractical

2 *The robbers' plan was not very* **practical**.

- workable, realistic, sensible, feasible, viable, achievable
  OPPOSITE impractical

3 *Do you have any* **practical** *experience of childminding?*

- real, actual, hands-on
  OPPOSITE theoretical

practically adverb
Keep going—we're **practically** *there!*

- almost, just about, nearly, virtually

practice noun
1 *We have extra football* **practice** *this week.*

- training, exercises, preparation, rehearsal, drill

2 *Is it the* **practice** *amongst ogres to eat grubs for breakfast?*

- custom, habit, convention, routine

in practice
What will the plan involve **in practice**?

- in effect, in reality, actually, really

practise verb
1 *My piano teacher asked me to* **practise** *for longer.*

- do exercises, rehearse, train, drill
- To practise just before the start of a performance is to warm up.

2 *My sister wants to* **practise** *veterinary medicine.*

- do, perform, carry out, put into practice, follow, pursue

praise verb
The critics **praised** *the actress for her outstanding performance.*

- commend, applaud, admire, compliment, congratulate, pay tribute to
- (*informal*) rave about
  OPPOSITE criticize

praise noun
She received a lot of **praise** *for her painting.*

- approval, admiration, compliments, congratulations, applause

prance verb
Milly started **prancing** *about in a silly way.*

- dance, skip, hop, leap, romp, cavort, caper, frolic, gambol

precarious adjective
1 *The diver was in a* **precarious** *situation, surrounded by sharks.*

- dangerous, perilous, risky

2 *Take care—that ladder looks* **precarious**!

- unsafe, unstable, unsteady, insecure, shaky, wobbly, rickety
  OPPOSITE secure

precede verb
A fireworks display **preceded** *the concert.*

- come before, go before, lead
  OPPOSITE follow, succeed

precious adjective
1 *Her most* **precious** *possession was an old photograph.*

- treasured, cherished, valued, prized, dearest, beloved

2 *The throne glittered with* **precious** *gems and gold.*

- valuable, costly, expensive, priceless
  FOR PRECIOUS STONES
  SEE **jewel, jewellery**
  OPPOSITE worthless

precise adjective
1 *Can you tell me the* **precise** *time, please?*

- exact, accurate, correct, true, right
  OPPOSITE rough

2 *The map gave* **precise** *directions for finding the treasure.*

- careful, detailed, specific, particular, definite
  OPPOSITE vague

predict verb
You can't **predict** *what may happen in the future.*

- forecast, foresee, foretell, prophesy

a
b
c
d
e
f
g
h
i
j
k
l
m
n
o
p
q
r
s
t
u
v
w
x
y
z

a
b
c
d
e
f
g
h
i
j
k
l
m
n
o
p
q
r
s
t
u
v
w
x
y
z

predictable adjective
*It was **predictable** that it would rain.*
- expected, foreseeable, likely, probable

OPPOSITE unpredictable

preface noun
*The story behind the book is explained in the **preface**.*
- introduction, prologue

prefer verb
*Would you **prefer** juice or lemonade?*
- rather have, go for, opt for, plump for, choose, fancy

preferable adjective
preferable to
*She finds country life **preferable to** living in the city.*
- better than, superior to, more attractive than, more suitable than

preference noun
1 *Sandy has a **preference** for sweet things.*
- liking, fancy, inclination

2 *My **preference** is to walk rather than take the bus.*
- choice, option, selection, pick, wish

prefix noun
OPPOSITE suffix

pregnant adjective
*One of the giraffes in the zoo is **pregnant**.*
- expecting a baby, carrying a baby
- (*informal*) expecting
- A pregnant woman is an expectant mother.

prehistoric adjective

> **WORD WEB**
>
> PREHISTORIC REMAINS YOU MIGHT VISIT
> barrow or tumulus, cromlech or stone circle, dolmen, hill fort, menhir or standing stone

- A person who studies prehistory by excavating and analysing remains is an archaeologist.
  NAMES OF PREHISTORIC PERIODS
- The best tools and weapons were made of stone in the Stone Age, of bronze in the Bronze Age, and of iron in the Iron Age.
- Formal names for the Old, Middle, and New Stone Ages are Palaeolithic, Mesolithic, and Neolithic periods.
- Prehistoric people who lived during the Stone Age were Neanderthals.
- Most of the earth's surface was covered with ice in the Ice Age.
  SEE ALSO **cave** noun
  SOME PREHISTORIC ANIMALS
  cave bear, dinosaur, glyptodon, ground sloth, sabre-toothed cat or smilodon, sabre-toothed squirrel, woolly mammoth, woolly rhino
- A person who studies fossils of prehistoric life is a palaeontologist.
  SEE ALSO **dinosaur**

prejudice noun
*The school has a policy against racial **prejudice**.*
- bias, discrimination, intolerance, narrow-mindedness, bigotry
- Prejudice against other races is racism.
- Prejudice against other nations is xenophobia.
- Prejudice against the other sex is sexism.

OPPOSITE fairness, tolerance

preliminary adjective
*They were knocked out in the **preliminary** round of the competition.*
- first, initial, introductory, early, opening, preparatory

prelude noun SEE **introduction**

premises plural noun
*Keep out—these are private **premises**.*
- buildings, property, grounds

preoccupied adjective
preoccupied with something
> She was so **preoccupied with** her work that she forgot the time.

- absorbed in, engrossed in, wrapped up in, intent on, obsessed with

prepare verb
> The museum staff are **preparing** for the new exhibition.

- get ready, make arrangements for, organize, plan, set up
- To prepare for a play is to rehearse.
- To prepare to take part in a sport is to train.

prepared adjective
> The knights were **prepared** to fight for the queen.

- be able, be ready, be willing

presence noun
> Your **presence** is required upstairs.

- attendance

present adjective
1 Is everyone **present**?
- here, in attendance, at hand
2 Who is the **present** world chess champion?
- current, existing

present noun
> What would you like for your birthday **present**?

- gift
- (informal) prezzie

present verb
1 The head **presents** the prizes on sports day.
- award, hand over
2 Our class is **presenting** a play about the Vikings.
- put on, perform, stage, mount
3 Dr Smart **presented** her amazing invention to the world.
- put forward, show, display, exhibit, make known

preserve verb
1 It's more difficult to **preserve** food in hot weather.
- keep, save, store

2 It's important to **preserve** wildlife.
- look after, protect, conserve, defend, safeguard, maintain
OPPOSITE destroy

press verb
1 **Press** the fruit through a sieve to get rid of the seeds.
- push, force, squeeze, squash, crush, shove, cram, compress
2 She **pressed** her blouse for the party.
- iron, flatten, smooth
3 Our friends **pressed** us to stay a bit longer.
- beg, urge, entreat, implore

press noun
1 We read about the competition in the **press**.
- newspapers, magazines
2 The **press** came to the opening of the new arts centre.
- journalists, reporters, the media

pressure noun
1 The nurse applied **pressure** to the wound.
- force, compression, squeezing, weight, load
2 In the final, the home team were under a lot of **pressure**.
- stress, strain, tension

prestige noun
> There's a lot of **prestige** in winning an Olympic medal.

- credit, glory, fame, honour, renown, distinction, status, kudos

presume verb
1 I **presume** you'd like something to eat.
- assume, take it, imagine, suppose, think, believe, guess
2 He wouldn't **presume** to tell her what to do!
- be bold enough, dare, venture

pretend verb
> She's not really crying—she's only **pretending**.

- put on an act, bluff, fake, sham, pose
- (informal) kid, put it on

pretend · adjective
*That's not a real spider—it's just a **pretend** one!*
- fake, false, artificial, made-up
OPPOSITE real

pretty adjective
*The doll was dressed in a **pretty** blue outfit.*
- attractive, beautiful, lovely, nice, pleasing, charming, dainty, picturesque, quaint
- (*informal*) cute
- A common simile is as pretty as a picture.
OPPOSITE ugly

prevent verb
1 *The driver could do nothing to **prevent** the accident.*
- stop, avert, avoid, head off
2 *The police **prevented** an attempted bank raid.*
- block, foil, frustrate, thwart
3 *There's not much you can do to **prevent** colds.*
- stave off, ward off

previous adjective
1 *The couple had met on a **previous** occasion.*
- earlier, former
2 *The **previous** owners of the house have gone abroad.*
- preceding
OPPOSITE subsequent

prey noun
*The lion killed its **prey**.*
- quarry, victim

prey verb
to prey on
*Owls **prey on** small animals.*
- hunt, kill, feed on

price noun
*What is the **price** of a return ticket to Sydney?*
- cost, amount, figure, expense, payment, sum, charge, rate
- The price you pay for a journey on public transport is a fare.
- The price you pay to send a letter is the postage.

- The price you pay to use a private road, bridge, or tunnel is a toll.

priceless adjective
1 *The museum contained many **priceless** antiques.*
- precious, rare, valuable, costly, expensive, dear
2 (*informal*) *The joke she told was **priceless**.*
- funny, amusing, comic, hilarious, witty

prick verb
*Jamie burst the balloon by **pricking** it with a pin.*
- pierce, puncture, stab, jab, perforate

prickle noun
*A hedgehog uses its **prickles** for defence.*
- spike, spine, needle, barb, thorn
- The prickles on a hedgehog or porcupine are also called quills.

prickly adjective
*Holly leaves are very **prickly**.*
- spiky, spiny, thorny, bristly, sharp, scratchy

pride noun
1 *Mr Dodds takes great **pride** in his garden.*
- satisfaction, pleasure, delight
2 *The medal winner was a source of great **pride** to his family.*
- self-esteem, self-respect, dignity, honour
3 ***Pride** comes before a fall.*
- arrogance, conceit, bigheadedness, vanity, snobbery
OPPOSITE humility

priest noun
*The **priest** conducted the wedding ceremony.*
- minister, vicar, pastor, padre
- A Buddhist religious leader is a lama.
- A Hindu or Sikh religious leader is a guru.
- A Jewish religious leader is a rabbi.
- A Muslim religious leader is an imam.
- An ancient Celtic priest was a Druid.

prim adjective
*Aunt Jemima is always very **prim** and proper.*
- prudish, strait-laced, formal, demure

primarily adverb
*The website is aimed **primarily** at teenagers.*
- chiefly, especially, mainly, mostly, predominantly, principally, above all

primary adjective
*Their **primary** aim was to win the match.*
- main, chief, principal, foremost, major, most important, top, prime
FOR PRIMARY COLOURS
SEE **colour** noun

prime adjective
1 *The penguins' **prime** concern is to protect their chicks.*
SEE **primary**
2 *The dish is made with **prime** cuts of meat.*
- best, superior, first-class, choice, select, top

primitive adjective
1 ***Primitive** humans were hunters rather than farmers.*
- ancient, early, prehistoric, primeval
OPPOSITE civilized
2 *These days steam engines seem very **primitive**.*
- crude, basic, simple, rudimentary, undeveloped
OPPOSITE advanced

prince, princess nouns SEE **royalty**

principal adjective
*The **principal** aim of the race is to raise money for charity.*
- main, chief, primary, foremost, most important, leading, major, dominant, fundamental, supreme, top

principle noun
*Both teams agreed to follow the **principles** of fair play.*
- rule, standard, code, ethic

print noun
1 *She found the tiny **print** difficult to read.*
- lettering, letters, printing, type, characters
2 *The detective searched the building for **prints**.*
- mark, impression, footprint, fingerprint
3 *Is that a **print** or an original painting?*
- copy, reproduction, duplicate

priority noun
*Traffic on the main road has **priority**.*
- precedence, right of way

prise verb
*He tried to **prise** the lid off the treasure chest.*
- lever, force, wrench

prison noun
*He was sentenced to six months in **prison**.*
- jail, imprisonment, confinement

prisoner noun
*The **prisoner** tried to escape from jail.*
- convict, captive, inmate
- A person who is held prisoner until some demand is met is a hostage.

private adjective
1 *Everything I write in my diary is **private**.*
- secret, confidential, personal, intimate
- Secret official documents are classified documents.
2 *Can we go somewhere a little more **private**?*
- quiet, secluded, hidden, concealed
OPPOSITE public

privilege noun
*Club members enjoy special **privileges**.*
- advantage, benefit, concession, right

privileged adjective
*She comes from a **privileged** family background.*
- advantaged, wealthy, fortunate, affluent, prosperous

a
b
c
d
e
f
g
h
i
j
k
l
m
n
o
p
q
r
s
t
u
v
w
x
y
z

prize noun

*Our team won first **prize** in the relay race.*

- award, reward, trophy
- Money that you win as a prize is your winnings.
- Prize money that keeps increasing until someone wins it is a jackpot.

prize verb

*Chrissie **prized** her grandmother's ring above all else.*

- treasure, value, cherish, hold dear, esteem, revere

OPPOSITE dislike

probable adjective

*A burst pipe was the most **probable** cause of the flood.*

- likely, feasible, possible, predictable, expected

OPPOSITE improbable

probe verb

1 *The submarine can **probe** the depths of the ocean.*
- explore, penetrate, see into, plumb
2 *Detectives **probed** the circumstances surrounding the crime.*
- investigate, inquire into, look into, examine, study

problem noun

1 *Our maths teacher set us a difficult **problem**.*
- puzzle, question
- (*informal*) brainteaser, poser
2 *I'm having a **problem** with my computer.*
- difficulty, trouble, snag, worry
- (*informal*) headache

procedure noun

*The recipe explains the **procedure** for making bread.*

- method, process, system, technique, way
- A procedure which you follow regularly is a routine.

proceed verb

1 *The sheep **proceeded** slowly along the path.*
- go on, advance, move forward, progress
2 *We advised them not to **proceed** with their plan.*
- go ahead, carry on

proceedings plural noun

*A thunderstorm interrupted the day's **proceedings**.*

- events, happenings, activities, affairs
- (*informal*) goings-on

proceeds plural noun

*They added up the **proceeds** from the jumble sale.*

- income, takings, money, earnings, profit

process noun

*The inventor showed us a new **process** for creating electricity.*

- method, procedure, operation, system, technique

process verb

*The dairy **processes** milk to make butter and cheese.*

- deal with, prepare, treat, refine, transform

procession noun

*The **procession** made its way slowly down the hill.*

- parade, march, column, line

proclaim verb

*The judges **proclaimed** that the winner was disqualified.*

- declare, announce, pronounce

prod verb

*Someone **prodded** me in the back with an umbrella.*

- poke, dig, jab, nudge, push

produce verb

1 *Some lorries **produce** a lot of fumes.*
- create, generate, cause, give rise to
2 *The tree **produced** a good crop of apples this year.*
- grow, yield
3 *The factory **produces** cars and vans.*
- make, manufacture, construct

4 *The referee's decision **produced** whistles from the crowd.*
- provoke, result in, arouse, stimulate

5 *The writers have **produced** an award-winning comedy.*
- compose, invent, think up

6 *The magician **produced** a rabbit from his hat.*
- bring out, present, reveal

produce noun
*The shop sells organic **produce**.*
- food, crops, fruit and vegetables

product noun
1 *The company launched a new range of beauty **products**.*
- item, article, substance

2 *The famine is the **product** of years of drought.*
- result, consequence, outcome, upshot

production noun
1 ***Production** at the factory has increased this year.*
- output

2 *We went to see a **production** of 'The Sound of Music'.*
- performance, show

productive adjective
1 *The soil here is rich and **productive**.*
- fertile, fruitful

2 *It wasn't a very **productive** meeting.*
- useful, valuable, worthwhile, constructive, profitable
- OPPOSITE unproductive

profession noun
*Nursing is a worthwhile **profession**.*
- career, job, occupation, work, employment, business

professional adjective
1 *The plans were drawn by a **professional** architect.*
- qualified, skilled, trained, experienced

2 *This is a very **professional** piece of work.*
- skilled, expert, proficient, competent, efficient
- OPPOSITE incompetent

3 *His ambition is to be a **professional** footballer.*
- paid, full-time
- OPPOSITE amateur

proficient adjective
*Olga is a **proficient** tap dancer.*
- skilful, skilled, accomplished, capable, expert, able
- OPPOSITE incompetent

profile noun SEE portrait

profit noun
*They sold the business and bought a yacht with the **profit**.*
- gain, surplus, excess
- The extra money you get on your savings is interest.
- OPPOSITE loss

programme noun
1 *We worked out a **programme** for sports day.*
- plan, schedule, timetable
- A list of things to be done at a meeting is an agenda.

2 *There was a really good **programme** on TV last night.*
- broadcast, show, production, transmission

progress noun
1 *I traced their **progress** on the map.*
- journey, route, movement, travels

2 *I'm not making much **progress** learning Dutch.*
- advance, development, growth, improvement, headway
- An important piece of progress is a breakthrough.

progress verb
*Work on the new building is **progressing** well.*
- proceed, advance, move forward, make progress, make headway, continue, develop, improve
- (informal) come along

prohibit verb
*Skateboarding is **prohibited** in the school grounds.*
- ban, forbid, outlaw, rule out, veto
- OPPOSITE permit, allow

a b c d e f g h i j k l m n o p q r s t u v w x y z

project noun
1 *We did a history **project** on the Victorians.*
- activity, task, assignment, piece of research
2 *There is a **project** to create a bird sanctuary in the area.*
- plan, proposal, scheme

project verb
1 *A narrow ledge **projects** from the cliff.*
- extend, protrude, stick out, jut out, overhang
2 *The lighthouse **projects** a beam of light.*
- cast, shine, throw out

prolong verb
*Our guests **prolonged** their visit by a few days.*
- extend, lengthen, make longer, stretch out, draw out
OPPOSITE shorten

prominent adjective
1 *The clown had a very **prominent** nose.*
- noticeable, conspicuous, obvious, striking, eye-catching
OPPOSITE inconspicuous
2 *He is a **prominent** Hollywood actor.*
- well-known, famous, celebrated, major, leading, notable, distinguished, eminent
OPPOSITE unknown

promise noun
1 *We had **promises** of help from many people.*
- assurance, pledge, guarantee, commitment, vow, oath, word of honour
2 *That young pianist shows **promise**.*
- potential, talent

promise verb
*Dad **promised** that we'd go camping this summer.*
- assure someone, give your word, guarantee, swear, take an oath, vow

promising adjective
1 *The weather looks **promising** for tomorrow.*
- encouraging, hopeful
2 *Sheena is a **promising** young singer.*
- bright, talented, gifted, budding
- (*informal*) up-and-coming

promote verb
1 *Gareth has been **promoted** to captain.*
- move up, advance, upgrade, elevate
2 *The singer is here to **promote** her new CD.*
- advertise, publicize, market, push, sell
- (*informal*) plug
3 *The school is trying to **promote** healthy eating.*
- encourage, foster, advocate, back, support

prompt adjective
*I received a **prompt** reply to my email.*
- punctual, quick, rapid, swift, immediate, instant
OPPOSITE delayed

prompt verb
*Having a dog **prompted** her to take more exercise.*
- cause, lead, induce, motivate, stimulate, encourage, provoke

prone adjective
1 *The victim was lying **prone** on the floor.*
- face down, on the front
- To lie face upwards is to be supine.
2 *He is **prone** to exaggerate his health problems.*
- inclined, apt, liable, likely

pronounce verb
1 *Try to **pronounce** the words clearly.*
- say, speak, utter, articulate, sound
2 *The doctor **pronounced** her fully recovered.*
- declare, announce, proclaim, judge

a
b
c
d
e
f
g
h
i
j
k
l
m
n
o
p
q
r
s
t
u
v
w
x
y
z

pronounced adjective

*She spoke with a **pronounced** Australian accent.*

- clear, marked, distinct, definite, noticeable, obvious, striking, unmistakable, prominent
  OPPOSITE imperceptible

proof noun

*There is no **proof** that he is a secret agent.*

- evidence, confirmation

prop noun

*The bridge is supported by steel **props**.*

- support, strut
- A stick to prop yourself on when you hurt a leg is a crutch.
- Part of a building which props up a wall is a buttress.

prop verb

*Kenny **propped** his bike against the kerb.*

- lean, rest, stand

to prop something up

*The shelf was **propped up** with sticks of wood.*

- support, hold up, reinforce

propel verb

*The steamboat was **propelled** by a huge paddlewheel.*

- drive forward, push forward, power, impel

proper adjective

1 *The nurse showed them the **proper** way to tie a bandage.*

- correct, right, accurate, precise, true, genuine
  OPPOSITE wrong, incorrect

2 *It's only **proper** that he should pay for the broken window.*

- fair, just, fitting, appropriate, deserved, suitable
  OPPOSITE inappropriate

3 *It's not **proper** to speak with your mouth full.*

- decent, respectable, tasteful
  OPPOSITE rude

4 *(informal) I looked a **proper** idiot wearing two different socks!*

- complete, total, utter, absolute, thorough

property noun

1 *This office deals with lost **property**.*

- belongings, possessions, goods

2 *The website lists **property** that is for sale in the city.*

- buildings, houses, land, premises

3 *Many herbs have healing **properties**.*

- quality, characteristic, feature, attribute, trait

prophecy noun

*The witch's **prophecy** came true.*

- prediction, forecast

prophesy verb

*The witch **prophesied** that there would be a great battle.*

- predict, forecast, foresee, foretell

proportion noun

1 *A large **proportion** of wild elephants live on nature reserves.*

- part, section, share, fraction

2 *What is the **proportion** of girls to boys in your class?*

- balance, ratio

proportions

*The dining hall was a room of large **proportions**.*

- measurements, size, dimensions

proposal noun

*What do you think of the **proposal** to build a skate park?*

- plan, project, scheme, suggestion, recommendation

propose verb

1 *He **proposed** a change in the rules.*

- suggest, ask for, recommend

2 *How do you **propose** to pay for the holiday?*

- intend, mean, plan, aim

3 *The class **proposed** two pupils to represent them on the school council.*

- nominate, put forward

a
b
c
d
e
f
g
h
i
j
k
l
m
n
o
p
q
r
s
t
u
v
w
x
y
z

proprietor noun
*Who is the **proprietor** of the bicycle shop?*
- manager, owner
- (*informal*) boss

prosecute verb
*Anyone caught shoplifting will be **prosecuted**.*
- bring to trial, charge, take to court
- To take someone to court to try to get money from them is to sue them.

prospect noun
1 *What are their **prospects** of winning the tournament?*
- chance, hope, expectation, likelihood, possibility, probability
2 *The hotel has a lovely **prospect** across the valley.*
- outlook, view, vista

prosper verb
*We expect our business to **prosper** this year.*
- do well, be successful, flourish, succeed, thrive, grow, boom
OPPOSITE fail

prosperity noun
*Tourism has brought **prosperity** to the region.*
- wealth, affluence, growth, success
- (*informal*) boom

prosperous adjective
*She used to be married to a **prosperous** businessman.*
- wealthy, rich, well-off, well-to-do, affluent, successful, thriving
OPPOSITE poor

protect verb
1 *A sentry was posted outside to **protect** the palace.*
- defend, guard, safeguard, keep safe, secure
2 *I wore a hat to **protect** myself from the sun.*
- shield, shade, screen, insulate

protection noun
*The waterproof hood gives **protection** from the rain.*
- shelter, cover, defence, insulation

protest noun
1 *There were **protests** at the plan to close the cinema.*
- complaint, objection
- A general protest is an outcry.
2 *Some streets will be closed for a **protest** in the city centre.*
- demonstration, march, rally
- (*informal*) demo

protest verb
*We wrote a letter **protesting** about the closure of the cinema.*
- complain, make a protest, object (to), take exception (to), express disapproval (of)

protrude verb
*His stomach **protrudes** above his waistband.*
- stick out, poke out, bulge, swell, project, stand out, jut out

proud adjective
1 *Jennie's father was very **proud** when she passed her music exam.*
- delighted (with), pleased (with)
- A common simile is as proud as a peacock.
2 *He's too **proud** to mix with the likes of us!*
- conceited, big-headed, arrogant, vain, haughty, self-important, snobbish, superior
- (*informal*) stuck-up
OPPOSITE humble

prove verb
*The evidence will **prove** that he is innocent.*
- confirm, demonstrate, establish, verify
OPPOSITE disprove

proverb noun SEE saying

provide verb
1 *We'll **provide** the juice if you bring the sandwiches.*
- bring, contribute, arrange for, lay on
- To provide food and drink for people is to cater for them.
2 *The ski centre can **provide** you with boots and skis.*
- supply, equip, furnish

a b c d e f g h i j k l m n o **p** q r s t u v w x y z

provisions plural noun
*We had enough **provisions** for two weeks.*
- food, rations, stores, supplies

provoke verb
1 *Don't do anything to **provoke** the lions!*
- annoy, irritate, anger, incense, infuriate, exasperate, tease, taunt, goad
- (*informal*) wind up
  OPPOSITE pacify
2 *The referee's decision **provoked** anger from the crowd.*
- arouse, produce, prompt, cause, generate, induce, stimulate, spark off, stir up, whip up

prowl verb
*Guard dogs **prowled** about the grounds of the palace.*
- roam, slink, sneak, creep, steal

prudent adjective
*It would be **prudent** to start saving some money.*
- wise, sensible, shrewd, thoughtful, careful, cautious
  OPPOSITE reckless, unwise

prune verb
*Mum **prunes** her roses every spring.*
- cut back, trim

pry verb
*I didn't mean to **pry**, but I overheard your conversation.*
- be curious, be inquisitive, interfere
- (*informal*) be nosy, nose about or around, snoop

to pry into something
*Mrs Snout was always **prying into** other people's business.*
- interfere in, meddle in, spy on
- (*informal*) poke your nose into

psychic adjective
*The sorceress was said to have **psychic** powers.*
- supernatural, telepathic

psychological adjective
*The doctor thinks her illness is **psychological**.*
- mental, emotional
  OPPOSITE physical

public adjective
1 *The **public** entrance is at the front of the gallery.*
- common, communal, general, open, shared
  OPPOSITE private
2 *The name of the author is now **public** knowledge.*
- well-known, acknowledged, published, open, general, universal
  OPPOSITE secret

public noun
the public
*This part of the castle is not open to **the public**.*
- people in general, everyone, the community, society, the nation

publication noun
*She's celebrating the **publication** of her first novel.*
- issuing, printing, production
- Various publications are books and magazines.

publicity noun
1 *Did you see the **publicity** for the book fair?*
- advertising, advertisements, promotion
2 *Famous people don't always enjoy **publicity**.*
- fame, exposure, limelight

publish verb
1 *The magazine is **published** every week.*
- issue, print, produce, bring out, release, circulate
2 *When will they **publish** the results?*
- announce, declare, disclose, make known, make public, report, reveal
- To publish information on radio or TV is to broadcast it.

a
b
c
d
e
f
g
h
i
j
k
l
m
n
o
p
q
r
s
t
u
v
w
x
y
z

a
b
c
d
e
f
g
h
i
j
k
l
m
n
o
P
q
r
s
t
u
v
w
x
y
z

pudding noun
*Do you want any **pudding**?*
- dessert, sweet
- (informal) afters
FOR TYPES OF PUDDING
SEE **food**

puff noun
1 *A **puff** of wind caught his hat.*
- gust, breath, flurry
2 *A **puff** of smoke rose from the chimney.*
- cloud, whiff

puff verb
1 *The dragon **puffed** green smoke from its nostrils.*
- blow out, send out, emit, belch
2 *By the end of the race I was **puffing**.*
- breathe heavily, pant, gasp, wheeze
3 *The sails **puffed** out as the wind rose.*
- become inflated, billow, swell

pull verb
1 *She **pulled** her chair nearer to the desk.*
- drag, draw, haul, lug, trail, tow
OPPOSITE push
2 *Be careful—you nearly **pulled** my arm off!*
- tug, rip, wrench, jerk, pluck
to pull out
1 *The dentist **pulled out** one of his teeth.*
- extract, take out, remove
2 *He had to **pull out** of the race.*
- back out, withdraw, retire
to pull someone's leg
*I hope you aren't **pulling my leg**!*
- make fun of you, play a trick on you, tease you
to pull through
*It was a bad accident, but the doctors expect him to **pull through**.*
- get better, recover, revive, survive
to pull up
*The bus **pulled up** at the traffic lights.*
- draw up, stop, halt

pulse noun
*You can feel the **pulse** of blood in your veins.*
- beat, throb, drumming

pump verb
*The fire brigade **pumped** water out of the cellar.*
- drain, draw off, empty

- To move liquid from a higher container to a lower one through a tube is to siphon it.

punch verb
1 *Mrs Rafferty **punched** the robber on the nose.*
- jab, poke, prod, thump
FOR OTHER WAYS OF HITTING
SEE **hit** verb
2 *I need to **punch** a hole through the card.*
- bore, pierce

punctual adjective
*The bus was **punctual** today.*
- in good time, on time, prompt
OPPOSITE late

punctuation noun

🕸 **WORD WEB**

PUNCTUATION MARKS
apostrophe, brackets, colon, comma, dash, exclamation mark, full stop, hyphen, question mark, quotation marks or speech marks, semicolon, square brackets

OTHER MARKS USED IN WRITING
accent, asterisk or star, bullet point, slash

---

puncture noun
1 *I had a **puncture** on the way home.*
- burst tyre, flat tyre
2 *I found the **puncture** in my tyre.*
- hole, leak

puncture verb
*A nail **punctured** my tyre.*
- perforate, pierce, deflate, let down

punish verb
*Those responsible for the crime will be **punished**.*
- penalize, discipline, chastise

punishment noun
*The **punishment** for dropping litter is a hefty fine.*
- penalty
- Punishing someone by taking their life is capital punishment or execution.

puny adjective
*Miles was rather a **puny** child.*
- delicate, weak, feeble, frail, weedy
OPPOSITE strong, sturdy

pupil noun
*There are 33 **pupils** in our class.*
- schoolchild, student, learner, scholar
- Someone who follows a great teacher is a disciple.

purchase verb
*I'm saving my pocket money to **purchase** a bike.*
- buy, pay for, get, obtain, acquire

purchase noun
1 *She opened her bag and examined her **purchases**.*
- acquisition
2 *The climbers had difficulty getting any **purchase** on the ice.*
- grasp, hold, leverage

pure adjective
1 *The bracelet is made of **pure** gold.*
- authentic, genuine, real
2 *He was talking **pure** nonsense.*
- complete, absolute, utter, sheer, total
3 *All our dishes are made from **pure** ingredients.*
- natural, wholesome
4 *They swam in the **pure**, clear water of the lake.*
- clean, fresh, unpolluted
OPPOSITE impure

purify verb
*You can't drink this water unless you **purify** it.*
- clean, make pure
- You destroy germs by disinfecting or sterilizing things.
- You take solid particles out of liquids by filtering them.
- To purify water by boiling it and condensing the vapour is to distil it.
- To purify crude oil is to refine it.

purpose noun
1 *Have you got a particular **purpose** in mind?*
- intention, aim, end, goal, target, objective, outcome, result

2 *What's the **purpose** of your invention?*
- point, use, usefulness, value

purposeful adjective
*Sam barged into the room with a **purposeful** look on her face.*
- determined, decisive, positive
OPPOSITE aimless

purse noun
*I always keep some loose change in my **purse**.*
- money bag, pouch
- A purse which holds paper money and credit cards is a wallet.

pursue verb
1 *The thief ran off, **pursued** by two police officers.*
- chase, follow, run after, tail, track, hunt, trail, shadow
2 *She wants to **pursue** a career as a dancer.*
- follow, undertake, practise, conduct, carry on, continue, maintain, proceed with

pursuit noun
1 *The **pursuit** of the criminals lasted for months.*
- hunt (for), search (for), tracking, chase, trail
2 *The family enjoy many outdoor **pursuits**.*
- activity, pastime, hobby, interest

push verb
1 *We **pushed** our way through the crowd.*
- shove, thrust, force, propel, barge, elbow, jostle
OPPOSITE pull
2 *Pete **pushed** his things into a bag.*
- pack, press, cram, crush, compress, ram, squash, squeeze
3 *They **pushed** him to work even harder.*
- pressurize, press, drive, urge, compel, bully
- (*informal*) lean on
4 *The actress is **pushing** her latest film.*
- promote, publicize, advertise
- (*informal*) plug

a
b
c
d
e
f
g
h
i
j
k
l
m
n
o
p
q
r
s
t
u
v
w
x
y
z

a
b
c
d
e
f
g
h
i
j
k
l
m
n
o
p
q
r
s
t
u
v
w
x
y
z

put verb

1 *You can **put** your schoolbags in the corner.*
- place, set down, leave, deposit, dump, stand

2 *The dog **put** its head on my lap.*
- lay, lean, rest

3 *I'll **put** some pictures on the wall.*
- attach, fasten, fix, hang

4 *Where are they planning to **put** the car park?*
- locate, situate

5 *They **put** guards outside the bank.*
- position, post, station

6 *I'm not sure of the best way to **put** this.*
- express, word, phrase, say, state

to put someone off
*The colour of the food **put** me **off** eating.*
- deter, discourage, distract

to put something off
*They **put off** their journey because of the fog.*
- delay, postpone, defer

to put something out
*The firefighters quickly **put out** the blaze.*
- extinguish, quench, smother

to put something up
1 *It doesn't take long to **put up** the tent.*
- set up, construct, erect

2 *I'm going to buy a new bike before they **put up** the price.*
- increase, raise

to put up with something
*I don't know how you **put up with** that noise.*
- bear, stand, tolerate, endure

puzzle noun

*Has anyone managed to solve the **puzzle**?*
- question, mystery, riddle, conundrum, problem
- (*informal*) brainteaser, poser

puzzle verb

1 *Phil was **puzzled** by the mysterious message.*
- confuse, baffle, bewilder, bemuse, mystify, perplex, fox

2 *We **puzzled** over the problem for hours.*
- ponder, think, meditate, worry, brood

puzzled adjective

*Why are you looking so **puzzled**?*
- confused, baffled, bewildered, mystified, perplexed

puzzling adjective

*There was something **puzzling** about the signature on the letter.*
- confusing, baffling, bewildering, mystifying, perplexing, mysterious, inexplicable
OPPOSITE straightforward

pyramid noun

WORD WEB

THINGS FOUND INSIDE ANCIENT EGYPTIAN PYRAMIDS
burial chamber, coptic jar, hieroglyphics, mummy (of a pharaoh), papyrus, sarcophagus

- A pyramid which does not have smooth sides is a stepped pyramid.

quaint adjective

*They stayed in a **quaint** thatched cottage.*
- charming, picturesque, sweet, old-fashioned, old-world

quake verb

*The ground **quaked** with the thud of the giant's footsteps.*
- shake, shudder, tremble, quiver, shiver, vibrate, rock, sway, wobble

qualification noun

1 *What kind of **qualification** do you need to be a vet?*
- diploma, certificate, degree, knowledge, training, skill

2 *The committee approved the plan, but with some **qualifications**.*
- condition, reservation

qualified adjective

1 *This job needs a **qualified** electrician.*
- experienced, skilled, trained, professional
- OPPOSITE amateur

2 *He received **qualified** praise for his efforts.*
- limited, cautious, half-hearted

qualify verb

1 *The licence **qualifies** him to work as a private detective.*
- authorize, permit, allow, entitle

2 *The first three runners will **qualify** to take part in the final.*
- get through, pass, be eligible

3 *She felt the need to **qualify** her remarks.*
- limit, modify, restrict, soften, weaken

quality noun

1 *We only use ingredients of the highest **quality**.*
- grade, class, standard

2 *The most obvious **quality** of rubber is that it stretches.*
- characteristic, feature, property, attribute, trait

quantity noun

1 *She receives a huge **quantity** of fan mail every week.*
- amount, mass, volume, bulk, weight
- (*informal*) load

2 *We recycled a large **quantity** of empty bottles.*
- number
- When you add up numbers, you get a sum or total.

quarrel noun

*We have **quarrels**, but really we are good friends.*
- argument, disagreement, dispute, difference of opinion, row, squabble, clash, tiff
- Continuous quarrelling is strife.
- A long-lasting quarrel is a feud or vendetta.
- A quarrel in which people become violent is a brawl or fight.

quarrel verb

*The twins **quarrelled** over who should sit in the front.*
- disagree, argue, row, squabble, bicker, clash, fight, fall out

to quarrel with something
*I can't **quarrel with** your decision.*
- disagree with, object to, take exception to, oppose

quarrelsome adjective

*Goblins can be very **quarrelsome** creatures.*
- bad-tempered, irritable, aggressive, argumentative
- OPPOSITE placid

quarry noun

1 *The **quarry** produces fine white marble.*
- SEE **mine**

2 *The lioness patiently stalked her **quarry**.*
- prey, victim

quarters plural noun

*This part of the house was once the servants' **quarters**.*
- accommodation, lodging, rooms, housing

quaver verb

*The boy's voice **quavered** with fear.*
- shake, tremble, waver, quake, quiver, falter

quay noun

*The ship unloaded its cargo onto the **quay**.*
- dock, harbour, pier, wharf, jetty, landing stage

a b c d e f g h i j k l m n o p **q** r s t u v w x y z

queasy adjective
The sea was rough and I began to feel a bit **queasy**.
- sick, ill, unwell, nauseous, groggy, green

queer adjective
1 *The engine made a* **queer** *rattling noise.*
- curious, strange, unusual, weird, funny, mysterious, puzzling
2 *There's something* **queer** *going on.*
- odd, peculiar, abnormal, suspicious, shady
- (*informal*) fishy
OPPOSITE normal, ordinary

quench verb
1 *The iced lemonade soon* **quenched** *her thirst.*
- cool, satisfy
2 *They dumped sand on the embers to* **quench** *the fire.*
- extinguish, put out, smother

query noun
If you have any **queries**, *please phone this number.*
- question, enquiry, problem

query verb
The manager **queried** *the referee's decision.*
- question, challenge, dispute, argue over, quarrel with, object to

quest noun
The knights set out on a **quest** *to find the enchanted tower.*
- search, hunt, expedition, mission

question noun
1 *Does anyone have any* **questions**?
- enquiry, query, problem
- A question which someone sets as a puzzle is a brain-teaser or conundrum or riddle.
- A series of questions asked as a game is a quiz.
- A set of questions which someone asks to get information is a questionnaire or survey.

2 *There's some* **question** *over the player's fitness.*
- uncertainty, doubt, argument, debate, dispute

question verb
1 *The detective decided to* **question** *the suspect.*
- ask, examine, interview, quiz, interrogate
- To question someone intensively is to grill them.
2 *He* **questioned** *the referee's decision.*
- challenge, dispute, argue over, quarrel with, object to, query

queue noun
There was a **queue** *of people outside the cinema.*
- line, file, column, string
- A long queue of traffic on a road is a tailback.

queue verb
Please **queue** *at the door.*
- line up, form a queue

quick adjective
1 *You'd better be* **quick**—*the bus leaves in 10 minutes.*
- fast, swift, rapid, speedy, hasty
- (*informal*) nippy
- A common simile is as quick as a flash.
OPPOSITE slow
2 *Do you mind if I make a* **quick** *phone call?*
- short, brief, momentary, immediate, instant, prompt, snappy
OPPOSITE long, lengthy
3 *She's very* **quick** *at mental arithmetic.*
- bright, clever, sharp, acute, alert
- (*informal*) on the ball
OPPOSITE slow

quicken verb
The front runners **quickened** *their pace.*
- accelerate, speed up, hurry up, hasten

quiet adjective
1 *The deserted house was still and **quiet**.*
- silent, noiseless, soundless
- A common simile is as quiet as a mouse.
  OPPOSITE noisy
2 *The children spoke in **quiet** whispers.*
- hushed, low, soft
- Something that is so quiet that you can't hear it is inaudible.
  OPPOSITE loud
3 *Amy has always been a **quiet** child.*
- shy, reserved, subdued, placid, uncommunicative, retiring, withdrawn,
  OPPOSITE talkative
4 *We found a **quiet** place for a picnic.*
- peaceful, secluded, isolated, restful, tranquil, calm, serene
  OPPOSITE busy

quieten verb
1 *The mother tried to **quieten** her baby.*
- calm, soothe, hush, pacify
2 *Turn this dial to **quieten** the volume.*
- deaden, muffle, mute, soften, suppress

quit verb
1 *She **quit** her teaching job to travel round the world.*
- leave, give up, resign from
- (*informal*) pack in
2 (*informal*) ***Quit** pushing me!*
- stop, cease, leave off

quite adverb
Take care how you use **quite**, as the two senses are almost opposites.
1 *The two puppies have **quite** different personalities.*
- completely, totally, utterly, entirely, absolutely, wholly
2 *They played **quite** well, but far from their best.*
- fairly, reasonably, moderately, rather

quiver verb
*The jelly **quivered** when the table was banged.*
- shake, wobble, quake, shiver, quaver, tremble, shudder, vibrate

quiz noun
*Our class took part in a general knowledge **quiz**.*
- test, competition, questionnaire, exam, examination

quiz verb
*The teacher **quizzed** us on our times tables.*
- question, ask, examine, interrogate

quota noun
*I've had my **quota** of chocolate for this week.*
- ration, share, portion, allowance, helping

quotation noun
*I copied a short **quotation** from the book.*
- extract, excerpt, passage, piece
- A piece taken from a newspaper is a cutting.
- A piece taken from a film or TV programme is a clip.

quote verb
*He **quoted** some lines from a poem.*
- recite, repeat

Rr

race noun
1 *We had a **race** to see who was the fastest runner.*
- competition, contest, chase
- A race to decide who will take part in the final is a heat.
2 *We belong to different **races** but we're all humans.*
- nation, people, ethnic group

a
b
c
d
e
f
g
h
i
j
k
l
m
n
o
p
q
r
s
t
u
v
w
x
y
z

race verb

1 *We raced each other to the end of the road.*
- have a race with, run against, compete with

2 *She had to race home because she was late.*
- run, rush, dash, hurry, sprint, fly, tear, whizz, zoom

rack noun

Cooking pots hung from a rack on the wall.
- frame, framework, shelf, support

racket noun

1 *A racket is used to hit the ball in tennis.*
- In cricket and other games you hit the ball with a bat.
- In golf you hit the ball with a club.

2 *Please stop making that awful racket!*
- noise, row, din, commotion, disturbance, uproar, rumpus

radiant adjective

The fairy queen beamed with a radiant smile.
- bright, dazzling, happy, cheerful, joyful, warm

radiate verb

1 *This fire radiates a lot of heat.*
- give off, send out, emit

2 *The bus routes radiate from the centre of town.*
- spread out

radical adjective

1 *They have made radical changes to school meals.*
- fundamental, drastic, thorough, sweeping
  OPPOSITE superficial

2 *The politician was known for her radical views.*
- extreme, revolutionary
  OPPOSITE moderate

rage noun

Derek slammed the door in a show of rage.
- anger, fury, indignation
- (*old use*) wrath
- A child's rage is a tantrum or temper.

rage verb

1 *He was still raging about the cost of the meal.*
- be angry, be fuming, seethe, rant

2 *The hurricane raged for three days.*
- blow, storm, rampage

ragged adjective

1 *They met a traveller wearing ragged clothes.*
- tattered, tatty, threadbare, torn, frayed, patched, ripped, shabby, worn out

2 *A ragged line of people waited in the rain.*
- irregular, uneven

raid noun

The enemy raid caught them by surprise.
- attack, assault, strike, onslaught, invasion, blitz

raid verb

1 *Long ago, Vikings raided the towns on the coast.*
- attack, invade, ransack, plunder, loot, pillage
- Someone who raids ships at sea is a pirate.
- Someone who raids and steals cattle is a rustler.

2 *Police raided the house at dawn.*
- descend on, rush, storm, swoop on

rail noun

The fence was made of iron rails.
- bar, rod, spar
- A fence made of rails is also called railings.

railway noun

 WORD WEB

VARIOUS TYPES OF RAILWAY
branch line, cable railway, funicular, main line, metro, monorail, mountain railway, tramway, underground railway

TYPES OF RAILWAY TRAIN
diesel, electric train, express, freight train or goods train, intercity, sleeper, steam train, tram, underground train

- Vehicles which run on the railway are locomotives and rolling stock.

PARTS OF A RAILWAY TRAIN
buffet car, carriage or coach, dining car, engine, goods van, guard's van, locomotive, sleeping car

THINGS YOU MIGHT SEE ON OR NEAR A RAILWAY
buffers, cutting, level crossing, platform, points, signals, signal-box, sleepers, station, track, trolley, tunnel, viaduct

- The rails which trains run on are the line or track.
- The end of the line is the terminus.

PEOPLE WHO WORK ON A TRAIN OR RAILWAY
conductor, driver, engineer, guard, porter, signalman, station manager, stationmaster, steward

rain noun
- A formal word for rain is precipitation.
- The rainy season in south and southeast Asia is the monsoon.
- When there is no rain for a long time you have a drought.

FOR WAYS TO DESCRIBE RAIN
SEE **weather** noun

raise verb
1 *Raise your hand if you need help.*
- hold up, put up, lift
2 *The box was too heavy for him to raise.*
- lift, pick up, elevate, hoist, jack up
3 *The Post Office is raising the price of stamps.*
- increase, put up
4 *The runners hope to raise £1000 for charity.*
- collect, gather, take in, make
5 *He raised some objections to the plan.*
- bring up, mention, put forward, present, introduce
6 *The doctor didn't want to raise their hopes.*
- encourage, build up, arouse
7 *It's hard work trying to raise a family.*
- bring up, care for, look after, nurture, rear

rally noun
Some demonstrators held a rally in the town square.
- demonstration, meeting, march, protest
- (informal) demo

ram verb
The car skidded and rammed into a lamp-post.
- bump, hit, strike, crash into, collide with, smash into

ramble verb
1 *They rambled round the country park.*
- walk, stroll, wander, roam, rove, range, hike, trek
2 *The speaker rambled on for hours.*
- chatter, babble, drift
- (informal) rabbit, witter

rambling adjective
We followed a rambling path through the forest.
- indirect, roundabout, twisting, winding, meandering,zigzag
OPPOSITE direct

rampage verb
An angry mob rampaged through the streets.
- run riot, run amok, go berserk, go wild, race about, rush about

random adjective
They picked a random selection of pupils.
- arbitrary, chance, haphazard, casual, unplanned
OPPOSITE deliberate

range noun
1 *There is a range of mountains to the south.*
- chain, line, row, series, string
2 *Supermarkets sell a wide range of goods.*
- variety, assortment, selection, choice, spectrum
3 *The shop caters for all age ranges from toddlers to teenagers.*
- span, scope

a
b
c
d
e
f
g
h
i
j
k
l
m
n
o
p
q
r
s
t
u
v
w
x
y
z

a
b
c
d
e
f
g
h
i
j
k
l
m
n
o
p
q
r
s
t
u
v
w
x
y
z

range verb
1 *Prices **range** from five to twenty euros.*
- vary, differ, extend, fluctuate
2 *Rows of jam jars were **ranged** on the shelf.*
- arrange, order, lay out, set out, line up
3 *Wild deer **range** over the hills.*
- wander, ramble, roam, rove, stray

rank noun
1 *The soldiers formed themselves into **ranks**.*
- column, line, file, row
2 *A black belt is the highest **rank** in judo.*
- grade, level, position, status
- To raise someone to a higher rank is to promote them.
- To reduce someone to a lower rank is to demote them.

ransack verb
1 *Mrs Hogg **ransacked** the house looking for her keys.*
- search, scour, rummage through, comb
- (*informal*) turn upside down
2 *Thieves had **ransacked** the building.*
- loot, pillage, plunder, wreck

rap verb
*Someone **rapped** urgently on the door.*
- knock, tap

rapid adjective
*The cyclists set off at a **rapid** pace.*
- fast, quick, speedy, swift, brisk
OPPOSITE slow

rare adjective
1 *These flowers are now very **rare** in the wild.*
- uncommon, unusual, infrequent, scarce, sparse
OPPOSITE common
2 *He has a **rare** ability to make people laugh.*
- exceptional, remarkable, special

rarely adverb
*Our next-door neighbour **rarely** goes out.*
- seldom, infrequently, hardly ever
OPPOSITE often

rash adjective
*Don't make any **rash** promises.*
- reckless, foolhardy, hasty, hurried, impulsive, unthinking
OPPOSITE careful

rash noun
1 *Rory had an itchy red **rash** on his leg.*
- spots
2 *There has been a **rash** of break-ins lately.*
- outbreak, series, succession, spate

rate noun
1 *The cyclists were pedalling at a furious **rate**.*
- pace, speed
2 *What's the usual **rate** for washing a car?*
- charge, cost, fee, payment, price, figure, amount

rate verb
*How do you **rate** their chance of winning?*
- judge, regard, consider, estimate, evaluate

rather adverb
1 *It's **rather** chilly today.*
- quite, fairly, moderately, slightly, somewhat, a bit, a little
2 *I'd **rather** not go out tonight.*
- preferably, sooner

ratio noun
*The **ratio** of boys to girls is about 50-50.*
- proportion, balance
- You can express a ratio as a percentage.

ration noun
*The pirates each had a daily **ration** of rum.*
- portion, quota, share, allowance, helping, measure
rations
*The astronauts took enough **rations** to last a month.*
- food, provisions, stores, supplies

ration verb
*During the war, the government had to **ration** food.*
- limit, restrict, share out, allot

rattle noun, verb
. FOR VARIOUS SOUNDS
SEE **sound** noun

rave verb
1 *Connie **raved** about the film she saw last week.*
• be enthusiastic, talk wildly
2 *The head **raved** on about their bad behaviour.*
• shout, rage, storm, yell, roar

ravenous adjective
*The children were **ravenous** after their walk.*
• hungry, starved, starving, famished

raw adjective
1 ***Raw** vegetables are supposed to be good for you.*
• uncooked
OPPOSITE cooked
2 *The factory imports a lot of **raw** materials from abroad.*
• crude, natural, unprocessed, untreated
OPPOSITE manufactured, processed
3 *Her knee felt **raw** after she fell off her bike.*
• red, rough, sore, tender, inflamed
4 *There was a **raw** wind blowing from the east.*
• bitter, cold, chilly, biting, freezing, piercing

ray noun
*A **ray** of light shone into the dark cave.*
• beam, shaft, stream

reach verb
1 *They hoped to **reach** Oxford by lunch time.*
• arrive at, go as far as, get to, make
2 *The appeal fund has **reached** its target.*
• achieve, attain
3 *I'm not tall enough to **reach** the top shelf.*
• get hold of, grasp, touch
to reach out
***Reach out** your hands.*
• extend, hold out, put out, stick out, stretch out

reach noun
1 *The shelf was just within his **reach**.*
• grasp
2 *The shops are within easy **reach**.*
• distance, range

react verb
*How did he **react** when he read the letter?*
• respond, behave, answer, reply

reaction noun
*What was her **reaction** when you said you were sorry?*
• response, answer, reply

read verb
*They couldn't **read** the doctor's handwriting.*
• make out, understand, decipher
• To read through something very quickly is to skim through it.
• To read here and there in a book is to dip into it.
• To read something intently is to pore over it.

readily adverb
1 *My friends **readily** agreed to help.*
• willingly, gladly, happily, eagerly
2 *The recipe uses ingredients which are **readily** available.*
• easily, conveniently, quickly

ready adjective
1 *When will tea be **ready**?*
• prepared, set, done, available, in place
OPPOSITE not ready
2 *He's always **ready** to help.*
• willing, glad, pleased, happy, keen, eager
OPPOSITE reluctant
3 *She's always got a **ready** reply.*
• quick, prompt, immediate
OPPOSITE slow

real adjective
1 *History is about **real** events.*
• actual, true, factual, verifiable
OPPOSITE fictitious, imaginary
2 *The necklace was made from **real** rubies.*
• authentic, genuine, bona fide, natural
OPPOSITE artificial, fake

3 *She doesn't often show her **real** feelings.*
- true, honest, sincere, genuine, heartfelt
  OPPOSITE insincere

realistic adjective
1 *The portrait of the artist is very **realistic**.*
- lifelike, true to life, faithful, convincing, recognizable
2 *It's not **realistic** to expect a puppy to be quiet.*
- feasible, practical, sensible, possible, workable
  OPPOSITE unrealistic

reality noun
*Stop daydreaming and face **reality**.*
- the facts, the real world, the truth

realize verb
*It took him a long time to **realize** what she meant.*
- understand, appreciate, grasp, comprehend, recognize, see
- (informal) catch on to, tumble to, twig

really adverb
1 *Are you **really** going to Peru?*
- actually, definitely, truly, in fact, certainly, genuinely, honestly
2 *I saw a **really** good film last night.*
- very, extremely, exceptionally

realm noun
*The king ruled the **realm** for fifty years.*
- country, kingdom, domain, empire

rear adjective
*They found seats in the **rear** coach of the train.*
- back, end, last
- The rear legs of an animal are its hind legs.
  OPPOSITE front

rear noun
*The buffet car is at the **rear** of the train.*
- back, end, tail-end
- The rear of a ship is the stern.

rear verb
1 *The couple have **reared** three children.*
- bring up, raise, nurture
2 *The deer **reared** their heads when they caught his scent.*
- hold up, lift, raise

reason noun
1 *What was the **reason** for the delay?*
- cause, grounds, explanation, motive, justification, excuse
2 *It was clear that the poor woman had lost her **reason**.*
- mind, sanity, senses, wits
- (informal) marbles
3 *They tried to make him see **reason**.*
- sense, common sense, logic

reason verb
to reason with someone
*We tried to **reason with** him, but he wouldn't change his mind.*
- argue with, persuade, talk round

reasonable adjective
1 *That seems like a **reasonable** plan.*
- sensible, intelligent, rational, logical, sane, sound
  OPPOSITE irrational
2 *They bought the house for a **reasonable** price.*
- fair, acceptable, average, moderate, respectable, normal, proper
  OPPOSITE excessive

reassure verb
*The doctor **reassured** her that the wound was not serious.*
- calm, comfort, encourage, hearten, give confidence to
  OPPOSITE threaten

rebel verb
*The king feared that the people would **rebel**.*
- revolt, rise up
- To rebel against the captain of a ship is to mutiny and someone who does this is a mutineer.
  OPPOSITE obey

rebellion noun
*The protest soon became a widespread **rebellion**.*
- revolt, revolution, uprising, resistance
- A rebellion on a ship is a mutiny.

rebound verb
*The ball **rebounded** off the wall.*
- bounce back, spring back
- If a bullet rebounds off a surface, it is said to ricochet.

recall verb
*Try to **recall** what happened.*
- remember, recollect, think back to

recede verb
*When the rain stopped, the flood **receded**.*
- go back, retreat, decline, subside, ebb

receive verb
1 *The captain went up to **receive** the winners' cup.*
- collect, take, accept, be given
- OPPOSITE give, present

2 *Some passengers **received** minor injuries.*
- experience, suffer, undergo, sustain
- OPPOSITE inflict

3 *We went to the front door to **receive** our visitors.*
- greet, meet, welcome

recent adjective
*We watch the news to keep up with **recent** events.*
- current, up-to-date, contemporary, new, the latest, fresh

reception noun
1 *The home crowd gave the team a friendly **reception**.*
- greeting, welcome

2 *Who are they inviting to the wedding **reception**?*
- party, gathering, celebration, function
- (*informal*) do

recipe noun
*I followed my granny's **recipe** for making apple pie.*
- directions, instructions
- The items you use for a recipe are the ingredients.

recital noun
*There will be a short **recital** of piano music at noon.*
- concert, performance

recite verb
*Zoe **recited** a poem she had written.*
- say aloud, read out, narrate

reckless adjective
*A man has been charged with **reckless** driving.*
- careless, irresponsible, mindless, thoughtless, negligent, foolhardy, rash, wild
- OPPOSITE careful

reckon verb
1 *I tried to **reckon** how much she owed me.*
- calculate, work out, add up, figure out, assess, estimate

2 *Do you **reckon** it's going to rain?*
- think, believe, guess, imagine, feel

recline verb
*Paula **reclined** lazily on the sofa.*
- lean back, lie, lounge, rest, stretch out, sprawl, loll

recognize verb
1 *I didn't **recognize** her with her new haircut.*
- identify, know, distinguish, make out, recall, recollect, remember

2 *He refused to **recognize** that he was to blame.*
- acknowledge, admit, accept, grant, concede, confess, realize

recoil verb
*Cloe **recoiled** as a spider scuttled towards her.*
- draw back, flinch, quail, wince, shrink back

a
b
c
d
e
f
g
h
i
j
k
l
m
n
o
p
q
r
s
t
u
v
w
x
y
z

recollect verb

1 *Do you **recollect** what happened?*
- remember, recall, have a memory of
2 *The two friends sat for hours **recollecting** the past.*
- reminisce about, think back to, cast your mind back to
OPPOSITE forget

recommend verb

1 *The doctor **recommended** a complete rest.*
- advise, counsel, propose, suggest, advocate, prescribe, urge
2 *The restaurant was **recommended** by a friend of mine.*
- approve of, endorse, praise, commend

record noun

*The zookeepers keep a **record** of the animals' diet.*
- account, report
- A record of daily events is a diary or journal.
- The record of a voyage at sea or in space is the log.
- The record of what happened at a meeting is the minutes.
- A record of people's names is a register.
- Records consisting of historical documents are archives.

record verb

1 *The concert is being **recorded** by the BBC.*
- tape, video
2 *She **recorded** our interview in a notebook.*
- write down, note, set down, put down, enter

recover verb

1 *It took a long time to **recover** after my illness.*
- get better, heal, improve, recuperate, pick up, mend, come round, pull through, revive, rally
2 *The police have **recovered** the stolen vehicles.*
- get back, retrieve, reclaim, repossess, find, trace

recovery noun

*The doctors were surprised at her speedy **recovery**.*
- healing, cure, revival, recuperation, convalescence

recreation noun

*What do you do for **recreation** around here?*
- fun, enjoyment, pleasure, relaxation, leisure, amusement, diversion, entertainment, play
- A particular activity you do as recreation is a hobby or pastime.

recruit noun

*The police **recruits** were very inexperienced.*
- beginner, learner, novice
- A recruit learning a trade is an apprentice or trainee.
- A recruit training to be in the armed services is a cadet.

recruit verb

*The book club has **recruited** two new members.*
- bring in, take on, attract, enrol
- To be recruited into the armed services is to enlist or sign on.

rectangle noun

- oblong

recur verb

*Go to the doctor if the symptoms **recur**.*
- happen again, come again, reappear, return

recycle verb

*You can **recycle** glass by putting it in the bottle bank.*
- reuse, reprocess, salvage, use again

red adjective

1 *I chose a **red** ribbon for my doll.*
- Something which is rather red is reddish.
- A common simile is as red as a beetroot.
2 *My nose and cheeks were **red** with cold.*
- flushed, glowing, rosy, ruddy, blushing
3 *Her eyes were **red** from lack of sleep.*
- bloodshot, inflamed, red-rimmed

a
b
c
d
e
f
g
h
i
j
k
l
m
n
o
p
q
r
s
t
u
v
w
x
y
z

4 *The fairy queen had flaming **red** hair.*
- ginger, auburn, coppery
- (*informal*) carroty

red adjective, noun

> **WORD WEB**
>
> SOME SHADES OF RED
> brick red, cherry, crimson, maroon, pillar-box red, pink, rose, ruby, scarlet, vermilion

reduce verb
*She's **reduced** the amount of sugar in her diet.*
- decrease, lessen, lower, cut, cut back, slash
- To reduce something by half is to halve it.
- To reduce the width of something is to narrow it.
- To reduce the length of something is to shorten or trim it.
- To reduce speed is to decelerate.
- To reduce the strength of a liquid is to dilute it.

  OPPOSITE increase

reel noun
*I bought a **reel** of white cotton thread.*
- spool

reel verb
1 *The blow made his head **reel**.*
- spin, whirl

2 *The injured man **reeled** as if he was drunk.*
- stagger, stumble, sway, rock, totter, lurch, roll

to reel off
*The chef **reeled off** a long list of ingredients.*
- recite, rattle off, fire off

refer verb
*The shop assistant **referred** me to another department.*
- hand over, pass on, direct, send

to refer to
1 *Please don't **refer to** this matter again.*
- mention, speak of, make reference to, allude to, bring up

2 *If you can't spell a word, **refer to** a dictionary.*
- look up, consult, go to, turn to

referee noun
*The **referee** blew his whistle.*
- umpire, adjudicator
- (*informal*) ref
- A person who helps the referee in football is a linesman or touch judge.

refill verb
*The waiter **refilled** our glasses of water.*
- top up
- To refill a fuel tank is to refuel.

reflect verb
1 *Cat's-eyes **reflect** the light from car headlights.*
- send back, throw back, shine back

2 *Their success **reflects** their hard work.*
- show, indicate, demonstrate, exhibit, reveal

to reflect on
*We need time to **reflect on** what to do next.*
- think about, contemplate, consider, ponder, mull over

reflection noun
1 *Gus could see his **reflection** in the pond.*
- image, likeness

2 *Their success is a **reflection** of their hard work.*
- indication, demonstration, evidence, result

3 *We need more time for **reflection**.*
- thinking, contemplation, meditation

reform noun
*They're making **reforms** to the school curriculum.*
- change, improvement, modification, amendment

refrain verb
to refrain from
*Please **refrain from** talking in the library.*
- avoid, abstain from, stop
- (*informal*) leave off, quit

a
b
c
d
e
f
g
h
i
j
k
l
m
n
o
p
q
r
s
t
u
v
w
x
y
z

a
b
c
d
e
f
g
h
i
j
k
l
m
n
o
p
q
r
s
t
u
v
w
x
y
z

refresh verb
1 *They refreshed themselves with a glass of lemonade.*
- cool, freshen, revive, restore, invigorate, stimulate

2 *Let me refresh your memory.*
- jog, prompt, prod

refreshing adjective
We went for a refreshing dip in the pool.
- reviving, invigorating, restorative, bracing, stimulating

refuge noun
1 *The climbers looked for refuge from the blizzard.*
- shelter, cover, protection, safety

2 *The outlaws stayed hidden in their mountain refuge.*
- hideaway, hideout, retreat, haven, sanctuary

refund verb
She asked them to refund her money.
- give back, pay back, repay, return

refuse verb
1 *Why did you refuse my offer of help?*
- decline, reject, turn down, say no to
  OPPOSITE accept

2 *They were refused permission to enter the building.*
- deny, deprive of
  OPPOSITE allow

refuse noun
The refuse was taken to the local tip.
- rubbish, garbage, trash, waste, litter, junk

regain verb
The patient began to regain consciousness.
- get back, get back to, return to

regard verb
1 *Do you still regard him as your friend?*
- think of, consider, judge, value

2 *The cat regarded us curiously.*
- look at, gaze at, stare at, eye, view, scrutinize, watch

regarding preposition
I must speak with you regarding a private matter.
- about, concerning, on the subject of, with reference to, with regard to

regardless adjective
regardless of
She dived into the water regardless of the danger.
- indifferent to, heedless of, not caring about, unconcerned about

region noun
1 *The Arctic and Antarctic are polar regions.*
- area, place, land, territory, part of the world

2 *There are two local radio stations serving this region.*
- area, district, neighbourhood, locality, vicinity, zone

register verb
1 *The parents registered the birth of their child.*
- record, set down, write down

2 *The thermometer registered a very high temperature.*
- show, indicate, display, read

regret verb
She regretted her decision to leave Ireland.
- be sorry for, repent, feel sad about

regular adjective
1 *Signs are placed at regular intervals along the cycle path.*
- evenly spaced, fixed
  OPPOSITE irregular, uneven

2 *The drummer kept up a regular rhythm.*
- constant, consistent, steady, uniform, unvarying
- A common simile is as regular as clockwork.
  OPPOSITE erratic

3 *Is this your regular route to school?*
- normal, usual, customary, habitual, ordinary, routine
  OPPOSITE unusual

4 *Craig is a **regular** customer at the sweet shop.*
- frequent, familiar, persistent
OPPOSITE rare, unusual

regulate verb
1 *Just turn the knob to **regulate** the volume.*
- control, set, adjust, alter, change, moderate
2 *The new roundabout is meant to **regulate** the traffic.*
- control, manage, direct, govern, monitor

regulation noun
*There are new **regulations** on school uniform.*
- rule, law, order, decree, requirement

rehearsal noun
*The actors had to learn their words before the **rehearsal**.*
- practice, preparation
- (*informal*) try-out
- A play rehearsal in which actors wear their costumes is a dress rehearsal.

rehearse verb
*We had to **rehearse** the scene all over again.*
- go over, practise, try out

reign verb
*Which British monarch **reigned** the longest?*
- be king or queen, be on the throne, govern, rule

reject verb
1 *At first, she **rejected** their offer of help.*
- decline, refuse, turn down, say no to
2 *As we picked the berries, we **rejected** any bad ones.*
- discard, get rid of, throw out, scrap
OPPOSITE accept

rejoice verb
*The people **rejoiced** when the wicked queen died.*
- celebrate, delight, be happy, exult
OPPOSITE grieve

relate verb
1 *Do you think the two crimes are **related**?*
- connect, link, associate
2 *The travellers **related** the story of their adventures.*
- tell, narrate, report, describe

relate to
*The letter **relates to** your great grandfather.*
- be about, refer to, have to do with, concern

relation noun
1 *The stolen car has no **relation** to the robbery.*
- connection, link, association, bond
2 *Are you a **relation** of hers?*
- relative, member of the family, kinsman or kinswoman
FOR MEMBERS OF A FAMILY
SEE **family**

relationship noun
1 *There is a **relationship** between your diet and health.*
- connection, link, association, bond
- The relationship between two numbers is a ratio.
2 *The twins have a close **relationship**.*
- friendship, attachment, understanding

relative noun SEE relation

relax verb
1 *I like to **relax** by listening to music.*
- unwind, rest, take it easy
2 *This exercise will **relax** your shoulder muscles.*
- loosen, ease
OPPOSITE tighten
3 *He **relaxed** his hold on the dog's leash.*
- slacken, loosen, ease, lessen, reduce
OPPOSITE tighten

relaxed adjective
*They liked the **relaxed** atmosphere of village life.*
- informal, casual, carefree, leisurely, easygoing, peaceful, restful, unhurried, calm
- (*informal*) laid-back
OPPOSITE tense, stressful

a
b
c
d
e
f
g
h
i
j
k
l
m
n
o
p
q
r
s
t
u
v
w
x
y
z

a
b
c
d
e
f
g
h
i
j
k
l
m
n
o
p
q
r
s
t
u
v
w
x
y
z

release verb

1 *The prisoners were **released** early.*
- free, let go, discharge, liberate, set free
- To release slaves is to emancipate them.
  OPPOSITE imprison

2 *The dog was tied up—who **released** him?*
- let loose, set loose, unfasten, unleash, untie

3 *The band will **release** their new CD in April.*
- issue, publish, put out

relent verb

*Her parents **relented** and let her stay up late.*
- give in, give way, yield, soften, weaken

relentless adjective

*The footballer faced **relentless** questions from the press.*
- constant, continuous, incessant, perpetual, persistent, never-ending, unrelenting, remorseless, ruthless

relevant adjective

1 *The detective noted everything that was **relevant** to the case.*
- applicable, pertinent, appropriate, suitable, significant, related, connected

2 *Don't interrupt unless your comments are **relevant**.*
- to the point
  OPPOSITE irrelevant

reliable adjective

1 *The king summoned his most **reliable** knights.*
- faithful, dependable, trustworthy, loyal, constant, devoted, staunch, true

2 *The secret agent always sent **reliable** information.*
- dependable, valid, trustworthy, safe, sound, steady, sure
  OPPOSITE unreliable

relief noun

1 *The pills gave some **relief** from the pain.*
- comfort, ease, help, release

2 *I watched a film for some light **relief** after work.*
- relaxation, rest

relieve verb

1 *The doctor said the pills would **relieve** the pain.*
- ease, help, lessen, diminish, relax, soothe, comfort

2 *We played cards to **relieve** the boredom of waiting.*
- reduce, lighten, dispel, counteract
  OPPOSITE intensify

religion noun

 WORD WEB

*People from all **religions** went to the service.*
- faith, belief, creed, denomination, sect

MAJOR WORLD RELIGIONS
Buddhism, Christianity, Hinduism, Islam, Judaism, Shintoism, Sikhism, Taoism, Zen

MAJOR RELIGIOUS FESTIVALS
Buddhist: Buddha Day, Nirvana Day; Christian: Lent, Easter, Christmas Day; Hindu: Holi, Diwali; Muslim: Ramadan, Eid; Jewish: Passover, Rosh Hashanah, Yom Kippur, Hanukkah; Sikh: Baisakhi, Birth of Guru Nanak
- The study of religion is divinity or theology.

FOR RELIGIOUS LEADERS
SEE **priest**

religious adjective

1 *The choir sang a selection of **religious** music.*
- sacred, holy, divine
  OPPOSITE secular

2 *My grandparents were very **religious**.*
- devout, pious, reverent, spiritual, godly
  OPPOSITE ungodly

relish verb
*He would **relish** the chance to appear on television.*
- enjoy, delight in, appreciate

reluctant adjective
*The old woman was **reluctant** to open the door.*
- unwilling, hesitant, slow, grudging, half-hearted, resistant
OPPOSITE eager

rely verb
*Are you sure that we can **rely** on their help?*
- depend on, count on, have confidence in, trust
- (informal) bank on

remain verb
1 *The boys were told to **remain** behind after school.*
- stay, wait, linger
- (informal) hang about
2 *It will **remain** warm and sunny all weekend.*
- continue, persist, keep on, carry on
3 *Little **remained** of the house after the fire.*
- be left, survive

remainder noun
*We played games for the **remainder** of the afternoon.*
- rest, what is left, surplus, remains

remains plural noun
*They cleared away the **remains** of the picnic.*
- remnants, leftovers, leavings, fragments, traces, scraps, debris
- The remains at the bottom of a cup are dregs.
- Remains still standing after a building has collapsed are ruins.
- Historic remains are relics.

remark verb
*He **remarked** that it was a nice day.*
- say, state, comment, note, declare, mention, observe
SEE ALSO **say**

remark noun
*They exchanged a few **remarks** about the weather.*
- comment, observation, word, statement, thought, mention

remarkable adjective
1 *He described his **remarkable** escape from the island.*
- amazing, extraordinary, astonishing, memorable, wonderful, incredible, unforgettable, breathtaking
2 *The young violinist shows **remarkable** skill for her age.*
- exceptional, notable, noteworthy, striking, outstanding, impressive, phenomenal
OPPOSITE ordinary

remedy noun
1 *There is no known **remedy** for his illness.*
- cure, treatment, medicine, therapy, relief
- A remedy to act against a poison is an antidote.
2 *We may have found a **remedy** for the problem.*
- solution, answer

remember verb
1 *Can you **remember** what she looked like?*
- recall, recollect, recognize, place
2 *He was trying to **remember** his lines for the play.*
- learn, memorize, keep in mind
OPPOSITE forget
3 *My granny likes to **remember** the old days.*
- reminisce about, think back to

remind verb
***Remind** me to buy a newspaper.*
- prompt, jog your memory
to remind you of something
*What does this tune **remind** you **of**?*
- make you think of, take you back to

a
b
c
d
e
f
g
h
i
j
k
l
m
n
o
p
q
r
s
t
u
v
w
x
y
z

reminder noun
1 *They sent him a **reminder** to pay the bill.*
• prompt, cue, hint, nudge
2 *The photographs are a **reminder** of our holiday.*
• souvenir, memento

reminiscent adjective
be reminiscent of something
*The tune is **reminiscent of** an old folk song.*
• remind you of, make you think of, call to mind

remnants plural noun
*They had to clear up the **remnants** of the party.*
• remains, scraps, traces, fragments, debris, leftovers

remorse noun
*He showed no **remorse** for stealing the money.*
• regret, repentance, guilt, guilty conscience, sorrow, shame

remote adjective
1 *The tour will explore a **remote** part of Brazil.*
• distant, faraway, isolated, cut-off, inaccessible, out-of-the-way, unfrequented
OPPOSITE accessible
2 *The chances of us winning are **remote**.*
• poor, slender, slight, small, faint, doubtful
OPPOSITE likely

remove verb
1 *Please **remove** your rubbish.*
• clear away, take away
2 *The rowdy passengers were **removed** from the bus.*
• throw out, turn out, eject, expel
• (informal) kick out
• To remove people from a house where they are living is to evict them.
• To remove a monarch from the throne is to depose him or her.

3 *The author decided to **remove** the last paragraph.*
• cut out, delete, erase, get rid of, do away with, eliminate
4 *The dentist **removed** my bad tooth.*
• extract, pull out, take out, withdraw
5 *The divers slowly **removed** their wetsuits.*
• take off, peel off, strip off, shed, cast off

render verb
1 *The shock **rendered** her speechless.*
• make, leave, cause to be
2 *Many volunteers **rendered** their assistance.*
• give, provide, offer, furnish, supply

renew verb
1 *The church roof has been completely **renewed**.*
• repair, renovate, restore, replace, rebuild, reconstruct, revamp, refurbish, overhaul
• (informal) do up
2 *We stopped for a cup of tea to **renew** our energy.*
• refresh, revive, restore, replenish, revitalize
3 *You must **renew** your passport before you go abroad.*
• bring up to date, update

renowned adjective
*The cafe is **renowned** for its homemade scones.*
• famous, celebrated, well-known, famed, noted, notable, acclaimed
OPPOSITE unknown

rent verb
*We **rented** a couple of bikes to tour the Lake District.*
• hire, charter, lease

repair verb
*It took them a week to **repair** the damaged car.*
• mend, fix, put right, patch up

repay verb
1 *I can **repay** you the money next week.*
• pay back, refund
2 *How can we ever **repay** your kindness?*
• return, reciprocate

repeat verb

1 *The parrot **repeated** everything he said.*
- say again, copy, duplicate, reproduce, echo

2 *The actors had to **repeat** the opening scene.*
- do again, redo

repeatedly adverb

*We warned them **repeatedly** about the danger.*
- again and again, over and over, regularly, time after time, frequently, often

repel verb

1 *The humans managed to **repel** the Martian invasion.*
- drive back, beat back, push back, fend off, resist

2 *This spray will **repel** wasps and other insects.*
- keep away, scare off, deter, ward off

3 *They were **repelled** by the smell of the dragon's lair.*
- disgust, revolt, sicken, offend
- (*slang*) turn you off

repellent adjective

*The princess found the ogre quite **repellent**.*
- disgusting, repulsive, revolting, hideous, horrible, loathsome, objectionable, foul, offensive, vile
- OPPOSITE attractive

replace verb

1 *The spy carefully **replaced** the missing document.*
- put back, return, restore, reinstate

2 *Who will **replace** the head teacher when she retires?*
- follow, succeed, take over from, take the place of

3 *I need to **replace** one of the tyres on my bike.*
- change, renew

replacement noun

*They found a **replacement** for the injured player.*
- substitute, standby, stand-in, reserve
- Someone who can take the place of an actor is an understudy.

replica noun

*In the garden, there's a **replica** of a Roman statue.*
- copy, reproduction, duplicate, model, imitation, likeness
- An exact copy of a document is a facsimile.

reply noun

*He has received no **replies** to his email.*
- response, answer, reaction, acknowledgement
- An angry reply is a retort.

reply verb

to reply to

*She took a long time to **reply to** my letter.*
- answer, respond to, give a reply to, react to, acknowledge

report verb

1 *The newspapers **reported** what happened.*
- give an account of, record, state, describe, announce, publish

2 *We were told to **report** to reception when we arrived.*
- present yourself, make yourself known, check in

3 *If you cause any damage, I'll **report** you to the police.*
- complain about, inform on, denounce

report noun

1 *There was a **report** in the paper about the crash.*
- account, record, story, article, description

2 *The deer were startled by the **report** of the gun.*
- bang, blast, crack, noise

reporter noun

*The film star was being interviewed by a TV **reporter**.*
- journalist, correspondent

represent verb

1 *The picture **represents** an ancient legend.*
- depict, illustrate, portray, picture, show, describe

a
b
c
d
e
f
g
h
i
j
k
l
m
n
o
p
q
r
s
t
u
v
w
x
y
z

a
b
c
d
e
f
g
h
i
j
k
l
m
n
o
p
q
r
s
t
u
v
w
x
y
z

2 *A dove is often said to* **represent** *peace.*
- stand for, symbolize

3 *He appointed a lawyer to* **represent** *him.*
- speak for

reprimand verb
He **reprimanded** *them for their bad behaviour.*
- reproach, scold, criticize
- (*informal*) tell off, tick off
OPPOSITE praise

reproduce verb
1 *The robot can* **reproduce** *a human voice.*
- copy, duplicate, imitate, simulate, mimic

2 *Mice* **reproduce** *very quickly.*
- breed, produce offspring, multiply, procreate
- Fish reproduce by spawning.
- To reproduce plants is to propagate them.

reproduction noun
1 *Vets have to know about animal* **reproduction**.
- breeding, procreation

2 *Is that an original painting or a* **reproduction**?
- copy, replica, imitation, likeness, duplicate, print
- A reproduction of something which is intended to deceive people is a fake or forgery.
- An exact reproduction of a document is a facsimile.

reptile noun

WORD WEB

SOME ANIMALS WHICH ARE REPTILES
alligator, chameleon, crocodile, gecko, iguana, lizard, salamander, slow-worm, snake, terrapin, tortoise, turtle
SEE ALSO snake

- A reptile found in myths and legends is the basilisk.
FOR OTHER ANIMALS
SEE animal

repulsive adjective
We were put off eating by the **repulsive** *smell.*
- disgusting, revolting, offensive, repellent, disagreeable, foul, repugnant, obnoxious, sickening, hateful, hideous, horrible, loathsome, objectionable, vile
OPPOSITE attractive

reputation noun
The singer's **reputation** *spread throughout the world.*
- fame, celebrity, name, renown, eminence, standing, stature

request verb
She has **requested** *a transfer to a different job.*
- ask for, appeal for, apply for, beg for, call for, entreat, implore, invite, pray for, seek

request noun
They have ignored our **request** *for help.*
- appeal, plea, entreaty, call, cry
- A request for a job or membership is an application.
- A request signed by a lot of people is a petition.

require verb
1 *They* **require** *a draw to win the championship.*
- need, must have

2 *Visitors are* **required** *to sign the register.*
- instruct, oblige, request, direct, order, command

rescue verb
1 *A helicopter was sent to* **rescue** *the trapped climbers.*
- free, liberate, release, save, set free
- To rescue someone by paying money is to ransom them.

2 *The divers* **rescued** *some items from the sunken ship.*
- retrieve, recover, salvage

resemblance noun
It's easy to see the **resemblance** *between the two sisters.*
- likeness, similarity, closeness
OPPOSITE difference

resemble verb

*The twins closely **resemble** their mother.*
- look like, be similar to
- (*informal*) take after

resent verb

*She **resents** having to work such long hours.*
- be annoyed about, take exception to, be resentful about, begrudge, grudge

reservation noun

1 *They saw giraffes on the wildlife **reservation**.*
- reserve, park, preserve, sanctuary

2 *We have a **reservation** for two nights in the hotel.*
- booking

3 *She had **reservations** about whether the plan would work.*
- doubt, misgiving, hesitation, qualm
- If you have reservations about something, you are sceptical about it.

reserve verb

1 *The astronauts had to **reserve** fuel for the return voyage.*
- keep, put aside, set aside, save, preserve, retain, hold back

2 *Have you **reserved** your seats on the train?*
- book, order, secure

reserve noun

1 *The climbers kept a **reserve** of food in their base camp.*
- stock, store, supply, hoard, stockpile
- A reserve of money is a fund or savings.

2 *They put him down as a **reserve** for Saturday's game.*
- substitute, standby, stand-in, replacement
- Someone who can take the place of an actor is an understudy.

3 *The wildlife **reserve** has a new baby rhino.*
- reservation, park, preserve, sanctuary

reserved adjective

1 *These seats are **reserved**.*
- booked, set aside, ordered

2 *She is too **reserved** to speak up for herself.*
- shy, timid, quiet, bashful, modest, retiring, reticent
OPPOSITE outgoing

residence noun

*The palace is the official **residence** of the queen.*
- dwelling, home, house
- (*old use*) abode

resident noun

*The **residents** of New York are proud of their city.*
- citizen, inhabitant, occupant
- A temporary resident in a hotel is a guest.
- A resident in rented accommodation is a boarder, lodger, or tenant.

resign verb

*The manager of the football team was forced to **resign**.*
- leave, quit, stand down, step down, give in your notice
- When a monarch resigns from the throne, he or she abdicates.

resist verb

1 *They were too weak to **resist** the sorcerer's magic.*
- stand up to, defend yourself against, withstand, defy, oppose, fend off
OPPOSITE yield to, surrender to

2 *I couldn't **resist** having another piece of chocolate.*
- avoid, hold back from, refuse
OPPOSITE give in, accept

resolve verb

1 *I **resolved** to try harder next time.*
- decide, determine, make up your mind

2 *They held a meeting to try to **resolve** the dispute.*
- settle, sort out, straighten out, end, overcome

a
b
c
d
e
f
g
h
i
j
k
l
m
n
o
p
q
r
s
t
u
v
w
x
y
z

a
b
c
d
e
f
g
h
i
j
k
l
m
n
o
p
q
r
s
t
u
v
w
x
y
z

resort noun
*As a last **resort**, we could always walk.*
- option, choice, course of action

resort verb
*He didn't want to **resort** to violence.*
- start using, turn to, fall back on, rely on, stoop to

resound verb
*The howling of the wolves **resounded** through the forest.*
- echo, boom

resources plural noun
1 *The country is rich in natural **resources**.*
- materials, raw materials, reserves
2 *The library has limited **resources** for buying CDs.*
- funds, money, capital, assets, means, wealth

respect noun
1 *Her colleagues have the deepest **respect** for her.*
- admiration, esteem, regard, reverence, honour
2 *Have some **respect** for other people's feelings.*
- consideration, sympathy, thought, concern
3 *In some **respects**, he's a better player than I am.*
- way, point, aspect, feature, characteristic, detail, particular

respect verb
1 *Everyone **respects** her for her courage.*
- admire, esteem, revere, honour, look up to, value
  OPPOSITE scorn, despise
2 *She tried to **respect** the wishes of her dead husband.*
- obey, follow, observe, adhere to, comply with
  OPPOSITE ignore

respectable adjective
1 *He came from a very **respectable** family.*
- decent, honest, upright, honourable, worthy

2 *I finished the race in a **respectable** time.*
- reasonable, satisfactory, acceptable, passable, adequate, fair, tolerable

respective adjective
*We all returned to our **respective** homes.*
- separate, individual, own, particular, personal, specific

respond verb
to respond to
*He didn't **respond to** my question.*
- reply to, answer, react to, acknowledge

response noun
*Did you get a **response** to your letter?*
- reply, answer, reaction, acknowledgement
- An angry response is a retort.

responsible adjective
1 *Parents are legally **responsible** for their children.*
- in charge
  OPPOSITE not responsible
2 *He's a very **responsible** sort of person.*
- reliable, sensible, trustworthy, dependable, conscientious, dutiful, honest
  OPPOSITE irresponsible
3 *Looking after people's money is a **responsible** job.*
- important, serious
4 *Who is **responsible** for all this mess?*
- to blame, guilty (of), at fault

rest noun
1 *The actors had a short **rest** in the middle of the rehearsal.*
- break, breather, breathing-space, pause, respite, lie-down, nap
2 *The doctor said the patient needed complete **rest**.*
- relaxation, leisure, inactivity, ease, quiet, time off

the rest
*Take a few sweets now, but leave **the rest** for later.*
- the remainder, the surplus, the others, the remains

rest verb
1 *I think we should stop and rest for a while.*
- have a rest, lie down, relax, lounge, have a nap
2 *Rest the ladder against the wall.*
- lean, prop, stand, place, support

restaurant noun

WORD WEB

SOME TYPES OF RESTAURANT
buffet, café, cafeteria, canteen, carvery, chip shop, coffee shop, diner, grill, ice-cream parlour, snack bar, steakhouse, takeaway, tea room, wine bar
- A French-style restaurant is a bistro.
- A restaurant which serves pizza is a pizzeria.

restful adjective
We spent a restful Sunday morning reading magazines.
- peaceful, quiet, relaxing, leisurely, calm, tranquil, undisturbed
OPPOSITE stressful

restless adjective
1 *The animals became restless during the storm.*
- agitated, nervous, anxious, edgy, fidgety, excitable, jumpy, jittery
OPPOSITE relaxed
2 *I'm tired—I had a restless night.*
- sleepless, troubled, disturbed, unsettled, interrupted
OPPOSITE restful

restore verb
1 *Please restore the book to its proper place on the shelf.*
- put back, replace, return
2 *My uncle loves to restore old cars.*
- renew, repair, renovate, fix, mend, rebuild
3 *They are going to restore the Sunday bus service.*
- bring back, reinstate
- To restore someone to health is to cure them.

restrain verb
1 *Dogs must be restrained on a lead in the park.*
- hold back, keep back, keep under control, subdue, repress, restrict
2 *She tried to restrain her anger.*
- control, curb, suppress, stifle

restrict verb
The new law restricts the sale of fireworks.
- control, limit, regulate
to restrict to
In a safari park, animals are not restricted to enclosures.
- confine to, enclose in, keep in, shut in, imprison in

result noun
1 *The water shortage is a result of a long drought.*
- consequence, effect, outcome, sequel (to), upshot
- The result of a game is the score.
- The result of a trial is the verdict.
2 *If you multiply 9 by 12, what is the result?*
- answer, product

result verb
The bruising on his leg resulted from a bad fall.
- come about, develop, emerge, happen, occur, follow, ensue, take place, turn out
to result in
Severe flooding resulted in chaos on the roads.
- cause, bring about, give rise to, lead to, develop into

resume verb
We'll resume work after lunch.
- restart, start again, recommence, proceed with, continue, carry on

a
b
c
d
e
f
g
h
i
j
k
l
m
n
o
p
q
r
s
t
u
v
w
x
y
z

retain verb
1 *Please **retain** your ticket.*
- hold on to, keep, preserve, reserve, save
- (*informal*) hang on to
OPPOSITE surrender
2 *This type of soil is good at **retaining** water.*
- hold in, keep in, hold back
OPPOSITE release

retire verb
1 *The manager plans to **retire** at the end of the season.*
- give up work, stop working
- To leave your job voluntarily is to resign.
2 *Mrs Doyle **retired** to her room with a headache.*
- withdraw, adjourn

retort verb
*'There's no need to be rude!' **retorted** Hannah.*
- reply, answer, respond, react
FOR OTHER WAYS TO SAY SOMETHING
SEE **say**

retreat verb
1 *The army **retreated** to a safe position.*
- move back, draw back, fall back, withdraw, retire
- To retreat in a shameful way is to run away or (*informal*) turn tail.
2 *The snail **retreated** into its shell.*
- shrink back, recoil

retrieve verb
*I had to climb the fence to **retrieve** our ball.*
- get back, bring back, fetch, recover, rescue, salvage

return verb
1 *We hope to **return** to Paris next summer.*
- go back, revisit
2 *My husband **returns** on Friday.*
- get back, come back, come home
3 *I **returned** the book to its rightful owner.*
- give back, restore
4 *Faulty goods may be **returned** to the shop.*
- send back, take back

5 *Please **return** the money I lent you.*
- give back, repay, refund
6 *We hoped that the fever would not **return**.*
- happen again, recur

return noun
1 *She looked forward to her friends' **return**.*
- reappearance, homecoming
2 *Did you get a good **return** from your investment?*
- profit, interest, gain

reveal verb
1 *The spy refused to **reveal** his real identity.*
- declare, disclose, make known, confess, admit, announce, proclaim, publish, tell
2 *She swept aside the curtain to **reveal** a secret door.*
- uncover, unveil, expose
OPPOSITE hide

revenge noun
*He sought **revenge** for the killing of his brother.*
- reprisal, vengeance
to take revenge on someone
*He declared that he would **take revenge on** them all.*
- get even with, repay
- (*informal*) get your own back on

revere verb
*The painter was greatly **revered** by his fellow artists.*
- admire, respect, honour, esteem, worship, adore
OPPOSITE despise

reverse noun
*The letter had a handwritten note on the **reverse**.*
- other side, back

reverse verb
1 *You can use tracing paper to **reverse** a drawing.*
- turn round, swap round, transpose, invert
2 *The driver tried to **reverse** into the parking space.*
- back, drive backwards, go backwards

a b c d e f g h i j k l m n o p q r s t u v w x y z

review noun

1 *They are carrying out a **review** of after-school clubs.*
- study, survey, examination, inspection

2 *We had to write **reviews** of our favourite books.*
- report, criticism, appraisal, critique

review verb

1 *The judge began to **review** the evidence.*
- examine, go over, study, survey, consider, assess, appraise, evaluate, weigh up

2 *He **reviews** the latest films for the Sunday paper.*
- criticize, write a review of

revise verb

1 *We **revised** the work we did last term.*
- go over, review, study

2 *The new evidence forced me to **revise** my opinion.*
- change, modify, alter, reconsider, re-examine

3 *The last chapter has been **revised** by the author.*
- correct, amend, edit, rewrite, update

revive verb

1 *The patient **revived** slowly after the operation.*
- come round, come to, recover, rally, wake up

2 *A cold drink will **revive** you.*
- refresh, restore, invigorate, bring back to life, revitalize

revolt verb

1 *The people **revolted** against the cruel king.*
- rebel, riot, rise up
- To revolt on a ship is to mutiny.

2 *They were **revolted** by the stench in the dungeon.*
- disgust, repel, sicken, nauseate, offend, appal

revolting adjective

*What is that **revolting** smell?*
- disgusting, foul, horrible, nasty, loathsome, offensive, obnoxious, repulsive, repugnant, sickening, nauseating, vile, unpleasant

OPPOSITE pleasant, attractive

revolution noun

1 *The **revolution** brought in a new government.*
- rebellion, revolt, uprising

2 *Computers brought about a **revolution** in the way people work.*
- change, transformation, shift

3 *One **revolution** of the earth takes 24 hours.*
- rotation, turn, circuit, cycle

revolutionary adjective

*The inventor had come up with a **revolutionary** design.*
- new, novel, innovative, radical

revolve verb

*The earth **revolves** once every 24 hours.*
- rotate, turn
- To revolve quickly is to spin or whirl.
- To move round something is to circle or orbit it.

reward noun

*There is a **reward** for finding the missing cat.*
- prize, bonus, payment, award, decoration

OPPOSITE punishment

reward verb

1 *The firefighters were **rewarded** for their bravery.*
- honour, decorate

2 *She was generously **rewarded** for her work.*
- compensate, repay

rewarding adjective

*Being a vet must be a **rewarding** job.*
- satisfying, pleasing, gratifying, worthwhile

OPPOSITE thankless

rhyme noun

*The children like listening to nursery **rhymes**.*
- poem, verse

a
b
c
d
e
f
g
h
i
j
k
l
m
n
o
p
q
r
s
t
u
v
w
x
y
z

rhythm noun
*We tapped our feet to the **rhythm** of the music.*
- beat, pulse
- The speed or type of rhythm of a piece of music is the tempo.
- The type of rhythm of a piece of poetry is its metre.

rich adjective
1 *They must be **rich** to live in a castle.*
- wealthy, affluent, prosperous, well-off, well-to-do
  OPPOSITE poor
2 *The palace was full of **rich** furnishings.*
- expensive, costly, luxurious, sumptuous, opulent, lavish, splendid, ornate
3 *The dancer wore a dress of a **rich** red colour.*
- deep, strong, vivid, intense
4 *The soil in this area is very **rich**.*
- fertile, productive

riches plural noun
*They acquired **riches** beyond their wildest dreams.*
- wealth, money, affluence, prosperity, fortune, treasure

rickety adjective
*Take care—that ladder looks **rickety**.*
- shaky, unsteady, unstable, wobbly, flimsy
  OPPOSITE solid

rid verb
*The new vaccine may **rid** the world of the disease.*
- clear, free, empty, strip, purge
to get rid of
*He decided to **get rid of** his old guitar.*
- dispose of, throw away or out, scrap
- (*informal*) dump

riddle noun
*They had to solve the **riddle** to find the treasure.*
- puzzle, mystery, question, conundrum, problem

ride verb
*My little brother is learning to **ride** a bike.*
- control, handle, manage, steer

ride noun
*They took us for a **ride** in their new car.*
- drive, run, journey, trip
- (*informal*) spin

ridicule verb
*The inventor was **ridiculed** for his wacky ideas.*
- laugh at, make fun of, mock, scoff at, jeer at, sneer at, taunt, tease, deride

ridiculous adjective
1 *My little sister looked **ridiculous** in high-heeled shoes.*
- silly, stupid, foolish, daft, absurd, funny, laughable
2 *That is a **ridiculous** price for a pair of trainers!*
- ludicrous, senseless, nonsensical, preposterous, outrageous, absurd, unreasonable, crazy
  OPPOSITE sensible

right adjective
1 *The entrance is on the the **right** side of the building.*
- The right side of a ship when you face the bow is the starboard side.
  OPPOSITE left
2 *Put up your hand if you got the **right** answer.*
- correct, accurate, true, exact
  OPPOSITE wrong
3 *She was waiting for the **right** moment to tell him.*
- proper, appropriate, fitting, suitable, ideal
  OPPOSITE wrong
4 *It's not **right** to steal.*
- fair, honest, decent, just, honourable, lawful, moral, upright, virtuous, ethical
  OPPOSITE wrong

right adverb
1 *Turn **right** at the corner.*
  OPPOSITE left
2 *Turn **right** round.*
- all the way, completely
3 *She stood **right** in the middle.*
- exactly, precisely
4 *Go **right** ahead.*
- directly, straight

right noun

1 *The post office is on the right along the High Street.*
OPPOSITE left

2 *People have the right to walk across the common.*
• freedom, liberty

3 *You don't have the right to tell me what to do.*
• authority, power

rigid adjective

1 *The tent was supported by a rigid framework.*
• solid, stiff, firm, hard

2 *The referee was rigid in applying the rules.*
• strict, inflexible, harsh, stern, uncompromising
OPPOSITE flexible

rigorous adjective

The detective carried out a rigorous investigation.
• thorough, careful, meticulous, painstaking

rim noun

Mrs Sharpe peered at us over the rim of her glasses.
• brim, edge, lip, brink

ring noun

1 *The children danced around in a ring.*
• circle, round, loop, circuit

2 *The wooden barrel had metal rings round it.*
• band, hoop

ring verb

1 *The whole area was ringed by a high fence.*
• surround, encircle, enclose, circle

2 *The doorbell rang.*
• chime, peal, toll, jangle, tinkle, sound, buzz
SEE ALSO **bell**

3 *Ring me tomorrow evening.*
• phone, call, telephone, ring up
• (*informal*) give a buzz

rinse verb

After shampooing your hair, rinse it in clean water.
• wash, clean, bathe, swill
• To rinse out a toilet is to flush it.

riot noun

The police moved in to stop the riot.
• commotion, disorder, disturbance, turmoil, uproar, uprising

riot verb

The crowds were rioting in the streets.
• run riot, run wild, run amok, rampage, revolt, rise up, rebel

rip verb

She snatched the letter and ripped it to pieces.
• tear

ripe adjective

Some of the plums on the tree are ripe now.
• mature, ready to eat
• To become ripe is to ripen.

ripple verb

The wind rippled the surface of the pond.
• ruffle, stir, disturb, make waves on

rise verb

1 *The kite rose high into the air.*
• climb, mount, fly up, ascend, soar
• When a plane rises into the air, it takes off.
• When a rocket rises into the air, it lifts off.
OPPOSITE descend

2 *The outer wall of the castle rose before us.*
• tower, loom, reach up, stick up

3 *House prices rose again last year.*
• go up, increase
OPPOSITE fall

4 *The audience rose and applauded wildly.*
• stand up, get up
OPPOSITE sit

a
b
c
d
e
f
g
h
i
j
k
l
m
n
o
p
q
r
s
t
u
v
w
x
y
z

a
b
c
d
e
f
g
h
i
j
k
l
m
n
o
p
q
r
s
t
u
v
w
x
y
z

rise noun

1 *There will be a* **rise** *in temperature over the next few days.*
- increase, jump
  OPPOSITE fall

2 *At the top of the* **rise** *they paused for a break.*
- hill, slope, ascent, incline, bank, ramp
- (*Scottish*) brae

risk verb

1 *If you place a bet, you* **risk** *losing the money.*
- chance, dare, gamble, venture

2 *The firefighter* **risked** *his life to save them.*
- endanger, put at risk, jeopardize, hazard

risk noun

1 *All outdoor activities carry an element of* **risk**.
- danger, hazard, peril

2 *Starting a business involves* **risk**.
- a gamble, uncertainty

3 *The forecast says there's a* **risk** *of snow.*
- chance, likelihood, possibility

risky adjective

Cycling on icy roads is **risky**.
- dangerous, hazardous, perilous, unsafe
  OPPOSITE safe

ritual noun

The temple was used for ancient religious **rituals**.
- ceremony, rite, service

rival noun

He has no serious **rival** *for the championship.*
- competitor, adversary, challenger, opponent, contender, contestant

rival verb

Few countries can **rival** *Scotland for mountainous scenery.*
- compete with, contend with

rivalry noun

There was fierce **rivalry** *between the two local teams.*
- competition, competitiveness, opposition
  OPPOSITE cooperation

river noun

- A small river is a stream or rivulet or (*Scottish*) burn.
- A small river which flows into a larger river is a tributary.
- The place where a river begins is its source.
- The place where a river goes into the sea is its mouth.
- A wide river mouth is an estuary or (*Scottish*) firth.
- The place where the mouth of a river splits before going into the sea is a delta.
- A river of ice is a glacier.

WRITING TIPS

You can use these words to describe a river.
- to describe *HOW A RIVER FLOWS*: cascade, eddy, flood, flow, glide, gush, meander, plunge, rush, snake, sweep, swirl, twist, wind
- to describe *HOW A RIVER SOUNDS*: babble, burble, gurgle, murmur, ripple, roar, splash, thunder

road noun

WORD WEB

KINDS OF ROAD FOR TRAFFIC
bypass, dual carriageway, highway, main road, motorway, one-way street, ring road, trunk road
- A road which is closed at one end is a dead-end.
- A private road up to a house is a drive.

KINDS OF ROAD IN TOWNS
alley, avenue, boulevard, crescent, cul-de-sac, lane, street, terrace
SEE ALSO **path**

roam verb

1 *We roamed about town aimlessly.*
* wander, ramble, drift, stroll, amble, meander

2 *Herds of wild deer roamed over the hills.*
* range, rove, prowl

roar noun, verb

The dragon lifted its might head and roared.
* bellow, cry, yell, bawl, howl, thunder

rob verb

The thieves planned to rob several banks in the city.
* steal from, break into, burgle, hold up, raid, loot, ransack, rifle

robber noun SEE thief

robbery noun SEE stealing

robe noun

* A kind of robe you might wear in your bedroom is a dressing gown or bathrobe.
* Robes worn by a priest are vestments.
* The robe worn by a monk or nun is a habit.
* A robe an official might wear at a ceremony is a gown.
* Robe is also a formal word for a woman's dress.

robot noun

> **WORD WEB**
>
> *The robot spoke in a metallic voice.*
> * automaton, android
> * A robot which is part-human is a cyborg.
>
> PARTS A ROBOT MIGHT HAVE
> antenna, buttons, computer brain or chip, control panel, flashing lights, arm or limb, gripper, laser, motor, sensor, wheels
>
> SOME WAYS TO DESCRIBE A ROBOT
> bionic, intelligent, machine-like, mechanical, metallic, super-human

robust adjective

1 *To be an explorer, you must be robust.*
* strong, vigorous, fit, hardy, healthy, rugged
* OPPOSITE weak

2 *I bought a robust pair of boots for hiking.*
* sturdy, tough, durable, hard-wearing
* OPPOSITE flimsy

rock noun

> **WORD WEB**
>
> *We clambered over the rocks on the seashore.*
> * boulder, stone
> * A small rock is a pebble.
> * A steep face of rock is a cliff or crag.
>
> SOME KINDS OF ROCK
> basalt, chalk, flint, granite, gypsum, lava, limestone, marble, quartz, sandstone, shale, slate
>
> * Rock from which metal or valuable minerals can be extracted is ore.
> * A layer of rock is a stratum.
> * A person who studies rocks is a geologist.

rock verb

1 *I rocked the baby's cradle to and fro.*
* sway, swing

2 *The ship rocked in the storm.*
* roll, toss, lurch, pitch, tilt, reel

rocky adjective

1 *Nothing was growing in the rocky ground.*
* barren, stony, pebbly

2 *Take care—that chair's a bit rocky.*
* rickety, shaky, unsteady, unstable, wobbly

rod noun

The framework is held together by steel rods.
* bar, rail, pole, strut, shaft, stick, spoke, staff

rodent noun FOR VARIOUS KINDS OF ANIMAL

SEE **animal**

rogue noun
Don't trust him—he's a rogue.
- rascal, scoundrel, villain, cheat, fraud, swindler

role noun
1 *Who is playing the lead role in the play?*
- character, part
2 *Each player has an important role in the team.*
- job, task, function, position

roll verb
1 *The wheels of the carriage began to roll.*
- move round, turn, revolve, rotate, spin, twirl, whirl
2 *Roll the paper around your finger.*
- curl, wind, wrap, twist, coil
- To roll up a sail on a yacht is to furl it.
3 *Roll the pastry into a large circle.*
- flatten, level out, smooth
4 *The ship rolled about in the storm.*
- pitch, rock, sway, toss, wallow, lurch

romantic adjective
1 *The film had a very romantic ending.*
- sentimental, emotional, tender
- (informal) soppy, mushy
2 *The life of an explorer sounds very romantic.*
- exotic, glamorous, exciting

romp verb
The children romped around the playground.
- leap about, run about, skip about, caper, frisk, frolic

roof noun
- The sloping beams in the framework of a roof are rafters.
- The overhanging edge of a roof is the eaves.
- A building without a roof is an open-air building.
- A vehicle without a roof is an open-top vehicle.

room noun
1 *How many rooms are there in your house?*
- An old word for room is chamber.
2 *Is there room in the car for another suitcase?*
- space, capacity

WORD WEB

ROOMS YOU MIGHT FIND IN A HOUSE OR FLAT
bathroom, bedroom, boxroom, conservatory, dining room, drawing room, hall, kitchen or kitchenette, landing, lavatory or toilet or (informal) loo, living room, lounge, nursery, pantry, parlour, scullery, sitting room, spare room or guest room, study, utility room

ROOMS YOU MIGHT FIND IN A SCHOOL
assembly hall, classroom, cloakroom, corridor, drama room, laboratory, lavatories or toilets or (informal) loos, library, music room, office, sickroom, staffroom, storeroom

- A small room in a monastery or prison is a cell.
- An underground room is a basement or cellar or vault.
- The space in the roof of a house is the attic or loft.
- A room where an artist works is a studio.
- A room where you wait to see a doctor or dentist is a waiting room.
- A room in a boarding school where pupils sleep is a dormitory.
- A room in a hospital for patients is a ward.

roomy adjective
The flat is surprisingly roomy inside.
- big, large, spacious, sizeable

root noun
We need to get to the root of the problem.
- origin, source, cause, basis, starting point

rope noun
The sailors threw a rope to the men in the water.
- cable, cord, line

- The ropes that support a ship's mast and sails are the rigging.
- A rope with a loop at one end used for catching cattle is a lasso.

rot verb

*The wooden fence had begun to **rot**.*

- decay, decompose, become rotten, crumble, disintegrate
- If metal rots it is said to corrode.
- If rubber rots it is said to perish.
- If food rots it is said to go bad or putrefy.

rotate verb

*The globe **rotates** on its axis.*

- revolve, turn, spin, pivot, wheel, swivel, twirl, twist, whirl

rotten adjective

1 *The window frame is **rotten**.*
- decayed, decaying, decomposed, crumbling, disintegrating
- Rotten metal is corroded or rusty metal.
  OPPOSITE sound

2 *The fridge smelled of **rotten** eggs.*
- bad, mouldy, mouldering, foul, putrid, smelly
  OPPOSITE fresh

3 (*informal*) *The weather has been **rotten** all week.*
- bad, unpleasant, disagreeable, awful, abysmal, dreadful, nasty
- (*informal*) lousy
  OPPOSITE good

rough adjective

1 *A **rough** track led to the farm.*
- bumpy, uneven, irregular, rocky, stony, rugged, craggy, jagged
  OPPOSITE even, smooth

2 *The sea was **rough** and the boat lurched from side to side.*
- stormy, turbulent, heaving
- If the sea is rough with small waves it is said to be choppy.
  OPPOSITE calm

3 *The woman wore a **rough** woollen cloak.*
- coarse, harsh, scratchy, bristly
  OPPOSITE soft

4 *The prisoners had suffered **rough** treatment.*
- harsh, severe, cruel, hard, tough, violent
  OPPOSITE gentle, mild

5 *I had only a **rough** idea of where we were.*
- approximate, vague, inexact, imprecise, hazy
  OPPOSITE exact

6 *Our guide made a **rough** sketch of the route.*
- quick, hasty, crude, basic
  OPPOSITE detailed, careful

roughly adverb

*The cinema can seat **roughly** a hundred people.*

- approximately, about, around, close to, nearly

round adjective

*Holly bushes have small **round** berries.*

- rounded, spherical
- A flat round shape is circular.

round noun

*Our team got through to the second **round** of the competition.*

- stage, heat, bout, contest, game

round verb

*The motorbike **rounded** the corner at top speed.*

- go round, travel round, turn

to round something off

*They **rounded** the evening **off** with some songs.*

- bring to an end, conclude, end, finish, complete

to round up people or things

*The captain **rounded up** his players.*

- assemble, gather, bring together, collect, muster, rally

roundabout adjective

*We went by a **roundabout** route to avoid the traffic.*

- indirect, circuitous, long, winding, twisting
  OPPOSITE direct

a
b
c
d
e
f
g
h
i
j
k
l
m
n
o
p
q
r
s
t
u
v
w
x
y
z

rouse verb
1 *We were **roused** by the sound of birds singing.*
- arouse, awaken, call, wake up
2 *He was a quiet man, not easily **roused** to anger.*
- provoke, agitate, excite, stimulate, stir up

route noun
*We drove home by the quickest **route**.*
- path, road, way, course, direction, journey

routine noun
1 *Brushing my teeth is part of my morning **routine**.*
- pattern, procedure, way, custom, habit, practice, order
2 *The ice-skaters practised their new **routine**.*
- act, programme, performance, number

row noun
1 *The gardener planted the vegetables in **rows**.* (rhymes with go)
- column, line, string, series, sequence
- A row of people waiting for something is a queue.
- A row of people walking behind each other is a file.
- A row of soldiers standing side by side on parade is a rank.
2 *The class next door was making a terrible **row**.* (rhymes with cow)
- noise, racket, din, commotion, disturbance, uproar, rumpus
3 *One of the pirates had a **row** with the captain.* (rhymes with cow)
- argument, fight, quarrel, squabble, disagreement, dispute

rowdy adjective
*Later in the evening, the party became **rowdy**.*
- noisy, unruly, wild, disorderly, boisterous, riotous
OPPOSITE quiet

royalty noun

> **WORD WEB**
> SOME MEMBERS OF A ROYAL FAMILY
> king, monarch, prince, princess, queen, queen mother, sovereign
> - The husband or wife of a royal person is a consort.
> - The way to address a king or queen is Your Majesty.
> - The way to address a prince or princess is Your Highness.
> SEE ALSO **ruler**

rub verb
1 *Kathy **rubbed** her sore elbow.*
- stroke, knead, massage
2 *I **rubbed** some suncream on my arms.*
- spead, smooth, smear, apply (to)
3 *These boots are **rubbing** against my ankles.*
- graze, scrape, chafe
4 *She **rubbed** the mirror until it gleamed.*
- polish, wipe, shine, buff
to rub something out
*Can you **rub out** those pencil marks?*
- erase, wipe out, delete, remove

rubbish noun
1 *Mike took the **rubbish** out to the bin.*
- refuse, waste, trash, garbage, junk, litter, scrap
2 *Don't talk **rubbish**!*
- nonsense, drivel, balderdash, piffle, gibberish, claptrap, gobbledegook
- (*informal*) rot, tripe, twaddle

rude adjective
1 *It's very **rude** to talk with your mouth full.*
- impolite, discourteous, disrespectful, impertinent, impudent, insolent, offensive, insulting, bad-mannered, ill-bred
- To be rude to someone is to insult or snub them.
- To be rude about sacred things is to be blasphemous or irreverent.
OPPOSITE polite

2 *Some of the jokes in the film are rather* **rude**.
- indecent, improper, offensive, coarse, crude

OPPOSITE decent, clean

ruffle verb
*The peacock shook and **ruffled** its tail feathers.*
- stir, ripple, rumple, tousle

ruin verb
*The storm had **ruined** the farmer's crops.*
- damage, destroy, spoil, wreck, devastate, demolish, lay waste, shatter

ruin noun
*When they lost the match, it was the **ruin** of their dream.*
- collapse, failure, breakdown
- Financial ruin is bankruptcy.

ruins
*Archaeologists have discovered the **ruins** of a Roman fort.*
- remains, remnants, fragments

ruined adjective
*Bats flew in and out of the **ruined** abbey.*
- wrecked, crumbling, derelict, dilapidated, tumbledown, ramshackle

rule noun
1 *Players must stick to the **rules** of the game.*
- law, regulation, principle
- A set of rules is a code.

2 *The country was formerly under French* **rule**.
- control, authority, command, power, government, reign

rule verb
1 *The Romans **ruled** a vast empire.*
- command, govern, control, direct, lead, manage, run, administer

2 *Queen Victoria continued to **rule** for many years.*
- reign, be ruler

3 *The umpire **ruled** that the batsman was out.*
- judge, decree, pronounce, decide, determine, find

ruler noun

> **WORD WEB**
>
> SOME KINDS OF RULER
> emir, emperor, empress, governor, head of state, king, lord, monarch, president, prince, princess, queen, sovereign
>
> - A person who rules while a monarch is too young or too ill to rule is a regent.
>
> SOME RULERS IN PAST TIMES
> caesar, pharaoh, raja or rani, sultan or sultana, tsar or tsarina

rummage verb
*I **rummaged** through my bag looking for my purse.*
- search, hunt, ransack, scour

rumour noun
*There was a **rumour** that the queen was a witch in disguise.*
- gossip, hearsay, talk
- (informal) tittle-tattle

run verb
1 *We **ran** as fast as our legs could carry us.*
- race, sprint, dash, tear, bolt, career, speed, hurry, rush, streak, fly, whiz, zoom, scurry, scamper, scoot
- To run at a gentle pace is to jog.
- When a horse runs, it gallops, canters, or trots

2 *Tears **ran** down the mermaid's cheeks.*
- stream, flow, pour, gush, flood, cascade, spill, trickle, dribble, leak

3 *That old sewing machine still **runs** well.*
- function, operate, work, go, perform

4 *My uncle **runs** a restaurant in Leeds.*
- manage, be in charge of, direct, control, supervise, govern, rule

5 *The High Street **runs** through the city centre.*
- pass, go, extend, stretch, reach

a b c d e f g h i j k l m n o p q r s t u v w x y z

to run away or **off**
The thieves ran off when they heard footsteps.
- bolt, fly, flee, escape, take off, hurry off
- (*informal*) make off, clear off, scarper

to run into
1 *Guess who I ran into the other day?*
- meet, come across, encounter
- (*informal*) bump into
2 *A cyclist skidded and ran into a tree.*
- hit, collide with

run noun
1 *She goes for a run in the park every morning.*
- A fast run is a dash, gallop, race, or sprint.
- A gentle run is a jog.
2 *We went for a run in the car.*
- drive, journey, ride
3 *They've had a run of good luck recently.*
- sequence, stretch, series
4 *The farmer built a new chicken run.*
- enclosure, pen, coop

runaway noun
- A person who has run away from the army is a deserter.
- A person who is running away from the law is a fugitive or outlaw.

runner noun
The runners were ready to start the race.
- athlete, competitor
- Someone who runs fast over short distances is a sprinter.
- Someone who runs to keep fit is a jogger.

runny adjective
This custard is too runny.
- watery, thin, liquid, fluid
OPPOSITE thick

rural adjective
They live in a peaceful rural area.
- country, rustic, agricultural, pastoral
OPPOSITE urban

rush verb
I rushed home with the good news.
- hurry, hasten, race, run, dash, fly, bolt, charge, shoot, speed, sprint, tear, zoom
- When cattle or other animals rush along together they stampede.

rush noun
1 *We've got plenty of time, so what's the rush?*
- hurry, haste, urgency
2 *There was a sudden rush of water.*
- flood, gush, spurt, stream, spate

rustic adjective
The village had a rustic charm.
- country, rural, pastoral, countrified

rut noun
The tractor left ruts along the track.
- furrow, groove, channel, trough

ruthless adjective
The pirates launched a ruthless attack.
- cruel, brutal, bloodthirsty, barbaric, heartless, pitiless, merciless, callous, ferocious, fierce, savage, vicious, violent
OPPOSITE merciful

Ss

sack noun
The farmer delivered a large sack of potatoes.
- bag, pack

sack verb
The manager threatened to sack the whole team.
- dismiss, discharge
- (*informal*) fire, give you the sack

sacred adjective

*The Koran is a **sacred** book.*
- holy, religious, divine, heavenly

sacrifice verb

1 *I **sacrificed** my lunch break to practise guitar.*
- give up, surrender, go without

2 *The ancient Greeks **sacrificed** animals to please the gods.*
- offer up, kill, slaughter

sad adjective

> **OVERUSED WORD**
>
> Try to vary the words you use for **sad**. Here are some other words you could use.
>
> - for a SAD MOOD or SAD PERSON :
>   unhappy, sorrowful, miserable, depressed, downcast, downhearted, despondent, crestfallen, dismal, gloomy, glum, blue, low, dejected, forlorn, desolate, doleful, wretched, woeful, woebegone, tearful, heartbroken, broken-hearted
>   *Mia felt **miserable** when her best friend moved away.*
>
> - If you are sad because you are away from home, you are homesick.
>   OPPOSITE happy
>
> - for a SAD STORY or SAD TUNE :
>   depressing, melancholy, mournful, moving, touching, plaintive, wistful
>   *The pirate related the **mournful** tale of Billy Bones.*
>   OPPOSITE cheering
>
> - for a SAD SITUATION or SAD NEWS :
>   unfortunate, unpleasant, painful, regrettable, lamentable, grim, serious, grave, tragic, grievous
>   *The letter contained some **painful** news.*
>   OPPOSITE cheerful, pleasant
>
> - for something that MAKES YOU FEEL SAD :
>   upsetting, distressing, heartbreaking, heart-rending, pitiful, pathetic
>   *It was **heartbreaking** to watch the injured bird.*

sadden verb

*The news of her friend's illness **saddened** her.*
- distress, upset, depress, grieve, disappoint
- (*informal*) break your heart
  OPPOSITE cheer up

sadness noun SEE **sorrow**

safe adjective

1 *The kitten was found **safe** and well in a neighbour's garden.*
- unharmed, unhurt, uninjured, undamaged, sound, intact
- (*informal*) in one piece
  OPPOSITE hurt, damaged

2 *They felt **safe** indoors as the storm raged outside.*
- protected, guarded, defended, secure
  OPPOSITE vulnerable

3 *The secret code is in **safe** hands.*
- reliable, trustworthy, dependable

4 *Is the tap water **safe** to drink?*
- harmless, uncontaminated, innocuous
  OPPOSITE dangerous

safety noun

*You must wear a seat belt for your own **safety**.*
- protection, security, well-being
  OPPOSITE danger

sag verb

*The sandwich was so full that it **sagged** in the middle.*
- sink, dip, droop, flop, slump

sail verb

1 *We **sailed** to Norway rather than going by air.*
- travel by ship
- To have a holiday sailing on a ship is to cruise.
- To begin a sea voyage is to put to sea or set sail.

2 *None of the survivors knew how to **sail** the ship.*
- pilot, steer, navigate

a
b
c
d
e
f
g
h
i
j
k
l
m
n
o
p
q
r
s
t
u
v
w
x
y
z

sailor noun

*The crew comprised three **sailors** and a cook.*

- seaman, seafarer, mariner, boatman
- A person who sails a yacht is a yachtsman or yachtswoman.

sake noun

for the sake of

*He put some money aside **for the sake of** his children.*

- for the good of, on behalf of, in the interests of, to help

salary noun

*The job has an annual **salary** of £30,000.*

- income, pay, earnings
- If your pay is paid week by week, it is called wages.

sale noun

*They made a lot of money from the **sale** of their house.*

- selling, marketing, vending
OPPOSITE purchase

salvage verb

*The crew tried to **salvage** some supplies from the wreck.*

- rescue, save, recover, retrieve, reclaim

same adjective

the same

1 *Each pirate was given **the same** ration of rum.*
- equal, identical, equivalent

2 *Everyone in the choir wore **the same** outfit.*
- matching, similar, alike, uniform

3 *Her feelings have remained **the same**.*
- unaltered, unchanged, constant
- Words which mean the same are synonymous.
OPPOSITE different

sample noun

*The detective asked for a **sample** of her handwriting.*

- specimen, example, instance, illustration, selection

sample verb

*Would you like to **sample** some home-made jam?*

- taste, test, try

sand noun

*We built a huge castle out of **sand** and seashells.*

- Hills of sand along the coast are dunes.

sands

*They played on the **sands** until the tide came in.*

- beach, shore

sane adjective

*No **sane** person would stand out in the pouring rain!*

- sensible, rational, reasonable
OPPOSITE insane

sarcastic adjective

*He made a **sarcastic** remark about my hat.*

- mocking, satirical, ironical, sneering, taunting

satisfaction noun

*He gets a lot of **satisfaction** from growing vegetables.*

- happiness, pleasure, enjoyment, contentment, fulfilment, sense of achievement, pride
OPPOSITE dissatisfaction

satisfactory adjective

*I'm afraid this work is not **satisfactory**.*

- acceptable, adequate, passable, good enough, tolerable, competent
- (*informal*) all right, up to scratch
OPPOSITE unsatisfactory

satisfy verb

*Nothing **satisfies** him—he's always complaining.*

- please, content, make you happy
- To satisfy your thirst is to quench or slake it.
OPPOSITE dissatisfy

saturate verb

*The heavy rainfall had **saturated** the ground.*

- soak, drench
- If something is saturated, it is said to be wringing wet.

saunter verb

*We **sauntered** slowly through the woods.*
- amble, stroll, wander, ramble
FOR OTHER WAYS TO WALK
SEE **walk** verb

savage adjective

1 *The invaders launched a **savage** attack on the town.*
- vicious, cruel, barbaric, brutal, bloodthirsty, pitiless, ruthless, merciless, inhuman
OPPOSITE humane
2 *A **savage** beast is said to live in the cave.*
- untamed, wild, ferocious, fierce
OPPOSITE domesticated

save verb

1 *They managed to **save** most of the books from the fire.*
- rescue, recover, retrieve, salvage
2 *The knight pledged to **save** the princess from the witch's curse.*
- protect, defend, guard, shield, preserve
3 *She **saved** him from making a fool of himself.*
- stop, prevent, deter
4 *I **saved** you a piece of my birthday cake.*
- keep, reserve, set aside, hold on to
5 *If you share a car, then you can **save** petrol.*
- be sparing with, conserve, use wisely

savings plural noun

*They used all their **savings** to go on a cruise.*
- reserves, funds, resources, investments

saw noun FOR VARIOUS TOOLS
SEE **tool**

say verb

1 *He found it hard to **say** what he meant.*
- express, communicate, put into words, convey
2 *I would like to **say** a few words before we start.*
- utter, speak, recite, read

⚠ **OVERUSED WORD**

Try to vary the words you use for **say**, especially in direct speech. Here are some other words you could use.

- to *SAY LOUDLY* :
call, cry, exclaim, bellow, bawl, shout, yell, roar
*'Land ahoy!' **bellowed** the cabin boy.*

- to *SAY QUIETLY* :
whisper, mumble, mutter
*'That woman,' I **whispered**, 'is a secret agent.'*

- to *SAY STRONGLY* :
state, announce, assert, declare, pronounce, insist, maintain, profess
*'I never cut my toenails,' the ogre **declared**.*

- to *SAY CASUALLY* :
remark, comment, observe, note, mention
*'It's very warm for this time of year,' Mr Lewis **remarked**.*

- to *SAY ANGRILY* :
snap, snarl, growl, thunder, bark, rasp, rant, rave
*'Give me that piece of paper!' **snapped** Miss Crabbit.*

- to *SAY SUDDENLY* :
blurt out
*'That's just a pretend dinosaur!' Ben **blurted out**.*

- to *SAY UNCLEARLY* :
babble, burble, gabble, stammer, stutter
*The stranger kept **babbling** about hidden treasure.*

- to *SAY IN SURPRISE* or *ALARM* :
gasp, cry, squeal
*'The tunnel is sealed! There's no way out!' **gasped** Alex.*

- to *SAY SOMETHING FUNNY* :
joke, quip, tease
*'Were you singing? I thought it was a cat,' **teased** my big sister.*

- to *GIVE AN ORDER* :
command, demand, order
*A voice outside **demanded**, 'Open the door at once!'*

a
b
c
d
e
f
g
h
i
j
k
l
m
n
o
p
q
r
s
t
u
v
w
x
y
z

- to *ASK A QUESTION*:
  enquire, demand, query
  'How do you spell your name?' the judge
  enquired.

- to *GIVE A REPLY*:
  answer, reply, respond, retort
  *'Certainly not!' **retorted** Lady Dimsley.*

- to *MAKE A REQUEST*:
  beg, entreat, implore, plead, urge
  *The mouse **pleaded**, 'Please let go off*
  my tail!'

- to *MAKE A SUGGESTION*:
  suggest, propose
  'Let's make them walk the plank,'
  ***suggested** Captain Hook.*

- to *SAY AGAIN*:
  repeat, reiterate, echo
  *The Martians **repeated**, 'Take us to your*
  leader!'

saying noun
'Many hands make light work' is a
*common **saying**.*
- expression, phrase, motto, proverb,
  catchphrase
- An overused saying is a cliché.

scamper verb
*The rabbits **scampered** away to*
safety.
- hurry, dash, run, rush, hasten,
  scuttle

scan verb
1 *The lookout **scanned** the horizon,*
  hoping to see land.
- search, study, survey, examine,
  scrutinize, stare at, eye
2 *I **scanned** through some magazines in*
  the waiting room.
- skim, glance at, flick through

scandal noun
1 *The waste of food after the party was a*
  ***scandal**.*
- disgrace, embarrassment, shame,
  outrage
2 *Some newspapers like to publish the*
  *latest **scandal**.*
- gossip, rumours, dirt

scanty adjective
*The villagers had only a **scanty** supply*
of water.
- limited, meagre, scarce, poor, sparse,
  inadequate, insufficient
- (*informal*) measly
  OPPOSITE plentiful

scar noun
*The warrior had a **scar** across his*
forehead.
- mark, blemish, wound

scar verb
*The injuries he received **scarred** him for*
life.
- mark, disfigure, deface

scarce adjective
*Water is very **scarce** in the desert.*
- hard to find, in short supply, lacking,
  sparse, scanty, rare, uncommon
- (*informal*) thin on the ground
  OPPOSITE plentiful

scarcely adverb
She was so tired that she could
***scarcely** walk.*
- barely, hardly, only just

scare noun
*The explosion gave them a nasty **scare**.*
- fright, shock, alarm

scare verb
*My brother tried to **scare** us by making*
ghost noises.
- frighten, terrify, petrify, alarm,
  startle, panic
  OPPOSITE reassure

scared adjective
When she heard the footsteps, Lily was
*too **scared** to move.*
- frightened, terrified, petrified,
  horrified, alarmed, fearful, panicky
  SEE ALSO afraid

scary adjective (*informal*)
*I had to close my eyes at the **scary** bits*
in the film.
- frightening, terrifying, horrifying,
  alarming, nightmarish, fearsome,
  chilling, spine-chilling, hair-raising,
  bloodcurdling, chilling, eerie, sinister

scatter verb
1 *She **scattered** the seeds on the ground.*
- spread, sprinkle, sow, strew, throw about, shower
OPPOSITE collect

2 *The animals **scattered** when the children ran towards them.*
- break up, separate, disperse, disband
OPPOSITE gather

scene noun
1 *The police arrived quickly at the **scene** of the crime.*
- location, position, site, place, situation, spot

2 *They were rehearsing a **scene** from the play.*
- episode, part, section, act

3 *I gazed out of the window at the moonlit **scene**.*
- landscape, scenery, view, sight, outlook, prospect, spectacle, setting, backdrop

4 *He didn't want to create a **scene** in the restaurant.*
- fuss, commotion, disturbance, quarrel, row

scenery noun
*We admired the **scenery** from the top of the hill.*
- landscape, outlook, prospect, scene, view, panorama

scent noun
*Rowena loves the **scent** of roses.*
- smell, fragrance, perfume, aroma
SEE ALSO **smell** noun, verb

sceptical adjective
*At first, I was **sceptical** about the legend of the ghost.*
- disbelieving, doubtful, doubting, unconvinced, dubious, incredulous, suspicious, uncertain, unsure
OPPOSITE trustful

schedule noun
*The athletes had a rigorous training **schedule**.*
- programme, timetable, plan, calendar, diary
- A schedule of topics to be discussed at a meeting is an agenda.
- A schedule of places to be visited on a journey is an itinerary.

scheme noun
*They worked out a **scheme** to raise some money.*
- plan, proposal, project, procedure, method, system

scheme verb
*The smugglers were **scheming** against each other.*
- plot, conspire, intrigue

school noun

WORD WEB

VARIOUS KINDS OF SCHOOL
academy, boarding school, comprehensive school, faith school, grammar school, high school, independent school, infant school, junior school, kindergarten, nursery school, preparatory or prep school, primary school, private school, public school, secondary school

FOR ROOMS IN A SCHOOL
SEE **room**

science noun

WORD WEB

SOME BRANCHES OF SCIENCE
aeronautics, anatomy, astronomy, biology, botany, chemistry, computer science, earth science, electronics, engineering, genetics, geology, information technology, mechanics, medicine, meteorology, physics, psychology, veterinary science, zoology

scoff verb
to scoff at
*Everyone **scoffed at** her ideas.*
- mock, ridicule, sneer at, jeer at, deride, make fun of, poke fun at

scold verb
*He **scolded** the paper boy for being late.*
- reprimand, reproach, tell off
- (informal) tick off

a
b
c
d
e
f
g
h
i
j
k
l
m
n
o
p
q
r
s
t
u
v
w
x
y
z

a
b
c
d
e
f
g
h
i
j
k
l
m
n
o
s
t
u
v
w
x
y
z

scoop verb

*We **scooped** out a moat for our sandcastle.*

- dig, gouge, scrape, excavate, hollow

scope noun

1 *The park offers plenty of **scope** for children to play.*

- opportunity, room, space, freedom, liberty

2 *These things are outside the **scope** of the project.*

- range, extent, limit, reach, span

scorch verb

*The dragon's breath **scorched** the wizard's beard.*

- burn, singe, sear, blacken, char

score noun

*We added up each other's **scores**.*

- marks, points, total
- *The final score is the* result.

score verb

1 *How many goals did you **score**?*

- win, get, make, gain, earn

2 *Some lines were **scored** into the bark of the tree.*

- cut, gouge, mark, scrape, scratch

scorn noun

*She dismissed my suggestion with **scorn**.*

- contempt, derision, disrespect, mockery, ridicule
- OPPOSITE admiration

scour verb

1 *He **scoured** the pan until it shone.*

- scrape, scrub, rub, clean, polish

2 *Edith **scoured** the room looking for her glasses.*

- search, hunt through, ransack, comb

scowl verb

*The witch **scowled** under her floppy black hat.*

- frown, glower

FOR OTHER FACIAL EXPRESSIONS

SEE **expression**

scramble verb

1 *The smugglers escaped by **scrambling** over the rocks.*

- clamber, climb, crawl, scrabble

2 *The children **scrambled** to get the best seats.*

- push, jostle, struggle, fight, scuffle

scrap noun

1 *They fed the **scraps** of food to the birds.*

- bit, piece, fragment, morsel, crumb, speck, particle

2 *He took a pile of **scrap** to the tip.*

- rubbish, waste, junk, refuse, litter
- Scraps of cloth are rags or shreds.

3 (*informal*) *There was a **scrap** between the two gangs.*

- fight, brawl, scuffle, tussle, squabble

scrap verb

1 *The author **scrapped** the last paragraph.*

- discard, throw away, abandon, cancel, drop, give up
- (*informal*) dump

2 (*informal*) *The cubs enjoy **scrapping** with each other.*

- fight, brawl, tussle, scuffle

scrape verb

1 *She **scraped** her knee when she fell over.*

- graze, scratch, scuff

2 *I tried to **scrape** the mud off my trainers.*

- rub, scour, scrub, clean

scrape noun

*My little brother is always getting into **scrapes**.*

- trouble, mischief
- (*informal*) jam, pickle

scratch verb

1 *Someone **scratched** the side of the car.*

- mark, score, scrape, gouge, graze

2 *The cat tried to **scratch** her.*

- claw

scratch noun

*Who made this **scratch** on the side of the car?*

- gash, groove, line, mark, scrape

scrawl verb
*She **scrawled** his phone number on a scrap of paper.*
- jot down, scribble, write

scream noun, verb
*A woman ran out of the house **screaming**.*
*We heard a woman's **scream** in the distance.*
- shriek, screech, shout, yell, cry, bawl, howl, wail, squeal, yelp

screen noun
*The room was divided into two by a **screen**.*
- curtain, partition, divider

screen verb
1 *Miss Bennett used a parasol to **screen** her from the sun.*
- shield, protect, shelter, shade, cover, hide, mask, veil

2 *All employees are **screened** before being appointed.*
- examine, investigate, test

scribble verb
*He **scribbled** his phone number on a scrap of paper.*
- scrawl, jot down, dash off, write
- To scribble a rough drawing, especially when you are bored, is to doodle.

script noun
- The script for a film is a screenplay.
- A handwritten or typed script is a manuscript.

scrub verb
*She **scrubbed** the floor clean.*
- rub, brush, clean, wash, scour

scruffy adjective
*Magnus wore an old jumper and **scruffy** jeans.*
- untidy, messy, ragged, tatty, tattered, worn-out, shabby
- **OPPOSITE** smart

scrutinize verb
*She **scrutinized** the handwriting on the letter.*
- examine, inspect, look at, study, investigate, explore

scuffle noun
*A **scuffle** broke out between rival fans.*
- fight, brawl, tussle, scrap, squabble

sculpture noun
*The temple was full of marble **sculptures**.*
- carving, figure, statue

sea noun

WORD WEB
- The very large seas of the world are called oceans.
- An area of sea partly enclosed by land is a bay or gulf.
- A wide inlet of the sea is a sound.
- A wide inlet where a river joins the sea is an estuary, or in Scotland a firth.
- A narrow stretch of water linking two seas is a strait.
- The bottom of the sea is the seabed.
- The land near the sea is the coast or the seashore.
- Creatures that live in the sea are marine creatures.

THINGS YOU MIGHT SEE ON THE SEA
breaker, iceberg, sea spray, surf, swell, waves; boat, cruise ship, ocean liner, yacht

SOME CREATURES THAT LIVE IN THE SEA
dolphin, eel, fish, killer whale, octopus, porpoise, seahorse, seal, sea lion, shark, squid, stingray, turtle, whale
SEE ALSO **seashore**

WRITING TIPS
You can use these words to describe **the sea**.
- to describe *A CALM SEA* :
calm, crystal clear, glassy, sparkling, tranquil, unruffled
- to describe *A ROUGH SEA* :
choppy, raging, rough, stormy, tempestuous, turbulent, wild
- *WAVES ON THE SEA* might:
billow, break, crash, heave, pound, roll, surge, swell, tumble, wash

a
b
c
d
e
f
g
h
i
j
k
l
m
n
o
p
q
r

s
t
u
v
w
x
y
z

seal verb
*The entrance to the burial chamber had been **sealed**.*
- close, fasten, shut, lock, secure
- To seal a leak is to plug it or stop it.

seam noun
1 *The **seam** on his trousers split.*
- join
2 *Geologists discovered a **seam** of coal.*
- layer, stratum

search verb
1 *He was **searching** for the book he had lost.*
- hunt, look, seek
- To search for gold or some other mineral is to prospect.
2 *The police **searched** the house but didn't find anything.*
- explore, scour, ransack, rummage through, comb
3 *Security staff **searched** all the passengers.*
- check, inspect, examine, scrutinize
- (informal) frisk

search noun
*After a long **search**, she found her keys.*
- hunt, look, check
- A long journey in search of something is a quest.

seashore noun

WORD WEB

*We explored the **seashore**, looking for shells and fossils.*
- seaside, beach, shore, coast

THINGS YOU MIGHT SEE ON THE SEASHORE
cave, cliff, coral reef, driftwood, dunes, lighthouse, mudflats, pebbles, rock pool, rocks, sand, seashell, seaweed, shingle
SEE ALSO **seaside**

CREATURES THAT LIVE ON THE SEASHORE
barnacle, clam, cockle, coral, crab, cuttlefish, jellyfish, limpet, mussel, oyster, prawn, razor shell, sea anemone, sea bird, seagull, sea urchin, shrimp, sponge, starfish, whelk

FOR NAMES OF SEA BIRDS
SEE **bird**

FOR OTHER SEA CREATURES
SEE **sea**

seaside noun

WORD WEB

*If it's sunny tomorrow, we might go to the **seaside**.*
- beach, sands, seashore

THINGS YOU MIGHT SEE AT THE SEASIDE
beach huts, funfair, harbour, ice-cream van, jetty, pier, promenade

- A town where you go to have fun by the sea is a seaside resort.

THINGS YOU MIGHT TAKE TO THE SEASIDE
beach ball, bucket and spade, deckchair, fishing net, snorkel, sunglasses, sunhat, sunshade, suncream, surfboard, surfsuit, swimming costume, towel, windbreak

THINGS YOU MIGHT DO AT THE SEASIDE
ball games, beachcombing, building sandcastles, collecting shells, fishing, paddling, scuba diving, snorkelling, sunbathing, surfing, swimming, water-skiing, windsurfing

season noun
*The hotels are full during the holiday **season**.*
- period, time

seat noun
*We found two empty **seats** at the back of the cinema.*
- chair, place
- A long seat for more than one person is a bench.
- A long wooden seat in a church is a pew.
- A seat on a bicycle or horse is a saddle.
- A special seat for a king or queen is a throne.

seat verb

1 The guests **seated** themselves around the table.
- place, position, sit down, settle

2 The theatre can **seat** two hundred people.
- have seats for, accommodate, hold, take

secluded adjective

They found a **secluded** beach for their picnic.
- quiet, isolated, private, lonely, remote, cut off, sheltered, hidden
OPPOSITE crowded

second adjective

Would anyone like a **second** helping of pudding?
- another, additional, extra, further

second noun

1 The magic potion only takes a **second** to work.
- instant, moment, flash
- (informal) jiffy, tick

2 Inga was **second** in the cross-country race.
- runner-up

second verb

We need someone to **second** the proposal.
- back, support

secondary adjective

She loves to run and winning is of **secondary** importance to her.
- lesser, lower, minor, inferior, subordinate

second-hand adjective

The shop sells **second-hand** computers.
- used, pre-owned
OPPOSITE new

secret adjective

1 The spy managed to get hold of a **secret** document.
- confidential, classified, restricted
- (informal) hush-hush

2 The detectives are part of a **secret** operation.
- undercover, covert

3 The things I write in my diary are **secret**.
- private, confidential, personal, intimate

4 The cook showed us a **secret** passageway into the castle.
- hidden, concealed, disguised
OPPOSITE public, open
FOR SECRET AGENTS
SEE **spy** noun

secretive adjective

Why is she being so **secretive** about her past?
- uncommunicative, tight-lipped, reticent, reserved, mysterious, quiet
- (informal) cagey
OPPOSITE communicative, open

section noun

The website has a special **section** aimed at children.
- part, division, sector, portion, segment, bit, fragment
- A section of a book is a chapter.
- A section from a piece of classical music is a movement.
- A section taken from a book or a long piece of music is a passage.
- A section of a journey is a stage.

sector noun

Soldiers occupied one **sector** of the town.
- area, part, district, region, section, zone

secure adjective

1 The ladder was not very **secure**.
- steady, firm, solid, fixed, fast, immovable

2 She is still trying to find a **secure** job.
- permanent, regular, steady

3 They bolted the doors to make the castle **secure**.
- safe, guarded, protected, defended
OPPOSITE insecure, unsafe

secure verb

1 The door wasn't properly **secured**.
- fasten, lock, seal, bolt

2 He managed to **secure** two tickets for the match.
- get hold of, acquire, obtain

a
b
c
d
e
f
g
h
i
j
k
l
m
n
o
p
q
r
s
t
u
v
w
x
y
z

security noun

*You must wear a seat belt for your own **security**.*

- protection, safety

see verb

1 *If you look closely, you might **see** a dragonfly.*

- catch sight of, spot, notice, observe, make out, distinguish, note, perceive, recognize, sight, spy
- To see something briefly is to glimpse it.
- To see an accident or some unusual event is to witness it.

2 *Did you **see** the news yesterday?*

- watch, look at, view

3 *You may **see** me in my office after work.*

- go to, report to

4 *I didn't expect to **see** you here!*

- meet, run into, encounter
- (*informal*) bump into

5 *Will we have time to **see** them on the way home?*

- visit, call on, drop in on

6 *I **see** what you mean.*

- understand, appreciate, comprehend, follow, grasp, realize, take in

7 *I find it hard to **see** him in the role of Peter Pan.*

- imagine, picture, visualize

8 *Please **see** that the windows are shut.*

- make sure, make certain, ensure

9 *I'll **see** what I can do.*

- think about, consider, ponder, reflect on, weigh up

10 *I'll **see** you to the door.*

- conduct, escort, accompany, guide, lead, take

to see to something

*Who's going to **see to** the refreshments?*

- deal with, attend to, take care of, sort out

seed noun

- The seed in an orange, lemon, etc., is a pip.
- The seed in a date, plum, etc., is a stone.

seek verb

1 *For many years he **sought** his long-lost brother.*

- search for, hunt for, look for

2 *The king **sought** only to make his daughter happy.*

- try, attempt, strive, want, wish, desire

seem verb

*Everything **seems** to be all right.*
*She is far more friendly than she **seems**.*

- appear, look, give the impression of being

seep verb

*Oil began to **seep** through the crack.*

- leak, ooze, escape, flow, dribble, trickle, soak

seethe verb

*The mixture in the cauldron began to **seethe**.*

- boil, bubble, foam, froth up

to be seething

*Greg **was seething** when I crashed his bike.*

- be angry, be furious, rage, storm

segment noun

*Divide the orange into **segments**.*

- section, portion, piece, part, bit, wedge, slice

seize verb

1 *The climber stretched out to **seize** the rope.*

- grab, catch, snatch, take hold of, grasp, grip, clutch

2 *The police **seized** the robbers as they left the bank.*

- arrest, capture
- (*informal*) collar, nab
- To seize someone's property as a punishment is to confiscate it.
- To seize someone's power or position is to usurp it.
- To seize an aircraft or vehicle during a journey is to hijack it.

seldom adverb

*It **seldom** rains in the desert.*

- rarely, infrequently
  OPPOSITE often

select verb
*They had to **select** a new captain.*
• choose, pick, decide on, opt for, settle on, appoint, elect

select adjective
*Only a **select** few were invited to the party.*
• privileged, chosen, special, hand-picked

selection noun
*The shop has a wide **selection** of rollerskates.*
• choice, range, variety, assortment

selfish adjective
*He's so **selfish** that he kept all the chocolate to himself.*
• greedy, mean, miserly, grasping, self-centred, thoughtless
OPPOSITE unselfish, generous

sell verb
*The corner shop **sells** newspapers and sweets.*
• deal in, trade in, stock, retail
• Uncomplimentary synonyms are peddle and hawk.
FOR PEOPLE WHO SELL THINGS
SEE **shop**
OPPOSITE buy

send verb
1 *I **sent** each of my friends a postcard.*
• post, mail, dispatch
2 *They plan to **send** a rocket to Mars.*
• launch, propel, direct, fire, shoot
to send for someone
*I think we should **send for** a doctor.*
• call, summon, fetch
to send something out
*The device was **sending out** weird noises.*
• emit, issue, give off, discharge

senior adjective
1 *She's one of the **senior** players in the squad.*
• older, long-standing, principal
2 *He is a **senior** officer in the navy.*
• high-ranking, superior
OPPOSITE junior

sensation noun
1 *She had a tingling **sensation** in her fingers.*
• feeling, sense
2 *The unexpected news caused a **sensation**.*
• excitement, thrill
• A sensation caused by something bad is an outrage or a scandal.

sensational adjective
1 *The newspaper printed a **sensational** account of the murder.*
• shocking, horrifying, startling, lurid
2 (informal) *Did you hear the **sensational** result of yesterday's match?*
• amazing, extraordinary, remarkable, fantastic, spectacular, stupendous

sense noun
1 *A baby learns about the world through its **senses**.*
• Your five senses are hearing, sight, smell, taste, and touch.
2 *A drummer needs to have a good **sense** of rhythm.*
• awareness, consciousness, perception, feeling (for)
3 *If you had any **sense** you'd stay at home.*
• common sense, intelligence, wisdom, wit, brains
4 *The **sense** of the word is not clear.*
• meaning, significance, import
to make sense of something
*They couldn't **make sense of** the garbled message.*
• understand, make out, interpret, follow

sense verb
1 *He **sensed** that she didn't like him.*
• be aware, realize, perceive, feel, guess, notice, suspect
2 *The device **senses** any change of temperature.*
• detect, respond to

369

senseless adjective

1 *Smashing the window was a **senseless** act.*
- foolish, stupid, crazy, daft, irrational, mad, illogical, pointless, futile
OPPOSITE sensible

2 *The blow on the head left the ogre **senseless**.*
- unconscious, knocked out
OPPOSITE conscious

sensible adjective

1 *It would be **sensible** to wait until the weather improves.*
- wise, intelligent, shrewd, rational, reasonable, careful, prudent, logical, sane, sound
OPPOSITE stupid

2 *You will need **sensible** shoes for the hiking trip.*
- comfortable, practical
OPPOSITE impractical

sensitive adjective

1 *She has **sensitive** skin which gets sunburnt.*
- delicate, tender, fine, soft

2 *Take care what you say—he's very **sensitive**.*
- easily offended, easily upset, touchy

3 *She's very **sensitive** towards other people.*
- tactful, considerate, thoughtful, sympathetic, understanding
OPPOSITE insensitive

sentence verb

*The judge **sentenced** him to five years in prison.*
- pass judgement on, pronounce sentence on, condemn

sentimental adjective

1 *He gets **sentimental** looking at old photographs.*
- emotional, nostalgic, tearful

2 *I hate **sentimental** messages on birthday cards.*
- romantic, tender
- (*informal*) soppy, mushy

sentry nouns

*He gave the password to the **sentry** at the gate.*
- guard, lookout, sentinel, watchman

separate adjective

1 *The zoo kept the male lions **separate** from the cubs.*
- apart, separated, distinct, independent
OPPOSITE together

2 *They slept in **separate** rooms.*
- different, detached, unattached
OPPOSITE attached, joined

separate verb

1 *The sheepdog **separated** the sheep from the lambs.*
- cut off, divide, fence off, isolate, keep apart, remove, segregate, set apart, take away
- To separate something which is connected to something else is to detach or disconnect it.
- To separate things which are tangled together is to disentangle them.
OPPOSITE combine, mix

2 *They walked along together until their paths **separated**.*
- split, branch, fork
OPPOSITE merge

3 *Her friend's parents have **separated**.*
- split up, break up, part company
- To end a marriage legally is to divorce.

sequence noun

*The detective tried to piece together the **sequence** of events.*
- order, progression, series, succession, string, chain, train

serene adjective

*The woman in the painting had a **serene** smile on her face.*
- calm, contented, untroubled, peaceful, quiet, placid, tranquil
OPPOSITE agitated

series noun

1 *We had to answer a **series** of questions in our exam.*
- succession, sequence, string, set, chain, train

2 *Are you watching the new **series** on TV?*
- serial

serious adjective

1 *His **serious** expression told them something was wrong.*
- solemn, sombre, unsmiling, grave, grim
- OPPOSITE cheerful

2 *She is writing a **serious** book about global warming.*
- learned, intellectual, scholarly
- (*informal*) heavy
- OPPOSITE light

3 *Are you **serious** about wanting to learn to ski?*
- sincere, genuine, in earnest

4 *This hospital ward is for people with **serious** injuries.*
- severe, acute, critical, bad, terrible, appalling, dreadful, major, grave
- OPPOSITE minor, trivial

servant noun

*This part of the house was where the **servants** lived.*
- attendant, retainer, helper, domestic, manservant, maid
- The chief manservant in a private house is a butler.
- The servant of a medieval knight was a page or squire.

serve verb

1 *The shopkeeper was busy **serving** customers.*
- help, assist, aid

2 *When everyone had sat down they **served** the first course.*
- give out, dish up, pass round, distribute

3 *This room will **serve** as a study.*
- be suitable, be useful, function

service noun

1 *The genie bowed and said he was glad to be of **service**.*
- help, assistance, aid, use, usefulness, benefit

2 *Their marriage **service** was held in the local church.*
- ceremony, ritual, rite
- A service in church is a meeting for worship.

3 *Mum says her car needs a **service**.*
- a check-over, maintenance, servicing

service verb

*The garage **serviced** her car.*
- maintain, check, repair, mend, overhaul

session noun

1 *We have a training **session** on Saturday mornings.*
- period, time

2 *The Queen will open the next **session** of Parliament.*
- meeting, sitting

set verb

1 *The removal men **set** the piano on the floor.*
- place, put, stand, position

2 *I helped Dad to **set** the table.*
- arrange, lay, set out

3 *Have they **set** a date for the wedding yet?*
- appoint, specify, name, decide, determine, choose, fix, establish, settle

4 *The jelly will **set** quicker in the fridge.*
- become firm, solidify, harden, stiffen

5 *The sun was just beginning to **set**.*
- do down, sink

to set about something
*We **set about** clearing the table immediately.*
- begin, start, commence

to set off

1 *The knights **set off** on their quest.*
- depart, get going, leave, set out, start out

2 *The burnt toast **set off** the smoke alarm.*
- activate, start, trigger

a
b
c
d
e
f
g
h
i
j
k
l
m
n
o
p
q
r
s
t
u
v
w
x
y
z

to set something out

*The information is clearly **set out** on the page.*

- lay out, arrange, display, present

to set something up

*They're trying to **set up** an after-school club.*

- establish, create, start, begin, introduce, organize

set noun

1 *There is a **set** of measuring spoons in the drawer.*
- collection, batch, kit

2 *Is there something wrong with the TV **set**?*
- apparatus, receiver

3 *Our class painted the **set** for the play.*
- scenery, setting

setting noun

*The house stood in a rural **setting**.*

- surroundings, location, place, position, site, background

settle verb

1 *The brothers tried to **settle** their differences.*
- resolve, sort out, deal with, end

2 *The cat had just **settled** on the sofa.*
- sit down, relax, rest

3 *A robin **settled** on a nearby branch.*
- land, alight

4 *The family is planning to **settle** in Canada.*
- emigrate (to), move (to), set up home

5 *You can see lots of fish when the mud **settles**.*
- sink to the bottom, clear, subside

6 *We'll **settle** the hotel bill in the morning.*
- pay, clear, square

to settle on

*Have you **settled on** a date for the wedding?*

- agree on, decide on, choose, name, fix

settlement noun

*There was once a Viking **settlement** in this area.*

- community, colony, encampment, village

settler noun

*The film is about early European **settlers** in America.*

- colonist, immigrant, pioneer

sever verb

*The couple decided to **sever** their relationship.*

- break off, end, terminate
- To sever a branch of a tree is to cut it off or remove it.
- To sever a limb is to amputate it.

several adjective

*The spy was able to adopt **several** disguises.*

- a number of, many, some, a few, various

severe adjective

1 *The jailer was very **severe** with the prisoners.*
- harsh, strict, hard, stern
  OPPOSITE lenient

2 *The traffic warden gave him a **severe** look.*
- unkind, unsympathetic, disapproving, grim
  OPPOSITE kind

3 *Ruby has a **severe** case of chickenpox.*
- bad, serious, acute, grave
  OPPOSITE mild

4 *The Arctic has a **severe** climate.*
- extreme, tough, harsh, hostile
- A severe frost is a sharp frost.
- Severe cold is intense cold.
- A severe storm is a violent storm.

sew verb

*Mum **sewed** a name tag onto my coat.*

- stitch, tack
- To sew a picture or design is to embroider it.
  SEE ALSO **needlework**

sex noun

*What **sex** is the hamster?*

- gender

shabby adjective
1 *The witch disguised herself in a **shabby** cloak.*
- ragged, scruffy, tattered, worn, worn-out, threadbare, frayed, tatty, seedy, dingy
OPPOSITE smart
2 *That was a **shabby** trick!*
- mean, nasty, unfair, unkind, dishonest, shameful, low, cheap

shade noun
1 *They sat in the **shade** of a chestnut tree.*
- shadow
2 *The porch had a **shade** to keep out the sun.*
- screen, blind, canopy
- A type of umbrella used as a sun shade is a parasol.
3 *The bathroom walls are a pale **shade** of blue.*
- hue, tinge, tint, tone, colour

shade verb
1 *Wearing a cap will **shade** your eyes from the sun.*
- shield, screen, protect, hide, mask
2 *He **shaded** the background of the picture with a pencil.*
- fill in, make darker, darken

shadow noun
*Her face was deep in **shadow**.*
- shade, darkness, gloom

shadow verb
*The detective was **shadowing** the suspect.*
- follow, pursue, tail, stalk, track, trail

shady adjective
1 *They found a **shady** spot under a tree.*
- shaded, shadowy, sheltered, dark, sunless
OPPOSITE sunny
2 *He took part in some **shady** business deals.*
- dishonest, disreputable, suspicious, dubious, suspect, untrustworthy
- (*informal*) fishy, dodgy
OPPOSITE honest

shaft noun
1 *Modern arrow **shafts** are made of wood.*
- spine, stick, pole, rod, staff
2 *He nearly fell into an old mine **shaft**.*
- pit, tunnel, hole
3 *A **shaft** of moonlight shone through the window.*
- beam, ray

shaggy adjective
*Llamas have long **shaggy** coats.*
- bushy, woolly, fleecy, hairy, thick

shake verb
1 *The hurricane made the whole house **shake**.*
- quake, shudder, shiver, rock, sway, totter, wobble, quiver, vibrate, rattle
2 *He was so upset that his voice was **shaking**.*
- tremble, quaver
3 *The giant **shook** his fist and growled angrily.*
- wave, brandish, flourish, wag, waggle, joggle
4 *They were **shaken** by the terrible news.*
- shock, startle, distress, upset, disturb, alarm, frighten

shaky adjective
1 *Be careful—the table is rather **shaky**.*
- unsteady, wobbly, insecure, rickety, flimsy, weak
2 *He was so nervous that his hands were **shaky**.*
- shaking, trembling, quivering
3 *He spoke in a **shaky** voice.*
- quavering, faltering, nervous, tremulous
OPPOSITE steady

shallow adjective
*The children paddled about in the **shallow** water.*
OPPOSITE deep

sham noun
*The story he told about his family was all a **sham**.*
- pretence, deception, lie

a b c d e f g h i j k l m n o p q r s t u v w x y z

a
b
c
d
e
f
g
h
i
j
k
l
m
n
o
p
q
r
s
t
u
v
w
x
y
z

shame noun
The guilty man hung his head in ***shame****.*
- disgrace, dishonour, humiliation, embarrassment, guilt

a shame
*It's **a shame** that you can't stay for longer.*
- a pity, unfortunate

shameful adjective
*The player was sent off for his **shameful** conduct on the pitch.*
- disgraceful, outrageous, scandalous, contemptible, despicable, wicked
OPPOSITE honourable

shape noun

WORD WEB
*The Halloween cake was in the **shape** of a bat.*
- form, figure
- A line showing the shape of a thing is the outline.
- A dark outline seen against a light background is a silhouette.
- A container for making things in a special shape is a mould.

FLAT SHAPES
circle, diamond, ellipse, heptagon, hexagon, oblong, octagon, oval, parallelogram, pentagon, polygon, quadrilateral, rectangle, rhombus, ring, semicircle, square, trapezium, triangle

THREE-DIMENSIONAL SHAPES
cone, cube, cylinder, hemisphere, polyhedron, prism, pyramid, sphere

shape verb
*The potter **shaped** the clay into a tall vase.*
- form, mould, fashion
- To shape something in a mould is to cast it.

share noun
*Each of the pirates got a **share** of rum.*
- ration, allowance, portion, quota, helping, division, part
- (*informal*) cut

share verb
*The robbers **shared** the loot between them.*
- divide, split, distribute, allot, allocate, deal out, ration out

sharp adjective
1 *Use a pair of **sharp** scissors.*
- keen, sharpened, razor-sharp
OPPOSITE blunt
2 *Barbed wire has **sharp** points all along it.*
- pointed, spiky, jagged
OPPOSITE smooth
3 *He felt a **sharp** pain in his side.*
- acute, piercing, stabbing
OPPOSITE dull
4 *Eagles have **sharp** eyes to see far in the distance.*
- keen, keen-sighted, observant, perceptive
OPPOSITE unobservant
5 *You need to focus the camera to get a **sharp** picture.*
- clear, distinct, well defined, crisp
OPPOSITE blurred
6 *Sherlock Holmes had a very **sharp** intelligence.*
- clever, quick, shrewd, perceptive
OPPOSITE dull, slow
7 *The bus slowed down before a **sharp** bend in the road.*
- abrupt, sudden, steep
- A bend that doubles back on itself is a hairpin bend.
OPPOSITE gradual
8 *The **sharp** frost killed our geraniums.*
- severe, extreme, intense, serious
OPPOSITE slight, mild
9 *This salad dressing is a bit **sharp**.*
- sour, tart, bitter
OPPOSITE mild, sweet

sharpen verb
*I need to **sharpen** these crayons.*
- make sharp, grind, whet, hone

shatter verb
1 *The ball **shattered** a window.*
- break, smash, destroy, wreck
2 *The windscreen **shattered** when a stone hit it.*
- break, splinter, disintegrate

sheaf noun
*She had a **sheaf** of papers in her hand.*
- bunch, bundle

sheath noun
*The knight put his sword back in its **sheath**.*
- casing, covering, sleeve
- A sheath for a sword or dagger is a scabbard.

shed noun
*They kept their lawnmower in the garden **shed**.*
- hut, shack, outhouse

shed verb
*A lorry **shed** its load on the motorway.*
- drop, let fall, spill, scatter

sheen noun
*He waxed the table to give it a nice **sheen**.*
- shine, polish, gloss, gleam, lustre

sheep noun
- A male sheep is a ram.
- A female sheep is a ewe.
- A young sheep is a lamb.
- Meat from sheep is mutton or lamb.
- The woolly coat of a sheep is its fleece.

sheer adjective
1 *The story he told was **sheer** nonsense.*
- complete, total, utter, absolute, pure
2 *Don't try to climb that **sheer** cliff.*
- vertical, perpendicular
3 *The ballgown was made of **sheer** silk.*
- fine, thin, transparent, see-through

sheet noun
1 *She started her diary on a fresh **sheet** of paper.*
- page, leaf, piece
2 *The pond was covered with a thin **sheet** of ice.*
- layer, film, covering, surface
3 *The glazier came to fit a new **sheet** of glass.*
- panel, pane, plate

shelf noun
*She put the books back on the **shelf**.*
- ledge, rack
- A shelf above a fireplace is a mantelpiece.

shell noun
*Tortoises have hard **shells**.*
- covering, case, casing, outside, exterior

shellfish noun

> **WORD WEB**
>
> SOME TYPES OF SHELLFISH
> barnacle, clam, cockle, conch, crab, crayfish, cuttlefish, limpet, lobster, mussel, oyster, prawn, razor shell, scallop, shrimp, whelk, winkle
> - Shellfish with legs such as crabs, lobsters, and shrimps are crustaceans.

shelter noun
*They reached **shelter** just before the storm broke.*
- cover, protection, safety, refuge, sanctuary

shelter verb
1 *The hedge **shelters** the garden from the wind.*
- protect, screen, shield, guard, defend, safeguard
2 *We **sheltered** from the rain under the trees.*
- hide, take refuge

shelve verb
*They had to **shelve** their plans for a summer holiday.*
- postpone, put off, defer, suspend
- (*informal*) put on ice

shield noun
*The trees act as an effective wind **shield**.*
- screen, barrier, defence, guard, protection
- The part of a helmet that shields your face is the visor.

shield verb
*The mother bear **shielded** her cubs from danger.*
- protect, defend, guard, safeguard, keep safe, shelter

a
b
c
d
e
f
g
h
i
j
k
l
m
n
o
p
q
r
s
t
u
v
w
x
y
z

a
b
c
d
e
f
g
h
i
j
k
l
m
n
o
p
q
r
s
t
u
v
w
x
y
z

shift verb

1 *I need some help to **shift** the furniture.*
- move, rearrange, reposition

2 *It was hard work **shifting** the mud off the tyres.*
- remove, dislodge, budge

shine verb

1 *A light **shone** from an upstairs window.*
- beam, glow, blaze, glare, gleam

FOR OTHER WAYS TO DESCRIBE LIGHT

SEE **light** noun

2 *He **shines** his shoes every morning.*
- polish, rub, brush

3 *She's good at all sports, but she **shines** at tennis.*
- be outstanding, excel, stand out

shiny adjective

*She polished the mirror until it was **shiny**.*
- shining, bright, gleaming, glistening, glossy, polished, burnished, lustrous
OPPOSITE dull

ship noun

FOR TYPES OF BOAT OR SHIP

SEE **boat**
- Ships that travel long distances at sea are ocean-going or seagoing ships.
- People who work on ships at sea are nautical or seafaring people.

ship verb

*The firm **ships** goods all over the world.*
- transport, send, post, mail

shirk verb

*He always **shirks** the unpleasant tasks.*
- avoid, evade, get out of, dodge, duck

shiver verb

*Ali waited outside, **shivering** with cold.*
- tremble, quiver, shake, shudder, quake

shock noun

1 *The news of his death came as a great **shock**.*
- blow, surprise, fright, upset

2 *People felt the **shock** of the explosion miles away.*
- bang, impact, jolt

3 *The driver involved in the accident was in a state of **shock**.*
- distress, trauma

shock verb

*The whole town was **shocked** by the news.*
- horrify, appal, startle, alarm, stun, stagger, shake, astonish, astound, surprise, dismay, upset
- A formal synonym is traumatize.

shoe noun

WORD WEB

SOME TYPES OF SHOE OR BOOT
ankle boot, ballet shoe, baseball boot, boot, brogue, clog, court shoe, espadrille, flip-flop, gymshoe, high-heel shoe, moccasin, mule, platform shoe, plimsoll, pump, sandal, slip-on, slipper, sneaker, stiletto, tap shoe, tennis shoe, trainer, wader, wellington or (*informal*) wellie

shoot verb

1 *Robin Hood **shot** an arrow into the air.*
- fire, discharge, launch, aim

2 *It is now illegal to hunt and **shoot** tigers.*
- fire at, hit, open fire on, gun down

3 *They watched the racing cars **shoot** past.*
- race, speed, dash, rush, streak, hurtle, fly, whiz, zoom

4 *Part of the film was **shot** in Canada.*
- film, photograph

shoot noun

*Young **shoots** grow in the spring.*
- bud, sprout

shop noun

WORD WEB

VARIOUS TYPES OF SHOP
boutique, corner shop, department store, hypermarket, market, shopping arcade, shopping centre, shopping mall, supermarket

shopping noun
*Just put the **shopping** in the boot of the car.*
- goods, purchases

shore noun SEE seashore

short adjective
1 *They live a **short** distance from the shops.*
- little, small
  OPPOSITE long
2 *It was a very **short** visit.*
- brief, quick, fleeting, hasty, temporary
  OPPOSITE long
3 *The troll was very **short** and fat.*
- small, tiny, little, squat, dumpy, diminutive, petite
  OPPOSITE tall
4 *The supply of water was getting **short**.*
- low, meagre, scant, limited, inadequate, insufficient
  OPPOSITE plentiful
5 *There is no need to be **short** with me!*
- abrupt, rude, sharp, curt, impolite, snappy
  OPPOSITE patient, polite

shortage noun
*The **shortage** of water is worrying.*
- scarcity, deficiency, lack, want, dearth
- A shortage of water is a drought.
- A shortage of food is a famine.

shortcoming noun
*As an actor, he has some **shortcomings**.*
- defect, failing, fault, weakness, limitation, drawback

shorten verb
*She had to **shorten** the essay because it was too long.*
- cut down, reduce, cut, trim, abbreviate, abridge, condense, compress, curtail
  OPPOSITE lengthen

shortly adverb
*The post should arrive **shortly**.*
- soon, before long, presently

shot noun
1 *I heard a noise like the **shot** of a pistol.*
- bang, blast, crack
2 *The archer was an excellent **shot**.*
- A person who is good at shooting with a gun is a marksman.
3 *The striker had an easy **shot** at the goal.*
- hit, strike, kick
4 *The photographer took some unusual **shots**.*
- photograph, picture, snap, snapshot
5 *(informal) We each had a **shot** at solving the riddle.*
- try, go, attempt
- *(informal)* bash

shout verb
*The ogre was **shouting** and stamping with rage.*
- call, cry out, bawl, yell, bellow, roar, howl, yelp, scream, screech, shriek
  OPPOSITE whisper

shove verb
*A man ran past and **shoved** me to the side.*
- push, thrust, force, barge, elbow, jostle, shoulder

shovel verb
*We **shovelled** the snow into a huge heap.*
- dig, scoop, shift, clear, move

show verb

1 *My uncle **showed** us his coin collection.*
- present, reveal, display, exhibit

2 *The photo **shows** my grandparents on holiday.*
- portray, picture, depict, illustrate, represent

3 *The dance tutor **showed** them what to do.*
- explain to, make clear to, instruct, teach, tell

4 *The evidence **shows** that he was right.*
- prove, demonstrate

5 *A nurse **showed** them into the waiting room.*
- direct, guide, conduct, escort, usher

6 *The signpost **shows** the way.*
- indicate, point out

7 *His vest **showed** through his shirt.*
- be seen, be visible, appear

to show off

*Walter is always **showing off**.*
- boast, brag, crow, gloat, swagger
- (*informal*) blow your own trumpet
- A person who shows off is a show-off.

show noun

1 *There is a **show** of artwork at the end of term.*
- display, exhibition, presentation

2 *There's a good **show** on at the theatre.*
- performance, production, entertainment

shower noun FOR VARIOUS TYPES OF RAIN

SEE **weather** noun

shower verb

*A passing bus **showered** mud over them.*
- spray, splash, spatter, sprinkle

showy adjective

*She was wearing very **showy** earrings.*
- gaudy, flashy, bright, loud, garish, conspicuous
OPPOSITE plain

shred noun

*The police couldn't find a **shred** of evidence.*
- bit, piece, scrap, trace

shreds

*The gale ripped the tent to **shreds**.*
- tatters, ribbons, rags, strips

shrewd adjective

*The spy was too **shrewd** to be caught.*
- clever, quick-witted, intelligent, sharp, cunning, crafty, artful, ingenious, wily, canny
OPPOSITE stupid

shriek noun, verb

*'Quick!' **shrieked** Alice. 'Open the door!'*
- cry, scream, screech, shout, howl, bawl, squeal, wail, yell

shrill adjective

*They heard the **shrill** sound of a whistle.*
- high, high-pitched, piercing, sharp, screechy
OPPOSITE low, soft

shrink verb

*My jeans have **shrunk** in the wash.*
- become smaller, contract
OPPOSITE expand

shrivel verb

*The plants **shrivelled** in the heat.*
- wilt, wither, droop, dry up, wrinkle, shrink

shroud verb

*The mountain was **shrouded** in mist.*
- cover, envelop, wrap, blanket, hide, conceal, mask, screen, veil

shrub noun

*She bought some **shrubs** at the garden centre.*
- bush

shudder verb

*They **shuddered** with fear when they heard the creature roar.*
- tremble, quake, quiver, shake, shiver

shuffle verb

1 *She **shuffled** along the corridor in her slippers.*
- shamble, scuffle, hobble, scrape

2 *Did you remember to **shuffle** the cards?*
- mix, mix up, jumble

shut verb
*Please **shut** the door behind you.*
- close, fasten, seal, secure, lock, bolt, latch
- To shut a door with a bang is to slam it.

to shut down
*The restaurant may have to **shut down**.*
- close down

to shut someone up
*He had been **shut up** in a dungeon for five years.*
- imprison, confine, detain

shut up (*informal*)
*I wish those people behind us would **shut up**!*
- be quiet, be silent, stop talking, hold your tongue

shy adjective
*The little girl was too **shy** to say anything.*
- bashful, timid, coy, reserved, hesitant, self-conscious, inhibited, modest
  OPPOSITE bold

sick adjective
1 *Katie is off school because she's **sick**.*
- ill, unwell, poorly, sickly, ailing, indisposed, off colour, peaky
  OPPOSITE healthy
2 *The sea was rough and the cabin boy felt **sick**.*
- nauseous, queasy

to be sick of
*I'm **sick of** this miserable weather!*
- be fed up with, be tired of, have had enough of

sicken verb
*They were **sickened** by the smell in the dungeon.*
- disgust, revolt, repel, offend
- (*informal*) turn your stomach

sickly adjective
*He has always been a **sickly** child.*
- unhealthy, weak, delicate, frail
  OPPOSITE healthy, strong

sickness noun SEE illness

side noun
1 *A cube has six **sides**.*
- face, surface
2 *The path runs along the **side** of the field.*
- edge, border, boundary, fringe, perimeter
- The side of a page is the margin.
- The side of a road is the verge.
3 *I could see both **sides** of the argument.*
- point of view, view, angle, aspect
4 *The football club has a strong **side** this year.*
- team

side verb
to side with someone
*Some of the townspeople **sided with** the enemy.*
- support, favour, take the side of, agree with, back

siege noun
*The town held out against the **siege** for months.*
- blockade

sift verb
***Sift** the flour to get rid of any lumps.*
- sieve, strain, filter

to sift through something
*The detective began to **sift through** the evidence.*
- examine, inspect, sort out, analyse, scrutinize, review

sigh noun, verb
*'I'll never be good at tennis,' **sighed** Libby.*
- moan, lament, grumble, complain

sight noun
1 *Weasels have sharp **sight** and excellent hearing.*
- eyesight, vision
2 *The woods in autumn are a lovely **sight**.*
- spectacle, display, show, scene
3 *By the third day, the ship was in **sight** of land.*
- view, range
4 *We went to London to see the **sights**.*
- attraction, landmark

a b c d e f g h i j k l m n o p q r s t u v w x y z

379

a
b
c
d
e
f
g
h
i
j
k
l
m
n
o
p
q
r
s
t
u
v
w
x
y
z

sight verb

*The lookout **sighted** a ship on the horizon.*

- see, spot, spy, make out, observe, notice, distinguish, recognize, glimpse

sign noun

1 *A **sign** pointed to the exit.*
- notice, placard, poster, signpost
- The sign belonging to a particular business or organization is a logo.
- The sign on a particular brand of goods is a trademark.

2 *The witch gave no **sign** that she was angry.*
- indication, clue, hint, warning

3 *The guard gave us a **sign** to pass through the gates.*
- signal, gesture, cue, reminder

sign verb

1 *Please **sign** your name on the form.*
- write, inscribe

2 *The club **signed** a new player last week.*
- take on, engage, recruit, enrol

signal noun

*The spy waited for the **signal** that all was clear.*

- sign, indication, prompt, cue
- A signal that tells you not to do something is a warning.

signal verb

*The pilot **signalled** that he was going to descend.*

- give a sign or signal, gesture, indicate, motion

significance noun

*What's the **significance** of that symbol?*

- importance, meaning, message, point, relevance

significant adjective

1 *The book describes the **significant** events of last century.*
- important, major, noteworthy, influential

2 *Global warming is having a **significant** effect on wildlife.*
- noticeable, considerable, perceptible, striking
- OPPOSITE insignificant

signify verb

1 *A red light **signifies** danger.*
- represent, stand for, symbolize, indicate, denote, mean

2 *The crew **signified** their agreement by raising their hands.*
- show, express, communicate, convey

silence noun

*There was **silence** while we sat the exam.*

- quiet, quietness, hush, stillness, calm, peace
- OPPOSITE noise

silence verb

*He **silenced** the audience by ringing a gong.*

- deaden, muffle, quieten, suppress
- To silence someone by putting something in or over their mouth is to gag them.

silent adjective

1 *At night, the desert was cold and **silent**.*
- quiet, noiseless, soundless, still, hushed
- Something you can't hear is inaudible.
- A common simile is as silent as the grave.
- OPPOSITE noisy

2 *Morris kept **silent** throughout the meeting.*
- quiet, speechless, mute
- (informal) mum
- To be too shy to speak is to be tongue-tied.
- OPPOSITE talkative

silky adjective

*Some types of rabbit have long, **silky** fur.*

- smooth, soft, fine, sleek, velvety

silly adjective

*It was **silly** of me to lock myself out of the house.*

- foolish, stupid, idiotic, senseless, thoughtless, brainless, unwise, unintelligent, half-witted, hare-brained, scatterbrained
- (*informal*) daft
OPPOSITE sensible

similar adjective

*The puppies are **similar** in appearance.*

- alike, identical, indistinguishable, matching, the same
OPPOSITE dissimilar, different

similar to

*The new book is **similar to** the previous one.*

- alike, close to, comparable to
OPPOSITE unlike, different from

similarity noun

*It's easy to see the **similarity** between the twins.*

- likeness, resemblance
OPPOSITE difference

simple adjective

1 *Can you answer this **simple** question?*
- easy, elementary, straightforward
OPPOSITE difficult
2 *The help file is written in **simple** language.*
- clear, plain, uncomplicated, understandable, intelligible
OPPOSITE complicated
3 *The girl wore a **simple** cotton dress.*
- plain, undecorated
OPPOSITE elaborate
4 *He enjoys **simple** pleasures like walking and gardening.*
- ordinary, unsophisticated, humble, modest, homely
OPPOSITE sophisticated

simply adverb

1 *I found his story **simply** unbelievable.*
- absolutely, wholly, completely, totally, utterly
2 *He won't eat peas **simply** because they're green!*
- just, merely, purely, only, solely

sin noun

*Some people believe that lying is a **sin**.*

- wrong, evil, wickedness, wrongdoing

sincere adjective

*Please accept my **sincere** apologies.*

- genuine, honest, true, truthful, real, earnest, wholehearted, frank
OPPOSITE insincere

sing verb

> **WORD WEB**
>
> SOME WAYS TO SING
> chant, chirp, croon, hum, trill, warble, yodel
>
> TYPES OF SINGING VOICE
> alto, baritone, bass, contralto, soprano, tenor, treble
>
> FOR KINDS OF MUSIC FOR SINGING
> SEE **song**

singe verb

*The iron was too hot and **singed** my T-shirt.*

- burn, scorch, sear, blacken, char

singer noun

*The band comprises two guitarists and a **singer**.*

- vocalist
- A group of singers is a choir or chorus.
- A member of a choir is a chorister.

single adjective

1 *We saw a **single** house high on the moors.*
- solitary, isolated
- When only a single example of something exists, it is unique.
2 *Miss Dempster was quite content to stay **single**.*
- unmarried
- An unmarried man is a bachelor.
- An unmarried woman is a spinster.

single verb

to single someone out

*They **singled her out** as the best player in the team.*

- pick out, select, choose, identify

a b c d e f g h i j k l m n o p q r s t u v w x y z

a
b
c
d
e
f
g
h
i
j
k
l
m
n
o
p
q
r
s
t
u
v
w
x
y
z

sinister adjective
*He looked up with a **sinister** smile on his face.*
- menacing, threatening, malevolent, evil, disturbing, unsettling, eerie
- (*informal*) creepy

sink verb
1 *The ship hit the rocks and **sank**.*
- go down, become submerged, founder, capsize
- To let water into a ship to sink it deliberately is to scuttle it.
2 *The sun began to **sink** below the horizon.*
- drop, fall, descend, subside, dip
- When the sun sinks to the horizon it sets.

sit verb
1 *Rachel **sat** on the sofa reading a magazine.*
- have a seat, settle down, rest, perch
- To sit on your heels is to squat.
- To sit to have your portrait painted is to pose.
2 *My brother is **sitting** his driving test next week.*
- take
- (*informal*) go in for

site noun
*This is the **site** of an ancient burial ground.*
- location, place, position, situation, setting, plot

site verb
*The new cinema will be **sited** in the middle of the town.*
- locate, place, position, situate

situated adjective
*The house is **situated** next to the park.*
- located, positioned

situation noun
1 *The house is in a pleasant **situation**.*
- location, locality, place, position, setting, site, spot

2 *I found myself in an awkward **situation**.*
- position, circumstances, condition, state of affairs
- A bad situation is a plight or predicament.
3 *She applied for a **situation** in the bank.*
- job, post, position, appointment

size noun
1 *What **size** is the garden?*
- dimensions, proportions, area, extent
2 *They were amazed by the sheer **size** of the pyramids.*
- scale, magnitude, immensity

sizeable adjective
*There is a **sizeable** reward for finding the stolen jewels.*
- large, considerable, substantial, fair-sized, decent, generous, worthwhile
OPPOSITE small

skeleton noun
1 *Inside the crypt, they found several human **skeletons**.*
- bones
2 *So far they've only put up the **skeleton** of the building.*
- frame, framework, shell

sketch noun
1 *She drew a quick **sketch** of her cat.*
- drawing, picture, outline
- A sketch you do while you think of other things is a doodle.
2 *The actors performed a comic **sketch**.*
- scene, turn, routine

sketch verb
*He **sketched** a rough design for the poster*
- draw, draft, outline, rough out

skid verb
*The postman **skidded** on the icy pavement.*
- slide, slip

skilful adjective
*Dickens was a **skilful** writer.*
- expert, skilled, accomplished, able, capable, talented, brilliant, clever, masterly, deft
- If you are skilful at a lot of things, you are versatile.
OPPOSITE incompetent

skill noun
*It takes a lot of **skill** to build a boat.*
- expertise, ability, aptitude, capability, competence, accomplishment, talent, proficiency, deftness

skim verb
*The stone **skimmed** across the surface of the pond.*
- glide, slide, skid, slip

to skim through
*Luke **skimmed through** the newspaper.*
- scan, look through, skip through, flick through

skin noun
*The cave people were dressed in animal **skins**.*
- coat, fur, hide, pelt
- The type of skin you have on your face is your complexion.
- Skin on fruit or vegetables is peel or rind.
- Skin that might form on top of a liquid is a coating, film, or membrane.

skinny adjective
*A **skinny** girl in bare feet answered the door.*
- thin, lean, bony, gaunt, lanky, scrawny, scraggy
OPPOSITE plump

skip verb
1 *The children **skipped** along the pavement.*
- hop, jump, leap, bound, caper, dance, prance
2 *I **skipped** the boring bits in the book.*
- pass over, miss out, ignore, omit, leave out

skirt verb
*The path **skirts** the playing field.*
- circle, go round, pass round

sky noun
*Clouds drifted slowly across the **sky**.*
- air, heavens

✏️ **WRITING TIPS**

You can use these words to describe **the sky**.
- to describe THE SKY BY DAY:
blue, clear, cloudless, cloudy, grey, overcast, stormy, sunless, sunny, thundery
SEE ALSO **weather** noun
- to describe THE SKY AT NIGHT:
moonless, moonlit, pitch-black, starless, starlit, starry, star-studded

---

slab noun
*The words were engraved on a **slab** of marble.*
- block, piece, tablet, slice, chunk, hunk, lump

slack adjective
1 *One of the ropes on the tent was **slack**.*
- loose, limp
OPPOSITE tight
2 *The team looked very **slack** in defence.*
- lazy, lax, negligent, casual, relaxed, easygoing
OPPOSITE alert

slacken verb
1 *The climber **slackened** the rope around his waist.*
- loosen, relax, release, ease off
OPPOSITE tighten
2 *The pace of the game **slackened** after half-time.*
- lessen, reduce, decrease, slow down
OPPOSITE increase

slam verb
*Don't **slam** the door!*
- bang, shut loudly

slant verb
1 *Her handwriting **slants** backwards.*
- lean, slope, tilt, incline, be at an angle

a b c d e f g h i j k l m n o **s** t u v w x y z

2 *He **slanted** his story to make it more dramatic.*
- distort, twist, warp

slant noun
1 *The floor of the caravan was at a **slant**.*
- slope, angle, tilt, incline, gradient
- A slant on a damaged ship is a list.
- A slanting line joining opposite corners of a square, etc., is a diagonal.
- A surface slanting up to a higher level is a ramp.

2 *The film brings a new **slant** to an old story.*
- point of view, angle, emphasis, bias

slap verb
*He **slapped** his hand against his thigh and laughed.*
- smack, strike, spank, hit, clout
- (*informal*) whack

slash verb FOR VARIOUS WAYS TO CUT THINGS
SEE **cut** verb

slaughter verb
*They had to **slaughter** the diseased cattle.*
- kill, butcher, massacre

slaughter noun
*The battle ended in terrible **slaughter**.*
- bloodshed, killing, massacre, butchery

slave verb
*They **slaved** all day to get the job done.*
- work hard, labour, toil, grind, sweat

slavery noun
*The prisoners were sold into **slavery**.*
- captivity, bondage
- OPPOSITE freedom

sledge noun
*We dragged our **sledges** up the snowy slope.*
- sled, toboggan
- A large sledge pulled by horses is a sleigh.
- A sledge used in winter sports is a bobsleigh.

sleek adjective
*Otters have **sleek** coats.*
- smooth, glossy, shiny, silky, soft, velvety
- OPPOSITE coarse

sleep verb
*The baby is **sleeping** in the next room.*
- be asleep, take a nap, doze
- (*informal*) snooze
- To go to sleep is to drop off or nod off.

sleep noun
*Mr Khan had a short **sleep** after lunch.*
- nap, rest, doze, catnap
- (*informal*) snooze, forty winks, shut-eye
- An afternoon sleep is a siesta.
- The long sleep some animals have through the winter is hibernation.

sleepless adjective
*The wanderers spent a **sleepless** night.*
- restless, wide awake
- The formal name for sleeplessness is insomnia.

sleepy adjective
*The giant was usually **sleepy** after dinner.*
- drowsy, tired, weary, heavy-eyed, lethargic, ready to sleep
- (*informal*) dopey
- OPPOSITE wide awake

slender adjective
1 *The ballerina had a **slender** figure.*
- slim, lean, slight, graceful, trim, svelte
- OPPOSITE fat

2 *The spider dangled on a **slender** thread.*
- thin, fine, fragile, delicate
- OPPOSITE thick

3 *They only had a **slender** chance of winning.*
- poor, slight, slim, faint, negligible, remote
- OPPOSITE good

4 *The team won by a **slender** margin.*
- narrow, small, slim
- OPPOSITE wide

slice verb
- To slice meat is to carve it.
  SEE ALSO **cut** verb

slick adjective
*He was very **slick** at shuffling cards.*
- skilful, artful, clever, cunning, deft, quick
  OPPOSITE clumsy

slide verb
*I like **sliding** down the chute in the playground.*
- glide, skid, slip, slither

slight adjective
1 *There's a **slight** problem with the computer.*
- minor, unimportant, insignificant, negligible, superficial, trifling, trivial
  OPPOSITE important
2 *The fairy was a **slight** creature, barely two inches tall.*
- delicate, fragile, frail, slender, slim, small, spare, thin, tiny
  OPPOSITE stout

slightly adverb
*She was **slightly** hurt in the accident.*
- a little, a bit, somewhat, rather
  OPPOSITE very, seriously

slim adjective
1 *A tall, **slim** figure appeared out of the fog.*
- graceful, lean, slender, spare, thin, trim
  OPPOSITE fat
2 *Their chances of winning are **slim**.*
- faint, poor, slight, slender, negligible, remote
  OPPOSITE good
3 *They won by a **slim** margin.*
- narrow, small, slender
  OPPOSITE wide

slimy adjective
*The floor of the tunnel was covered with **slimy** mud.*
- slippery, slithery, sticky, oozy
- (*informal*) gooey, icky

sling verb
*Robin Hood **slung** his quiver over his shoulder.*
- throw, cast, fling, hurl, pitch, heave, toss, lob
- (*informal*) chuck

slink verb
*The spy **slunk** away without being seen.*
- slip, sneak, steal, creep, edge, sidle

slip verb
1 *The paper boy **slipped** on the ice.*
- skid, slither, skate
2 *The lifeboat **slipped** into the water.*
- glide, slide
3 *Marion **slipped** out while everyone was talking.*
- sneak, steal, slink, tiptoe, creep, edge, sidle

slip noun
1 *She wrote her phone number on a **slip** of paper.*
- piece, scrap
2 *The pianist made a tiny **slip** at the start of the concert.*
- mistake, error, fault, blunder, gaffe, lapse

to give someone the slip
*The robber **gave them all the slip**.*
- escape, get away, run away

slippery adjective
*Take care—the floor is **slippery**.*
- slithery, slippy, smooth, glassy
- A surface slippery with frost is icy.
- A surface slippery with grease is greasy or oily.
- A common simile is as slippery as an eel.

slit noun
*The archers shot arrows through the **slits** in the castle wall.*
- opening, chink, gap, slot, split, tear, cut

slit verb FOR VARIOUS WAYS TO CUT THINGS
  SEE **cut** verb

a
b
c
d
e
f
g
h
i
j
k
l
m
n
o
p
q
r
s
t
u
v
w
x
y
z

slither verb
*The rattlesnake **slithered** through the long grass.*
- slide, slip, glide, slink, snake

slope verb
*The beach **slopes** gently down to the sea.*
- fall or rise, incline, bank, shelve

slope noun
1 *It was hard work pushing my bike up the **slope**.*
- hill, rise, bank, ramp
- An upward slope is an ascent.
- A downward slope is a descent.
2 *Rain runs down the roof because of the **slope**.*
- incline, slant, tilt, gradient

sloppy adjective
1 *For breakfast, there was a bowl of steaming, **sloppy** porridge.*
- runny, slushy, watery, liquid, wet
- (informal) gloopy
2 *His handwriting is very **sloppy**.*
- untidy, messy, careless, slovenly, slapdash, slipshod

slot noun
1 *To use the phone, put a coin into the **slot**.*
- slit, chink, hole, opening
2 *The programme has been moved from its usual **slot**.*
- time, spot, space, place

slouch verb
*Enid sat at her desk, **slouched** over the computer.*
- hunch, stoop, slump, droop, flop

slow adjective
1 *Tortoises move at a **slow** but steady pace.*
- unhurried, leisurely, gradual, plodding, dawdling, sluggish
2 *They took the train to London, followed by a **slow** bus journey.*
- lengthy, prolonged, drawn-out, tedious
3 *The prisoner was **slow** to answer.*
- hesitant, reluctant, tardy
OPPOSITE quick

slow verb
to slow down
Slow down—you're driving too fast!
- go slower, brake, reduce speed
OPPOSITE accelerate

sludge noun
*They cleared a lot of **sludge** out of the pond.*
- muck, mud, ooze, slime
- (informal) gunk

slump verb
1 *Sales of music CDs have **slumped** recently.*
- decline, fall, drop, plummet, plunge, crash, collapse
2 *The professor **slumped** into an armchair.*
- flop, collapse, sink, sag, slouch

slump noun
*There was a **slump** in trade after Christmas.*
- collapse, drop, fall, decline
- A general slump in trade is a depression or recession.
OPPOSITE boom

sly adjective
*The chess player knew several **sly** moves.*
- crafty, cunning, artful, clever, wily, tricky, sneaky, devious, furtive, secretive, stealthy, underhand
- A common simile is as sly as a fox.
OPPOSITE straightforward

smack verb
*He **smacked** the other player on the head by accident.*
- slap, strike, hit, cuff
- (informal) whack
FOR OTHER WAYS OF HITTING
SEE **hit** verb

small adjective

⚠ **OVERUSED WORD**
Try to vary the words you use for **small**. Here are some other words you could use.
- for a *SMALL OBJECT*:

- little, tiny, minute, compact, miniature, microscopic, minuscule, mini, baby
(*informal*) teeny, titchy, dinky
(*Scottish*) wee
OPPOSITE big, large
*Moles have incredibly **tiny** eyes and ears.*
- for a SMALL PERSON:
little, short, petite, slight, dainty, diminutive
(*informal*) pint-sized
*A **petite** little elf was standing on a toadstool.*
OPPOSITE big, tall, large
- for a SMALL HELPING or SMALL PORTION:
meagre, inadequate, insufficient, paltry, scanty, stingy, skimpy
(*informal*) measly
OPPOSITE large, generous, ample
*For breakfast there was stale bread with a **meagre** scraping of butter.*
- for a SMALL CHANGE or SMALL PROBLEM:
minor, unimportant, insignificant, trivial, trifling, negligible
OPPOSITE major, substantial
*The writers made some **trivial** changes to the script.*

smart adjective

1 *Everyone looked **smart** at the wedding.*
- elegant, well-dressed, well-groomed, stylish, spruce, fashionable, chic, neat, trim
- To make yourself smart is to smarten up.
OPPOSITE scruffy
2 *They booked a table in a very **smart** restaurant.*
- fashionable, high-class, exclusive, fancy
- (*informal*) posh
3 *The detective made a very **smart** move.*
- clever, ingenious, intelligent, shrewd, crafty
OPPOSITE stupid
4 *The cyclists set off at a **smart** pace.*
- fast, quick, rapid, speedy, swift, brisk
OPPOSITE slow

smart verb

*The smoke from the barbecue made our eyes **smart**.*
- hurt, sting, prick, prickle, tingle

smash verb

*A vase fell off the table and **smashed** to pieces on the floor.*
- break, crush, shatter, crack
- When wood smashes it splinters.
- To smash something completely is to demolish or destroy or wreck it.

to smash into
*A lorry had **smashed into** the side of a bus.*
- crash into, collide with, bang into, bump into

smear verb

*The chef **smeared** butter over the cooking dish.*
- spread, wipe, plaster, rub, dab, smudge, daub

smear noun

*There were **smears** of paint all over the carpet.*
- streak, smudge, blotch, splodge, splotch, daub, mark

smell noun

1 *The air was filled with the **smell** of roses.*
- scent, aroma, perfume, fragrance
2 *The **smell** of mouldy cheese was unbearable.*
- odour, stench, stink, reek, whiff
- (*informal*) pong, niff

smell verb

1 *I could **smell** something baking in the oven.*
- scent, sniff
- (*informal*) get a whiff of
2 *After walking all day, my feet were beginning to **smell**.*
- stink, reek
- (*informal*) pong

WRITING TIPS

You can use these words to describe how something smells.
- to describe something which SMELLS GOOD:
fragrant, aromatic, perfumed, scented, sweet-smelling
*The garden was planted with **sweet-smelling** herbs.*

a
b
c
d
e
f
g
h
i
j
k
l
m
n
o
p
q
r
s
t
u
v
w
x
y
z

a
b
c
d
e
f
g
h
i
j
k
l
m
n
o
p
q
r
s
t
u
v
w
x
y
z

- **to describe something which**
  SMELLS BAD :
  smelly, stinking, evil-smelling,
  foul-smelling, musty, odorous,
  reeking, rotten, fetid, foul
  (*informal*) stinky, pongy, whiffy
  *The witch stirred the **evil-smelling** brew.*

smile verb, noun
*The stranger **smiled** and introduced himself.*
- grin, beam
- To smile in a silly way is to simper.
- To smile in a self-satisfied way is to smirk.
- To smile in an insulting way is to sneer.

smoke noun
*Puffs of green **smoke** came from the dragon's nostrils.*
- fumes, gas, steam, vapour
- The smoke given out by a car is exhaust.
- A mixture of smoke and fog is smog.

smoke verb
1 *The bonfire was still **smoking** next morning.*
- smoulder
2 *A man stood silently **smoking** a cigar.*
- puff at

smooth adjective
1 *This part of the road is **smooth** and good for cycling.*
- flat, even, level
  OPPOSITE uneven
2 *In the early morning, the lake was perfectly **smooth**.*
- calm, still, unruffled, undisturbed, glassy
  OPPOSITE rough
3 *Otters have **smooth** and shiny coats.*
- silky, sleek, velvety
  OPPOSITE coarse
4 *The journey by train is very quick and **smooth**.*
- comfortable, steady
  OPPOSITE bumpy
5 *Stir the cake mixture until it is **smooth**.*
- creamy, flowing, runny
  OPPOSITE lumpy

smooth verb
*Charlotte stood up and **smoothed** her dress.*
- flatten, level, even out
- To smooth cloth you can iron or press it.
- To smooth wood you can plane or sand it.

smother verb
1 *Pythons **smother** their prey to death.*
- suffocate, choke, stifle
2 *The pudding was **smothered** with cream.*
- cover, coat

smoulder verb SEE burn

smudge noun
*There were **smudges** of ink all over the page.*
- smear, blot, streak, stain, mark

smudge verb
*Don't **smudge** the icing on the cake!*
- smear, blur, streak

snack noun
*I usually bring an apple or banana for a **snack**.*
- bite, refreshments
- (*informal*) nibble
- A snack in the middle of the morning is sometimes called elevenses.

snag noun
*We've hit a **snag** with our holiday plans.*
- problem, difficulty, obstacle, hitch, complication, setback

snake noun

WORD WEB
*The **snake** coiled itself round a branch.*
- serpent

SOME KINDS OF SNAKE
adder, anaconda, boa constrictor, cobra, grass snake, mamba, puff adder, python, rattlesnake, sand snake, sea snake, sidewinder, tree snake, viper

- A route or river that twists like a snake is said to be serpentine.

snap verb
1 *A twig **snapped** under one of my boots.*
- break, crack

2 *The dog **snapped** at the postman's ankles.*
- bite, nip

3 *Mr Baker was in a bad mood and **snapped** at everyone.*
- snarl, bark

snare noun
*A bird had got caught in the **snare**.*
- trap

snarl verb
1 *The guard dog **snarled** as we approached.*
- growl, bare its teeth

2 *'Go away!' **snarled** a voice inside the cave.*
- snap, growl, thunder, bark

snatch verb
*The thief **snatched** the jewels and ran off.*
- grab, seize, grasp, pluck, wrench away, wrest away

sneak verb
*I managed to **sneak** in without anyone seeing.*
- slip, steal, creep, slink, tiptoe, sidle, skulk

sneaky adjective
*That was a really **sneaky** trick.*
- sly, underhand, cunning, crafty, devious, furtive, untrustworthy
- OPPOSITE honest

sneer verb
to sneer at
*He **sneered at** my first attempts to ice-skate.*
- make fun of, mock, ridicule, scoff at, jeer at, deride

sniff noun, verb FOR VARIOUS SOUNDS
SEE **sound** noun

snigger verb
*Please stop **sniggering** at the back of the room.*
- laugh, giggle, titter, chuckle

snip verb
*The mermaid **snipped** off a lock of her hair.*
- cut, chop, clip, trim

snippet noun
*We could hear **snippets** of their conversation.*
- piece, fragment, bit, scrap, morsel, snatch

snivel verb
*For goodness' sake, stop **snivelling**!*
- cry, sob, weep, sniff, whimper, whine

snobbish adjective
*She's too **snobbish** to mix with us.*
- arrogant, pompous, superior, haughty
- (*informal*) stuck-up, snooty, toffee-nosed
- OPPOSITE humble

snoop verb
*They caught a man **snooping** round the office.*
- sneak, pry, poke, rummage, spy

snort noun, verb FOR VARIOUS SOUNDS
SEE **sound** noun

snout noun
*Aardvarks have long, narrow **snouts**.*
- muzzle, nose

snub verb
*She **snubbed** the neighbours by not inviting them to the party.*
- insult, offend, be rude to, brush off
- (*informal*) put down

snug adjective
*Lucy was tucked up **snug** in bed.*
- cosy, comfortable, warm, relaxed
- (*informal*) comfy
- A common simile is as snug as a bug in a rug.
- OPPOSITE uncomfortable

soak verb
1 *Days of rain had **soaked** the cricket pitch.*
- wet thoroughly, drench, saturate

2 *Leave the beans to **soak** in water overnight.*
- steep, immerse, submerge

soaking adjective

*My socks are absolutely **soaking**!*

- wet through, drenched, dripping, wringing, saturated, sodden, sopping, soggy
- Ground that has been soaked by rain is waterlogged.

soar verb

1 *The seagull spread its wings and **soared** into the air.*
- climb, rise, ascend, fly, wing

2 *House prices have continued to **soar**.*
- go up, rise, increase, shoot up

sob verb

*Tina threw herself on the bed, **sobbing** loudly.*

- cry, weep, bawl, blubber, shed tears, snivel

sober adjective

1 *He drank a little wine, but he stayed **sober**.*
- clear-headed
OPPOSITE drunk

2 *The funeral was a **sober** occasion.*
- serious, solemn, sombre, grave, dignified, sedate
OPPOSITE light-hearted, frivolous

sociable adjective

*Our new neighbours are very **sociable**.*

- friendly, outgoing, amiable, hospitable, neighbourly
OPPOSITE unfriendly

social adjective

1 *Elephants are **social** animals.*
- People and creatures who like to be in groups or communities are said to be gregarious.
OPPOSITE solitary

2 *The club organized several **social** activities.*
- communal, community, public, group

society noun

1 *Ancient Egypt was a **society** ruled by pharaohs.*
- community, civilization

2 *Mrs Burns is head of the local music **society**.*
- association, group, organization, club

3 *She enjoys the **society** of her friends.*
- companionship, company, fellowship, friendship

soft adjective

1 *The kittens can only eat **soft** food.*
- pulpy, spongy, squashy
- (*informal*) squidgy
OPPOSITE hard, dry

2 *My head sank into the **soft** pillow.*
- supple, pliable, springy, yielding, flexible
OPPOSITE firm, rigid

3 *The rabbit's fur felt very **soft**.*
- smooth, silky, sleek, velvety, downy, feathery
OPPOSITE coarse

4 *A **soft** breeze stirred the leaves.*
- gentle, light, mild, delicate
OPPOSITE rough, strong

5 *The smugglers spoke in **soft** whispers.*
- quiet, low, faint
OPPOSITE loud

6 *It was hard to see clearly in the **soft** light.*
- subdued, muted, pale, dim, low
OPPOSITE bright, dazzling

7 *You are being too **soft** with that puppy.*
- lenient, easygoing, tolerant, indulgent
OPPOSITE strict, tough

soggy adjective

1 *The pitch was **soggy** after all the rain.*
- wet, drenched, soaked, saturated, sodden, waterlogged

2 *The bread in my sandwich had become **soggy**.*
- moist, soft, pulpy, squelchy
- (*informal*) squidgy
OPPOSITE dry

soil noun

*The plants grow best in well-drained **soil**.*

- earth, ground, land
- Good fertile soil is loam.
- The fertile top layer of soil is topsoil.

soil ➡ sombre

soil verb
*My jeans were **soiled** with mud and grass stains.*
- dirty, make dirty, stain, muddy, tarnish

soldier noun
*Three **soldiers** stood guard outside the building.*
- serviceman or servicewoman
- A soldier paid to fight for a foreign country is a mercenary.
- An old word for a soldier is warrior.
- Soldiers who use big guns are the artillery.
- Soldiers who fight on horseback are the cavalry.
- Soldiers who fight on foot are the infantry.
  SEE ALSO **armed services**

sole adjective
*The castaway was the **sole** inhabitant of the island.*
- only, single, one, solitary, lone, unique

solemn adjective
1 *The butler always had a **solemn** expression on his face.*
- serious, grave, sober, sombre, unsmiling, glum
  OPPOSITE cheerful
2 *The coronation was a **solemn** occasion.*
- formal, dignified, grand, stately, majestic, pompous
  OPPOSITE frivolous

solid adjective
1 *A cricket ball is **solid**.*
  OPPOSITE hollow
2 *The water turned into **solid** ice.*
- hard, firm, dense, compact, rigid, unyielding
- A common simile is as solid as a rock.
  OPPOSITE soft
3 *The bars of the climbing frame are quite **solid**.*
- firm, robust, sound, strong, stable, sturdy
  OPPOSITE weak, unstable

4 *The crown was made of **solid** gold.*
- pure, genuine
5 *He got **solid** support from his team-mates.*
- firm, reliable, dependable, united, unanimous
  OPPOSITE weak, divided

solidify verb
*The lava from the volcano **solidifies** as it cools.*
- harden, become solid, set, stiffen
  OPPOSITE soften, liquify

solitary adjective
1 *He was a **solitary** man and rarely spoke to others.*
- isolated, secluded, lonely, unsociable
- To be solitary is to be alone.
  OPPOSITE sociable.
2 *There was a **solitary** tree in the middle of the field.*
- single, sole, one, only

solitude noun
*On the island, there was total peace and **solitude**.*
- privacy, seclusion, isolation, loneliness

solve verb
*The professor was trying to **solve** an ancient riddle.*
- interpret, explain, answer, work out, find the solution to, unravel, decipher

sombre adjective
1 *The hall was decorated in **sombre** shades of grey.*
- dark, dull, dim, dismal, dingy, drab, cheerless
  OPPOSITE bright
2 *A messenger arrived with a **sombre** look on his face.*
- gloomy, serious, grave, sober, sad, melancholy, mournful
  OPPOSITE cheerful

a b c d e f g h i j k l m n o p q r s t u v w x y z

a
b
c
d
e
f
g
h
i
j
k
l
m
n
o
p
q
r
s
t
u
v
w
x
y
z

song noun

WORD WEB

SOME KINDS OF SONG
anthem, aria, ballad, calypso, carol, chant, ditty, folk song, hymn, jingle, lament, lay, love song, lullaby, madrigal, nursery rhyme, pop song, psalm, rap, round, shanty, spiritual

- A play or film that includes many songs is a musical.
- A song from a musical is a number.
- The words for a song are the lyrics.

FOR OTHER MUSICAL TERMS
SEE **music**

soon adverb
*Dinner will be ready **soon**.*
- before long, in a minute, shortly, presently, quickly

soothe verb
1 *The quiet music **soothed** her nerves.*
- calm, comfort, relax, pacify
2 *This cream will **soothe** the pain.*
- ease, lessen, relieve

soothing adjective
*They played **soothing** music.*
- calming, relaxing, restful, peaceful, gentle, pleasant

sophisticated adjective
1 *Diana looked very **sophisticated** in her ballgown.*
- grown-up, mature, cultivated, cultured, refined
OPPOSITE naïve
2 *She has a **sophisticated** digital camera.*
- advanced, complex, complicated, intricate, elaborate
OPPOSITE primitive, simple

sorcerer, sorceress nouns SEE
magic noun

sore adjective
*My feet are still **sore** from the walk.*
- painful, aching, hurting, smarting, tender, sensitive, inflamed, raw, red

sore noun
*A nurse put ointment on the **sore**.*
- wound, inflammation, swelling

sorrow noun
1 *He felt great **sorrow** at leaving his children behind.*
- sadness, unhappiness, misery, woe, grief, anguish, despair, distress, heartache, heartbreak, melancholy, gloom, depression, desolation, wretchedness
- Sorrow because of someone's death is mourning.
- Sorrow at being away from home is homesickness.
OPPOSITE happiness
2 *She expressed her **sorrow** for what she had done.*
- regret, remorse, repentance, apologies

sorry adjective
1 *Scott said he was **sorry** for losing my football.*
- apologetic, regretful, remorseful, ashamed (of), repentant
OPPOSITE unapologetic
2 *We felt **sorry** for the villagers who had lost their homes.*
- sympathetic, pitying, understanding, compassionate
OPPOSITE unsympathetic

sort noun
*What **sort** of music do you like?*
- kind, type, variety, form, nature, style, genre, category, order, class
- A sort of animal is a breed or species.

sort verb
*The books are **sorted** according to their subjects.*
- arrange, organize, class, group, categorize, classify, divide
OPPOSITE mix

to sort something out

*They managed to **sort out** their disagreement.*

- settle, resolve, clear up, cope with, deal with

sound noun

WORD WEB

*We heard the **sound** of footsteps approaching.*

- noise, tone
- A loud, harsh sound is a din or racket.

SOUNDS MADE BY PEOPLE

bawl, bellow, boo, boom, cackle, chortle, clap, croak, cry, gasp, groan, gurgle, hiccup, hiss, howl, hum, moan, murmur, puff, scream, shout, shriek, sigh, sing, sniff, snore, snort, sob, splutter, stammer, stutter, wail, wheeze, whimper, whine, whisper, whistle, whoop, yell, yodel

SEE ALSO **say**

FOR SOUNDS MADE BY ANIMALS AND BIRDS

SEE **animal, bird**

SOUNDS MADE BY THINGS

bang, blare, beep, bleep, boom, buzz, chime, chink, chug, clang, clank, clash, clatter, click, clink, clunk, crack, crackle, crash, creak, crunch, ding, drone, drum, fizz, grate, gurgle, jangle, jingle, patter, peal, ping, plop, pop, purr, putter, rattle, ring, rumble, rustle, scrunch, sizzle, slam, snap, squeak, squelch, swish, throb, thud, thunder, tick, ting, tinkle, twang, whirr, whoosh, whistle, whiz, zoom

WRITING TIPS

You can use these words to describe a **sound**.

- to describe a *PLEASANT SOUND*: dulcet, harmonious, mellifluous, melodious, sweet

*I heard the **sweet** strains of a harp playing.*

- to describe an *UNPLEASANT SOUND*: grating, harsh, jarring, piercing, rasping, raucous, shrill, thin, tinny

*A **raucous** fight was going out outside.*

sound verb

*A trumpet **sounded** in the distance.*

- make a noise, resound, be heard

sound adjective

1 *The walls of the fortress seemed **sound**.*
- firm, solid, stable, safe, secure, intact, undamaged
  OPPOSITE unsound, unstable

2 *She gave us some **sound** advice.*
- good, sensible, wise, reasonable, trustworthy
  OPPOSITE unwise

3 *The travellers returned safe and **sound**.*
- strong, well, fit, healthy
  OPPOSITE weak, unfit

sour adjective

1 *These apples are a bit **sour**.*
- tart, bitter, sharp, acid
  OPPOSITE sweet

2 *The guard opened the door with a **sour** look on his face.*
- cross, bad-tempered, grumpy, disagreeable, peevish

source noun

*The vet has found the **source** of the infection.*

- origin, start, starting point, head, root, cause
- The source of a river or stream is usually a spring.

south noun, adjective, adverb

- The parts of a continent or country in the south are the southern parts.
- To travel towards the south is to travel southward or southwards or in a southerly direction.
- A wind from the south is a southerly wind.
- A person who lives in the south of a country is a southerner.

sow verb
- To sow seeds in the ground is to plant them.
- To sow an area of ground with seeds is to seed it.

space noun
1 *There wasn't much **space** to move about.*
- room, freedom, scope
2 *He peered through the tiny **space** in the curtains.*
- gap, hole, opening, break
- A space without any air in it is a vacuum.
- A space of time is an interval or period.
3 *The astronauts will spend ten days in **space**.*
- outer space

🕸 **WORD WEB**

- Everything that exists in space is the universe or cosmos.
- Distances in space stretch to infinity.
- Travel to other planets is interplanetary travel.
- Travel to other stars is interstellar travel.
- Travel to other galaxies is intergalactic travel.
- A traveller in space is an astronaut.
- In stories, beings from other planets are aliens or extraterrestrials.
  SEE ALSO **alien, astronaut**

NATURAL OBJECTS FOUND IN SPACE
asteroid, black hole, comet, constellation, galaxy, meteor, meteorite, Milky Way, moon, nebula, nova, planet, red dwarf, red giant, shooting star, solar system, star, sun, supernova
SEE ALSO **moon, planet**

WORDS TO DO WITH TRAVEL IN SPACE
blast-off, countdown, launch, mission, orbit, re-entry, rocket, satellite, spacecraft, spaceship, space shuttle, space station, spacesuit, spacewalk

---

- A robot spacecraft is a probe.
- A vehicle which can travel on the surface of a planet is a buggy or rover.

THINGS YOU MIGHT FIND ON A SPACESHIP
booster rocket, bridge, cargo bay, capsule, computer, docking bay, fuel tank, heat shield, instrument panel, life-support system, module, pod, solar panel

THINGS A SPACESHIP MIGHT DO
blast off, burn up, drift off-course, land, lift off, malfunction, orbit, re-enter the earth's atmosphere, splash down, touch down

---

spacious adjective
*The living room is **spacious** and bright.*
- big, large, roomy, sizeable
  OPPOSITE small, cramped

span noun
*The bridge has a **span** of 200 metres.*
- breadth, extent, length, width, distance, reach
- A span of time is a period or stretch.

span verb
*A rickety footbridge **spanned** the river.*
- cross, stretch over, extend across, straddle, bridge, traverse

spare verb
1 *Can you **spare** any money for a good cause?*
- afford, part with, give, provide, do without
2 *Gretel begged the witch to **spare** her brother.*
- show mercy to, pardon, reprieve, let off, release, free

spare adjective
1 *The **spare** tyre is in the boot.*
- additional, extra, reserve, standby
2 *Have you any **spare** change?*
- leftover, surplus, odd, remaining, unused, unwanted
3 *The ghostly figure was tall and **spare**.*
- lean, thin, slender, slim, trim

a b c d e f g h i j k l m n o p q r s t u v w x y z

spark noun
*There was a **spark** of light as he struck the match.*
- flash, gleam, glint, flicker, sparkle

sparkle verb
*The diamond ring **sparkled** in the sunlight.*
- glitter, glisten, glint, twinkle

sparse adjective
*In the desert, vegetation is very **sparse**.*
- scarce, scanty, scattered, inadequate, infrequent
OPPOSITE plentiful

spatter verb
*The bus **spattered** mud all over us.*
- splash, spray, sprinkle, scatter, shower

speak verb
*The robot opened its mouth and began to **speak**.*
- communicate, express yourself, say something, talk, utter

speaker noun
- A person who gives a talk is a lecturer.
- A person who makes formal speeches is an orator.
- A person who speaks on behalf of an organization is a spokesperson.

spear noun
- A spear used in whaling is a harpoon.
- A spear thrown as a sport is a javelin.
- A spear carried by a medieval knight on horseback was a lance.

special adjective
1 *Are you keeping the champagne for a **special** occasion?*
- important, significant, memorable, noteworthy, momentous, exceptional, extraordinary, out-of-the-ordinary
OPPOSITE ordinary
2 *My granny has her own **special** way of making porridge.*
- unique, individual, characteristic, distinctive, different, peculiar
3 *You need a **special** camera to film underwater.*
- particular, specific, proper, specialized

speciality noun
*The chef's **speciality** is sticky toffee pudding.*
- strength, strong point, expertise, forte

specific adjective
*The treasure map gave **specific** directions.*
- detailed, precise, exact, definite, particular, clear-cut
OPPOSITE general, vague

specify verb
*Please **specify** your shoe size.*
- be specific about, identify, name, define

specimen noun
*The police asked for a **specimen** of his handwriting.*
- sample, example, illustration, instance

speck noun
*She brushed a **speck** of dust from her shoes.*
- bit, dot, spot, fleck, grain, particle, trace, mark
SEE ALSO **bit**

speckled adjective
*A brown, **speckled** egg lay on the nest.*
- flecked, spotted, spotty, mottled
- If you have a lot of brown spots on your skin you are freckled.
- Something with patches of colour is dappled or patchy.

spectacle noun
*The fireworks for Diwali will be a great **spectacle**.*
- display, show, performance, exhibition, extravaganza

spectacles plural noun SEE **glasses**

spectacular adjective
1 *The acrobats gave a **spectacular** performance.*
- dramatic, exciting, impressive, thrilling, magnificent, sensational

2 *The tulips are **spectacular** at this time of year.*
- eye-catching, showy, splendid, breathtaking, colourful

spectator noun
- The spectators at a show are the audience.
- The spectators at a football match are the crowd.
- A person watching TV is a viewer.
- If you see an accident or a crime you are an eyewitness or witness.
- If you just happen to see something going on you are a bystander or onlooker.

speech noun
1 *His **speech** was slurred and he looked tired.*
- speaking, talking, articulation, pronunciation

2 *She was invited to give an after-dinner **speech**.*
- talk, address, lecture, oration
- A talk in church is a sermon.
- Speech between actors in a play is dialogue.
- A speech delivered by a single actor is a monologue.

speechless adjective
*She was **speechless** with surprise.*
- dumbstruck, dumbfounded, tongue-tied

speed noun
1 *Could a spaceship travel faster than the **speed** of light?*
- pace, rate
- A formal synonym is velocity.
- The speed of a piece of music is its tempo.
- To increase speed is to accelerate.
- To reduce speed is to decelerate.

2 *They finished clearing up with amazing **speed**.*
- quickness, rapidity, swiftness
OPPOSITE slowness

speed verb
*The skiers **sped** down the mountain.*
- race, rush, dash, dart, hurry, hurtle, career, fly, streak, tear, shoot, zoom, zip

speedy adjective
*They sent their best wishes for a **speedy** recovery.*
- fast, quick, swift, rapid, prompt, brisk
OPPOSITE slow

spell noun
1 *A magic **spell** had turned the knight into a toad.*
- charm, incantation
- Making magic spells is sorcery, witchcraft, or wizardry.
FOR OTHER WORDS TO DO WITH MAGIC
SEE **magic** noun

2 *We're hoping for a **spell** of dry weather.*
- period, interval, time, stretch, run

spend verb
1 *Have you **spent** all your pocket money already?*
- pay out, use up, get through, exhaust
- (*informal*) fork out, shell out
- To spend money unwisely is to fritter or squander it.

2 *She **spends** a lot of time working in the garden.*
- pass, occupy, fill
- To spend time doing something useless is to waste it.

sphere noun
1 *The earth has the shape of a **sphere**.*
- ball, globe, orb

2 *He's an expert in the **sphere** of photography.*
- subject, area, field

spherical adjective
*The earth is **spherical**.*
- round, ball-shaped

spice noun

WORD WEB

SOME SPICES USED IN COOKING
allspice, aniseed, bayleaf, capsicum, aniseed, cardamom, cayenne, chilli, cinnamon, cloves, coriander, cumin, curry powder, ginger, juniper, mace, nutmeg, paprika, pepper, pimento, saffron, sesame, turmeric

spicy adjective
*The meat was cooked in a **spicy** chilli sauce.*
- hot, peppery, fiery

spike noun
*His shirt got caught on a metal **spike**.*
- point, prong, spear, stake, barb

spill verb
1 *Katie **spilled** her juice all over the table.*
- overturn, upset, tip over
2 *Milk **spilled** onto the floor.*
- overflow, pour, slop, slosh, splash
3 *The treasure chest fell open, **spilling** gold coins everywhere.*
- shed, tip, scatter, drop

spin verb
*The rear wheels of the jeep **spun** round.*
- turn, rotate, revolve, whirl, twirl

spine noun
1 *Your **spine** runs down the middle of your back.*
- backbone, spinal column
- The bones in your spine are your vertebrae.
2 *A porcupine has sharp **spines**.*
- needle, quill, point, spike, bristle

spiral noun
*The staircase wound upwards in a long **spiral**.*
- coil, twist, corkscrew, whorl
- A tight spiral of swirling air or water is a vortex.

spirit noun
1 *He carried a charm to keep evil **spirits** away.*
- ghost, ghoul, phantom, spectre, demon
  SEE ALSO **ghost**
2 *The orchestra played the piece with great **spirit**.*
- energy, liveliness, enthusiasm, vigour, zest, zeal, fire
3 *There is a real **spirit** of cooperation in the team.*
- feeling, mood, atmosphere

spiritual adjective
*The Dalai Lama is the **spiritual** leader of Tibet.*
- religious, holy, sacred
  OPPOSITE worldly

spite noun
*I believe that she ripped my book out of **spite**.*
- malice, spitefulness, ill will, ill feeling, hostility, bitterness, resentment, venom

spiteful adjective
*He made some really **spiteful** comments.*
- malicious, malevolent, ill-natured, hostile, venomous, vicious, nasty, unkind
  OPPOSITE kind

splash verb
1 *The bus **splashed** water over us.*
- shower, spray, spatter, sprinkle, squirt, slop, slosh, spill
- (*informal*) splosh
2 *The children **splashed** about in the playing pool.*
- paddle, wade, dabble, bathe

splendid adjective
1 *There was a **splendid** banquet on the eve of the wedding.*
- magnificent, lavish, luxurious, impressive, imposing, grand, great, dazzling, glorious, gorgeous, elegant, rich, stately, majestic
2 *That's a **splendid** idea!*
- excellent, first-class, admirable, superb, wonderful, marvellous

splendour noun
*They admired the **splendour** of the cathedral.*
- magnificence, glory, grandeur, majesty, richness, brilliance, spectacle

splinter noun
*There were **splinters** of glass all over the floor.*
- fragment, sliver, chip, flake

splinter verb
*The glass **splintered** into pieces.*
- shatter, smash, fracture, chip, crack, split

a
b
c
d
e
f
g
h
i
j
k
l
m
n
o
p
q
r
s
t
u
v
w
x
y
z

a
b
c
d
e
f
g
h
i
j
k
l
m
n
o
p
q
r
s
t
u
v
w
x
y
z

split verb

1 *He **split** the log in two.*
- chop, cut up, crack open, splinter

2 *He **split** his trousers climbing over the fence.*
- rip open, tear

3 *The pirates **split** the gold between them.*
- distribute, share out

4 *The path **splits** here.*
- branch, fork, separate

to split up
*The search party decided to **split up**.*
- break up, part, separate, divide
- If a married couple splits up, they may divorce.

split noun

*He had a **split** in the seat of his trousers.*
- rip, tear, slash, slit

spoil verb

1 *Bad weather **spoiled** the holiday.*
- ruin, wreck, upset, mess up, mar, scupper

2 *The grafitti **spoils** the look of the new building.*
- damage, harm, hurt, disfigure, deface

3 *His parents have **spoiled** him since he was a baby.*
- indulge, pamper, make a fuss of

spoken adjective

*Her **spoken** French is excellent.*
- oral

OPPOSITE written

spongy adjective

*The mossy ground felt **spongy** to walk on.*
- soft, springy, squashy, absorbent, porous

spontaneous adjective

*The audience broke into **spontaneous** applause.*
- unplanned, impromptu, unrehearsed, voluntary, impulsive, instinctive, natural
- An action done without any conscious thought is a reflex action.

spoon noun SEE cutlery

sport noun

WORD WEB

*I enjoy playing **sport** at the weekend.*
- exercise, games

TEAM SPORTS INCLUDE
American football, baseball, basketball, bowls, cricket, football or soccer, hockey, lacrosse, netball, polo, rounders, rugby, volleyball, water polo

INDIVIDUAL SPORTS INCLUDE
angling, archery, athletics, badminton, billiards, boxing, bowling, canoeing, climbing, croquet, cross-country running, cycling, darts, diving, fencing, golf, gymnastics, horse racing, jogging, judo, karate, motor racing, mountaineering, orienteering, pool, rowing, sailing, show jumping, snooker, squash, surfing, swimming, table tennis, tae kwon do, tennis, waterskiing, weightlifting, windsurfing, wrestling

FOR INDIVIDUAL ATHLETIC EVENTS
SEE **athletics**

WINTER SPORTS INCLUDE
bobsleigh, curling, ice hockey, ice skating, skiing, snowboarding, speed skating, tobogganing

PEOPLE WHO TAKE PART IN SPORT
athlete, coach, competitor, player, sportsman or sportswoman

PLACES WHERE SPORT TAKES PLACE
arena, field, ground, park, pitch, pool, ring, rink, run, slope, stadium, track

sporting adjective

*It was **sporting** of him to admit the ball was out.*
- sportsmanlike, fair, generous, honourable

OPPOSITE unsporting

spot noun

1 *There were several **spots** of paint on the carpet.*
- mark, stain, blot, blotch, smudge, dot, fleck, speck

- Small brown spots on your skin are freckles.
- A small dark spot on your skin is a mole.
- A mark you have had on your skin since you were born is a birthmark.
- A small round swelling on your skin is a pimple.
- A lot of spots is a rash.

2 *We felt a few **spots** of rain.*
- drop, blob, bead

3 *Here's a nice **spot** for a picnic.*
- place, position, location, site, situation, locality

spot verb

1 *Nina **spotted** her friend in the crowd.*
- see, sight, spy, catch sight of, notice, observe, make out, recognize, detect

2 *The tyres were **spotted** with mud.*
- mark, stain, blot, spatter, fleck, speckle, mottle

spotless adjective
*Mr Travis washed his car until it was **spotless**.*
- clean, unmarked, immaculate, gleaming
OPPOSITE dirty

spout verb
*Molten lava and ash **spouted** from the volcano.*
- gush, spew, pour, stream, spurt, squirt, jet

sprawl verb

1 *We **sprawled** on the lawn.*
- flop, lean back, lie, loll, lounge, recline, relax, slouch, slump, spread out, stretch out

2 *New houses have started to **sprawl** across the countryside.*
- spread, stretch

spray verb
*A passing bus **sprayed** mud over us.*
- shower, spatter, splash, sprinkle, scatter

spray noun

1 *We gave the plants a **spray** of water with the hose.*
- shower, sprinkling, fountain, mist

2 *She picked a **spray** of snowdrops from the garden.*
- bunch, posy

spread verb

1 *I **spread** the map on the table.*
- lay out, open out, fan out, unfold, unfurl, unroll

2 *The milk spilled and **spread** all over the floor.*
- expand, extend, stretch, broaden, enlarge, swell

3 *The school website is a good way of **spreading** news.*
- communicate, circulate, distribute, transmit, make known, pass on, pass round

4 *She **spread** jam on a piece of toast.*
- smear

5 *He **spread** the seeds evenly over the ground.*
- scatter, strew

sprightly adjective
*My granny is quite **sprightly** for her age.*
- lively, energetic, active, agile, nimble, frisky, spry
OPPOSITE inactive

spring verb
*Suddenly a rabbit **sprang** over the fence.*
- jump, leap, bound, hop, vault
- When a cat springs at a mouse, it pounces.

to spring up
*Weeds **spring up** quickly in damp weather.*
- appear, develop, emerge, shoot up, sprout

springy adjective
*The bed felt soft and **springy**.*
- bouncy, elastic, stretchy, flexible, pliable
OPPOSITE rigid

sprinkle verb
*She **sprinkled** flakes of chocolate over the cake.*
- scatter, shower, spray, dust, powder

a
b
c
d
e
f
g
h
i
j
k
l
m
n
o
p
q
r
s
t
u
v
w
x
y
z

sprout verb

*The seeds will **sprout** if they are warm and damp.*

- grow, germinate, shoot up, spring up, develop, emerge

spruce adjective

*He looked very **spruce** in a clean white shirt.*

- smart, well-dressed, well-groomed, elegant, neat, trim

OPPOSITE scruffy

spur verb

to spur someone on

*The cheers of the crowd **spurred on** the athletes.*

- egg on, encourage, inspire, prompt, stimulate, urge

spurt verb

*Water **spurted** from the hole in the pipe.*

- gush, spout, shoot out, stream, squirt, jet

spy noun

WORD WEB

*The **spy** was on a top-secret mission.*
- agent, secret agent
- The work of a spy is spying or espionage.
- A spy who works for two rival countries or organizations is a double agent
- An informal name for a spy who works undercover is a mole.

THINGS A SPY MIGHT DO

adopt a disguise or cover, assume a secret identity, carry out a secret mission, crack or decipher a code, gather intelligence, keep someone under surveillance, report to headquarters, uncover an enemy agent, work undercover

SEE ALSO **code**

THINGS A SPY MIGHT USE OR CARRY

coded message, false passport, hidden camera or microphone, listening device, motion detector, night-vision goggles, password, torch, walkie talkie

A SPY'S MISSION MIGHT BE

clandestine, covert, secret, stealthy, surreptitious, top-secret, undercover (*informal*) cloak-and-dagger, hush-hush

spy verb

*The lookout **spied** a ship on the horizon.*

- see, sight, spot, catch sight of, notice, observe, make out, detect

squabble verb

*The twins are always **squabbling** in the car.*

- argue, fight, quarrel, bicker, wrangle

squalid adjective

*The prisoners were kept in a **squalid** underground cell.*

- degrading, dingy, dirty, filthy, foul, mucky, nasty, unpleasant

OPPOSITE clean

squander verb

*He **squandered** his money on an expensive watch.*

- waste, fritter away, misuse
- (*informal*) blow

OPPOSITE save

square adjective

*All the tiles have **square** corners.*

- right-angled
- A pattern of squares is a chequered pattern.

squarely adverb

*The ball hit him **squarely** in the face.*

- directly, straight, head on

OPPOSITE obliquely

squash verb

1 *My sandwich got **squashed** at the bottom of my schoolbag.*

- crush, flatten, press, compress, mangle
- To squash food deliberately is to mash or pulp or purée it.

2 *We **squashed** our sleeping bags into our rucksacks.*

- squeeze, stuff, force, cram, pack, ram

squat verb

We squatted on the ground to watch the puppet show.
- crouch, sit

squat adjective

The alien had a squat little body on three short legs.
- dumpy, stocky, plump, podgy, portly

squeak, squeal nouns, verbs FOR VARIOUS SOUNDS

SEE **sound** noun

squeeze verb

1 *She squeezed the water out of the sponge.*
- press, wring, compress, crush

2 *Five of us squeezed into the back of the car.*
- squash, cram, crowd, stuff, push, ram, shove, wedge

3 *Holly squeezed her sister affectionately.*
- clasp, hug, embrace, cuddle
- To squeeze something between your thumb and finger is to pinch it.

squirm verb

The guinea pig squirmed out of the vet's grasp.
- wriggle, writhe, twist

squirt verb

My little brother made the tap water squirt all over me.
- spurt, spray, gush, spout, shoot, jet

stab verb

1 *He stabbed the sausage with his fork.*
- spear, jab, pierce, impale

2 *She stabbed a finger at him.*
- stick, thrust, push, jab

stab noun

Jake felt a sudden stab of pain in his chest.
- pang, prick, sting

stable adjective

1 *The ladder doesn't look very stable.*
- steady, secure, firm, fixed, solid, balanced
OPPOSITE wobbly, shaky

2 *He's been in a stable relationship for years.*
- steady, established, lasting, durable, strong
OPPOSITE temporary

stack noun

There were stacks of books all over the floor.
- pile, heap, mound, tower
- Another word for a stack of hay is a rick or hayrick.

stack verb

Stack the papers on the desk.
- gather, assemble, collect, heap up, pile up

staff noun

There was a party at the hospital for all the staff.
- workers, employees, personnel, workforce, team
- The staff on a ship or aircraft are the crew.

stage noun

1 *They went up on the stage to collect their prizes.*
- platform

2 *The final stage of the journey was made by coach.*
- leg, step, phase, portion, stretch

3 *At this stage in her life, she wants to try something new.*
- period, point, time, juncture

stagger verb

1 *The wounded knight staggered and fell.*
- reel, stumble, lurch, totter, sway, falter, waver, wobble

2 *We were staggered at the size of the pyramid.*
- amaze, astonish, astound, surprise, flabbergast, stupefy, startle, stun

a
b
c
d
e
f
g
h
i
j
k
l
m
n
o
p
q
r
s
t
u
v
w
x
y
z

a
b
c
d
e
f
g
h
i
j
k
l
m
n
o
p
q
r
s
t
u
v
w
x
y
z

stagnant adjective
*Mosquitoes swarmed around the pool of **stagnant** water.*
- still, motionless, static
OPPOSITE flowing, fresh

stain noun
*There were several coffee **stains** on the tablecloth.*
- mark, spot, blot, blotch, blemish, smear, smudge

stain verb
1 *Her trainers were **stained** with mud.*
- discolour, mark, soil, dirty, blacken, tarnish
2 *The wood can be **stained** a darker shade.*
- dye, colour, paint, tint, tinge

stairs plural noun
*The **stairs** up to the front door were worn with age.*
- steps
- A set of stairs taking you from one floor to another is a flight of stairs, or a staircase or stairway.
- A moving staircase is an escalator.
- A handrail at the side of a starircase is a banister.

stake noun
*The fence was made from sharp wooden **stakes**.*
- pole, post, stick, spike, stave, pile

stale adjective
*The bread had gone **stale**.*
- dry, hard, old, mouldy, musty
OPPOSITE fresh

stalk noun
*The recipe requires half a **stalk** of celery.*
- stem, shoot, twig

stalk verb
1 *The cheetah **stalked** its prey.*
- hunt, pursue, track, trail, follow, shadow, tail
2 *Miss Foster turned and **stalked** out of the room.*
- stride, strut
FOR OTHER WAYS TO WALK
SEE **walk** verb

stall verb
*The man was **stalling** to give his friends time to escape.*
- play for time, delay, hesitate, hedge

stammer verb
*Angela went red and started **stammering**.*
- stutter, falter, stumble, splutter

stamp verb
1 *He **stamped** on the flower by mistake.*
- step, tread, trample
2 *The librarian **stamped** my library book.*
- mark, print
- To stamp a postmark on a letter is to frank it.
- To stamp a mark on cattle with a hot iron is to brand them.

stamp noun
*I put a first-class **stamp** on the letter.*
- A person who studies or collects stamps is a philatelist.

stampede noun
*When the bell went, there was a **stampede** towards the door.*
- charge, rush, dash, rout

stand verb
1 *The newborn pup was too weak to **stand**.*
- get to your feet, get up, rise
2 *They **stood** the ladder against the wall.*
- put, place, set, position, station, erect
3 *The offer still **stands**.*
- remain valid, be unchanged, continue
4 *I can't **stand** the smell any longer.*
- bear, abide, endure, put up with, tolerate, suffer

to stand for something
1 *She won't **stand for** any nonsense.*
- put up with, tolerate, accept, allow, permit
2 *What do these initials **stand for**?*
- mean, indicate, signify, represent

to stand out
*Among all the photographs, this one really **stood out**.*
- catch your eye, stick out, be prominent

to stand up for someone
*He always **stands up for** his friends.*
- support, defend, side with, speak up for
- (*informal*) stick up for

stand noun
- A three-legged stand for a camera or telescope is a tripod.
- A stand for a Bible or other large book is a lectern.
- A stand to put a statue on is a pedestal or plinth.

standard noun
1 *Their writing is of a very high **standard**.*
- grade, level, quality
2 *He considered the book good by any **standard**.*
- guidelines, ideal, measurement, model
3 *The soldiers carried their **standard** proudly.*
- colours, flag, banner

standard adjective
*The teacher showed us the **standard** way to write a letter.*
- normal, usual, common, conventional, typical, customary, accepted, approved, established, orthodox, regular, traditional
- OPPOSITE abnormal

standby noun
*We need a **standby** in case someone drops out.*
- reserve, substitute, replacement

standstill noun
to come to a standstill
*The traffic had **come to a standstill**.*
- stop moving, draw up, halt, stop

staple adjective
*Rice is the **staple** food in many countries.*
- chief, main, principal, standard, basic

star noun
1 *Astronomers study the **stars**.*
FOR OBJECTS FOUND IN SPACE
SEE **space**
FOR SIGNS OF THE ZODIAC
SEE **zodiac**

- A word meaning 'to do with stars' is stellar.
- A night sky in which you can see stars is starry or star-studded.
- A mark in the shape of a star in a piece of writing is an asterisk.
2 *Several Hollywood **stars** attended the premiere of the film.*
- celebrity, idol, superstar

stare verb
*The guard **stared** straight ahead, not blinking.*
- gaze, gape, peer, look
to stare at someone
*The wolf was **staring** hungrily **at** us.*
- gaze at, gawp at, goggle at, eye, ogle, scrutinize, watch
- To stare angrily at someone is to glare at them.

start verb
1 *The new course will **start** in the autumn.*
- begin, commence
- (*informal*) get going, get cracking, kick off
- OPPOSITE finish, end
2 *We are planning to **start** a book club.*
- create, set up, establish, found, institute, originate, introduce, initiate, open, launch
- OPPOSITE close
3 *The horses **started** when the gun went off.*
- jump, flinch, jerk, twitch, recoil, wince

start noun
1 *Try not to miss the **start** of the film.*
- beginning, opening, introduction, commencement
- OPPOSITE end, close, finish
2 *She has been with the theatre company right from the **start**.*
- beginning, outset, creation, inception, birth, dawn, launch
3 *The explosion gave us all a nasty **start**.*
- jump, jolt, shock, surprise

startle verb
*The sudden noise **startled** the deer.*
- alarm, panic, frighten, scare, make you start, make you jump, surprise, take you by surprise

starve verb
*Many animals will **starve** if the drought continues.*
- die of starvation, go hungry
- To choose to go without food is to fast.

starving adjective (*informal*)
*What's for dinner? I'm **starving**!*
- hungry, famished, ravenous
- To be slightly hungry is to be peckish.

state noun
1 *The roof of the cottage is in a bad **state**.*
- condition, shape
- The state of a person or animal is their fitness or health.
2 *He gets into a terrible **state** before an exam.*
- panic, fluster
- (*informal*) flap
3 *The queen is the head of **state**.*
- country, nation

state verb
*Her passport **states** that she is an Australian citizen.*
- declare, announce, report, say, proclaim, pronounce, communicate

stately adjective
*The royal banquet will be a **stately** occasion.*
- grand, dignified, formal, imposing, majestic, noble, splendid

statement noun
*The prime minister made a **statement** to the press.*
- announcement, declaration, communication, report, testimony

station noun
1 *Does the train stop at the next **station**?*
- The station at the end of a line is the terminus.
  FOR OTHER WORDS TO DO WITH TRAINS
  SEE **railway**

2 *He was taken to the police **station** for questioning.*
- depot, headquarters
3 *There are two local radio **stations**.*
- channel

station verb
*A lookout was **stationed** on the roof of the building.*
- place, position, put, stand, situate, locate

stationary adjective
*The bus was stuck behind a **stationary** vehicle.*
- still, static, unmoving, immobile, motionless, standing, at rest
  OPPOSITE moving

statue noun
*There is a **statue** of Lord Nelson in Trafalgar Square.*
- figure, sculpture, carving
- A small statue is a statuette.

status noun
*Slaves had a very low **status** in Ancient Rome.*
- rank, level, position, grade, importance, prestige

staunch adjective
*The Black Knight was a **staunch** ally of the prince.*
- firm, strong, faithful, loyal, true, reliable, dependable, steadfast, trusty
  OPPOSITE unreliable

stay verb
1 *Can you **stay** there while I park the car?*
- wait, hang about, remain
  OPPOSITE leave, depart
2 *We tried to **stay** warm by stamping our feet.*
- keep, carry on being, continue
3 *Do you plan to **stay** in America for long?*
- live, reside, dwell, lodge, settle, stop

stay noun
*Our friends came for a short **stay**.*
- visit, stopover, holiday, break

steady adjective
1 *You need a **steady** hand to be a surgeon.*
- stable, balanced, settled, secure, fixed, firm, fast, solid
- A common simile is as steady as a rock.
OPPOSITE unsteady, shaky
2 *The plants need a **steady** supply of water.*
- continuous, uninterrupted, non-stop, consistent
OPPOSITE intermittent
3 *The runners kept up a **steady** pace.*
- regular, constant, even, smooth, rhythmic, unvarying
OPPOSITE irregular

steady verb
*The crew managed to **steady** the yacht.*
- balance, stabilize

steal verb
1 *The thieves **stole** several valuable paintings.*
- rob, thieve, take, lift, make off with
- (*informal*) pinch, nick, swipe, snaffle
2 *The children **stole** quietly upstairs.*
- creep, sneak, tiptoe, slip, slink

stealing noun
*The police have accused him of **stealing**.*
- robbery, theft
- Stealing from someone's home is burglary or housebreaking.
- Stealing from a shop is shoplifting.
- Stealing small things is pilfering.

stealthy adjective
*We heard **stealthy** footsteps going upstairs.*
- furtive, secretive, surreptitious, sly, sneaky, underhand
OPPOSITE conspicuous, open

steam noun
*Clouds of **steam** were coming from the cauldron.*
- vapour, mist, haze
- Steam on a cold window is condensation.

steamy adjective
1 *The climate in a jungle is hot and **steamy**.*
- humid, muggy, close, damp, moist
2 *She wiped the **steamy** mirror.*
- misty, hazy, cloudy

steep adjective
*The bus inched its way slowly up the **steep** slope.*
- abrupt, sudden, sharp
- A cliff or drop which is straight up and down is sheer or vertical.
OPPOSITE gradual, gentle

steer verb
*She **steered** the car into the parking space.*
- direct, guide
- To steer a vehicle is to drive it.
- To steer a boat is to navigate or pilot it.

stem noun
*The gardener pulled out the dead **stems**.*
- stalk, shoot, twig, branch
- The main stem of a tree is its trunk.

stem verb
*Chloe blinked, trying to **stem** the flow of her tears.*
- stop, check, hold back, restrain, curb

step noun
1 *The baby took her first **steps** yesterday.*
- footstep, pace, stride
2 *Be careful not to trip on the **step**.*
- doorstep, stair
- A set of steps going from one floor of a building to another is a staircase.
- A folding set of steps is a stepladder.
- The steps of a ladder are the rungs.
3 *The first **step** in making a cake is to weigh the ingredients.*
- stage, phase, action

step verb
*Don't **step** in the puddle!*
- put your foot, tread, walk, stamp, trample

a b c d e f g h i j k l m n o p q r **s** t u v w x y z

to step something up

*They have **stepped up** security at the airport.*

- increase, intensify, strengthen, boost

sterile adjective

1 *Very little grows in the **sterile** soil of the desert.*

- barren, dry, arid, infertile, lifeless
OPPOSITE fertile

2 *The nurse put a **sterile** bandage on the wound.*

- sterilized, disinfected, germ-free, antiseptic, hygienic, clean,
OPPOSITE infected

stern adjective

*The coach gave each of the players a **stern** look.*

- disapproving, unsmiling, severe, strict, hard, harsh, grim
OPPOSITE lenient

stew verb FOR WAYS TO COOK FOOD
SEE **cook** verb

stick noun

1 *They collected **sticks** to make a fire.*

- twig, branch, stalk

2 *The elderly patient walked with a **stick**.*

- cane, rod, staff, pole
- A stick used by a conductor is a baton.
- A stick carried by a police officer is a truncheon.
- A magic stick used by a witch or fairy is a wand.

stick verb

1 *He **stuck** his fork into the potato.*

- poke, prod, stab, thrust, dig, jab

2 *She tried to **stick** the broken pieces of china together.*

- glue, paste, cement, bond, join, fasten

3 *The stamp wouldn't **stick** to the envelope.*

- adhere, attach, cling

4 *The wheels of the caravan **stuck** fast in the mud.*

- jam, wedge, become trapped

5 (informal) *I can't **stick** people who're always complaining.*

- put up with, stand, tolerate, bear, abide, endure

to stick out

*The shelf **sticks out** too far.*

- jut out, poke out, project, protrude

to stick up for someone (informal)

*She **stuck up for** him when he was in trouble.*

- support, defend, side with, stand up for, speak up for

sticky adjective

1 *Someone had left a blob of **sticky** toffee on the chair.*

- tacky, gummy, gluey
- (informal) gooey, icky

2 *I don't like hot **sticky** weather.*

- humid, muggy, clammy, close, steamy, sultry
OPPOSITE dry

3 (informal) *The pirates came to a **sticky** end.*

- grisly, gruesome, horrible, nasty, unpleasant

stiff adjective

1 *Stir the flour and water to a **stiff** paste.*

- firm, hard, solid
- A common simile is as stiff as a poker.
OPPOSITE soft

2 *He mounted the picture on **stiff** card.*

- rigid, inflexible, thick
OPPOSITE pliable

3 *Her muscles were **stiff** after the long walk.*

- aching, achy, painful, taut, tight
OPPOSITE supple

4 *The team will face **stiff** competition in the final.*

- strong, powerful, tough, difficult
OPPOSITE easy

5 *His **stiff** manner made him hard to talk to.*

- unfriendly, cold, formal, awkward, wooden
OPPOSITE relaxed

6 *The judge imposed a **stiff** penalty.*

- harsh, severe, strict, hard
OPPOSITE lenient

7 *A **stiff** breeze was blowing.*

- strong, brisk, fresh
OPPOSITE gentle

stifle verb

1 *We were almost **stifled** by the fumes from the exhaust pipe.*
- choke, suffocate, smother
- To kill someone by stopping their breathing is to strangle or throttle them.

2 *She tried to **stifle** a yawn.*
- suppress, muffle, hold back, repress, restrain

still adjective

1 *The prisoner sat **still** and said nothing.*
- motionless, unmoving, stationary, static, inert

2 *It was a beautiful **still** evening.*
- calm, peaceful, quiet, tranquil, serene, hushed, silent, noiseless, windless

still verb

*I breathed deeply to try to **still** my nerves.*
- calm, quieten, soothe, lull
OPPOSITE agitate

stimulate verb

1 *Her travels **stimulated** her to write a book.*
- encourage, inspire, spur

2 *The exhibition **stimulated** my interest in painting.*
- arouse, rouse, stir up, kindle, excite, provoke, trigger
OPPOSITE discourage

sting verb

1 *One of the campers was **stung** by a wasp.*
- bite, nip

2 *The smoke made our eyes **sting**.*
- smart, hurt, prick, prickle, tingle

stingy adjective (*informal*)

*He's too **stingy** to give anyone a birthday card.*
- mean, miserly, selfish, uncharitable
- (*informal*) tight-fisted, penny-pinching
OPPOSITE generous

stink verb

*The dungeon **stank** of unwashed bodies.*
- reek, smell
SEE ALSO **smell** verb

stink noun

*The mouldy cheese gave off a dreadful **stink**.*
- odour, stench, reek, bad smell

stir verb

1 ***Stir** the mixture until it is smooth.*
- mix, beat, blend, whisk

2 *The giant **stirred** in his sleep.*
- move slightly, shift, toss, turn

to stir something up

*The bandits were always **stirring up** trouble.*
- arouse, encourage, provoke, set off, trigger, whip up

stir noun

*The news caused quite a **stir**.*
- fuss, commotion, excitement, hullabaloo

stock noun

1 ***Stocks** of food were running low.*
- supply, store, reserve, hoard, stockpile

2 *The shopkeeper arranged his new **stock**.*
- goods, merchandise, wares

3 *The duke is descended from royal **stock**.*
- descent, ancestry, family, line

stock verb

*Most supermarkets now **stock** organic food.*
- sell, carry, trade in, deal in, keep in stock

stocky adjective

*The wrestler had a strong **stocky** body.*
- dumpy, squat, thickset, solid, sturdy
OPPOSITE thin

stodgy adjective

1 *The pudding was rich and **stodgy**.*
- heavy, solid, starchy, filling
OPPOSITE light

2 *I'm finding the book a bit **stodgy**.*
- boring, dull, uninteresting, slow, tedious
OPPOSITE lively

a
b
c
d
e
f
g
h
i
j
k
l
m
n
o
p
q
r
s
t
u
v
w
x
y
z

a
b
c
d
e
f
g
h
i
j
k
l
m
n
o
p
q
r
s
t
u
v
w
x
y
z

stomach noun
*He rolled over and lay on his **stomach**.*
- belly, gut, paunch
- (*informal*) tummy
- The part of the body that contains the stomach is the abdomen.

stomach verb
*I can't **stomach** watching horror films.*
- stand, bear, put up with, tolerate, take

stone noun
*The columns of the temple were carved from **stone**.*
- A large lump of stone is a rock.
- A large rounded stone is a boulder.
- Small rounded stones are pebbles.
- A mixture of sand and small stones is gravel.
- Pebbles on the beach are shingle.
- Round stones used to pave a path are cobbles.

FOR PRECIOUS STONES
SEE **jewel, jewellery**

stony adjective
1 *The waves broke over the **stony** beach.*
- pebbly, rocky, shingly
OPPOSITE sandy
2 *There was a **stony** silence in the room.*
- unfriendly, cold, hostile, frosty, icy
OPPOSITE warm, friendly

stoop verb
*We had to **stoop** to go through the tunnel.*
- bend, duck, bow, crouch

stop verb
1 *I'll go into town when the rain **stops**.*
- end, finish, cease, conclude, terminate
OPPOSITE start
2 *Can you **stop** talking for a minute?*
- give up, cease, suspend, quit, leave off, break off
- (*informal*) knock off, pack in
OPPOSITE continue, resume
3 *Guards, **stop** that man!*
- hold, detain, seize, catch, capture, restrain
4 *You can't **stop** me from going.*
- prevent, obstruct, bar, hinder

5 *How do you **stop** this machine?*
- turn off, immobilize
6 *The bus will **stop** at the school gates.*
- come to a stop, halt, pull up, draw up
7 *If you tighten the valve, it will **stop** the leak.*
- close, plug, seal, block up, bung up

stop noun
1 *Everything suddenly came to a **stop**.*
- end, finish, conclusion, halt, standstill
2 *They drove down through France, with a short **stop** in Paris.*
- break, pause, stopover, rest

store verb
*Squirrels need to **store** food for the winter.*
- save, set aside, stow away, hoard, reserve, stockpile
- (*informal*) stash

store noun
1 *The building is now used as a grain **store**.*
- storeroom, storehouse, repository, vault
- A store for food is a larder or pantry.
- A store for weapons is an armoury or arsenal.
2 *He kept a large **store** of wine in the cellar.*
- hoard, supply, quantity, stock, stockpile, reserve
3 *He's the manager of the local grocery **store**.*
SEE **shop**

storey noun
*The new building has six **storeys**.*
- floor, level, tier

storm noun
1 *Crops were damaged in the heavy **storms**.*
- squall, blizzard, gale, thunderstorm, hurricane, typhoon
- An old word for storm is tempest.
- When a storm begins to develop it is brewing.
SEE ALSO **weather** noun

2 *Plans to close the library caused a* ***storm*** *of protest.*
- outburst, outcry, uproar, clamour

storm verb
The soldiers ***stormed*** *the castle.*
- charge at, rush at

stormy adjective
1 *It was a dark,* ***stormy*** *night.*
- blustery, squally, tempestuous, wild, windy, rough, choppy, gusty, raging
OPPOSITE calm
2 *Fighting broke out at the end of a* ***stormy*** *meeting.*
- bad-tempered, quarrelsome, turbulent, violent

story noun

WORD WEB
1 *Peter Pan is a* ***story*** *about a boy who never grew up.*
- tale
- (*informal*) yarn

VARIOUS KINDS OF STORY
adventure story, bedtime story, crime story, detective story, fable, fairy tale, fantasy, folk tale, ghost story, horror story, legend, love story, mystery, myth, narrative poem, novel, parable, romance, saga, science fiction or SF, short story, spy story, thriller
- Invented stories are fiction.

FOR OTHER TYPES OF WRITING
SEE **writing**

2 *The book tells the* ***story*** *of her childhood in New York.*
- account, history, narrative
- A story of a person's life is a biography.
- The story of your life told by yourself is your autobiography.
3 *It was the front-page* ***story*** *in all the papers.*
- article, item, feature, report, piece
4 (*informal*) *Have you been telling* ***stories*** *again?*
- lie, fib

stout adjective
1 *The doctor was a* ***stout*** *man with grey hair.*
- fat, plump, chubby, dumpy, tubby, portly, stocky, beefy, burly
OPPOSITE thin
2 *You will need a pair of* ***stout*** *walking boots.*
- strong, sturdy, tough, robust, sound, substantial
OPPOSITE weak
3 *The enemy put up a* ***stout*** *resistance.*
- brave, courageous, spirited, plucky, determined, staunch, resolute, firm
OPPOSITE cowardly

stow verb
They ***stowed*** *the boxes in the attic.*
- store, put away, pack, pile, load

straight adjective
1 *They walked in a* ***straight*** *line.*
- direct, unswerving
- A common simile is as straight as an arrow.
OPPOSITE crooked
2 *It took a long time to get the room* ***straight***.
- neat, orderly, tidy
OPPOSITE untidy
3 *She found it difficult to get a* ***straight*** *answer from him.*
- honest, plain, frank, straightforward
OPPOSITE indirect, evasive

straightforward adjective
The cake recipe is fairly ***straightforward***.
- simple, plain, uncomplicated, easy, clear, direct
OPPOSITE complicated

strain verb
1 *The dog was* ***straining*** *at its lead.*
- pull, tug, stretch, haul
2 *People were* ***straining*** *to see what was going on.*
- struggle, strive, make an effort, try, attempt
3 *Take it easy and don't* ***strain*** *yourself.*
- weaken, exhaust, wear out, tire out, tax

a
b
c
d
e
f
g
h
i
j
k
l
m
n
o
p
q
r
s
t
u
v
w
x
y
z

strain noun
*The **strain** of her job was making her ill.*
- stress, tension, worry, anxiety, pressure

strand noun
*The **strands** of the wool began to unravel.*
- fibre, filament, thread

stranded adjective
1 *A whale lay **stranded** on the beach.*
- run aground, beached, marooned
2 *He was **stranded** in London without any money.*
- abandoned, deserted, helpless, lost, stuck
- (*informal*) high and dry

strange adjective
1 *A **strange** thing happened this morning.*
- funny, odd, peculiar, unusual, abnormal, curious, extraordinary, remarkable, singular, uncommon
OPPOSITE ordinary, everyday
2 *Did you hear **strange** noises in the night?*
- mysterious, puzzling, baffling, mystifying, perplexing, bewildering, inexplicable
3 *The professor showed us his **strange** inventions.*
- weird, eccentric, peculiar, bizarre
- (*informal*) oddball, wacky
4 *I find it hard to get to sleep in a **strange** bed.*
- unfamiliar, unknown, new, alien
OPPOSITE familiar

stranger noun
*A **stranger** stopped us and asked for directions to the castle.*
- newcomer, outsider, visitor, foreigner

strangle verb
*The victim had been **strangled**.*
- throttle

strap noun
*The trunk was fastened with a leather **strap**.*
- belt, band

strategy noun
*The schoool has a **strategy** to deal with bullying.*
- plan, policy, procedure, approach, scheme, programme

stray verb
*Some sheep had **strayed** onto the road.*
- wander, drift, roam, rove, straggle, meander, ramble

streak noun
1 *The horse had a white **streak** on his muzzle.*
- band, line, stripe, strip, smear, stain
2 *There is a **streak** of meanness in his character.*
- element, trace

streak verb
1 *Rain had begun to **streak** the window.*
- smear, smudge, stain, line
2 *A group of motorbikes **streaked** past.*
- rush, speed, dash, fly, hurtle, flash, tear, zoom

stream noun
1 *The climbers dipped their feet in a cool mountain **stream**.*
- brook, rivulet
- (*Scottish*) burn
2 *The raft was carried along with the **stream**.*
- current, flow, tide
3 *A **stream** of water poured through the hole.*
- cataract, flood, gush, jet, rush, torrent
4 *The museum had a steady **stream** of visitors.*
- series, string, line, succession

stream verb
*Warm sunlight **streamed** through the window.*
- pour, flow, flood, issue, gush, spill

street noun SEE **road**

strength noun
1 *Hercules was said to have enormous **strength**.*
- power, might, muscle, brawn, toughness, force, vigour

2 *The main **strength** of the team is in scoring goals.*
- strong point, asset, advantage
OPPOSITE weakness

strengthen verb

1 *Regular exercise **strengthens** your muscles.*
- make stronger, build up, toughen, harden

2 *Concrete was used to **strengthen** the tunnel.*
- fortify, reinforce, bolster, prop up
OPPOSITE weaken

strenuous adjective

1 *We are making **strenuous** efforts to recycle our rubbish.*
- determined, strong, vigorous, energetic, resolute
OPPOSITE feeble

2 *The doctor told him to avoid **strenuous** exercise.*
- hard, tough, difficult, demanding, tiring, exhausting
OPPOSITE easy

stress noun

1 *The hospital staff were working under a lot of **stress**.*
- strain, pressure, tension, worry, anxiety

2 *My piano teacher puts great **stress** on the need to practise.*
- emphasis, importance, weight

stress verb

*She **stressed** the need for absolute secrecy.*
- emphasize, draw attention to, highlight, underline

stretch verb

1 *He **stretched** the rubber band until it snapped.*
- expand, extend, draw out, pull out, elongate, lengthen

2 *She **stretched** her arms wide.*
- extend, open out, spread out

3 *The road **stretched** into the distance.*
- continue, extend

stretch noun

1 *He had a two-year **stretch** in the army.*
- spell, period, time, stint

2 *There are often accidents on this **stretch** of road.*
- section, length, piece

3 *It's a beautiful **stretch** of countryside.*
- area, tract, expanse, sweep

strict adjective

1 *The club has **strict** rules about who can join.*
- rigid, inflexible
- (*informal*) hard and fast
OPPOSITE flexible

2 *The sergeant was known for being **strict** with his men.*
- harsh, severe, stern, firm
OPPOSITE lenient

3 *He used the word in its **strict** scientific sense.*
- exact, precise, correct
OPPOSITE loose

stride noun

*The robot took two **strides** forward.*
- pace, step

strike verb

1 *Roy **struck** his head on the low ceiling.*
- bang, bump, hit, knock, thump, collide with
- (*informal*) wallop, whack

2 *The enemy could **strike** again at any time.*
- attack

3 *The clock **struck** one.*
- chime, ring

striking adjective

*The most **striking** feature of the mermaid was her iridescent tail.*
- conspicuous, noticeable, prominent, remarkable, memorable, extraordinary, outstanding, impressive
OPPOSITE inconspicuous

string noun

1 *She tied some **string** round the parcel.*
- rope, cord, twine
FOR MUSICAL INSTRUMENTS WITH STRINGS
SEE **music**

a b c d e f g h i j k l m n o p q r s t u v w x y z

411

2 *They have received a **string** of complaints.*
- series, succession, chain, sequence

string verb
*We **strung** the fairy lights on the Christmas tree.*
- hang, arrange, thread

stringy adjective
*This meat is very **stringy**.*
- chewy, fibrous, tough
- OPPOSITE tender

strip verb
1 *Lottie **stripped** the paper off her present.*
- peel, remove
- OPPOSITE cover, wrap

2 *He **stripped** and got into the bath.*
- get undressed, undress
- OPPOSITE dress

strip noun
*In front of the house was a narrow **strip** of grass.*
- band, length, ribbon, piece, bit

stripe noun
*The tablecloth was white with blue **stripes**.*
- line, strip, band, bar

strive verb
*Each athlete **strives** to do his or her best.*
- try hard, aim, attempt, endeavour

stroke noun
1 *He split the log with a single **stroke**.*
- blow, hit, action, movement, effort

2 *She added a few quick pencil **strokes** to her drawing.*
- line, mark

stroke verb
*Jess was curled up on the sofa, **stroking** the cat.*
- pat, caress, rub, touch, fondle, pet

stroll verb
*The children **strolled** quietly home.*
- walk slowly, amble, saunter
- SEE ALSO **walk** verb

strong adjective

⚠️ **OVERUSED WORD**

Try to vary the words you use for **strong**. Here are some other words you could use.

- for a *STRONG PERSON* or *STRONG BODY*:
  powerful, muscular, mighty, well-built, beefy, brawny, burly, strapping
  *Crocodiles have **powerful** jaws.*
- A common simile is as strong as an ox.
  OPPOSITE weak, puny
- for *STRONG MATERIAL*:
  robust, sturdy, tough, hard-wearing, durable, stout, substantial
  *The tent is made from **hard-wearing** material.*
  OPPOSITE thin, flimsy
- for a *STRONG LIGHT* or *STRONG COLOUR*:
  bright, brilliant, dazzling, glaring
  *The fugitive was caught in the **glaring** beam of a searchlight.*
  OPPOSITE weak, pale
- for a *STRONG FLAVOUR* or *STRONG SMELL*:
  overpowering, pronounced, pungent, piquant
  *I smelt the **pungent** aroma of roasting coffee.*
  OPPOSITE faint, slight
- for a *STRONG ARGUMENT* or *STRONG CASE*:
  convincing, persuasive, effective, sound, solid, valid
  *The police have **solid** evidence of his guilt.*
  OPPOSITE weak, feeble, flimsy
- for a *STRONG INTEREST* or *STRONG SUPPORTER*:
  enthusiastic, keen, passionate, fervent, avid, zealous
  *Zelda takes a **keen** interest in fashion.*
  OPPOSITE slight

structure noun
1 *The pagoda is a magnificent* **structure**.
- building, construction, framework
2 *Can you explain the* **structure** *of the poem?*
- design, plan, shape, arrangement, organization

struggle verb
1 *The captives* **struggled** *to get free.*
- strain, strive, wrestle, writhe about, tussle, fight, battle
2 *The expedition had to* **struggle** *through a snowstorm.*
- stagger, stumble, flounder, labour

struggle noun
1 *The rebels surrendered without a* **struggle**.
- fight, battle, combat, clash, contest
2 *It was a* **struggle** *to keep going in the blazing heat.*
- effort, exertion, problem, difficulty

stubborn adjective
She's too **stubborn** *to admit that she was wrong.*
- obstinate, pig-headed, strong-willed, uncooperative, inflexible, wilful
- A common simile is as stubborn as a mule.
  OPPOSITE compliant

stuck-up adjective (*informal*)
Nobody likes Ernest—he's so **stuck-up**.
- arrogant, conceited, haughty, proud, snobbish, superior
- (*informal*) snooty, toffee-nosed
  OPPOSITE humble

stud verb
studded with
The lid of the chest was **studded with** *jewels.*
- inlaid with, encrusted with

student noun
- A student at school is a pupil.
- An old word for a pupil is scholar.

studious adjective
Sadiq is a quiet, **studious** *boy.*
- hard-working, diligent, scholarly, academic, bookish

study verb
1 *He went to university to* **study** *medicine.*
- learn about, read, research into
2 *The spy* **studied** *the document carefully.*
- examine, inspect, analyse, investigate, look closely at, scrutinize, survey
3 *She has to* **study** *for her exams.*
- revise, cram
- (*informal*) swot

stuff noun
1 *What's that sticky* **stuff** *on the carpet?*
- matter, substance
2 *You can put your* **stuff** *in one of the lockers.*
- belongings, possessions, things, gear

stuff verb
1 *We managed to* **stuff** *everything into the boot of the car.*
- pack, push, shove, squeeze, ram, compress, force, cram, jam
2 *The cushions are* **stuffed** *with foam rubber.*
- fill, pad

stuffy adjective
1 *Open a window—it's* **stuffy** *in here.*
- airless, close, muggy, humid, stifling, musty, unventilated
  OPPOSITE airy
2 *I found the book a bit* **stuffy**.
- boring, dull, dreary, pompous, stodgy
  OPPOSITE lively

stumble verb
1 *He* **stumbled** *on a tree root and twisted his ankle.*
- trip, stagger, totter, flounder, lurch
2 *The actress* **stumbled** *over her words.*
- stammer, stutter, falter, hesitate

to stumble across something
I **stumbled across** *some old photos.*
- come across, encounter, find, unearth, discover

a
b
c
d
e
f
g
h
i
j
k
l
m
n
o
p
q
r
s
t
u
v
w
x
y
z

stump verb

*The detective was **stumped** by the case.*
- baffle, bewilder, perplex, puzzle, fox, mystify, outwit, defeat
- (*informal*) flummox

stun verb

1 *The pilot was alive but **stunned**.*
- daze, knock out, knock senseless, make unconscious

2 *The whole town was **stunned** by the news.*
- amaze, astonish, astound, shock, stagger, stupefy, bewilder, dumbfound

stunt noun

*The acrobats performed breathtaking **stunts**.*
- feat, exploit, act, deed, trick

stupid adjective

1 *Trolls are often very **stupid**.*
- foolish, unintelligent, dense, dim, dim-witted, brainless, dumb, slow, thick, feeble-minded, half-witted, simple, simple-minded, dopey, dull

2 *It would be **stupid** to go snowboarding without a helmet.*
- senseless, mindless, idiotic, unwise, foolhardy, silly, daft, crazy, mad
- OPPOSITE intelligent

sturdy adjective

1 *Shetland ponies are short and **sturdy**.*
- stocky, strong, robust, athletic, brawny, burly, healthy, hefty, husky, muscular, powerful, vigorous, well-built
- OPPOSITE weak

2 *She bought some **sturdy** walking boots.*
- durable, solid, sound, substantial, tough, well made
- OPPOSITE flimsy

stutter verb

*He tends to **stutter** when he's nervous.*
- stammer, stumble, falter

style noun

1 *I don't like that **style** of jeans.*
- design, pattern, fashion

2 *The book is written in an informal **style**.*
- manner, tone, way, wording

3 *The actress always dresses with great **style**.*
- elegance, stylishness, taste, sophistication

stylish adjective

*Jacqueline always wears **stylish** clothes.*
- fashionable, elegant, chic, smart, sophisticated, tasteful
- (*informal*) trendy, snazzy
- OPPOSITE unfashionable

subdue verb

1 *The army managed to **subdue** the rebels.*
- beat, conquer, defeat, overcome, overpower, crush, vanquish

2 *Jason tried hard to **subdue** his anger.*
- suppress, restrain, repress, check, hold back, curb, control

subject noun

1 *Do you have any strong views on the **subject**?*
- matter, issue, question, point, theme, topic

2 *Her passport shows that she is a British **subject**.*
- citizen, national

subject verb

*The press **subjected** him to a string of questions.*
- expose, submit, lay open

submerge verb

1 *The submarine **submerged** slowly.*
- dive, go down, go under
- OPPOSITE surface

2 *The tsunami **submerged** several coastal villages.*
- engulf, flood, drown, immerse, inundate, swallow up

submit verb

1 *The swordsman finally **submitted** to his opponent.*
- give in, surrender, yield

2 *You need to **submit** a membership form to join the club.*
- give in, hand in, present

subordinate adjective
*He began as a police officer of **subordinate** rank.*
- junior, lesser, lower, inferior
OPPOSITE superior, higher

subscribe verb
to subscribe to
*She **subscribes to** several good causes.*
- contribute to, donate to, give to, support

subsequent adjective
*I missed the first episode and two **subsequent** ones.*
- later, succeeding, following, ensuing, next
OPPOSITE previous

subside verb
1 *One side of the old cottage has started to **subside**.*
- sink, settle
2 *After three days, the flood waters began to **subside**.*
- go down, fall, recede, decline, ebb
3 *The pain will eventually **subside**.*
- decrease, diminish, lessen, die down, dwindle

substance noun
1 *The spaceship was made from an alien **substance**.*
- material, matter, stuff
2 *What was the **substance** of the book?*
- theme, essence, gist, subject matter

substantial adjective
1 *They have made **substantial** improvements to the city.*
- considerable, significant, sizeable, worthwhile, big, large, generous
OPPOSITE small
2 *There is a **substantial** fence to keep out wild animals.*
- strong, sturdy, solid, robust, hefty, durable, sound, well-built
OPPOSITE flimsy

substitute verb
*You can **substitute** margarine for butter in the recipe.*
- exchange, swap, switch
You can also say: **margarine can take the place of butter**, or **you can replace butter with margarine.**

to substitute for someone
*He **substituted for** the injured goalkeeper.*
- stand in for, take the place of, deputize for

substitute noun
*The manager brought on a **substitute** during extra time.*
- replacement, reserve, standby, stand-in
- A substitute for a sick actor is an understudy.

subtle adjective
1 *There was a **subtle** smell of roses in the air.*
- faint, slight, mild, delicate
2 *His jokes are too **subtle** for most people.*
- ingenious, sophisticated
3 *I tried to give her a **subtle** hint.*
- gentle, tactful, indirect
OPPOSITE obvious

subtract verb
*If you **subtract** 5 from 20, you will have 15 left.*
- take away, deduct, remove
OPPOSITE add

suburbs plural noun
*A new rail service will link the city to the **suburbs**.*
- outskirts, outer areas, fringes
- The suburbs of large towns are also known as suburbia.

succeed verb
1 *You have to work hard if you want to **succeed**.*
- be successful, do well, prosper, flourish, thrive
- (*informal*) make it
2 *Everyone hoped that the plan would **succeed**.*
- be effective, produce results, work
- (*informal*) catch on
OPPOSITE fail
3 *Edward VII **succeeded** Queen Victoria.*
- come after, follow, take over from, replace

a
b
c
d
e
f
g
h
i
j
k
l
m
n
o
p
q
r
s
t
u
v
w
x
y
z

success noun
1 *She talked about her **success** as an actress.*
• achievement, attainment, fame
2 *They congratulated the team on their **success**.*
• victory, win, triumph
3 *The group's last CD was a great **success**.*
• hit, bestseller
• (*informal*) winner
4 *The **success** of the mission depends on the astronauts.*
• effectiveness, successful outcome, completion
OPPOSITE failure

successful adjective
1 *She owns a very **successful** chain of restaurants.*
• thriving, flourishing, booming, prosperous, profitable, popular
2 *The supporters cheered the **successful** team.*
• winning, victorious, triumphant
OPPOSITE unsuccessful

succession noun
*Arthur received a **succession** of mysterious emails.*
• series, sequence, run, string, chain

successive adjective
*It rained on seven **successive** days.*
• consecutive, uninterrupted
You can also say: **it rained on several days in succession.**

suck verb
to suck something up
*A sponge will **suck up** water.*
• soak up, draw up, absorb

sudden adjective
1 *Maria felt a **sudden** urge to burst into song.*
• unexpected, unforeseen, impulsive, rash, quick
OPPOSITE expected
2 *The bus came to a **sudden** halt.*
• abrupt, sharp, swift
OPPOSITE gradual

suffer verb
1 *He **suffers** terribly with his back.*
• feel pain, hurt

2 *He will **suffer** for his crime.*
• be punished, pay
3 *The home team **suffered** a humiliating defeat.*
• experience, undergo, go through, endure, stand, bear, tolerate

suffering noun
*The people endured great **suffering** during the war.*
• hardship, deprivation, misery, anguish, pain, distress

sufficient adjective
*The castaways had **sufficient** food for a five days.*
• enough, adequate, satisfactory
OPPOSITE insufficient

suffix noun
OPPOSITE prefix

suffocate verb
*The firefighters were nearly **suffocated** by the fumes.*
• choke, stifle
• To stop someone's breathing by squeezing their throat is to strangle or throttle them.
• To stop someone's breathing by covering their nose and mouth is to smother them.

suggest verb
1 *Mum **suggested** going to the zoo.*
• propose, advise, advocate, recommend
2 *Her comments **suggest** that she's not happy.*
• imply, hint, indicate, signal

suggestion noun
*They didn't like his **suggestion**.*
• proposal, plan, idea, proposition, recommendation

suit verb
1 *Would it **suit** you to stay here overnight?*
• be convenient for, be suitable for, please, satisfy
OPPOSITE displease
2 *His new haircut doesn't **suit** him.*
• look good on, become, flatter

suitable adjective

1 *Please wear clothes **suitable** for wet weather.*

- appropriate, apt, fitting, suited (to), proper, right
  OPPOSITE unsuitable

2 *Is this a **suitable** time to have a chat?*

- convenient, acceptable, satisfactory
  OPPOSITE inconvenient

sulk verb

*I was **sulking** because I wasn't allowed to play outside.*

- be sullen, mope, brood, pout

sulky adjective

*Ron had turned into a **sulky** teenager.*

- moody, sullen, brooding, moping, mopey

sullen adjective

*Beth slouched on the sofa, looking **sullen**.*

- sulky, moody, bad-tempered, mopey, morose, surly, sour
  OPPOSITE cheerful, good-tempered

sum noun

1 *The **sum** of 2 and 2 is 4.*

- total, result

2 *They lost a large **sum** of money.*

- amount, quantity

sums

*Desmond is good at doing **sums**.*

- adding up, arithmetic
- (*informal*) maths
  FOR OTHER MATHEMATICAL TERMS
  SEE **mathematics**

sum verb

to sum up

SEE **summarize**

summarize verb

*Can you **summarize** the main points of the story?*

- sum up, outline, review
- (*informal*) recap

summary noun

*We each wrote a **summary** of the poem.*

- synopsis, précis, outline

summit noun

*The **summit** of the mountain was shrouded in mist.*

- top, cap, peak, tip
  OPPOSITE base

summon verb

*The king **summoned** his knights from far and wide.*

- call, send for, order to come, bid to come
- To ask someone politely to come is to invite them.

sun noun

*They went out into the garden to sit in the **sun**.*

- sunshine, sunlight
- To sit or lie in the sun is to sunbathe.

sunlight noun

*Most plants can only grow in **sunlight**.*

- daylight, sun, sunshine
- Rays of light from the sun are sunbeams.

sunny adjective

1 *It was a beautiful **sunny** day.*

- fine, clear, cloudless
  SEE ALSO **weather** noun
  OPPOSITE cloudy

2 *The flat has a large, **sunny** living room.*

- bright, sunlit, cheerful
- A place that gets a lot of sunshine is sunbaked.
  OPPOSITE gloomy

sunrise noun

*The magic spell wears off at **sunrise**.*

- dawn, daybreak
  OPPOSITE sunset

sunset noun

*They arranged to meet in the churchyard at **sunset**.*

- sundown, dusk, twilight, evening, nightfall
  OPPOSITE sunrise

a b c d e f g h i j k l m n o p q r s t u v w x y z

a
b
c
d
e
f
g
h
i
j
k
l
m
n
o
p
q
r
s
t
u
v
w
x
y
z

superb adjective

Brazil scored another superb goal.

- excellent, outstanding, exceptional, remarkable, impressive, magnificent, marvellous, splendid, tremendous, wonderful
- (*informal*) brilliant, fantastic, terrific, fabulous, sensational, super

  FOR OTHER WAYS TO DESCRIBE SOMETHING GOOD

  SEE **good**

superficial adjective

1 *The scratch on his leg was only superficial.*
- on the surface, shallow, slight
  OPPOSITE deep

2 *The book gives a very superficial view of history.*
- simple, trivial, lightweight, shallow, frivolous, casual
  OPPOSITE thorough, profound

superfluous adjective

Cut away the superfluous fat from the meat.

- excess, surplus, spare, redundant, unwanted
  OPPOSITE necessary

superior adjective

1 *A colonel is superior in rank to a captain.*
- senior, higher, greater

2 *They only sell chocolate of superior quality.*
- first-class, first-rate, top, top-notch, choice, select, better

3 *I don't like her superior attitude.*
- arrogant, haughty, snobbish, stuck-up, self-important
- (*informal*) snooty
  OPPOSITE inferior

supernatural adjective

The fortune-teller claimed to have supernatural powers.

- magic, magical, miraculous
  OPPOSITE natural

supervise verb

Children must be supervised by an adult in the park.

- oversee, superintend, watch over, be in charge of, be responsible for, direct, manage
- To supervise candidates in an exam is to invigilate.

supple adjective

The moccasins are made of supple leather.

- flexible, pliable, soft
  OPPOSITE stiff, rigid

supplementary adjective

There is a supplementary charge for postage.

- additional, extra

supply verb

The art shop can supply you with brushes and paints.

- provide, equip, furnish

supply noun

They had a good supply of fuel for the winter.

- quantity, stock, store, reserve

supplies

We bought supplies for the camping trip.

- provisions, stores, rations, food, necessities

support noun

1 *She thanked them for their support.*
- assistance, backing, aid, cooperation, encouragement, help

2 *The cinema was reopened with support from local businesses.*
- donations, contributions, sponsorship

3 *The supports prevented the wall from collapsing.*
- prop, brace
- A support for a shelf is a bracket.
- A support built against a wall is a buttress.
- A support for someone with an injured leg is a crutch.
- A bar of wood or metal supporting a framework is a strut.
- A support put under a board to make a table is a trestle.

support verb

1 *The rope couldn't support his weight.*
- bear, carry, stand, hold up

2 *The beams support the roof.*
- prop up, strengthen, reinforce

3 *His friends supported him when he was in trouble.*
- aid, assist, help, back, encourage, stand by, stand up for, rally round

4 *She had to work to support her family.*
- maintain, keep, provide for

5 *He supports several local charities.*
- donate to, contribute to, give to

6 *Which team did you support in the World Cup?*
- be a supporter of, follow

supporter noun

1 *The home supporters cheered their team.*
- fan, follower

2 *She is a well-known supporter of animal rights.*
- champion, advocate, backer, defender

suppose verb

1 *I suppose you want to borrow some money.*
- expect, presume, assume, guess, believe, think

2 *Suppose a spaceship landed in your garden!*
- imagine, pretend, fancy

to be supposed to do something
The bus is supposed to leave at 9 o'clock.
- be meant to, be due to, be expected to, ought to

suppress verb

1 *He managed to suppress his anger.*
- check, hold back, contain, control, repress, restrain, curb, bottle up, stifle
- To suppress ideas for political or moral reasons is to censor them.

2 *The army suppressed the rebellion.*
- crush, quash, quell, put down, stamp out, stop, subdue

supreme adjective
Her supreme achievement was winning a gold medal.
- greatest, highest, best, outstanding, top

sure adjective

1 *I'm sure that I'm right.*
- certain, convinced, confident, definite, positive
- OPPOSITE unsure, uncertain

2 *He's sure to phone tonight.*
- bound, certain
- OPPOSITE unlikely

3 *A high temperature is a sure sign of illness.*
- clear, definite, true, undoubted, undeniable
- OPPOSITE unclear, doubtful

surface noun

1 *The surface of Mars is barren and rocky.*
- exterior, outside
- The surface of something may be covered with a crust or shell or skin.
- A thin surface of expensive wood on furniture is a veneer.
- OPPOSITE centre

2 *A dice has dots on each surface.*
- face, side
- OPPOSITE inside

3 *Oil floated on the surface of the water.*
- top
- OPPOSITE bottom

surface verb

1 *The road is surfaced with cobbles.*
- cover, coat

2 *The head of an alligator surfaced in the river.*
- rise to the surface, come up, emerge, appear
- (*informal*) pop up

surge verb

1 *Massive waves surged around the tiny raft.*
- rise, roll, swirl, heave, billow

2 *The crowd surged forward.*
- rush, push, sweep

a
b
c
d
e
f
g
h
i
j
k
l
m
n
o
p
q
r
s
t
u
v
w
x
y
z

surly adjective
*The first mate was a **surly** fellow called Flint.*
- bad-tempered, unfriendly, sullen, sulky, grumpy, churlish

surpass verb
*It will be hard to **surpass** last year's performance.*
- beat, exceed, do better than, outdo

surplus noun
*Farmers have produced a **surplus** of apples this year.*
- excess, glut, surfeit, oversupply
OPPOSITE shortage, lack

surprise noun
*The news that Sara was married came as a **surprise**.*
- amazement, astonishment, revelation, shock, wonder
- (*informal*) bombshell

surprise verb
1 *I was **surprised** by how well she could sing.*
- amaze, astonish, astound, stagger, startle, stun, take aback, take by surprise, dumbfound
- (*informal*) bowl over, flabbergast
2 *He **surprised** the burglars as they came through the window.*
- discover, come upon, catch unawares, catch offguard, catch red-handed

surprised adjective

WRITING TIPS
- Someone who FEELS SURPRISED might: have eyes bulging out of their head, have eyes on the end of stalks, jump out of their skin, stare wide-eyed
- Something which SURPRISES YOU might:
knock you for six, knock your socks off, knock you sideways, make your eyes pop
FOR THINGS YOU MIGHT SAY WHEN SURPRISED
SEE **exclamation**

---

surprising adjective
*There are a **surprising** number of errors in the book.*
- amazing, astonishing, astounding, extraordinary, remarkable, incredible, staggering, startling, stunning, unexpected
OPPOSITE predictable

surrender verb
1 *The band of outlaws refused to **surrender**.*
- admit defeat, give in, yield, submit, capitulate,
2 *Please **surrender** your ticket to the driver.*
- give, hand over

surround verb
1 *The garden was **surrounded** by a stone wall.*
- enclose, fence in, wall in
2 *The pack of wolves **surrounded** its prey.*
- encircle, ring, hem in, besiege

surroundings plural noun
*The hotel is set in very pleasant **surroundings**.*
- setting, location, environment

survey noun
1 *They did a **survey** of local leisure facilities.*
- review, investigation, study
- A survey to count the population of an area is a census.
2 *The builders did a **survey** of the house.*
- inspection, examination

survey verb
1 *You can **survey** the whole valley from the top of the tower.*
- view, look over, look at, observe
2 *They **surveyed** the damage done by the storm.*
- inspect, examine, scrutinize, study
3 *The builders will need to **survey** the area.*
- map out, plan out, measure

survive verb
1 *He managed to **survive** alone on the island for six months.*
- stay alive, last, live, keep going, carry on, continue
  OPPOSITE die
2 *Ada **survived** her husband by twenty years.*
- outlast
3 *Will the birds **survive** this cold weather?*
- endure, withstand, live through, weather

suspect verb
1 *The police **suspected** his motives.*
- doubt, mistrust, have suspicions about
2 *I **suspect** that the shop will be closed on Sundays.*
- expect, imagine, presume, guess, sense, fancy

suspend verb
1 *The meeting was **suspended** until the next day.*
- adjourn, break off, discontinue, interrupt
2 *For the party, we **suspended** balloons from the ceiling.*
- hang, dangle, swing

suspense noun
*The film was a thriller, full of action and **suspense**.*
- tension, uncertainty, anticipation, expectancy, drama, excitement

suspicion noun
*I have a **suspicion** that he is lying.*
- feeling, hunch, inkling, intuition, impression

suspicious adjective
1 *There is something about him which makes me **suspicious**.*
- doubtful, distrustful, mistrustful, unsure, uneasy, wary
  OPPOSITE trusting
2 *What do you make of his **suspicious** behaviour?*
- questionable, suspect, dubious, shady
- (*informal*) fishy

sustain verb
1 *Squirrels store nuts to **sustain** them through the winter.*
- keep going, nurture, provide for
2 *The runners couldn't **sustain** the high speed.*
- keep up, maintain
3 *Will the bridge **sustain** his weight?*
- support, bear, carry, stand

swagger verb
*The lead actor **swaggered** about on stage.*
- strut, parade

swallow verb
*The bread was so dry that it was hard to **swallow**.*
- gulp down
FOR OTHER WAYS TO EAT AND DRINK
SEE **eat, drink** verb
to swallow something up
*As it climbed higher, the rocket was **swallowed up** by the clouds.*
- envelop, engulf, cover over, absorb

swamp verb
*A huge wave threatened to **swamp** the ship.*
- overwhelm, engulf, inundate, flood, submerge

swamp noun
*Much of the land near the coast is **swamp**.*
- marsh, bog, mire, fen, quicksand, quagmire

swan noun
- A female swan is a pen.
- A male swan is a cob.
- A young swan is a cygnet.

swap or **swop** verb
*We **swapped** seats so I could sit in the aisle.*
- change, exchange, switch, substitute

swarm verb
*Hundreds of people **swarmed** around the film star.*
- crowd, flock
to swarm with
*The garden is **swarming with** ants.*
- be overrun by, be crawling with, be infested with, teem with

a
b
c
d
e
f
g
h
i
j
k
l
m
n
o
p
q
r
s
t
u
v
w
x
y
z

sway verb
*The tall grass **swayed** in the breeze.*
- wave, swing, rock, bend, lean

swear verb
1 *The knight **swore** that he would protect the unicorn.*
- pledge, promise, vow, give your word, take an oath

2 *The player **swore** when he bashed his knee.*
- curse

sweat verb
*He **sweats** a lot in hot weather.*
- perspire

sweaty adjective
*When I'm nervous, my palms get **sweaty**.*
- sweating, perspiring, clammy, sticky, moist

sweep verb
1 *She **swept** the floor with an old broom.*
- brush, clean, dust

2 *The bus **swept** past.*
- shoot, speed, zoom

to sweep something away
1 *He tried to **sweep away** the rubbish.*
- clear away, get rid of, remove

2 *The flood **swept away** several houses.*
- destroy, flatten, level

sweet adjective
1 *The pudding is too **sweet** for me.*
- sickly, sugary, sweetened, syrupy
  OPPOSITE acid or bitter or savoury

2 *The **sweet** smell of roses filled the room.*
- fragrant, pleasant
  OPPOSITE foul

3 *Fergus heard the **sweet** sound of a harp.*
- melodious, pleasant, soothing, tuneful
  OPPOSITE ugly

4 *What a **sweet** little cottage!*
- attractive, charming, dear, lovely, pretty, quaint
  OPPOSITE unattractive

sweet noun
1 *The bag contained a mixture of **sweets**.*
- An American word is candy.
- A formal word for sweets is confectionery.

2 *We had rhubarb crumble for **sweet**.*
- dessert, pudding

sweet noun

WORD WEB

SOME KINDS OF SWEET
barley sugar, boiled sweet, bull's-eye, butterscotch, candyfloss, caramel, chewing gum, chocolate, fruit pastille, fudge, humbug, liquorice, lollipop, marshmallow, marzipan, mint or peppermint, nougat, rock, tablet, toffee, Turkish delight

swell verb
*The balloon **swelled** as it filled with hot air.*
- expand, inflate, bulge, grow, enlarge, puff up, billow
  OPPOSITE shrink

swelling noun
*He had a painful **swelling** on his foot.*
- inflammation, lump, bump, growth
- A tumour is a serious swelling on the body.

swerve verb
*The car **swerved** to avoid a hedgehog.*
- turn aside, veer, dodge, swing

swift adjective
1 *They set off at a **swift** pace.*
- fast, quick, rapid, speedy, brisk, lively

2 *She received a **swift** reply to her email.*
- quick, fast, immediate, instant, prompt, speedy, snappy
  OPPOSITE slow

swim verb

WORD WEB

*We **swam** in the sea on our holiday.*
- go swimming, bathe, take a dip

VARIOUS SWIMMING STROKES
backstroke, breaststroke, butterfly, crawl, doggy-paddle

PLACES WHERE YOU CAN SWIM
baths, leisure pool, lido, paddling pool, swimming bath or swimming pool

CLOTHING FOR SWIMMING
bathing costume, bathing suit, bikini, swimming cap, swimming costume, swimsuit, trunks

OTHER EQUIPMENT FOR SWIMMING
armbands, flippers, float, goggles, nose-clip, rubber ring, snorkel

swindle verb
*He **swindled** them out of a lot of money.*
- cheat, trick, dupe, fleece
- (*informal*) con, diddle

swing verb
1 *A glass chandelier **swung** from the ceiling.*
- hang, dangle, sway, flap, wave about

2 *She **swung** round when I called her name.*
- turn, twist, veer, swerve

swipe verb
*The polar bear **swiped** the seal with its paw.*
- swing at, hit, strike, slash

FOR OTHER WAYS TO HIT THINGS
SEE **hit** verb

swirl verb
*Clouds of dust **swirled** up in the desert wind.*
- spin, twirl, whirl, churn

switch verb
1 *Please remember to **switch** off the light.*
- turn

2 *The teams will **switch** ends at half-time.*
- change, swap, exchange, shift

swivel verb
*The dentist **swivelled** round in her chair.*
- spin, turn, twirl, pivot, revolve, rotate

swollen adjective
*My feet were **swollen** from walking all day.*
- inflamed, bloated, puffed up, puffy

swoop verb
*The owl **swooped** and caught the mouse.*
- dive, drop, plunge, plummet, descend, pounce

swop verb SEE **swap**

sword noun

WORD WEB

*Athena raised her shield and drew her **sword**.*
- blade

SOME TYPES OF SWORD
broadsword, cutlass, foil, rapier, sabre, scimitar

- **Fighting with swords is** fencing or swordsmanship.
- **A person who fences with a sword is a** swordsman **or** swordswoman.

FOR OTHER WEAPONS
SEE **weapon**

symbol noun
*The dove is a **symbol** of peace.*
- sign, emblem, image
- The symbols we use in writing are characters or letters.
- The symbols used in ancient Egyptian writing were hieroglyphics.
- The symbol of a club or school is their badge.
- The symbol of a firm or organization is their logo.

symbolize verb
*The dove **symbolizes** peace.*
- represent, stand for, signify, indicate, mean, denote

a
b
c
d
e
f
g
h
i
j
k
l
m
n
o
p
q
r
s
t
u
v
w
x
y
z

sympathetic adjective
*They were **sympathetic** when my mother was ill.*
- understanding, compassionate, concerned, caring, comforting, kind, supportive
OPPOSITE unsympathetic

sympathize verb
to sympathize with
*We **sympathized with** those who had lost their homes.*
- be sympathetic towards, be sorry for, feel for, commiserate with

sympathy noun
*Did you feel any **sympathy** for the characters in the story?*
- understanding, compassion, pity, fellow-feeling, tenderness

synonym noun
*'Cheerful' is a **synonym** of 'happy'.*
OPPOSITE antonym

synthetic adjective
*Nylon is a **synthetic** material.*
- artificial, man-made, manufactured, imitation
OPPOSITE natural

system noun
1 *The city has an archaic transport **system**.*
- organization, structure, network, framework
- (*informal*) set-up
2 *Do you understand the new cataloguing **system**?*
- procedure, process, scheme, arrangement, method, routine

systematic adjective
*Inspector Giles works in a **systematic** way.*
- methodical, logical, orderly, organized, scientific
OPPOSITE unsystematic

table noun FOR ITEMS OF FURNITURE
SEE **furniture**

tablet noun
1 *The doctor prescribed some **tablets** for the pain.*
- pill, capsule, pellet
2 *There was a stone **tablet** above the entrance to the tomb.*
- slab, plaque
3 *He put a **tablet** of powder in the washing machine.*
- block, piece, bar, chunk

tack verb
1 *The carpet needs to be **tacked** down.*
- nail, pin
2 *She **tacked** up the hem of her skirt.*
- sew, stitch

tackle verb
1 *They left him to **tackle** the washing-up.*
- cope with, deal with, attend to, handle, manage, grapple with
2 *Another player **tackled** her and got the ball.*
- challenge, intercept, take on

tackle noun
1 *The referee said it was a fair **tackle**.*
- challenge, interception
2 *He kept his fishing **tackle** in a special case.*
- gear, equipment, apparatus, kit

tactful adjective
*She gave him a **tactful** reminder about her birthday.*
- subtle, discreet, diplomatic, sensitive, thoughtful
OPPOSITE tactless

tactics plural noun
*They discussed their **tactics** for the next game.*
- moves, manoeuvres, plan of action
- An overall plan for a game or battle is a strategy.

tag noun
*The price is marked on the **tag**.*
- label, sticker, ticket

tag verb
*Every item is **tagged** with a price label.*
- identify, label, mark

to tag along with someone
*She **tagged along with** them when they left.*
- accompany, follow, go with, join

to tag something on
*He **tagged on** a PS at the end of his letter.*
- add, attach, tack on

tail noun
*He joined the **tail** of the queue.*
- end, back, rear

tail verb
*The detective **tailed** the suspect to this address.*
- follow, pursue, track, trail, shadow, stalk

to tail off
*The number of tourists **tails off** in October.*
- decrease, decline, lessen, diminish, dwindle, wane

take verb
1 *Naomi **took** her sister's hand.*
- clutch, clasp, take hold of, grasp, grip, seize, snatch, grab
2 *The soldiers **took** many prisoners.*
- catch, capture, seize, detain
3 *Someone has **taken** my pen.*
- steal, remove, make off with
- (*informal*) swipe, pinch
4 *The guide will **take** you to the edge of the forest.*
- conduct, escort, lead, accompany
5 *The bus **took** us right to the station.*
- bring, carry, convey, transport
6 *It'll **take** two people to lift that table.*
- need, require

7 *The caravan can **take** six people.*
- hold, contain, accommodate, have room for
8 *He couldn't **take** the heat of the midday sun.*
- bear, put up with, stand, endure, tolerate, suffer, stomach
9 *He **took** their names and addresses.*
- make a note of, record, write down
10 *The magician asked me to **take** a card.*
- pick, choose, select
11 ***Take** 2 from 8 and you get 6.*
- subtract, take away, deduct

to take someone in
*Everyone was **taken in** by his disguise.*
- fool, deceive, trick, cheat, dupe, hoodwink

to take off
*The space shuttle **took off** on time.*
- lift off, depart

to take something off
*Please **take off** your coat.*
- remove, strip off, peel off

to take part in something
*Would you like to **take part in** the show?*
- participate in, be involved in, join in

to take place
*When did the accident **take place**?*
- happen, occur, come about

to take something up
*She has recently **taken up** tap dancing.*
- begin to do, start learning

tale noun
*Pinocchio is a **tale** about a boy made of wood.*
- story, narrative, account
- (*informal*) yarn
FOR VARIOUS KINDS OF STORY
SEE **story**

talent noun
*She has a great **talent** for music.*
- gift, ability, aptitude, skill, flair, knack
- Unusually great talent is genius.

talented adjective
*He's a very **talented** dancer.*
- gifted, able, accomplished, capable, skilled, skilful, clever, brilliant
- If you are talented in several ways, you are versatile.

a
b
c
d
e
f
g
h
i
j
k
l
m
n
o
p
q
r
s
t
u
v
w
x
y
z

a
b
c
d
e
f
g
h
i
j
k
l
m
n
o
p
q
r
s
t
u
v
w
x
y
z

talk verb
1 *Doug was trying to teach his parrot to* **talk***.*
- speak, say things, communicate, express yourself
2 *The two old friends had a lot to* **talk** *about.*
- discuss, converse, chat, chatter, gossip
- (*informal*) natter
3 *The prisoner refused to* **talk***.*
- give information, confess
  FOR OTHER WAYS TO SAY THINGS
  SEE **say**

talk noun
1 *I need to have a* **talk** *with you soon.*
- conversation, discussion, chat
- The talk between characters in a story is the dialogue.
2 *There is a* **talk** *about Egyptian art at lunchtime.*
- lecture, presentation, speech, address
- A talk in church is a sermon.

talkative adjective
You're not very **talkative** *this morning.*
- chatty, communicative, vocal, forthcoming, articulate
- An informal name for a talkative person is a chatterbox.

tall adjective
1 *Jasmine is* **tall** *for her age.*
- big
  OPPOSITE short
2 *Singapore has many* **tall** *buildings.*
- high, lofty, towering, soaring, giant
- Buildings with many floors are high-rise or multi-storey buildings.
  OPPOSITE low

tally verb
to tally with
Her story didn't **tally with** *her husband's.*
- agree with, correspond with, match

tame adjective
1 *The guinea pigs are* **tame** *and used to people.*
- domesticated, broken in, docile, gentle, obedient, manageable
  OPPOSITE wild
2 *The film seems very* **tame** *nowadays.*
- dull, boring, tedious, bland, unexciting, uninteresting.
  OPPOSITE exciting

tame verb
They were trying to **tame** *a wild horse.*
- break in, subdue, master, control

tamper verb
to tamper with something
Someone has been **tampering with** *the lock.*
- meddle with, tinker with, fiddle about with, interfere with

tan verb
Do you **tan** *easily in the sun?*
- get a tan, go brown
- If your skin goes red in the sun, you get sunburn.

tang noun
You can taste the **tang** *of oranges in the soup.*
- sharpness, zest, zing

tangle verb
1 *Her sewing threads were all* **tangled** *together.*
- entangle, twist, knot, jumble, muddle
- Tangled hair is dishevelled or matted hair.
2 *Dolphins can get* **tangled** *in fishing nets.*
- catch, trap, ensnare

tangle noun
The computer cables have got into a **tangle***.*
- muddle, jumble, knot, twist, confusion

tap verb
Someone **tapped** *three times on the door.*
- knock, rap, strike

tape noun

*The stack of old letters was tied up with **tape**.*

- ribbon, braid, binding

target noun

1 *Her **target** was to swim thirty lengths.*
- goal, aim, objective, intention, purpose, hope, ambition
2 *She was the **target** of his jokes.*
- object, victim, butt

tarnish verb

1 *The bronze sculptures had **tarnished** with age.*
- discolour, corrode
- When iron corrodes it rusts.
2 *The scandal **tarnished** his reputation.*
- stain, taint, blot, spoil, mar

tart adjective

*Lemons have a **tart** taste.*
- sharp, sour, acid, tangy
OPPOSITE sweet

task noun

1 *The robot was given a number of **tasks** to do.*
- job, chore, exercise, errand
2 *The soldiers' **task** was to capture the hill.*
- assignment, mission, duty, undertaking

taste verb

1 ***Taste** the soup to see if it needs salt.*
- sample, try, test, sip
2 *The curry **tastes** quite mild.*
  FOR WAYS TO DESCRIBE HOW FOOD TASTES
  SEE **food**

taste noun

1 *I love the **taste** of ginger.*
- flavour
2 *May I have a **taste** of the cheese?*
- mouthful, bite, morsel, nibble, bit, piece, sample
3 *Her **taste** in clothes is a bit odd.*
- choice, preference, discrimination, judgement

tasteful adjective

*The room was decorated in **tasteful** colours.*
- refined, cultivated, smart, stylish, artistic, elegant, attractive
OPPOSITE tasteless

tasteless adjective

1 *He apologized for making a **tasteless** remark.*
- crude, tactless, indelicate, inappropriate
OPPOSITE tasteful
2 *The sprouts were overcooked and **tasteless**.*
- flavourless, bland, insipid
OPPOSITE flavourful

tasty adjective

*That pie was very **tasty**.*
- delicious, appetizing
SEE ALSO **food**
OPPOSITE unappetizing

tattered adjective

*Some of the blankets were worn and **tattered**.*
- ragged, ripped, torn, frayed, tatty, threadbare
OPPOSITE smart

taunt verb

*The gladiator **taunted** his opponent.*
- barrack, insult, jeer at, laugh at, make fun of, mock, ridicule, sneer at

taut adjective

*Make sure the rope is **taut**.*
- tight, tense, stretched
OPPOSITE slack

teach verb

*My dad is **teaching** me to play the guitar.*
- educate, inform, instruct
- To teach people to play a sport is to coach or train them.
- To teach one person at a time or a small group is to tutor them.

a b c d e f g h i j k l m n o p q r s t u v w x y z

teacher noun
*We have a new ballet **teacher**.*
- tutor, instructor, trainer
- Someone who teaches you to play a sport is a coach.
- In the past, a woman who taught children in a private household was a governess.

team noun
*She's been picked for the junior hockey **team**.*
- side

tear verb
1 *The tree branch **tore** a hole in our kite.*
- rip, snag, gash, shred, split, slit
2 *He **tore** home to watch his favourite TV programme.*
- run, rush, dash, hurry, race, sprint, speed
SEE ALSO **run** verb

tear noun
*There was a **tear** in one of the sails.*
- cut, rip, rent, split, gash, hole, opening, slit, gap

tease verb
*They **teased** him about his new haircut.*
- taunt, make fun of, poke fun at, mock, ridicule, laugh at

technical adjective
*The computer manual uses **technical** language.*
- specialized, scientific, advanced

technique noun
1 *The archaeologists use modern **techniques**.*
- method, procedure, approach
2 *The pianist's **technique** was flawless.*
- skill, expertise, art, craft

tedious adjective
*It was a **tedious** journey by bus.*
- boring, dreary, dull, tiresome, monotonous, unexciting, uninteresting
OPPOSITE exciting

teem verb
to teem with
*The pond **teemed with** tadpoles.*
- be overrun by, be crawling with, be infested with, swarm with

teenager noun
*The film is designed to appeal to **teenagers**.*
- adolescent, youth

telephone verb
*He **telephoned** to say that he'd be late.*
- phone, call, ring, dial

tell verb
1 ***Tell** us what you can see.*
- describe, explain, reveal, report, say, state
2 ***Tell** me when you are ready.*
- let you know, inform, notify, announce, communicate
3 *He **told** them to stop making so much noise.*
- order, command, direct, instruct
4 *We **told** each other scary ghost stories.*
- narrate, relate
5 *He **told** me he would buy the tickets.*
- assure, promise
6 *She couldn't **tell** where she was in the dark.*
- make out, recognize, identify, perceive
7 *Can you **tell** one twin from the other?*
- distinguish, separate
to tell someone off
*She **told them off** for being late.*
- scold, reprimand, reproach
- (*informal*) tick off

temper noun
1 *Mr Black had been in a bad **temper** all morning.*
- mood, humour, state of mind
2 *The chef is always flying into a **temper**.*
- rage, fury, fit of anger, tantrum
to lose your temper
*When she **loses her temper**, her cheeks go red.*
- get angry, get annoyed, fly into a rage
SEE ALSO **angry**

temperature noun FOR UNITS FOR
MEASURING TEMPERATURE
SEE **measurement**

tempestuous adjective
*There was a **tempestuous** storm at sea.*
- stormy, squally, rough, raging,
turbulent, wild
OPPOSITE calm

temple noun FOR PLACES WHERE
PEOPLE WORSHIP
SEE **building**

temporary adjective
*They made a **temporary** shelter for the
night.*
- makeshift, provisional
OPPOSITE permanent

tempt verb
*Can I **tempt** you to have more pudding?*
- coax, entice, persuade, attract
- To tempt someone by offering
them money is to bribe them.
- To tempt an animal into a trap is to
lure it.

tend verb
1 *One of the campers was left to **tend** the
fire.*
- mind, watch over, maintain
2 *Ned spends a lot of time **tending** his
garden.*
- take care of, cultivate, manage
3 *Nurses **tended** those who were injured.*
- care for, attend to, look after, nurse,
treat

to tend to do something
*She **tends to** worry too much.*
- be inclined to, be liable to, be apt to

tendency noun
*He has a **tendency** to be lazy.*
- inclination, leaning, predisposition

tender adjective
1 *Frost may damage **tender** plants.*
- delicate, fragile
OPPOSITE hardy, strong
2 *Cook the meat slowly until it is **tender**.*
- soft, succulent, juicy
OPPOSITE tough
3 *The bruise is still **tender**.*
- painful, sensitive, sore

4 *She gave him a **tender** smile.*
- affectionate, kind, loving, caring,
warm-hearted, compassionate,
sympathetic, fond
OPPOSITE uncaring

tennis noun

> **WORD WEB**
>
> WAYS TO HIT A TENNIS BALL
> lob, serve, slice, smash, volley; drop
> shot, backhand, forehand
>
> SCORING USED IN A TENNIS MATCH
> love, deuce, advantage, break point,
> match point, tiebreak; game, set
>
> OTHER TERMS USED IN TENNIS
> ace, ballboy or ballgirl, court,
> doubles, net, racket or racquet,
> service, singles, umpire

tense adjective
1 *The muscles in her shoulders were
tense.*
- taut, tight, strained, stretched
2 *The crowd were **tense** as they waited to
hear the results.*
- anxious, nervous, apprehensive,
edgy, on edge, fidgety, jumpy, jittery
- (*informal*) uptight
3 *It was a **tense** moment for all of us.*
- nerve-racking, stressful, worrying
OPPOSITE relaxed

tension noun
1 *Can you check the **tension** on the
guy-ropes?*
- tightness, tautness
2 *The **tension** of waiting was almost
unbearable.*
- stress, strain, anxiety, nervousness,
suspense, worry

tent noun

> **WORD WEB**
>
> SOME KINDS OF TENT
> big top or circus tent, dome tent,
> frame tent, marquee, pop-up tent,
> tipi or teepee, tunnel tent, wigwam,
> yurt
- The ropes which hold down a tent
are the guys or guy-ropes.

a
b
c
d
e
f
g
h
i
j
k
l
m
n
o
p
q
r
s
t
u
v
w
x
y
z

a
b
c
d
e
f
g
h
i
j
k
l
m
n
o
p
q
r
s
t
u
v
w
x
y
z

term noun
1 *He was sentenced to a **term** in prison.*
• period, time, spell, stretch, session
2 *The book has a glossary of technical **terms**.*
• word, name, expression

terrible adjective
*We heard there had been a **terrible** accident.*
• awful, dreadful, horrible, appalling, shocking, ghastly, horrific, frightful
FOR OTHER WAYS TO DESCRIBE SOMETHING BAD
SEE **bad**

terrific adjective (*informal*)
1 *The footprint of the yeti was a **terrific** size.*
• big, huge, immense, enormous, giant, gigantic, colossal, massive
SEE ALSO **big**
2 *She's a **terrific** tennis player.*
• excellent, first-class, first-rate, superb, marvellous, wonderful
• (*informal*) brilliant, fantastic, fabulous

terrify verb
*The dogs were **terrified** by the thunder.*
• frighten, scare, startle, alarm, panic, horrify, petrify

territory noun
*We had now entered uncharted **territory**.*
• land, area, ground, terrain, country, district, region, sector, zone
• A territory which is part of a country is a province.

terror noun
*Her eyes filled with **terror** as she described the ghost.*
• fear, fright, horror, panic, alarm, dread

test noun
*How did you do in the maths **test**?*
• exam, examination, assessment, appraisal, evaluation
• A set of questions you answer for fun is a quiz.
• A test for a job as an actor or singer is an audition.
• A test to find the truth about something is an experiment or trial.

test verb
1 *I made an appointment to have my eyes **tested**.*
• examine, check, evaluate, assess, screen
2 *He is **testing** a new formula for invisibile ink.*
• experiment with, try out, trial

text noun
1 *The lawyer studied the **text** of the document.*
• wording, words, content
2 *She quoted a **text** from Shakespeare.*
• passage, extract, quotation

textiles plural noun SEE **cloth**

texture noun
*Silk has a smooth **texture**.*
• feel, touch, quality, consistency
FOR WAYS TO DESCRIBE TEXTURE
SEE **feel** verb

thankful adjective
to be thankful for something
*The travellers were **thankful for** her help.*
• grateful for, appreciative of, pleased about, relieved about
OPPOSITE ungrateful

thanks plural noun
*She sent them a card to show her **thanks**.*
• gratitude, appreciation

thaw verb
1 *The snowman gradually began to **thaw**.*
• melt, dissolve
2 *Leave frozen food to **thaw** before cooking it.*
• defrost, unfreeze
OPPOSITE freeze

theatre noun

WORD WEB

PARTS OF A THEATRE
auditorium, balcony, bar, boxes, box office, circle, dress circle, dressing rooms, foyer, gallery, orchestra pit, stage, stalls

PEOPLE WHO PERFORM OR WORK IN A THEATRE

actor, actress, ballerina, dancer, director, dresser, make-up artist, musician, producer, prompter, scene shifter, stage manager, understudy, usher or usherette

- A person who writes plays for the theatre is a dramatist or playwright.

PEFORMANCES YOU MIGHT SEE AT A THEATRE

ballet, comedy, dance, drama, farce, mime, musical, opera, pantomime, play, puppet show

theft noun
*He was found guilty of **theft**.*
- robbery, stealing

FOR VARIOUS KINDS OF THEFT

SEE **stealing**

theme noun
*What is the **theme** of the poem?*
- subject, topic, idea, gist, argument

theory noun
1 *The detective has a **theory** about the case.*
- explanation, hypothesis, view, belief, idea, notion, suggestion
2 *She bought a book about musical **theory**.*
- laws, principles, rules

therapy noun
*She tried several **therapies** to cure her headaches.*
- treatment, remedy

thick adjective
1 *The Roman wall was about 2 metres **thick**.*
- wide, broad
2 *The cabin was made from **thick** logs of wood.*
- stout, chunky, heavy, solid, substantial
OPPOSITE thin, slender
3 *The explorers hacked their way through the **thick** jungle.*
- dense, close, compact

4 *His boots got stuck in a **thick** layer of mud.*
- deep, heavy
OPPOSITE thin, shallow
5 *The guide spoke with a **thick** Polish accent.*
- heavy, noticeable
OPPOSITE slight
6 *(informal) Fortunately, the giant was rather **thick**.*
- stupid, brainless, foolish
OPPOSITE intelligent

thief noun
*The police managed to catch the **thief**.*
- robber
- Someone who steals from people's homes is a burglar or housebreaker.
- Someone who steals from people in the street is a pickpocket.
- Someone who steals from shops is a shoplifter.
- Someone who used to steal from travellers was a highwayman.

thin adjective
1 *The prisoners were dreadfully **thin**.*
- lean, skinny, bony, gaunt, spare, slight, underweight
- Someone who is thin and tall is lanky.
- Someone who is thin but strong is wiry.
- Someone who is thin but attractive is slim or slender.
- Thin arms or legs are spindly.
- A common simile is as thin as a rake.
OPPOSITE fat
2 *The fairy wore a **thin** cloak of spider's silk.*
- fine, light, delicate, flimsy, sheer, wispy
- A thin line is a fine or narrow line.
- A thin book is a slim book.
OPPOSITE thick
3 *The icing should be **thin** enough to spread.*
- runny, watery
OPPOSITE thick

thin verb
*You can **thin** the paint with a little water.*
- dilute, water down, weaken

to thin out

*The crowd **thinned out** later in the day.*
- diminish, disperse

thing noun

1 *What's that green **thing** on the floor?*
- item, object, article

2 *We had a lot of **things** to talk about.*
- matter, affair, detail, point, factor

3 *A lot of **things** had happened since we spoke.*
- event, happening, occurrence, incident

4 *I have only one **thing** left to do.*
- job, task, act, action

things

*Put your **things** in one of the lockers.*
- belongings, possessions, stuff, equipment, gear

think verb

1 ***Think** before you do anything rash.*
- consider, contemplate, reflect, deliberate, reason
- To think hard about something is to concentrate on it.
- To think quietly and deeply about something is to meditate.
- To keep thinking anxiously about something is to brood on it.

2 *Do you **think** this is a good idea?*
- believe, feel, consider, judge, conclude

3 *What do you **think** this ring is worth?*
- reckon, suppose, imagine, estimate, guess, expect

to think about something

*I need some more time to **think about** it.*
- consider, reflect on, ponder, muse on, mull over

to think something up

*They **thought up** a good plan.*
- invent, make up, conceive, concoct, devise

thirsty adjective

*They were **thirsty** after their long walk.*
- dry, parched
- If someone is ill through lack of fluids, they are dehydrated.

thorn noun

*The florist cut the **thorns** off the rose stems.*
- prickle, spike, needle, barb

thorny adjective

1 *He scratched his arm on a **thorny** rose bush.*
- prickly, spiky, spiny, sharp, bristly, scratchy

2 *They discussed the **thorny** problem for hours.*
- tricky, difficult, complicated, hard, perplexing, ticklish

thorough adjective

1 *The doctor gave him a **thorough** examination.*
- comprehensive, full, rigorous, careful, methodical, systematic, meticulous, painstaking, conscientious
  OPPOSITE superficial

2 *He's made a **thorough** mess of things!*
- complete, total, utter, absolute, downright

thought noun

1 *She gave a lot of **thought** to the problem.*
- consideration, deliberation, study

2 *The detective spent some time in **thought**.*
- thinking, contemplation, reflection, meditation

3 *What are your **thoughts** on modern art?*
- opinion, belief, idea, notion, conclusion

thoughtful adjective

1 *Mr Levi had a **thoughtful** expression on his face.*
- pensive, reflective, absorbed, preoccupied
  OPPOSITE blank, vacant

2 *She added some **thoughtful** comments in the margin.*
- well-thought-out, careful, conscientious, thorough
  OPPOSITE careless

3 *It was very **thoughtful** of you to visit me in hospital.*
- caring, considerate, kind, friendly, good-natured, unselfish
  OPPOSITE thoughtless

thoughtless adjective
*It was **thoughtless** of him to mention her dead husband.*
- inconsiderate, insensitive, uncaring, unthinking, negligent, ill-considered, rash
  OPPOSITE thoughtful

thrash verb
1 *The rider **thrashed** and spurred his horse to go faster.*
- hit, beat, whip, flog
- (*informal*) whack, wallop

2 *The crocodile **thrashed** its tail in the mud.*
- swish, flail, jerk, toss

3 (*informal*) *The visitors **thrashed** the home side 6—0.*
- beat, defeat, trounce

thread noun
1 *There was a loose **thread** hanging from her dress.*
- strand, fibre

2 *Do you sell embroidery **thread**?*
- cotton, yarn, wool, silk
- Sewing thread is wound onto a reel or spool.

threat noun
1 *She made a **threat** about phoning the police.*
- warning

2 *Earthquakes are a constant **threat** in California.*
- danger, menace, hazard, risk

threaten verb
1 *The bandits **threatened** him when he tried to escape.*
- make threats against, menace, intimidate, terrorize, bully, browbeat

2 *The forecast **threatened** rain.*
- warn of

3 *Wild tigers are **threatened** with extinction.*
- endanger, put at risk

three noun
- A group of three musicians is a trio.
- Three babies born at the same time are triplets.
- A shape with three sides is a triangle.
- To multiply a number by three is to triple it.

thrifty adjective
*Wendy had been **thrifty** and saved her pocket money.*
- careful, economical, frugal, prudent, sparing
  OPPOSITE extravagant

thrill noun
*Kim loves the **thrill** of rock climbing.*
- adventure, excitement, sensation, tingle
- (*slang*) buzz, kick

thrill verb
*The thought of seeing a real shark **thrilled** him no end.*
- excite, exhilarate, electrify, rouse, stir, stimulate
  OPPOSITE bore

thrilled adjective
*I was **thrilled** to be invited to the wedding.*
- delighted, pleased, excited, overjoyed, ecstatic

thrive verb
*Tomato plants **thrive** in greenhouses.*
- do well, flourish, grow, prosper, succeed

thriving adjective
*He runs a **thriving** restaurant in town.*
- successful, prosperous, booming, healthy, profitable
  OPPOSITE unsuccessful

throb verb
*She could feel the blood **throbbing** through her veins.*
- beat, pound, pulse, pulsate

a b c d e f g h i j k l m n o p q r s **t** u v w x y z

throng noun
*There were **throngs** of people on the street.*
- crowd, swarm, horde

throttle verb
*My tie was so tight that it nearly **throttled** me!*
- strangle, choke

throw verb
1 *I **threw** some bread into the pond for the ducks.*
- fling, cast, pitch, sling, toss
- (*slang*) bung, chuck
- To deliver the ball in cricket or rounders is to bowl.
- To throw the shot in athletics is to put the shot.
- To throw something high in the air is to lob it.
- To throw something heavy is to heave it.
- To throw something with great force is to hurl it.
- If someone throws a lot of things at you, they pelt you
2 *The horse **threw** its rider.*
- throw off, shake off, dislodge
to throw away
*We **threw away** a pile of old junk.*
- get rid of, dispose of, discard, scrap
- (*informal*) dump, ditch

thrust verb
1 *Drew **thrust** his hands into his pockets.*
- push, force, shove
2 *The bandit **thrust** at him with a dagger.*
- lunge, jab, prod, stab, poke

thump verb
*'Silence!' he rasped, **thumping** his fist on the table.*
- bang, bash, pound, hit, strike, knock, rap
- (*informal*) whack, wham

thunder noun, verb
*We could hear **thunder** in the distance.*
- A burst of thunder is a clap, crack, peal, or roll of thunder.
SEE ALSO **weather** noun

thunderous adjective
*The speech was greeted by **thunderous** applause.*
- deafening, loud, resounding, booming
OPPOSITE quiet

tick verb
*A clock was **ticking** in the background.*
FOR VARIOUS WAYS TO MAKE SOUNDS
SEE **sound** noun
to tick someone off (*informal*)
*She **ticked him off** for talking in class.*
- tell off, reprimand, reproach, scold

ticket noun
1 *They got free **tickets** for the concert.*
- pass, permit, token, voucher, coupon
2 *What does it say on the price **ticket**?*
- label, tag, tab

tide noun
*The beach is completely covered at high **tide**.*
- When the tide is coming in it is flowing or incoming.
- When the tide is going out it is ebbing or outgoing.
- The tide is fully in at high tide and fully out at low tide.

tidy adjective
*Mr Rackham likes to keep his office **tidy**.*
- neat, orderly, uncluttered, trim, smart, spruce, straight
OPPOSITE untidy

tie verb
1 *Zoe **tied** a pink ribbon round the parcel.*
- bind, fasten, hitch, knot, loop, secure
- To tie up a boat is to moor it.
- To tie up an animal is to tether it.
OPPOSITE untie
2 *The two teams are still **tied**.*
- be equal, be level, draw

tight adjective
1 *The lid was too **tight** for him to unscrew.*
- firm, fast, secure
- If it is so tight that air cannot get through, it is airtight.

- If it is so tight that water cannot get through, it is watertight.
  OPPOSITE loose
2 *They squeezed into the **tight** space.*
- cramped, compact, small, narrow, poky, snug
  OPPOSITE spacious
3 *Make sure that the ropes are **tight**.*
- taut, tense, stretched, rigid
- A common simile is as tight as a drum.
  OPPOSITE slack
4 *He can be very **tight** with his money.*
- mean, miserly, stingy
  OPPOSITE generous

tighten verb
1 *She **tightened** her grip on his hand.*
- increase, strengthen, tense, stiffen
2 *You need to **tighten** the guy ropes.*
- make taut, pull tighter, stretch
3 *He tried to **tighten** the screw.*
- make tighter, screw up
  OPPOSITE loosen

till verb
*Farmers use tractors to **till** the land.*
- cultivate, farm, plough, dig

tilt verb
*The caravan **tilted** to one side.*
- lean, incline, tip, slant, slope, angle
- When a ship tilts to one side, it lists.

timber noun
*He bought some **timber** to build a shed.*
- wood, lumber, logs, planks

time noun
1 *Is this a convenient **time** to talk?*
- moment, occasion, opportunity
2 *Autumn is my favourite **time** of the year.*
- phase, season
3 *He spent a short **time** living in China.*
- period, while, term, spell, stretch
4 *Shakespeare lived in the **time** of Elizabeth I.*
- era, age, days, epoch, period
5 *Please try to keep **time** with the music.*
- tempo, beat, rhythm

on time
*Please try to be **on time**.*
- punctual, prompt

WORD WEB

UNITS FOR MEASURING TIME
second, minute, hour, day, week, fortnight, month, year, decade, century, millennium

INSTRUMENTS USED TO MEASURE TIME
clock, eggtimer, hourglass, pocket watch, stopwatch, sundial, timer, watch, wristwatch

---

timetable noun
*I looked at the **timetable** on the bus stop.*
- schedule, programme, rota

timid adjective
*At first, the mermaid was too **timid** to say anything.*
- shy, bashful, modest, nervous, fearful, shrinking, retiring, sheepish
- A common simile is as timid as a mouse.
  OPPOSITE brave, confident

tingle verb
*My ears were **tingling** with the cold.*
- prickle, sting, tickle

tingle noun
1 *She felt a **tingle** in her foot.*
- prickling, stinging, tickle, tickling, pins and needles
2 *He felt a **tingle** of excitement.*
- thrill, sensation, quiver, shiver

tinker verb
*He **tinkered** with the computer to get it to work.*
- fiddle, play about, dabble, meddle, tamper

tint noun
*The paint was white with a faint **tint** of blue.*
- colour, hue, shade, tone
  FOR NAMES OF COLOURS
  SEE **colour** noun

a b c d e f g h i j k l m n o p q r s **t** u v w x y z

a
b
c
d
e
f
g
h
i
j
k
l
m
n
o
p
q
r
s
t
u
v
w
x
y
z

tiny adjective
*The ladybird was so **tiny** that you could hardly see it.*
- little, minute, miniature, microscopic, minuscule
- (*informal*) teeny, titchy
- OPPOSITE big, large

tip noun
1 *The **tip** of his nose felt cold.*
- end, point
- The tip of an ink pen is the nib.
2 *The **tip** of the mountain was covered in snow.*
- cap, peak, top, summit, pinnacle, crown
3 *He gave them some useful **tips** on first aid.*
- hint, piece of advice, suggestion, clue, pointer
4 *They took a load of rubbish to the **tip**.*
- dump, rubbish heap

tip verb
1 *Have you **tipped** the waiter?*
- give a tip to, reward
2 *The caravan **tipped** to one side.*
- lean, tilt, incline, slope, slant
- When a ship tips slightly to one side, it lists.
- When a ship tips right over, it capsizes.
3 *Sophie **tipped** the box of crayons onto the table.*
- empty, turn out, dump, unload

to tip over
*He **tipped** the milk jug **over** by accident.*
- knock over, overturn, topple, upset

tiptoe verb FOR VARIOUS WAYS TO WALK
SEE **walk** verb

tire verb
to tire someone out
*Running in the playground had **tired** us all **out**.*
- exhaust, wear out
OPPOSITE refresh, invigorate

tired adjective
*Have a lie down if you're **tired**.*
- exhausted, fatigued, weary, worn out, listless, sleepy, drowsy
- (*informal*) all in

to be tired of something
*I'm **tired of** watching TV.*
- bored with, fed up with, sick of
- If you are not interested in anything, you are apathetic.

tiring adjective
*Digging the garden is **tiring** work.*
- exhausting, fatiguing, demanding, difficult, hard, laborious, tough
OPPOSITE refreshing

title noun
1 *She couldn't think of a **title** for the story.*
- name, heading
- The title above a newspaper story is a headline.
- A title or brief description next to a picture is a caption.
2 *The form asks you to fill in your name and **title**.*
- form of address, designation, rank
- The ordinary title used before a man's name is Mr.
- The ordinary title used before a woman's name is Miss or Mrs or Ms.
- A polite way to address someone whose name you don't know is sir or madam.
FOR ROYAL TITLES
SEE **royalty**

toast verb
***Toast** the bread on one side.*
FOR VARIOUS WAYS TO COOK
SEE **cook** verb

together adverb
1 *They walked to school **together**.*
- side by side, hand in hand
2 *The choir sang the first verse **together**.*
- all at once, at the same time, simultaneously, in chorus, in unison
OPPOSITE independently, separately

toil verb
*They had been **toiling** all day in the fields.*
- work hard, labour, sweat, slave
- (*informal*) grind, slog

toilet noun
*Can you tell me where the **toilet** is?*
- lavatory, WC, bathroom
- (*informal*) loo

token noun
1 *You can exchange this **token** for a free drink.*
- voucher, coupon, ticket, counter
2 *They gave her a card as a **token** of their thanks.*
- sign, symbol, mark, expression, indication, proof, reminder

tolerant adjective
*Molly was very **tolerant** towards other people.*
- understanding, easygoing, open-minded, sympathetic, charitable, forgiving, lenient, indulgent, long-suffering
OPPOSITE intolerant

tolerate verb
1 *He won't **tolerate** sloppy writing.*
- accept, permit, put up with
2 *Cactus plants can **tolerate** extreme heat.*
- bear, endure, stand, abide, suffer, stomach
- (*informal*) stick

tomb noun
*Inside the **tomb** were several ancient skeletons.*
- burial chamber, crypt, grave, mausoleum, sepulchre, vault
- An underground passage containing several tombs is a catacomb.
- A tomb is often marked by a tombstone, gravestone, or headstone.
SEE ALSO **pyramid**

tone noun
1 *There was an angry **tone** to her voice.*
- note, sound, quality, intonation, manner

2 *The room is painted in subtle **tones**.*
- colour, hue, shade, tint
3 *Eerie music created the right **tone** for the film.*
- feeling, mood, atmosphere, spirit, effect

tool noun

WORD WEB

*There's a box of **tools** in the garage.*
- implement, utensil, device, gadget, instrument

TOOLS THAT ARE USED FOR WOODWORK
awl, chisel, clamp, drill, gimlet, hammer, jigsaw, plane, rasp, sander, saw, set square, T-square, vice

TOOLS THAT ARE USED IN THE HOME
broom, brush, ladder, mop, needle, pliers, scissors, screwdriver, tape measure, tweezers

FOR COOKING UTENSILS
SEE **cook** verb

TOOLS THAT ARE USED FOR GARDENING OR FARMING
dibber or dibble, fork, hoe, lawnmower, pitchfork, rake, roller, scythe, secateurs, shears, shovel, sickle, spade, strimmer, trowel

TOOLS YOU MIGHT USE ON A BIKE OR CAR
Allen key, jack, lever, pump, spanner, wrench

OTHER TOOLS
axe, chain saw, crowbar, file, hacksaw, hatchet, mallet, paintbrush, pallet knife, penknife, pick, pickaxe, punch, sledgehammer, stapler

tooth noun

WORD WEB
TEETH IN A PERSON'S MOUTH
canine tooth, eyetooth, incisor, molar, wisdom tooth
- A dog's or wolf's canine tooth is a fang.

a b c d e f g h i j k l m n o p q r **t** u v w x y z

- A long tooth that sticks out of an animal's mouth is a tusk.

THINGS A DENTIST MIGHT FIT TO YOUR TEETH

braces, bridge or bridgework, crown, dentures, plate

SOME PROBLEMS PEOPLE HAVE WITH THEIR TEETH

cavity, decay, plaque, tartar, toothache

SEE ALSO **dentist**

WRITING TIPS

You can use these words to describe **teeth** or **jaws**:

- jagged, serrated, razor-sharp, needle-sharp, pincer-like

- TEETH may:
bite, chew, grind, munch, chomp, gnash, snap, tear, rip, puncture

- A fierce animal or creature might bare its teeth or bare its fangs.

---

top noun
1 *They climbed to the **top** of the hill.*
- peak, summit, tip, crown, crest, head
OPPOSITE bottom, base
2 *The desk **top** was covered with newspapers.*
- surface
3 *The **top** of the jar was screwed on tightly.*
- lid, cap, cover, covering

top adjective
1 *Their office is on the **top** floor.*
- highest, topmost, uppermost, upper
OPPOSITE bottom, lowest
2 *She got **top** marks in her exam.*
- most, best, highest
3 *The skiers set off at **top** speed.*
- greatest, maximum
4 *He is one of Europe's **top** chefs.*
- best, leading, finest, foremost, principal, superior
OPPOSITE junior

top verb
1 *Mum **topped** the cake with fudge icing.*
- cover, decorate, garnish, crown

2 *The athlete is hoping to **top** her personal best.*
- beat, better, exceed, outdo, surpass

topic noun
*What was the **topic** of the conversation?*
- subject, talking-point, issue, matter, question

topical adjective
*The website often discusses **topical** issues.*
- current, recent, up-to-date

topple verb
1 *The books were piled too high and **toppled** over.*
- fall, tumble, overbalance, collapse
2 *The gale **toppled** their TV aerial.*
- knock down, overturn, upset
3 *The rebels plotted to **topple** the king.*
- overthrow, bring down, remove from office

torment verb
1 *He was **tormented** by bad dreams.*
- afflict, torture, plague, distress
2 *He told them to stop **tormenting** the other children.*
- annoy, bother, harass, pester, tease, bully
- To torment someone continually is to persecute or victimize them.

torrent noun
*A **torrent** of water flowed down the hill.*
- flood, gush, rush, stream, cascade

torrential adjective
*They got caught in a **torrential** rainstorm.*
- heavy, violent
- Torrential rain is a cloudburst, deluge, or downpour.
SEE ALSO **weather** noun

toss verb
1 *He **tossed** a coin into the wishing-well.*
- throw, cast, hurl, fling, pitch, sling
- (*informal*) chuck
2 *Let's **toss** a coin to see who'll go first.*
- flip, spin

3 *The little boat **tossed** about in the storm.*
- lurch, pitch, roll, heave, rock, bob

4 *She **tossed** and turned, unable to get to sleep.*
- thrash about, flail, writhe, wriggle

total noun
*A **total** of 15 million people live in Tokyo.*
- sum, whole, entirety, amount

total adjective
1 *The bill shows the **total** amount due.*
- full, complete, whole, entire

2 *The party was a **total** disaster.*
- complete, utter, absolute, thorough, downright, sheer

total verb
*The donations **total** almost 300 euros.*
- add up to, amount to, come to, make

totter verb
*The child **tottered** across the floor.*
- stagger, stumble, reel, wobble
FOR VARIOUS WAYS TO WALK
SEE **walk** verb

touch verb
1 *Some animals don't like to be **touched**.*
- feel, handle, stroke, fondle, caress, pat, pet

2 *The car just **touched** the gatepost.*
- brush, graze, contact

3 *The speed of the racing car **touched** 200 miles per hour.*
- reach, rise to

4 *I was **touched** by the poem that she wrote.*
- move, affect, stir

to touch on something
*Your letter **touched on** the issue of payment.*
- refer to, mention, raise

touch noun
1 *I felt a light **touch** on my arm.*
- pat, stroke, tap, caress, contact

2 *Working with animals requires a special **touch**.*
- sensitivity, understanding, feel, knack, manner

3 *There's a **touch** of frost in the air.*
- hint, trace, suggestion

touchy adjective
*Be careful what you say—he's very **touchy**.*
- easily offended, sensitive, irritable, quick-tempered

tough adjective
1 *You'll need **tough** shoes for hiking.*
- strong, sturdy, robust, durable, stout, hard-wearing, substantial
- Common similes are as tough as nails and as tough as old boots.
OPPOSITE flimsy

2 *The meat was very **tough**.*
- chewy, leathery, rubbery
OPPOSITE tender

3 *They played against **tough** opposition.*
- strong, stiff, powerful, resistant, determined, stubborn
OPPOSITE weak, feeble

4 *The police deal with some **tough** criminals.*
- rough, violent, vicious, hardened

5 *It was a **tough** job to clean the oven.*
- demanding, laborious, strenuous, gruelling, tiring, exhausting
OPPOSITE easy

6 *The crossword puzzle was too **tough** for him.*
- difficult, hard, puzzling, baffling, knotty, thorny
OPPOSITE easy

tour noun
*They went on a sightseeing **tour**.*
- journey, trip, excursion, expedition, outing, drive, ride

tourist noun
*The cathedral was full of **tourists**.*
- sightseer, holidaymaker, traveller, visitor

tournament noun
*She reached the semi-final of the chess **tournament**.*
- championship, competition, contest, series

tow verb
*Horses used to **tow** barges up and down the river.*
- pull, tug along, drag, haul, draw

a b c d e f g h i j k l m n o p q r s t u v w x y z

a
b
c
d
e
f
g
h
i
j
k
l
m
n
o
p
q
r
s
t
u
v
w
x
y
z

tower noun
- A small tower on a castle or other building is a turret.
- A church tower is a steeple.
- The pointed structure on a steeple is a spire.
- The top part of a steeple with a bell is a belfry.
- The tall tower of a mosque is a minaret.

tower verb
to tower above something
*The castle **towers above** the village.*
- rise above, stand above, dominate, loom over

town noun
- A town with its own local council is a borough.
- A large and important town is a city.
- Several towns that merge into each other are a conurbation.
- A word meaning 'to do with a town or city' is urban.
- The people who live in a town are the townspeople.
  SEE ALSO **city**

toxic adjective
*The flask contained a **toxic** gas.*
- poisonous, deadly, lethal, harmful
  OPPOSITE harmless

toy noun

WORD WEB
SOME TOYS YOU MIGHT PLAY WITH
ball, balloon, bicycle, board game, building bricks, computer or video game, construction kit, doll, doll's house, frisbee, hoop, jigsaw, kaleidoscope, kite, marbles, model, playing cards, puppet, puzzle, rattle, rocking horse, rollerblades, rollerskates, skateboard, skipping rope, teddy bear, top, train set, yo-yo

SEE ALSO **game**

trace noun
1 *The burglar left no **trace** of his presence.*
- evidence, sign, mark, indication, hint, clue, track, trail,
- A trace left by an animal might be its footprint or scent or spoor.
2 *They found **traces** of blood on the carpet.*
- tiny amount, drop, spot

trace verb
*She is trying to **trace** her distant ancestors.*
- track down, discover, find, uncover, unearth

track noun
1 *A rough **track** leads past the farm.*
- path, pathway, footpath, trail
2 *They followed the deer's **tracks** for miles.*
- footprint, footmark, trail, scent
3 *They are laying the **track** for a new railway.*
- line, rails
4 *The athletes are warming up on the **track**.*
- racetrack, circuit, course

track verb
*Astronomers are **tracking** the path of the comet.*
- follow, trace, pursue, chase, tail, trail, hunt, stalk
to track someone or **something down**
*They **tracked down** the owner of the car.*
- find, discover, trace, hunt down, sniff out, run to ground

tract noun
*They had to cross a **tract** of desert.*
- area, expanse, stretch

trade noun
1 *The **trade** in antiques has been booming recently.*
- business, dealing, buying and selling, commerce, the market
2 *He is still learning his **trade** as a plumber.*
- craft, skill, occupation, profession, business

trade verb
to trade in something
*The company **trades in** second-hand computers.*
- deal in, do business in, buy and sell
FOR PEOPLE WHO SELL THINGS
SEE **shop**

tradition noun
*It's a **tradition** to sing 'Auld Lang Syne' on New Year's Eve.*
- custom, convention, habit, routine, fashion

traditional adjective
1 *The African drummers wore **traditional** costumes.*
- national, regional, historical
2 *They chose to have a **traditional** wedding.*
- conventional, customary, established, time-honoured, habitual, typical, usual

traffic noun FOR TYPES OF TRAFFIC
SEE **vehicle**

tragedy noun
1 *'Romeo and Juliet' is a **tragedy**.*
OPPOSITE comedy
2 *The accident at sea was a terrible **tragedy**.*
- disaster, catastrophe, calamity, misfortune

tragic adjective
1 *He died in a **tragic** accident.*
- catastrophic, disastrous, calamitous, terrible, appalling, dreadful, unfortunate, unlucky
2 *She had a **tragic** expression on her face.*
- sad, sorrowful, mournful, grief-stricken, pitiful, woeful, wretched, pathetic
OPPOSITE comic, happy

trail noun
1 *We walked along a **trail** through the woods.*
- path, pathway, track, route
2 *The police were on the **trail** of the bank robbers.*
- track, chase, hunt, pursuit
- The trail left in the water by a ship is its wake.

trail verb
1 *The detective **trailed** the suspect all day.*
- follow, chase, tail, track, pursue, shadow, stalk, hunt
2 *She **trailed** her suitcase behind her.*
- pull, tow, drag, draw, haul
3 *He is already **trailing** behind the front runners.*
- fall behind, lag, straggle, dawdle

train noun
1 *They travelled to Johannesburg by **train**.*
FOR WORDS TO DO WITH TRAINS
SEE **railway**
2 *It was a strange **train** of events.*
- sequence, series, string, chain, succession

train verb
1 *He **trains** the football team every Saturday.*
- coach, instruct, teach, tutor
2 *They are **training** hard for the Commonwealth Games.*
- practise, exercise, prepare yourself
- (*informal*) work out
3 *The archer **trained** his arrow on the target.*
- aim (at), point (at), level (at)

trainer noun
1 *Their **trainer** makes them work hard.*
- coach, instructor, teacher, tutor
2 *These **trainers** are for indoor use.*
FOR TYPES OF SHOE OR BOOT
SEE **shoe**

tramp verb
*They **tramped** across the muddy fields.*
- march, hike, trek, trudge, plod, stride
FOR OTHER WAYS TO WALK
SEE **walk** verb

trample verb
*Don't **trample** the flowers!*
- crush, flatten, squash, tread on, walk over, stamp on

trance noun
*The fortune-teller was lost in a **trance**.*
- daydream, daze, dream

a
b
c
d
e
f
g
h
i
j
k
l
m
n
o
p
q
r
s
t
u
v
w
x
y
z

- One way to be in a trance is to be hypnotized.
- Unconsciousness caused by an illness or accident is a coma.

tranquil adjective

1 *They led a **tranquil** life in the country.*
- calm, peaceful, quiet, restful, serene, sedate
- (*informal*) laid-back
OPPOSITE eventful, busy

2 *The sea was **tranquil** after the storm had passed.*
- calm, placid, still, undisturbed, unruffled

transfer verb

*Some paintings have been **transferred** to the new gallery.*
- move, remove, shift, relocate, convey, hand over

transform verb

*They **transformed** the attic into an office.*
- change, alter, turn, convert, adapt, modify

translate verb

*She **translates** Russian poetry into English.*
- interpret, convert
- A person who translates a foreign language is an interpreter or translator.
- An expert in languages is a linguist.

transmit verb

1 *The spy **transmitted** her messages in code.*
- send, communicate, relay, emit, broadcast
- To transmit a programme on radio or TV is to broadcast it.
OPPOSITE receive

2 *Can the disease be **transmitted** to humans?*
- pass on, spread, carry

transparent adjective

*The box had a **transparent** lid.*
- clear
- (*informal*) see-through

- Something which is not fully transparent, but allows light to shine through, is translucent.

transport verb

*The goods are **transported** to Europe by sea.*
- take, carry, convey, ship, transfer, move, bring, fetch, haul, shift

transport noun

WORD WEB

METHODS OF TRANSPORT

TRANSPORT BY AIR
aeroplane, airship, helicopter, hot-air balloon
SEE ALSO **aircraft**

TRANSPORT BY ROAD
bicycle, bus, car, coach, horse, jeep, lorry, minibus, taxi, van
SEE ALSO **vehicle**

TRANSPORT BY RAIL
monorail, train, tram, underground
SEE ALSO **railway**

TRANSPORT BY WATER
barge, boat, canoe, ferry, punt, raft, ship, yacht
SEE ALSO **boat**

FOR VARIOUS WAYS TO TRAVEL
SEE **travel**

trap noun

1 *The animal was caught in a **trap**.*
- snare, net, noose, booby trap
2 *The police set up a **trap** to catch the robbers.*
- ambush

trap verb

*They tried to **trap** the mouse.*
- capture, catch, snare, corner

trash noun

1 *He put the **trash** into the bin.*
- rubbish, waste, garbage, junk, litter, refuse
2 *Don't listen to that **trash**!*
- nonsense

travel verb

WORD WEB

*She prefers to **travel** to work by bus.*

- go, journey, move along, proceed, progress

VARIOUS WAYS TO TRAVEL

cruise, cycle, drive, fly, go by rail, hike, hitch-hike, motor, pedal, ramble, ride, roam, row, sail, tour, trek, voyage, walk, wander

- When birds travel from one country to another they migrate.
- When people travel to another country to live there they emigrate.

FOR METHODS OF TRANSPORT

SEE **transport**

PEOPLE WHO TRAVEL AS A WAY OF LIFE

itinerant, nomad, traveller

OTHER PEOPLE WHO TRAVEL

astronaut, commuter, cyclist, driver or motorist, explorer, hitch-hiker, holidaymaker, motorcyclist, passenger, pedestrian, pilot or aviator, rambler or walker, sailor, tourist

- A person who travels to a religious place is a pilgrim.
- A person who travels illegally on a ship or plane is a stowaway.
- A person who likes travelling round the world is a globetrotter.

treacherous adjective

1 *His **treacherous** plan was to ambush them as they escaped.*

- disloyal, traitorous, deceitful, double-crossing, faithless, false, unfaithful, untrustworthy
- A treacherous person is a traitor.
OPPOSITE loyal

2 *The roads are often **treacherous** in winter.*

- dangerous, hazardous, perilous, unsafe, risky
OPPOSITE safe

tread verb

*Please **tread** carefully.*

- step, walk, proceed

to tread on

*Don't **tread on** the wet cement!*

- walk on, step on, stamp on, trample, crush, squash

treasure noun

*The **treasure** was buried somewhere on the island.*

- hoard, riches, wealth, fortune
- A hidden store of treasure is a cache.

FOR THINGS YOU MIGHT FIND AS TREASURE

SEE **coin** noun, **jewel**, **jewellery**

treasure verb

*She **treasures** the photograph of her grandmother.*

- cherish, prize, value

treat verb

1 *The old woman had always **treated** him kindly.*

- behave towards, deal with

2 *She is being **treated** for minor injuries.*

- give treatment to
- To treat a wound is to dress it.
- To treat an illness or wound successfully is to cure or heal it.

3 *Let me **treat** you by buying you dinner.*

- give you a treat, pay for

treatment noun

1 *The hospital is for the **treatment** of sick animals.*

- care, nursing, healing

2 *He is trying a new **treatment** for back pain.*

- remedy, therapy, medication
- Emergency treatment at the scene of an accident is first aid.

FOR KINDS OF MEDICAL TREATMENT

SEE **medicine**

3 *The sculpture has been damaged by careless **treatment**.*

- handling, use, care, management

treaty noun

*The two sides signed a peace **treaty**.*

- agreement, pact, contract

a b c d e f g h i j k l m n o p q r s t u v w x y z

a b c d e f g h i j k l m n o p q r s t u v w x y z

tree noun

 WORD WEB
- Trees which lose their leaves in winter are deciduous.
- Trees which have leaves all year round are evergreen.
- Trees which grow cones are conifers.
- A young tree is a sapling.
- Small, low trees are bushes or shrubs.
- Miniature trees grown in small containers are bonsai trees.

SOME VARIETIES OF TREE
alder, ash, aspen, baobab, banyan, bay, beech, birch, cedar, chestnut, cypress, elder, elm, eucalyptus, fir, flame tree, hawthorn, hazel, holly, jujube, juniper, larch, lime, maple, oak, olive, palm, pine, plane, poplar, redwood, rowan, spruce, sycamore, tamarind, willow, yew

FOR NAMES OF FRUIT TREES
SEE **fruit**

PLACES WHERE TREES GROW
forest, grove, jungle, plantation, spinney, thicket, wood, woodland
- An area covered with trees is a wooded area.
- A small group of trees is a copse or coppice.
- An area planted with fruit trees is an orchard.

tremble verb
*The little fairy was **trembling** with cold.*
- shake, shiver, quake, quiver, shudder

tremendous adjective
1 *They heard a **tremendous** roar issue from the cave.*
- big, enormous, great, huge, immense, massive, mighty, fearful
2 *Winning the cup was a **tremendous** achievement.*
- marvellous, magnificent, wonderful, superb, terrific, sensational, spectacular, stupendous, extraordinary, outstanding

tremor noun
*A **tremor** in her voice showed she was nervous.*
- trembling, shaking, quavering, quivering, vibration, wobble

trend noun
1 *There is a general **trend** towards healthier eating.*
- tendency, movement, shift, leaning
2 *This type of computer game is the latest **trend**.*
- fashion, style, craze, fad, vogue

trial noun
1 *Scientists are conducting **trials** on a new space probe.*
- test, experiment
2 *The **trial** will be heard in a crown court.*
- case, hearing
- A military trial is a court martial.

triangular adjective
- A triangular shape is three-cornered or three-sided.

tribe noun SEE **family**

trick noun
1 *Stephie played a **trick** on her brother.*
- joke, practical joke, prank
- Tricks which a magician performs are conjuring tricks.
2 *The Trojans never guessed that the wooden horse was a **trick**.*
- deception, pretence, fraud, cheat, hoax
- (*informal*) con

trick verb
*He **tricked** them into believing he was a police officer.*
- deceive, dupe, fool, hoodwink, cheat, swindle
- (*informal*) con

trickle verb
*Water **trickled** from the tap.*
- dribble, drip, leak, seep, ooze
OPPOSITE gush

tricky adjective
1 *There were a couple of **tricky** questions in the exam.*
- difficult, complicated, awkward, intricate, involved, ticklish
OPPOSITE straightforward, easy

2 *Redbeard is a **tricky** person to deal with.*
- crafty, cunning, sly, wily

trigger verb
*The burnt toast **triggered** the smoke alarm.*
- activate, set off, switch on, start

trim adjective
*Mr Stanley always keeps his garden **trim**.*
- neat, orderly, tidy, well-kept, smart, spruce
  OPPOSITE untidy

trim verb
1 *He asked the barber to **trim** his beard.*
- cut, clip, shorten, crop, neaten, tidy
2 *The cuffs of the blouse are **trimmed** with lace.*
- edge, decorate, adorn

trip noun
*They went on a **trip** to the seaside.*
- journey, visit, outing, excursion, jaunt, expedition

trip verb
1 *He **tripped** on the loose carpet.*
- catch your foot, stumble, fall, slip, stagger
2 *Little Red Riding Hood was **tripping** happily along.*
- run, skip

triumph noun
*The team celebrated their **triumph** at the Olympic Games.*
- victory, win, success, conquest

triumphant adjective
1 *They cheered the **triumphant** team.*
- winning, victorious, conquering, successful
  OPPOSITE unsuccessful
2 *'I've solved the riddle!' said Nat with a **triumphant** smile.*
- elated, exultant, joyful, gleeful, jubilant

trivial adjective
*Don't bother me with **trivial** details.*
- unimportant, minor, insignificant, trifling, negligible, petty, silly, slight, frivolous
  OPPOSITE important

troop noun
*A **troop** of horse riders crossed the river.*
- group, band, party, body, company

troop verb
*The children **trooped** along the road.*
- march, parade, walk, proceed
- To walk one behind the other is to file along.

troops plural noun SEE **armed services**

trophy noun
*My friend, Marnie, won a **trophy** for gymnastics.*
- award, prize, cup, medal

trouble noun
1 *The family has had a lot of **trouble** recently.*
- difficulty, hardship, suffering, unhappiness, distress, misfortune, pain, sadness, sorrow, worry
2 *The police dealt with **trouble** in the crowd.*
- disorder, unrest, disturbance, commotion, fighting, violence
3 *The **trouble** with this computer is that it's very slow.*
- problem, difficulty, disadvantage, drawback

to take trouble
*He **took trouble** to remember all our names.*
- bother, make an effort, take pains

trouble verb
1 *What's **troubling** you?*
- distress, upset, bother, worry, concern, pain, torment, vex
2 *I don't want to **trouble** her if she's busy.*
- disturb, interrupt, bother, pester
3 *Nobody **troubled** to tidy up the room.*
- bother, make an effort, take trouble

troublesome adjective
1 *Do you find the heat **troublesome**?*
- annoying, irritating, trying, tiresome, bothersome, distressing, inconvenient, upsetting

a
b
c
d
e
f
g
h
i
j
k
l
m
n
o
p
q
r
s
t
u
v
w
x
y
z

2 *There are two **troublesome** teenagers in the family.*
- badly behaved, disorderly, rowdy, unruly, disobedient
  OPPOSITE helpful

trousers plural noun FOR ITEMS OF CLOTHING
  SEE **clothes**

truce noun
*The two sides agreed on a **truce**.*
- ceasefire, armistice, peace

true adjective
1 *Do you think the newspaper report is **true**?*
- accurate, correct, right, factual, authentic, undeniable
  OPPOSITE untrue, false
2 *This is a **true** copy of my birth certificate.*
- genuine, real, actual, faithful, exact
  OPPOSITE false
3 *Esther has always been a **true** friend.*
- faithful, loyal, constant, devoted, sincere, steady, trustworthy, dependable, reliable
  OPPOSITE unreliable

trunk noun
1 *The **trunk** of a palm tree can bend in the wind.*
- stem, stock
2 *Push up from the ground, keeping your **trunk** straight.*
- torso, body, frame
3 *The magician kept his things in a huge travelling **trunk**.*
- chest, case, box, crate, suitcase, coffer

trust verb
1 *I **trusted** her to keep my identity a secret.*
- rely on, depend on, count on, bank on, believe in, be sure of, have confidence in, have faith in
2 *I **trust** you are well.*
- hope

trust noun
1 *The director has **trust** in her acting ability.*
- belief, confidence, faith

2 *They put their lives in the **trust** of the pilot.*
- responsibility, safe-keeping, hands

trustworthy adjective
*Sir Boldwood was a **trustworthy** ally of the king.*
- reliable, dependable, loyal, trusty, true, honourable, responsible
  OPPOSITE untrustworthy

truth noun
1 *The detective doubted the **truth** of her story.*
- accuracy, authenticity, correctness, genuineness, reliability, truthfulness, validity
  OPPOSITE inaccuracy or falseness
2 *Are you sure you're telling the **truth**?*
- facts
  OPPOSITE lies

truthful adjective
1 *She is normally a **truthful** person.*
- honest, frank, sincere, straight, straightforward, reliable, trustworthy
2 *He gave a **truthful** answer.*
- accurate, correct, proper, right, true, valid
  OPPOSITE dishonest

try verb
1 *I'm going to **try** to beat my dad at chess.*
- aim, attempt, endeavour, make an effort, strive, struggle
2 *Would you like to **try** a larger size?*
- test, try out, evaluate, experiment with

try noun
1 *We may not succeed, but it's worth a **try**!*
- attempt, effort, go, shot
2 *Would you like a **try** of my mango smoothie?*
- trial, test, taste

trying adjective
*The way he keeps asking questions is very **trying**.*
- tiresome, irritating, annoying, wearing, wearisome

a b c d e f g h i j k l m n o p q r s **t** u v w x y z

tub noun

*We shared a large **tub** of popcorn between us.*

- pot, drum, barrel, cask, vat

tube noun

*Roll the paper into a **tube**.*

- cylinder, pipe
- A flexible tube is a hose.
- A tube which liquid pours out of is a spout.

tuck verb

*He **tucked** his t-shirt into his jeans.*

- push, insert, stuff

tuft noun

*The goat stood munching on a **tuft** of grass.*

- clump, bunch

tug verb

1 *It annoys me when my brother **tugs** my hair.*

- pull, yank, jerk, pluck, wrench

2 *We **tugged** the sledge up the hill.*

- drag, pull, tow, haul, lug, draw, heave

tumble verb

*The boy slipped and **tumbled** into the water.*

- topple, drop, fall, pitch, flop, stumble, plummet

tumult noun

*He had to shout to be heard above the **tumult**.*

- noise, uproar, commotion, clamour, din, racket, rumpus, hubbub

tumultuous adjective

*The spectators broke into **tumultuous** applause.*

- noisy, wild, enthusiastic, uproarious
- OPPOSITE subdued

tune noun

*Can you play the **tune** to 'Happy Birthday'?*

- melody, song, air, theme

tunnel noun

- A tunnel dug by rabbits is a burrow.
- A system of burrows is a warren.
- A tunnel in a mine is a gallery.
- A tunnel beneath a road is a subway or underpass.

tunnel verb

*Badgers use their strong front paws to **tunnel** for food.*

- burrow, dig, excavate

turmoil noun

*The whole country was in **turmoil**.*

- chaos, upheaval, uproar, disorder, unrest, commotion, disturbance, ferment, pandemonium
- OPPOSITE calm, peace

turn verb

1 *A wheel **turns** on its axle.*

- go round, revolve, rotate, roll, spin, swivel, pivot, twirl, whirl

2 *The van **turned** into a side street.*

- change direction, corner
- To turn unexpectedly is to swerve or veer off course.
- If you turn to go back in the direction you came from, you do a U-turn.
- If marching soldiers change direction, they wheel.

3 *He **turned** a curious shade of green.*

- become, go, grow

4 *They **turned** the attic into a spare bedroom.*

- convert, adapt, change, alter, modify, transform, develop

to turn something down

*She **turned down** the offer of a part in the play.*

- decline, refuse, reject

to turn something on or **off**

*He **turned on** the radio.*

- switch on or off

to turn out

*Everything **turned out** well in the end.*

- end up, come out, happen, result

to turn over

*The boat **turned over**.*

- capsize, overturn, turn upside down, flip over, keel over

to turn up

*A friend **turned up** unexpectedly.*

- arrive, appear, drop in

a
b
c
d
e
f
g
h
i
j
k
l
m
n
o
p
q
r
s
t
u
v
w
x
y
z

turn noun
1 *She gave the handle a **turn**.*
- twist, spin, whirl, twirl
- A single turn of wheel is a revolution.
- The process of turning is rotation.
2 *The house is just past the next **turn** in the road.*
- bend, corner, curve, angle, junction
- A sharp turn in a country road is a hairpin bend.
3 *It's your **turn** to do the washing up.*
- chance, opportunity, occasion, time, slot, go
4 *Everyone had to do a **turn** in the show.*
- act, performance, scene, sketch
5 (*informal*) *Seeing the skeleton gave her quite a **turn**.*
- fright, scare, shock, start, surprise

turret noun SEE **tower** noun

twig noun
*They gathered **twigs** to make a fire.*
- stick, branch, stalk, stem, shoot

twin noun
*This vase is a **twin** of the one in the museum.*
- double, duplicate, lookalike, match, clone

twinkle verb
*The stars **twinkled** in the sky.*
- sparkle, shine, glitter, glisten, glimmer, glint

twirl verb
1 *The dancers **twirled** faster and faster.*
- spin, turn, whirl, revolve, rotate, pirouette
2 *He paced up and down, **twirling** his umbrella.*
- twiddle, twist

twist verb
1 *She **twisted** a bandage round her wrist.*
- wind, loop, coil, curl, entwine
2 ***Twist** the handle to open the door.*
- turn, rotate, revolve, swivel
3 *The road **twists** through the hills.*
- wind, weave, curve, zigzag
4 *He **twisted** and turned in his sleep.*
- toss, writhe, wriggle

5 *I tried to **twist** the cap off the bottle.*
- unscrew
6 *Heat can **twist** metal out of shape.*
- bend, buckle, warp, crumple, distort

twisted adjective
*The trunk of the olive tree was **twisted** with age.*
- knarled, warped, buckled, misshapen, deformed

twitch verb
*The dog **twitched** in his sleep.*
- jerk, jump, start, tremble

two noun
- Two musicians playing or singing together is a duet.
- Two people or things which belong together are a couple or a pair.
- To multiply a number by two is to double it.

type noun
1 *What **type** of films do you like to watch?*
- kind, sort, variety, category, class, genre
2 *The book was printed in large **type**.*
- print, lettering, letters, characters

typical adjective
1 *The weather is **typical** for this time of year.*
- normal, usual, standard, ordinary, average, predictable, unsurprising
OPPOSITE unusual
2 *The pointed arch is **typical** of Gothic architecture.*
- characteristic, representative
OPPOSITE uncharacteristic

Uu

ugly adjective
1 *The princess had to kiss a fat, **ugly** toad.*
- grotesque, hideous, unattractive, repulsive, revolting, monstrous
  OPPOSITE beautiful
2 *The room was filled with **ugly** furniture.*
- unattractive, unsightly, displeasing, tasteless, horrid, nasty
  OPPOSITE beautiful
3 *The crowd was in an **ugly** mood.*
- unfriendly, hostile, menacing, threatening, angry, dangerous
  OPPOSITE friendly

ultimate adjective
*Her **ultimate** goal is to be a writer.*
- eventual, final
  OPPOSITE initial

umpire noun SEE **referee**

un- prefix

WRITING TIPS

To find synonyms for words beginning with un- which are not listed below, try the following. Look up the word to which un- has been added, then add un- or the word not to its synonyms. For example, to find synonyms for unable, you would look up able and then work out the synonyms not allowed, unwilling, etc.

---

unanimous adjective
*It was a **unanimous** decision.*
- collective, joint, united
- A decision where most but not all people agree is a majority decision.

unattractive adjective SEE **ugly**

unavoidable adjective
*The accident was **unavoidable**.*
- inevitable, bound to happen, certain, destined

unaware adjective
unaware of
*They were **unware of** the dangers that lay ahead.*
- ignorant of, oblivious to, unconscious of

unbearable adjective
*The stench in the cave was **unbearable**.*
- unendurable, intolerable, impossible to bear

unbelievable adjective
1 *The account of the UFO sighting was **unbelievable**.*
- unconvincing, unlikely, far-fetched, improbable, incredible
2 *She scored an **unbelievable** goal.*
- amazing, astonishing, extraordinary, remarkable, sensational, phenomenal

uncertain adjective
1 *I was **uncertain** what to do next.*
- unsure, doubtful, in two minds, unclear
2 *They are facing an **uncertain** future.*
- indefinite, unknown, undecided, unpredictable
  OPPOSITE certain

unclean adjective SEE **dirty**

unclear adjective SEE **uncertain**

uncomfortable adjective
1 *She complained that her shoes were **uncomfortable**.*
- restrictive, cramped, hard, stiff, tight, tight-fitting
2 *He spent an **uncomfortable** night sleeping on the floor.*
- restless, troubled, disagreeable, uneasy
  OPPOSITE comfortable

uncommon adjective SEE **unusual**

a
b
c
d
e
f
g
h
i
j
k
l
m
n
o
p
q
r
s
t
u
v
w
x
y
z

unconscious adjective

1 *The patient had been **unconscious** for two days.*
- If you are unconscious because of a hit on the head, you are knocked out.
- If you are unconscious for an operation, you are anaesthetized.
- If you are unconscious because of an accident or illness, you are in a coma.

2 *She's **unconscious** of the effect she has on other people.*
- ignorant, unaware

3 *They laughed at her **unconscious** slip of the tongue.*
- accidental, unintended, unintentional
- OPPOSITE conscious

unconscious of

*He's **unconscious of** all the trouble he's caused.*
- unaware of, ignorant of, oblivious to

uncover verb

1 *Archaeologists have **uncovered** two more skeletons.*
- dig up, unearth, expose, reveal, show, disclose
- To uncover your body is to strip or undress.

2 *He **uncovered** the truth about his family's past.*
- detect, discover, come across
- OPPOSITE cover up, hide

undergo verb

*Wizards have to **undergo** rigorous training.*
- go through, be subjected to, experience, put up with, endure

undermine verb

*Losing the race could **undermine** her confidence.*
- weaken, lessen, reduce, destroy, ruin
- OPPOSITE support, boost

understand verb

1 *I don't **understand** what you mean.*
- comprehend, grasp, follow, see, take in, realize, appreciate, recognize, work out, fathom

2 *Can you **understand** this writing?*
- read, interpret, make out, make sense of
- To understand something in code is to decode or decipher it.

3 *I **understand** they're moving to Sydney.*
- believe, hear

understanding noun

1 *The robot has limited powers of **understanding**.*
- intelligence, intellect, sense, judgement

2 *The course will increase your **understanding** of science.*
- appreciation, awareness, knowledge, comprehension, grasp,

3 *The two sides reached an **understanding**.*
- agreement, deal, settlement, arrangement, accord

4 *She treats her patients with **understanding**.*
- sympathy, compasssion, consideration

understanding adjective

*Martha is an **understanding** person.*
- sympathetic, caring, friendly, kind, helpful, open-minded, tolerant

undertake verb

1 *She was asked to **undertake** a secret mission.*
- take on, accept, tackle, handle

2 *He **undertook** to pay all the costs.*
- agree, consent, promise, guarantee, commit yourself

underwear noun

- underclothes, underclothing, undergarments
- (*informal*) undies
- Women's underclothes are lingerie.

FOR ITEMS OF UNDERWEAR

SEE **clothes**

undo verb

1 *I'll have to **undo** this row of knitting.*
- unfasten, untie, unravel, loosen, release
- To undo stitching is to unpick it.

2 *Sue **undid** the wrapping on the parcel.*
- open, unwrap, unfold, unwind, unroll, unfurl

3 *The good witch tried to **undo** the spell.*
- reverse, cancel out, wipe out

undoubtedly adverb
*She is **undoubtedly** our best player.*
- definitely, certainly, surely, doubtless, of course

undress verb
*He **undressed** quickly and got into bed.*
- get undressed, take off your clothes, strip
OPPOSITE dress

unearth verb
1 *The dog **unearthed** an old bone.*
- dig up, uncover

2 *She **unearthed** some old diaries in the attic.*
- find, discover, come across, stumble upon, track down

uneasy adjective
1 *I had an **uneasy** feeling that something was wrong.*
- anxious, nervous, apprehensive, tense, troubling, upsetting, worrying
OPPOSITE confident

2 *Our guest passed an **uneasy** night.*
- restless, unsettled, uncomfortable, disturbed
OPPOSITE comfortable

unemployed adjective
*Since the factory closed, he has been **unemployed**.*
- out of work, jobless
- (*informal*) on the dole
- To be unemployed because there is not enough work to do is to be redundant.
OPPOSITE employed, working

uneven adjective
1 *The ground was very **uneven** in places.*
- rough, bumpy, rutted
OPPOSITE smooth

2 *Their performance has been **uneven** this season.*
- erratic, inconsistent, irregular, variable, unpredictable
OPPOSITE consistent

3 *It was a very **uneven** contest.*
- one-sided, unbalanced, unequal, unfair
OPPOSITE balanced

unexpected adjective
*Her reaction was totally **unexpected**.*
- surprising, unforeseen, unpredictable, unplanned
OPPOSITE expected

unfair adjective
1 *Do you think that the umpire's decision was **unfair**?*
- unjust, unreasonable, wrong, one-sided, imbalanced, impartial, biased
OPPOSITE fair, just

2 *I felt that her criticism of my work was **unfair**.*
- undeserved, unmerited, uncalled-for, unjustified
OPPOSITE fair, deserved

unfaithful adjective SEE disloyal

unfamiliar adjective
*The astronauts looked on an **unfamiliar** landscape.*
- stange, unusual, curious, novel, alien
unfamiliar with
*They were **unfamiliar with** the local customs.*
- unaccustomed to, unused to, unaware of

unfit adjective
1 *She used to be **unfit** before she took up swimming.*
- out of condition, unhealthy
OPPOSITE fit

2 *He is **unfit** to be left in charge of the house.*
- unsatisfactory, unsuitable, incompetent, inadequate

unfortunate adjective
1 *The **unfortunate** couple had lost all their possessions.*
- unlucky, poor, unhappy, hapless, wretched, ill-fated

2 *The goalkeeper made one **unfortunate** error.*
- disastrous, calamitous, unwelcome
OPPOSITE fortunate, lucky

3 He made an **unfortunate** remark about her cooking.

- regrettable, inappropriate, tactless, unsuitable, untimely

unfriendly adjective
The housekeeper greeted us with an **unfriendly** glare.

- unwelcoming, inhospitable, unsympathetic, unkind, impolite, uncivil, unhelpful, hostile, cold, cool, distant, standoffish, aloof, unsociable, unneighbourly
OPPOSITE friendly, amiable

ungrateful adjective
Don't be so **ungrateful**.

- unappreciative, unthankful
OPPOSITE grateful

unhappy adjective
You look **unhappy**—what's the matter?

- brokenhearted, dejected, depressed, desolate, despairing, dismal, distressed
- (informal) down, downcast, downhearted, forlorn, gloomy, glum, grave, heartbroken, in low spirits, miserable, regretful, sad, sorrowful, sorry, tearful, troubled, upset, wistful, woeful, wretched
OPPOSITE happy

unhealthy adjective
1 One of the calves has been **unhealthy** since birth.

- unwell, ill, sick, diseased, infirm, sickly, poorly, weak, delicate, feeble, frail
OPPOSITE healthy, strong

2 He eats an **unhealthy** diet of junk food.

- unwholesome, unnatural, harmful, unhygienic
OPPOSITE healthy, wholesome

unhelpful adjective
The shop assistant was most **unhelpful**.

- uncooperative, unfriendly, inconsiderate, reluctant to help
OPPOSITE helpful

unidentified adjective
An **unidentified** aircraft was spotted at night.

- unknown, unrecognized, unspecified, unnamed, anonymous, nameless
OPPOSITE named

uniform noun
The guards at the Tower of London wear fancy **uniforms**.

- costume, outfit, regalia, livery

uniform adjective
The greenhouse is kept at a **uniform** temperature.

- consistent, regular, even, unvarying, identical, similar, the same
OPPOSITE different, varying

unify verb
The new president tried to **unify** the country.

- unite, bring together, harmonize, combine, integrate, join, merge, amalgamate
OPPOSITE separate

unimportant adjective
Don't worry about **unimportant** details.

- insignificant, minor, trivial, trifling, irrelevant, secondary, slight, small, negligible, worthless, petty
OPPOSITE important

uninhabited adjective
The island had been **uninhabited** for centuries.

- unoccupied, empty, deserted, abandoned
OPPOSITE inhabited, populated

uninteresting adjective SEE **boring**

union noun
The city was formed by the **union** of two neighbouring towns.

- uniting, joining, integration, combination, merger, amalgamation, fusion
- A union of two rivers is a confluence.
- A union of two countries is their unification.
- A union of two people is a marriage or partnership.

unique adjective
*Each person's fingerprints are **unique**.*
- distinctive, different, individual, special, peculiar
- (*informal*) one-off

unit noun
*The bookcase is built up from separate **units**.*
- piece, part, bit, section, segment, element, component, module
  FOR UNITS OF MEASUREMENT
  SEE **measurement**

unite verb
1 *King Bluetooth **united** the kingdoms of Denmark and Norway.*
- combine, join, merge, link, integrate, unify, amalgamate, bring together
  OPPOSITE separate
2 *People of all ages **united** to celebrate Chinese New Year.*
- collaborate, cooperate, join forces
- To unite to do something bad is to conspire.
  OPPOSITE compete

universal adjective
*Scientists have made a discovery of **universal** importance.*
- general, widespread, global, worldwide

unjust adjective SEE **unfair**

unkind adjective
*It was a thoughtless and **unkind** remark.*
- callous, hard-hearted, cruel, thoughtless, heartless, uncaring, unfeeling, inconsiderate, unsympathetic, unfriendly, uncharitable, harsh, mean, nasty, selfish, spiteful, vicious, malicious
  OPPOSITE kind

unknown adjective
1 *The letter was in an **unknown** hand.*
- unidentified, unrecognized
  OPPOSITE known
2 *The author of the story is **unknown**.*
- anonymous, nameless, unnamed, unspecified
  OPPOSITE named

3 *The explorers entered **unknown** territory.*
- unfamiliar, alien, foreign, undiscovered, unexplored, uncharted
  OPPOSITE familiar
4 *The part was played by an **unknown** actor.*
- little known, unheard of, obscure
  OPPOSITE famous

unlike adjective
*The food was **unlike** anything I had tasted before.*
- different from, distinct from
  OPPOSITE similar (to)

unlikely adjective
*No-one believed her **unlikely** excuse.*
- unbelievable, unconvincing, improbable, implausible, incredible, far-fetched
  OPPOSITE likely

unlucky adjective
1 *Some people think that 13 is an **unlucky** number.*
- unfavourable, ill-omened, ill-starred, jinxed
2 *By an **unlucky** chance, their plan was discovered.*
- unfortunate, unwelcome, untimely
  OPPOSITE lucky

unmarried adjective
- If you are unmarried, you are single.
- If your marriage has been legally ended, you are divorced.
- An unmarried man is a bachelor.
- An unmarried woman is a spinster.

unmistakable adjective
*There was an **unmistakable** smell of burnt toast.*
- distinct, distinctive, clear, obvious, plain, telltale

unnatural adjective
1 *It's **unnatural** for it to snow in April.*
- unusual, abnormal, odd, strange, weird, bizarre
2 *Some of the acting in the film was a bit **unnatural**.*
- stiff, stilted, unrealistic, forced, self-conscious

a
b
c
d
e
f
g
h
i
j
k
l
m
n
o
p
q
r
s
t
u
v
w
x
y
z

3 *Her hair was an **unnatural** orange colour.*

- artificial, synthetic, man-made, manufactured
OPPOSITE natural

unnecessary adjective
*I'm deleting any **unnecessary** files from my computer.*

- inessential, non-essential, uncalled for, unwanted, excessive, superfluous, surplus, extra, redundant
OPPOSITE necessary

unoccupied adjective
1 *Since the fire, the flats have been **unoccupied**.*

- empty, uninhabited, deserted, unused, vacant
OPPOSITE occupied

2 *The bathroom is **unoccupied**.*

- available, vacant
OPPOSITE engaged

unpleasant adjective
1 *Mr Smallweed was a thoroughly **unpleasant** man.*

- disagreeable, unfriendly, unkind, bad-tempered, nasty, malicious, spiteful, hateful

2 *Being lost in the jungle had been an **unpleasant** experience.*

- uncomfortable, disagreeable, awful

3 *The smell from the drain was very **unpleasant**.*

- disgusting, foul, repulsive, revolting, horrible, horrid, repellent, offensive, objectionable
SEE ALSO bad
OPPOSITE pleasant

unpopular adjective
*The new manager was **unpopular** at first.*

- disliked, hated, despised, unloved
OPPOSITE popular

unreal adjective
*Everything seemed **unreal**, as if in a dream.*

- imaginary, made-up, fictitious, false, pretend
OPPOSITE real

unsafe adjective SEE dangerous

unsatisfactory adjective
*The repairs to the roof were **unsatisfactory**.*

- unacceptable, inadequate, disappointing, displeasing, poor, incompetent, insufficient
OPPOSITE satisfactory

unseen adjective SEE invisible

unsteady adjective
*The table was a bit **unsteady**.*

- unstable, shaky, wobbly, insecure, unbalanced, rickety
OPPOSITE stable, steady

unsure adjective SEE uncertain

untidy adjective
1 *Our house is the one with the **untidy** garden.*

- messy, disorderly, cluttered, jumbled, tangled, littered, chaotic
- (*informal*) higgledy-piggledy, topsy-turvy

2 *His work was **untidy** and full of mistakes.*

- careless, disorganized, slapdash
- (*informal*) sloppy

3 *She arrived looking **untidy** and flustered.*

- dishevelled, bedraggled, rumpled, unkempt, scruffy, slovenly
OPPOSITE tidy

untrue adjective SEE false

unusual adjective
1 *The weather was **unusual** for the time of year.*

- abnormal, out of the ordinary, exceptional, remarkable, extraordinary, odd, peculiar, singular, strange, unexpected, irregular, unconventional, unheard-of
OPPOSITE ordinary

2 *Ebenezer is an **unusual** name.*

- uncommon, rare, unfamiliar
OPPOSITE common

unwell adjective SEE ill

unwilling adjective SEE reluctant

unwise adjective SEE **foolish**

upheaval noun
Moving to a new house causes such an upheaval.
- disruption, disturbance, upset, commotion, fuss

uphill adjective
1 *The last part of the road is uphill.*
- upward, ascending, rising
2 *Finding a job proved to be an uphill struggle.*
- hard, difficult, tough, strenuous, laborious, arduous, exhausting, gruelling, taxing

upkeep noun
The upkeep of a car can be expensive.
- care, maintenance, running

upper adjective
My bedroom is on the upper floor.
- higher, upstairs
OPPOSITE lower

upright adjective
1 *The car seat should be in an upright position.*
- erect, perpendicular, vertical
OPPOSITE horizontal
2 *He is an upright member of the local community.*
- honest, honourable, respectable, reputable, moral, virtuous, upstanding, principled, trustworthy
OPPOSITE corrupt

uproar noun
The meeting ended in uproar.
- chaos, confusion, disorder, commotion, turmoil, pandemonium, mayhem, rumpus, furore

upset verb
1 *Something in the letter had upset her.*
- distress, trouble, disturb, displease, unsettle, offend, dismay, grieve, fluster, perturb
2 *Bad weather upset the train timetable.*
- disrupt, interfere with, interrupt, affect, throw out
3 *The baby upset a whole bowl of cereal.*
- knock over, spill, tip over, topple
4 *A fallen tree branch upset the canoe.*
- overturn, capsize

upset noun
1 *He is off school with a stomach upset.*
- illness, ailment
- (*informal*) bug
2 *They caused a major upset by winning 7–0.*
- shock, surprise, upheaval

upside-down adjective
1 *I can't read the writing if it's upside-down.*
- wrong way up, inverted
- (*informal*) topsy-turvy
2 (*informal*) *Everything in her life seemed to be upside-down.*
- in a mess, chaotic, disorderly, jumbled
- (*informal*) higgledy-piggledy
OPPOSITE orderly

up to date adjective
Note that you write **up-to-date** immediately before a noun.
1 *The spacecraft uses up-to-date technology.*
- new, modern, present-day, recent, current, the latest, advanced, cutting-edge
OPPOSITE out of date or or out-of-date
2 *Her clothes are always up to date.*
- fashionable, stylish, contemporary
- (*informal*) trendy, hip
OPPOSITE old-fashioned

upward adjective
He started on the steep, upward climb.
- uphill, ascending, rising
OPPOSITE downward

urban adjective
Most of the population live in urban areas.
- built-up, densely populated
OPPOSITE rural

urge verb
He urged her to reconsider her decision.
- advise, counsel, appeal to, beg, implore, plead with, press
- To urge someone to do something is also to advocate or recommend it.
to urge someone on
The fans urged their team on.
- encourage, spur on, egg on
OPPOSITE discourage

urge noun

*I had a sudden **urge** to burst into song.*

- impulse, compulsion, longing, wish, yearning, desire, itch
- (*informal*) yen

urgent adjective

1 *She had **urgent** business in New York.*

- pressing, immediate, essential, important, top-priority
  OPPOSITE unimportant

2 *He spoke in an **urgent** whisper.*

- anxious, insistent, earnest

usable adjective

1 *The lift is not **usable** today.*

- operating, working, functioning, functional
  OPPOSITE unusable

2 *This ticket is **usable** only on certain trains.*

- valid, acceptable,
  OPPOSITE invalid

use verb

1 *She **used** a calculator to add up the figures.*

- make use of, employ, utilize
- To use your knowledge is to apply it.
- To use your muscles is to exercise them.
- To use a musical instrument is to play it.
- To use an axe or sword is to wield it.
- To use people or things selfishly is to exploit them.

2 *Can you show me how to **use** the photocopier?*

- operate, work, handle, manage

3 *You've **used** all the hot water.*

- use up, go through, consume, exhaust, spend

use noun

1 *Would these books be any **use** to you?*

- help, benefit, advantage, profit, value

2 *A sonic screwdriver has many **uses**.*

- function, purpose, point

useful adjective

1 *A flask is **useful** for keeping food warm.*

- convenient, handy, effective, efficient, practical

2 *The website offers some **useful** advice.*

- good, helpful, valuable, worthwhile, constructive, invaluable
  OPPOSITE useless

useless adjective

1 *This old vacuum cleaner is **useless**.*

- ineffective, inefficient, impractical, unusable
  OPPOSITE useful, effective

2 *Her advice was completely **useless**.*

- worthless, unhelpful, pointless, futile, unprofitable, fruitless
  OPPOSITE useful

3 (*informal*) *I'm **useless** at drawing.*

- bad, poor, incompetent
- (*informal*) rubbish, hopeless
  OPPOSITE good

user-friendly adjective

*The computer manual isn't very **user-friendly**.*

- easy to use, straightforward, uncomplicated, understandable

usual adjective

1 *I'll meet you at the **usual** time.*

- normal, customary, familiar, habitual, regular, standard

2 *It's **usual** to knock before entering.*

- common, accepted, conventional, traditional
  OPPOSITE unusual

utensil noun

*A row of cooking **utensils** hung on the wall.*

- tool, implement, device, gadget, instrument, appliance
  FOR VARIOUS TOOLS
  SEE **tool**

utter adjective

*They stared at the unicorn in **utter** amazement.*

- complete, total, absolute, sheer, downright, out-and-out

utter verb

*The robot could only **utter** a few phrases.*

- say, speak, express, pronounce, put into words

vacancy noun

*They have a **vacancy** for a trainee journalist.*

- job, opening, post, position, situation

vacant adjective

1 *The house over the road is still **vacant**.*
- unoccupied, uninhabited, deserted
  OPPOSITE occupied

2 *The receptionist gave me a **vacant** stare.*
- blank, expressionless, mindless, absent-minded, deadpan
  OPPOSITE alert

vacuum noun

- A trade name used as a synonym for a vacuum cleaner is Hoover.
- A trade name used as a synonym for a vacuum flask is Thermos.

vague adjective

1 *The directions she gave me were rather **vague**.*
- indefinite, imprecise, broad, general, ill-defined, unclear, woolly
  OPPOSITE exact, detailed

2 *A **vague** shape could be seen through the mist.*
- blurred, indistinct, obscure, dim, hazy, shadowy
  OPPOSITE definite

vain adjective

1 *The duchess was **vain** about her appearance.*
- arrogant, proud, conceited, haughty, self-satisfied
  OPPOSITE modest

2 *He made a **vain** attempt to tidy the room.*
- unsuccessful, ineffective, useless, worthless, fruitless, futile, pointless
  OPPOSITE successful

valid adjective

1 *The ticket is **valid** for three months.*
- current, legal, approved, authorized, official, permitted, suitable, usable

2 *She made several **valid** points.*
- acceptable, reasonable, sound, convincing, genuine, legitimate
  OPPOSITE invalid

valley noun

*A rocky path meandered through the **valley**.*

- vale, dale, dell, gorge, gully, hollow, pass, ravine, canyon
- (*Scottish*) glen

valuable adjective

1 *Apparently the painting is very **valuable**.*
- expensive, costly, dear, precious, priceless

2 *He gave her some **valuable** advice.*
- useful, helpful, constructive, good, worthwhile, invaluable
  OPPOSITE worthless
  Notice that **invaluable** is not the opposite of **valuable**.

value noun

1 *The house has recently increased in **value**.*
- price, cost, worth

2 *He stressed the **value** of taking regular exercise.*
- advantage, benefit, merit, use, usefulness, importance

a
b
c
d
e
f
g
h
i
j
k
l
m
n
o
p
q
r
s
t
u
v
w
x
y
z

a
b
c
d
e
f
g
h
i
j
k
l
m
n
o
p
q
r
s
t
u
v
w
x
y
z

value verb

1 *He had always **valued** her advice.*
- appreciate, respect, esteem, have a high opinion of, set great store by
- To value something highly is to prize or treasure it.

2 *A surveyor was sent to **value** the house.*
- price, cost, rate, evaluate, assess

van noun FOR VARIOUS VEHICLES

SEE **vehicle**

vanish verb

*With a flick of his wand, the wizard **vanished** into thin air.*
- disappear, go away, fade, dissolve, disperse
OPPOSITE appear

vanity noun

*His **vanity** is such that he never admits he's wrong.*
- arrogance, pride, conceit, self-esteem, self-importance

vapour noun

*Thick clouds of **vapour** poured from the volcano.*
- smoke, fumes, steam, gas
- Vapour hanging in the air is haze, fog, mist, or smog.
- When something turns to vapour it vaporizes.

variable adjective

*The temperature is **variable** at this time of year.*
- changeable, varying, fluctuating, erratic, inconsistent, uncertain, unpredictable, unsteady, unstable
- If your loyalty to friends is variable, you are fickle.
OPPOSITE constant

variation noun

*There are huge **variations** in age within the group.*
- difference, alteration, change, fluctuation, shift

variety noun

1 *The centre offers a **variety** of leisure activities.*
- assortment, mixture, array

2 *The supermarket has over thirty **varieties** of pasta.*
- kind, sort, type, make, brand
- A variety of animal is a breed or species.

3 *There is not much **variety** in her choice of words.*
- variation, change, difference, diversity

various adjective

*The hats are available in **various** colours.*
- different, several, assorted, varying, differing, a variety of, diverse

vary verb

1 *The length of daylight **varies** with the seasons.*
- change, alter, differ, fluctuate

2 *They **vary** the menu from week to week.*
- change, modify, adjust, alter

vast adjective

1 *The miser accumulated a **vast** fortune.*
- large, huge, enormous, great, immense, massive

2 *A **vast** stretch of water lay between them and dry land.*
- broad, wide, extensive, sweeping
OPPOSITE small, tiny

vault verb

to vault over something
*He **vaulted over** the fence.*
- jump over, leap over, bound over, spring over, clear, hurdle

vault noun

*The gold was stored in the **vaults** of the bank.*
- strongroom, treasury
- An underground part of a house is a cellar.
- A room underneath a church is a crypt.

veer verb

*The car suddenly **veered** to the left.*
- change direction, swerve, turn

vegetable noun

WORD WEB

GREEN VEGETABLES
broccoli, Brussels sprout, cabbage, cauliflower, Chinese cabbage, kale, spinach

ROOT VEGETABLES
beetroot, carrot, parsnip, radish, sugar beet, swede, sweet potato, turnip

LEGUMES OR PULSES
broad bean, butter bean, chickpea, French bean, kidney bean, lentil, mangetout or sugar pea, pea, runner bean, soya bean

OTHER VEGETABLES
artichoke, asparagus, aubergine, celeriac, celery, courgette, garlic, leek, marrow, mushroom, okra, onion, pepper, potato, pumpkin, shallot, squash, sweetcorn, water chestnut, yam

vegetarian noun

- A person who doesn't eat any animal products is a vegan.
- An animal that feeds only on plants is a herbivore.
- The opposite—a person or animal that eats flesh—is a carnivore.

vegetation noun

*The rainforest is filled with lush **vegetation**.*
- foliage, greenery, growth, plants, undergrowth

vehicle noun

WORD WEB

VEHICLES WHICH CARRY PEOPLE
bus, cab, camper, car or motorcar, caravan, coach, jeep, minibus, minicab, people carrier, rickshaw, taxi, train, tram, trolleybus
SEE ALSO **aircraft, bicycle, boat, car, railway**

VEHICLES USED FOR WORK
ambulance, bulldozer, dustcart, fire-engine, hearse, HGV or heavy goods vehicle, horsebox, lorry, milkfloat, removal van, pick-up truck, police car, steamroller, tank, tanker, tractor, truck, van

VEHICLES WHICH TRAVEL ON SNOW OR ICE
sled or sledge, sleigh, skidoo, snowplough, toboggan

OLD HORSE-DRAWN VEHICLES
carriage, cart, chariot, coach, gig, stagecoach, trap, wagon

veil verb

*Her face was partly **veiled** by a scarf.*
- cover, conceal, hide, mask, shroud

vein noun

- A tube in the body that carries blood away from the heart is an artery.
- Veins and arteries are blood vessels.
- Delicate hairlike blood vessels are capillaries.

velocity noun

*A rocket travels at great **velocity** through space.*
- speed, rate, swiftness

vengeance noun

*The knight swore **vengeance** on his enemies.*
- revenge, retribution, retaliation
OPPOSITE forgiveness

venomous adjective

*The adder is Britain's only **venomous** snake.*
- poisonous
OPPOSITE harmless

vent noun

*A **vent** in the roof lets the smoke out.*
- gap, hole, opening, outlet, slit
to give vent to
*She **gave vent to** her anger.*
- express, let go, release

a
b
c
d
e
f
g
h
i
j
k
l
m
n
o
p
q
r
s
t
u
v
w
x
y
z

a
b
c
d
e
f
g
h
i
j
k
l
m
n
o
p
q
r
s
t
u
v
w
x
y
z

venture noun

*His first business **venture** was a disaster.*
- enterprise, undertaking, project, scheme

venture verb

*They **ventured** out into the snow.*
- journey, set forth, dare to go

verdict noun

*What was the jury's **verdict**?*
- conclusion, decision, judgement, opinion

verge noun

*Don't park on the **verge** of the road.*
- side, edge, margin
- A stone or concrete edging beside a road is a kerb.
- The flat strip of road beside a motorway is the hard shoulder.

verify verb

*Several witnesses **verified** his statement.*
- confirm, prove, support
- (*informal*) check out

versatile adjective

*He's a very **versatile** musician.*
- adaptable, resourceful, many-sided, all-round, flexible

verse noun

1 *Most of the play is written in **verse**.*
- rhyme
- The rhythm of a line of verse is its metre.
- Something written in verse is poetry or a poem.
  SEE ALSO **poem**

2 *We need to learn the first two **verses** of the poem by heart.*
- stanza

version noun

1 *The two newspapers gave different **versions** of the accident.*
- account, description, story, report

2 *It's an English **version** of a French play.*
- adaptation, interpretation
- A version of something which was originally in another language is a translation.

3 *A new **version** of the computer game will be released in May.*
- design, model, form, variation

vertical adjective

*The fence posts must be **vertical**.*
- erect, perpendicular, upright
- A vertical drop is a sheer drop.
  OPPOSITE horizontal

very adverb

*Carl is a **very** talented juggler.*
- extremely, highly, enormously, exceedingly, truly, intensely, especially, particularly, remarkably, unusually, uncommonly, outstandingly, really
- (*informal*) terribly
  OPPOSITE slightly

vessel noun

1 *A fishing **vessel** has gone missing in the North Sea.*
- boat, ship, craft
  FOR TYPES OF BOAT OR SHIP

  SEE **boat**

2 *Archaeologists found clay **vessels** at the site.*
- pot, dish, bowl, jar, bottle, container

blood vessels
- Blood vessels are your arteries, capillaries, and veins.

veto verb

*The council **vetoed** the proposal for a skatepark.*
- reject, turn down, rule out, say no to, disallow, refuse, ban, forbid, prohibit
  OPPOSITE approve

vex verb

*It **vexed** her that he'd forgotten her birthday.*
- annoy, irritate, make you cross, upset, anger, exasperate

vibrate verb

*I pulled a lever and the whole engine began to **vibrate**.*
- shake, shudder, tremble, throb, judder, quake, quiver, rattle

vicious adjective

1 *This was once the scene of a **vicious** murder.*

- brutal, barbaric, violent, bloodthirsty, cruel, merciless, pitiless, ruthless, callous, inhuman, malicious, sadistic, atrocious, barbarous, murderous, villainous, wicked

2 *Male baboons can be **vicious** if provoked.*

- fierce, ferocious, violent, savage, wild

victim noun

1 *Ambulances took the **victims** to hospital.*

- casualty
- Victims of an accident are also the injured or the wounded.
- A person who dies in an accident is a fatality.

2 *The hawk carried its **victim** in its talons.*

- prey

victor noun

*Who were the **victors** in the battle?*

- winner, conqueror, champion

victorious adjective

*A trophy was presented to the **victorious** team.*

- winning, triumphant, conquering, successful, top, first
  OPPOSITE defeated

victory noun

*Hannibal won several **victories** over the Romans.*

- win, success, triumph
  OPPOSITE defeat

view noun

1 *There's a good **view** from the top of the hill.*

- outlook, prospect, scene, panorama, scenery

2 *What are your **views** on animal testing?*

- opinion, thought, attitude, belief, conviction, idea, notion

in view of something

In view of the circumstances, they gave her a refund.

- because of, as a result of, considering, taking account of

view verb

1 *Thousand of tourists come to **view** Niagara Falls each year.*

- look at, see, watch, observe, regard, contemplate, gaze at, inspect, survey, examine, eye

2 *Wanda **viewed** her cousin with extreme dislike.*

- think of, consider, regard

viewer noun

- People who view a performance are the audience or spectators.
- People who view something as they happen to pass by are bystanders or onlookers or witnesses.

vigilant adjective

*A lookout has to be **vigilant** at all times.*

- alert, watchful, attentive, wary, careful, observant, on the lookout, on your guard
  OPPOSITE negligent

vigorous adjective

1 *She does an hour of **vigorous** exercise every week.*

- active, brisk, energetic, enthusiastic, lively, strenuous

2 *I gave the door a **vigorous** push.*

- forceful, powerful, mighty

3 *He was a **vigorous** man in the prime of life.*

- healthy, strong
  OPPOSITE feeble

vigour noun

*When they sighted land, they began to row with **vigour**.*

- energy, force, spirit, vitality, gusto, verve, enthusiasm, liveliness, zeal, zest

a
b
c
d
e
f
g
h
i
j
k
l
m
n
o
p
q
r
s
t
u
v
w
x
y
z

461

vile ➡ vision

vile adjective

1 *The professor gave us a vile concoction to drink.*
- disgusting, repulsive, revolting, foul, horrible, loathsome, offensive, repellent, sickening, nauseating
  OPPOSITE pleasant

2 *Murder is a vile crime.*
- dreadful, despicable, appalling, contemptible, wicked, evil

villain noun

Detectives are on the trail of an infamous villain.
- criminal, offender, rogue, wrongdoer
- An informal word for the villain in a story is baddy.
  SEE ALSO criminal noun
  OPPOSITE hero

violate verb

The bowler was penalized for violating the rules.
- break, disobey, infringe, flout, disregard, ignore

violation noun

He's guilty of a violation of the rules.
- breach, breaking, offence (against)
- A violation of the rules of a game is a foul or an infringement.

violence noun

1 *The marchers protested against the use of violence.*
- fighting, might, war, brute force, barbarity, brutality, cruelty, savagery
  OPPOSITE non-violence, pacifism

2 *The violence of the storm uprooted trees.*
- force, power, strength, severity, intensity, ferocity, fierceness, fury, rage
  OPPOSITE gentleness, mildness

violent adjective

1 *There were violent clashes in the streets.*
- aggressive, forceful, rough, fierce, frenzied, vicious, brutal
  OPPOSITE gentle, mild

2 *The bridge was washed away in a violent storm.*
- severe, strong, powerful, forceful, raging, tempestuous, turbulent, wild
  OPPOSITE weak, feeble

virtually adverb

It's virtually impossible to tell if the letter is genuine.
- almost, nearly, practically, as good as, in effect

virtue noun

1 *She has the virtue of a saint!*
- goodness, decency, honesty, integrity, righteousness, uprightness, worthiness, morality

2 *One virtue of living in the country is that it's quiet.*
- advantage, benefit, asset, good point, merit, strength
  OPPOSITE vice

virtuous adjective

She had always tried to lead a virtuous life.
- good, honest, honourable, innocent, just, law-abiding, moral, praiseworthy, pure, righteous, trustworthy, upright, worthy
  OPPOSITE wicked

visible adjective

There were no visible signs that the door had been forced.
- noticeable, obvious, conspicuous, clear, distinct, evident, apparent, perceptible, recognizable, detectable
  OPPOSITE invisible

vision noun

1 *He began to have problems with his vision.*
- eyesight, sight

2 *The soothsayer saw a vision of the future.*
- apparation, dream, hallucination
- Something travellers in the desert think they see is a mirage.

3 *As an artist, she has great vision.*
- foresight, imagination, insight

visit verb

*They're **visiting** friends in Toronto for a few days.*

- call on, come to see, drop in on, go to see, pay a call on, stay with

visit noun

1 *My grandmother is coming for a **visit**.*
- call, stay

2 *We are planning a short **visit** to Paris.*
- trip, excursion, outing

visitor noun

1 *They've got some Polish **visitors** staying with them.*
- guest, caller

2 *Rome welcomes millions of **visitors** every year.*
- tourist, holidaymaker, sightseer, traveller

visualize verb

*I can't **visualize** her with curly hair.*

- imagine, picture, envisage, see

vital adjective

*It is **vital** that you remember the secret password.*

- essential, crucial, imperative, important, necessary, indispensable
OPPOSITE unimportant

vitality noun

*That painting of sunflowers bursts with **vitality**.*

- energy, life, liveliness, spirit, animation, exuberance, vigour, zest

vivid adjective

1 *Gaugin often painted in **vivid** colours.*
- bright, colourful, strong, intense, vibrant, dazzling, brilliant, glowing, striking, showy

2 *He gave a **vivid** description of his travels in Mexico.*

- lively, clear, powerful, evocative, imaginative, dramatic, lifelike, realistic, graphic
OPPOSITE dull

voice noun

*The robot spoke with a slow, metallic **voice**.*

- speech, tone, way of speaking
FOR TYPES OF SINGING VOICE
SEE **sing**

WRITING TIPS

You can use these words to describe a **voice**:

- croaky, droning, gruff, high-pitched, husky, low, shrill, soft-spoken, squeaky, throaty
*A **gruff** voice cried, 'Who dares to enter my cave?'*

---

voice verb

*He **voiced** several objections to the plan.*

- express, communicate, put into words, speak

volcano noun

- Molten rock that builds up inside a volcano is magma.
- Molten rock that pours from a volcano is lava.
- Lava and ash pouring from a volcano is an eruption.
- A volcano that often erupts is an active volcano.
- A volcano that can no longer erupt is an extinct volcano.
- A scientist who studies volcanoes is a vulcanologist.

volume noun

1 *We had to measure the **volume** of the jug.*
- capacity, size, dimensions

2 *They struggle to cope with the **volume** of fan mail they receive.*
- amount, quantity, bulk, mass

3 *The full encyclopedia consists of twenty **volumes**.*
- book, tome

a b c d e f g h i j k l m n o p q r s t u v w x y z

a
b
c
d
e
f
g
h
i
j
k
l
m
n
o
p
q
r
s
t
u
v
w
x
y
z

voluntary adjective
*She does **voluntary** work for a charity.*
- optional, unpaid
OPPOSITE compulsory

volunteer verb
*No-one **volunteered** to do the washing-up.*
- offer, put yourself forward, be willing

vomit verb
*The seasickness made him want to **vomit**.*
- be sick, heave, retch
- (*informal*) throw up

vortex noun SEE **spiral**

vote verb
*Everyone has a right to **vote** in the election.*
- cast your vote
to vote for someone or **something**
*I haven't decided who to **vote for**.*
- choose, opt for, nominate, elect

vote noun
*The results of the **vote** will be known tomorrow.*
- ballot, election, poll, referendum

voucher noun
*You can exchange this **voucher** for a free drink.*
- coupon, ticket, token

vow verb
*He **vowed** never to reveal the genie's name.*
- pledge, promise, guarantee, swear, give your word, take an oath

vow noun
*The mermaid took a **vow** to leave the sea forever.*
- pledge, promise, oath, word

voyage noun
- A holiday voyage is a cruise.
- A voyage across a channel or sea is a crossing.
- A long voyage is a sea passage.
FOR OTHER WAYS TO TRAVEL
SEE **travel**

vulgar adjective
1 *The new colour scheme just looks **vulgar** to me.*
- tasteless, unsophisticated, cheap, tawdry
- (*informal*) tacky
OPPOSITE tasteful
2 *The book sometimes uses **vulgar** language.*
- indecent, offensive, rude, coarse
OPPOSITE decent

vulnerable adjective
*As night fell, the outlaws were in a **vulnerable** position.*
- defenceless, exposed, unguarded, unprotected, at risk
OPPOSITE safe

waddle verb
*A pair of geese **waddled** along the path.*
- toddle, totter, shuffle, shamble, wobble

wade verb
1 *Is it safe to **wade** in the river?*
- paddle, wallow
2 *She had piles of paperwork to **wade** through.*
- toil, labour, work, plough

wag verb
*The dog was eagerly **wagging** its tail.*
- move to and fro, shake, swing, wave, waggle, wiggle

wage noun
*How much is your weekly **wage**?*
- earnings, income, pay, pay packet
- A fixed regular amount you are paid for work is a salary.

wage verb
*The Greeks **waged** a long war against Troy.*
- carry on, conduct, fight

wail verb
*Upstairs, the baby began to **wail**.*
- cry, howl, bawl, cry, moan, shriek

wait verb
*Please **wait** here until I get back.*
- remain where you are, stay, stop, rest, pause, linger
- (*informal*) hang about or around, hold on

wait noun
*There was a long **wait** before the show began.*
- interval, pause, delay, hold-up

wake, waken verbs
1 *Hagor the giant **woke** from a deep sleep.*
- awake, awaken, become conscious, come round, rise, arise, stir, wake up
2 *The alarm clock **woke** me at 6 a.m.*
- rouse, arouse, awaken, disturb

walk verb

 OVERUSED WORD
Try to vary the words you use for walk. Here are some other words you could use.
- to *WALK SLOWLY*:
amble, crawl, creep, dodder, pace, plod, saunter, step, stroll, wander
*I **sauntered** down the lane, humming a tune.*

- to *WALK UNSTEADILY*:
hobble, limp, lope, lurch, shamble, shuffle, stagger, stumble, toddle, totter, waddle
*A squat little troll **shuffled** towards the forest.*

- to *WALK HEAVILY* or *LOUDLY*:
clump, pound, stamp, traipse, tramp, trudge, wade
*The robot **clumped** its way up the stairs.*

- to *WALK QUIETLY*:
mince, pad, patter, prowl, slink, stalk, steal, tiptoe
*The burglar **slunk** away into the shadows.*

- to *WALK SMARTLY* or *PROUDLY*:
march, parade, stride, strut, swagger, trot
*Captain Flint **swaggered** on board the ship.*

- to *WALK A LONG DISTANCE*:
hike, trek, ramble
*They are planning to **trek** across the Himalayas.*

- to *WALK IN A GROUP*:
file, troop
*The children **trooped** into the classroom.*

walk noun
1 *We went for a **walk** in the country.*
- stroll, saunter, ramble, hike, trek, tramp, trudge
2 *There are some lovely **walks** through the forest.*
- path, route

walker noun
- When you walk along the street, you are a pedestrian.
- If you go for long walks, you are a hiker or rambler.

wall noun
*A crumbling stone **wall** surrounded the cottage.*
- barricade, barrier, fortification, embankment
- A wall to hold back water is a dam or dyke.
- A low wall along the edge of a roof is a parapet.
- A wall built on top of a mound of earth is a rampart.
- A wall or fence made of sticks is a stockade.

a
b
c
d
e
f
g
h
i
j
k
l
m
n
o
p
q
r
s
t
u
v
w
x
y
z

wallow verb
1 *Hippos like to **wallow** in mud.*
• roll about, flounder, wade, lie, loll
2 *He is **wallowing** in all the attention.*
• revel, take delight, bask

wand noun
*The fairy gave a flick of her magic **wand**.*
• stick, rod, baton, staff
FOR OTHER WORDS TO DO WITH MAGIC
SEE **magic** noun

wander verb
1 *Sheep **wandered** about the hills.*
• stray, roam, rove, range, ramble, meander, travel, walk
2 *We must have **wandered** off the path.*
• stray, turn, veer, swerve

wane verb
1 *At sunset, the light began to **wane**.*
• fade, fail, dim
OPPOSITE brighten
2 *Her enthusiasm **waned** after a while.*
• decline, decrease, lessen, diminish, subside, weaken, dwindle
OPPOSITE strengthen

want verb
1 *He desperately **wants** to win a medal.*
• wish, desire, long, hope
2 *Gayle had always **wanted** a pony of her own.*
• wish for, desire, fancy, crave, long for, yearn for, hanker after, pine for, set your heart on, hunger for, thirst for
3 *That floor **wants** a good scrub.*
• need, require

want noun
1 *The hotel staff saw to all their **wants**.*
• demand, desire, wish, need, requirement
2 *The plants died from **want** of water.*
• lack, need, absence

war noun
*The **war** between the two countries lasted many years.*
• fighting, warfare, conflict, strife, hostilities
SEE ALSO **fight** noun

ward verb
to ward off someone or **something**
1 *He put up his shield to **ward off** the blow.*
• avert, block, check, deflect, turn aside, parry
2 *The charm was intended to **ward off** bad luck.*
• fend off, drive away, repel, keep away, push away

wares plural noun
*The market traders displayed their **wares**.*
• goods, merchandise, produce, stock, commodities

warlike adjective
*The Picts were said to be a **warlike** people.*
• aggressive, fierce, violent, hostile, quarrelsome, militant
OPPOSITE peaceful

warm adjective
1 *It was a **warm** September evening.*
• Weather which is unpleasantly warm is close or sultry.
• Water or food which is only just warm is lukewarm or tepid.
• A common simile is as warm as toast.
OPPOSITE cold
2 *Sandy put on a **warm** jumper.*
• cosy, thick, woolly
OPPOSITE thin
3 *The fans gave the singer a **warm** welcome.*
• friendly, warm-hearted, welcoming, kind, affectionate, genial, amiable, loving, sympathetic
OPPOSITE unfriendly

warm verb
*She sat by the fire, **warming** her hands and feet.*
• heat, make warmer, thaw out
OPPOSITE chill

warn verb

*The guide **warned** us to keep to the path.*

- advise, caution, alert, remind
- To warn people of danger is to raise the alarm.

warning noun

1 *There was no **warning** of the danger ahead.*

- sign, signal, indication, advance notice

2 *The traffic warden let him off with a **warning**.*

- caution, reprimand

warp verb

*The wheel is slightly **warped** with age.*

- bend, buckle, twist, curl, bend out of shape, distort

warrior noun SEE fighter

wary adjective

*The cat is always **wary** when strangers are around.*

- cautious, distrustful, suspicious, careful, watchful, attentive, vigilant, on your guard
- OPPOSITE reckless

wash verb

1 *It took Rapunzel a long time to **wash** her hair.*

- clean
- To wash something with a cloth is to mop, sponge, or wipe it.
- To wash something with a brush is to scrub it.
- To wash something in clean water is to rinse, sluice, or swill it.
- To wash yourself all over is to bath or shower.

2 *Waves **washed** over the beach.*

- flow, splash

waste verb

*Let's not **waste** any more time.*

- squander, misuse, throw away, fritter away
- OPPOSITE save

waste noun

*A lot of household **waste** can be recycled.*

- rubbish, refuse, trash, garbage, junk, litter
- Waste food is leftovers.
- Waste metal is scrap.

wasteful adjective

*It's **wasteful** to cook more food than you need.*

- extravagant, uneconomical, prodigal, lavish, spendthrift
- OPPOSITE economical, thrifty

watch verb

1 *I could sit and **watch** the sea for hours.*

- gaze at, look at, stare at, view, contemplate

2 ***Watch** how the batsman holds the bat.*

- observe, take notice of, keep your eyes on, pay attention to, attend to, heed, note

3 *Could you **watch** my bag for a few minutes?*

- keep an eye on, keep watch over, guard, mind, look after, safeguard, supervise, tend

to watch out

***Watch out**—there's a car coming!*

- be careful, pay attention, beware, take care, take heed

watch noun FOR INSTRUMENTS USED TO MEASURE TIME

SEE **time**

watchful adjective

*She kept a **watchful** eye on the baby.*

- alert, attentive, observant, vigilant, careful, sharp-eyed, keen

water noun

 WORD WEB

SOME AREAS OF WATER
brook, (*Scottish*) burn, canal, lake, lido, (*Scottish*) loch, ocean, pond, pool, reservoir, river, rivulet, sea, stream

a
b
c
d
e
f
g
h
i
j
k
l
m
n
o
p
q
r
s
t
u
v
w
x
y
z

a
b
c
d
e
f
g
h
i
j
k
l
m
n
o
p
q
r
s
t
u
v
w
x
y
z

- Animals and plants which live in water are aquatic.

SPORTS PLAYED IN OR NEAR WATER
angling, canoeing, deep-sea diving, diving, kayaking, rafting, rowing, sailing, snorkelling, swimming, surfing, water polo, waterskiing, windsurfing

---

WRITING TIPS

You can use these words to describe how water moves:
- bubble, cascade, dribble, drip, flood, flow, froth, gurgle, gush, jet, ooze, overflow, ripple, roll, run, seep, shower, spill, spatter, splash, spout, spray, sprinkle, spurt, squirt, stream, surge, sweep, swirl, swish, trickle, well up

SEE ALSO **flow** verb

---

water verb
*Please remember to **water** the plants.*
- wet, irrigate, sprinkle, dampen, moisten, soak, drench

watery adjective
1 *The soup was **watery** and tasteless.*
- weak, thin, runny, diluted, watered down
2 *Chopping onions makes my eyes **watery**.*
- tearful, wet, damp, moist

wave verb
1 *The tall grass **waved** in the breeze.*
- move to and fro, sway, swing, flap, flutter
2 *I tried to get their attention by **waving** a newspaper.*
- shake, brandish, flourish, twirl, wag, waggle, wiggle

wave noun
1 *We watched the **waves** break on the shore.*
- breaker, roller, billow
- A very small wave is a ripple.
- A huge wave caused by an earthquake is a tidal wave or tsunami.

- A number of white waves following each other is surf.
- The top of a wave is the crest or ridge.
2 *A **wave** of anger spread through the crowd.*
- surge, outbreak

waver verb
1 *She **wavered** about whether to send the letter.*
- hesitate, dither, falter, be uncertain, think twice
2 *The candle flame **wavered** in the draught.*
- flicker, quiver, tremble, shake, shiver

wavy adjective
*The mermaid combed her long **wavy** hair.*
- curly, curling, rippling, winding, zigzag
OPPOSITE straight

way noun
1 *Can you show me the **way** to the bus station?*
- direction, route, road, path
2 *Is your house a long **way** from here?*
- distance, journey
3 *This is the best **way** to make porridge.*
- method, procedure, process, system, technique
4 *What a childish **way** to behave!*
- manner, fashion, style
5 *In some **ways**, the brothers are very alike.*
- respect, particular, feature, detail, aspect
6 *Things are in a bad **way**.*
- state, condition

weak adjective
1 *The footbridge was old and **weak** in places.*
- fragile, flimsy, rickety, shaky, unsound, unsteady, unsafe, decrepit
2 *The patient was too **weak** to walk very far.*
- feeble, frail, ill, sickly, infirm, delicate, puny

3 *The nobles plotted against the* **weak** *king.*

- timid, spineless, ineffective, powerless, useless

4 *The film was fun, but the plot was a bit* **weak**.

- feeble, lame, unsatisfactory, unconvincing

5 *He asked for a mug of* **weak** *tea.*

- watery, diluted, tasteless, thin
- (*informal*) wishy-washy
  OPPOSITE **strong**

weaken verb

1 *Too much water will* **weaken** *the flavour.*

- reduce, lessen, diminish, sap, undermine

2 *The storm had* **weakened** *overnight.*

- decrease, decline, die down, fade, dwindle, ebb away, wane
  OPPOSITE **strengthen**

weakness noun

1 *He pointed out the* **weakness** *in their plan.*

- fault, flaw, defect, imperfection, weak point

2 *Eve has a* **weakness** *for toffee apples.*

- liking, fondness
- (*informal*) soft spot
  OPPOSITE **strength**

wealth noun

The family had acquired its **wealth** *from coal.*

- fortune, money, riches, affluence, prosperity
  OPPOSITE **poverty**

a wealth of

There's **a wealth of** *information on the Internet.*

- lots of, plenty of, an abundance of, a profusion of

wealthy adjective

They say that he comes from a very **wealthy** *family.*

- rich, well-off, affluent, prosperous, moneyed, well-to-do
- (*informal*) flush, loaded
  OPPOSITE **poor**

weapon noun

WORD WEB

- Weapons in general are weaponry or arms.
- A collection or store of weapons is an armoury or arsenal.

VARIOUS WEAPONS
bayonet, blowpipe, bomb, dagger, gun, hand-grenade, harpoon, machine-gun, missile, mortar, pistol, revolver, rifle, shell, sword, torpedo, truncheon
SEE ALSO **sword**

SOME WEAPONS USED IN THE PAST
battering ram, battleaxe, blunderbuss, bow and arrow, cannon, catapult, crossbow, javelin, lance, longbow, musket, pike, spear, staff, tomahawk, trident

wear verb

1 *Can I* **wear** *my new dress to the party?*

- dress in, be dressed in, have on

2 *The rug in the hallway is starting to* **wear**.

- fray, wear away, wear out

3 *Those tyres have* **worn** *well.*

- last, endure, survive

to wear off

The pain will **wear off** *soon.*

- die down, disappear, ease, fade, lessen, moderate, subside, weaken

weary adjective

The children were **weary** *after the long walk.*

- tired, worn out, exhausted, fatigued, flagging
- (*informal*) all in

weather noun

WORD WEB

- The typical weather in a particular area is the climate.
- A person who studies and forecasts the weather is a meteorologist.

a b c d e f g h i j k l m n o p q r s t u v **w** x y z

SOME TYPES OF WEATHER
fog: mist, (*Scottish*) haar, haze, smog;
ice and snow: blizzard, frost, hail, ice,
sleet, snowstorm
light rain: drizzle, shower
heavy rain: cloudburst, deluge,
downpour, monsoon, torrent
sun: drought, heatwave, sunshine
storm: squall, tempest
light wind: breeze, gust
strong wind: cyclone, gale, hurricane,
tornado, typhoon, whirlwind

SEE ALSO **sky**, **wind** noun

WRITING TIPS

You can use these words to
describe weather.

- to describe *CLOUDY WEATHER*:
dull, grey, overcast, sunless
- to describe *COLD WEATHER*:
arctic, bitter, chilly, frosty, icy, nippy,
perishing, raw, snowy, wintry
- to describe *SNOW*:
crisp, powdery, slushy
- to describe *HOT WEATHER*:
baking, humid, melting, roasting,
sizzling, sticky, sultry, sweltering
- to describe *STORMY WEATHER*:
rough, squally, tempestuous,
turbulent, violent, wild
- *THUNDER* may:
boom, crash, resound, roar, rumble
- to describe *SUNNY WEATHER*:
bright, cloudless, fair, fine, springlike,
summery, sunny, sunshiny
- to describe *WET WEATHER*:
damp, drizzly, raining cats and dogs,
showery, spitting, torrential
- *RAIN* may:
lash or pelt down, pour, teem
(*informal*) bucket, tip down
- to describe *WINDY WEATHER*:
biting, blowy, blustery, breezy,
gusty
- *WIND* may:
batter, blast, buffet, howl, moan,
wail

weather verb
*Somehow, the tiny ship **weathered** the storm.*
- survive, withstand, endure, come through

weave verb
*A messenger **weaved** his way through the crowd.*
- wind, zigzag, twist and turn

web noun
*A **web** of tunnels lay under the castle.*
- net, network, mesh

wedding noun

 WORD WEB
*She was a bridesmaid at her cousin's **wedding**.*
- marriage
- A formal word for a wedding is nuptials.

PEOPLE WHO MAY BE INVOLVED IN A WEDDING
best man, bride, bridegroom,
bridesmaid, groom, maid or matron
of honour, page, registrar, usher,
wedding guests

SEE ALSO **marry** verb

wedge verb
*The door was **wedged** open with an old shoe.*
- jam, stick

weep verb
*Dierdre buried her face in her hands and began to **weep**.*
- cry, sob, shed tears
- To weep noisily is to bawl or blubber.
- To weep in an annoying way is to snivel or whimper.

weigh verb
to weigh someone down
1 *Many troubles **weighed** him **down**.*
- bother, worry, trouble, distress, burden
2 *She was **weighed down** with shopping.*
- load, burden, lumber

to weigh something up
*The detective **weighed up** the evidence.*
- consider, assess, evaluate, examine, study, ponder

weight noun
*Take care when lifting heavy **weights**.*
- load, mass, burden
FOR UNITS FOR MEASURING WEIGHT
SEE **measurement**

weighty adjective
1 *He lifted a **weighty** volume off the shelf.*
- heavy, bulky, cumbersome
OPPOSITE light
2 *They had **weighty** matters to discuss.*
- important, serious, grave, significant
OPPOSITE unimportant, trivial

weird adjective
1 ***Weird** noises have been heard in the tower at midnight.*
- eerie, ghostly, unearthly, mysterious, uncanny, unnatural
- (*informal*) spooky, creepy
OPPOSITE ordinary, natural
2 *My big sister has a **weird** taste in music.*
- strange, odd, peculiar, bizarre, curious, quirky, eccentric, outlandish, unconventional, unusual
- (*informal*) wacky, way-out
OPPOSITE conventional

welcome noun
*The landlady gave us a friendly **welcome**.*
- greeting, reception

welcome adjective
1 *A cup of tea would be very **welcome**.*
- pleasant, pleasing, agreeable, appreciated, desirable, acceptable
OPPOSITE unacceptable
2 *You're **welcome** to use my bike.*
- allowed, permitted, free
OPPOSITE forbidden

welcome verb
1 *An elderly butler **welcomed** us at the door.*
- greet, receive, meet, hail
2 *We **welcome** suggestions from the public.*
- appreciate, accept, like, want

welfare noun
*Her only concern was the **welfare** of her children.*
- well-being, good, benefit, interests

well adverb
1 *The whole team played **well** on Saturday.*
- ably, skilfully, expertly, effectively, efficiently, admirably, marvellously, wonderfully
OPPOSITE badly
2 *It's cold outside, so you'd better wrap up **well**.*
- properly, suitably, correctly, thoroughly, carefully
3 *I know her brother **well**.*
- closely, intimately, personally

well adjective
*Mrs Orr looks surprisingly **well** for her age.*
- healthy, fit, strong, sound, robust, vigorous, lively, hearty
OPPOSITE ill

well-known adjective
*A **well-known** athlete will open the new sports shop.*
- famous, celebrated, prominent, notable, renowned, distinguished, eminent
OPPOSITE unknown, obscure

west noun, adjective, adverb
- The parts of a continent or country in the west are the western parts.
- To travel towards the west is to travel westward or westwards.
- A wind from the west is a westerly wind.

wet adjective
1 *Archie took off his **wet** clothes and had a hot bath.*
- damp, soaked, soaking, drenched, dripping, sopping, wringing wet
2 *The pitch was too **wet** to play on.*
- waterlogged, saturated, sodden, soggy, dewy, muddy, boggy
3 *Take care—the paint is still **wet**.*
- runny, sticky, tacky

a b c d e f g h i j k l m n o p q r s t u v w x y z

4 *It was cold and **wet** all afternoon.*
- rainy, showery, pouring, drizzly, misty
  SEE ALSO **weather** noun
  OPPOSITE dry

wet verb
__Wet__ the clay before you start to mould it.
- dampen, moisten, soak, water
  OPPOSITE dry

wheel noun
- A small wheel under a piece of furniture is a caster.
- The centre of a wheel is the hub.
- The outer edge of a wheel is the rim.

wheel verb
1 *A pair of seagulls **wheeled** overhead.*
- circle, orbit
2 *The column of soldiers **wheeled** to the right.*
- swing round, turn, veer, swerve

whiff noun
*I caught a **whiff** of coffee as I walked past the café.*
- smell, scent, aroma

while noun
*You may need to wait a **while** for the next train.*
- period, time, spell

whimper, **whine** verbs
*A dog **whimpered** in the corner of the room.*
- cry, moan

whip verb
1 *The jockey **whipped** his horse to make it go faster.*
- beat, hit, lash, flog, thrash
2 *__Whip__ the cream until it is thick.*
- beat, whisk

whirl verb
*The snowflakes **whirled** in the icy wind.*
- turn, twirl, spin, twist, circle, spiral, reel, pirouette, revolve, rotate

whisk verb
__Whisk__ the egg yolks together in a bowl.
- beat, whip, mix, stir

whisper verb
*What are you two **whispering** about?*
- murmur, mutter, mumble
  OPPOSITE shout

whistle noun, verb FOR VARIOUS SOUNDS
  SEE **sound** noun

white adjective, noun

WORD WEB

SOME SHADES OF WHITE
cream, ivory, off-white, platinum, silvery, snow-white
- When coloured things become whiter they become bleached or faded.
- When someone turns white with fear they blanch or turn pale.
- Hair that is white with age is hoary.
- Something which is rather white is whitish.
- Common similes are as white as a sheet, as white as chalk, and as white as snow.

whole adjective
1 *I haven't read the **whole** book yet.*
- complete, entire, full, total, unabbreviated
  OPPOSITE incomplete
2 *The dinosaur skeleton appears to be **whole**.*
- in one piece, intact, unbroken, undamaged, perfect
  OPPOSITE broken, in pieces

wholesome adjective
*Pets should be fed a **wholesome** diet.*
- healthy, nutritious, nourishing
  OPPOSITE unhealthy

wholly adverb
*I'm not **wholly** convinced by his story.*
- completely, totally, fully, entirely, utterly, thoroughly
  OPPOSITE partly

wicked adjective

1 *Cinderella had a **wicked** stepmother.*
- evil, cruel, vicious, villainous, detestable, mean, corrupt, immoral, sinful, foul, vile
  OPPOSITE good, virtuous

2 *They hatched a **wicked** scheme to take over the world.*
- evil, fiendish, malicious, malevolent, diabolical, monstrous, deplorable, dreadful, shameful

3 *The goblin had a **wicked** grin on his face.*
- mischievous, playful, impish, naughty

wide adjective

1 *The hotel is close to a **wide** sandy beach.*
- broad, expansive, extensive, large, spacious
  OPPOSITE narrow

2 *She has a **wide** knowledge of classical music.*
- comprehensive, vast, wide-ranging, encyclopedic
  OPPOSITE limited

widely adverb

*The story of Cinderella is **widely** known.*
- commonly, everywhere, far and wide

widespread adjective

*There is **widespread** interest in the new engine design.*
- general, extensive, universal, wholesale
- Something which spreads over the whole world is global or worldwide.
  OPPOSITE uncommon

width noun

*The room is about eight feet in **width**.*
- breadth
- The distance across a circle is its diameter.

wield verb

*The lumberjack was **wielding** his axe.*
- brandish, flourish, hold, use

wife noun

*Katherine is Mr Gray's second **wife**.*
- Another word for a person's wife or husband is their spouse.

wild adjective

1 *I don't like seeing **wild** animals in captivity.*
- undomesticated, untamed
  OPPOSITE tame

2 *The hedgerow was full of **wild** flowers.*
- natural, uncultivated
  OPPOSITE cultivated

3 *To the west is a **wild** and mountainous region.*
- rough, rugged, uncultivated, uninhabited, desolate
  OPPOSITE cultivated

4 *The crowd were **wild** with excitement.*
- riotous, rowdy, disorderly, unruly, boisterous, excited, noisy, uncontrollable, hysterical
  OPPOSITE calm, restrained

5 *The weather looked **wild** outside.*
- blustery, windy, gusty, stormy, turbulent, tempestuous
  OPPOSITE calm

wilful adjective

1 *He was very **wilful** as a child.*
- obstinate, stubborn, strong-willed, pig-headed

2 *There is a fine for **wilful** damage to trees.*
- deliberate, intentional, planned, conscious

will noun

*They seem to have lost the **will** to win.*
- desire, wish, determination, resolution, will-power, resolve, purpose

willing adjective

1 *She is always **willing** to help.*
- eager, happy, pleased, ready, prepared

2 *I need a couple of **willing** volunteers.*
- enthusiastic, helpful, cooperative, obliging
  OPPOSITE unwilling

a
b
c
d
e
f
g
h
i
j
k
l
m
n
o
p
q
r
s
t
u
v
w
x
y
z

a
b
c
d
e
f
g
h
i
j
k
l
m
n
o
p
q
r
s
t
u
v
w
x
y
z

wilt verb
*The flowers **wilted** in the heat.*
- become limp, droop, flop, sag, fade, shrivel, wither
OPPOSITE flourish

wily adjective
*The player was outwitted by his **wily** opponent.*
- clever, crafty, cunning, shrewd, scheming, artful, sly, devious

win verb
1 *Who do you think will **win**?*
- come first, be victorious, succeed, triumph, prevail
- To win against someone is also to beat, conquer, defeat or overcome them.
OPPOSITE lose
2 *She **won** first prize in the poetry competition.*
- get, receive, gain, obtain, secure
- (*informal*) pick up, walk away with

wind noun
- A gentle wind is a breath, breeze, or draught.
- A violent wind is a cyclone, gale, hurricane, or tornado.
- A sudden unexpected wind is a blast, gust, puff, or squall.
SEE ALSO **weather** noun

wind instruments
FOR MUSICAL INSTRUMENTS
SEE **music**

wind verb
1 *She **wound** the wool into a ball.*
- coil, loop, roll, turn, curl
2 *The road **winds** up the hill.*
- bend, curve, twist and turn, zigzag, meander

window noun
- The glass in a window is a pane.
- A semicircular window above a door is a fanlight.
- A window in a roof is a skylight.
- A decorative window with panels of coloured glass is a stained-glass window.
- A person whose job is to fit glass in windows is a glazier.

windy adjective
1 *It was a cold, **windy** day.*
- breezy, blustery, gusty, squally, stormy
OPPOSITE calm
2 *This spot is too **windy** for a picnic.*
- windswept, exposed, draughty
OPPOSITE sheltered

wink verb
1 *My friend **winked** at me and smiled.*
- To shut and open both eyes quickly is to blink.
2 *The lights **winked** on and off.*
- flash, flicker, sparkle, twinkle

winner noun
*The **winner** was presented with a silver cup.*
- victor, prizewinner, champion, conqueror
OPPOSITE loser

winning adjective
*The **winning** team went up to receive their medals.*
- victorious, triumphant, conquering, successful, top-scoring, champion
OPPOSITE losing

wintry adjective
*It was a grey, **wintry** day.*
- cold, frosty, freezing, bitter, icy, snowy

wipe verb
*I **wiped** the table with a cloth.*
- rub, clean, polish, mop, swab, sponge
to wipe something out
*Pompeii was **wiped out** by the eruption of Mount Vesuvius.*
- destroy, annihilate, exterminate, get rid of

wire noun
*Several **wires** protruded from the robot's head.*
- cable, lead, flex
- A system of wires is wiring.

wisdom noun
*She's a woman of great **wisdom**.*
- sense, judgement, understanding, intelligence, common sense, good sense, insight, reason

wise adjective
1 *The soothsayer was very old and **wise**.*
- sensible, reasonable, intelligent, perceptive, knowledgeable, rational, thoughtful
2 *I think you made a **wise** decision.*
- good, right, proper, sound, fair, just, appropriate
  OPPOSITE foolish

wish noun
*Her dearest **wish** was to travel to the Amazon.*
- desire, want, longing, yearning, hankering, craving, urge, fancy, hope, ambition
- (*informal*) yen

wish verb
*I **wish** that everyone would sit still for a minute!*
- If you wish something would happen, you can say that you want or would like it to happen.

to wish for
*The genie asked him what he **wished** for.*
- desire, want, crave, fancy, long for, yearn for, hanker after

wisp noun
*She blew a **wisp** of hair away from her face.*
- shred, strand

wistful adjective
*She gave a **wistful** sigh as she read the letter.*
- sad, melancholy, thoughtful, pensive

wit noun
1 *Ogres are creatures with very little **wit**.*
- intelligence, cleverness, brains, sharpness, understanding
2 *The filmscript sparkled with **wit**.*
- humour, comedy, jokes
3 *Charlie is regarded as the class **wit**.*
- joker, comedian, comic

witch, witchcraft nouns SEE
magic noun

withdraw verb
1 *The general **withdrew** his troops.*
- call back, recall
  OPPOSITE send in

2 *She **withdrew** her offer of help.*
- take back, cancel, retract
  OPPOSITE make, present
3 *The wolves **withdrew** into the forest.*
- retire, retreat, draw back, fall back, back away
  OPPOSITE advance
4 *He **withdrew** his hands from his pockets.*
- draw back, pull back, take away, remove
  OPPOSITE put out, extend
5 *Some competitors **withdrew** at the last minute.*
- pull out, back out, drop out
  OPPOSITE enter

wither verb
*The flowers had **withered** and died.*
- shrivel, dry up, shrink, wilt, droop, sag, flop
  OPPOSITE flourish

withhold verb
*The police believe he is **withholding** information.*
- hold back, keep back, refuse
  OPPOSITE grant

withstand verb
*Penguins can **withstand** extreme cold.*
- bear, endure, stand up to, tolerate, cope with, survive, resist, weather

witness noun
*A **witness** said that the car was going too fast.*
- bystander, observer, onlooker, eyewitness, spectator

witty adjective
*He gave a **witty** account of his schooldays.*
- humorous, amusing, comic, funny
  OPPOSITE dull

wizard noun
1 *The **wizard** cast a spell over the whole palace.*
- magician, sorcerer, enchanter
  SEE ALSO magic noun
2 *My sister is a **wizard** with computers.*
- expert, specialist, genius
- (*informal*) whizz

a
b
c
d
e
f
g
h
i
j
k
l
m
n
o
p
q
r
s
t
u
v
w
x
y
z

wobble verb
1 *The cyclist **wobbled** all over the road.*
- sway, totter, tetter, waver, rock
2 *The jelly **wobbled** as I carried the plate.*
- shake, tremble, quake, quiver, vibrate

wobbly adjective
1 *The baby giraffe was a bit **wobbly** on its legs.*
- shaky, tottering, unsteady
2 *This chair is a bit **wobbly**.*
- loose, rickety, rocky, unstable, unsafe
OPPOSITE steady

woman noun
- A polite word for a woman is lady.
- A married woman is a wife.
- A woman who has children is a mother.
- An unmarried woman is a spinster.
- A woman whose husband has died is a widow.
- A woman on her wedding day is a bride.
- A woman who is engaged to be married is a fiancée.
- Words for a young woman are girl and lass.
- Old words for a young woman are maid and maiden.

wonder noun
1 *The sight of the Taj Mahal filled them with **wonder**.*
- admiration, awe, reverence, amazement, astonishment
2 *It's a **wonder** that he is still alive.*
- marvel, miracle

wonder verb
*I **wonder** why she left in such a hurry.*
- be curious about, ask yourself, ponder, think about
to wonder at
*People **wondered at** the acrobat's skill.*
- marvel at, admire, be amazed or astonished by

wonderful adjective
1 *It's **wonderful** what computers can do these days.*
- amazing, astonishing, astounding, incredible, remarkable, extraordinary, marvellous, miraculous, phenomenal
2 *We had a **wonderful** time at the party.*
- excellent, splendid, great, superb, delightful
- (*informal*) brilliant, fantastic, terrific, fabulous, super
OPPOSITE ordinary

wood noun
1 *All the furniture in the room was made of **wood**.*
- timber, lumber, planks, logs
2 *We followed a nature trail through the **wood**.*
- woodland, woods, forest, trees
SEE ALSO **tree**

wood noun

> **WORD WEB**
> KINDS OF WOOD OFTEN USED TO MAKE THINGS
> ash, balsa, beech, cedar, chestnut, ebony, elm, lime, mahogany, oak, pine, rosewood, sandalwood, spruce, teak, walnut
> - A person who makes things from wood is a carpenter or wood-carver.
> - A person whose job is to cut down trees for wood is a lumberjack.

wooden adjective
1 *They sat down on a **wooden** bench.*
- wood, timber
2 *The acting was a bit **wooden** at times.*
- stiff, lifeless, awkward, unnatural, unemotional, expressionless

woolly adjective
1 *He wore a **woolly** hat with a bobble on top.*
- wool, woollen
- Clothes made of wool, such as hats and scarves, are woollens.
2 *Mammoths were like elephants with **woolly** coats.*
- thick, fleecy, furry, downy, fuzzy, hairy, shaggy, soft, cuddly
3 *Some parts of the plot were rather **woolly**.*
- vague, confused, unclear, unfocused, hazy, indefinite, uncertain

word noun

1 *What's the French **word** for 'birthday'?*
- expression, term
- All the words you know are your vocabulary.

2 *You gave me your **word**.*
- promise, assurance, guarantee, pledge, vow

3 *There has been no **word** from him for several weeks.*
- news, message, information

word verb

*I spent ages trying to **word** the letter correctly.*
- express, phrase, put into words
- The way that you word something is the wording or phrasing.

work noun

1 *Digging the garden involves a lot of hard **work**.*
- effort, labour, toil, exertion

2 *Do you have any **work** to do this weekend?*
- task, assignment, chore, job, homework, housework

3 *What kind of **work** does she do?*
- occupation, employment, job, profession, business, trade, vocation

FOR VARIOUS KINDS OF WORK

SEE **job**

work verb

1 *She's been **working** in the garden all day.*
- be busy, exert yourself, labour, toil, slave

2 *He **works** in the bookshop on Saturdays.*
- be employed, have a job, go to work

3 *My watch isn't **working**.*
- function, go, operate

4 *Is the DVD player easy to **work**?*
- operate, run, use, control, handle

to work out

*Things didn't quite **work out** as planned.*
- turn out, happen, emerge, develop

to work something out

*Can anyone **work out** this sum?*
- answer, calculate, solve, explain, figure out

worker noun

*The biscuit factory employs around 200 **workers**.*
- employee
- All the workers in a business or factory are the staff or workforce.

FOR PEOPLE WHO DO SPECIFIC JOBS

SEE **job**

world noun

1 *Antarctica is a remote part of the **world**.*
- earth, globe

2 *Scientists are searching for life on other **worlds**.*
- planet

worried adjective

*You look **worried**. Is something the matter?*
- anxious, troubled, uneasy, distressed, disturbed, upset, apprehensive, concerned, bothered, tense, strained, nervous
- OPPOSITE relaxed

worry verb

1 *There's no need to **worry**.*
- be anxious, be troubled, be disturbed, brood, fret

2 *It **worried** her that he hadn't replied to her letter.*
- trouble, distress, upset, concern, disturb

3 *Don't **worry** her now—she's busy.*
- bother, annoy, disturb, pester, harass
- (*informal*) badger, bug

worry noun

1 *He's been a constant source of **worry** to her.*
- anxiety, distress, uneasiness, vexation

2 *I don't want to add to your **worries**.*
- trouble, concern, burden, care, problem

worsen verb

1 *Moving the patient may **worsen** the pain.*
- make worse, aggravate

2 *The weather had **worsened** overnight.*
- get worse, deteriorate, degenerate
- OPPOSITE improve

a
b
c
d
e
f
g
h
i
j
k
l
m
n
o
p
q
r
s
t
u
v
w
x
y
z

a
b
c
d
e
f
g
h
i
j
k
l
m
n
o
p
q
r
s
t
u
v
w
x
y
z

worship verb

1 *Ancient Egyptians **worshipped** the sun god, Ra.*
- pray to, glorify, praise

FOR PLACES WHERE PEOPLE WORSHIP

SEE **building**

2 *She adores her sons and they **worship** her.*
- adore, be devoted to, look up to, love, revere, idolize

worth noun

*This ring was once an object of great **worth**.*
- value, merit, quality, significance, importance

worthless adjective

*It's nothing but a **worthless** piece of junk.*
- useless, unusable, valueless
- (*informal*) trashy

OPPOSITE valuable

worthwhile adjective

*It may be **worthwhile** to get a second opinion.*
- helpful, useful, valuable, beneficial, profitable

OPPOSITE useless

worthy adjective

*They gave the money to a **worthy** cause.*
- good, worthwhile, deserving, praiseworthy, admirable, commendable, respectable

OPPOSITE unworthy

wound noun

*He is being treated in hospital for a head **wound**.*
- injury, cut, gash, graze, scratch, sore

FOR OTHER TYPES OF WOUND

SEE **injury**

wound verb

*The fox was **wounded** in the leg and bleeding.*
- injure, hurt, harm

wrap verb

1 *She **wrapped** the presents in shiny gold paper.*
- cover, pack, enclose, enfold, swathe
- To wrap water pipes is to insulate or lag them.

2 *The mountain was **wrapped** in mist.*
- cloak, envelop, shroud, surround, hide, conceal

wreathe verb

*The tree was **wreathed** in fairy lights.*
- encircle, festoon, surround, adorn, decorate

wreck verb

1 *His bicycle was **wrecked** in the accident.*
- demolish, destroy, crush, smash, shatter, crumple

2 *The injury **wrecked** her chances becoming a dancer.*
- ruin, spoil

wreckage noun

*Divers have discovered the **wreckage** of an old ship.*
- debris, fragments, pieces, remains
- The wreckage of a building is rubble or ruins.

wrench verb

*The giant **wrenched** the door off its hinges.*
- pull, tug, prise, jerk, twist, force
- (*informal*) yank

wrestle verb

*He **wrestled** with the thief as he tried to escape.*
- struggle, tussle, grapple

wretched adjective

1 *I lay in bed with flu feeling **wretched**.*
- miserable, unhappy, woeful, pitiful, unfortunate

2 *The **wretched** computer has frozen again!*
- annoying, maddening, exasperating, useless

wriggle verb

*The prisoner managed to **wriggle** out of his bonds.*

- twist, writhe, squirm, worm your way

wring verb

1 *She **wrung** the water out of her skirt.*

- press, squeeze, twist

2 *He **wrung** her hand enthusiastically.*

- shake, clasp, grip, wrench

wringing wet

*My towel is **wringing wet**.*

- soaked, drenched, dripping, sopping, saturated

wrinkle noun

*The old hag's face was covered in **wrinkles**.*

- crease, fold, furrow, line, ridge, crinkle, pucker, pleat
- A small hollow on someone's skin is a dimple.

wrinkle verb

*The creature **wrinkled** its nose and sniffed.*

- pucker up, crease, crinkle, crumple, fold

OPPOSITE smooth

write verb

1 *My granny **wrote** a diary when she was a girl.*

- compile, compose, draw up, set down, pen
- To write letters or emails to people is to correspond with them.
- To write a rough version of a story is to draft it.

2 *He **wrote** his address on the back of an envelope.*

- jot down, note, print, scrawl, scribble
- To write on a document or surface is to inscribe it.
- To write your signature on something is to autograph it.

writer noun

- A person who writes books is an author.
- A person who writes novels is a novelist.

- A person who writes plays is a dramatist or playwright.
- A person who writes scripts for films or television is a scriptwriter or screenwriter.
- A person who writes poetry is a poet.
- A person who writes about someone else's life is a biographer.
- A person who writes for newspapers is a correspondent, journalist, or reporter.
- A person who writes music is a composer.

writhe verb

*The wounded man was **writhing** in agony.*

- thrash about, twist, squirm, wriggle

writing noun

1 *Can you read the **writing** on the envelope?*

- handwriting
- Untidy writing is a scrawl or scribble.
- The art of beautiful handwriting is calligraphy.

2 *The **writing** on the stone was very faint.*

- inscription

3 *(often plural)* *She introduced me to the **writings** of Roald Dahl.*

- literature, works

WORD WEB

VARIOUS FORMS OF WRITING AND LITERATURE

autobiography, biography, children's literature, comedy, crime or detective story, diary, drama or play, essay, fable, fairy story or fairy tale, fantasy, fiction, film or TV script, folk tale, ghost story, historical fiction, history, journalism, legend, letters or correspondence, lyrics, myth, newspaper article, non-fiction, novel, parody, philosophy, poetry or verse, prose, romance, satire, science fiction or (*informal*) sci-fi, spy story, thriller, tragedy, travel writing, western

a
b
c
d
e
f
g
h
i
j
k
l
m
n
o
p
q
r
s
t
u
v
w
x
y
z

writing noun

> ### ✏ WRITING TIPS
>
> You can use these words to describe **a piece of writing**.
>
> - to describe the LANGUAGE or STYLE:
>   elegant, literary, ornate, poetic; colloquial, informal, slangy; formal, old-fashioned; hard-boiled, sparse
> - (*uncomplimentary*) banal, dry, insipid, lacklustre, monotonous, plodding, prosaic
>   *The author uses **poetic** words, like 'cornucopia'.*
>
> - to describe a CHARACTER:
>   hero, heroine, protagonist, narrator, villain; believable, convincing, lifelike, realistic, strong, well-drawn; feeble, thin, unbelievable, unconvincing, weak
>   *Mr Scruggs is a thoroughly **convincing** villain.*
>
> - to describe the SETTING:
>   atmospheric, moody; alien, exotic, fanciful, fantastic, fictitious, made-up, imaginary, strange, unfamiliar; eerie, spooky, weird; accurate, authentic, familiar, realistic, recognizable, true to life
>   *The story is set on an **imaginary** planet.*
>
> - to describe the STORYLINE or PLOT:
>   action-packed, dramatic, dynamic, engrossing, entertaining, eventful, fast-paced, gripping, hair-raising, intriguing, mind-boggling, page-turning, spellbinding, thrilling, rip-roaring; creative, imaginative, intriguing, moving, thought-provoking, well-crafted; amusing, diverting, entertaining, hilarious, humorous; romantic, sentimental
>
> - (*uncomplimentary*) dull, insipid, unimaginative, uneventful; absurd, far-fetched, ludicrous, ridiculous, unbelievable, unlikely
>   *Finn's adventures are **dramatic** and at times moving.*
>
> - to describe the ENDING:
>   climax, conclusion, finale, cliffhanger; electrifying, nail-biting, sensational, spectacular, surprising, unexpected
>
> *The book keeps you guessing until the **sensational** finale.*
>
> - (*uncomplimentary*) banal, clichéd, predictable, trite, unsatisfying, abrupt

wrong adjective

1 *It was **wrong** to take the book without asking.*
- bad, dishonest, irresponsible, immoral, sinful, wicked, criminal, unfair, unjust

2 *His calculations were all **wrong**.*
- incorrect, mistaken, inaccurate

3 *Did I say the **wrong** thing?*
- inappropriate, unsuitable, improper

4 *There's something **wrong** with the TV.*
- faulty, defective, not working, out of order
  OPPOSITE right

to go wrong
> *The professor's plan began to **go wrong**.*
- fail, backfire
- (*informal*) flop, go pear-shaped
  OPPOSITE succeed

Yy

yacht noun FOR TYPES OF BOAT OR SHIP
SEE **boat**

yard noun
A solitary tree stood in the middle of the yard.
- court, courtyard, enclosure

yearly adjective
I'm due for my yearly dental check-up.
- annual

yearn verb
to yearn for something
She yearned for some peace and quiet.
- want, wish for, desire, long for, pine for
- (*informal*) be dying for

yell verb
I yelled to attract their attention.
- call out, cry out, shout, bawl, bellow

yellow adjective, noun

WORD WEB

SOME SHADES OF YELLOW
amber, chrome yellow, cream, gold, golden, lemon, tawny
- **Something which is rather yellow is** yellowish.

yelp verb FOR SOUNDS MADE BY ANIMALS
SEE **animal**

yield verb
1 *In the end, her parents yielded and let her go out.*
- give in, give way, concede, surrender, admit defeat, submit, compel
2 *The apple trees yielded a good crop of fruit.*
- bear, grow, produce, supply, generate

yield noun
They got a good yield from the orchard this year.
- crop, harvest, produce, return

young adjective
1 *A lot of young people went to the concert.*
- youthful, juvenile
OPPOSITE older, mature
2 *I think this book is a bit young for you.*
- childish, babyish, immature, infantile
OPPOSITE adult, grown-up
- A young person is a child or youngster.
- A young adult is an adolescent or youth.
- A very young child is a baby or infant.
- A young bird is a chick, fledgling, or nestling.
- Young fish are fry.
- A young plant is a cutting or seedling.
- A young tree is a sapling.
FOR OTHER YOUNG ANIMALS AND BIRDS
SEE **animal, bird**

young plural noun
The mother bird returned to feed her young.
- offspring, children, young ones, family
- A family of young birds is a brood.
- A family of young cats or dogs is a litter.

youth noun
1 *In her youth, she had been a keen tennis player.*
- childhood, boyhood or girlhood, adolescence, teens
2 *The fight was started by a group of youths.*
- adolescent, youngster, juvenile, teenager, young adult

youthful adjective
The magic potion will keep you eternally youthful.
- young, youngish, vigorous, sprightly, young-looking

a b c d e f g h i j k l m n o p q r s t u v w x **y** z

481

Zz

a
b
c
d
e
f
g
h
i
j
k
l
m
n
o
p
q
r
s
t
u
v
w
x
y
z

zero noun

*Four minus four makes **zero**.*

- nothing, nought
- A score of zero in football is nil; in cricket it is a duck, and in tennis it is love.

zest noun

*Uncle Arthur has a great **zest** for life.*

- enthusiasm, eagerness, enjoyment

zigzag verb

*The road **zigzags** up the hill.*

- wind, twist, meander

zodiac noun

 WORD WEB

THE SIGNS OF THE ZODIAC ARE
Aquarius (or the Water-Carrier),
Aries (or the Ram), Cancer (or the
Crab), Capricorn (or the Goat),
Gemini (or the Twins), Leo (or the
Lion), Libra (or the Scales), Pisces (or
the Fish), Sagittarius (or the Archer),
Scorpio (or the Scorpion), Taurus (or
the Bull), Virgo (or the Virgin)

zone noun

*No-one may enter the forbidden **zone**.*

- area, district, region, sector, locality, neighbourhood, territory, vicinity

zoo noun

*Which is your favourite animal in the **zoo**?*

- menagerie, safari park, wildlife reserve, nature reserve, zoological gardens

FOR ANIMALS YOU MIGHT SEE IN A ZOO

SEE **animal**

ecome a Word Explorer!

u don't need a map and a compass to be an explorer. You can explore
e world of **words** equipped with your thesaurus. For example, you can:

- explore the differences between **synonyms**

- explore effects like **simile** and **alliteration**

- explore ways to **build words**

- explore ideas to improve your **story writing** and other writing

Explore: Basic writing skills

Punctuation

Punctuation makes writing easier to read and understand. You should use
these basic punctuation marks in your writing:

> a **full stop** (.) comes at the end of a sentence
>
> a **comma** (,) separates items in a list, or parts of a sentence:
> > *Hedgehogs eat slugs, snails, and worms.*
> > *After four days at sea, we sighted land.*
>
> an **apostrophe** (') shows that a letter is missing, or tells you who
> something belongs to:
> > *Don't enter the dragon's lair!* [= Do not enter the lair of the
> > dragon!]

These punctuation marks are especially useful for writing dialogue in a story:

> **quotation marks** (' ' " ") come before and after words that a
> character says:
> > *"My name," said the knight, "is Sir Joustalot."*
>
> a **question mark** (?) comes at the end of a question:
> > *"How old are you?" I asked the wizard.* ▶

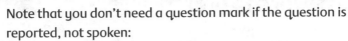

Note that you don't need a question mark if the question is reported, not spoken:

> *I asked the wizard how old he was.*

An exclamation mark comes after a shout, or shows that a character is excited:

> *"Wow! Look at the size of that crater!"*

Explorer tip

The Word Web panel for punctuation lists various punctuation marks that you might use or come across. You will find more tips on writing dialogue and using exclamations in the Explore: Writing stories section too.

Confusable words

Take extra care when you use any of these **confusable words** in your writing. Although the words in each group sound alike, they each have a different *spelling* (some with an apostrophe) and a different *meaning*. If you choose the wrong one, your writing will not make sense.

its		The crocodile snapped **its** jaws.
it's	[= it is]	**It's** a blustery day.
your		When is **your** birthday?
you're	[= you are]	**You're** all invited to my party.
their		The pirates rattled **their** swords.
there		**There** are only two chocolates left.
they're	[= they are]	**They're** coming for tea tomorrow.

Note the three different spellings in this example:

> *"Where are the penguins?"*
> *"**They're** over **there**, feeding **their** chicks."*

Explore: Synonyms

The main job of a thesaurus is to list **synonyms**. Synonyms are words which mean the same – or nearly the same – as each other, like *big* and *huge*, or *horrible* and *nasty*.

Sometimes, you can choose between a few synonyms. A giant's nose might be *huge* or *immense* or *colossal* or *mammoth*: you can swop the words around and it makes no difference to the meaning.

Other synonyms are more limited and only fit in certain contexts. For example:
- formal or informal synonyms (*yummy* is an informal synonym of *delicious*)
- synonyms which are special cases (*trunk* and *casket* are special types of box).

Examples

In a piece of schoolwork, you might write:
> The cake was **delicious** / **tasty**.

But in your diary or an email, you could write instead:
> The cake was **scrumptious** / **yummy**!

In a story, you might write:
> The magician carried his things in a **trunk**.
> The treasure was sealed in a wooden **casket**.

Explorer tip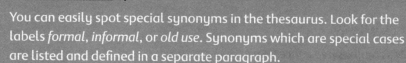

You can easily spot special synonyms in the thesaurus. Look for the labels *formal*, *informal*, or *old use*. Synonyms which are special cases are listed and defined in a separate paragraph.

Explore: Overused words

Words like *bad*, *big*, and *nice* are very useful, but they can make your writing boring if you use them too often. If you choose a synonym which is more unusual, it will make your writing more interesting.

Examples

Instead of making a fairy simply *beautiful*, try describing her as *radiant* or *resplendent*.

Is a *big ogre* scary enough? If not, transform it into a *hulking* or *monstrous ogre*.

Explorer tip

You can easily spot **overused words** in the thesaurus. They are treated in special panels and have this symbol next to them: ⚠ There is a complete list of **overused words** at the front of the thesaurus.

Explore: Similes

This thesaurus notes common **similes** like *as fit as a fiddle*. But you can also make up your own, using your thesaurus for ideas.

Similes are useful for describing how a character looks or sounds, or how a landscape appears.

Examples

*Miss Mullins had a face **like a soggy sponge**.*
*The dragon's eyes were **as dark as a moonless night**.*
*The waves crashed **like cymbals** on the shore.*

imiles allow you to mix and match: you can describe a person like an imal (*Mr Scruggs scuttled off like a spider*), or an animal like a thing (*the hake sprang up like a jack-in-the-box*).

imiles can also make your writing individual. Lots of people may describe road as *bumpy*, but you may be the only person to say it is *as bumpy as he back of a crocodile*.

Explorer tip

The **animal** and **bird** panels list ways to describe animals and birds. But you can also use these words in similes to describe people.

Explore: Idioms

An **idiom** is a phrase that doesn't mean exactly the same as the words in it. For example, *to be in hot water* is an idiom which means 'to be in trouble' (not to be in actual hot water).

Idioms can make your writing more lively. But be careful: your writing can look clichéd if you use too many!

Example

A character in your story has just seen a ghost. How do you describe their reaction?

Anita **blanched** and stood **rooted to the spot**.
She **had goosebumps** all over and began to **tremble like a leaf**.

Explorer tip

You will find suggestions for idioms and other words to use in the **writing tips** panels for **afraid**, **angry**, and **surprised**.

Explore: Special effects

Word Explorer

Some words come with their own sound effects. These are called **onomatopoeic** words, and they sound like the thing they are describing. Using a sound-effect word can give an extra zing to your writing.

> ## Example
>
> You are describing footsteps on a path.
>
> On a dry, stony path, the footsteps might *crunch*, but on a muddy path, they would *squelch*.
>
> A child's feet might *patter* on the path, whereas a giant's feet would *thud*.

Explorer tip

You will find lots of sound-effect words in the **word web** panel for **sound**.

A sound effect that you can create yourself is **alliteration**, which means using two or more words which start with the same sound. This is especially useful in poetry, but can also be effective in story writing.

> ## Example
>
> You are writing a poem about food. Use alliteration to make it *crispy and crumbly*, or maybe *sweet and sticky*.
>
> If the food is disgusting, you might describe it as *slimy and sloppy*, or even *mouldy and mushy*!

Explorer tip

You will find words to describe both delicious *and* disgusting food in the **writing tips** panel for **food**.

Explore: Word building

Have you ever thought about making up a word? You can add to the words in your thesaurus by creating your own.

Try building a new word by starting with a word you know, or a word you have found in the thesaurus, and adding one of these *suffixes* (endings) to it:

-ish	*purplish*, *shortish*, *hairyish*
-less or **-free**	a *flowerless* garden, a *chocolate-free* chin
-like	a *ghost-like* shadow, a *swan-like* neck
-proof	a *sword-proof* shield, a *magic-proof* castle
-y	a *lemony* pudding, a *herby* flavour

You can also build *compounds* by joining two whole words together. Here are a few suggestions for words to use, but you can also try out your own:

-feeling	*rough-feeling* skin
-looking	*scary-looking* teeth
-smelling	a *musty-smelling* room
-sounding	an *eerie-sounding* wail

Example

You are describing a dragon. You could give it:

> *lidless* eyes
> *bat-like* wings
> *sour-smelling* breath
> *fire-emitting* nostrils

Explore: Writing stories

Before you write:

1 Plan your story. Think about setting, the characters, and the action.
2 Share the story with a friend before you write. Would you want to read this story? Would your friend? Change your plan if necessary.

While you are writing:

3 Keep to your plan.
4 Write in sentences and think about punctuation.
5 Don't forget paragraphs. If you need to begin a sentence with an adverbial clause of time (e.g. Later that day... When it was all over...) or place (e.g. Outside...In the woods) you probably need to start a new paragraph.

After you have written the first draft:

6 Use a dictionary to check your spelling.
7 Use a thesaurus to make sure you have chosen the best words.
8 Look at the overused words list. Try to use other words.
9 Can you add in some details about your characters to increase your reader's interest in them?
10 Can you add more information about your setting to help your reader 'see' it in their minds?

Creating a setting: *Place*

The first thing to decide is *where* your story takes place. For example:
    does the action happen *at sea* or *on a desert island*?
    is it set in an *ancient castle* or in *outer space*?

Once you have a general setting, you can draw your readers' attention to details such as trees or buildings, animals or birds, or even mythological creatures.

Explorer tip

Look up these panels for ideas for where your story takes place:
    **cave   desert   island   jungle   landscape   mountain
    planet   polar   river   sea   seashore   seaside   space**

Look up more specific panels, such as **boat**, **castle**, **ice**, and **tree**, for more *features* to include in your setting.

Creating a setting: *Time*

You also need to tell your readers *when* your story takes place. For example:

- does it take place in *late spring* or in *early autumn*?
- does it begin at *dusk* or at *dawn*?
- is it set in the *present* day, in *ancient* times, or even in the *future*?

Explorer tip

Look up the panels for **season**, **day**, **night**, and **time** for words to describe when your story takes place.

Creating a setting: *Atmosphere and weather*

Once you've settled on the place and time, you can start to think about the atmosphere. What is the weather like? For example:

- is the sky *cloudy* or *cloudless*?
- is the wind *blustery* or *breezy*?
- is a storm *brewing*?

Explorer tip

You will find useful weather words in the main panels for **weather**, as well as in the entries for **ice**, **rain**, **sky**, **snow**, **sun**, and **wind**.

You can also look up **hot** and **cold** for more ways to describe temperature.

Describing a character

Describing how your characters look, sound (and even smell!) will make them more believable and vivid. Think about the details which make people different from each other. For example:

- are your characters *lean* and *lanky*, or *short* and *squat*?
- is their hair *straight* and *stringy*, or *fine* and *frizzy*?
- are they more likely to *scowl* and *grimace*, or to *beam*?

Explorer tip

Look up the panels for **body**, **expression**, **eye**, **face**, **hair**, **nose**, and **voice** to get ideas for how your characters might look and sound.

Look at the **clothes** panel for things that your characters might wear.

Typical characters

Some types of story require certain characters. For example, a detective story needs a detective, and a pirate story needs at least one pirate. A number of the word web panels focus on typical story characters like these. They are rather like dressing-up boxes with words (rather than costumes) with which to dress up your characters. For example:

- **detective** lists things a detective might look for (*fingerprints*, *suspect*)
- **astronaut** lists places an astronaut might visit (*moonbase*, *spacelab*)

These **Word Web** panels don't list *everything* a detective or astronaut might do, but they do list *typical* things and can give you ideas for writing your own mystery story or space story.

> **Explorer tip**
>
> You will find ideas for typical story characters in these panels:
>
> **astronaut   criminal   detective   explorer
> fairy   ghost   knight   pirate   robot   spy**
>
> The **magic** panel also has suggestions for **witches** and **wizards**.

Imaginary creatures

If your characters are not human, it is even more important to let your readers know how they look and sound. Not all aliens and ogres are alike, so be sure to describe *your* imaginary creatures in detail.

You can make an imaginary monster vivid by giving it body parts of real animals, for example the head of a snake, the wings of a bat, and the legs of a beetle.

> ### Example
>
> You are writing a space story. How do you describe your alien creatures?
> *The aliens had **insect-like bodies**, with **spindly legs** and **spiky antennae**. Their **scaly backs** were patterned with **purple blotches**. They spoke to each other in **high-pitched screeches**.*

Describing action

When you describe what your characters do, try to be specific. For example

- how do your characters move? Do they *scurry* quickly, *glide* gracefully, or *slink* stealthily?
- do they *tap* gently on a door, or *pound* it insistently?
- do they *nibble* their food politely, or *gobble* it greedily?

There is nothing wrong with using simple words like *move*, *hit*, and *eat*. But your writing will be more interesting if you use more colourful verbs at times

Example

You are writing a detective story. How does your main character act?
*Inspector Giles **paced** slowly round the room, **twitching** his moustache. He **inspected** the broken window and **peered** closely at the stains on the carpet.*

Explorer tip

The panels for **eat**, **drink**, **look**, **move**, and **walk** list many different ways that your characters might act.

You will find even more action words in the entries for **hit** and **run**.

Look up the **animal** or **bird** panels for ways that creatures might move.

Writing dialogue

the word "say"

The words that your characters say in the story is the *dialogue*. When you are writing dialogue, try not to use the verb **say** each time. Your story will be more interesting if you vary the words which report what each character says.

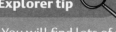

Example

> *"Stop that racket!"* **snapped** Miss Grump

and *"Don't look now, but there's a ghost behind us,"* **whispered** Evie

sound far more interesting than simply
> *said Miss Grump* and *said Evie.*

Explorer tip

You will find lots of suggestions for words to use instead of *say* in the **overused word** panel for **say**.

exclamations

Lively dialogue can bring the characters in your story to life. Try using *exclamations* at exciting moments in your story.

Example

A character in your story suddenly gets angry or annoyed. What should he or she say?
> *"**Blast** that parrot!" said Captain Cutlass with an evil leer.*
> *"**Bother!** The magic potion is wearing off!" said Megan, frowning*

Explorer tip

You will find ideas for what a character who is angry or annoyed, or surprised or alarmed might say in the panel at **exclamation**.

Explore: Writing non-fiction

Your thesaurus can help you with **non-fiction** writing, too. For example:

- how can you describe a *book* you have read, or a *place* you have visited?
- what words can you use to report a *sports match*?
- what words can you use in a *recipe* for cooking?

Example 1

You are writing a book review. How do you describe the way that the book ends?

> '*Smugglers Cove*' hurtles towards a **gripping finale**. The final chapter is a **nail-biting** description of a sea chase.

Example 2

You are writing a report of a football match. How do you describe the winning goal?

> Martinez **dribbled** the ball past two **defenders**, then **chipped** it across to the **captain** who **blasted** it into the back of the net.

Explorer tip

You will find useful words and phrases to describe a book in the **writing tips** panel for **writing**.

You will find words that are used in various sports in the **word web** panels for **football**, **tennis**, etc. You can also get ideas for how a player might hit or throw a ball in the **writing tips** panel for **ball**.

e **Word Web** panels in the thesaurus include lists of related words
hich can give you ideas or information for a project on that topic.

Example

You are writing a project on animals. Look up the **animal** panel to
find:

- animals that live on land (*aardvark*, *zebra*) or in the sea (*dolphin*,
  whale)
- names of young animals (*cub*, *pup*)
- names of animal body parts (*claw*, *snout*)
- names of wild animal homes (*earth*, *warren*)

Explorer tip

You can easily spot word webs in the thesaurus. They are treated in
special panels and have this symbol next to them:

There is a complete list of **word web** panels at the front of the
thesaurus.

explore further . . .

Like a good explorer, be prepared to follow a trail. **Cross references** in the
word webs will help you to find other panels with related information. For
example, the panel for **dinosaur** points you also to **prehistoric**, where
you will find a list of other prehistoric animals.

You may want to explore your topic further by looking up the listed words
in a dictionary or an encyclopedia.

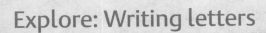
Explore: Writing letters

When you are writing a letter or email, think about *who* you are writing to, and *why*: that will help you decide what type of letter to write. For example:
- you might write a formal letter to a teacher, but an informal email to a friend
- you might send informal invitations to your birthday party, but receive a formal invitation to a wedding

If a character in your story writes a letter, it should also fit with the person and situation you are describing. For example:
- a medieval knight would write an elaborate, formal letter to a king
- a spy might send a hasty, informal email to headquarters

Here are some tips for writing both formal and informal types of letter.

In a **formal letter**, you should:
- write in complete sentences
- avoid short forms like *don't* and *I'm* (use *do not* and *I am*)
- avoid informal words and phrases, such as *thanks* (use *thank you* instead)
- begin with *Dear*, and end with *Yours sincerely* or *Yours truly*
- call the person you are writing to by their family name or title (if you don't know their name, call them *Sir* or *Madam*)

> Dear Prince Charming,
>
> Thank you for your invitation to the Palace Ball on Saturday. Unfortunately I am unable to come, as I must stay at home all evening to sweep the floors. Please accept my apologies.
>
> Yours sincerely,
> Cinderella

formal letters and emails are often chatty in tone, as if you were
~eaking rather than writing the words.

■ an **informal letter**, you might:
  use incomplete sentences
  use short forms like *don't* and *I'm*
  use informal words and phrases, such as *terrific* or *thanks*
• use exclamation marks when you (or your characters) are excited
• begin with *Dear* or *Hello* or *Hi* (or just a name), and end with *Yours* or *Best wishes*
• call the person you are writing to by their first or given name, or by a nickname

---

Dear Cinders

Just had a terrific idea! Meet me at the kitchen door at 6pm on Sat. Bring a pumpkin and a few mice.

Yours
Fairy Godmother

Explorer tip

The **word web** panel for **communication** lists some types of message you might write.

Look up **title** in the thesaurus for ways to address people you are speaking to or writing to.